Professional Ethics

Professional Ethics

THE CITY
LAW SCHOOL
CITY, UNIVERSITY OF LONDON
—— EST 1894 ——

Authors

Nigel Duncan, Professor Emeritus of Legal Education, The City Law School
Oliver Hanmer, Director of Regulatory Assurance, Bar Standards Board
John-Paul MacNamara, Barrister, Lecturer, The City Law School

Editor

John-Paul MacNamara, Barrister, Lecturer, The City Law School

Series Editor

Julie Browne, Associate Professor of Law, The City Law School

OXFORD
UNIVERSITY PRESS

OXFORD
UNIVERSITY PRESS

Great Clarendon Street, Oxford, OX2 6DP,
United Kingdom

Oxford University Press is a department of the University of Oxford.
It furthers the University's objective of excellence in research, scholarship,
and education by publishing worldwide. Oxford is a registered trade mark of
Oxford University Press in the UK and in certain other countries

Seventeenth edition 2016
Eighteenth edition 2018
Nineteenth edition 2020

Published in the United States of America by Oxford University Press
198 Madison Avenue, New York, NY 10016, United States of America

British Library Cataloguing in Publication Data
Data available

ISBN 978–0–19–285795–8

Printed and bound in the UK by
TJ Books Limited

FOREWORD

These manuals have been written by a combination of practitioners and members of staff of The City Law School (formerly the Inns of Court School of Law), and are designed primarily to support training on the Bar Course, wherever it is taught. They provide an extremely useful resource to assist in acquiring the skills and knowledge that practising barristers need.

This series of manuals exemplifies the practical and professional approach that is central to Bar training.

I congratulate the authors on the excellent standard of these manuals, and I am grateful to Oxford University Press for their ongoing and enthusiastic support.

Professor Andrew Stockley
Dean
The City Law School
City, University of London
2022

PREFACE

Since 2010, students joining the Bar Course have sat a separate assessment in Professional Ethics. The Bar Standards Board was concerned that this topic should play a more prominent role in the training of barristers and the use of a separate assessment reflects that. The Professional Ethics module will prepare you for your career with the rigour that is required in an age of high public scrutiny and expectation. The importance that the profession places in professional ethics is further exemplified by the introduction of the professional ethics assessment during pupillage and the additional ethics training required as part of the new practitioner programme.

The barristers' Code of Conduct, while it remains the primary reference point, is no longer sufficient to indicate the far-reaching ethical considerations that should inform a barrister's working life. Ethics denotes a much wider scope for the values that underpin the profession. The Code itself underwent a drastic rewriting as it entered its ninth edition, coming into effect in January 2014. The Code is an integral part of a new Handbook, the entirety of which needs to be considered and absorbed by barristers. There are now outcomes, rules, and guidance set down throughout the Handbook, not simply in the Code of Conduct itself.

This is a time of great change for the Bar and for the way it is regulated. The Legal Services Act 2007 has led to new ways of working for solicitors and barristers with the introduction of multidisciplinary teams known as Alternative Business Structures (ABSs). Barristers will be regulated under the terms of the new Handbook but may also find themselves in situations where they also need to comply with other professional codes, most obviously that issued by the Solicitors Regulation Authority. The increasing public prominence of both the Bar Council and the Bar Standards Board, through their websites and other publications, indicates a concern to demonstrate transparency and public accountability in a profession that has often been criticised in the past. Many of those criticisms are unjustified. But if the Bar is to be proof against all challenges, the highest ethical standards are required. A proper approach to ethics in a specialist area can only arise through thorough knowledge and an understanding of the relevant sources. We are members of an honourable and highly reputable profession. It is incumbent upon us to maintain the reputation of the Bar and to conduct ourselves accordingly.

The aim of this manual is to give you the necessary grounding. By studying the manual and by putting to use what you have read in the exercises and discussions that take place throughout the Bar Course, you should be in a position to make an informed decision on any ethical problem that arises in the course of your practice. There will always be areas of uncertainty, though. If ethics were easy, the world would be a different place. But with thoughtful application of what you learn, you will be in a position to choose the best of a number of possible options and be able to justify your choice.

As a barrister you will have weighty responsibilities. You have a duty to the court and a duty to your client. You also have a duty to the public at large to help maintain confidence in the legal profession. Problems most commonly arise when these duties appear to conflict. Decisions on professional ethics can be difficult. They will be even more difficult when you are dealing with real clients. So make the most of this year of preparation. Maintaining professional ethics and working to professional standards are central to everything you will do in practice.

John-Paul MacNamara
Barrister,
Lecturer,
The City Law School,
City, University of London

ACKNOWLEDGEMENTS

Grateful acknowledgement is made to the publishers of copyright material which appears in this book, namely the Bar Standards Board, <http://www.barstandardsboard.org.uk>, for kind permission to reproduce sections from *The Bar Standards Board Handbook* fourth edition (as at February 2020), including Sections A, B, C, and D of the Code of Conduct of the Bar for England and Wales (ninth edition), Scope of Practice, Bar Training Rules, and the CPD rules; and the Bar Standard Board Code Guidance, available at <https://www.barstandardsboard.org.uk/regulatory-requirements/bsb-handbook/code-guidance/>.

Much of the original text was written by Robert McPeake, now an Emeritus Fellow of City, University of London.

GUIDE TO USING THIS BOOK

The Bar Manuals series includes a range of tools and features to aid your learning. This guide will outline the approach to using this book, and help you to make the most out of each of the features within.

Practical-based approach

The authors have taken a practical-based approach to Professional Ethics at the Bar. This manual uses realistic examples of ethical dilemmas that may confront a barrister.

The code and beyond

The manual looks beyond the Code to consider related issues such as the scope of practice in a more liberal legal profession. There is also coverage of the requirements placed on barristers under the Proceeds of Crime Act 2002.

Core texts

Extracts from the barristers' Code of Conduct, and other essential content from the BSB Handbook, are included in Appendices to this manual. Where content in the Handbook has not yet been approved by the Legal Services Board, it is scored through to indicate this status.

OUTLINE CONTENTS

DETAILED CONTENTS

Introduction

1.1 A time of change

In a previous edition of this manual, we wrote that

> you are hoping to join this profession at a time of change. The courts, for example, are no longer the exclusive adversarial platforms for barristers, but are now open to freelance solicitor advocates, in-house solicitors, and the employed Bar. In the course of your career you may find yourself working closely with non-lawyers in a 'Legal Disciplinary Practice', a new form of business structure permitted by the Legal Services Act 2007. You may act as a mediator or arbitrator, in addition to your court practice. Furthermore, the nature of your work is likely to change rapidly, with an increasing emphasis on the interpretation of regulations and the defining of quality standards. In these changing times, there is nothing more important to practice at the Bar than maintaining the highest standards with respect to the way in which barristers conduct themselves, and the regard in which they are held by their peers, the judges before whom they appear, their instructing solicitors, their clients, and members of the public with whom they come into contact during their professional lives.

Those words still hold good today, some ten years later. Of course, in addition to being well thought of by others, the barrister should demonstrate that he or she holds those others in high regard as well. It has also become clearer that we should add *colleagues* to the list of others to whom we should pay regard, as more barristers enter the world of work in Alternative Business Structures (ABSs). It is possible that a barrister will be working as a manager in an ABS, perhaps with other barristers and solicitors around but also perhaps managing, or being managed by, someone who is not qualified as a lawyer—for example, an accountant. We should also reflect on the fact that there will not always be an instructing solicitor, someone to support the barrister and provide such a valuable link with, and sometimes a buffer against, the lay client. These days, many barristers are engaging in direct access work, either public access or licensed access, where there is no instructing solicitor to act as an intermediary. These relationships raise many new challenges, to which the barrister needs to be alert.

These changing times are also reflected in other ways, sometimes rather contentiously. Some years ago, our regulatory body the Bar Standards Board ('BSB') moved, in partnership with the Solicitors Regulation Authority and the Chartered Institute of Legal Executives, to establish the Quality Assurance Scheme for Advocates or 'QASA'. This was intended to create a benchmarking scheme to ensure that advocates, from whatever branch of the legal services sector, have attained a specific level of competence for the work they are undertaking. It was to be rolled out initially for those in criminal practice. However, opinion was divided amongst those legal professionals who would be affected by QASA, and there was opposition, resulting in a legal challenge in the courts (see *R (on the application of Lumsdon and others) v Legal Services Board* [2015] UKSC 41). Although the challenge failed in the courts, QASA was subsequently dropped in 2017, at least by the BSB. At the same time, members of the profession took the unprecedented step of refusing 'returned' work and not attending court, in protest about cuts to public funding. Scenes of barristers standing outside Crown Courts, bewigged and somewhat embarrassed, appeared on national news channels. In 2018, we again saw dissent and challenge against public spending plans, with the Criminal Bar Association calling for its members to refuse new instructions in publicly funded cases from April 2018. In early April 2020, with the Covid-19 pandemic upon us, one read of chambers and law firms announcing their closure with continuing funding issues compounded by the collapse in work and consequently income whilst fixed costs remain. At the same time, another effect of the pandemic is that more courts are trying to manage their work using virtual hearings, with lawyer and client in different physical locations and neither in the same place as the judge. On 13 March 2022, the Criminal Bar Association released the results of their members' ballot: 94 per cent of the 1,908 Criminal Bar Association members who voted, confirmed that they would withdraw their goodwill and decline to accept return work from 11 April 2022 unless the government increases their remuneration under the Advocates' Graduated Fee Scheme (AGFS) by 25 per cent each year on claims submitted from that date.

So, in a nutshell, the profession does not stand still. The environment in which we work is changing, quite fundamentally, in many ways. Public scrutiny and our accountability are increasingly important. The BSB introduced significant new 'transparency rules' in 2019, designed to make one's terms of service and pricing structures much more visible to potential clients, whether professional or lay client. Barristers certainly need to find their 'sea legs', in new circumstances and potentially working with other professionals and finding that they are expected to adhere to other sets of ethical behaviours, sometimes as well as or instead of their own code of conduct. The need for new entrants to the profession to begin their careers with a solid ethical foundation is probably more important now than ever before.

1.2   A new Code of Conduct

In 2013, the BSB introduced the ninth edition of the Code of Conduct. The most recently published version (version 4.6 at the time of writing) came into effect on 31 December 2020. The ninth edition is radically different from earlier iterations of the Code; according to the then-Chair of the BSB, Baroness Deech,

> superfluous rules have been stripped away and others modernised. The Handbook's approach is less prescriptive, with more focus and guidance on what the outcome of a rule should be, rather than attempting to define how a barrister should act in every situation.

The BSB wanted to move from the previous rule-focused scheme and the Handbook describes its approach to regulation as 'risk-focused' (I5.2). This approach is intended to assist in preventing misconduct in the first place, and to avoid any recurrence of less serious non-compliance. At the same time, it is intended to ensure that action to enforce the Code is 'reserved for the most serious cases of non-compliance'—specifically those cases where there are 'considerable consequences for the client and the public interest'.

The new Code is part of a new BSB Handbook. The overall structure of the Handbook splits the content into six parts. Part 1 introduces the Handbook, whilst Part 2 is the Code of Conduct. Part 3 addresses the scope of practice and the role and functions of the BSB in terms of authorising and licensing entities to provide legal services. Part 4 sets out the Qualification Rules, Part 5 is the Enforcement Regulations, and Part 6 gives the definitions. The Handbook is available as a download from the BSB website at <https://www.barstandardsboard.org.uk/the-bsb-handbook.html>. Relevant sections from the Code of Conduct and other relevant extracts from the BSB Handbook are set out in the Appendices to this manual, as it stood on 22 March 2022. We have focused on the most important parts, previously used by the BSB for its centrally set Professional Ethics assessment on the Bar Professional Training Course. We are now into a post-BPTC era and Professional Ethics is now being assessed both in the Bar training course with a provider-set assessment and again during pupillage with a centrally set assessment, but it seems sensible to use the former requirements as a guide to the content of this manual. Some sections of the Handbook which were not assessable are also included where this seems to be helpful for understanding a topic.

The Code of Conduct contains five components—the Core Duties (see **1.3**), outcomes, rules, guidance, and regulations.

The Code (and Handbook) uses a particular tripartite reference system for its content. For example:

rC4 Your duty to act in the best interests of each client is subject to your duty to the court.

The first component in the indicator shows the nature of the statement. So, outcomes appear as 'o', always in lower case; rules (and regulations) appear as 'r'; and guidance is shown as 'g'. The next component shows the relevant section within the Handbook, so the Code of Conduct is in Part 2 but its indicator is 'C', always in upper case. Similarly, the indicator for Part 1 'Introduction' is 'I'; for Part 3 'Scope of Practice' it is 'S'; Part 4 'Qualification Rules' uses 'Q'; and Part 5 'Enforcement' uses 'E'. The third and final component in the indicator is always a number and runs sequentially through each part of the Handbook. So, to return to our example, 'rC4', we can see that this is a rule; it is in Part 2 'Code of Conduct', and it is the fourth rule in that part.

The core duties apply to all barristers, and sometimes to others; compliance with these duties is mandatory. The outcomes are descriptive and supply the thinking behind the rules, why a rule is necessary. They should assist with understanding the rules and the guidance. Compliance with the outcomes is not mandatory but, when a breach of the rules is being considered, the relevant outcomes will be taken into account. Rules are there to supplement the core duties, where it is felt that specific rules are required. The Introduction to the Handbook makes it clear that the Conduct Rules (those relating to the Code of Conduct in Part 2) are not intended to be exhaustive, so that in any specific situation where no Conduct Rule applies, one should still refer to the Core Duties. Even where there is a specific Conduct Rule that applies, compliance with that may not be sufficient—as the Introduction states 'compliance with the Rules alone will not necessarily be sufficient to comply with the Core Duties' (I6.3.a). Guidance, as its title implies, is there to assist in interpreting the rules, not least through giving examples of the behaviour that is expected (but is not mandatory). However, the guidance in the Handbook is not exhaustive; other documents are published from time to time which supplement the Handbook.

1.3 The ten Core Duties

The first thing to note about the Code is that it lays down ten 'Core Duties' for every barrister to attend to. Specifically, these apply to all BSB regulated persons, except where the Code provides otherwise. A 'BSB regulated person' includes all practising barristers, 'second six' pupils, and registered European lawyers. The Core Duties also apply to unregistered barristers, some of them apply all of the time, such as CD5 and CD9, others will apply when an unregistered barrister provides legal services to clients; an 'unregistered barrister' is someone who has been called to the Bar by an Inn of Court and has not ceased to be a member of the Bar but does not currently hold a practising certificate (see Part 6 of the Handbook). For example, in 2017 an unregistered barrister who was identifiable as a barrister used Twitter to post a tweet that was described as 'racially charged and derogatory to women'. He was subsequently reprimanded and fined £1,000 for a breach of CD5 (see below). The core duties are:

CD1   You must observe your duty to the court in the administration of justice [CD1].

CD2   You must act in the best interests of each client [CD2].

CD3   You must act with honesty and integrity [CD3].

CD4   You must maintain your independence [CD4].

CD5   You must not behave in a way which is likely to diminish the trust and confidence which the public places in you or in the profession [CD5].

CD6   You must keep the affairs of each client confidential [CD6].

CD7   You must provide a competent standard of work and service to each client [CD7].

CD8   You must not discriminate unlawfully against any person [CD8].

CD9   You must be open and co-operative with your regulators [CD9].

CD10 You must take reasonable steps to manage your practice, or carry out your role within your practice, competently and in such a way as to achieve compliance with your legal and regulatory obligations [CD10].

The Code makes it clear that whilst the ten are not presented in order of precedence, nevertheless there will be circumstances where one core duty does take priority. In fact, CD1 overrides any other core duty where they are inconsistent (gC1). The Code is also clear that CD2 is subordinate to the obligations imposed by CDs 3, 4, and 8.

A BSB regulated person or an unregistered barrister may face disciplinary proceedings where the BSB considers that (a) that person has breached one or more of the core duties and (b) such proceedings are in accordance with the Code's enforcement policy.

1.4 The Code and the Bar Course

This manual is designed to support students through their time on the Bar Course and specifically to help them to prepare for the assessment that they will undertake on Professional Ethics as a part of the Bar Course.

Prior to 2020–1, the assessment in Professional Ethics was an assessment set centrally by the BSB, through its Central Examinations Board. From September 2020 onwards, the BSB has split the assessment of Professional Ethics into two parts. The first part will be taken whilst on the Bar Course and it will be a locally set assessment. This means that the timing and format of that assessment will be determined by the institution where the student is taking the Bar Course. The second part will be centrally set by the BSB and will be taken during the pupillage stage of training for the Bar. For this manual, the focus is on the central areas set out in the Code of Conduct, but there is also some coverage given to other areas where it is hoped that this will assist student comprehension of professional ethics. The current version of the BSB Handbook (v.4.6) deals in Part 4 with the Bar Qualification Rules. Outcome oC1 in Part 4 makes it clear that a central purpose of the Qualification Rules is to enable those people who qualify as barristers to meet the requirements of the Professional Statement. The Professional Statement describes a Threshold Standard as 'the knowledge, skills and attributes that all barristers should have on "day one" of practice' (according to the BSB website). This comes at the completion of pupillage and thus for Professional Ethics not all of it has to be addressed and satisfied by that locally set assessment. On the subject of Ethics, the Professional Statement says:

1.16 Comply with regulatory requirements set down by the Bar Standards Board, including the Code of Conduct.

They will clearly understand a barrister's Core Duties and apply them in all aspects of their work.
Barristers should:

(a) Identify the most recent Code of Conduct and other applicable rules and regulations relevant to their practice and the conduct of any matters they are dealing with.
(b) Recognise potential ethical situations and identify ethical issues.
(c) Be aware of and make effective use of relevant guidance, advice and support regarding ethical issues.
(d) Behave ethically and consistently act in accordance with the Code of Conduct and other applicable rules and regulations.

1.17 Know how to conduct themselves appropriately in court.

They will know and use the required dress, accepted forms of address, formalities of proceedings and established conventions and customs in each forum where they represent clients.
Barristers should:

(a) Use the required dress, accepted forms of address, observe formalities of proceedings and follow established conventions and customs in each forum where they represent clients.

1.18 Only accept work which they believe they are competent to undertake.

They will be able to assess the level of their own knowledge, skills and attributes, to enable them to make an informed judgement on the acceptance of work and have the resilience to decline to act where necessary.

Barristers should:

(a) Recognise and operate within the limits of their competence.
(b) Explain clearly the limits of their competence and knowledge to relevant others.
(c) Consult relevant others, where appropriate.
(d) Make an informed judgement on the level of knowledge, skills and attributes required in a particular case.
(e) Decline to act where the Code of Conduct requires them to do so.

There are other provisions within the Professional Statement that are also relevant to professional ethics and conduct; these will be referred to at the appropriate points in subsequent chapters.

In addition to the Handbook and the Professional Statement, there are other BSB Guidance documents on ethics topics. Currently, these include the following (all issued in October 2019 unless indicated otherwise):

- Supporting Information for Chambers BSB Handbook Equality Rules
- *Guidance on Practising Rules and Requirements*
  - Unregistered Barristers Guidance (barristers without practising certificates)—supplying legal services and holding out
  - Guidance for barristers supervising immigration advisers
  - Public access guidance for barristers
  - Conducting Litigation Guidance

- *Guidance on the Administration of a Barrister's Practice*
  - First tier complaints handling guidance
  - Referral and marketing arrangements guidance
  - Confidentiality guidance
  - Investigating and collecting evidence and taking witness statements guidance
  - After the event insurance guidance
  - Chambers closure guidance
  - Referral and marketing arrangements guidance

- *Guidance on the Professional Conduct of Barristers*
  - Reporting serious misconduct of others guidance
  - Social media guidance
  - Guidance on clash of hearing dates (Listings)
  - Pilot harassment support schemes waivers guidance

- *Additional Guidance*
  - Guidance on the Transparency Rules
  - Authorisation to practice section on the BSB website
  - Practising certificate, including fees.

Other assessable documentation which originates outside the BSB and is relevant to professional ethics includes:

- the Code for Crown Prosecutors, 8th edition, October 2018
- the Farquharson Guidelines—the Role of Prosecution Advocates
- provisions on money-laundering and terrorist financing; see currently Anti-Money Laundering Guidance for the Legal Sector, accessible on the BSB website.

1.5 Structure of the manual

The manual is organised to reflect the structure of the Code of Conduct. Specifically, we have taken the five sets of 'conduct rules' as our template. Thus, we have chapters on:

- you and the court (**chapter 2**)
- behaving ethically (**chapter 3**)
- you and your client (**chapter 4**)
- you and your regulator (**chapter 5**)
- you and your practice (**chapter 6**).

This should allow us to concentrate on the Code. However, other parts of the Handbook are also important and assessable and these will be picked up in **chapter 7** onwards, looking at the scope of practice, practising certificates, Qualification Rules, and continuing professional development.

You and the court

2.1 Making sure that the legal system works properly

Extract from the Professional Statement:

2.1 Act with the utmost integrity and independence at all times, in the interests of justice, representing clients with courage, perseverance and fearlessness.

2.2 Be honest in their dealings with others.

2.3 Be aware and active in the pursuit of equality and respect for diversity, not tolerating unlawful discrimination, in themselves or others.

2.4 Ensure their work does not incur unnecessary fees.

2.5 Adopt a reflective approach to their work, enabling them to correct errors and admit if they have made mistakes.

2.6 Ensure they practise with adaptability and flexibility, by being self-aware and self-directed, recognising and acting upon the continual need to maintain and develop their knowledge and skills.

There are five outcomes for the 'You and the court' section of the Code of Conduct. The aim is essentially to provide a guarantee that the public interest is served by having a robust and transparent legal system, not one that is affected by lawyers seeking partisan benefit or advantage. The outcomes seek both substantive justice and the appearance of justice in the legal system. So, oC2 requires 'the proper administration of justice' to be served whilst oC5 insists that the public must be enabled to have 'confidence in the administration of justice and in those who serve it'. The advocates who appear before the court owe duties to the court but the system itself cannot function properly unless the lay client and anyone who is professionally connected to the litigation also abides by their own obligations. An example of this might be the disclosure obligations in civil litigation, where lay clients sometimes struggle to see the benefit to themselves of disclosing to their opponent evidence that is relevant to the dispute but damaging to their case. Outcome oC4 makes the point that both the advocates in court and others who are conducting litigation owe duties to the court and there will be occasions when these duties will override the duties owed to the lay client. It is important that both advocates and clients clearly understand the scope of those duties and what situations may give rise to a client's interests effectively being set aside. Here, we can begin to see one of the frequent areas for ethical dilemmas to arise—the pinch point where the barrister's public obligations run into conflict with their private, client-facing, obligations.

Probably the key outcome is oC1—that the court can trust the information that is given to it, whether by someone conducting litigation (perhaps through filing documents at court) or by an advocate at court, either making submissions or calling evidence. In a sense, this harks back to long-standing duties owed by barristers not to mislead the court (and see rC3.1) and not to devise evidence but this outcome is rather wider than that. Finally, oC3 recognises that the interests of lay clients are of course to be protected but only to the extent that this is compatible with the core duties and with oC1 and oC2; see also rC4. In other words, the interests of any individual client are subservient to justice and the wider public interest in the proper administration of justice. This reflects Core Duty 1 and its primacy over all other provisions, outlined in gC1.1.

The requirement not to be partisan is reflected in rC3 which states that you are to 'act with independence in the interests of justice'. This will include being independent of any pressure being placed upon you by a client (whether lay or professional), by anyone else involved in conducting the litigation, or by any third party (including the judge). This obligation can be difficult for lay clients to understand, not least because they are often paying for your services and feel that your interests should align with theirs; that you should be arguing to win for them, not striving for justice. It is rather an abstract concept and it may be helpful to look at some of the more specific rules and guidance on this point.

2.2   Independence in the interests of justice

As an advocate instructed in a case, you will be privy to certain information—some of it (typically factual and specific to this case) will have come from the lay client and some of it (typically legal and normative) you will have acquired independently of the client.

2.2.1   Factual information

When factual information is presented to the court by an advocate, often the court will have to take on trust that the information is genuine as it has no way of testing the veracity. Of course, this does not apply to trials, where the veracity of the evidence is a key determinant in the outcome. But, in essence, as the court has to trust the advocate not to mislead it, so the advocate has to trust the lay client not to mislead him or her.

The court may ask itself—has counsel just said something 'on instructions'—that is, based on information that has come from the client or a witness but which has not been presented to the court as evidence? Or has counsel just made something up? Of course, clients and witnesses may well make up evidence and allegations from time to time and the advocate has to trust them not to do so, to an extent. The system breaks down without the element of trust. Whilst it can be useful to play 'devil's advocate' in a conference, to see what answers the client will give to challenging questions from the opponent, it is not a function of the advocate to play 'private detective' and investigate the truthfulness of the instructions he has received from the lay client, to go behind the client's back.

2.2.2   Legal information

Is the law conclusively on one side's favour in a court hearing? Do both parties' advocates know the same cases and statutes? Suppose one party's advocate is more up to date on the relevant law than the advocate acting for the other party? We might say that this is as it should be, the more up-to-date advocate is better informed and should be able to take advantage of her more accurate legal knowledge. That is certainly how her client would see things. But suppose her more accurate legal knowledge means that she knows about an authority that damages her arguments and makes it more likely that the *opponent* will succeed? Then, the instinct of the lay client may be to keep this quiet—if the opposition advocate doesn't know about this authority, that's his and his client's problem and they should both take the consequences. Of course, the difficulty with this is that the court should stand impartial and seek to make the correct decision, both in law and fact.

2.2.3   Disclosure obligations

Although it is typically the position in an adversarial system like ours that the parties decide what evidence to present to the court, the advocate cannot knowingly present false evidence nor can the advocate withhold material evidence (at least it should be disclosed to the opponent before the hearing). Using false evidence or hiding material evidence would not promote a factually correct decision. Similarly, it is not a requirement that the advocates present every single case and statutory principle that they can find on the point under argument; apart from anything else, there would be replication, court time would be wasted, and costs incurred unnecessarily. So, the advocates will winnow out the marginal, the old, and the less persuasive legal authorities before they come to court but what they must not do is knowingly present a false legal argument. The argument would be false if there is an authority which contradicts or undermines their argument. This is not an insistence that the advocate must know every single case and piece of legislation relevant to the argument—we do not seek perfection! But it does mean that if the advocate actually knows of an authority that damages his argument, he must bring it to the court's attention and not set it aside. Either he considers that the authority is fatal to his client's case; if so, his client's position is unarguable and he should abandon it. Or he considers that he can properly distinguish the adverse authority, in which case that is what he should endeavour to do. Here, we begin to see one of the big issues with professional ethics—the element of self-policing, or perhaps having the proper 'values'—who will know whether you were aware of a damaging legal authority and ignored it, or if you were simply ignorant of it? The former is unethical, the latter is negligent but not unethical. Usually, only the individual advocate can tell the difference.

2.3 The advocate must not mislead the court

2.3.1 The advocate's knowledge and belief

This is a clear example of the requirement of professional independence, that one's representation of a party and his interests is overridden by the interests of justice. Rule rC3 makes it clear that the advocate must not mislead the court, knowingly or recklessly, or attempt to do so (see also rC9.1 for a broader example of the duty not to mislead). One example of this is the obligation to 'take reasonable steps to ensure that the court has before it all relevant decisions and legislative provisions' (rC3.4). Thus, we seek to maximise the chance of a legally sound and just decision from the court. Also, the advocate must not make submissions to the court or any other sort of statement which he knows are untrue or misleading. If his client instructs him to do this, he must refuse. This could cover both legal and factual points. More plainly fact-based is the requirement not to ask a witness questions which suggest facts that the advocate knows, or is instructed by his client, are false or misleading (rC6.1). This is most obviously demonstrated in cross-examination, where the advocate is putting his client's case to an opposing witness. Suppose the witness testifies that she sent an email to the barrister's client but she is unable to produce evidence of the email in court; there is just her oral testimony as to its existence and content. If the cross-examiner has previously been told privately by his client that he did receive such an email from the witness but he deleted it, then the cross-examiner cannot ask questions of the witness which suggest that no such email existed or was ever sent by her to the client.

It is important not to confuse knowledge with belief. The guidance under these rules (gC6) makes it clear that the advocate does not need to turn detective or pretend to be omniscient; you do not have to believe that what your client tells you in his instructions is factually true. Suppose your client tells you that it isn't him on the CCTV recording; you may view the recording and feel very strongly that it definitely looks very much like him and his appearance is so unusual that you cannot imagine it could have been anyone else. Nevertheless, you must present his case based on *his* instructions, not on *your* intuition or belief. Of course, if the client says 'Look at me there on the CCTV! Of course, I'm going to tell the court that it's not me, see what I can get away with', you cannot call him as a witness to say that it does not show him— now you *know* that would be a lie. So, your knowledge is important but your belief is irrelevant here. That should be clear. Where things become a little grey is when we introduce the idea of *recklessness*. This crops up in various areas of substantive law, most obviously criminal law. Here in professional ethics, though, it is applied to the advocate, not to the client. Rule rC3.1 says that the advocate must not mislead the court knowingly or recklessly. Guidance gC4 expands on this—recklessness means 'being indifferent to the truth, or not caring whether something is true or false'. One might be tempted to say that this imposes certain additional obligations on the advocate—to turn detective, to cross-examine one's client, to establish 'the truth', regardless of the client's interests in the outcome of the case. If the advocate is to 'care' whether something that he is responsible for putting before the court is true or not, shouldn't he test it? Do some investigating himself? Play devil's advocate? The simple answer, it is suggested, is 'no' to all of the above. What it ought to mean is that the advocate has to keep his wits about him and not let things pass into evidence which, if he had been paying attention, he would have spotted as problematic and then considered. This is the sort of thing that is much more of a danger inside the courtroom than outside. In the heat of the moment, the cut and thrust, the need for the advocate to be concentrating on so many things, you can just lose your focus. Then the witness says something unexpected in the witness box and it's gone in as evidence, possibly without you even realising its significance. So, we would suggest that this is really what the obligation not to be reckless means in effect—pay attention! If you do not, then at least you should try to rectify matters if you realise later what has happened. Hence, the Professional Statement says at 2.5(c) that the barrister should identify their errors of judgment, omissions, and mistakes 'and take appropriate action'.

Guidance gC4 makes it clear that these obligations run throughout the lifespan of the case. If you discover later that you have unwittingly misled the court, you have to correct the position; failure to do so would mean that you are now knowingly misleading the court. This may mean making a statement to the court, withdrawing a particular claim or assertion, perhaps recalling a witness for further questioning to correct a point, or having to withdraw from the case completely.

2.3.2 Respecting client confidentiality whilst not misleading the court

The advocate has a fundamental obligation to respect the confidentiality of information imparted by the client or gathered whilst working for the client; see Core Duty 6. This information may also be covered by legal professional privilege (see the *Evidence* manual); where it is privileged, it will be exempt from the usual disclosure obligations. However, the confidentiality requirement may come into conflict with the obligation not to mislead the court. Remember that the obligation not to mislead the court falls within Core Duty 1, and that takes precedence over any other Core Duty. It is quite easy to envisage a situation where your client gives you information which is relevant to the litigation but which they do not wish to disclose to anyone else, certainly not the opponent or the court. This information may come in the form of verbal instructions or perhaps a document or a copy of an email. There are four possible situations here:

1. The information is not protected by legal professional privilege and must be disclosed to the opponent as usual; the client agrees to the disclosure; or

2. The information is not protected by legal professional privilege and must be disclosed to the opponent as usual; the client refuses to agree to the disclosure; or

3. The information is protected by legal professional privilege and need not be disclosed to the opponent; and there is no danger of the court being misled by reason of the information being withheld; or

4. The information is protected by legal professional privilege and so need not be disclosed to the opponent but there is a risk that the court may be misled if the information is withheld.

In situations 1 and 3, there is no problem, this shows the system running as it is designed to. In situation 2, the disclosure regime is malfunctioning. In situation 4, there is no issue with the disclosure regime but there is nevertheless a problem in that incorrect factual information may be given to the court and thus the court may be misled.

2.3.2.1 Non-disclosure of a document

The most obvious example of situation 2 is where your client has a document which predates the proceedings and is perhaps an email between claimant and defendant evidencing a business deal, or a copy of an invoice, the content of which is prejudicial to his case. Therefore, he does not want it to be disclosed. Under rC3.5, the advocate must ensure that his 'ability to act independently is not compromised'. His duty to the court takes priority and so the advocate must advise the client to disclose the document. If the client refuses permission, the advocate cannot reconcile his conflicting duties and is in a dilemma.

2.3.2.2 Non-disclosure of guilt

Probably the most obvious example of situation 4 is the criminal case where the accused tells his advocate that he is guilty of the crime but wants to plead not guilty. How is the advocate to handle this in court?

2.3.2.3 Solutions

These are tricky situations—so what is the solution? First, the advocate should not breach the client's confidentiality. It is not acceptable for the advocate to take it upon herself to make an unsanctioned disclosure. So, if your client refuses to allow the document to be disclosed, you should not disclose it (gC13). Likewise, if your client insists on pleading not guilty, you should not go into court and inform the court that he has told you that he committed the crime (gC9.1). Thereafter, the solutions diverge somewhat.

If the client refuses to disclose the document, the advocate has no alternative but to withdraw from the case (gC13); the conflict between the obligations is irreconcilable. This is straightforward. See also rC25.

If the client insists on pleading not guilty, the defence can put the prosecution to proof. In a criminal trial, the burden of proof is on the prosecution and the defence advocate can legitimately test the reliability of the prosecution evidence through cross-examination, and then make a closing argument that the burden of proof has not been discharged. In this way, the defence advocate is not advancing an alternative explanation which he knows (because of his client's instructions) to be false. Thus, the advocate is not actively presenting false information or a false hypothesis to the court but merely challenging the information and hypothesis offered by the prosecution (gC9.2). However, if the defence advocate were to call evidence, or suggest through cross-examination, that the accused had not committed the offence, then this would be actively misleading the court and constitute a breach of Core Duty 1 (gC10). This distinction can be difficult to justify.

It becomes more difficult if we look at rC6. This says that the advocate must not make a submission which, on his instructions, he knows to be false. Applying that to our situation, the defence advocate *can* make a closing speech that challenges the prosecution evidence but he *cannot* explicitly assert that the accused is innocent, because he knows this to be untrue. Rule rC6 also says that the advocate must not present evidence which he knows to be, or is instructed is, untrue; the rule goes on—'unless you make clear to the court the true position as known by or instructed to you'. This seems to suggest a positive obligation on the advocate to breach the client's confidentiality. It is submitted that this is not a correct interpretation of the rule. In effect, as you cannot breach the confidentiality, the rule is really saying that you simply cannot present that false evidence to the court. This interpretation is supported by gC11 which states that where there is a risk of the court being misled if confidential information is not disclosed, the advocate should seek the client's permission to disclose it. If that permission is not given, then the advocate must cease to act for the client and withdraw from the case. Guidance gC11 explicitly states that, in this position, when you withdraw 'you must not reveal the information to the court'.

2.3.2.4 Non-disclosure of criminal record

Another example of the fourth situation occurs, again, in a criminal setting. Suppose that you are representing the defendant. The evidence disclosed by the prosecution to you and to the court indicates that there are no previous convictions recorded against the defendant. But suppose that your client tells you that the prosecution has got it wrong, and that he does have a previous conviction? Guidance gC12 addresses this in the context of a sentencing hearing. Clearly, the defendant's criminal record *could* be relevant to determination of the sentence at the hearing. So if the court is unaware of the true position, it may impose the wrong sentence; it will have been misled. Conversely, if any offender is a man of good character—has no criminal record—then this will be a strong mitigating factor for the defence advocate to rely upon in the plea in mitigation. So the defendant in our example will be motivated to keep the court in the dark about the truth. The guidance distinguishes two situations, with the distinction turning on the presence or absence of a mandatory sentence.

The first situation arises where a mandatory sentence should be imposed if the court knew the true position; for example, where the defendant *in fact* has two previous convictions for domestic burglary and now awaits sentence on his third, so in law he should receive a mandatory minimum sentence of three years' imprisonment. If this defendant refuses to allow his advocate to disclose the true position, the court will inevitably fail to pass the sentence which the law requires it to pass. The advocate must advise the defendant that if he refuses to sanction disclosure of the true position to the court, then the advocate has no choice and must withdraw from the case, but preserving client confidentiality.

The second situation is where no mandatory sentence is in play. If this defendant refuses to allow disclosure of his true record, the advocate can continue to act for him but will be limited in what he can say on the defendant's behalf. The advocate must not mislead the court and so cannot assert that the defendant is of good character. This powerful potential mitigating factor will be lost here, as it should be. The advocate needs to advise the client that if the court asks her a direct question—for example, 'Is it correct, Miss Green, that your client has never been in any trouble with the courts before?'—then she cannot mislead the court and so, if the defendant were not to permit this question to be answered truthfully, the advocate would have no choice but must withdraw at that point. What this tends to produce is a tactical discussion between advocate and client before the hearing begins and where, having advised the client of these various scenarios, the advocate asks the client whether or not the true position may be disclosed. If the client agrees to disclosure, the ethical dilemma is removed. In fact, disclosure might be beneficial to the client: the true position may emerge anyway during or even after the hearing and the correct sentence would then be imposed, so why not get some credit for being frank? Candour can be a mitigating factor too.

2.4 The advocate must not abuse his role

This requirement is specifically stated in rC3.2 and expanded upon in rC7.1–4.

2.4.1 Insulting people

It would be an abuse of one's role to make a statement or ask a question *merely* with the aim of insulting, humiliating, or annoying a witness (or any other person). If you have a different aim but your question or statement may have the incidental effect of insulting, etc, you will not be prohibited from asking it.

One example might be taken from the criminal prosecution of two sisters, Elisabetta and Francesca Grillo, in 2013. The two women had been personal assistants employed by a couple, Charles Saatchi and Nigella Lawson, to assist with the family and in particular Ms Lawson and the children. In December 2013, the sisters were tried in the Crown Court on a charge of fraud, having spent over £650,000 on credit cards belonging to Lawson and Saatchi. Their defence was that Nigella Lawson had agreed to their spending. This would seem rather unbelievable at first blush, so they supplied a motive for her to agree with their spending, namely that they had agreed in return not to inform her husband about her cocaine use. Clearly then, in order to run that defence, it would be necessary for the defence advocate to cross-examine Nigella Lawson on her drug consumption. The result of that was that when Ms Lawson was called as a prosecution witness, she was subjected to lengthy cross-examination about her personal life, her relationship with Charles Saatchi, her previous marriage to John Diamond, and her consumption of illegal drugs, an experience that she subsequently described as 'deeply disturbing' and one that had 'maliciously vilified' her (according to BBC News, 20 December 2013). We should note that the trial judge did not prevent this line of cross-examination; indeed, it was essential to the sisters' defence. They were acquitted but even if they had not been, this would still have been a central and highly relevant line of questioning to put to this witness *notwithstanding* that it left her distressed, facing a possible police investigation, and with an embargo on entering the USA due to her admissions of drug-taking.

2.4.2 Making a serious allegation against someone

This is closely connected to the preceding obligation. An advocate must not make a serious allegation against any person (not simply someone who is a witness in the proceedings), or, in particular, suggest that someone else is guilty of the crime with which the advocate's client is charged, unless that allegation is relevant either to the client's case or to a witness's credibility. In addition, there must be reasonable grounds to support the allegation, although usually it will be sufficient to have instructions from the client that the allegations are true. Finally, if the allegations concern someone who is not a party to the proceedings, the advocate should not name them in open court unless it is reasonably necessary to do so. That is no doubt because they are not present or represented in the proceedings and so are unable to defend themselves or protect their reputation.

2.4.3 Putting your case

Rule rC7.2 makes it clear that the advocate will not be allowed to make a serious allegation about a witness whom the advocate has had the chance to cross-examine unless he gave that witness the chance to answer the allegation during cross-examination. This is commonly known as the duty to 'put your case'. Again, one can see that this is connected to the preceding two points: it is by definition a serious allegation and so it needs to be both relevant to the client's case and based on reasonable grounds (rC7.3); further, if it satisfies those requirements, it may be insulting or annoying but it will be a topic which is necessary to address in the proceedings (rC7.1). So, what does this specific rule add?

There are two key points here. First, if you want to make a serious allegation against someone who is appearing as a witness in the proceedings, you must give them the chance to give their account of the allegation. They may accept the allegation but offer an innocent explanation for it, or they may deny it, or they may just agree with it. The point here is that the advocate has to give them the chance to respond to the allegation. This is partly a matter of fairness but it is also a matter of allowing the court to hear both sides on the point, the better to make an informed decision. Secondly, if the advocate fails to 'put the case' and to give the witness a chance to respond, then the advocate will not be allowed to rely on that allegation. Thus, the point will be barred and any argument that is based upon the allegation cannot be made in the proceedings. This can be quite damaging to one's case, of course. If need be, and if it is possible to do so, one might ask for the witness to be recalled to the witness box so that the point can be addressed properly. In effect, the advocate would be asking for permission to re-open cross-examination and so, if permission is granted, the advocate who called the witness should be allowed a further opportunity to re-examine on any matters arising from the new questioning. The judge may decide not to recall the witness, though, and if so then the point is lost. If the judge does allow the witness to be recalled, the cross-examiner may find himself liable for wasted costs, flowing from the original failure. The obligation to put your case to material witnesses in cross-examination is so fundamental that a failure to do so will almost certainly be an innocent oversight, rather than a deliberate attempt to dodge the matter.

2.4.4 Personal opinions

This is fairly straightforward. The advocate is simply required to present the evidence in accordance with his instructions from the client (subject to not misleading the court, of course). The law is whatever case law and statutes say it is. No one is concerned with the advocate's belief in the evidence, as noted earlier. Nor is it relevant whether the advocate agrees with the legal principles being advanced in the proceedings. The law is the law and one can argue about its scope, its applicability, and its interpretation but no one is interested in the advocate's opinion of whether it is good or bad law. So, rC7.4 states that the advocate must not put forward his *personal* opinion of the facts or the law *unless* the court invites him to do so or he is required to do so by law.

Behaving ethically

3.1 Introduction

The outcomes here build upon those seen in **chapter 2**. Once again, we see the emphasis on the need to ensure the proper administration of justice, whilst the best interests of the client are re-iterated. In addition, this time we must ensure access to justice, so this section looks at how that is to be achieved. Those who are regulated by the BSB must maintain the standards of honesty, integrity, and independence which run throughout these provisions (see CD3 and 4). In order to maintain these standards, it is necessary to understand them; to assist the advocate, it is important that the client understands these obligations as well (oC9). Finally, regulated persons must ensure that they do not engage in unlawful discrimination themselves and they should also take steps to avoid discrimination occurring in their practices. So, for example, they need to look at chambers' policies and procedures and make sure that these are non-discriminatory (see CD8; also, the Supporting Information for Chambers BSB Handbook Equality Rules).

The Professional Statement includes the following:

2.3 Be aware and active in the pursuit of equality and respect for diversity, not tolerating unlawful discrimination, in themselves or others.

They will understand the law on equality and the need to value differences between members of society and apply that understanding in the workplace through taking positive steps to confront and tackle discrimination, whether in themselves, in others or in the structures of that workplace.

Barristers should:

(a) Actively observe and uphold the law on equality, diversity and discrimination.

(b) Be alert to the potential for unconscious bias.

(c) Take active steps to act fairly and inclusively and show respect to others.

(d) Identify situations where there is a risk of breach of the law on equality and diversity.

(e) Promote diversity in the workplace and where appropriate challenge others if their behaviour does not comply with the spirit of the law relating to equality, diversity and discrimination.

3.2 Honesty, integrity, and independence

These three requirements are established directly by Core Duties 3 and 4. Rule rC8 goes further and states that an advocate must not do anything that could be seen by a member of the public as undermining these professional standards (and see CD5 for the importance of public perception). So, the appearance of honesty is just as important as actually behaving honestly. Indeed, so important are these standards that gC14 advises us that the advocate's duty to act in the best interests of the client is subservient not only to CD1 (duty to the court) but also to CD3 and 4 (reinforced by rC16, in section C3 'You and your client').

As one might expect, there are several more specific rules to assist the advocate (especially in rC9). In order to act with honesty and integrity, the advocate *must not*:

- knowingly or recklessly mislead *anyone* or attempt to do so (cf rC3.1—not mislead the court)

- draft a statement of case, a witness statement, an affidavit, or any other document which contains:
  - any statement of fact which is unsupported by his client or by his instructions
  - any contention which he does not consider to be properly arguable
  - any allegation of fraud, unless the advocate has (i) clear instructions from the client to make this allegation and (ii) reasonably credible material to establish an arguable case of fraud
  - any statement of fact which is not what he reasonably believes the witness would say if giving evidence orally (this applies when drafting witness statements or affidavits)
- encourage a witness to give evidence which is misleading or untruthful (cf rC6.2—not knowingly call an untruthful witness)
- rehearse, practise, or coach a witness on the evidence that they will give
- communicate about the case with any witness (including the client) whilst they are giving their evidence, unless the opponent or court gives permission to do so
- make or offer any payment to any witness which is contingent on either the evidence they will give or the outcome of the case
- propose or accept any fee arrangement which is illegal (see rC9; for example, paying or receiving a referral fee).

3.3 Money, gifts, and the advocate

Plainly, a number of the don'ts set out in 3.2 relate to money and it is easy to see how one's independence might be affected (or at least be reasonably seen to be affected) by dealings with money, or its equivalent. So, the guidance here indicates that the barrister must not offer or give a commission or a referral fee to a client or professional client or an intermediary, regardless of the amount involved (and see rC10; but note that gC21 provides a very limited exception for an *employed* barrister—he may pay or receive a referral fee where permitted to do so by either his employer or the approved regulator). The barrister should also avoid giving them gifts, other than items of modest value, or giving or lending them money; and should not accept any money from them unless it is payment for professional services or reimbursement of expenses. This can be a challenge to a barrister who wants to help a client in distress. For example, in 2014 an experienced junior barrister who was representing a client in a criminal case gave the client £300 when she told him that she could not afford to buy food or pay for electricity. Subsequently, he gave her a further £2,000 so that she could buy clothes and take a course at college. One might regard these as acts of charity. However, the matter came before a disciplinary tribunal which found the barrister to have acted in breach of two Core Duties—CD4 on maintaining one's independence and CD5 relating to public confidence in barristers.

If the barrister is offered a gift, and this does sometimes happen, she should assess the size of the gift and the circumstances in which it is being offered, and she should then consider how acceptance of the gift might appear to others, bearing in mind the need to be independent and have integrity. If the circumstances are such that it might lead others to question her independence, the gift should be politely declined. Always be courteous. The gift may be offered by a current client, a former client, or a prospective client and arguably the decision whether or not to accept may be partly dependent on which of these categories applies. Of course, the gift may be offered by a professional client or someone else with whom the barrister has a professional connection or who wishes to have such a connection with the barrister. As the circumstances shift, so may the proper decision on acceptance or refusal.

It sometimes happens that at the conclusion of a successful case, the client offers to treat his lawyers to a slap-up meal. In many instances, that may mean at best a curry at the local

Indian; on rare occasions, it may mean an opportunity to indulge in fine dining. In both instances the same principles apply—whether one is being entertained in this way, or offering it to another, how might it appear to an outsider? If it could reasonably be seen as compromising the barrister's independence, it should not take place.

The guidance suggests that these sorts of dilemmas are perhaps more pertinent to the self-employed barrister (gC21).

3.4   Other ways to compromise your independence and integrity

Engaging in criminal conduct is an obvious way to fall foul of CD3 (acting with honesty and integrity) and CD5 (behaving in a way likely to diminish public confidence in oneself or in the profession). *Minor* criminal offences are unlikely to count here; this term is defined in Part 6 (and gC28) as including (a) fixed-penalty road traffic offences in the UK, (b) offences anywhere which are dealt with in a substantially similar way as a fixed-penalty offence, or (c) an offence whose main ingredient is the unlawful parking of a motor vehicle. As can be seen then, these are very minor crimes indeed. Sadly, barristers are not immune from engaging in more serious behaviour as well. For example, just in March 2020, three barristers were sanctioned for infringing CD5 by being convicted of (i) breaching a non-molestation order, (ii) assaulting another, and (iii) assaulting another and then failing to surrender to custody at the magistrates' court.

Engaging in seriously offensive or discreditable conduct towards third parties is likely to damage one's integrity (gC25.4). This might include comments on social media, so one should pay attention to the BSB Guidance document on the use of social media. For example, in 2019 a barrister was suspended from practice for breaching CD5; a disciplinary tribunal found that he had posted a number of 'offensive and disparaging' comments about a member of the public on a Facebook chat forum, including matters of a sexual and/or violent nature.

Behaving dishonestly will necessarily affect one's commitment to honesty. So, lying to a client would be an obvious example. However, we must keep dishonesty and integrity distinct from each other. In *Wingate & Evans v Solicitors Regulation Authority and SRA v Malins* [2018] EWCA Civ 366, the Court of Appeal held that dishonesty and a lack of integrity are not the same thing. In fact, in the context of a professional code of conduct, 'integrity' is 'a useful shorthand to express the higher standards which society expects from professional persons and which the professions expect from their own members . . . Integrity connotes adherence to the ethical standards of one's own profession. That involves more than mere honesty . . .'. Nevertheless, there are limits—the court observed that one's duty to act with integrity 'does not require professional people to be paragons of virtue. In every instance, professional integrity is linked to the manner in which that particular profession professes to serve the public.' Although these conjoined appeals both involved solicitors, the principles clearly also apply to the Bar. For example, in 2015 a barrister persuaded her clerk to write to an instructing solicitor, saying that the barrister could not accept a brief because the hearing clashed with a hospital appointment to undergo a medical procedure. That was untrue and its purpose was to enable the barrister to attend a different professional appointment. By causing the statement to be made, the barrister fell foul of CD3—the duty to act with honesty, and with integrity, as well as CD5. The result of the statement was that the solicitor, the court, and other party were all misinformed (to put it nicely) and that hearing was adjourned. Thus, in addition, there was another breach of CD5 and the court had been misled, knowingly or recklessly, contrary to rC3.1.

Unlawfully victimising someone or harassing them is likely to be seen as not acting with integrity or diminishing public confidence and trust. If one victimises or harasses another on the basis of a protected characteristic (within the Equality Act definitions), then this would infringe provisions in the BSB Equality Rules Handbook, as well as probably being 'serious misconduct' within gC96 and illegal. See also rC12. More generally, harassment can be a criminal offence, contrary to the Protection from Harassment Act 1997. For example, in 2017 a barrister was convicted of two offences of harassment against his partner, resulting in a suspended prison sentence. That was, of course, also a breach of CD5 and it led subsequently to him being disbarred from the profession.

Abusing one's professional position is wrong; an example of how this might be done is to fall foul of the 'do you know who I am?' syndrome. So, using chambers notepaper to write to the man who services your partner's car, to complain about the cost of the new tyres, might be seen as an abuse. If you are dealing with someone in your professional capacity, then of course they need to know what that capacity is. If you are dealing with someone in your personal capacity, you should not try to intimidate them by referring to your profession. You may well have legal knowledge that they don't, and of course you can use that. But what you mustn't do is try to bully people because 'I'm a barrister, I'll have you know.' See gC26.

Apart from criminal behaviour and the 'abuse' situations identified earlier, usually the BSB is not interested in a barrister's personal or private life unless it might diminish the trust placed by the public in the barrister or the profession as a whole (see CD5).

3.5 Media comment

Since 2013, the BSB's position is that barristers have freedom of expression so that 'the starting point is that barristers are free to make comments to or in the media'. This freedom is nevertheless constrained by various considerations: first, the need to act in the client's best interests; secondly, the need to preserve one's professional independence and integrity; thirdly, the need to not conduct oneself in such a way as to diminish public trust and confidence in the individual barrister or the profession; finally, the need to preserve the confidentiality of the client unless given permission to make a particular disclosure. All of these elements are present in the Code of Conduct (and see gC22).

Practising barristers are under no prohibition from expressing a personal opinion in the media relating to any current or future proceedings in which they are briefed, or their past cases. The point is made though that practising barristers must still ensure that any comment they make does not, and is not seen as, undermining their professional independence. Furthermore, comments should not bring the profession, or a fellow barrister, into disrepute. Important points include the need for each barrister to weigh up the nature and type of proceedings involved, the stage that has been reached, and the need to ensure that any comment could not prejudice the administration of justice. The barrister should also consider whether any comment might require the client's consent because of issues around confidentiality or professional privilege. An ill-judged comment could cause unintended harm to the client's interests. Finally, the barrister should remember that although he is now generally free to comment to the media, he is under no obligation to do so and could not be criticised for declining an invitation to comment. If the barrister is instructed by the client to make a statement to the media on the client's behalf, this is quite a different situation but the barrister still should probably bear in mind all of the factors identified above. The barrister also needs to be aware that comments that relate to current or future proceedings could seriously prejudice those proceedings. Should this occur, the barrister may face contempt proceedings but it is possible that he or she may also face costs consequences as well as possibly having to withdraw from the case. Proceed with caution.

3.6 Referral fees

As noted earlier, referral fees are generally unacceptable for BSB regulated persons. This is stated plainly in rC10—you must not pay or receive referral fees. *Referral fee* is defined in Part 6 as 'any payment or other consideration made in return for the referral of professional instructions by an intermediary'. In another era, this might have been described as 'touting for business' or 'you scratch my back and I'll scratch yours'. As the Professional Practice Committee of the Bar Council put it in 2012, at best referral fees can limit a client's choice of advocate, at worst they can lead to a client receiving a substandard service; where a solicitor expects a referral fee to be paid by a barrister in return for instructing them, that solicitor will be incentivised to brief advocates based on economic criteria rather than on which advocate would provide the best representation for the lay client (legalfutures.co.uk, 30 October 2012). Anyway, it is forbidden and gC29 makes it clear that getting involved with such payments is inconsistent with the barrister's obligations under Core Duties 2, 3, 4, and possibly 5!

If that is not enough, the legal position should deter the barrister from any meddling with referral fees. If the case is publicly funded, then the standard terms of the Legal Aid Agency's Unified Contract expressly prohibit a contract holder from paying or receiving a referral fee; the lay client's knowledge of and/or consent to the payment of the fee is irrelevant. Furthermore, regardless of how a case is being funded, a referral fee to which the lay client has not consented may constitute a bribe and would thus be a criminal offence under the Bribery Act 2010—clearly not something the barrister should be involved with. Finally, if the case involves a claim for damages in a personal injury or fatality matter, then referral fees and inducements are prohibited by the Legal Aid, Sentencing and Punishment of Offenders Act 2012, s 56 (see also Criminal Justice and Courts Act 2015, s 58). See gC30.

There are exceptions though. Payment for the provision of a particular service, for example a barrister's clerks' fees, are not referral fees. This would also cover payments for advertising and publicity, where they are payable regardless of whether any work is generated for the barrister as a result. However, where a payment is linked to, or conditional upon, or will vary in amount according to, the receipt of instructions—these usually *are* referral fees and are prohibited. Applying those criteria, we can see that clerks' fees are an exceptional arrangement. Guidance gC31.3 states that the fact that a fee varies with the amount of work received does not necessarily make it a referral fee, so long as it is a genuine payment for a marketing service and the person who provides that service is not directing work to one lawyer rather than another, according to who is paying him more. See gC29–32; also the BSB guidance on referral 'Referral and marketing arrangements guidance', issued October 2019.

3.7 Giving an undertaking

This is relatively straightforward. When a barrister gives an undertaking in the course of conducting litigation, then he must comply with it either by an agreed deadline or else within a reasonable period of time (rC11). He should also have adequate insurance cover for any liability he may incur as a result of giving the undertaking (gC33). In other words, an undertaking is a serious matter, not to be given lightly, and with potentially damaging consequences if it is not adhered to.

3.8 **Non-discrimination**

Core Duty 8 prohibits unlawful discrimination. Rule rC12 unpacks this to make it crystal clear. The barrister must not discriminate unlawfully against, or victimise or harass, any other person on grounds of:

- race
- colour
- ethnic or national origin
- nationality
- citizenship
- sex
- gender re-assignment
- sexual orientation
- marital or civil partnership status
- disability
- age
- religion or belief
- pregnancy and maternity.

The Handbook guidance gC34 refers the reader to supporting information on the BSB Handbook Equality Rules. Guidance gC34 also refers to rule rC110, in section D1.2 of Part 2. This section (which is not itself assessable) deals with equality and diversity. Briefly, rC110 requires the barrister to take reasonable steps to ensure that his or her chambers have a written policy statement on equality and diversity accompanied by a written implementation plan and that numerous specific requirements are complied with in chambers. These include: the use of fair and objective criteria in recruitment and selection processes (clearly relevant to pupillage and tenancies as well as the appointment or dismissal of chambers' employees), the appointment of (at least) one equality and diversity officer, fair access to work (including the fair distribution of work opportunities amongst pupils and members of chambers), policies on parental leave and flexible working, and a written anti-harassment policy.

It is important not to confuse these rules, which are about non-discrimination in its usual sense, with rule rC28. This rule is titled 'Requirement not to discriminate' but it does not address non-discrimination on the protected characteristics. Its aim is a broader one—to provide that a barrister must not withhold his services from a prospective client where his reason for doing so is either:

(a) that the client is objectionable to him or to a section of the public or

(b) that the conduct, opinion, or beliefs of the prospective client are unacceptable to him or to a section of the public or

(c) based on the source of any financial support which is being given to the client in connection with the proceedings.

For example, a barrister may feel that publicly funded work does not pay as well as work which is paid for by a client. However, to turn work down on that basis is not permissible. See gC88.

3.9 Foreign work

As defined in Part 6 of the Handbook, *foreign work* means legal services (of whatever nature) which relate to court or other legal proceedings which are taking place (or are contemplated to do so) outside England and Wales. It also covers legal services related to any matter, or contemplated matter, which is not subject to the law of England and Wales, where there are no such proceedings. *Legal services* include providing legal advice, representation, and drafting or settling any statement of case, witness statement, or other legal document.

The Handbook at rC13 requires a barrister who undertakes foreign work to abide by any applicable rule of conduct which is laid down either by the law or by any national or local Bar of the place where the work is to be performed and the place where any proceedings or matters to which the work relates are taking place, unless any such rule is inconsistent with anything required by the Core Duties.

For example, English-qualified barrister George provides legal advice in Athens to a client who is being sued in Delaware, USA. George must comply with Greek legal requirements on lawyers' conduct and the professional requirements of the Greek Bar and the Athens Bar. George must also comply with the equivalent obligations under US federal provisions and the Delaware state Bar. Unlikely as it is that anything here will be incompatible with the BSB Core Duties, in the event of a conflict George must abide by the Core Duties.

If George had got this work as the result of soliciting work outside of England and Wales, then he should take care to do it in ways that would not be prohibited for members of the local Bar where the soliciting took place. The onus is on George to inform himself about the relevant conduct rules. See rC14 and gC35.

You and your client

4.1 Introduction

Extract from the Professional Statement:

> 3.1 **Understand and exercise their duty to act in the best interests of their client.**
>
> They will apply this core barrister's duty in every case except where it conflicts with their duty to the court in the administration of justice.
>
> Barristers should:
>
> (a) Provide a competent standard of work and service to each client [CD7].
>
> (b) Identify the client's best interests in accordance with the client's lawful instructions.
>
> (c) Recognise and evaluate any conflict between the client's best interests and their duty to the court, their obligation to act with honesty and integrity and to maintain their independence.
>
> (d) Ensure that subject to (c) above they do not act contrary to the client's lawful instructions.
>
> (e) Act in accordance with the Code of Conduct and other applicable rules and regulations.

Part 2, section C3 'You and your client' is a fundamentally important section of the Handbook and the Code of Conduct. The relationship between barrister and client lies at the core of what we do and how we do it. It is of course reflected in Core Duty 2—'you must act in the best interests of each client'. As we have seen already in earlier chapters, this Core Duty is subservient to others, not least the duty owed to the court, but also the need to act with honesty and integrity, and to maintain your independence. This hierarchy is made explicit in rC16. The balance between these core duties is a thread running throughout the Handbook Part 2, section C3. Probably, from the client's perspective, the 'bottom line' here is to be found in the two outcomes oC10 and 11: clients must receive a competent standard of work and service, and their best interests must be protected and promoted by those who act for them.

4.2 Personal responsibility

Any practising barrister is personally responsible for his own conduct (how he behaves towards others as well as how he conducts his life) and for his professional work. It matters not whether he is a self-employed barrister in chambers or is acting in an employed capacity. This does not mean that particular tasks cannot be delegated or outsourced but the barrister remains personally responsible for the work done. Similarly, the barrister is responsible for the service provided to the client by others who represent him, such as his clerks. Making any necessary adjustments, these principles apply equally to pupils and to registered European lawyers. See further rC20 and guidance gC64–8.

4.3   Duty to act in the best interests of your client

4.3.1   Introduction

As noted earlier, the obligation to act in your client's best interests comes in Core Duty 2. One aspect of this is the obligation to promote fearlessly and by all proper and lawful means the best interests of the client (rC15.1). This obligation has been carried straight over from the previous edition of the Code of Conduct. As well as applying CD2, it also picks up CD4 as the duty to be independent could include resisting external pressures to advise or act in a particular way that contradicts what you perceive to be in the client's best interests. We should also note that the duty under CD2 is to act in the *best* interests of the client, thus there may be some need to consider and prioritise competing interests of the client; it is also slightly paternalistic in that the barrister may justifiably substitute his own opinion for the client's opinion about what is in the client's best interests.

The need to be independent and free from pressure in order to do the best by the client is also shown by rC15.2–4. Here, we see that the barrister must put the client's best interests above his own and regardless of any consequences which may befall him or anyone else. The barrister is not to allow anyone—for example, a professional client or an employer—to limit his own discretion as to how best to serve the client's interests. If the barrister can see that he is likely to be compromised in his representation of a *prospective* client because of instructions he has received from other current or former clients (often related to his knowledge of confidential information, see **4.5**), he must not accept the new instructions—he cannot operate with limitations (rC21.1). These rules put the barrister into a very powerful yet responsible and isolated position vis-à-vis the client once he has accepted the instructions to act for the client. The need to act in a client's best interests is perhaps heightened when the barrister represents a vulnerable client; it may even be that additional expertise is required (oC14; gC41; and see **4.7**).

4.3.2   Not misleading the client

According to the Handbook, it is always in the client's best interests to be informed about *who* is working on their case, *what* they are doing, and *how* they will be doing it (rC19 and gC53). The barrister must explain clearly to the client the nature and scope of the legal services he will be providing and the terms on which those services will be provided. The client must get a clear statement that the barrister is entitled to provide those services. It must be clear who will do the work on the case and the basis on which the work will be charged. Care needs to be taken on this point where any work is done by a pupil or a 'devil' (gC59). 'Devilling' describes an arrangement whereby one member of chambers arranges for some of his work to be undertaken by a fellow member (his 'devil' and usually more junior) on the basis that he will pay the fellow member for the work, and he will remain responsible to the client for that work as if he had done it himself. A pupil must be careful not to hold himself out to other people as if he were a member of chambers or permit himself to appear as such, for example in the information publicly displayed at the entrance to chambers. Clients must not be misled over a pupil's status (gC62). Finally, a client or prospective client must not be misled about the extent of any insurance cover in case of professional negligence by the barrister (gC60).

It is possible that a client may be misled about some of these matters by the appearance of a chambers' 'brand', perhaps when paying a visit to chambers' premises or looking on the chambers' website. The Handbook suggests that this is a particular concern where 'unsophisticated lay clients' are dealing directly with 'a set of chambers' (gC56). So, there needs to be special care taken by a set of chambers whose members undertake public access work. There may be a large pool of such clients and the potential for confusion may not be limited to situations where the client is a public access client (see **chapter 7**). In any event, the possibility of being misled can be reduced if the chambers (or the individual barrister) explains that the members of chambers are not responsible for each others' work but are self-employed individuals. A similar problem can arise through advertising, so care needs to be taken there too. The Handbook advises that special care should be taken about comparative advertising as this 'may often be regarded as misleading' (gC57). At least one notable practising barrister has fallen foul of this, making claims on websites which he was unable to substantiate (his website contained a client testimonial that he could 'get Stevie Wonder a driver's licence') and subsequently facing disciplinary hearings for breaching Core Duty 5.

Concern from a different perspective about the need to have clarity for clients has led to another significant change that was made by the BSB in 2019—the introduction of new 'Transparency Rules'.

4.3.3 The Transparency Rules

Influenced by a recommendation from the Competition and Markets Authority that legal regulators should 'deliver a step change in standards of transparency for consumers', the BSB introduced new 'Transparency Rules'. These came through amendments to the Handbook (new section Part 2, D6) and further guidance documents. These changes took effect in July 2019. In essence, their aim is, as oC36 states, that:

> Clients are provided with appropriate information to help them make informed choices and understand the price and service they will receive.

There are mandatory transparency rules which must be followed by all self-employed barristers, chambers, and BSB entities. They apply to the website of the self-employed barrister or chambers. The website must:

- State that professional, licensed access, and/or lay clients (as appropriate) may contact the barrister/chambers/BSB entity to get a quotation for legal services
- Give contact details
- State the models most commonly used by the barrister/chambers/BSB entity for pricing legal services (for example, fixed fee or hourly rate)
- State those practice areas where the barrister/chambers/BSB entity most commonly provides legal services
- State the legal services that are most commonly provided and identify factors that can affect the timescale within which those services are provided
- Display 'regulated by the Bar Standards Board' on the homepage
- Display information about the complaints procedure, any right to complain to the Legal Ombudsman, how to do so, and any time limits for a complaint
- Link to the Legal Ombudsman's website on decision data and to the Barristers' Register page on the BSB website.

In addition to the mandatory rules for all, there are further transparency rules for those barristers who undertake public access work. Here, the website must link to the BSB website and the 'Public access guidance for lay clients' page. Where a barrister offers his services for advice and representation in the following areas:

- Employment Tribunal cases
- financial disputes arising out of divorce
- immigration appeals (First-Tier Tribunal)
- Inheritance Act advice
- licensing applications for business premises
- personal injury claims
- summary-only motoring offences
- winding-up petitions

there will be specific additional transparency requirements to meet.

In summary, the public access barrister's website must then:

- state which pricing models are being used (for example, fixed fee or hourly rate)
- give indicative fees and identify any factors that might cause a variation in them
- state whether the fees include VAT
- state any likely additional costs (for example, court fees), what would be covered and either the cost or, if estimating, the typical range for such costs
- identify and describe the relevant public access services, showing key stages and an indicative timescale for them.

4.3.4 Conflicts of interest

There are several relationships which *could* give rise to a conflict of interest, or at least the risk of one. There could be a conflict between the client's interest and:

- the interests of the barrister
- the interests of another client of the barrister—whether past, present, or prospective
- the interests of the professional client, if there is one
- the interests of anyone else.

That the barrister's interests are subservient to those of the client can be seen, for example, in oC16, which states that a barrister must not accept, refuse, or return instructions where this would have an adverse effect on the administration of justice, access to justice, or the best interests of the client. Further, rC17 requires the barrister to consider whether the client's best interests are served by having different legal representation (that could include someone other than this barrister) and, if the barrister considers this to be so, he *must* advise the client of this opinion. This applies where the barrister considers that he should be replaced by another (perhaps more senior, more junior, or just one with different expertise)—an obvious example of putting the client first. It also applies where the barrister thinks that the client needs to be represented by more lawyers, or fewer, or by different solicitors. The latter may arise where the barrister thinks that the solicitor has been professionally negligent. Where this occurs, the barrister must tell the client about this; this is an example of giving primacy to the client's interests over those of the professional client (gC51). There is a particular example of this point when handling public access work: the barrister must consider whether the client should instruct a solicitor, either as well as the barrister or instead of the barrister. This may be a live issue where the work necessary to conduct the litigation is beyond the client's ability to discharge it effectively and the barrister is not authorised by the BSB to conduct litigation (see gC50 and **chapter 7**).

There is also a potential connection to the question of public funding. Public access work does not attract public funding, so any public access client will be paying privately for their barrister's services. However, if the lay client is eligible for public funding, they can apply for it and, if successful, they will be able to instruct a solicitor. Note: not a barrister. It may be that the solicitor will instruct a barrister but it may not be the same one as represented the client originally. So, in this chain of events, the public access barrister will lose the case (and the income) but the client will save money. Hence, it is an obligation on the public access barrister to consider at an early stage, and to keep under consideration, whether the client is eligible for public funding and if so to advise the client to that effect.

The barrister must not accept any instructions where there is a conflict between the barrister's own interests and those of his prospective client (rC21.2). Note that although rC21.2 refers to the *personal* interests of the barrister, this is typically understood as limited to his or her financial or pecuniary interests (for example, bank accounts, company shareholdings, or business interests) and it does not include, for example, the barrister's political beliefs or party affiliations, or recreational activities.

Where there is a conflict between the interests of a prospective client and those of an existing or past client, the barrister must not accept the new instructions unless all affected clients give informed consent to him acting for the new client (rC21.3). The same principle applies where a conflict arises between the interests of two or more current clients, or two or more prospective clients (gC37). The barrister must make full disclosure to everyone of the nature and extent of the conflict in order for them to (possibly) give their informed consent to his continuing to act. It may be that he can continue to act for all clients or only some of them but all must consent to him continuing. If one client does not consent, the barrister must refuse the instructions or return them, as appropriate (see further gC69, rC25, rC27). The duty to respect client confidentiality may mean that the barrister cannot make the necessary full disclosure to each client (see rC15.5 and **4.5**). In this situation, there is no possibility of informed consent, and the barrister will have no alternative but to refuse or return at least one set of instructions. It is important to bear in mind that the barrister has to be able to act in the best interests of each client as if he is the barrister's only client (see gC37); this applies generally but is particularly important where the barrister is acting (or has been sent instructions to act for) multiple clients in the same proceedings. In the situation where instructions are returned, the barrister would be under a duty to explain to the client(s) his reasons for withdrawal (see rC27) but would need to be oblique to maintain client confidentiality.

4.4 Providing a competent standard of work and service

Core Duty 7 obliges the barrister to provide a competent standard of work and service to each client. As we will see in **4.6**, notions of competence under this heading cross over into issues of when a barrister can properly refuse to accept instructions, as well as representing the need to act in the client's best interests (CD2). So, rC21.8–9 make it clear that a barrister must not accept any instructions where he is not competent to tackle the matter or lacks the experience necessary to do so. Also, he must refuse the instructions if he does not have enough time to do what needs to be done, unless it will nevertheless be in the client's best interests for him to accept the instructions and do his best to provide a competent level of service. This is only likely to apply where there is very little time left either to find an alternative barrister or for any such barrister to get to court or do whatever work is needed.

So, time management is important for barristers and it is a key aspect of providing a competent standard of work and service. If a barrister realises that he will be unable to complete the work that he has been instructed to do by an agreed deadline, or within a reasonable time if there is no specific deadline, he must tell the professional client (or the lay client if dealing directly with him). Obviously, concomitant with this is the obligation to read one's instructions promptly upon receipt in order to consider the question of how much time will be required to perform the work to a competent standard. Guidance gC38.4 highlights this duty and makes the additional point that timely reading of one's instructions is vital because there will often be a time limit for action or even a limitation period that might expire soon. If the barrister delays reading the case papers, by the time he realises the proximity of the deadline, it may already be too late. Clearly, it will not be in the client's interests to let those deadlines pass unfulfilled as the consequences may be extremely problematic for the client. The main aim here is to enable the client to make alternative arrangements so far as is possible or take any other steps which could protect the interests of the client (such as applying for an adjournment or an extension of time). The barrister has the same duty to inform others in situations where he realises that he simply will be unable to fulfil his commitment to the client at all; typically, this will arise where he has a diary clash and needs to be in two places at once. One of the clients will need to be informed—it may be possible to apply for an adjournment of the hearing or there may be a need to instruct another barrister to attend it. See generally rC18 and note that the BSB has issued a guidance document on avoiding diary clashes and how to handle one if it arises. This is related to CD10—the duty to take reasonable steps to manage your practice.

No less important in terms of standard of service to the client is the need to advise and explain matters to each client in terms that they will understand, regardless of whether this is done orally in a meeting or through providing written advice. This will have special significance when dealing with a vulnerable client (see **4.7**). When advising any type of client, sometimes bad news has to be given. This may need to be done face-to-face, either at court or at a meeting in chambers or in the offices of the professional client. Clearly, it will help the client if the possibility of the negative advice has been flagged up in advance as one would want to minimise any distress or upset that the client may feel on being told the bad news. It would also help if the barrister gives some thought to how the advice might affect the client and perhaps arranges for the meeting to be somewhere private, certainly if it takes place at a court building. In any event, the barrister should be mindful of the likely impact on the client and his possible reactions; try to see things from the client's perspective. The barrister should always act with courtesy and that is no less important in this type of situation. See generally gC38; also the Professional Statement at 3.3 'Respond appropriately to those from diverse backgrounds and to the needs and sensitivities created by individual circumstances'. Also Professional Statement 3.4 'Treat all people with respect and courtesy, regardless of their background or circumstances'.

The barrister is providing a specialist and expert service to each client and therefore needs to keep up to date and be well informed about legal developments. It is also necessary to maintain and seek to improve one's skill sets. This is another facet of the obligation to provide a competent service and standard of work. It really should go without saying that this process must go on continually throughout a professional career but the BSB has set down requirements for barristers to observe concerning their continuing professional development needs ('CPD'; see further **chapter 11** and the Professional Statement at 2.6). Guidance gC39 makes the point that CPD only establishes a base level for maintenance and improvement—in terms of maintaining one's ability to provide a competent standard of service, the barrister may well need to do more. Specific examples are given, of the need to undertake specialist training before the barrister can undertake advisory work at police stations or can handle public access work. Really these are forms of what might be called 'gateway' training, where the barrister cannot undertake that type of work at all until he or she is properly and effectively trained to do so. Perhaps the spirit of the guidance here is that the barrister should always be seeking to improve her knowledge, her know-how, and her abilities, to make the best of herself. If she can continue to do this it will be to the benefit of all her clients.

4.5 Client confidentiality

Extract from the Professional Statement:

> 4.5 Maintain the confidentiality of their client's affairs, adopting secure technology where appropriate.

Confidentiality is another matter of fundamental importance, as reflected in Core Duty 6—the barrister 'must keep the affairs of each client confidential'. To an extent, we have considered this matter already, as it can easily arise in the context of a conflict of interest between clients where it may mean that new instructions cannot be accepted due to the possible jeopardy to a current or former client's confidential information which requires protection. The duty is clearly a continuing one that carries on after the relationship of barrister and client has formally ended. The duty is fleshed out more in Part 2, section C3 of the Handbook; see, for example, rC15.5—the barrister 'must protect the confidentiality of each client's affairs, except for such disclosures as are required or permitted by law or to which your client gives informed consent'.

This obligation can cause tensions with CD1 (duty to the court) and CD2 (duty to protect best interests of the client) in particular. We have considered some aspects of this already, in **chapter 2** (for example, gC8–13, in the context of the duty not to mislead the court). Guidance now makes it clear that 'confidentiality is central to the administration of justice' (gC42). There is an echo here of CD1, where the duty owed to the court is 'in the administration of justice'. But the dilemma for the barrister is that there may be occasions where respecting client confidentiality leads to either the risk or the actuality that the court will be misled. The key principle is that, generally, the barrister must always respect the client's confidentiality; the same applies to the pupil of (or someone 'devilling' for) a self-employed barrister (gC46). In a position of dilemma, the Code solution is usually for the barrister to walk away—to return one's instructions and withdraw from the case. See, for example, rC25.2–3 (further at **4.6.3**). The solution is *not* to take it upon oneself to make the disclosure without the client's consent.

There are exceptions, though. As gC42 states, confidentiality will be respected in 'normal circumstances'. Rule rC15.5 itself allows disclosures to be made when they are 'required or permitted by law' regardless of client consent, as well as disclosures where the client gives informed consent. The latter of course does not impact on the client's expectation of confidentiality as the client has waived it in those circumstances. In terms of situations where *unsanctioned* disclosure is required or permitted by law, the Handbook gives two examples. First, where the anti-money laundering provisions in the Prevention of Crime Act 2002 require a barrister to report to the authorities concerns about possible money laundering activities undertaken by or on behalf of the client; see further **chapter 12**. Secondly, where the Handbook itself requires disclosure in breach of confidentiality—this may arise in the context of reporting *oneself* to the BSB for possible misconduct. The situation is different when considering reporting someone else for serious misconduct. A distinction needs to be made between confidential information and that which is subject to legal professional privilege—they are not the same thing. See further rC64, gC93, and rC66; **chapter 8**.

Another situation of practical concern for barristers is where the lay client is in receipt of public funding and the barrister discovers that the financial statement made by the client has understated his finances, to the extent that he may not actually be entitled to receive public funding at all. In this situation, the barrister should advise the client to inform the Legal Aid Agency of the true position. Given the likely loss of public funding if he follows this advice, and the likely consequent loss of his legal representative, the lay client may decide not to follow that advice. In this situation, the barrister has no choice and must withdraw from the case—the lay client is refusing to make a disclosure that the barrister has advised he must make (rC25.1). But the barrister's duty goes further than this—regulations made under the legal aid legislation make it clear that the lawyer is now under a duty to make the necessary disclosure to the Legal Aid Agency, *regardless* of the client's wishes. See, for example, SI 2013/457:

> *The relationship between a provider [lawyer] and a legally aided person, and any privilege arising out of that relationship, does not preclude the provider from disclosing relevant information to the Lord Chancellor or the Director for the purposes of enabling or assisting them to carry out their functions under Part 1 of the [Legal Aid, Sentencing, and Punishment of Offenders] Act [2012].*

Before leaving this topic, we must take note of rC21.4 and rC30: the barrister must not accept instructions where there is a real risk that a current (or former) client's confidential information will be relevant to a prospective client's case and the need to respect the existing confidentiality means that the barrister cannot act in the best interests of the prospective client. Further, in these circumstances, the 'cab rank' rule will not apply and the barrister is free (in fact, he is required) to decline the instructions from the prospective client (see rC21.4).

4.6 Accepting and returning instructions

As we have seen already in this chapter, there may be situations where the barrister cannot take on a case, for example due to a lack of competence in the subject matter or because of a conflict of interest. There will also be situations that arise only after the barrister has accepted the instructions and has perhaps begun to work on the case or has even done a substantial amount of work on it. A fatal problem may even occur in mid-trial. To an extent, the obligation to *accept* instructions finds its most obvious form in the existence and scope of the 'cab rank' rule (see **4.6.5**). What we will look at first are those circumstances where, for one reason or another, the barrister must in fact *refuse* to accept new instructions.

4.6.1   When the barrister must refuse instructions

This is governed primarily by rC21. The barrister is under an obligation not to accept instructions where:

- as the result of the instructions that one has from a current or former client, the barrister would not be able to act in the best interests of the prospective client
- there is a conflict of interest (or a real risk of one) between the barrister and the prospective client
- there is a conflict of interest (or a real risk of one) between current or former clients and the prospective client (and informed consent is not forthcoming from all clients involved)
- the barrister could not act in the best interests of the prospective client because of a real risk that confidential information of another client is relevant and that other client does not sanction its use or disclosure
- the instructions from the lay or professional client seek to restrict the barrister's freedom to use his own authority and discretion over matters in court, or for other reasons there is a real prospect that he may be unable to maintain his independence
- the instructions would require the barrister to break the law or act in breach of his obligations under the Handbook, contrary to his obligation to the administration of justice
- the work required by the instructions is work that the barrister is not authorised or accredited to carry out (for example, the conduct of litigation, where the barrister does not have the necessary litigation extension to his practising certificate; see **10.3.6**)
- the barrister is not competent to handle the work required by the instructions or lacks the experience to do so (a reflection of the requirement to provide a competent level of work)—this will be an especially important consideration when the prospective client is vulnerable (gC71; and see **4.7**)
- the barrister does not have enough time to deal with the matter, unless it would still be in the prospective client's best interests for him to undertake the work.

We can see that this list includes challenges to the barrister's independence (rC21.10). The Handbook gives the example of a barrister who receives instructions to act as the advocate for a client but there is a risk that the barrister may be called as a significant witness in the case. This barrister should not accept the instructions here unless his withdrawal might jeopardise the client's interests; if so, then he should not withdraw. This is likely to be a potential problem where the issue arises very shortly before the relevant hearing (possible non-acceptance of instructions) or in the course of a trial (possible withdrawal, having previously accepted the instructions). See gC73.

The final point in our list—refusing work where you do not have enough time—has an important exception, concerned with protecting the client's best interests as far as possible in the circumstances. Guidance gC72 makes the point that sometimes a barrister will receive instructions so late in the day or so close to the deadline or court hearing that 'no suitable, competent advocate would have adequate time to prepare'. In this situation, there would be no purpose in refusing to take the case, other than to cause even more delay and leave the client either with no representation at all or with a barrister even less prepared than this one could be.

4.6.2   Setting the terms on which instructions are accepted

Please read this section in conjunction with the section on the new Transparency Rules (at **4.3.3**).

4.6.2.1   Notifying the terms

When a barrister first accepts instructions in a matter, it is important to give written confirmation of the acceptance to either the professional client (if there is one) or the lay client; an email will suffice (see rC22). This confirmation must include the terms on which the barrister is acting and the basis on which he will charge the client, and the procedure for making a complaint about poor service, should that become relevant (gC78). Alternatively, the confirmation can direct the relevant client to the barrister's terms of service on chambers' website or to the standard terms of service which are set out on the Bar Council website (gC75). The confirmation ought to be provided before work commences unless it is for some reason not reasonably practical to do so (rC24). The barrister's clerk can give the confirmation on his behalf (gC77).

4.6.2.2 Varying the terms

If the client subsequently varies the instructions, there is no need to serve a fresh confirmation of acceptance as you will be deemed to have accepted on the same terms as before, unless it is specified to the contrary. See generally rC22–4 and gC75–82.

However, where a fundamental change is made to the basis of the barrister's remuneration, this should be treated as though the original instructions have been withdrawn and an offer of new instructions on different terms has been made (see gC87). In these circumstances, the barrister must first decide whether he is bound to accept the new instructions under the 'cab rank' rule. If he is so obliged, then he must accept them and that is an end to it. If he decides that he is not so obliged, then he may refuse the new instructions if he so chooses. If he does refuse the new instructions, this is not a return or withdrawal pursuant to rule rC25 or rC26 (see **4.6.3**) as the original instructions have been withdrawn by the client. On the 'cab rank' rule, see further **4.6.5**.

4.6.3 Returning your instructions

This topic can be divided into two sets of situations—those where the instructions *must* be returned, and those where they *may* be returned. The Handbook sometimes uses '*may*' where it plainly means '*must*' but here it is important to distinguish the two clearly.

4.6.3.1 The instructions *must* be returned

Rule rC25 deals with situations where the barrister must return his instructions. It begins by cross-referencing all of the situations identified already where the barrister must not accept instructions (see rC21 and **4.6.1**). If one of these situations arises post-acceptance, then the same principle applies—the barrister must cease to act for the client and promptly return the instructions, including physically returning any paperwork supplied by the client. Rule rC25 adds three more situations to the original list:

- If the case is publicly funded but it becomes apparent to the barrister that this funding has been obtained wrongly, by either false or inaccurate information being supplied to the Legal Aid Agency, the barrister must draw this to the client's attention. If the client fails to take immediate action to rectify the position, the barrister must withdraw. (See also **4.5** on breaching client confidentiality in order to inform the Legal Aid Agency.)

- If the barrister becomes aware of information which his duty to the court requires him to disclose (remember that the barrister must not mislead the court), again, the barrister must draw this fact to the client's attention. If the client refuses to sanction the disclosure, the barrister must withdraw. (Here, the barrister must continue to respect client confidentiality.)

- If, during the course of the case, the barrister learns of a document which should have been disclosed as part of the usual disclosure requirements in the case but it has in fact not been disclosed, the need to disclose it should be drawn to the client's attention. If the client then fails either to disclose it himself, or to permit the barrister to disclose it, then the barrister must withdraw. (Again, client confidentiality must continue to be respected in this situation.)

Note that, in each of these three situations, the problem can be rectified by the client either making the appropriate disclosure or permitting the barrister to do so. Where neither of these events happens, the solution is usually *not* for the barrister to make an unsanctioned disclosure but instead he should withdraw from the case. Although the Handbook does not say so, the problem with public funding is actually an exception to the normal obligation to maintain client confidentiality. As we saw earlier, client confidentiality can be breached where required by law and this is a situation where the law does require that.

See further **4.6.4** on how to manage a withdrawal from a case.

4.6.3.2   The instructions *may* be returned

This situation is governed by rule rC26. The use of the term '*may*' in this rule might denote some element of discretion or choice on the part of the barrister. This interpretation is reinforced by the guidance gC83 which states that when the barrister makes a decision under rule rC26 he should ensure that the client is not adversely affected by withdrawal because there is insufficient time for the client to find other adequate legal assistance. If the client is likely to be adversely affected, then the barrister probably ought not to withdraw. That is subject to the overriding duty to the court which may mean that, regardless of the potential adverse effect to the client, the barrister actually has no alternative but to withdraw.

Rule rC26 sets out the grounds for possible withdrawal as follows:

- the professional conduct of the barrister is being called into question
- the client consents to withdrawal
- the barrister is a self-employed barrister and either
    - despite all reasonable efforts being made to avoid it, a hearing has become fixed for a date which he has already marked in his professional diary as one on which he is unavailable or
    - the barrister becomes unable reasonably to carry out the instructions because of illness, injury, pregnancy, childbirth, a bereavement, or something similar to any of these situations or
    - the barrister is unavoidably required to perform jury service
- the barrister's fees are not paid when due, the client has been notified of this fact, given the chance to rectify it, told of the likely consequences should he fail to rectify it, and he has failed to do so
- the barrister becomes aware of material which is relevant to the matter on which he is instructed but the material is confidential (or contained in privileged documents belonging) to another person
- the barrister is conducting litigation (performing the type of tasks that a solicitor would usually be doing, in a public access case), the client does not consent to the barrister ceasing to act in the matter but the court has approved the barrister's application to 'come off the record'
- there is 'some other substantial reason' for withdrawal (this reason for withdrawal can only be exercised subject to rC27–9).

The barrister should not use the 'non-availability' ground above (essentially the 'diary clash') to break an agreement to provide legal services in order to attend or fulfil a non-professional engagement of any kind other than those identified above. See guidance gC85.

There is a rather obscure reference in the list to the barrister becoming aware of another person's confidential or privileged information. This in fact covers the situation where the barrister has come into possession of such material inadvertently, typically where it has been sent to him (or sent to his instructing solicitor and then passed on to him) by the other side in error. This might include, and on occasion has included, confidential or privileged information such as unused witness statements, counsel's notes from a client conference, instructions to counsel, and counsel's written advice to the client. The guidance gC86 rather vaguely instructs the reader to have regard to relevant case law, including *English & American Insurance Co Ltd and ors v Herbert Smith* (1987) NLJ 148 and *Ablitt v Mills & Reeve (A Firm) and anor* (The Times 24 October 1995). What these cases might be said to indicate is that if the barrister realises the nature of what he has *before* reading it, he should not read it at all but should send it back to the other person unread. If he decides to read it, or begins to read it before realising its nature, there is a grave risk that when he does notify the opponent of the situation (remember he must not mislead any person: rC9.1), the opponent may apply for an injunction to prevent the barrister from continuing to act in the matter. So, in a sense, this reason for withdrawal is a little like the barrister sending himself off the field of play before the referee (or judge) does so!

4.6.3.3   Withdrawal of the professional client

There is a further situation to be aware of, although it is not addressed by either rC25 or rC26 and so it does not appear in the lists in **4.6.3.1** or **4.6.3.2**. Guidance gC84 applies where a barrister is working on a referral basis, meaning that he has been instructed by a professional client on behalf of a lay client. In this situation, if the professional client withdraws for any reason then the barrister is no longer instructed in the matter and cannot continue to act for the lay client. There are two exceptions to this requirement to cease to act—either (i) the barrister is then appointed to act for the lay client by the court that is dealing with the matter or (ii) he receives and accepts new instructions (from a new professional client or perhaps on a public access basis) to represent the lay client.

In a similar position under the old Code of Conduct, it was said that the barrister had 'a complete discretion' whether or not to carry on representing the lay client in this situation. Clearly, that position has been modified in the present scheme. If an offer of new instructions is forthcoming, no doubt this will need to be considered afresh but that should be done by applying the usual principles set out in rule rC21 (**4.6.1**) and subject to the 'cab rank' rule (**4.6.5**). Only if the court seeks to appoint the barrister might it still be said that he has a free choice of whether or not to accept the appointment as gC84 makes it clear that the 'cab rank' rule will not apply in this situation.

4.6.4   **How to handle withdrawal or the return of instructions**

4.6.4.1   The explanation

Rule rC27 states that, notwithstanding rules rC25 and 26, the barrister must not cease to act or return his instructions unless either he has his lay client's consent to this action or he has clearly explained, either to the professional client or lay client, his reasons for doing so. Given that often the lay client will be reluctant to see 'his' barrister departing the scene, either metaphorically or actually, a clear explanation is likely to be the usual method of handling the matter.

Plainly, rule rC25 says that the barrister must withdraw and offers plenty of cogent examples of situations where that makes perfect sense. It would be illogical to then give the lay client the power of veto over the barrister's withdrawal. That is not what rC27 does. It is suggested that it does not have that effect on the application of rule rC26 either. So, the upshot is that, whenever a barrister is withdrawing under either rC25 or rC26, he must first explain to the client(s) what he is doing and why. If after that has been done, the lay client consents, so be it. If he does not consent, that has no effect on the matter at all and the barrister will still withdraw.

4.6.4.2   Passing on the baton

When the barrister does withdraw, the lay client will be unrepresented (or at least under-represented) at least temporarily. No doubt, if so advised, he will seek to instruct another barrister to replace the one who has gone. What must not happen now is that the departing barrister simply returns his instructions to another barrister; it is not within his competence to make such a decision for the client(s). He can, of course, *suggest* to the client another particular barrister who he feels could properly represent the client instead of himself. Whether the client acts on that suggestion probably depends on the state of the relationship between the client and the departing barrister at that point. If and only if the lay or professional client consents to it can the departing barrister return his instructions to another one (see rC27.2). Otherwise, the departing barrister must do nothing else in the matter but simply return all case materials to the professional or lay client, as applicable.

4.6.5   The 'cab rank' rule and non-discrimination

The Handbook commences this subject with the non-discrimination principle (see rC28) and so shall we. In the course of one's professional practice, the barrister will probably encounter clients, lay and professional, for whom he does not care, or who he considers are unpleasant individuals. It may be that a prospective client has attracted considerable notoriety and public disapproval, and the barrister is afraid of the consequences for himself if he were to accept instructions to represent this individual and somehow be seen by a section of the public as being 'representative of' or in sympathy with this unattractive individual. The Bar has long held to the entirely commendable ideal that everyone is entitled to competent legal representation, regardless of their own nature, the nature of their case, the allegations against them, and a lawyer's personal feelings about them.

Nowadays, we have the Equality Act 2010 to provide a degree of protection against discrimination on the basis of a protected characteristic. That of course applies to the acceptance or refusal of instructions to provide legal services, just as it applies elsewhere. Rule rC28 sets out a broader principle though; it declares that the barrister must not withhold legal services for any of the following reasons:

- the nature of the case is objectionable to him or to any section of the public
- the conduct, opinions, or beliefs of the prospective client are unacceptable to him or to any section of the public
- the basis of funding for the instructions is not acceptable to him.

Generally, this should be quite clear and straightforward. The only matter which should require further explanation is the third prohibited reason—the financial basis for funding the case. In essence, what this says is that the barrister cannot refuse to take a publicly funded case, simply for that reason. See further guidance gC88.

The 'cab rank' rule is, it is suggested, something of which the Bar can rightly be proud (see rC29). The Legal Services Board ('LSB') commissioned research into the rule; the fascinating report that was published in January 2013 suggested that the rule was widely ignored or evaded, served no real purpose, and should be scrapped. The report noted, however, that the Bar 'strongly subscribes to it'. In response, the BSB published its own study, produced by barristers from Fountain Court chambers. In turn, this suggested that removal of the rule would constitute a major threat to justice. The then-Chair of the BSB, Baroness Deech, said that the rule gave everyone the chance to be represented by a barrister of their choice, which ought to help to ensure a fair trial. She added that the report's evidence showed that the rule protected the consumer (that is, the clients) and not the barrister, although the report did show that the rule helped to protect barristers from the wrath of the community as well. The Bar Council also published a report, written by Sir Sydney Kentridge QC, which was somewhat critical of the LSB's report, suggesting that its authors did not 'see the Bar as an honourable profession whose members generally obey the ethical rules of their profession, and who do not seek to evade them. Indeed, throughout the [LSB] Report one finds not merely hostility to the ['cab rank'] rule but hostility to the Bar and sneers at its ethical pretensions.' After these responses, the LSB agreed to look at the rule once more. As the Handbook was given LSB approval in 2013, some months after that exchange took place, one would assume that the LSB is content for the rule to remain in place in the form that it takes in Part 2, section C3. All three reports are available on the respective websites of the LSB, BSB, and the Bar Council.

As its name implies, if a barrister is available for hire, much like a London hackney cab with its yellow 'taxi' sign illuminated, then he must accept any client who hails him. Of course, it is a little more complicated than getting a taxi, although both barrister and cabbie will have areas into which they will not venture, like south of the river, for example. So, let us examine how the 'cab rank' rule operates for barristers.

The relevant rule is rC29. It is important to note at the outset that we are looking only at *referral* work—the rule only applies to self-employed barristers who receive instructions (the case is 'referred') from a professional client on behalf of a client. Therefore, it does not apply to public access work. 'Professional client' is to be given a broad interpretation; it should not be read as simply synonymous with 'solicitor'. This means that the 'cab rank' rule applies whenever a barrister is instructed by an authorised person who is regulated by another approved regulator. See the BSB guidance on the 'cab rank' rule: professional clients may be authorised persons even though they are not authorised by the Solicitors Regulation Authority, so long as they are regulated by another approved regulator.

If the instructions are appropriate to the barrister's experience, seniority, and field of practice then, unless there is a specific reason to disapply the 'cab rank' rule under rC30 (see **4.6.6**), the barrister must accept the instructions. This is the position regardless of the client's identity, the nature of the case, whether the client is paying privately or publicly, and irrespective of any belief or opinion that the barrister may have formed about the prospective client's character, reputation, conduct, cause, guilt, or innocence. This may well require the barrister to separate the personal from the professional; even a client that the barrister finds to be utterly unsympathetic and whose case is quite distasteful must be represented properly; indeed, this client must be represented 'fearlessly' and using 'all proper and lawful means' to protect his best interests (rC15.1). One might say that the 'cab rank' rule is a central plank of the commitment of both barrister and Bar to the administration of justice.

Having said that, as noted earlier, there are situations where the rule must be disapplied and it is to these that we now turn.

4.6.6   Disapplying the 'cab rank' rule

There are several grounds on which the 'cab rank' rule must be disapplied; they are set out in rule rC30.

First, the 'cab rank' rule is subordinate to rule rC21—all of those situations where the barrister must not accept instructions, largely on public interest grounds such as conflict of interest or maintenance of client confidentiality (see **4.6.1**). The 'must not accept' in rC21 overrides the 'must accept' in rC29.

Secondly, the 'cab rank' rule can be disapplied if the instructions require the barrister to perform an activity or provide a service 'other than in the course of their ordinary working time'. This is not explained in the guidance but it is tentatively suggested that it has its origins in the equality provisions as applied to the Bar. If one looks at the BSB Handbook Equality Rules (a separate publication which supports the Handbook), one can see that there are provisions in there about equality and diversity, obviously, but also specifically also covering issues around fair access to work, parental leave, and flexible and part-time working. It may be that this ground for disapplication is aimed at giving barristers with non-professional commitments the ability to juggle more of the demands on their time. Certainly, it has traditionally been the position that a self-employed barrister would work on a case for as long as it took; the notion of the EU Working Time Directive applying to such individuals would be well wide of the mark. But this mindset may be disadvantageous to some, especially those who simply cannot devote every waking moment to their professional practice. This ground for refusal may be an attempt to allow some degree of work/life balance to be achieved.

Thirdly, the rule can be disapplied if acceptance of the instructions would result in a diary clash. There needs to be another commitment already in the diary for this ground to apply.

Fourthly, the barrister cannot be obliged to accept the instructions if they create a significant potential for professional negligence liability, such that it could exceed the cover which is reasonably available and which is likely to be available for that barrister. This is quite a pragmatic reason to set aside the rule but it protects the client as well as the barrister.

Fifthly, there is no obligation to accept the instructions if doing so would require the barrister to undertake any foreign work, or to act for a foreign lawyer. Both of these terms are defined in Part 6 of the Handbook. A foreign lawyer is defined as 'a person who is a member, and is entitled to practice as such, of a legal profession regulated within a jurisdiction outside of England and Wales and who is not an authorised person for the purposes of the LSA'. The Handbook offers no guidance on this ground; presumably it is justified by the likely lack of competence on the part of the barrister. If he is in fact competent to undertake the work, then he can choose to do so.

Sixthly, the identity of the *professional* client may be a reason for not having to accept the instructions. If the professional client is instructing you as a lay client and thus not in their professional capacity, then the rule does not apply to these facts (because you would not be instructed on a referral basis). Next, if the professional client is not accepting liability for the barrister's fees, there is no obligation to accept the work. Why would you? Next, but related to the preceding reason, the barrister may refuse instructions if the professional client represents 'an unacceptable credit risk', in the barrister's reasonable opinion. Typically, this will arise if he is on the Bar Council's list of Defaulting Solicitors, that is solicitors who are problem payers. See gC91A.

Seventhly, the barrister can refuse to take a case if he has not been offered a proper fee for his services. What constitutes a proper fee is initially for the barrister to decide, usually in consultation with his clerk. Factors to consider include: how complex and difficult the case looks; how long it is likely to take; the barrister's ability, experience, and seniority; and the expenses that he will incur if he accepts the instructions (gC90). If a fee has been proposed by the professional client but the barrister does not respond within a reasonable time, then he cannot refuse the instructions on this ground (rC30.8). So, the onus will be on the barrister to act promptly or face being stuck with a poorly paid case. However, if the instructions are offered on the basis of either a conditional fee agreement or a damages-based agreement, then the barrister is entitled to refuse the instructions on the ground of not being offered a proper fee (gC91).

Eighthly, the barrister can refuse instructions where his fees have not been agreed (subject to the same caveat about prompt responses as above with the 'proper' fee exception). He can also refuse where he required his fee to be paid prior to acceptance of the instructions and the fee has not been paid. Lastly, he can refuse where acceptance would mean that he is required to act other than on the Standard Contractual Terms for the Supply of Legal Services by Barristers to Authorised Persons 2012, as published on the Bar Council's website, or on his own published standard terms of work (if applicable). None of these last three reasons for refusal can be used where the barrister is to be paid by either the Legal Aid Agency (public funding) or the Crown Prosecution Service.

In conclusion, this is rather a miscellany of grounds and it is impossible to see a common thread to them all. Most of them do seem to be justifiable in their own circumstances, aside perhaps from the foreign work embargo. It really is just a matter of knowing the list and therefore when the 'cab rank' rule could be disapplied. It is suggested that, given the Bar's strong attachment to the rule, it should be disapplied very infrequently, despite the long list of situations permitting a barrister to do just that.

4.7 Dealing with a vulnerable client

4.7.1 Barristers and vulnerable clients

It is important for barristers to know how to deal with vulnerable clients. Outcome oC14, under 'You and your client' in the BSB Handbook, stipulates that the barrister must be careful to ensure that the interests of vulnerable clients are considered and their needs are met. Guidance gC41 goes on to point out that *any* client may be unfamiliar with legal proceedings; he or she may also find them 'difficult and stressful'. The barrister bears a greater responsibility to consider such matters where the client is vulnerable. Communication is important as is managing expectations—the barrister should do what is reasonable here. Unnecessary distress for the client should be avoided if at all possible; where a topic or task is likely to cause distress but it is unavoidable, consideration should be given to how such distress might be minimised and the topic or task handled with sensitivity.

4.7.2   Vulnerability factors

According to the BSB guidance on public access, there are several factors which may mean that a client—or prospective client—is vulnerable. This is a particularly important issue for the 'public access' barrister to consider since there will only be the barrister and the lay client, and no professional client is involved. However, even where a barrister is instructed by a professional client on behalf of a vulnerable client, the vulnerability is still present and will need to be managed properly.

'Vulnerability' is to be interpreted *widely* but it can include factors falling within the 'protected characteristics' under the Equality Act. See the list of examples in para 25 of the public access guidance document. But it can also include the client's finances—can he or she bear the likely costs of litigation, for example? The client may be homeless, involved with substance abuse, an addict, illiterate, or traumatised by the matter at issue (for example, a case including a violent or sexual assault).

4.7.3   Public access work or a solicitor?

The lay client will need to take on the tasks that are usually performed by a solicitor unless the public access barrister is authorised to conduct litigation. The barrister will only be so authorised if he or she has a litigation extension to their full practising certificate. If the public access barrister does not have a litigation extension, one important consideration in deciding whether to accept the instructions from a public access client will be whether it is in the prospective client's best interests to instruct a solicitor (who *will* be able to undertake those tasks) instead of the barrister directly.

The fact that a prospective client is vulnerable does not mean automatically that he or she cannot be taken on as a public access client. It does mean that the barrister needs to identify any factors that make the client vulnerable and consider what steps will need to be taken so that the client has proper support and can fully understand any information—including legal advice—that the barrister passes on to him or her.

4.7.4   Rejecting instructions to act on behalf of a vulnerable client

Where the barrister is self-employed in private practice and is instructed by a professional client on behalf of a vulnerable client then, if the 'cab rank' rule in rC29 applies to the work, the barrister is obliged to accept it. The fact that the client is vulnerable is not of itself a valid reason for refusing the work.

However, rC30 states that the 'cab rank' rule is subject to any requirement imposed by rC21 to refuse the work. Rule rC21.8 says that the barrister must not accept instructions where he or she is not competent to handle the matter or otherwise does not have enough experience to handle it. Guidance gC71 explains that the competence and experience of the barrister includes his or her ability to work with vulnerable clients. Since vulnerable clients come in a wide variety of circumstances, this can only be determined on a case-by-case (or client-by-client) basis. The point here is that the vulnerable client is to be protected from representation by an incompetent or inexperienced barrister, not to excuse a barrister from having to represent a vulnerable client.

The 'cab rank' rule does not apply to public access practitioners, but rC28 does. So again, if the public access barrister is competent and capable of dealing with a vulnerable client, and it is not in that person's best interest to act through solicitors, then the work should not be refused purely on the basis that the client is vulnerable.

4.7.5   Interacting with a vulnerable client

Communication may be a particular problem when dealing with a vulnerable client. It may be that someone else is needed to facilitate communication with the client. This may be an interpreter for someone who does not speak or understand English. It may be someone who has a unique expertise for communicating with the client through previous experience. Often, this person will be a family member or someone from the client's community or circle of close friends.

Whilst the involvement of such a person may expedite effective communication, it is important to be aware of issues around client confidentiality and the potential for conflicts of interest to arise—a family member may find it difficult to be truly independent and objective, for example. Where the 'interpreter' is also directly involved in the proceedings, it will need very serious consideration as to whether that person is an appropriate channel of communication or whether there is a risk that they have their own interests to serve so that things get 'lost in translation'. Where there is an obvious danger of a conflict of interest arising between the client and the 'interpreter', or of confidential information being 'leaked', a different solution to the communication problem must be found.

4.7.6   The vulnerable client and complaints

Vulnerable clients have the same rights to complain about their barrister as everyone else, of course. The complaints procedure that a set of chambers must have in place needs to be both 'convenient and easy to use' (para 17, first tier complaints handling guidance). This applies, for example, where a client may need to act through another person to communicate their complaint, but the procedure should also enable vulnerable clients who wish to make their complaint themselves. So, complaints should be able to be made by telephone, or by email, or in writing, perhaps even in person at chambers—as the BSB guidance says, 'by any reasonable means'.

You and your regulator

5.1 Introduction

The regulator here is the Bar Standards Board. Part 2, section C4, is intended to enable the BSB to perform its regulatory functions effectively. Specific aspects include ensuring that those regulated by the BSB pass the 'fit and proper person' test and continue to do so; also, that serious misconduct is reported to the BSB and that the BSB can effectively investigate such reports.

It is important that there is public confidence in those persons who are regulated by the BSB (oC22). The BSB has to be able to get the information that it needs in order to be able to regulate effectively. With this in mind, any regulated person must respond promptly (rC64; gC92) to the BSB, whether this relates to a requirement to provide information to it or to compliance with any decision or sentence imposed by it (or another body operating within the disciplinary or 'fitness to practise' frameworks). The information that is requested may relate to oneself or to any other BSB regulated person. Most importantly, the BSB may request client information that is covered by legal professional privilege ('LPP'). See gC93. Without any sense of irony, the Handbook goes on to state that a barrister is entitled to withhold from the BSB any material that is privileged in his own hands; for example, any legal advice that he has received about his own position in relation to a disciplinary matter.

5.2 Reporting oneself to the BSB

We highlighted in **5.1** the need to *react* swiftly to requests or decisions made by the BSB. Here, we start to look at the duty to be proactive. It can apply to one's own circumstances or to instances of serious misconduct by another barrister or registered European lawyer (see **5.3**).

As we shall see in **chapter 11**, where we look at qualifying as a barrister, there are certain requirements and standards that an aspiring barrister must meet. Of necessity, these standards cannot be lowered once one has qualified. So, many of the matters that must be disclosed to the BSB by those who aspire to become barristers and which ultimately may prevent them from fulfilling their ambition are also to be found in the Handbook Part 2, section C4.

5.2.1 What must be reported

The onus is on the barrister (or BSB regulated person) to tell the BSB if any of the following situations arises, and to do so promptly:

- He is charged with an indictable offence in England and Wales, or with an offence of comparable gravity anywhere else
- He is convicted of, or accepts a caution for, any criminal offence anywhere in the world, other than a 'minor criminal offence' (one which may be dealt with by a fixed penalty or where the major element of the crime is unlawful parking)
- He knows that he (or an entity of which he is a manager) is the subject of disciplinary or other regulatory action by a regulator
- He is a manager of a non-BSB regulated entity which is subject to an intervention by its regulator
- He is a registered European lawyer and he knows that his home regulator is investigating his conduct, or has charged him with a disciplinary offence, or has made

a finding of professional misconduct against him, or his authorisation to practise is withdrawn or suspended in his home state

- He is made bankrupt or is disqualified from being a company director, or such proceedings are initiated against him, or he enters into an arrangement with his creditors
- He has had winding-up or administration proceedings initiated against him
- He has had an administrator, an administrative receiver, receiver or liquidator appointed in respect of him
- He has been authorised to practise by another approved regulator
- He has committed serious misconduct.

Where he considers that he has committed serious misconduct, he ought to take reasonable steps to mitigate its effects (gC94).

According to rC65.2 and guidance gC94.1, a 'spent' conviction or caution does not need to be reported to the BSB under rC65 (applying the provisions of the Rehabilitation of Offenders Act 1974). However, unless the conviction or caution becomes 'spent' immediately upon being imposed, then the BSB has to be notified 'promptly'. This is therefore likely to be a rarely applied exception to the reporting obligation. The group that are most likely to benefit will be those who have not yet begun their Bar Course. The period before they fell under the aegis of the BSB may have been long enough for the conviction or caution to become 'spent'.

5.2.2 What is serious misconduct

There is a list of what can constitute 'serious misconduct' in Part 2, at gC96, but this is not exhaustive. Many of the entries are quite obvious and infringe Core Duties but some are rather more surprising. 'Serious misconduct' includes:

- dishonesty
- assault or harassment
- trying to access confidential information relating to the opponent's case, including his instructions, without consent
- trying to access confidential information relating to someone else in chambers, whether a member, an employee, or a pupil, without consent
- encouraging a witness to give untruthful or misleading evidence
- knowingly or recklessly misleading a court or an opponent, or attempting to do so
- being under the influence of drink or drugs whilst in court
- conduct that poses a serious risk to the public
- failing to promptly report to the BSB the fact that proceedings have been started to disqualify you from being a director, or that you have been so disqualified, or similar situations regarding administration or winding-up proceedings
- reporting, or threatening to report, another barrister to the BSB under rC66 (see **5.3**) not for genuine reasons but as a litigation tactic or with some other abusive motivation (perhaps to please one's client) (and see rC67)
- failing to report yourself to the BSB or to report another barrister to the BSB where you have reasonable grounds to suspect that he is guilty of serious misconduct.

5.3 Reporting others to the BSB

5.3.1 The obligation to report another barrister

The obligation under rC66 on barrister A is only to report serious misconduct by barrister B where there are reasonable grounds to believe that barrister B is guilty of such misconduct (see **5.2.2**) and barrister A has a genuine and reasonably held belief to that effect (rC66–7). So, the reporting barrister A's actions must be justifiable both objectively and subjectively. The obligation on barrister A to report also applies where B is not a barrister but instead is a registered European lawyer. However, the obligation to report is subject to barrister A's duty to keep his client's affairs confidential. There are several other circumstances where a report need not be made, even if the barrister would be objectively and subjectively justified in making a report. See **5.3.2**.

5.3.2   When you need not report to the BSB

No report need be made if the barrister considers that the facts are likely to have come to the attention of the BSB independently, by virtue of the fact that the matters that have led him to believe there has been serious misconduct by another are in the public domain. This sounds a little bit like discouraging 'nosy neighbours', as misconduct that happens in the public eye (in court, for example) may well be reported by the media (see also gC99). Also, misconduct that is apparent in court may well be the subject of a report to the BSB by the judge hearing the proceedings. The barrister also has no duty to report if he is aware that the barrister who would be the subject of the possible serious misconduct report has already reported themselves to the BSB. Where the events that led the barrister to learn of another's serious misconduct are covered by their (presumably their client's) legal professional privilege, there is no duty to report and presumably one should in fact not report as to do so would breach the privilege. Finally, it is in the public interest that barristers are encouraged to make use of Bar Council advice helplines (for example, the ethics helpline and the pupillage helpline); it is also important that when they do so, they are frank and open and the Bar Council person advising them is able to give them fully informed advice. Thus, any BSB authorised person working on such a helpline who receives information in confidence has no duty to report to the BSB any misconduct which is thus disclosed to them (see also gC100). However, they are expected to encourage the caller to self-report to the BSB. See generally rC68.

5.3.3   Deciding whether or not to report another

If a situation arises where you think that there has been 'serious misconduct' by another barrister, be careful to consider the full circumstances before making a decision to report them. These circumstances may include:

- whether confidential matters, including their instructions, might be relevant to any assessment of the conduct
- if the other person has been given the chance to explain themselves (and if they have not, why not do that now?)
- any explanation that the other person has given, or could give, for their conduct
- if the conduct has been brought up in any litigation where it occurred, or may yet be raised there (and again, if it could be but has not been raised, why not do that now?).

Having considered the circumstances with care, you should now decide whether or not you have reasonable grounds to believe that there has been serious misconduct. Do you have material that you feel establishes 'a reasonably credible case of serious misconduct'? If so, then the duty under rC66 to report the other person is triggered. Bear in mind that not all misconduct is 'serious'. According to the BSB Guidance document on reporting serious misconduct, this is a matter of judgment and may be determined according to the particular circumstances of the situation. It may not just be a question of what has happened but a matter of the degree to which a Handbook obligation has been broken. For example, discrimination related to a protected characteristic may be serious misconduct but whether it actually is will apparently be determined according to the severity and impact of the discriminatory conduct. So, situations that may look similar superficially may be treated differently following investigation. However, the BSB Guidance document says that it is 'strongly in the public interest that the BSB is made aware of any serious misconduct'. With that nudge in mind, the Guidance says that if you remain unsure whether or not it is serious misconduct, you ought to 'err on the side of caution' and report it. See also generally gC97–102. However, incompetence (whilst possibly breaching Core Duties

2 and 7) is not generally seen by the BSB as raising a question of 'serious misconduct' unless either it is 'so serious that it poses a serious risk to the public' or it would have a detrimental effect on public trust and confidence in the legal profession. See BSB Guidance, para 26.

5.3.4 Freedom to report

The Bar is a close-knit profession, and gossip and rumours can move fast and cause long-lasting consequences. This is one reason to think carefully before reporting another barrister. The effects can be felt not just by the individual whose conduct has been reported but also by the reporter. Thus, rC69 makes it clear that no one is to be victimised for reporting another in good faith (and compare rC67). This may be of particular significance for barristers at the bottom of the 'food chain'—pupils and the very junior practitioner. Particularly, pupils want to be seen as 'team players' and will be very conscious that making a report against a member of those chambers (not all 'serious misconduct' occurs in court) may become known by those who will soon be making a decision about whether to offer that pupil (or another one) a tenancy or permanent seat in that set of chambers. Possibly the pressure will be even greater on a pupil when the barrister that they are considering reporting is their pupil supervisor. Nevertheless, such considerations will probably still affect a pupil's decision whether or not to report as a subsequent decision by chambers to offer someone else the tenancy may easily be explained on other grounds. The BSB Guidance recognises these pressures and suggests that a pupil, or very junior practitioner, may initially want to discuss the matter with others, perhaps the pupil supervisor (unless they are the potential subject of the report, of course), head of chambers, or head of legal practice (if there is one available).

It may be, of course, that the suspected misconduct directly affects the person who seems to be under a duty to report it—for example, a pupil who feels that he or she has been harassed by their pupil supervisor. The BSB Guidance is clear that even where the misconduct affects the barrister personally, they are still under the duty to report it to the BSB. But where the BSB receives a report of discrimination, harassment, or victimisation, it will act with sensitivity and will consult with the victim before acting. In such circumstances, should the misconduct be reported by someone other than the victim, the BSB is unlikely to take any action against the victim for a perceived 'failure' to report, contrary to rC66. Nevertheless, the Guidance asks victims to reflect on the fact that in the absence of a report now, someone else may be the victim later.

5.4 The Legal Ombudsman

If a barrister's client is unhappy with the service given by the barrister, they can complain. In the first instance, they should complain to the barrister using the chambers' complaints procedure (see **chapter 8**). If either no timely action is taken (allow at least eight weeks, according to the Legal Ombudsman website), or the client is unhappy with the final outcome, they have six months in which they can go to the Legal Ombudsman. The Ombudsman will then investigate the complaint; an investigator will be appointed and will first try to resolve the complaint informally and amicably, involving both client and barrister. Only if this fails will a recommendation report be produced; again, if the barrister and the client agree with the recommendation, the matter will be closed informally. If there is no agreement by both, then the matter will go to the Ombudsman for a formal decision. In order to facilitate the Ombudsman's procedures, it is incumbent on barristers to give 'all reasonable assistance' to the Ombudsman, when requested to do so (rC71). The rule is not explicitly limited to the barrister who is the subject of the complaint. For further information on the Legal Ombudsman scheme, see <http://www.legalombudsman.org.uk/>.

You and your practice

6.1 Introduction

This is quite a broad section, covering issues such as handling client money, professional insurance, outsourcing, and entering into an association with others. It also looks at how the self-employed barrister's practice should be administered, and the administration of chambers and of BSB authorised bodies. The last two topics are contained in rC89–90 and rC91–5, respectively.

The key outcome here is that the barrister's practice has to be run in a competent manner, it has to be compliant with the Core Duties, and to ensure that everyone working around the barrister—his clerks, employees, and pupils—understands and adheres to what they need to do so that the barrister meets his obligations under the Handbook (oC24).

6.2 Client money

6.2.1 The key principle

It has long been the tradition of the Bar that barristers do not handle client money. Even looking at the traditional design of the barrister's gown shows this—with the almost invisible pocket that is supposedly meant for payment, stitched onto the back of the gown where the barrister cannot really see it. The idea is that the client can just slip the money in and the barrister takes it on trust that the agreed, or a reasonable, sum has been paid. Of course, that system has not been used for centuries, if at all. The attitude of the Bar towards client money can perhaps be illustrated by the fact that until relatively recently a barrister's professional fee was described as an 'honorarium', a sort of tip or reward for doing a good job and it could not be sued for as a sum due under a contract. Also, for the self-employed barrister, it was her clerk who dealt with fees—first agreeing a fee with solicitors, then demanding it via a fee note and collecting it before transferring it onto the barrister. The situation has changed over the last few years but the Bar still has a very strict policy when it comes to keeping barristers apart from money and specifically money in which the client has an interest.

So, we can see in rC73 a very strong statement about barristers and their clients' money:

> Except where you are acting in your capacity as a manager of an authorised (non-BSB) body, you must not receive, control or handle client money apart from what the client pays you for your services.

Not only can the barrister himself not handle client money but he cannot hold it through anyone else (gC103). De facto control is also prohibited (gC104).

6.2.2 What is client money?

This is defined in Part 6 and it covers money and other assets:

- which the client owns beneficially or
- which has been provided by, or for the benefit of, the client or
- which is intended by someone else to be transmitted to the client.

It does *not* include a fixed fee which has been paid to the barrister in advance; nor does it cover money which belongs to the employer of an employed barrister. It does not cover money paid in settlement of an accrued debt. Of these, probably the most problematic is the fixed fee paid in advance. Guidance gC106 is very explicit that this is not client money but the fact that gC107 goes on to explain this in greater detail suggests that the position can be confusing so we shall consider it further in **6.2.3**.

6.2.3 The fixed fee

The *fixed fee* referred to in this section of the Handbook basically relates to privately funded work. We can begin with the idea that a barrister should only be paid for the work that she has done and that the rate for that work is likely to vary according to factors such as the nature and complexity of the case, its duration, the time spent on it by the barrister, and the expertise that she has. We might note in passing that all such factors should be clearly identified on the website of the barrister and/or chambers under the BSB's Transparency Rules (see **chapter 4**). There are essentially three ways that a barrister's remuneration can be paid: (i) in arrears after the work has been completed (which is really the traditional method), (ii) from time to time (where the work is spread over a substantial period and it would be difficult to manage cash flow without some money coming in), and (iii) in advance.

The norm is method (i)—payment at the end of the case. Essentially, the barrister is extending credit to the client in this situation. The same point applies to method (ii). That should not pose problems for payment. Usually, when the self-employed barrister is instructed by a professional client (typically a solicitor), the professional client is responsible for the barrister's fee. The professional client will usually be 'put in funds' by the client—that is, money is paid upfront by the lay client to the solicitor; it will be used by the solicitor to pay various expenses, including the barrister's fee, and should be sufficient for that purpose. That is not an issue for the barrister as he is not handling the lay client's money and it is not an issue for the professional client as they are subject to different rules about handling client money. Handling client money is a daily occurrence for solicitors and a necessary part of their practice; they have to be trained in how to handle it and account for it—such training is not a normal part of training for the Bar.

Where this becomes more problematic is when there is no professional client, no intermediary between the barrister and the lay client. So really, we are looking at public access work here, where a lay client is directly instructing the barrister. No one has been 'put in funds' here so there is no guarantee for the public access barrister that money will be available at the end of the case to pay her fees. Payment in arrears seems less advisable here. The temptation for the barrister is that she seeks in effect to be 'put in funds' herself by the lay client. She may ask for payment in advance and, in order to make that more acceptable to the lay client, she may ask for a fixed fee to be paid. This can be attractive to a lay client as they know precisely what their own legal fees are going to be and so they can budget.

The risk with the fixed fee paid in advance is that someone is likely to feel short-changed at the end of the matter: either the barrister thinks that she has undercharged when she looks at the work she has put into the case, or the client feels that he has overpaid the barrister. The likely compromise solution is that the barrister will seek a fixed fee at the upper range of what she would expect to be paid for the anticipated work and will assure the client that, once the work has been completed, whatever balance is left from the fixed fee after her actual fee has been calculated and deducted will then be repaid to the client. In essence, the barrister's fee is capped but the actual fee might eventually turn out to be less than the cap. Both barrister and client ought to be happy here—the barrister has guaranteed that she will receive the payment for her work and the client is reassured that he will only end up paying for the work that has been done for him. At this point, we can see the dilemma for the barrister: she is now holding client money. She has not yet done the work so she hasn't earned her fee and, if she is agreeing with the client to repay any surplus, there is a real risk that a court may think that she is holding some of the money on trust for the lay client. This is exactly what rC73 prohibits, of course.

The Handbook addresses this in gC107. As long as several criteria are satisfied, there will be no breach of the rule:

- There must be a clear written agreement between the barrister and the client, made in advance, as to the way that payment will work (see also rC22)
- The agreement must stipulate that:
  - the barrister's fee for any work will be calculated according to the time spent on it
  - a fixed fee will be paid by the lay client in advance, such fee being a reasonable payment for the work to be done
  - once the work has been done, any difference between the fixed fee and the fee that has actually been earned will be repaid by the barrister to the client and
  - the difference between the two will *not* be held on trust by the barrister for the client
- The lay client must be one who can reasonably be expected to understand the implications of the agreement.

The barrister should also give consideration to whether such an agreement is in the client's best interests (CD2) and whether the client fully understands its implications. The guidance states that where the amount of work that will be needed is unclear, it may be better to agree a scheme of staged payments, to be paid as the proceedings continue, rather than a fixed fee paid in advance. The guidance advises that a barrister 'should take extreme care if contracting with a client in this way'. If the barrister abuses the position by overestimating the sum likely to be due to himself, sets the fixed fee too high and thus holds more money than is reasonable at the start of the case, he is very likely to be found to be holding client money and thus in breach of rC73.

6.2.4 Third party services

As noted earlier, the barrister is forbidden to have even de facto control over a client's money (gC104). Thus, having the ability to determine the use or destination of funds, whether paid by or for the benefit of the client or intended by another party to be transmitted to your client, will breach the prohibition. This is so regardless of whether or not the funds are (a) beneficially owned by the client and (b) held in an account of the barrister.

In light of this, if the barrister uses a third party payment service in order to make payments either to, from, or on behalf of the client, she must take care to ensure that the arrangement will not result in her handling client money. She should only use the third party service to make payments to, from, or on behalf of the client for legal services; she should carry out reasonable checks to make sure that use of this service is consistent with her duties to act both competently and in her client's best interests (rC74; gC109–11). This will include ensuring that the third party payment service is authorised or regulated as a payment service by the Financial Conduct Authority ('FCA'), and that the service is 'in good standing' with the FCA (gC110).

6.3 Insurance

As one might expect, a barrister must have adequate insurance cover for the legal services he provides (rC76.1). The BSB may stipulate a minimum level of insurance cover and/or minimum terms for the insurance that must be taken out by 'BSB authorised persons'. This category covers practising barristers, pupils in their 'second six', and registered European lawyers.

When acting as a self-employed barrister (a practising barrister who is self-employed), the barrister must belong to the Bar Mutual Indemnity Fund (or 'BMIF'); see rC77. As a member of the BMIF, it is your obligation promptly to pay the insurance premiums and supply such information as BMIF requires (rC78). However, if a pupil is covered by his pupil supervisor's professional insurance then the pupil does not need to be a member of BMIF. A registered European lawyer will not need to have his own insurance where he can demonstrate to the BSB either that he is covered by insurance taken out in his home state, or that he is covered by a guarantee that has been provided in accordance with the rules of his home state.

If the barrister is working in an authorised (non-BSB) body, the insurance cover that the body must have will be determined by its approved regulator (gC115). An employed barrister working for a non-authorised body need not be insured if he is only providing legal services to his employer. If he is providing legal services to other people as part of his job, then he needs to consider whether his employer's insurance cover is adequate to cover claims made in respect of those services, including any pro bono work (gC116).

6.4 Associations with others

The principle here is quite simple—you cannot avoid the obligations placed upon you as an individual simply by practising in an 'association' (rC79; gC118). 'Association' is defined in Part 6 to cover the situation where several 'BSB authorised individuals' are practising as a set of chambers. A 'BSB authorised individual' is anyone that the BSB has authorised to undertake reserved legal activities. This can be a practising barrister, a 'second six' pupil, or a registered European lawyer. There is also an 'association' where BSB authorised persons and people who are not such 'persons' share premises and/or costs and/or use a common means for obtaining or distributing work in such a way that the association is not required to be authorised as an entity under the Legal Services Act 2007.

Where a barrister is in such an association (typically, in a set of chambers), the BSB must be notified and supplied with whatever details are required (rC80). The barrister should not enter into an association with anyone where, simply by being associated with him, the barrister may reasonably be considered as bringing the profession into disrepute, or diminishing public trust in himself and the profession—to do so would clearly be a breach of CD5; see also gC126, gC131.

To protect clients (and barristers) from a possible conflict of interest, where the barrister proposes to refer a client to an organisation in which he has a 'material commercial interest', he must inform the client in writing about that interest before making the referral and keep a record of all such referrals in case the BSB wishes to review them. He should only make the referral where it is in the client's best interest (gC124). Similarly, if an organisation in which the barrister has a material commercial interest is proposing to refer a client to the barrister, then the barrister (not the organisation) must make a written declaration of his interest to the client before accepting the referral and keep a record of all such referrals, as well as having a clear agreement with the organisation addressing how any conflicts of interest are to be resolved. A 'material commercial interest' is defined as one where an objective and fully informed observer would reasonably conclude that it might potentially influence the barrister's judgment (rC81–5). The guidance states that the purpose behind these rules is to ensure that clients and the public are not confused by such associations (gC120); it should always be clear to a client who is responsible for doing the work and how and by whom that person is being regulated.

6.5 Outsourcing

In the same way that being in an association does not absolve the barrister from his individual obligations under the Handbook (see **6.4**), neither does outsourcing any support services in connection with his supply of legal services. He remains responsible for compliance and must ensure that the outsourcing contract between himself and the third party protects client confidentiality to a similar degree as provided in the Handbook, as well as complying with any other obligations which may be affected by the outsourcing (see rC86).

This rule does not apply where the barrister instructs a pupil or 'devil' to undertake work on his behalf; see instead rC15 (see **chapter 3**). This is not outsourcing and the barrister himself (not the pupil or the 'devil') will continue to owe obligations to the client under Core Duties 2, 7, and 8; see gC129.

6.6 Administration and conduct of self-employed practice

This is covered in the Handbook at rC87–8. A barrister must take reasonable steps to ensure that his practice is administered efficiently and properly and that proper records are kept (rC87). Records relevant to any fees charged or claimed must be kept at least until either the fees are paid or any determination or assessment of costs has been done and the time for an appeal has passed (or the appeal has been determined), whichever comes later. The client should be provided with enough detail of the work done as is reasonably necessary to justify the fees charged (rC88).

6.7 Administration of chambers

This is covered in the Handbook at rC89–90.

The thrust of the rules here is that the onus is on the individual barrister to ensure that chambers' administration is competent and efficient, that chambers has appointed someone to liaise with the BSB about any regulatory requirements, that chambers does not employ someone who has been disqualified from such employment, that pupils and pupillages are dealt with properly, and that there are proper arrangements for managing any conflicts of interest that arise and ensuring that clients' affairs remain confidential (rC89–90).

7

Dealing with the client without a solicitor: public access and licensed access work

7.1 Introduction

It almost goes without saying that there are particular pressures involved in dealing directly with the client. Most barristers are unused to the proximity of the client, there may be issues around the conduct of litigation—what is involved, who is responsible—and of course there may be concerns about client money. It follows that in order to be operating in the public interest, it is important that barristers undertaking this type of work possess the necessary skills and experience (oC30). Proper records need to be kept of all such work and appropriate systems need to be in place for this (oC31). See generally Part 2, D2, of the Handbook.

It is important to make sure that clients only use public access to instruct a barrister when this is in their best interests and they have a full understanding of what they will need to do as the matter progresses. So, there will inevitably need to be an introductory contact where these issues are explored and then resolved, either with the client continuing to instruct the barrister as a public access client, or moving to a more traditional relationship and instructing a professional client, who may then handle the matter themselves instead of the barrister or may instruct a barrister (it need not be the original barrister).

The BSB has produced detailed guidance on public access work—for barristers, their clerks, and lay clients. See 'Public access guidance for barristers' on the BSB website, last updated October 2019.

One of the important matters raised by this guidance is the need to be alert for signs of money laundering. Responsibility for ensuring compliance with the Proceeds of Crime Act 2002 and the Money Laundering, Terrorist Financing and Transfer of Funds (Information on the Payer) Regulations 2017 remains at all times with the barrister and cannot be delegated to the barrister's clerk. The guidance notes that a barrister is most likely to undertake work that falls within the ambit of the Regulations when acting in one of the following ways:

(i)   as a tax adviser, as per reg 11(d) in the Regulations;

(ii) by participating in a financial or real property transaction by assisting a client in planning or executing a transaction that involves buying or selling real property or a business entity, or in relation to the creation, operation, or management of a company, trust, or a similar structure;

(iii) acting as a trust or company service provider, as per reg 12(2) of the Regulations.

7.2 Public access work

7.2.1 Qualification to do public access work

In order to accept public access work, a barrister must hold a full practising certificate, so it follows that a pupil barrister cannot undertake public access work, at any stage of pupillage.

In addition, the barrister must have satisfactorily completed the appropriate training to do such work, be registered with the Bar Council (acting through the BSB) as a public access practitioner, and have adequate insurance cover. See rC120 and BSB Public Access Guidance, para 3.

It follows that a pupil barrister cannot undertake public access work because he or she will either have no practising certificate (in their 'first six') or only a provisional practising certificate (in their 'second six'). However, a very junior barrister who has successfully completed his pupillage can do such work. If a barrister of less than three years' standing wishes to undertake public access work, then he must fulfil an additional requirement. He must have an experienced 'qualified person' available to guide and support him in his work. The 'qualified person' here must be someone who themselves is registered with the Bar Council for public access work and who meets the criteria in rS22. These criteria require the qualified person both to have been entitled to practise and to have practised as a barrister (not as a pupil) for at least six of the preceding eight years. The qualified person must also have made such practice their primary occupation for the previous two years, and they must have been entitled to exercise a right of audience before every court in relation to all types of proceedings. See further rC121 and rS22.

7.2.2 Accepting public access instructions

By definition, there is no professional client involved here. It follows that the 'cab rank' rule does not apply here and no barrister is obliged to accept any public access instructions. Nevertheless, he must still comply with his obligations under CD8, rC12, and rC28.

Before accepting public access instructions, the barrister must take reasonable steps to check whether it would be in the client's interests (or in the interests of justice) to instruct a solicitor or other form of professional client instead (rC122). This is a continuing obligation; if the barrister subsequently forms the opinion that it would be in the client's interests (or in the interests of justice) to instruct a solicitor or other professional client instead of himself, he must tell the client this and he must withdraw from the case unless the client acts on his advice by instructing a solicitor or other professional client to act on his behalf (rC123). The barrister must also check that the client is able to make an informed decision about whether to apply for public funding or to go ahead with the public access instructions (rC120.3). This is an important requirement—public access work for the Bar is privately paid; it cannot be publicly funded.

The BSB Guidance notes that the initial contact between the prospective client and the barrister will probably come in the form of a telephone call or email from the prospective client. Alternatively, the barrister's clerk may handle the initial contact; it is also possible that instructions from the prospective client will come in writing. In any event, a record needs to be started. It will be necessary to get an address for the client since he must be sent a client care letter, setting out (for example) standard terms and conditions and information on how to complain about poor service (rC125). A preliminary meeting may be needed, to help the barrister decide whether or not to accept the instructions. This may also be necessary to comply with the statutory requirements around money laundering and terrorist financing. The client may be vulnerable and this will need to be assessed carefully since it will affect how the barrister manages the case, if accepted. Issues around vulnerability may be associated with protected characteristics falling under the Equality Act 2010. The barrister will need to reflect on the level of support that the client is likely to require when making a decision about accepting or refusing the instructions. He will need to ensure that he does not refuse them because of a protected characteristic, or indeed for any reason that would put him in breach of rC28.

Once the barrister has accepted the public access instructions, he must inform the client forthwith, clearly and in writing, of:

- the work that he has agreed to perform and the fact that, in performing it, he will be subject to the conduct rules and scope of practice rules, in Parts 2 and 3 of the Handbook
- the fees which the barrister proposes to charge for the work or the basis on which the fee will be calculated
- the contact arrangements for the barrister
- the barrister's complaints procedure

- the fact that the barrister may be prevented from completing the work if a conflict of interest arises or there is a real risk that by maintaining confidential information of another client, he may not be able to act in the public access client's best interests and what can be expected of him in that situation. Typically, this means that the barrister will withdraw from the case (rC21).

See rC125. Further, the client must be told that the barrister is not allowed to perform the functions of a solicitor in relation to the conduct of this litigation, unless the barrister actually has been authorised by the BSB to do so (via a litigation extension to the practising certificate; see **chapter 10**). There is a model letter on the BSB website that will cover all of the foregoing matters (and see rC126).

Unless otherwise agreed, the barrister is entitled to take and keep copies of all documents sent by the client but must return all documents received if and when the client demands their return, whether or not he has been paid for any work done (so the barrister has no lien over the paperwork). On the other hand, the barrister need not deliver any documents he has drafted until he has been paid for all work done for the client.

Having accepted public access instructions, the barrister must keep a record of the case. This must include the dates that the instructions were received and accepted, the client's name, the case name, and the dates of all subsequent correspondence, for example when an advice was sent or when there was a telephone conversation (rC128). Thereafter, either the barrister or the client must retain, for a minimum of seven years after the date when the last work was done on the case, copies of all instructions, the originals or copies (or a list) of all documents enclosed with the instructions, copies of all written advice and documents drafted, and notes of all conferences and telephone advice given (rC129).

7.2.3   Withdrawing from a public access case

Withdrawal is a little more complicated in public access work. There is a contract between the barrister and the client; this will have been agreed when the barrister accepted the instructions. According to the BSB Guidance, unless withdrawal from the case is justified by reference to obligations imposed by the BSB Handbook, withdrawal carries the risk of putting the barrister in breach of his contract with the client (para 38). The Guidance points out that a simple 'difference of opinion' between barrister and client is not likely to make withdrawal an appropriate step to take. So, if the client quite legitimately rejects the barrister's advice on, say, case tactics or a settlement offer, this will not of itself justify withdrawing from the case. Likewise, if the client makes a minor complaint about service to the barrister, this will probably not justify withdrawal. It will, however, be prudent and in the interests of both barrister and client for a record to be made and its contents agreed, where possible, of any such disagreement or complaint.

See generally Part 2, section D2.1, rC119–31 and paras 40–1 of the Guidance document.

7.3   Licensed access work

This was originally launched in 1990, when it was known as direct professional access. The basic idea was that certain professions, such as accountants and surveyors, might be capable of and interested in instructing barristers without using a solicitor as an intermediary. The scheme has been extended since then and is now known as licensed access. This work is governed by the Licensed Access Guidelines. A licensed access client is any person or organisation that has applied to the BSB and been approved as such a client in accordance with the Regulations. Once approved, the BSB will issue the licence.

A self-employed barrister can accept instructions from a licensed access client if, and only if, the client is identified at the time of giving the instructions and at the same time the barrister checks that the client holds a valid licence from the BSB (rC134). This can be done by the client sending the barrister a copy of the licence that has been issued by the

BSB; alternatively, the barrister can simply check the list of licensed access clients that the BSB publishes on its website. The licence can vary considerably, as to its terms, its duration, and the type of matter on which the licensed client can instruct a barrister, so when a licensed access client seeks to instruct a barrister, the barrister will need to check the terms of the licence. If the barrister and his chambers are not able to provide the services that the licensed access client requires, he should not accept the instructions (rC135.1). If the barrister considers that it is in the client's best interests (or in the interests of justice) that an intermediary (such as a solicitor) be instructed, either in addition to the barrister or in substitution for him, he should decline the licensed access instructions (rC135.2). If the barrister, at any subsequent time, forms such an opinion, he should inform the client forthwith in writing; unless the client follows that advice as soon as is reasonably practicable, the barrister must cease to act in the matter (rC138).

When a barrister accepts instructions from a licensed access client, he must promptly send the client a statement that the instructions have been accepted on the standard terms previously agreed in writing with the client. If this does not apply, then the barrister must send the client a written copy of the agreement, setting out the terms on which he has agreed to do the work and specifying the basis on which he is to be paid. In any event, the client must be told that the barrister is not allowed to perform the functions of a solicitor in relation to the conduct of litigation, unless of course he has been authorised by the BSB to do so (via a litigation extension to his practising certificate). See rC137.

Having accepted the instructions, if the barrister at any point considers that there are substantial grounds to believe that the client has failed to comply with the terms of their licence, that failure shall be reported to the BSB forthwith (rC139).

The barrister must keep a case record for licensed access work (rC140). Either the barrister or the licensed access client must retain, for seven years following the date of the last item of work done, copies of the instructions, a list of all documents enclosed with the instructions, copies of all written advice and documents drafted, and notes of all conferences and telephone advice given (rC141).

See Part 2, section D2.2; rC132–4.

7.4 Barristers and immigration advisers

Under the Immigration and Asylum Act 1999, as amended, a barrister can act as a supervisor for the purpose of providing immigration advice and services (see 'Barristers supervising immigration advisers guidance'). From the client's perspective, such advice is likely to come from an immigration adviser, with the barrister remaining in the background, supervising the adviser, and having no direct role in the adviser–client relationship. However, the BSB considers that the supervisory role of the barrister is something relied upon by the client with the result that the barrister is personally responsible for the work undertaken by the adviser. This will be seen as a form of public access work and it should therefore not be undertaken unless the barrister is registered as a public access practitioner and satisfies the criteria to undertake public access work.

When acting as a supervisor, the barrister must comply with all relevant provisions of the Code of Conduct, including the Core Duties. This will include informing the client in writing when instructed (or at the next reasonable opportunity) of the right to make a complaint if dissatisfied with the service received (see rC99). It will also include providing for the client, in writing, the terms and basis on which instructions have been accepted. In particular, the client must not be misled about the status of an immigration adviser.

Before starting any supervision, the barrister has to notify the BSB of his intention to do so; see rC80. He should ensure that any immigration adviser that he proposes to supervise is professionally competent and do due diligence to ensure that the Office of the Immigration Services Commissioner has not refused or cancelled the registration of the adviser and that the adviser is not disqualified, suspended, or prohibited from practice. See rC85A.

8

Complaints

8.1 Introduction

We need to distinguish between complaints about non-compliance with the Core Duties and other provisions of the Handbook, and complaints about poor service.

Complaints about breaches of the Handbook are made to the BSB; the procedure is addressed in Part 5 of the Handbook, entitled 'Enforcement Regulations'. However, Part 5 is beyond the remit of this manual. What we need to focus on is in the Handbook at Part 2, section D1.1—this is the *complaints rules*. The difference between the two is basically that Part 5 handles issues about non-compliance with the Handbook whilst the complaints rules are there for a client to complain about the *legal service* he received from his barrister. If a client does complain to the BSB about the service provided by their barrister, then the BSB must refer it on to the Legal Ombudsman without further consideration. The rest of this chapter will confine itself to the *complaints rules* under Part 2, section D1.1. Reference will also be made to the current BSB Guidance on First Tier Complaints Handling, issued in October 2019. In effect, 'first tier' refers to complaints made to chambers.

8.2 The complaints rules

8.2.1 Different types of complaint

The BSB says that there are three types of complaint—about poor service, about misconduct, and about professionally negligent work. Misconduct matters should go to the BSB as per the Enforcement Regulations. Professional negligence should probably be addressed through legal proceedings against the barrister. The complaints rules address complaints about poor level of service. As we know, the barrister has a duty to provide the client with a competent level of work and service (CD7). It is possible that a single complaint may raise several issues—perhaps around poor service but also misconduct. It is not really appropriate for chambers to conduct its own investigation into allegations of misconduct (and these may need to be referred to the BSB anyway if they could be 'serious misconduct'; rC66) but chambers should still investigate the service elements of the complaint. The fact that it is a 'mixed' complaint would not justify inaction.

8.2.2 Information for the client

Basically, clients must be told clearly that they can complain if they are unhappy with the service they have received and they must be informed about how to make that complaint. Any complaint must be addressed promptly and the client must be kept updated about its progress (oC26–7, Part 2 D1).

When a barrister is instructed, he must inform the client in writing of:

(i) his right to complain, how to complain and to whom, and any time limits for doing so,

(ii) any right to complain to the Legal Ombudsman if he is dissatisfied with the outcome, and he must be given details of how to contact the Ombudsman, and

(iii) the name and web address of an ADR body that has been approved to handle unresolved complaints.

If it is impractical to provide this information when instructed, it must be given at the next appropriate opportunity (rC99; see also rC102).

In the case of referral work (that is, involving a professional client), the client should be told that he does not need to go through solicitors to raise a complaint but can complain to the barrister's chambers directly. It is not necessary to give a *professional* client the written information in a separate letter but it should be provided in the ordinary terms of reference supplied when the barrister accepts instructions in the matter.

Chambers' complaints procedure should also be displayed on chambers' literature and its website (see rC103).

8.2.3   The procedure for making a complaint

The procedure for making a complaint should be convenient and easy to use but each set of chambers is free to devise its own system (there are model complaints procedures in the BSB Guidance document in Appendix 1). The system should recognise and make provision for complaints by clients who are vulnerable or have disabilities; generally, the system should allow for a complaint to be made 'by any reasonable means' (BSB Guidance, para 17). When a complaint is received, it must be acknowledged promptly, telling the complainant who will be dealing with it and their role in chambers. The complainant must be given a copy of chambers' complaints procedure and a deadline by which they will next hear from chambers about the complaint (rC104; the overall deadline should not exceed eight weeks from the date the complaint was made: para 52 of the Guidance document).

Once a complaint has been dealt with by chambers, the complainant must be given written notice of any right that they have to complain to the Legal Ombudsman, how to do so, and any time limit (rC105). They will also need to be reminded of the possibility of going to ADR (Guidance, paras 11 and 13). Presumably, this information is only likely to be of any relevance where the complaint has been rejected or the complainant is dissatisfied for some other reason.

All records relating to complaints must be kept confidential (rC106) and material should be disclosed only for the purpose of dealing with the complaint, or where chambers conducts an internal review to improve its complaints handling, or where the BSB requires the information for an audit. A record should be kept for six years from the date on which the complaint was resolved (rC108).

8.2.4   Going to the Legal Ombudsman

Many, but not all, complaints about poor service will also fall within the jurisdiction of the Legal Ombudsman ('LeO'). This will then represent a second chance for a complaint to be made. The LeO recognises certain types of complainant—the most obvious one is the individual. But a client that is a micro-business can complain, as can a charity with an annual net income of less than £1 million. A public body cannot complain to the LeO. Where a solicitor (or other professional client) instructed the barrister on behalf of a client, only the client can complain to the LeO (as long as they meet the criteria); the solicitor cannot make the complaint on their behalf (but once the client has made the complaint to the LeO, he may authorise another, for example a solicitor, to act for him in pursuing the complaint).

The subject matter of the complaint does not have to be about a 'reserved legal activity' but it must be about service. This could be the service that was provided, or the service that was offered, or even the service that was refused (Scheme Rules for the LeO, part 2). Particular examples given on the LeO website include:

- **Costs:** the costs were unclear or different from the original estimate
- **Delay:** no clear reason for the work taking longer than expected
- **Poor information:** a process was not well explained, or there was not enough information for a consumer to make an informed choice

8.2.5   **Going to ADR**

Under the Alternative Dispute Resolution for Consumer Disputes (Amendment) Regulations 2015, any complaint that remains unresolved following chambers internal procedures can be referred to ADR. The client must be given clear information about this. A reference to ADR may only be made where both client and barrister agree to do so. On 24 October 2019, the Legal Ombudsman decided to discontinue its pilot scheme of using mediation services to settle complaints. The number of cases where both parties wished to use mediation was as low as 8 per cent and of that 8 per cent, mediation was successful in only half of the cases that engaged in it. If the barrister and the client use an arbitration scheme, the outcome will be legally binding and the parties will need to agree to this. In itself, this does not prevent the client from then making a complaint to the Legal Ombudsman. However, the Legal Ombudsman reserves the right to dismiss any complaint if it feels that a comparable independent complaints (or costs-assessment) scheme has already dealt with the same issue satisfactorily.

See further the BSB Guidance on First Tier Complaints Handling, para 14.

The unregistered barrister

9.1 Introduction

An unregistered barrister is a barrister who has been called to the Bar by an Inn of Court, has not subsequently ceased to be a member of the Bar but who does *not* hold a practising certificate. The practising certificate could be a full practising certificate, a provisional one, a limited one, a European lawyer's practising certificate, or a temporary one issued by the Bar Council. Rule rI7 states that the BSB Handbook applies to unregistered barristers. The Handbook Part 2, section D, sets out the rules which apply to particular groups of regulated people. D4 covers unregistered barristers. There is also a BSB Guidance document, last updated in October 2019, to which reference should be made.

The Core Duties apply to unregistered barristers as appropriate; in particular Core Duties 5 and 9 apply to them at all times. However, the Conduct Rules in Part 2 do not apply to them, except where the rules state clearly that they do so apply. Other rules that *do apply* to unregistered barristers include:

- rC3.5: must ensure the ability to act independently is not compromised
- rC4: duty to act in client's best interests is subordinate to the duty owed to the court
- rC8: must not do anything which could reasonably be seen by the public to undermine one's honesty, integrity, and independence
- rC16: duty to act in client's best interests is subordinate to duty to the court, obligation to act with honesty and integrity, and to maintain one's independence
- rC19: must not mislead clients about nature and scope of legal services being provided, the terms on which they are being provided, who is legally responsible, whether one is entitled to supply the services, whether one is regulated and if so by whom, and the extent to which one is covered by insurance. This is probably the key provision for the unregistered barrister
- rC64–70: in summary, rules relating to the relationship between the barrister and the Bar Standards Board.

See rC1.2, and note that the guidance that accompanies these rules also applies to the unregistered barrister.

9.2 The unregistered barrister and the inexperienced client

We saw above that, under rC19, the unregistered barrister must not supply misleading information to any client. Particular provisions apply to any unregistered barrister who is supplying legal services to an 'inexperienced' client (rC144). An 'inexperienced' client is typically any individual, but also includes others who would have the right to complain to the Legal Ombudsman *if* the barrister was a practising barrister. This includes micro-enterprise businesses, charities with an annual net income of less than £1 million, trustees of a trust with assets valued at less than £1 million, clubs or associations managed by their members with an annual net income of under £1 million, or the personal representative or beneficiary of the estate of a deceased who had not themselves complained to the Legal Ombudsman. A micro-business is one with fewer than ten employees and a turnover or assets that do not exceed €2 million.

An 'inexperienced' client who receives legal services from an unregistered barrister needs to understand that the barrister is not subject to the same regulatory framework as a practising barrister, so that the safeguards are not the same. So, the client must be told that the barrister is not acting as a barrister (this means as a *practising* barrister), that he is not subject to certain parts of the Code and the Handbook, and that in the event of a complaint to the BSB, it will only be considered if it relates to the Core Duties or those specific parts of the Handbook that apply to the unregistered barrister. The inexperienced client must also be told that the unregistered barrister is not covered by professional indemnity insurance (unless he is so covered, but this will not be via the Bar Mutual Indemnity Fund), and that the client has the right to complain, how to do so and to whom, and any deadline for doing so, but that he has no right to complain to the Legal Ombudsman about the legal services being supplied (rC144).

The obligations to inform the inexperienced client, as set out above, do not apply where the unregistered barrister supplies legal services as an employee or manager of a regulated entity, or of a body which is regulated by a professional body or regulator. The notice requirements also will not apply where the unregistered barrister is authorised by another approved regulator, or is supplying legal services on a voluntary or part-time basis at a legal advice centre. See rC145. Finally, the notice requirements will not apply where you supply legal services in accordance with S13 and S14. S13 refers to when you are practising as a foreign lawyer; and you do not: (a) give advice on English Law; or (b) supply legal services in relation to any proceedings or contemplated proceedings in England and Wales (other than as an expert witness on foreign law). S14 refers to when you are authorised and permitted to carry on reserved legal activities for another approved regulator; and you hold yourself out as a barrister or a registered European lawyer (as appropriate) other than as a manager or employee of a BSB entity; and when supplying legal services to any person for the first time, you inform them clearly in writing at the earliest opportunity that you are not practising as a barrister or a registered European lawyer.

9.3 The unregistered barrister and the provision of legal services

An unregistered barrister is able to supply 'legal services' but must not engage in any 'reserved legal activities'. These terms are defined in the Legal Services Act 2007. The most obvious forms of reserved legal activity for a barrister are (i) exercising rights of audience and (ii) conducting litigation. A practising barrister with a practising certificate can exercise rights of audience before courts and, if he has a 'litigation extension' to his practising certificate, he could 'conduct litigation'. If an unregistered barrister engaged in these reserved legal activities, he would be committing a crime under the Legal Services Act 2007. On the important subject of reserved legal activities, see further **chapter 10**.

The unregistered barrister is allowed to represent clients at a tribunal hearing, since this does not involve any exercise of a right of audience. Furthermore, the unregistered barrister is allowed to act as a mediator, to lecture on law, and to write law books, since these activities are not even regarded as legal services.

However, if the legal services that are provided by an unregistered barrister include immigration advice and services, there is a separate issue. Under the Immigration and Asylum Act 1999, it is a crime to provide immigration advice or services unless one is authorised to do so by the Office of the Immigration Services Commissioner ('OISC'). Practising barristers are automatically authorised to provide this service but an unregistered barrister is not. He could still apply to the OISC for authorisation but would need to meet the statutory criteria.

When an unregistered barrister provides legal services, then all of the Core Duties will apply, as well as rC4, 5, 19, 144, and 145 (see BSB Guidance, para 7).

9.4 Holding yourself out as a barrister

It is not permitted to practise as a barrister unless you hold a practising certificate (see rS8). If you hold yourself out as a barrister whilst providing legal services, this would amount to practising as a barrister (rS9). You would be considered to have held yourself out as a barrister if you described yourself as a barrister to a client, perhaps on a business card or headed notepaper or on your website, or if you attended court robed as a barrister and sat in the seats reserved for barristers. Furthermore, you would be breaking rC19—misleading anyone to whom you supply, or offer to supply, legal services about your status and the safeguards for them.

There used to be 'safe havens' for barristers without a practising certificate—they could describe themselves as a 'non-practising barrister' or a 'barrister-at-law'. The BSB does not allow these descriptions to be used now, as they may easily confuse clients or prospective clients as to the true status of the individual and any associated safeguards. However, if the unregistered barrister is *not* supplying legal services, there is no prohibition on describing himself as a barrister—the dangers foreseen by rC19 will not arise.

See further the BSB unregistered barristers guidance, last updated in October 2019.

The scope of practice

10.1 Introduction

Part 3 of the Handbook covers the scope of practice and the authorisation and licensing rules. Of the five substantive sections, we shall only consider Part 3B—the scope of practice rules and Part 3C—the fundamentals of the rules about practising certificates. Much of the rest of Part 3 is concerned with either registered European lawyers or BSB entities, both of which lie outside the scope of this manual.

We should note that, as we have moved from Part 2 to Part 3 of the Handbook, so the reference has altered—from 'C' to 'S', or from Conduct to Scope. So, the rules here appear as 'rS6', for example. It is mostly rules in Part 3, with no outcomes and very little Handbook guidance provided.

10.2 Scope of practice

Section B is fairly short but quite important. It addresses what work you are allowed to do and the circumstances under which it must be done. It covers the provision of legal services and reserved legal activities; these are crucial elements within the regulatory framework set up by the Legal Services Act 2007 ('LSA 2007').

10.2.1 Reserved legal activities and legal services

'Reserved legal activities' are ones which are regulated by the LSA 2007 and a person (including an unincorporated body and a body corporate) can only carry on a reserved legal activity if entitled to do so (LSA 2007, s 12; rS6 in Section 3B of the Handbook). One is entitled to do so if *authorised* or exempt (LSA 2007, s 13; see **10.2.2**). The following are the reserved legal activities under LSA 2007, s 12:

- exercising a right of audience in a court
- the conduct of litigation
- reserved instrument activities
- probate activities
- notarial services
- oath administration.

The first of these 'reserved activities' is straightforward but it is important to note that it is more limited than simply 'advocacy'. As well as appearing in court, 'advocacy' may also encompass appearance at a tribunal or in a form of ADR but these two are not 'reserved legal activities' and hence one would not need a practising certificate to undertake them. The second 'reserved activity'—'conducting litigation'—can be summarised as the sort of litigation work that is traditionally carried out by solicitors (see further **10.3.6**). Probate activities and the administration of oaths are also reasonably familiar work, albeit ones that are not often carried out by most self-employed barristers. 'Reserved instrument activities' is probably the most vague term here; it is defined in LSA 2007, Sch 2, as 'preparing any instrument of transfer or charge for the purposes of the Land Registration Act 2002', or making an application or lodging a document for registration under that Act, or preparing any other instrument relating to real or personal property for the purposes of the law of England and Wales. It also includes preparing a contract for the sale or other disposition of land, other than in a will or other form of testamentary disposal. The Bar Council does not authorise any barrister to perform notarial activities (see, for example, BSB Unregistered Barristers Guidance, section 3).

'Legal services' are defined in Part 6 as including giving legal advice; representing a client; and drafting or settling a statement of case, witness statement, affidavit, or other legal document. They do not include sitting as a judge, acting as a mediator, giving free legal advice to friends, being a 'libel reader' for the press, teaching law, or writing law books or articles.

10.2.2   Authorisation to carry out reserved legal activities

An 'authorised person' is defined in LSA 2007, s 18, as a person who is authorised to carry on a reserved legal activity by an approved regulator. Part 6 of the Handbook has several overlapping definitions of persons who are 'authorised'. A 'BSB authorised person' means BSB authorised individuals as well as BSB entities. A 'BSB authorised individual' is any individual who is authorised by the BSB to carry on reserved legal activities; this includes practising barristers and 'second six' pupils, and registered European lawyers.

To a great extent, authorisation by the BSB really turns on whether or not an individual has a practising certificate.

If you supply 'legal services' and either:

- you are an individual and have a practising certificate
- you hold yourself out as a barrister or a registered European lawyer or
- you manage, or own, an authorised (non-BSB) body and are required by the regulator of that body to hold a practising certificate issued by the Bar Council

then you are practising as a barrister or a registered European lawyer. If you are an individual and *do not* have a practising certificate, then you must not practise as a barrister or a registered European lawyer, and you are *not* authorised by the BSB to carry out any reserved legal activity.

A 'first six' pupil is not eligible for a practising certificate. The 'scope of practice' rules do not prevent a 'first six' pupil from accepting a noting brief for court, if permission to do so is granted by either his pupil supervisor or head of chambers (rS11). A noting brief is simply that—the pupil sits in court and makes a note of the evidence being given and any reasoned judgment given by the judge in a ruling; it is a passive role.

10.2.3   Providing reserved legal activities and other legal services

We should note that, as well as the BSB, other regulators have their own systems; for example, under the Solicitors Regulation Authority, solicitors are authorised to undertake reserved legal activities. We should also note that an unregistered barrister (one without a practising certificate) can provide legal services which do not constitute a reserved legal activity. In so doing, the unregistered barrister needs to be careful not to be holding himself out as 'a barrister' since that will connote someone with a practising certificate and all that that entails. Otherwise, as the BSB guidance on unregistered barristers states:

> Legal services, other than reserved legal activities, can be supplied by anyone and are not subject to any special statutory regulation. It would therefore be disproportionate to impose regulatory requirements on unregistered barristers who supply such services just because they are barristers, except where there would otherwise be a clear risk to their potential clients. (Unregistered Barristers Guidance, para 6)

Currently, for our purposes, the BSB recognises four capacities in which one may carry on a reserved legal activity or provide other legal services: first, as a self-employed barrister; secondly, as the manager of an authorised (non-BSB) body or as an 'employed barrister (authorised non-BSB body)'; thirdly, as an 'employed barrister (non-authorised body)'; and, fourthly, as a registered European lawyer; see rS16. (There are two further categories that relate to BSB entities but they are outside the scope of this manual.) We will examine each in turn but, before doing so, we should note two points.

First, a 'second six' pupil will have a provisional practising certificate and may supply legal services or exercise any right which he has by virtue of being a barrister (for example, a right of audience) but only if granted permission to do so by either his pupil supervisor, head of chambers, or head of legal practice (rS19).

Secondly, if you are a barrister of less than three years' standing and you either:

(i)   supply legal services, or

(ii)   exercise any right of audience, or

(iii) conduct litigation,

then generally you will need to have as your principal place of practice (i) a set of chambers or (ii) an office of an organisation. In both instances, there must be a more experienced lawyer who is readily available to guide you (a 'qualified person'). Obviously, exercising a right of audience or conducting litigation are 'reserved legal activities' and thus forbidden to the unregistered barrister. But an unregistered barrister may lawfully supply legal services that are not reserved legal activities and he will therefore need to have satisfied these criteria (principal place of practice and 'qualified person') for his first three years. See rS20–2 for details.

10.2.3.1   Scope of practice as a self-employed barrister

The first matter to consider here is—who can instruct you? Essentially, you may only supply legal services if you are instructed (i) by a court, (ii) by a professional client, (iii) by a licensed access client, or (iv) in any other situation you may supply legal services only if the matter is public access work or relates to the conduct of litigation (rS24). If you have a licensed access client, you must abide by the licensed access rules; see **7.3**. To accept public access instructions, you must be entitled to do so, have notified the BSB that you are willing to accept such work, and abide by the public access rules; see **7.2**. Where you are instructed to conduct litigation, you must have a litigation extension to your practising certificate (see **10.3.6**) and have informed the BSB that you are willing to accept instructions from lay clients.

Secondly, in summary, you must not undertake the management, administration, or general conduct of a client's affairs (rS25). Traditionally, this is solicitors' work, not done by barristers. Usually, we are neither trained nor qualified to offer these services. There is an exception—where this is 'foreign work', performed by you at a base outside England and Wales (rS26). 'Foreign work' is defined as offering or providing legal services that relate to either (i) legal proceedings taking place or contemplated to take place outside England and Wales (for example, Scotland) or (ii) where there are no actual or contemplated legal proceedings, any matter (actual or contemplated) which is not subject to the law of England and Wales.

10.2.3.2   Scope of practice as an employed barrister (non-authorised body)

This is covered by Part 3, B7 of the BSB Handbook. It applies where a practising barrister is employed by a non-authorised body under a contract of employment, or on a fixed-term contract for services, or by virtue of an office under the Crown (a civil servant), or by an EU institution (EU civil servant) and who supplies legal services as a barrister in the course of employment.

This practising barrister may only supply legal services as follows:

- to his employer, or to staff of his employer on matters concerning that person's employment
- if he is employed by a public authority, to another public authority where his employer has made arrangements to supply legal services as the other authority's agent
- if he is employed in a government department, to any government minister
- if he is employed by a trade association, to a member of the association
- if he is performing the functions of a Justices' clerk, to the Justices
- if he is employed at a Legal Advice Centre, he can supply legal services to its clients

- if he works pro bono or is employed by the Legal Aid Agency, he may supply legal services to members of the public
- if he is employed by a foreign lawyer, to any client of his employer if the legal services consist of 'foreign work' (any legal services relating either to legal proceedings taking place outside England and Wales, or to any matter not subject to the law of England and Wales).

10.2.3.3 Scope of practice for registered European lawyers

If a registered European lawyer is working in either of the two preceding categories (**10.2.3.1** or **10.2.3.2**), then the equivalent limitations that would have applied if he was practising as a barrister in that category shall equally apply to him in his practice (rS16.6).

10.2.3.4 Legal advice centres

For the time being, Legal Advice Centres are allowed to provide reserved legal activities without being authorised to do so (gS11). We have already seen that an employed barrister may supply legal services to Legal Advice Centres (**10.2.3.2**). You may also supply legal services at a Centre on a voluntary or part-time basis. In these situations, you will be treated as though you were employed by the Centre and the Handbook will apply as appropriate (rS41).

Where you are so treated as an employee, with the exception of a salary paid to you by the Centre, you must not receive any fee or reward for providing legal services to any client of the Centre. You must have no financial interest in the Centre and any fees that come in for legal services provided by you must accrue and be paid to the Centre or to charity, as prescribed by the Lord Chancellor (currently the Access to Justice Foundation). See rS42.

A self-employed barrister who also does work for a Centre does not need to tell the BSB that he is doing so (gS10).

See generally Part 3, section B9.

10.3 Practising certificates

10.3.1 Who is covered and what can they have

Two categories of lawyer can apply for a practising certificate—barristers and registered European lawyers. In both cases, they must not be currently suspended from practice or have been disbarred. Since 1 April 2015, they must also meet one of the following conditions:

- within the previous five years, they have
  - held a practising certificate or
  - satisfactorily completed either the first six months of pupillage or the full 12 months (or been exempted from the requirement to complete either period) or
- have complied with whatever training requirements have been laid down by the BSB.

Assuming that the above factors are satisfied, the lawyer can then aim for one of four different practising certificates—the full certificate, the provisional, the limited certificate, or the registered European lawyer's certificate. Each has separate qualifying criteria. We shall examine each in turn.

10.3.2 The full practising certificate

This authorises the barrister to exercise a right of audience before every court, covering all proceedings. A 'right of audience' means the right to appear before and address a court, and the right to call and examine witnesses; see LSA 2007, Sch 2, para 3.

There are four alternative ways to be eligible for the full certificate. First, the barrister has completed the full 12 months of pupillage satisfactorily. Secondly, the barrister has been exempted from the need to complete 12 months' pupillage. Thirdly, on 30 July 2000, the barrister was entitled to exercise full rights of audience by virtue of being a barrister. Finally, the barrister was called to the Bar before 1 January 2002 and, before 31 March 2012, the barrister had (i) notified the Bar Council that he wished to exercise rights of audience before every court and covering all proceedings, and (ii) complied with training requirements as laid down by the Bar Council or BSB (or had been informed that he need not comply with such requirements). Obviously, the usual method will be the first here—satisfactory completion of 12 months in pupillage. See rS46.1.

10.3.3   The provisional practising certificate

The BSB now refers to the 'first six' as the 'non-practising period'. It calls the 'second six' the 'practising period'. The provisional practising certificate authorises a 'second six' pupil to exercise a right of audience before every court, covering all proceedings. In order to get the certificate, the pupil must have completed their non-practising period satisfactorily (or been exempted from it) and be registered with the BSB as a pupil in their 'practising period' at the time of applying for the certificate. See rS46.2 and further the BSB guidance for pupils, within the Authorisation to practice section on the BSB website.

10.3.4   The limited practising certificate

The limited certificate only allows a barrister to exercise any rights of audience which he had by reason of being a barrister and was entitled to exercise on 30 July 2000. A barrister is entitled to this certificate if he was called to the Bar before 1 January 2002 and is otherwise unable to meet the eligibility requirement for a full certificate (see **10.3.2**; rS46.3).

10.3.5   The registered European lawyer's practising certificate

A 'registered European lawyer' is a European lawyer who has been registered as such, seemingly by the Bar Standards Board and by one of the Inns of Court (Part 6 of the Handbook but see **10.4**).

The certificate allows the lawyer to engage in the same reserved legal activities as a full practising certificate allows a barrister, except that the European lawyer can only exercise a right of audience or conduct litigation (see **10.3.6**) if he acts in conjunction with a solicitor or barrister who is entitled to practise in the relevant forum and who can legitimately exercise that right. There is also a limited class of European lawyers who can be paid to produce an instrument creating or transferring an interest in land.

10.3.6   Litigation extensions—conducting litigation

10.3.6.1   What is 'conducting litigation'?

A litigation extension can be added to a practising certificate (other than a provisional one) where the certificate holder wants to be able to 'conduct litigation'. This will allow the holder to conduct litigation in every court and for all proceedings. A registered European lawyer will need to be 'paired up' as mentioned in **10.3.5**. The ability to 'conduct litigation' has the same meaning as in the LSA 2007, Sch 2, para 4—it means that one can issue, commence, prosecute, and defend proceedings before any court in England and Wales, and perform any necessary ancillary functions. In essence, conducting litigation means to do the tasks that a solicitor would usually do.

The BSB Guidance on conducting litigation, last issued in October 2019, identifies the following as 'conducting litigation' and thus off limits for a barrister unless one holds a litigation extension:

(a) starting court proceedings by filing details of the claim at court (for example, claim form and particulars of claim) or making an application for a court order (this would not include the hearing of an application);

(b) filing an acknowledgement of proceedings;

(c) filing documents at courts (for example, an expert report);

(d) serving documents on another party to proceedings (for example, an expert report);

(e) giving your professional address as the client's address for service;

(f) signing off on a disclosure list;

(g) laying an information at the Magistrates' Court;

(h) issuing a notice of appeal.

However, there are many tasks that one might think would fall within the spirit of the list above and yet which have traditionally been done by barristers or their clerks. Those that are regarded by the BSB as not 'conducting litigation' and thus permitted to be done by a barrister without holding a litigation extension, include:

(a) conducting correspondence on behalf of a client (to do this, the barrister must be satisfied that this is in the client's best interests, that the barrister has adequate systems, experience, and resources to manage the correspondence, and adequate insurance cover for this work). Where the opponent is legally represented, the correspondence should be directed to those lawyers;

(b) lodging documents at court for a hearing (this is permissible where it is ancillary to the barrister's appearance at a hearing, for example a chronology or a case summary, skeleton arguments, or a criminal defence statement);

(c) covering an application to fix a trial date (usually done by the barrister's clerk);

(d) liaison with the opponent or the court over the preparation of a court order;

(e) signing a statement of truth on behalf of a client (but take care to comply with Civil Procedure Rules Part 22 PD, para 3.8);

(f) instructing an expert witness on behalf of a client;

(g) discharging a duty or a courtesy to the court—this could be supplying a list of dates to avoid, offering corrections to the content of a draft judgment, or writing to explain an absence from court.

10.3.6.2 Eligibility for a litigation extension

A barrister is eligible for a litigation extension if he satisfies the criteria in rS47. He must usually be of more than three years' standing, know the relevant procedural requirements well enough to be able to conduct litigation competently, and have the necessary administrative systems set up so that he can provide legal services direct to clients and cover the administrative demands involved in conducting litigation.

Where the barrister is of less than three years' standing, he can still have a litigation extension but only if his principal place of business is in chambers, which is also the principal place of business of a 'qualified person' who is on hand to provide guidance as necessary. Alternatively, his principal place of practice can be in the office of an organisation where an employee, manager, partner, or director is a 'qualified person' who will be on hand to provide swift guidance (rS47.2.b).

A 'qualified person' for conducting litigation is defined in Part 3, section B2, rS22.3. Put simply, it is a fairly senior barrister who himself has the right to conduct litigation and who has practised as a barrister for at least six of the preceding eight years. He must have made his practice his primary occupation for the last two years and he must not act as a qualified person to more than two other people. He must not have been designated by the BSB as unsuitable to act as a qualified person.

See further the BSB conducting litigation guidance—the current version of which was issued in October 2019.

10.3.6.3 What you can do with a litigation extension

Obviously, holding a litigation extension authorises the barrister to 'conduct litigation'. The meaning of that has been explored earlier, at **10.3.6.1**. In addition, we should note that in the course of conducting litigation, the barrister may find herself giving an undertaking, either to do or not do something. Where the undertaking involves an agreed timescale, it should be adhered to. Otherwise, any action that needs to be taken to comply with the undertaking should be taken within a reasonable time (rC11).

The fact that one has a litigation extension does not remove the prohibition against holding client money (see rC73). It also does not remove the prohibition against undertaking 'the general management, administration, or conduct of a client's affairs' (rS25). However, it is now possible for the barrister with a litigation extension to instruct another barrister on behalf of his client; this may seem an odd course of action but perhaps the other barrister has a particular specialisation which the current one does not have (see BSB Guidance, para 7).

10.3.6.4 When you do not need a litigation extension

Obviously, if you do not propose to 'conduct litigation', then you will not need a litigation extension to your practising certificate. But if you do need to conduct litigation, you may not need a litigation extension. There are two situations where a barrister may conduct litigation without obtaining a litigation extension. First, an employed barrister who was authorised to conduct litigation under the previous Code of Conduct (the 8th edition) retains that authorisation, so long as he remains in employed practice and the entity for which he works is itself authorised by the BSB to conduct litigation. Secondly, primary legislation may permit a barrister to conduct litigation. For example, Crown Prosecutors are entitled under the Prosecution of Offences Act 1985 to conduct litigation in connection with their role within the Crown Prosecution Service. Barristers employed in the Treasury Solicitors office, or a government department, are able to conduct litigation within the scope of their employment 'because of historic and current legislation' (see BSB Guidance, para 9).

10.3.7 Applying for a practising certificate

10.3.7.1 Generally

Essentially what is required here is to:

- complete the application form
- provide all information required
- pay the appropriate fee.

See rules rS48–9.

There are slightly different requirements for the information to be provided, depending on whether one is applying for a practising certificate or a litigation extension.

The applicant is personally responsible for the content of the application and, of course, no application should be submitted unless the applicant believes it contains full and accurate information.

The fee varies, according to the income earned in the preceding calendar year. For example, if income earned was £30,000 or less, the fee for a 2022–3 practising certificate is £100; for income between £30,001 and £60,000, the fee is £253.

10.3.7.2 Provisional practising certificates

Once a pupil has completed their first six months of pupillage (or 'non-practising period'), they should confirm satisfactory completion to the BSB and register a 'second six' pupillage with the BSB. (See also **10.5** on Youth Court work.) They will then be entitled to a *provisional* practising certificate. If the pupil supervisor is not available, the pupil can ask the head of chambers or director of pupil training to sign the 'certificate of completion or exemption of the non-practising period'. The certificate should still identify the pupil supervisor. Once the BSB is satisfied that everything is in place, it will issue a practising certificate, confirming that the pupil is now authorised to undertake reserved legal activities from a specified date. This procedure takes place on an online portal, MyBar; the practising certificate is simply stored on MyBar as a pdf file. See also rS11.

10.3.7.3 Moving from a provisional practising certificate to a full one

The BSB will require confirmation of satisfactory completion for the 'second six'. The BSB will then send details on how to change one's status from pupil to either practising barrister or unregistered barrister, as appropriate. Where the pupil is changing their status to practising barrister, the BSB will then issue a full practising certificate.

If the pupil barrister has completed their 'second six' but not obtained a tenancy in chambers, they may sometimes move on to a status known informally as a 'third six'. The BSB considers this as a period of practice and not as pupillage. The 'third six' barrister will therefore need to obtain a full practising certificate, in the manner set out above.

10.4 Registration of European lawyers

This is covered in the Handbook at Part 3, section D. The rules relating to the registration of 'European Lawyers' are set out in rS78–80. Following the United Kingdom's departure from the European Union the rules regarding the registration of 'European Lawyers' have changed and you will note the provisions relate to the registration of a *Qualified Swiss Lawyer*. The implications and specificity of these provisions are beyond the scope of this manual. Suffice it to say, our departure from the European Union has had a significant impact on the rules relating to European Lawyer registration.

As an alternative to registration, the European lawyer may decide to apply to be called to the Bar, in which case he will not be practising under his home professional title but will instead be practising as a barrister. See the Bar Qualification Manual on the BSB website for further information.

10.5 Youth Court work

Registration with the BSB is required for the barrister who wishes to undertake work in the Youth Court in the next 12 months; see rS59.6. This provision was introduced following a review into the standards of advocacy in the Youth Court in 2015. Essentially, the barrister is now asked to make a declaration that they possess the necessary specialist skills, knowledge, and attributes 'to work effectively with young people' (see further the BSB guide to Youth Proceedings competences, published February 2017 on the BSB website).

Registration is done through the MyBar portal. It may happen that a barrister who had not registered is unexpectedly instructed to perform work in the Youth Court; if so, he should register with the BSB within 28 days of accepting those instructions. If the barrister is a pupil in their practising period ('second six') they will be asked on registering for their provisional practising certificate whether they expect to undertake work in the Youth Court during the 'practising period' of pupillage. If the pupil answered that question in the negative and then the unexpected happens, they should email PupillageRecords@BarStandardsBoard.org.uk within 28 days.

11

Continuing professional development

11.1 Introduction

The rules on continuing professional development ('CPD') are to be found in Part 4 of the Handbook.

The BSB takes CPD very seriously. Every practising barrister must submit an annual declaration to the BSB, confirming that he has completed his CPD requirement. Looking at the reports of professional misconduct findings on the BSB website over recent years, it would seem that this is one of the more frequent reasons for a barrister to find himself the subject of disciplinary proceedings. So, clearly the BSB does check up that barristers are meeting their CPD obligations and takes action when it finds a shortcoming. Measures reported against non-compliant barristers include fines, suspension, and even disbarment.

Since January 2017, there has been a new scheme for CPD. We shall focus on rules rQ130–5 (the whole section on CPD is rQ130–8). Some of these provisions need not concern us further as they apply to people who were barristers on 1 October 2001, which takes us outside the scope of the manual. This leaves us with the following:

- rQ130—definitions
- rQ132—affects those barristers on the New Practitioner Programme ('NPP')—and gQ2
- rQ133—affects barristers on the Established Practitioners Programme ('EPP')
- rQ134—sets out the requirements for a barrister on the EPP—and gQ3–5
- rQ135—the obligation to produce one's CPD plan and record for inspection by the BSB.

11.2 The New Practitioner Programme

We need to start with some definitions (see rQ130). A 'calendar year' begins on 1 January and concludes on 31 December of the same year. A 'pupillage year' is any calendar year in which the barrister was a pupil, even if just for one day. CPD will not kick in for this barrister until 1 January of the year following any pupillage year. Assuming that the barrister now holds a practising certificate (if not, he can forget about CPD), then he will be in the New Practitioner Programme. This covers barristers in their first three calendar years of practice (post-pupillage). During this three-year period, the barrister must complete a minimum of 45 hours of CPD (rQ132). For the types of activity that count as CPD, reference should be made to the NPP guidance (see gQ2). There is no annual requirement for CPD in the NPP.

11.3 The Established Practitioner Programme

The Established Practitioner Programme ('EPP') takes over once the barrister has completed the NPP. There is now an annual CPD obligation (rQ130.4), specifically any EPP barrister holding a practising certificate during any part of a calendar year has to undertake CPD (rQ133). In order to meet this obligation, the EPP barrister must do the following (rQ134):

- he must prepare a written CPD plan. This should set out his learning objectives (defined in rQ130.8) and the types of CPD activities that he plans to undertake during the calendar year
- he has to keep a written record of
  - the activities undertaken
  - his reflection on those activities
  - any variation from what was planned
  - his assessment of his learning objectives for the future
- he must keep the record of his CPD plan and completed activities for three years and
- he must submit an annual declaration of completion of CPD to the BSB, in the form specified.

Further guidance on how to plan, undertake, and record one's CPD is given in the CPD Guidance (gQ3). There is no minimum number of hours' CPD that a barrister has to do. Instead, it is up to the individual to determine what he needs to do to satisfy the CPD requirements (gQ4). Compliance with these requirements will be monitored by the BSB (gQ4) and the barrister must produce his CPD plan and record at the request of the BSB (rQ135). As the Handbook states, the 'underlying principle behind the requirement to plan CPD and set learning objectives is that barristers consider their own circumstances and development needs when they complete CPD activities. This best ensures that activities completed contribute to the development of the barrister's practice' (gQ5).

The Proceeds of Crime Act 2002

12.1 The problem posed by the Proceeds of Crime Act 2002

Since it came into force, the Proceeds of Crime Act 2002 ('POCA 2002') has caused considerable anxiety for lawyers. Following the decision of the Court of Appeal in *Bowman v Fels* [2005] EWCA Civ 226, the main remaining area of concern for lawyers is the reporting obligation under s 330 when working in 'the regulated sector'. However, there is also the need to advise the client when he or she is at risk of liability under s 327 and/or s 329. Further new legislation appeared subsequently, in the form of the Money Laundering, Terrorist Financing and Transfer of Funds (Information on the Payer) Regulations 2017 (as amended), which came into force on 26 June 2017. HM Treasury has decided that there should be one set of anti-money laundering (AML) guidance for the legal sector in England, Wales, Scotland, and Northern Ireland. The current legal sector AML guidance can be found here; <https://www.barstandardsboard.org.uk/for-barristers/compliance-with-your-obligations/anti-money-laundering-counter-terrorist-financing/aml-guidance.html>.

The guidance is separated into two parts, with Part 1 providing general guidance for the legal sector whilst Part 2 is intended to provide more tailored AML guidance for specific types of legal practices or practitioners. Part 2a of the current AML guidance is specifically written to reflect the type of work that barristers typically engage in, the risks they are exposed to, and contains several useful FAQs and case studies to assist with interpreting the relevant legislation. Barristers are required to read Part 2a in the first instance, drawing on Part 1 for further detail where relevant. Both parts of the guidance documents are voluminous and therefore it is tentatively suggested that the rest of this chapter may suffice for the purposes of a reader of this manual. When embarking on the post-Bar Course stage of your professional career, whether self-employed or perhaps as an employee of an LLP, you would be well advised to visit the BSB website once more and embark on a more concentrated reading of the material that you find there.

To discuss the legislation, this chapter uses the specific example of financial relief. Financial relief is the process by which divorcing spouses obtain financial resolution of their affairs from the court. However, that should make it no less applicable to other situations. In financial relief, the client is in practice obliged to tell his or her adviser about all of his or her assets and income because of the obligation to the court of full and frank disclosure. The problem is that this process may disclose that some of those assets are the proceeds of crime.

In order for there to be proceeds of crime, somebody (usually the client or another party in the context of legal proceedings) must have engaged in 'criminal conduct' (s 340(2)). It is not necessary that he or she has actually been convicted of an offence, and your client does not necessarily need to have personally engaged in the criminal conduct, only (for example) to be in possession of criminal property (see **12.2.2**).

It may be that the client has, for example, been involved in mainstream drug dealing. More commonly, there may be issues of tax evasion; for example, the client receives money 'cash in hand'. This is not in itself 'criminal conduct'—anyone can pay their bills in cash or by cheque—but it becomes an offence if he or she fails to disclose these earnings to HM Revenue & Customs. Tax evasion is a crime, as is benefit fraud.

A number of problems face the lawyer as a result of the POCA 2002. First, there are the 'principal offences' under Part VII of the POCA 2002 (ss 327, 328, and 329) and the secondary offences under ss 333A–D (tipping off) and s 342 (prejudicing an investigation). The lawyer will need to advise the client of potential liability under these sections. There is a *small* residual risk of lawyers being liable under s 328 despite the judgment in *Bowman*. Secondly, since 15 December 2007, lawyers have been subject to the Money Laundering Regulations, and thus may be a 'relevant person' in terms of the Regulations, while also being in the 'regulated sector' in terms of the Act (as defined by Sch 9—definitions of these terms are the same in the Act and the Regulations). Being in the regulated sector exposes lawyers to the risk of criminal liability for breach of s 330 of the POCA 2002 (that is, failure to disclose). The risks are more acute for solicitors owing to the nature of their work (after all, they usually have first, and continuous, contact with the client and handle the client's money) but, for certain types of work, the Bar is also under specific obligations and at risk of criminal liability.

12.2   Principal offences

12.2.1   Key differences between the principal and secondary offences

Sections 327, 328, and 329 set out the principal offences in Part VII of the POCA 2002. They differ from the secondary offences (considered later) in a number of key respects:

- Disclosure in respect of the principal offences is 'authorised disclosure' under s 338 (not 'protected disclosure' under s 337 which relates to the secondary offences).

- The disclosure defence under s 338 requires not only 'authorised disclosure' but also the 'appropriate consent' under s 335. Section 337 does not require a consent because of the fundamental difference in the duties between ss 327–9 and 330: in ss 327–9, disclosure is made in order to exonerate the discloser from criminal responsibility for what he or she would otherwise do; s 330 on the other hand is a general duty (arising from the fact of one's practice in the regulated sector) to disclose the fact that someone is involved in money laundering and in that sense is separate from any activity with which the discloser himself is involved.

12.2.2   Definitions

'Criminal conduct' is defined in s 340(2) (s 340 is in fact the definition section for Part VII of the POCA 2002). It covers conduct which would constitute an offence in any part of the UK—so, for example, tax evasion is a criminal offence in UK law. It also covers conduct which occurs abroad but would be an offence in the UK if it had occurred there, but in those circumstances defendants charged under ss 327, 328, 329, and 330 may be able to take advantage of the defences in those sections. These provide that if the defendant knew or believed on reasonable grounds that the relevant conduct had occurred in a particular country or territory outside the UK, *and* that conduct was not criminal according to *local* laws at the time it occurred, *and* it was not conduct of a type prescribed by order of the Secretary of State, the defendant has not committed the offence.

'Criminal property' (s 340(3)) is that which constitutes 'a person's benefit from criminal conduct or . . . represents such a benefit (in whole or part and whether directly or indirectly)', and the alleged offender (that is, the person accused of facilitating money laundering, etc) knows or suspects that it constitutes or represents such a benefit.

If, for example, in a financial relief claim, the matrimonial home had been partially paid for by 'criminal property' in the form of unpaid tax monies—say, by paying the mortgage instalments partly with these monies—the house could 'represent' the benefit from criminal conduct. The same might be the case for other assets.

12.2.3   Sections 327, 328, and 329

Sections 327, 328, and 329 of the POCA 2002 may affect your client, and the client will need to be advised of this. Section 327 provides that:

> *(1) A person commits an offence if he—*
>> *(a) conceals criminal property;*
>> *(b) disguises criminal property;*

> (c) *converts criminal property;*
>
> (d) *transfers criminal property;*
>
> (e) *removes criminal property from England and Wales or from Scotland or from Northern Ireland.*
>
> . . .
>
> (3) *Concealing or disguising criminal property includes concealing or disguising its nature, source, location, disposition, movement or ownership, or any rights with respect to it.*

Section 328 provides that:

> (1) *A person commits an offence if he enters into or becomes concerned in an arrangement which he knows or suspects facilitates (by whatever means) the acquisition, retention, use or control of criminal property by or on behalf of another person.*

As discussed later, 'being concerned in an arrangement' was once thought to include involvement in litigation which resulted in a settlement or an order of the court in relation to proceeds of crime. The Court of Appeal in *Bowman* made it quite clear that s 328 is not intended to affect 'the ordinary conduct of litigation by legal professionals. That includes any step taken by them in litigation from the issue of proceedings and the securing of injunctive relief or a freezing order up to its final disposal by judgment', and that such activities are not to be regarded as 'being concerned in an arrangement'. Subject to the points made at **12.7.2** et seq, s 328 now clearly does not apply to the involvement of a lawyer in litigation or the resolution of litigation by agreement.

However, the client may still have committed the offence in relation to an arrangement over property, *independent of the litigation process*, for example a sham property transaction designed to conceal the proceeds of crime.

Section 329 provides:

> (1) *A person commits an offence if he—*
>
> (a) *acquires criminal property;*
>
> (b) *uses criminal property;*
>
> (c) *has possession of criminal property.*

For example, a wife in a financial relief claim who had not personally committed the criminal offence of tax evasion could potentially be accused of the s 329 offence—acquiring, using, or possessing criminal property—if the house that she jointly owns with her tax-evading husband was bought with money he had not declared to tax—unless she makes an authorised disclosure under s 338. The husband could conceivably be accused of both s 327 and s 329 offences, as well as tax evasion itself. In order to protect herself, the wife should make an 'authorised disclosure' under s 338.

12.2.4   Defences to the principal offences

The client (and the barrister, in the rare situation that disclosure is required of him) can obtain a complete defence by making an 'authorised disclosure' under s 338 (in the manner prescribed by s 339), *and* by getting the 'appropriate consent' (s 335) to carrying out an activity that may result in a person committing a principal money laundering offence as contained in Part VII of the POCA 2002.

Generally speaking, disclosure is to the National Crime Agency ('NCA'). The way that consent works is as follows:

- The NCA may consent within seven days of disclosure being made, in which case the client can continue with the act or transaction in question.

- If not, the client is required to wait for seven working days from the working day after disclosure. Once that period has passed without a notice of refusal from the NCA, the consent is deemed and the client can continue with the act or transaction.

- If the NCA gives notice of refusal within the seven-day period, there is then a moratorium period of 31 calendar days from the day on which refusal is received. This 31-day period may be extended, on application, by up to six months. Thereafter, the client is free to continue with the act or transaction.

Specific guidance can be found in paras 174–201 of Part 2a of the current legal sector AML guidance.

12.2.5   Does s 328 apply to the activities of lawyers?

The judgment in *Bowman* was handed down by the Court of Appeal on 8 March 2005. It is authority of considerable public importance since this was the first full examination by the Court of Appeal of the impact of the POCA 2002 on legal professional privilege between lawyer and client. It effectively overrules *P v P (Ancillary Relief; Proceeds of Crime)* [2003] EWHC Fam 2260.

12.2.5.1   Background

Prior to this decision, the word 'arrangement' was believed to cover litigation, including settlement of such litigation by agreement. Where a lawyer knew or suspected that money or assets being the subject of litigation were the proceeds of crime, then he or she could only escape criminal liability under s 328 by making an 'authorised disclosure'—in other words, by notifying the NCA of the suspected criminal activity and obtaining the appropriate consent to proceed with the arrangement. For lawyers, it seemed that the fundamental principle of legal professional privilege had been fatally undermined—not only would a lawyer be obliged to report suspected money laundering by the other party, but he or she would also be compelled to make disclosure to a third party of suspected money laundering by his or her own client.

12.2.5.2   The central question in *Bowman*

The Court of Appeal identified the following issues (para 24):

- whether s 328 applied to the ordinary conduct of legal proceedings at all

- whether Parliament could have been taken, without using clear words to that effect, to have intended to override the very important principles of legal professional privilege.

12.2.5.3   The decision in *Bowman*

The Court of Appeal concluded as follows:

- (para 83) Section 328 is not intended to affect 'the ordinary conduct of litigation by legal professionals. That includes any step taken by them in litigation from the issue of proceedings and the securing of injunctive relief or a freezing order up to its final disposal by judgment.' In other words, conducting litigation does not involve 'becoming concerned in an arrangement' within the meaning of s 328, and s 328 is therefore inapplicable to such activities.

- (para 87) The Court of Appeal further stated that even if the above conclusion was wrong, it was quite clear that on a proper construction s 328 does not override legal professional privilege.

- (paras 99 and 100) The Court of Appeal also came to the view that resolution of the whole, or any aspect of, legal proceedings by agreement would equally be outside the scope of s 328.

Clearly, this guidance has brought considerable clarity to an area which caused enormous concern to lawyers involved in litigation when the POCA 2002 was first enacted. A lawyer can advise and represent a client in the vast majority of situations without fear of being obliged to breach legal professional privilege by reporting suspected money laundering to the authorities. However, there remain some situations where s 328 could apply to lawyers. These are discussed at **12.7**.

12.3   Secondary offences

12.3.1   The Money Laundering, Terrorist Financing and Transfer of Funds (Information on the Payer) Regulations 2017

A barrister acting in the course of business who is a 'relevant person' as defined in the Regulations will be subject to additional requirements and liability. Barristers most likely to fall within the ambit of the Regulations are members of the Chancery Bar involved in non-contentious advisory work, especially in relation to business or taxation or property transactions and the setting up of companies and trusts.

12.3.1.1   When is counsel deemed to be a 'relevant person'?

Regulation 8(2) sets out a list of relevant persons, including at (c) 'tax advisers' and at (d) 'independent legal professionals'. 'Independent legal professional' is further defined in reg 12(1) as being a firm or sole practitioner providing legal or notarial services in financial or real property transactions concerning: at (a) the buying and selling of real property or business entities; and at (e) the creation, operation, or management of trusts, companies, or similar structures. Barristers may also engage the Regulations by way of acting as a 'trust or company service provider' as per reg 12(2).

The Regulations are transaction based; therefore counsel has to consider for every piece of work undertaken whether he or she is a relevant person.

Barristers must be astute to determine whether any particular piece of work undertaken by them falls within the Regulations, as an error in this regard and consequential failure to implement the requisite systems will result in the commission of a criminal offence, punishable by a fine or up to two years' imprisonment.

12.3.1.2   Additional requirements under the Regulations

The additional requirements for a relevant person when conducting business include the carrying out of:

- risk management practices
- due diligence procedures
- reliance and record-keeping procedures
- internal reporting procedures and training of employees.

The final set of requirements above are of less significance to the Bar than to other businesses in the regulated sector, because barristers in private practice are individuals, neither employing nor acting in association with any other person and are solely responsible for their own professional practice. Most of these latter requirements either do not apply or such individuals are exempted.

In terms of due diligence, record-keeping, and identification procedures, this will usually have been carried out by the UK solicitor or other regulated professional, and counsel's duty will often be discharged by ensuring that in the instructions a letter or certificate is included which confirms that the relevant process has been carried out. Where this is not the case, a barrister must carry out his own checks. The essence of due diligence is that the relevant person must know who they are representing, and obtain information as to the lay client's intention and purpose for instructing counsel. Guidance in respect of these matters can be found in paras 57–172 of Part 2a of the current legal sector AML guidance.

12.3.2   Liability under s 330 for barristers operating within the regulated sector

Since barristers are considered to be in the 'regulated sector', they are open to criminal liability under s 330, which is the offence of 'failure to disclose' by a person in the 'regulated sector'. However, the section includes a defence relating to legal privilege, which means that it will not catch most barristers engaged in the ordinary conduct of litigation. Section 330(1)–(5) (as amended) reads as follows:

(1) A person commits an offence if the conditions in subsections (2) to (4) are satisfied.

(2) The first condition is that he—

  (a) knows or suspects, or

  (b) has reasonable grounds for knowing or suspecting,

  that another person is engaged in money laundering.

(3) The second condition is that the information or other matter—

  (a) on which his knowledge or suspicion is based, or

(b) which gives reasonable grounds for such knowledge or suspicion

came to him in the course of a business in the regulated sector.

(3A) The third condition is—

(a) that he can identify the other person mentioned in subsection (2) or the whereabouts of any of the laundered property, or

(b) that he believes, or it is reasonable to expect him to believe, that the information or other matter mentioned in subsection (3) will or may assist in identifying that other person or the whereabouts of any of the laundered property.

(4) The fourth condition is that he does not make the required disclosure to—

(a) a nominated officer, or

(b) a person authorised for the purposes of this Part by the Director General of the National Crime Agency,

as soon as practicable after the information or other matter mentioned in subsection (3) comes to him.

(5) The required disclosure is a disclosure of—

(a) the identity of the other person mentioned in subsection (2), if he knows it,

(b) the whereabouts of the laundered property, so far as he knows it, and

(c) the information or other matter mentioned in subsection (3).

Note first that, unlike in other parts of Part VII, the standard is objective, not subjective. If you have failed to 'know' or 'suspect' personally, you can be liable if there were 'reasonable grounds' on which you should have known or suspected. In other words, the 'moron' defence (that the grounds were there but you simply failed to notice them) is not available to you.

So, for any piece of work you do, you have to consider your obligations under s 330. If the conditions in ss 2–4 apply then, subject to the defences described below, you may have an obligation to make a 'protected' disclosure under s 337.

12.3.3 Defences

There are in fact two defences available for a failure to disclose under s 330(6):

- you have a reasonable excuse for not making disclosure
- you are a professional legal adviser and the information (the identity of the other person in subsection (2), or the whereabouts of the laundered property, or the information or matter in subsection (3)) has come to you in privileged circumstances.

In other words, there is a legal professional privilege defence to s 330. Section 330(10) clarifies the circumstances in which it applies. However, it is to some degree limited by s 330(11), which provides that legal professional privilege will not apply where 'information . . . is communicated or given with the intention of furthering a criminal purpose'. It is not clear whose intention is relevant for the purposes of this section. Given the wide manner in which criminal behaviour prohibited by ss 327, 328, and 329 is drafted, the lawyer will have to look very closely at what the client is intending to achieve in communicating information to the lawyer. Certainly, in telling you that her husband is taking cash in hand and not declaring it for tax purposes, a financial relief client probably is not intending to further a criminal purpose; rather she is telling you this in order to maximise her recovery in the financial relief—the sole or dominant purpose of her giving you this information being the conduct of the family proceedings. Further guidance can be found in paras 236–50 of Part 2a of the current legal sector AML guidance.

If you do make disclosure under s 337 ('protected disclosure'), provided that you comply with the conditions of s 337, you will be protected against litigation by the client for breaching confidentiality by s 337(1). Check that you have (or should have) suspicion based on real grounds, as opposed to mere speculation, or you may be at risk that your disclosure is not in accordance with s 337 and thus leave yourself vulnerable to successful litigation by the client.

12.4   Other secondary offences

There are two other secondary offences which merit consideration. These arise particularly in the context of discussing the issue of disclosure with the client.

12.4.1   Sections 333A–D—'tipping off'

The offence of 'tipping off' has been amended and now only applies within the regulated sector. Essentially, it relates to a situation where you know or suspect that a disclosure has been made (for example, your solicitor has made a disclosure already). The offence cannot be committed in relation to a disclosure that is yet to be made (as to which, see s 342 below). Where you 'make a disclosure which is likely to prejudice any investigation which might be conducted' as a result of the primary disclosure, you may be guilty of an offence. The 'disclosure' you make could be to your client, or to the other side, the point being that by revealing what you know or intend to do, you could enable a criminal or money launderer to cover his or her tracks, conceal the evidence, etc. Defences are available—those most likely to be relevant to a barrister are set out in s 333D. Disclosure to the Bar Council or to further a proper investigation is permissible as is disclosure made without knowing or suspecting that it might prejudice an investigation under the Act. Also permitted is a disclosure made to your client and 'for the purpose of dissuading the client from engaging in conduct amounting to an offence' (s 333D(2)(b)). It is not clear how this will work in practice; it is submitted that its purpose is to enable the avoidance of an absurd, 'quasi-entrapment' scenario, where a legal adviser would be forced to stand dumbly by and watch a client commit a criminal offence that is bound to be detected, which would not be committed at all if the adviser could advise the client as to the reality of the situation.

12.4.2   Section 342—prejudicing an investigation

Unlike ss 333A–D, this offence *can* be committed in advance of a disclosure being made, and relates to conduct, including making disclosures, which could prejudice an investigation which is being made or is contemplated. (Other conduct could include, for example, concealing or falsifying or destroying relevant documents.)

A variety of defences are available, including legal professional privilege. Again, legal professional privilege is limited where there is an intention to further a criminal purpose, and again the relevant intention is that of the lawyer.

In the circumstances, it may be hard to see how a lawyer could be considered to be furthering a criminal intention of his own (in relation to 'tipping off' and the prejudicing of investigation offences) in simply advising a client of the state of the law with regard to his or her position, for example the risk of the client committing an offence under s 329.

12.5   Penalties

12.5.1   Section 334

Sections 327, 328, and 329	on summary conviction, imprisonment of up to six months or a fine or both; on indictment, a fine or imprisonment of up to 14 years.
Sections 330 and 333A–D	on summary conviction, imprisonment of up to six months or a fine or both; on indictment, a fine or imprisonment of up to five years.

12.5.2 Section 342

Section 342   on summary conviction, imprisonment of up to six
                                   months or a fine or both; on indictment, a fine or
                                   imprisonment of up to five years.

Clearly, it pays to get it right. And note that the mere fact that you advise the solicitor that
he has a reporting obligation under the POCA 2002 does not discharge your own obligations.
However, it is perfectly possible to make joint disclosure to the NCA on the part of the solicitor, counsel, and possibly the client. In addition, the NCA's predecessor entity, the Serious
Organised Crime Agency, indicated in its guidance that if a solicitor has made a report in
advance of instructing counsel and counsel's report would be based on the exact same facts,
there is no obligation on counsel to report further.

12.6 Sources of useful information

(a) The Bar Standards Board (<https://www.barstandardsboard.org.uk/regulatory-
    requirements/anti-money-laundering-and-counter-terrorist-financing/>)—the
    website provides resources to assist with barristers' obligations under the Regu-
    lations. You can access the legal sector AML guidance from here as well.

(b) *Bowman v Fels* [2005] EWCA Civ 226 can be accessed through the Court Service website
    (<https://www.gov.uk/government/organisations/hm-courts-and-tribunals-service>)—
    search under the 'Legal/Professional' section—or go directly to <http://www.bailii.org>.

(c) National Crime Agency (<https://nationalcrimeagency.gov.uk/what-we-do/crime-
    threats/money-laundering-and-terrorist-financing>)—for information such as how
    to go about making a report, and for NCA guidance.

12.7 Areas in which counsel remains at risk of liability under the POCA 2002

The decision in *Bowman v Fels* [2005] EWCA Civ 226 has provided considerable clarity on an
issue of acute concern to litigators. However, lawyers still need to tread carefully in certain
areas—and in others, confusion remains. References to paragraph numbers in the following
are to paragraphs in *Bowman*.

12.7.1 Section 330 and the regulated sector

Lawyers will have to continue to keep possible liability under s 330 in mind when operating
in the regulated sector (principally in relation to financial and real estate transactions). This
will be of particular concern to certain sectors of the Bar, such as tax specialists and Chancery practitioners who are routinely involved in such work—although every lawyer needs to
be aware of the potential application of s 330, since it is transaction based; in other words,
its applicability depends on the subject matter of every individual transaction rather than
the lawyer's general area of work. It may well be that specialist Bar associations issue future
guidance specific to their areas in relation to s 330 obligations. Of course, availability of the
legal professional privilege defence is likely to mean that you are very rarely obliged to report
money laundering by the client. As pointed out in para 16 (Part 2a of the AML guidance),
it is apparent from the reasoning in *Bowman* that the ordinary conduct of litigation or its
consensual resolution does not fall within the 'regulated sector' for the purposes of s 330
in any event, and so s 330 really only applies to non-contentious advisory work within the
'regulated sector'.

12.7.2   Negotiation and agreement in the absence of issued proceedings

At paras 99–102, the Court of Appeal considered resolution of the whole, or part, of legal proceedings by agreement. The obvious point was made that if the ordinary conduct of litigation was to be treated as outside the scope of s 328, as the court had already concluded, then it would be inconsistent and illogical to nevertheless treat any step in such proceedings taken by *agreement*, or a settlement of the litigation obtained by agreement, as subject to s 328. Given the considerable emphasis on resolution of litigation by agreement not only in domestic law (the 'Woolf reforms') but also in international law, the court concluded that consensual steps—including final resolution by agreement—were not subject to s 328.

However, the court indicated (para 101) that the situation might be different where the agreed settlement was *independent* of litigation. The court was careful to use the phrase 'in a litigious context' when discussing consensual agreement. This appears to extend to situations of *existing or contemplated legal proceedings* only. As the court pointed out (para 101), this is in line with the language of the relevant European directives, as well as relevant sections of the POCA 2002. It does, however, leave something of a grey area. Surely a lawyer with his or her client's interests foremost in their mind will attempt to negotiate a settlement without recourse to legal proceedings. At what point would a court regard him or her as negotiating in the context of 'contemplated' legal proceedings (and thus beyond the reach of s 328)? Will lawyers have to threaten legal proceedings as a first step to attempting negotiation in all cases in order to escape the confines of s 328?

There is considerable emphasis on the use and observance of pre-action protocols since the Woolf reforms. It is suggested that observance of such protocols (the purpose of which is to avoid litigation where possible by agreed settlement) could, and would, be considered by a court as negotiation in the context of contemplated legal proceedings. Clearly, legal proceedings are the likely result if negotiation under the protocol fails, and protocols additionally have as their aim the efficient preparation of the case for litigation in the event of failed negotiation. It may be that this aspect of the applicability, or not, of s 328 will serve to emphasise and increase use of the protocols.

12.7.3   Sham litigation

While not expressing a concluded view on the point, the Court of Appeal referred to the possibility that s 328 could potentially apply to lawyers in the situation where they were:

> concerned with a settlement which did not reflect the legal and practical merits of the parties' respective positions in the proceedings, and was known or suspected to be no more than a pretext for agreeing on the acquisition, retention, use or control of criminal property. (para 102)

This would be an entirely logical position on the basis of the court's interpretation of the legislation. First, s 330, used by the court to illuminate the intentions of the legislator in respect of s 328, clearly provides for a situation where legal professional privilege does not apply (s 330(11)), whereby if the client intends to further a criminal purpose (such as concealing proceeds of crime) in communicating the relevant information to his lawyer, privilege does not attach and the lawyer working in the regulated sector must report. Secondly, recital 17 of the 2001 Directive (Directive 2001/97/EC amending Council Directive 91/308/EEC on prevention of the use of the financial system for the purpose of money laundering), on which the court placed so much reliance in interpreting the applicability of s 328 to litigation, states:

> *legal advice remains subject to the obligation of professional secrecy unless the legal counsellor is taking part in money laundering activities, the legal advice is provided for money laundering purposes, or the lawyer knows that the client is seeking legal advice for money laundering purposes.*

The consequences are that a lawyer conducting litigation must be astute to the possibility that the litigation is a sham in order to pursue money laundering. A good indication might be that the settlement did not substantially reflect the merits of each side's case. The Court of Appeal further made the point that this still leaves the question of at what point the s 328 offence could be said to have been committed by the lawyer. In paras 67 and 68 of the judgment, the court took the view that an offence under s 328 could not have been committed until the 'arrangement' was actually made.

12.7.4   Transactions resulting from the judgment

The Court of Appeal stated at para 59 that:

> while legal advice may be given in any area, one would not often expect legal professionals assisting in the planning or execution of or acting for a client in respect of a financial or real estate transaction of a kind specified in Article 2a(5) to have received from, or obtained on, their client relevant information 'in the course of performing their task of defending or representing that client in, or concerning judicial proceedings'.

This viewpoint is doubtless entirely accurate in relation to many situations. However, the question arises, what is the position in relation to the 'fruits' of litigation? More often than not, the implementation of an order, or an agreed resolution to litigation, will involve lawyers in transactions—financial, commercial, real property. An example could be a financial relief case, involving the transfer of a house, or a shareholding, to one of the parties. This is clearly within the meaning of 'transaction' in Art 2a(5) of the 2001 Directive, and therefore subject to s 330. Quite often (if not always), the law firms involved in the litigation will be those dealing with the transactions required to finally resolve the dispute. To what degree could the knowledge of a client's wrongdoing gained by the litigation team be imputed to the team dealing with the transactions flowing from resolution of the litigation? Or perhaps even more acutely, what about the situation of a sole practitioner dealing with the litigation and the transactions flowing from it?

One answer to this dilemma seems to depend on how one interprets the reference to 'ordinary course of litigation' in the judgment. If it includes those transactions required to give effect to the order or agreement, then the difficulty is removed. Support for such an interpretation comes from para 62 of the judgment. Reference is made to the function of litigation—'resolving the rights and duties of two parties according to law'. Such 'resolution' would be threatened if parties were deterred from litigating due to a fear of a report of their activities at the stage of actually effecting the remedy obtained. More importantly, the court's reference to assets, being proceeds of money laundering, being 'retained *or used to satisfy any liability according to the outcome of proceedings*' seems to suggest that execution of the order or agreement would not be 'carrying out' a 'transaction' relating to money laundering.

Of course, such transactions, subject as they are to s 330, will benefit from the defence in s 330(6) and (10)—that the information has come to the lawyer in privileged circumstances and so disclosure will not be required. However, under s 330(11), privilege will afford no defence to the obligation to disclose if the client's purpose in communicating the information is a criminal purpose, and it may well be here that the problem arises.

12.7.5   Conclusion

Clearly, *Bowman* and its subsequent consideration has provided considerable clarity to lawyers in terms of their obligations under ss 328 and 330 of the POCA 2002 and the Money Laundering Regulations 2017 and to their clients in terms of legal professional privilege. However, some caution may still be required with regard to the situations suggested herein. As ever, it is crucial that you are familiar with, and remain up to date with, suitable professional guidance.

13

The letter and spirit of the Code: Professional ethics and personal values

13.1 The lawyer joke

> *A layperson, an accountant and a lawyer were all asked: 'What do two and two make?'*
> *The layperson replied: 'Four, of course.'*
> *The accountant replied: 'Four—or five.'*
> *The lawyer replied: 'What do you want it to make?'*

Lawyers are the butt of many jokes, many of which flow from a perception that lawyers are capable of acting quite unethically in pursuit of their client's interests. While this perception has, fortunately, never developed in the UK to the extent that it has in the USA, the characteristics of practice in common law jurisdictions expose lawyers to many ethical dilemmas, and responses to these vary. This chapter (and indeed this manual) will provide you with some answers, but in other areas it will simply provide you with a framework within which you will still have to make your own decisions. In these cases it should provide you with tools and ideas that may help you to arrive at conclusions that satisfy the ethical demands of practice.

The issues have been neatly presented by Ross Cranston:

> An important policy issue is the extent to which the Code of Conduct ought to be infused by wider ethical notions. There are two aspects to this. One is encapsulated in the question: 'Can a good lawyer be a bad person?'. In other words, are the standards in the Code of Conduct untenable when laid alongside ethical thought or common morality? The second aspect is that if there is a discrepancy between the Code of Conduct and secular ethical thought, what is special about barristers that exempts them from the precepts of the latter? To put it another way, how is it that barristers can decide ethically on a course of action for a client which is different from that which they would adopt for themselves?

> (Cranston, R (ed), *Legal Ethics and Professional Responsibility* (Oxford: Clarendon Press, 1996))

The Bar Standards Board recognises this dilemma. Amongst the things it requires you to achieve on the Bar Course are 'knowledge and understanding of the philosophical issues and purposes underpinning ethical behaviour'. This and the following quotation are from the Bar Qualification Manual Part 2, p 63, 'Professional Ethics', available at <https://www.barstandardsboard.org.uk/uploads/assets/ef96719e-7616-4433-923906aef673494d/bqmpart2b-b2bptcsyllabus2018-19.pdf#page=63&zoom=100,92,97>. More specifically, you are expected to 'understand and appreciate the core professional values which underpin practice at the Bar of England and Wales, particularly the additional moral responsibilities held by the profession (over and above the population in general) due to decision-making roles, functions and authority which are key to practice at the Bar'.

13.2 The Code of Conduct

The Bar Code of Conduct can be found in Part 2 of the BSB Handbook. It provides you with the duties, rules, and guidance that should inform all aspects of your practice at the Bar. It differs from a statute (the form of rule with which you will probably be most familiar) in that it contains Core Duties as well as Conduct Rules, that these are supported by Guidance, and, finally, that each section of the Conduct Rules is supported by the Outcomes that the rules are designed to achieve. These are valuable sources of assistance in interpretation.

These distinctive characteristics should remind you that you should not approach the Code as you would any other piece of legislation. Why should you not do so? It stems from the underlying principle within UK substantive law that all actions are permitted unless they are forbidden. Thus Acts that regulate behaviour are to be construed in a restrictive manner and loopholes may properly be exploited.

For example, the Theft Act 1968, s 9 provides:

(1) A person is guilty of burglary if:

    (a)   he enters any building or part of a building as a trespasser and with intent to commit any such offence as is mentioned in subsection (2) below; or

    (b)   having entered any building or part of a building as a trespasser, he steals or attempts to steal anything in the building or that part of it or inflicts or attempts to inflict on any person therein any grievous bodily harm.

(2) The offences referred to in subsection (1)(a) above are offences of stealing anything in the building or part of a building in question, of inflicting on any person therein any grievous bodily harm . . . therein, and of doing unlawful damage to the building or anything therein.

Your client has entered a building as a trespasser but with no particular intention and, once inside, decides to do unlawful damage to property within the building. Your advice to him should be to plead not guilty to a charge of burglary. This is because his actions fall within neither paragraph of the subsection even though his actions have produced the same result as behaviour that would lead to guilt (had he formed the intention to cause the damage before, rather than after entering the building). This conclusion may be hard for a layperson to understand but would be natural to any lawyer versed in statutory interpretation.

To adopt the same approach to following the Code may enable you to avoid successful disciplinary proceedings by the BSB. In other words, in so far as it acts in an analogous manner to a criminal statute, the Code may be treated in the same way. However, to approach the Code in this way could carry dangers for the reputation of the profession. Your interpretation of the Code should be informed by the desire to achieve its indicated outcomes and by ethical values, and where the Code permits a variety of responses your choice between them should be similarly informed. This is why the BSB requires that you understand these underpinning values.

An example of how the Code regulates your professional response arises from rC9:

(2) you must not draft any statement of case, witness statement, affidavit or other document containing:

. . .

    (c)   any allegation of fraud, unless you have clear instructions to allege fraud and you have reasonably credible material which establishes an arguable case of fraud;

The concept of 'reasonably credible material' inherently carries a degree of subjectivity. Suppose that you have been instructed by your lay client that the opponent has been perpetrating a fraud. It is not uncommon for hostility between the parties to lead to all sorts of allegations that are discovered later to be impossible of formal proof. That being the case, it would be unwise to incorporate such an allegation into any draft on the client's assertion alone. What, however, if the client (who has behaved in a temperate manner throughout) tells you that the opposing party has admitted to committing fraud, but no other independent evidence is available? What if, in addition, the client is prepared to make a statement of truth in respect of this allegation? Would such a statement be 'reasonably credible material' given that it is in essence no more than the original assertion presented formally in a way that is admissible in court? Should you still insist on some independent evidence?

In practical terms you would doubtless advise your professional client to seek independent evidence to corroborate your lay client's oral evidence before settling a statement of case that contained an allegation of fraud. If it is not forthcoming, should you pursue the allegation? The guidance section of this part of the Code offers no further assistance. The outcomes (oC6–9) are too general to help further. The assertion of an intemperate client would clearly be inadequate (it is the mischief the rule is designed to avoid). To rely on a statement of truth may be sufficient to avoid a finding of misconduct (although if there were no other evidence the client should be advised of the dangers of pressing the matter in court: a wasted costs order may loom). However, to refuse to incorporate such an allegation in those circumstances will upset your client, and is likely to upset them more if the allegations are in fact well founded. You must not let your independence be compromised (rC8), yet you should act in the best interests of your client (CD2 and rC15).

No doubt you should err on the side of caution and advise that further evidence should be obtained if possible, but it may not be available. Moreover, if, after settling the statement of case, it becomes clear that there is no credible evidence of fraud (for example, the opposing party may have made the admission to provoke a reaction or as an act of bravado) or if other facts come to light showing that the allegation of fraud has no prospect of success, you will no doubt recognise that the fraud allegation should no longer be pursued. It is submitted that the proper approach is not to seek a 'way around' the provisions of the Code, but to consider underlying values, so that your response is likely to assist to maintain the Bar's reputation as a thoroughly ethical profession (CD5). Fortunately, problems as awkward as this should not be a daily occurrence, and you should remember that advice will be available from your head of chambers or from the Bar Council.

An understanding of the underpinning values will give you a basis for deciding ethical questions beyond what the Code provides. Remember that behaviour prohibited by the Code is not made acceptable by a contrary underpinning value, but an underpinning value might validate conduct upon which the Code is silent or in circumstances that generate conflict between its provisions. Ultimately, where, having thought through matters in this degree of depth, you remain uncertain as to the proper way of proceeding, you should contact the Bar Council Ethical Enquiries Service available for advice in emergencies. Note that this service is only available for barristers and not for students.

13.3 Underpinning values

Here are a number of values that may be said to underpin the Code of Conduct. It is not intended to be exhaustive:

- justice
- respect for the law
- client autonomy
- confidentiality
- honesty.

How these values apply to the demands of practice at the Bar may best be understood by reading them in the context of the core principles identified by the Bar Standards Board in an earlier edition of the Code of Conduct (NB: eighth edition of the Bar Code of Conduct (obsolete since 2014)). These were:

- the principle of professional independence
- the principle of integrity
- the principle of duty to the court
- the principle of loyalty to the lay client
- an understanding of the problems and perception of conflict of interest
- the principle of non-discrimination on grounds of race, colour, ethnic or national origin, nationality, citizenship, sex, sexual orientation, marital status, disability, age, religion or belief and
- commitment to maintaining the highest professional standards of work, to the proper and efficient administration of justice, and to the Rule of Law.

13.3.1   Conflict in underpinning values

Conflict between values is inherent in legal practice. Lord Reid makes this clear in his opinion in *Rondel v Worsley* [1969] 1 AC 191, 227:

> Every counsel has a duty to his client fearlessly to raise every issue, advance every argument and ask every question, however distasteful, which he thinks will help his client's case. But, as an officer of the court concerned with the administration of justice, he has an overriding duty to the court, to the standards of his profession, and to the public, which may and often does lead to a conflict with his client's wishes or what the client thinks are his personal interests.

Consider a concrete situation. If your client in a criminal matter has provided you with information that is relevant (but adverse) to their case you will be faced with a conflict between maintaining confidentiality and not misleading the court. A perusal of the Code will throw up relevant provisions.

The Core Duties, in particular:

CD1 -

You must observe your duty to the *court* in the administration of justice

CD2 -

You must act in the best interests of each *client*

CD3 -

You must act with honesty, and with integrity

CD4 -

You must maintain your independence

CD5 -

You must not behave in a way which is likely to diminish the trust and confidence which the public places in you or in the profession

CD6 -

You must keep the affairs of each *client* confidential

Also:

rC3 -

You owe a duty to the *court* to act with independence in the interests of justice. This duty overrides any inconsistent obligations which you may have (other than obligations under the criminal law). It includes the following specific obligations which apply whether you are acting as an advocate or are otherwise involved in the conduct of litigation in whatever role (with the exception of Rule C3.1 below, which applies when acting as an advocate):

1 - you must not knowingly or recklessly mislead or attempt to mislead the *court*;

2 - you must not abuse your role as an advocate;

3 - you must take reasonable steps to avoid wasting the *court's* time;

4 - you must take reasonable steps to ensure that the *court* has before it all relevant decisions and legislative provisions;

5 - you must ensure that your ability to act independently is not compromised.

rC4 -

Your duty to act in the best interests of each *client* is subject to your duty to the *court*.

rC5 -

Your duty to the *court* does not require you to act in breach of your duty to keep the affairs of each *client* confidential.

These rules are helpful in identifying what is expected in relation to each of the underlying values. However, they provide little guidance as to how conflicts should be resolved. While on the one hand your duty to the court is described as overriding (rC3), it does not require breach of client confidentiality (rC5). Rule rC6 provides further detail:

rC6 -

Your duty not to mislead the court will include the following obligations:

you must not:

> a - make submissions, representations or any other statement; or
>
> b - ask questions which suggest facts to witnesses which you know, or are instructed, are untrue or misleading.

2 - you must not call witnesses to give evidence or put affidavits or witness statements to the *court* which you know, or are *instructed*, are untrue or misleading, unless you make clear to the *court* the true position as known by or instructed to you.

The Code then provides further guidance:

gC6 -

You are obliged by CD2 to promote and to protect your *client's* interests so far as that is consistent with the law and with your overriding duty to the *court* under CD1. Your duty to the court does not prevent you from putting forward your *client's* case simply because you do not believe that the facts are as your *client* states them to be (or as you, on your client's behalf, state them to be), as long as any positive case you put forward accords with your *instructions* and you do not mislead the *court*. Your role when acting as an advocate or conducting litigation is to present your *client's* case, and it is not for you to decide whether your *client's* case is to be believed.

gC7 -

For example, you are entitled and it may often be appropriate to draw to the witness's attention other evidence which appears to conflict with what the witness is saying and you are entitled to indicate that a *court* may find a particular piece of evidence difficult to accept. But if the witness maintains that the evidence is true, it should be recorded in the witness statement and you will not be misleading the *court* if you call the witness to confirm their witness statement. . . .

gC8 -

As set out in Rule C5, your duty to the *court* does not permit or require you to disclose confidential information which you have obtained in the course of your *instructions* and which your client has not authorised you to disclose to the *court*. However, Rule rC6 requires you not knowingly to mislead the *court*. There may be situations where you have obligations under both these rules.

In fact, the conflict identified occurs so regularly in practice that a proper way of responding is well established. You will not necessarily be required to withdraw unless your client wishes you to present information you now know (as opposed to believe) to be incorrect. Your precise duties will depend on the nature of the information being withheld. This may range from a full confession to dishonesty in obtaining public funding (where you may have a statutory duty to disclose) or an indication of past offences of which the prosecution appears to be unaware. You will find detailed guidance as to how to respond ethically to these different situations in the Code of Conduct.

By contrast, in civil litigation the demands of the Civil Procedure Rules and the overriding obligation expect full and frank disclosure during the pre-trial procedures. Thus, obligations of disclosure differ as between civil and criminal cases. This itself throws up an important value, associated with client autonomy and justice. Our adversarial system of justice requires as close as possible an approach to equality of arms. The assumption is that representation by competent and qualified lawyers achieves that equality. In a civil matter the parties are to some extent equal (although one may be able to spend more money than the other in preparing the case and, because of the reduction in the availability of public funding since the Legal Aid, Sentencing and Punishment of Offenders Act 2012, this inequality is often extreme). In a criminal matter, however, it is normal to find individuals (often impecunious and possibly facing loss of liberty) with all the forces and resources of a powerful state arranged against them. This goes some way to explaining:

- the 'cab rank' rule (rC29), which requires barristers to accept any case which is within their competence and ability to undertake (there are exceptions—see rC30) and

- the lesser expectations to disclose adverse factual information in criminal, as opposed to civil matters (given that the task is for the prosecution to prove the case, not for the defendant to prove his innocence).

So, your response to a clash of underlying values may need to differ depending on the context. You may find yourself in a situation where you face such a clash of values or where you are challenged by a client holding different values to your own. Consider the following situations.

EXAMPLE

What if my client is impecunious and facing a wealthy opponent?

For example, you are acting pro bono for an unemployed client who claims to have been unfairly dismissed for fighting at work. Your professional client instructs you to contact the respondent's lawyers in order to seek a settlement. The evidence from a number of witnesses and from personnel records suggests that your client had, indeed, been fighting, had done so on many occasions, and was only dismissed after proper warnings had been given. In conference, however, your client continues to deny the allegation while offering no explanation for the evidence against him. You are confident that should the matter proceed to trial your client will lose. You are, however, aware that many cases can result in a technical finding of unfair dismissal for procedural failings, even if the compensation in such cases is likely to be minimal. Your lay client has indicated that he is willing to accept £4,000 in settlement. You recognise, moreover, that for the employer to defend the claim, should you make many demands on them for disclosure or further questions, will cost them well over £4,000.

Should you contact the employer, pointing out that the hearing will be a long one and that you will be requiring considerable disclosure of documents and answers to detailed questions about personnel practices in the firm, suggesting that your client will withdraw the case if they pay £4,000 in settlement? To do so would promote the value of client autonomy and (by subverting the normal consequences of inequalities in wealth) promote a particular view of social justice.

Should you, instead, avoid putting that pressure on the employer when negotiating, recognising that this might make it less likely that the employer will settle for £4,000? To do so would promote the values of respect for the law and a particular (but different) perception of justice.

The Code does not prevent either course, provided you are acting on your client's instructions after giving proper advice. This is thus one example where your own values may have an impact on your choice of whether to use the 'we'll make this expensive for you' tactic.

What if my client is seeking to achieve, by instructing me, a goal which I regard as immoral?

For example, your clients, who are a couple seeking to have an exceptionally bright child, wish to carry out genetic checks to screen out any foetuses that appear not to be intelligent. You feel strongly that this is an abuse of the genetic research that has been done. Although the motive appears to be one that is forbidden under the relevant legislation you understand that similar checks (which are permitted) can indirectly provide information that would enable them to screen for intelligence.

Should you simply advise them that their proposed course of action would contravene the law and that they should not therefore attempt to pursue it? To do so may promote the value of (your particular view of) morality. This itself will be based on a value such as the integrity of the individual (in this case the newly conceived child).

Should you, instead, indicate how they might achieve their goal without technically breaking the law? To do so would promote the value of client autonomy.

When considering the propriety of your response you must remember that your duty is to act for your client and you should not make moral judgments about your client's actions. You should also consider what your client needs to know in order to make a properly informed decision. These principles are addressed in the Code and clearly prioritise the value of client autonomy.

What if my client is seeking to achieve, by instructing me, a goal which involves a breach of the law?

For example, you are instructed by solicitors to advise a corporate client which wishes to reduce some of its production costs. The proposed savings will significantly increase the risk of a release of toxic chemicals into a river. Such a release will constitute a breach of regulations designed to protect the environment and expose the client company to the risk of fines. However, you are aware that the local authority with responsibility for enforcing those regulations is extremely short of finance and is unable to make regular checks. A minor release is therefore unlikely to be noticed, although it will probably be environmentally damaging.

Should your advice be to explain the legal situation and simply point out that the proposed cost reductions place the company at risk of committing an illegal action for which they might suffer a penalty? To do so may promote the value of respect for the law.

Should your advice extend to your assessment of the very small risk of discovery? To do so may promote the value of client autonomy.

Does the principle indicated in the previous example (that you should not make moral judgments about your client's actions) apply equally here, when the proposed action involves your client committing a criminal offence? The Code indicates that you must do nothing dishonest or bring the profession into disrepute. Incitement to break the law clearly falls within that concept. You can therefore protect yourself from breach of the Code by giving clear advice not to break the law. However, you may be doing that in the realistic knowledge that your client may well ignore you and break the law. Note that if this has occurred to you it is probably your own sensitivity to ethical issues that alerts you to the risk that this may have the effect of indirectly inciting a breach of the law.

You will see that none of these three examples produces a single, clearly correct answer. Regrettably, this may well arise in practice. I have my personal preferences as to the most appropriate response in each case, but you may well take a different view. Any such difference will flow in part from the personal values that you or I espouse. For this reason we need to be aware of those values and how they impact on our responses when faced with ethical dilemmas (as we undoubtedly will be). At the same time it is important that we remember that we must not apply our personal values unrestrained. As barristers, we are bound by the Code and that recognition may assist when you are faced with a conflict of potentially applicable values. You cannot justify a departure from the clear requirements of the Code by pleading an inconsistent personal value, no matter how strongly you espouse it.

13.4 Role morality

One concept which may assist in resolving conflicts of this sort is that of role morality. A lawyer may be required to do something for a client which she could not morally justify doing for herself. That proposition may initially appear to be wrong, or at least counterintuitive. However, it is explained to a degree by the recognition that the basis of litigation in the UK is adversarialism. The lawyer is the skilled partisan advocate of the client and is (in theory) opposed by a similarly skilled partisan advocate for the opponent. The neutral decision-maker is neither lawyer but the tribunal.

This concept only works if the lawyer is genuinely partisan and the parties are equitably resourced. A client whose lawyer adopts a neutral role will be severely disadvantaged if opposed by a client whose lawyer adopts a partisan approach. In order to shoulder this burden properly, lawyers may well have to seek to achieve conclusions of which they disapprove, or carry out actions that they would not carry out on their own behalf. To justify this, many have introduced the idea of 'role morality'. This concept prioritises the value of client autonomy and is the source of the 'cab rank' rule (see rC29). Many lawyers regard it as enabling them to do for their clients what they would not do for themselves.

It may have surprising consequences. As Boon and Levin point out:

Paradoxically, whilst lawyers are expected to act cooperatively, altruistically and ethically when dealing with their clients, they are expected to be uncooperative, selfish and possibly unethical in pursuing the objectives of their clients. This creates considerable moral strain . . .

(Boon, A and Levin, J, *The Ethics and Conduct of Lawyers in England and Wales,* 2nd edn (Oxford: Hart, 2008) at 192)

That moral strain will alert you to the fact that while the concept of role morality may justify your doing for your client what you would not do for yourself, it does not give you guidance as to how far you can go. Take an example.

EXAMPLE

It may well be that if you clearly owed a debt you would not take advantage of the limitation provisions to evade it. However, would you apply the same moral judgment if it were your client who owed the debt? Suppose, for example, your client is very short of money and had forgotten the debt, which is owed to a large corporation? Suppose, instead, your client is the large corporation and the person owed the debt is impecunious?

Your view may be identical in those two situations or you may regard their relative wealth as a key issue. That is a matter for you. However, identifying the issue should make it clear that role morality, while potentially justifying actions which you would feel uncomfortable about on your own behalf, does not resolve questions about whether a particular course of action is ethically acceptable. For that, once again, you need to follow the Code and, where necessary, consider your underlying values.

The underpinning principle here is client autonomy. The Code permits you to do whatever your client wants provided that it is not illegal, you are not dishonest, and you give the court the full benefit of your knowledge of the law, whether helpful to your case or not. Equally, you must provide your client with advice that helps him or her to take an informed decision as to whether to pursue a case or not. It would be improper (as with the second example at **13.3.1**) to prioritise your views over those of your client. There is nothing to stop you identifying ethical considerations to your client, but the decision must remain with the client.

The adversarial nature of the UK legal system may be some justification for a barrister behaving differently in professional and personal contexts, but it also carries its own limits to professional behaviour. Because (unlike in an inquisitorial system) the court does not have the resources to explore the truth for itself, it relies on the honesty of advocates and their ability to research the law fully. This is the source of the requirements not to mislead the court and to cite authorities that go against your client's interests. This should identify two insights:

(a) A claim to role morality does not justify all behaviour. A balance between conflicting values must still be maintained. This is clear from the Marre Report (para 6.1):

The client is frequently acting under physical, emotional or financial difficulties and may well wish to take every step he can, whether legal or extra-legal, to gain advantage over the other party. In this situation the lawyer has a special duty and responsibility to advise his client as to the legal and ethical standards which should be observed and not to participate in any deception or sharp practice.

(Lady Marre, CBE, *A Time for Change: Report of the Committee on the Future of the Legal Profession* (London: General Council of the Bar and Council of the Law Society, 1998))

This is helpful guidance, but leaves much to the individual lawyer.

(b) No advocate will be able to meet the standards expected unless the requisite knowledge, understanding, and skills have been mastered. The knowledge, understanding, and skills that you have acquired in your undergraduate study and which you are now developing on your Bar Course are central to your effectively meeting the demands of an adversarial system. Competence itself is an ethical issue.

For further discussions of role morality, see Nicolson, D and Webb, J, *Professional Ethics: Critical Interrogations* (Oxford: OUP, 2000) at 169–71.

13.5 Ethical behaviour and self-interest

It is often said that ethical behaviour is in the individual lawyer's best interest because 'the Bar is a small profession and your reputation will quickly get around'. Barely hidden behind this assertion is the suggestion that if you acquire a reputation for poor ethical standards opponents will not trust you and you will find it increasingly difficult to meet your clients' needs. This may be true. However, it is important to recognise that ethics and self-interest should not be equated.

Some help may be available from the recognition that taking a long-term view of self-interest is highly likely to be an ethically safer approach than taking a short-term view. Thus, an approach which ensures that you have a reputation for honesty is likely to enable you to represent many future clients in negotiation. It is also therefore likely to enhance your long-term income. Willingness to deceive an opponent may achieve something your current client values but will inhibit your ability to come to desirable solutions for future clients. Not only would this inhibit long-term income, it would involve a breach of the Code (rC8, rC9).

One other aspect of self-interest is worth addressing here. You have an interest in your profession continuing to be perceived as in good ethical standing. If you comply with the provisions of the Code, this will preserve you from the risk of disciplinary proceedings. However, where the Code provides a framework within which different courses of action are permitted you should be alert to maintain the highest possible ethical standards.

This insight helps us to identify those aspects of self-interest that will assist us to maintain high ethical standards, but relying on self-interest is altogether insufficient. It ignores most of the underpinning values that we have identified earlier and leaves the individual lawyer without ethical guidance. Thus it remains necessary to comply with the requirements of the Code and to consider its underpinning values in those situations where conflicts nevertheless arise.

13.6 The lawyer joke again

So which of the three was acting most ethically? I have no problem with the layperson's response and am sufficiently ignorant to accept that there may be justification for the accountant's response. However, to judge the lawyer I need to go back to my core values again. If I prioritise client autonomy, this lawyer may be responding perfectly correctly. There are few situations in reality where one simple answer is the only one available. The lawyer here is seeking the client's instructions as to what the desired outcome is. It may be that that outcome is not legally available, in which case the lawyer should advise the client to that effect. It may be readily available, in which case the lawyer is in the fortunate position of giving the client good news. It is just as likely, however, that the answer is somewhere between the two. How far should you go to achieve the client's desired result? That is a matter of your professional responsibility. The Code of Conduct (gC15) provides guidance:

> Other rules deal with specific aspects of your obligation to act in your *client's* best interests (CD2) while maintaining honesty, integrity (CD3) and independence (CD4), such as rule C21.10 (not acting where your independence is compromised), rule C10 (not paying or accepting *referral fees*) and C21 (not acting in circumstances of a conflict of interest or where you risk breaching one *client's* confidentiality in favour of another's).

which makes it clear that you should not allow your personal values to override the requirements of the Code. However, within the boundaries provided by the Code, the Guidance available on the Bar Council and Bar Standards Board websites, and always remembering the availability of the Ethical Queries Helpline, the final decision is your responsibility.

SUGGESTED FURTHER READING

Andrew Boon: *The Ethics and Conduct of Lawyers in England and Wales*, 3rd edn (Oxford: Hart, 2014). This is the most authoritative of the books suggested and explores the principles underlying the ethics of solicitors and barristers. It looks critically at the conflicts that may arise and the ways in which the ethical principles apply in different areas of lawyers' work.

Andrew Boon: *Lawyers' Ethics and Professional*

Responsibility (Oxford: Hart, 2015). This is a student text that has the advantage of many examples and problems to help you to understand the ethical dilemmas that lawyers may encounter.

Adrian Evans: *The Good Lawyer: A Student Guide to Law and Ethics* (Cambridge: CUP, 2014). Although written from an Australian perspective, this book addresses the same issues as the UK-published books and takes your personal values as its starting point. It also contains many examples and problems.

Donald Nicolson and Julian Webb: *Professional Legal Ethics: Critical Interrogations* (Oxford: OUP, 2000). This is a more theoretical book that provides a wide-ranging and critical analysis of the ethical principles of the English legal professions.

Professional conduct problems

Question 1

A solicitor seeks to instruct you to act for notoriously bad landlords in an action for possession of premises occupied by a highly regarded charitable organisation. The case is likely to draw adverse publicity. You hold yourself out to act in landlord and tenant cases, you have no connection with either party or with the premises, you have no conflicting professional commitment, and the fee offered is a proper fee for you and for the case. Your clerk tells you that he wishes you to refuse the instructions because:

(a) it is chambers' policy not to act for landlords and

(b) he fears that your normal professional clients will be reluctant to instruct you in future cases as their clients (tenants, consumers, etc) would refuse to have as counsel one who had acted for these particular claimants.

What do you do?

Question 2

You are instructed in a family law matter. You act for a white father whose former wife, who is also white, is now cohabiting with a black African boyfriend. Your client instructs you to resist her application for contact with the parties' son on grounds which you consider to be racist. Can you refuse to put forward instructions even if wrapped up as seeking to avoid 'exposing his son to a cultural environment totally alien to him . . .'?

Question 3

You have successfully appeared for the claimants in an action where the unsuccessful defendants now wish to seek a Part 20 indemnity or contribution from a third party who was not a party to the original action. The defendants' solicitors were impressed with your performance and want you to be able to use your knowledge of the case against the third party. Do you accept the instructions?

Question 4

A solicitor, who regularly instructs you and your chambers, telephones you and instructs you to attend at a particular police station where a lay client is about to be interviewed and to advise the client as necessary. The solicitor undertakes to pay you a proper fee. If the matter leads to a charge or charges being preferred, the brief is likely to come into chambers for someone of your experience.

(a) Can you act?

(b) Would it make any difference if the brief would certainly be beyond your competence?

Question 5

You have received and accepted instructions to appear in case 'A' (a civil case fixed to be heard on 20 April). You have done a lot of preparatory work upon it and have seen the professional and lay clients in conference on a number of occasions. You have also accepted instructions to defend in a serious criminal case (case 'B'), expected to be tried in the week beginning 1 April and to last for five days, but which may well go on longer. Before you have conferred with the client in case 'B', you learn that it will not be heard until the week beginning 15 April. Both solicitors assert priority and both clients are anxious to have your services. Which case do you do? Why?

Question 6

You have represented your client successfully in court. After the hearing, the client stuffs a £20 note in your pocket and tells you to enjoy a drink on him.

(a) Do you keep the money?

(b) Would it make any difference if your client instead sent you a bottle of whisky?

Question 7

(a) The defendant in a rape case instructs you that sexual intercourse took place between him and the victim with her consent. At trial, he tells you that he did not have sexual intercourse with her and gives you names of alibi witnesses.

(b) Your client has mental health problems. His instructions differ each time you speak to him.

What should you do in these circumstances?

Question 8

You act for the claimant in civil proceedings. In the course of his evidence-in-chief, he produces several documents from his pocket which he alleges support his claim. You have never seen them before nor have they been disclosed to the defence. What do you do?

Question 9

You receive a set of instructions to advise and settle civil proceedings for a claimant from X and Co, a firm of solicitors who have instructed you on a number of occasions and are among your best clients. It is apparent that they have been negligent in handling the claimant's affairs. It appears to you that the claimant's chances have not been badly affected and he is likely to succeed in the litigation, but he has at least been prejudiced in the sense that, if the relevant matter 'surfaces' in the litigation, the defendants will be able to make use of it to reduce the damages or to obtain a better settlement than would otherwise have been open to them. (For example, there has been a failure to secure evidence relevant to proving the amount of the claimant's loss and damage.) What, if anything, should you do?

Question 10

You are defending in a trial at the Crown Court. In the course of giving his evidence, the defendant makes an allegation which, although it is in your instructions, you had not put to the victim. It is apparent that it should have been, and the victim has gone on holiday and cannot be recalled. The judge is furious. What do you do?

Question 11

You are asked to advise, in conference, upon the acceptability of an offer of £3,000 in settlement of your client's claim for damages in a personal injury case. The medical report, which has been disclosed to the defence, is now ten months old. In the course of the conference, your client informs you that the doctor's prognosis was unduly pessimistic as his condition has improved since the report was prepared. In the circumstances, the offer is generous and more than your client is likely to receive from the court.

(a) What advice do you give?
(b) Would it make any difference if the client's information was contained in a more recent, but undisclosed, medical report?

Question 12

You are instructed to represent the defendant in proceedings for damages for breach of contract. Upon your arrival at court, your instructing solicitor informs you that one of your witnesses has just telephoned his office to say that she is ill and cannot attend court to give evidence. Her testimony is vital to the defendant's case. You have no option but to seek an adjournment. At that moment, your opponent approaches you and asks if he can have a word with you. He indicates that he has witness difficulties and invites you to agree to an adjournment of the hearing for two weeks. In so doing:

(a) Do you inform your opponent and the court of your own witness difficulties?
(b) If not, do you make an application for the claimant to pay the defendant's costs thrown away by the adjournment?

APPENDIX 1
EXCERPTS FROM THE BAR STANDARDS BOARD HANDBOOK

THE BAR STANDARDS BOARD HANDBOOK

Version 4.6

December 2020

Bar Standards Board

Part 2

The Code of Conduct

OUTLINE CONTENTS

BSB Handbook

Part 2: Code of Conduct

Part 2 - A. Application   Rules

rC1

Who?

.1 Section 2.B (Core Duties): applies to all *BSB regulated persons* and *unregistered barristers* except where stated otherwise, and references to "you" and "your" in Section 2.B shall be construed accordingly.

.2 Section 2.C (Conduct Rules):

.a Applies to all *BSB regulated persons*.

.b Rules rC3.5, rC4, rC8, rC16, rC19 and rC64 to rC70 (and associated guidance to those rules) and the guidance on Core Duties also apply to *unregistered barristers*. If an *unregistered barrister* practises as a *barrister* as set out in rS9 then those rules which apply to practising barristers shall also apply.

References to "you" and "your" in Section 2.C shall be construed accordingly

.3 Section 2.D (Specific Rules): applies to specific groups as defined in each sub-section and references to "you" and "your" shall be construed accordingly.

rC2

When?

.1 Section 2.B applies when practising or otherwise providing *legal services*. In addition, CD5 and CD9 apply at all times.

.2 Section 2.C applies when practising or otherwise providing *legal services*. In addition, rules rC8, rC16 and rC64 to rC70 and the associated guidance apply at all times.

.3 Section 2.D applies when practising or otherwise providing *legal services*.

.4 Sections 2.B, 2.C and 2.D only apply to *registered European lawyers* in connection with professional work undertaken by them in that capacity in England and Wales.

Part 2 - B. The Core Duties   Core Duties

CD1 You must observe your duty to the court in the administration of justice [CD1].

CD2 You must act in the best interests of each client [CD2].

CD3 You must act with honesty, and with integrity [CD3].

CD4 You must maintain your independence [CD4].

CD5 You must not behave in a way which is likely to diminish the trust and confidence which the public places in you or in the profession [CD5].

CD6 You must keep the affairs of each client confidential [CD6].

CD7 You must provide a competent standard of work and service to each client [CD7]

CD8 You must not discriminate unlawfully against any person [CD8].

CD9 You must be open and co-operative with your regulators [CD9].

CD10 You must take reasonable steps to manage your practice, or carry out your role within your practice, competently and in such a way as to achieve compliance with your legal and regulatory obligations [CD10].

BSB Handbook

Guidance to the Core Duties   [Guidance]

gC1

The Core Duties are not presented in order of precedence, subject to the following:

.1 CD1 overrides any other core duty, if and to the extent the two are inconsistent. Rules rC3.5 and rC4 deal specifically with the relationship between CD1, CD2 and CD4 and you should refer to those rules and to the related Guidance;

.2 in certain other circumstances set out in this Code of Conduct one Core Duty overrides another. Specifically, Rule rC16 provides that CD2 (as well as being subject to CD1) is subject to your obligations under CD3, CD4 and CD8.

gC2

Your obligation to take reasonable steps to manage your *practice*, or carry out your role within your *practice*, competently and in such a way as to achieve compliance with your legal and regulatory obligations (CD10) includes an obligation to take all reasonable steps to mitigate the effects of any breach of those legal and regulatory obligations once you become aware of the same.

gC2A

Your obligation to be open and co-operative with your regulators (CD9) includes being open and co-operative with all relevant regulators and ombudsman schemes, including but not limited to approved regulators under the Legal Services Act 2007 and the Legal Ombudsman.

Part 2 - C. The Conduct Rules   [Rules]

Part 2 - C1. You and the court   [Rules]

Outcomes C1-C5   [Outcomes]

oC1

The *court* is able to rely on information provided to it by those conducting litigation and by advocates who appear before it.

oC2

The proper administration of justice is served.

oC3

The interests of *clients* are protected to the extent compatible with outcomes oC1 and oC2 and the Core Duties.

oC4

Both those who appear before the *court* and *clients* understand clearly the extent of the duties owed to the *court* by advocates and those conducting litigation and the circumstances in which duties owed to *clients* will be overridden by the duty owed to the *court*.

oC5

The public has confidence in the administration of justice and in those who serve it.

Rules C3-C6   [Rules]

BSB Handbook The BSB Handbook - Version 4.6

rC3

You owe a duty to the *court* to act with independence in the interests of justice. This duty overrides any inconsistent obligations which you may have (other than obligations under the criminal law). It includes the following specific obligations which apply whether you are acting as an advocate or are otherwise involved in the conduct of litigation in whatever role (with the exception of Rule C3.1 below, which applies when acting as an advocate):

.1 you must not knowingly or recklessly mislead or attempt to mislead the *court*;

.2 you must not abuse your role as an advocate;

.3 you must take reasonable steps to avoid wasting the *court's* time;

.4 you must take reasonable steps to ensure that the *court* has before it all relevant decisions and legislative provisions;

.5 you must ensure that your ability to act independently is not compromised.

rC4

Your duty to act in the best interests of each *client* is subject to your duty to the *court*.

rC5

Your duty to the *court* does not require you to act in breach of your duty to keep the affairs of each *client* confidential.

Not misleading the court

rC6

Your duty not to mislead the *court* will include the following obligations:

.1 you must not:

.a make submissions, representations or any other statement; or

.b ask questions which suggest facts to witnesses

which you know, or are instructed, are untrue or misleading.

.2 you must not call witnesses to give evidence or put affidavits or witness statements to the *court* which you know, or are *instructed*, are untrue or misleading, unless you make clear to the *court* the true position as known by or instructed to you.

Guidance to Rules C3-C6 and relationship to CD1-CD2 | Guidance |

gC3

Rules rC3 – rC6 set out some specific aspects of your duty to the *court* (CD1). See CD1 and associated Guidance at gC1.

gC4

As to your duty not to mislead the court:

.1 knowingly misleading the *court* includes being complicit in another person misleading the court;

.2 knowingly misleading the *court* also includes inadvertently misleading the court if you later realise that you have misled the *court*, and you fail to correct the position;

.3 recklessly means being indifferent to the truth, or not caring whether something is true or false; and

.4 the duty continues to apply for the duration of the case.

gC5

Your duty under Rule rC3.4 includes drawing to the attention of the *court* any decision or provision which may be adverse to the interests of your *client*. It is particularly important where you are appearing against a litigant who is not legally represented.

BSB Handbook

gC6

You are obliged by CD2 to promote and to protect your *client's* interests so far as that is consistent with the law and with your overriding duty to the *court* under CD1. Your duty to the *court* does not prevent you from putting forward your *client's* case simply because you do not believe that the facts are as your *client* states them to be (or as you, on your *client's* behalf, state them to be), as long as any positive case you put forward accords with your *instructions* and you do not mislead the *court*. Your role when acting as an advocate or conducting litigation is to present your *client's* case, and it is not for you to decide whether your *client's* case is to be believed.

gC7

For example, you are entitled and it may often be appropriate to draw to the witness's attention other evidence which appears to conflict with what the witness is saying and you are entitled to indicate that a *court* may find a particular piece of evidence difficult to accept. But if the witness maintains that the evidence is true, it should be recorded in the witness statement and you will not be misleading the *court* if you call the witness to confirm their witness statement. Equally, there may be circumstances where you call a hostile witness whose evidence you are instructed is untrue. You will not be in breach of Rule rC6 if you make the position clear to the *court*. See, further, the guidance at gC14.

gC8

As set out in Rule rC5, your duty to the *court* does not permit or require you to disclose confidential information which you have obtained in the course of your *instructions* and which your client has not authorised you to disclose to the *court*. However, Rule rC6 requires you not knowingly to mislead the *court*. There may be situations where you have obligations under both these rules.

gC9

Rule rC4 makes it clear that your duty to act in the best interests of your *client* is subject to your duty to the *court*. For example, if your *client* were to tell you that they have committed the crime with which they were charged, in order to be able to ensure compliance with Rule rC4 on the one hand and Rule rC3 and Rule rC6 on the other:

.1 you would not be entitled to disclose that information to the *court* without your *client's* consent; and

.2 you would not be misleading the *court* if, after your *client* had entered a plea of 'not guilty', you were to test in cross-examination the reliability of the evidence of the prosecution witnesses and then address the jury to the effect that the prosecution had not succeeded in making them sure of your *client's* guilt.

gC10

However, you would be misleading the *court* and would therefore be in breach of Rules rC5 and rC6 if you were to set up a positive case inconsistent with the confession, as for example by:

.1 suggesting to prosecution witnesses, calling your *client* or your witnesses to show; or submitting to the jury, that your *client* did not commit the crime; or

.2 suggesting that someone else had done so; or

.3 putting forward an alibi.

gC11

If there is a risk that the *court* will be misled unless you disclose confidential information which you have learned in the course of your *instructions*, you should ask the *client* for permission to disclose it to the *court*. If your *client* refuses to allow you to make the disclosure you must cease to act, and return your *instructions*: see Rules rC25 to rC27 below. In these circumstances you must not reveal the information to the *court*.

gC12

For example, if your *client* tells you that they have previous *convictions* of which the prosecution is not aware, you may not disclose this without their consent. However, in a case where mandatory sentences apply, the non-disclosure of the previous *convictions* will result in the *court* failing to pass the sentence that is required by law. In that situation, you must advise your *client* that if consent is refused to your revealing the information you will have to cease to act. In situations where mandatory sentences do not apply, and your *client* does not agree to disclose the previous *convictions*, you can continue to represent your *client* but in doing so must not say anything that misleads the court. This will constrain what you can say in mitigation. For example, you could not advance a positive case of previous good character knowing that there are undisclosed prior *convictions*. Moreover, if the *court* asks you a direct question you must not give an untruthful answer and therefore you would have to withdraw if, on your being asked such a question, your *client* still refuses to allow you to answer the question truthfully. You should explain this to your *client*.

BSB Handbook

gC13

Similarly, if you become aware that your *client* has a document which should be disclosed but has not been disclosed, you cannot continue to act unless your *client* agrees to the disclosure of the document. In these circumstances you must not reveal the existence or contents of the document to the *court*.

Rule C7 - Not abusing your role as an advocate   Rules

rC7

Where you are acting as an advocate, your duty not to abuse your role includes the following obligations:

.1 you must not make statements or ask questions merely to insult, humiliate or annoy a witness or any other person;

.2 you must not make a serious allegation against a witness whom you have had an opportunity to cross-examine unless you have given that witness a chance to answer the allegation in cross-examination;

.3 you must not make a serious allegation against any person, or suggest that a person is guilty of a crime with which your *client* is charged unless:

.a you have reasonable grounds for the allegation; and

.b the allegation is relevant to your *client's* case or the credibility of a witness; and

.c where the allegation relates to a third party, you avoid naming them in open *court* unless this is reasonably necessary.

.4 you must not put forward to the *court* a personal opinion of the facts or the law unless you are invited or required to do so by the *court* or by law.

Part 2 - C2. Behaving ethically   Rules

Outcomes C6-C9 Outcomes

oC6

Those regulated by the *Bar Standards Board* maintain standards of honesty, integrity and independence, and are seen as so doing.

oC7

The proper administration of justice, access to justice and the best interests of *clients* are served.

oC8

Those regulated by the *Bar Standards Board* do not discriminate unlawfully and take appropriate steps to prevent *discrimination* occurring in their practices.

oC9

Those regulated by the *Bar Standards Board* and *clients* understand the obligations of honesty, integrity and independence.

Rules C8-C9 - Honesty, integrity and independence Rules

BSB Handbook

rC8

You must not do anything which could reasonably be seen by the public to undermine your honesty, integrity (CD3) and independence (CD4).

rC9

Your duty to act with honesty and with integrity under CD3 includes the following requirements:

.1 you must not knowingly or recklessly mislead or attempt to mislead anyone;

.2 you must not draft any statement of case, witness statement, affidavit or other document containing:

.a any statement of fact or contention which is not supported by your *client* or by your *instructions*;

.b any contention which you do not consider to be properly arguable;

.c any allegation of fraud, unless you have clear instructions to allege fraud and you have reasonably credible material which establishes an arguable case of fraud;

.d (in the case of a witness statement or affidavit) any statement of fact other than the evidence which you reasonably believe the witness would give if the witness were giving evidence orally;

.3 you must not encourage a witness to give evidence which is misleading or untruthful;

.4 you must not rehearse, practise with or coach a witness in respect of their evidence;

.5 unless you have the permission of the representative for the opposing side or of the *court*, you must not communicate with any witness (including your *client*) about the case while the witness is giving evidence;

.6 you must not make, or offer to make, payments to any witness which are contingent on their evidence or on the outcome of the case;

.7 you must only propose, or accept, fee arrangements which are legal.

Guidance to Rules C8-C9 and relationship to CD1-CD5   `Guidance`

gC14

Your honesty, integrity and independence are fundamental. The interests of justice (CD1) and the *client's* best interests (CD2) can only be properly served, and any conflicts between the two properly resolved, if you conduct yourself honestly and maintain your independence from external pressures, as required by CD3 and CD4. You should also refer to Rule rC16 which subjects your duty to act in the best interests of your *client* (CD2) to your observance of CD3 and CD4, as well as to your duty to the *court* (CD1).

gC15

Other rules deal with specific aspects of your obligation to act in your *client's* best interests (CD2) while maintaining honesty, integrity (CD3) and independence (CD4), such as rule rC21.10 (not acting where your independence is compromised), rule rC10 (not paying or accepting *referral fees*) and rC21 (not acting in circumstances of a conflict of interest or where you risk breaching one *client's* confidentiality in favour of another's).

gC16

Rule C8 addresses how your conduct is perceived by the public. Conduct on your part which the public may reasonably perceive as undermining your honesty, integrity or independence is likely to diminish the trust and confidence which the public places in you or in the profession, in breach of CD5. Rule C9 is not exhaustive of the ways in which CD5 may be breached.

gC17

In addition to your obligation to only propose, or accept, fee arrangements which are legal in Rule C9.7, you must also have regard to your obligations in relation to referral fees in Rule rC10 and the associated guidance.

Examples of how you may be seen as compromising your independence

gC18

The following may reasonably be seen as compromising your independence in breach of Rule 8 (whether or not the circumstances are such that Rule rC10 is also breached):

BSB Handbook

.1 offering, promising or giving:

.a any commission or referral fee (of whatever size) – note that these are in any case prohibited by Rule rC10 and associated guidance; or

.b a gift (apart from items of modest value),

to any *client, professional client* or other *intermediary*; or

.2 lending money to any such *client, professional client* or other *intermediary*; or

.3 accepting any money (whether as a loan or otherwise) from any *client, professional client* or other *intermediary*, unless it is a payment for your professional services or reimbursement of expenses or of disbursements made on behalf of the *client*;

gC19

If you are offered a gift by a current, prospective or former *client, professional client* or other *intermediary*, you should consider carefully whether the circumstances and size of the gift would reasonably lead others to think that your independence had been compromised. If this would be the case, you should refuse to accept the gift.

gC20

The giving or receiving of entertainment at a disproportionate level may also give rise to a similar issue and so should not be offered or accepted if it would lead others reasonably to think that your independence had been compromised.

gC21

Guidance gC18 to gC20 above is likely to be more relevant where you are a *self-employed barrister*, a *BSB entity*, an *authorised (non-BSB) individual*, an *employed barrister (BSB entity)* or a *manager* of a *BSB entity*. If you are a *BSB authorised individual* who is a an employee or *manager* of an *authorised (non-BSB) body* or you are an *employed barrister (non-authorised body)* and your *approved regulator* or *employer* (as appropriate) permits payments to which Rule rC10 applies, you may make or receive such payments only in your capacity as such and as permitted by the rules of your *approved regulator* or *employer* (as appropriate). For further information on referral fees, see the guidance at gC32).

Media comment

gC22

The ethical obligations that apply in relation to your professional practice generally continue to apply in relation to media comment. In particular, *barristers* should be aware of the following:

• Client's best interests: Core Duty 2 and Rules C15.1-.2 require a barrister to promote fearlessly and by all proper and lawful means the lay *client's* best interests and to do so without regard to their own interests.

• Independence: Core Duties 3 and 4 provide that you must not permit your absolute independence, integrity and freedom from external pressures to be compromised.

• Trust and confidence: Core Duty 5 provides that you must not behave in a way which is likely to diminish the trust and confidence which the public places in you or the profession.

• Confidentiality: Core Duty 6 and Rule C15.5 require you to preserve the confidentiality of your lay client's affairs and you must not undermine this unless permitted to do so by law or with the express consent of the lay client.

Examples of what your duty to act with honesty and integrity may require

gC23

Rule rC9 sets out some specific aspects of your duty under CD3 to act with honesty and also with integrity.

gC24

In addition to the above, where the other side is legally represented and you are conducting correspondence in respect of the particular matter, you are expected to correspond at all times with that other party's legal representative – otherwise you may be regarded as breaching CD3 or Rule C9.

BSB Handbook

Other possible breaches of CD3 and/or CD5

gC25

A breach of Rule rC9 may also constitute a breach of CD3 and/or CD5. Other conduct which is likely to be treated as a breach of CD3 and/or CD5 includes (but is not limited to):

.1 subject to Guidance C27 below, breaches of Rule rC8;

.2 breaches of Rule rC10;

.3 criminal conduct, other than *minor criminal offences* (see Guidance C27);

.4 seriously offensive or discreditable conduct towards third parties;

.5 dishonesty;

.6 unlawful *victimisation* or *harassment*; or

.7 abuse of your professional position.

gC26

For the purposes of Guidance gC25.7 above, referring to your status as a *barrister*, for example on professional notepaper, in a context where it is irrelevant, such as in a private dispute, may well constitute abuse of your professional position and thus involve a breach of CD3 and/or CD5.

gC27

Conduct which is not likely to be treated as a breach of Rules rC8 or rC9, or CD3 or CD5, includes (but is not limited to):

.1 *minor criminal offences*;

.2 your conduct in your private or personal life, unless this involves:

.a abuse of your professional position; or

.b committing a *criminal offence*, other than a *minor criminal offence*.

gC28

For the purpose of Guidance C27 above, *minor criminal offences* include:

.1 an offence committed in the United Kingdom which is a fixed-penalty offence under the Road Traffic Offenders Act 1988; or

.2 an offence committed in the United Kingdom or abroad which is dealt with by a procedure substantially similar to that for such a fixed-penalty offence; or

.3 an offence whose main ingredient is the unlawful parking of a motor vehicle.

Rule C10 - Referral fees   `Rules`

rC10

You must not pay or receive *referral fees*.

Guidance to Rule C10 and relationship to CD2-CD5   `Guidance`

gC29

Making or receiving payments in order to procure or reward the referral to you by an intermediary of professional *instructions* is inconsistent with your obligations under CD2 and/or CD3 and/or CD4 and may also breach CD5.

gC30

Moreover:

BSB Handbook

.1 where public funding is in place, the *Legal Aid Agency's* Unified Contract Standard Terms explicitly prohibit contract-holders from making or receiving any payment (or any other benefit) for the referral or introduction of a *client*, whether or not the lay *client* knows of, and consents to, the payment;

.2 whether in a private or publicly funded case, a *referral fee* to which the *client* has not consented may constitute a bribe and therefore a *criminal offence* under the Bribery Act 2010;

gC31

Referral fees and inducements (as defined in the Criminal Justice and Courts Act 2015) are prohibited where they relate to a claim or potential claim for damages for personal injury or death or arise out of circumstances involving personal injury or death personal injury claims: section 56 Legal Aid, Sentencing and Punishment of Offenders Act 2012 and section 58 Criminal Justice and Courts Act 2015. Rule rC10 does not prohibit proper expenses that are not a reward for referring work, such as genuine and reasonable payments for:

.1 clerking and administrative services (including where these are outsourced);

.2 membership subscriptions to ADR bodies that appoint or recommend a person to provide mediation, arbitration or adjudication services; or

.3 advertising and publicity, which are payable whether or not any work is referred. However, the fact that a fee varies with the amount of work received does not necessarily mean that that it is a *referral fee*, if it is genuinely for a marketing service from someone who is not directing work to one provider rather than another, depending on who pays more.

gC32

Further guidance is available on the BSB's website.

Rule C11 - Undertakings | Rules |

rC11

You must within an agreed timescale or within a reasonable period of time comply with any undertaking you give in the course of conducting litigation.

Guidance to Rule C11 | Guidance |

gC33

You should ensure your insurance covers you in respect of any liability incurred in giving an undertaking.

Rule C12 - Discrimination | Rules |

rC12

You must not discriminate unlawfully against, victimise or harass any other person on the grounds of race, colour, ethnic or national origin, nationality, citizenship, sex, gender re-assignment, sexual orientation, marital or civil partnership status, disability, age, religion or belief, or pregnancy and maternity.

Guidance to Rule C12 | Guidance |

gC34

Rules rC110 and associated guidance are also relevant to equality and diversity. The BSB's Supporting Information on the BSB Handbook Equality Rules is available on the BSB website.

BSB Handbook   The BSB Handbook - Version 4.6

Rules C13-C14 - Foreign work   `Rules`

rC13

In connection with any *foreign work* you must comply with any applicable rule of conduct prescribed by the law or by any national or local Bar of:

.1 the place where the work is or is to be performed; and

.2 the place where any proceedings or matters to which the work relates are taking place or contemplated; unless such rule is inconsistent with any requirement of the Core Duties.

rC14

If you solicit work in any jurisdiction outside England and Wales, you must not do so in a manner which would be prohibited if you were a member of the local Bar.

Guidance to Rules C13-14   `Guidance`

gC35

When you are engaged in *cross border activities* within a *CCBE State* other than the UK, you must comply with the rules at 2.D5 which implement the part of the *Code of Conduct for European Lawyers* not otherwise covered by this Handbook as well as with any other applicable rules of conduct relevant to that particular *CCBE State*. It is your responsibility to inform yourself as to any applicable rules of conduct.

Part 2 - C3. You and your client   `Rules`

Outcomes C10-C20   `Outcomes`

oC10

Clients receive a competent standard of work and service.

oC11

Clients' best interests are protected and promoted by those acting for them.

oC12

BSB authorised persons do not accept instructions from *clients* where there is a conflict between their own interests and the *clients'* or where there is a conflict between one or more *clients* except when permitted in this *Handbook*.

oC13

Clients know what to expect and understand the advice they are given.

oC14

Care is given to ensure that the interests of vulnerable *clients* are taken into account and their needs are met.

BSB Handbook   The BSB Handbook - Version 4.6

oC15

Clients have confidence in those who are instructed to act on their behalf.

oC16

Instructions are not accepted, refused, or returned in circumstances which adversely affect the administration of justice, access to justice or (so far as compatible with these) the best interests of the *client*.

oC17

Clients and *BSB authorised persons* and *authorised (non-BSB) individuals* and *managers* of *BSB entities* are clear about the circumstances in which *instructions* may not be accepted or may or must be returned.

oC18

Clients are adequately informed as to the terms on which work is to be done.

oC19

Clients understand how to bring a *complaint* and *complaints* are dealt with promptly, fairly, openly and effectively.

oC20

Clients understand who is responsible for work done for them.

Rules C15-C16 - Best interests of each client, provision of a competent standard of work and confidentiality   `Rules`

---

rC15

Your duty to act in the best interests of each *client* (CD2), to provide a competent standard of work and service to each *client* (CD7) and to keep the affairs of each *client* confidential (CD6) includes the following obligations:

.1 you must promote fearlessly and by all proper and lawful means the *client's* best interests;

.2 you must do so without regard to your own interests or to any consequences to you (which may include, for the avoidance of doubt, you being required to take reasonable steps to mitigate the effects of any breach of this *Handbook*);

.3 you must do so without regard to the consequences to any other person (whether to your *professional client, employer* or any other person);

.4 you must not permit your *professional client, employer* or any other person to limit your discretion as to how the interests of the *client* can best be served; and

.5 you must protect the confidentiality of each *client's* affairs, except for such disclosures as are required or permitted by law or to which your *client* gives informed consent.

rC16

Your duty to act in the best interests of each *client* (CD2) is subject to your duty to the *court* (CD1) and to your obligations to act with honesty, and with integrity (CD3) and to maintain your independence (CD4).

Guidance to Rules C15-C16 and relationship to CD2 and CD6-CD7   `Guidance`

---

gC36

Your duty is to your *client*, not to your *professional client* or other *intermediary* (if any).

gC37

Rules rC15 and rC16 are expressed in terms of the interests of each *client*. This is because you may only accept *instructions* to act for more than one *client* if you are able to act in the best interests of each *client* as if that *client* were your only *client*, as CD2 requires

BSB Handbook

of you. See further Rule rC17 on the circumstances when you are obliged to advise your *client* to seek other legal representation and Rules rC21.2 and rC21.3 on conflicts of interest and the guidance to those rules at gC69.

gC38

CD7 requires not only that you provide a competent standard of work but also a competent standard of service to your *client*. Rule rC15 is not exhaustive of what you must do to ensure your compliance with CD2 and CD7. By way of example, a competent standard of work and of service also includes:

.1 treating each *client* with courtesy and consideration; and

.2 seeking to advise your *client*, in terms they can understand; and

.3 taking all reasonable steps to avoid incurring unnecessary expense; and

.4 reading your instructions promptly. This may be important if there is a time limit or limitation period. If you fail to read your instructions promptly, it is possible that you will not be aware of the time limit until it is too late.

gC39

In order to be able to provide a competent standard of work, you should keep your professional knowledge and skills up to date, regularly take part in professional development and educational activities that maintain and further develop your competence and performance and, where you are a *BSB entity* or a *manager* of such body, you should take reasonable steps to ensure that *managers* and employees within your organisation undertake such training. Merely complying with the Continuing Professional Development requirements may not be sufficient to comply with Rule rC15. You should also ensure that you comply with any specific training requirements of the *Bar Standards Board* before undertaking certain activities – for example, you should not attend a police station to advise a suspect or interviewee as to the handling and conduct of police interviews unless you have complied with the following training requirements imposed by the *Bar Standards Board*: *barristers* undertaking publicly funded police station work under a criminal contract must comply with the training requirements specified by the Legal Aid Agency. *Barristers* undertaking privately funded police station work must complete the Police Station Qualification ("PSQ") and (if they do not hold higher rights of audience) the Magistrates Court Qualification. Similarly, you should not undertake public access work without successfully completing the required training specified by the *Bar Standards Board*.

gC40

In addition to Guidance gC38 above, a *BSB entity* or a *manager* of such body should ensure that work is allocated appropriately, to *managers* and/or employees with the appropriate knowledge and expertise to undertake such work.

gC41

You should remember that your *client* may not be familiar with legal proceedings and may find them difficult and stressful. You should do what you reasonably can to ensure that the *client* understands the process and what to expect from it and from you. You should also try to avoid any unnecessary distress for your *client*. This is particularly important where you are dealing with a vulnerable *client*.

gC42

The duty of confidentiality (CD6) is central to the administration of justice. *Clients* who put their confidence in their legal advisers must be able to do so in the knowledge that the information they give, or which is given on their behalf, will stay confidential. In normal circumstances, this information will be privileged and not disclosed to a *court*. CD6, rC4 and Guidance gC8 and gC11 to gC13 provide further information.

gC43

Rule rC15.5 acknowledges that your duty of confidentiality is subject to an exception if disclosure is required or permitted by law. For example, you may be obliged to disclose certain matters by the Proceeds of Crime Act 2002. Disclosure in those circumstances would not amount to a breach of CD6 or Rule rC15.5 In other circumstances, you may only make disclosure of confidential information where your *client* gives informed consent to the disclosure. See the Guidance to Rule rC21 at gC69 for an example of circumstances where it may be appropriate for you to seek such consent.

gC44

There may be circumstances when your duty of confidentiality to your *client* conflicts with your duty to the *court*. Rule rC4 and Guidance gC8 and gC11 to gC13 provide further information.

BSB Handbook   The BSB Handbook - Version 4.6

gC45

Similarly, there may be circumstances when your duty of confidentiality to your *client* conflicts with your duty to your regulator. Rule rC64 and Guidance gC92 in respect of that rule provide further information. In addition, Rule rC66 may also apply.

gC46

If you are a *pupil* of, or are *devilling* work for, a *self-employed barrister*, Rule rC15.5 applies to you as if the *client* of the *self-employed barrister* was your own *client*.

gC47

The section You and Your Practice, at 2.C5, provides for duties regarding the systems and procedures you must put in place and enforce in order to ensure compliance with Rule rC15.5.

gC48

If you are an *authorised individual* or a *manager* working in a *BSB entity* your personal duty to act in the best interests of your *client* requires you to assist in the redistribution of *client* files and otherwise assisting to ensure each *client's* interests are protected in the event that the *BSB entity* itself is unable to do so for whatever reason (for example, insolvency).

Rule C17   Rules

rC17

Your duty to act in the best interests of each *client* (CD2) includes a duty to consider whether the *client's* best interests are served by different legal representation, and if so, to advise the *client* to that effect.

Guidance to Rule C17   Guidance

gC49

Your duty to comply with Rule rC17 may require you to advise your *client* that in their best interests they should be represented by:

.1 a different advocate or legal representative, whether more senior or more junior than you, or with different experience from yours;

.2 more than one advocate or legal representative;

.3 fewer advocates or legal representatives than have been instructed; or

.4 in the case where you are acting through a *professional client*, different *solicitors*.

gC50

Specific rules apply where you are acting on a public access basis, which oblige you to consider whether *solicitors* should also be instructed. As to these see the public access rules at Section 2.D2 and further in respect of *BSB entities* Rule S28 and the associated guidance.

gC51

CD2 and Rules rC15.5 and rC17 require you, subject to Rule rC16, to put your *client's* interests ahead of your own and those of any other person. If you consider that your *professional client*, another *solicitor* or *intermediary*, another *barrister*, or any other person acting on behalf of your *client* has been negligent, you should ensure that your *client* is advised of this.

Rule C18   Rules

rC18

Your duty to provide a competent standard of work and service to each *client* (CD7) includes a duty to inform your *professional client*, or your

---

BSB Handbook

client if instructed by a *client*, as far as reasonably possible in sufficient time to enable appropriate steps to be taken to protect the *client's* interests, if:

.1 it becomes apparent to you that you will not be able to carry out the *instructions* within the time requested, or within a reasonable time after receipt of *instructions*; or

.2 there is an appreciable risk that you may not be able to undertake the *instructions*.

Guidance to Rule C18   [Guidance]

gC52

For further information about what you should do in the event that you have a clash of listings, please refer to our guidance which can be accessed on the *Bar Standards Board's* website.

Rule C19 - Not misleading clients and potential clients   [Rules]

rC19

If you supply, or offer to supply, *legal services*, you must not mislead, or cause or permit to be misled, any person to whom you supply, or offer to supply, *legal services* about:

.1 the nature and scope of the *legal services* which you are offering or agreeing to supply;

.2 the terms on which the *legal services* will be supplied, who will carry out the work and the basis of charging;

.3 who is legally responsible for the provision of the services;

.4 whether you are entitled to supply those services and the extent to which you are regulated when providing those services and by whom; or

.5 the extent to which you are covered by insurance against claims for professional negligence.

Guidance to Rule C19   [Guidance]

gC53

The best interests of *clients* (CD2) and public confidence in the profession (CD5) are undermined if there is a lack of clarity as to whether services are regulated, who is supplying them, on what terms, and what redress *clients* have and against whom if things go wrong. Rule rC19 may potentially be infringed in a broad variety of situations. You must consider how matters will appear to the *client*.

gC54

Clients may, by way of example, be misled if *self-employed barristers* were to share premises with *solicitors* or other professionals without making sufficiently clear to *clients* that they remain separate and independent from one another and are not responsible for one another's work.

gC55

Likewise, it is likely to be necessary to make clear to *clients* that any entity established as a "ProcureCo" is not itself able to supply *reserved legal activities* and is not subject to regulation by the *Bar Standards Board*.

gC56

A set of *chambers* dealing directly with unsophisticated lay *clients* might breach Rule rC19 if its branding created the appearance of an entity or *partnership* and it failed to explain that the members of *chambers* are, in fact, self-employed individuals who are not responsible for one another's work.

BSB Handbook

gC57

Knowingly or recklessly publishing advertising material which is inaccurate or likely to mislead could also result in you being in breach of Rule rC19. You should be particularly careful about making comparisons with other persons as these may often be regarded as misleading.

gC58

If you carry out public access work but are not authorised to *conduct litigation*, you would breach Rule rC19 if you caused or permitted your *client* to be misled into believing that you are entitled to, or will, provide services that include the *conduct of litigation* on behalf of your *client*.

gC59

If you are a *self-employed barrister*, you would, for example, likely be regarded as having breached Rule rC19 if you charged at your own hourly rate for work done by a *devil* or *pupil*. Moreover, such conduct may well breach your duty to act with honesty and also with integrity (CD3).

gC60

If you are an *unregistered barrister*, you would breach Rule rC19 if you misled your *client* into thinking that you were providing *legal services* to them as a *barrister* or that you were subject to the same regulation as a *practising barrister*. You would also breach the rule if you implied that you were covered by insurance if you were not, or if you suggested that your *clients* could seek a remedy from the *Bar Standards Board* or the *Legal Ombudsman* if they were dissatisfied with the services you provided. You should also be aware of the rules set out in Section D4 of this Code of Conduct and the additional guidance for *unregistered barristers* available on the *Bar Standards Board* website.

gC61

Rule C19.3 is particularly relevant where you act in more than one capacity, for example as a *BSB authorised individual* as well as a manager or employee of an *authorised (non BSB) body*. This is because you should make it clear to each *client* in what capacity you are acting and, therefore, who has legal responsibility for the provision of the services.

gC62

If you are a *pupil*, you should not hold yourself out as a member of *chambers* or permit your name to appear as such. You should ensure the *client* understands your status.

gC63

A number of other rules impose positive obligations on you, in particular circumstances, to make clear your regulatory status and the basis and terms on which you are acting. See, for example, Rule rC23 and guidance gC74.

Rule C20 - Personal responsibility | Rules |

rC20

Where you are a *BSB authorised individual*, you are personally responsible for your own conduct and for your professional work. You must use your own professional judgment in relation to those matters on which you are instructed and be able to justify your decisions and actions. You must do this notwithstanding the views of your *client*, *professional client*, *employer* or any other person.

Guidance to Rule C20 | Guidance |

gC64

It is fundamental that *BSB authorised individuals* and *authorised (non-BSB) individuals* are personally responsible for their own conduct and for their own professional work, whether they are acting in a self-employed or employed capacity (in the case of *BSB authorised individuals*) or as an employee or *manager* of a *BSB entity* (in the case of *authorised (non-BSB) individuals*).

BSB Handbook   The BSB Handbook - Version 4.6

gC65

Nothing in Rule rC20 is intended to prevent you from delegating or outsourcing to any other person discrete tasks (for example, research) which such other person is well-equipped to provide. However, where such tasks are delegated or outsourced, you remain personally responsible for such work. Further, in circumstances where such tasks are being outsourced, Rule rC86 which deals with outsourcing, must be complied with.

gC66

You are responsible for the service provided by all those who represent you in your dealings with your *client*, including your clerks or any other employees or agents.

gC67

Nothing in this rule or guidance prevents a *BSB entity* from contracting on the basis that any civil liability for the services provided by a *BSB regulated individual* lies with the *BSB entity* and the *BSB regulated individual* is not to be liable. However, any such stipulation as to civil liability does not affect the regulatory obligations of the *BSB regulated individual* including (but not limited to) that of being personally responsible under Rule rC20 for the professional judgments made.

gC68

See, further, guidance to Rule rC19, as regards work by *pupils* and *devils* Rule rC15, gC124 and Rule rC86 (on outsourcing).

Rule C21 - Accepting instructions   `Rules`

rC21

You must not accept *instructions* to act in a particular matter if:

.1 due to any existing or previous *instructions* you are not able to fulfil your obligation to act in the best interests of the prospective *client*; or

.2 there is a conflict of interest, or real risk of conflict of interest, between your own personal interests and the interests of the prospective *client* in respect of the particular matter; or

.3 there is a conflict of interest, or real risk of conflict of interest, between the prospective *client* and one or more of your former or existing *clients* in respect of the particular matter unless all of the *clients* who have an interest in the particular matter give their informed consent to your acting in such circumstances; or

.4 there is a real risk that information confidential to another former or existing *client*, or any other person to whom you owe duties of confidence, may be relevant to the matter, such that if, obliged to maintain confidentiality, you could not act in the best interests of the prospective *client*, and the former or existing *client* or person to whom you owe that duty does not give informed consent to disclosure of that confidential information; or

.5 your instructions seek to limit your ordinary authority or discretion in the conduct of proceedings in *court*; or

.6 your instructions require you to act other than in accordance with law or with the provisions of this *Handbook*; or

.7 you are not authorised and/or otherwise accredited to perform the work required by the relevant *instruction*; or

.8 you are not competent to handle the particular matter or otherwise do not have enough experience to handle the matter; or

.9 you do not have enough time to deal with the particular matter, unless the circumstances are such that it would nevertheless be in the *client's* best interests for you to accept; or

.10 there is a real prospect that you are not going to be able to maintain your independence.

Guidance to Rule C21   `Guidance`

gC69

Rules rC21.2, rC21.3 and rC21.4 are intended to reflect the law on conflict of interests and confidentiality and what is required of you

BSB Handbook

by your duty to act in the *client's* best interests (CD2), independently (CD4), and maintaining *client* confidentiality (CD6). You are prohibited from acting where there is a conflict of interest between your own personal interests and the interests of a prospective *client*. However, where there is a conflict of interest between an existing *client* or *clients* and a prospective *client* or *clients* or two or more prospective *clients*, you may be entitled to accept instructions or to continue to act on a particular matter where you have fully disclosed to the relevant *clients* and prospective *clients* (as appropriate) the extent and nature of the conflict; they have each provided their informed consent to you acting; and you are able to act in the best interests of each *client* and independently as required by CD2 and CD4.

gC70

Examples of where you may be required to refuse to accept *instructions* in accordance with Rule rC21.7 include:

.1 where the *instructions* relate to the provision of litigation services and you have not been authorised to *conduct litigation* in accordance with the requirements of this *Handbook*;

.2 removed

.3 where the matter would require you to conduct correspondence with parties other than your *client* (in the form of letters, faxes, emails or the like), you do not have adequate systems, experience or resources for managing appropriately such correspondence and/or you do not have adequate insurance in place in accordance with Rule rC75 which covers, amongst other things, any loss suffered by the *client* as a result of the conduct of such correspondence.

gC71

Competency and experience under Rule rC21.8 includes your ability to work with vulnerable *clients*.

gC72

Rule rC21.9 recognises that there may be exceptional circumstances when *instructions* are delivered so late that no suitable, competent advocate would have adequate time to prepare. In those cases you are not required to refuse *instructions* as it will be in the *client's* best interests that you accept. Indeed, if you are obliged under the cab rank rule to accept the *instructions*, you must do so.

gC73

Rule rC21.10 is an aspect of your broader obligation to maintain your independence (CD4). Your ability to perform your duty to the *court* (CD1) and act in the best interests of your *client* (CD2) may be put at risk if you act in circumstances where your independence is compromised. Examples of when you may not be able to maintain your independence include appearing as an advocate in a matter in which you are likely to be called as a witness (unless the matter on which you are likely to be called as a witness is peripheral or minor in the context of the litigation as a whole and is unlikely to lead to your involvement in the matter being challenged at a later date). If it appears that you are likely to be a witness on a material question of fact, and therefore must withdraw from a case as there is a real prospect that you are not going to be able to maintain your independence (Rules C21.10 and C25), you must also comply with Rule C27.

gC74

Where the *instructions* relate to public access or licensed access work and you are a *self-employed barrister* you will also need to have regard to the relevant rules at 2.D2. If you are a *BSB entity*, you should have regard to the guidance to Rule S28.

Rules C22-C24 - Defining terms or basis on which instructions are accepted   `Rules`

rC22

Where you first accept *instructions* to act in a matter:

.1 you must, subject to Rule rC23, confirm in writing acceptance of the *instructions* and the terms and/or basis on which you will be acting, including the basis of charging;

.2 where your instructions are from a *professional client*, the confirmation required by rC22.1 must be sent to the *professional client*;

.3 where your instructions are from a *client*, the confirmation required by rC22.1 must be sent to the *client*.

.4 if you are a *BSB entity*, you must ensure that the terms under which you accept instructions from *clients* include consent from clients to disclose and give control of files to the *Bar Standards Board* or its agent in circumstances where the conditions in rS113.5 are met.

rC23

In the event that, following your acceptance of the *instructions* in accordance with Rule rC22, the scope of the *instructions* is varied by the relevant *client* (including where the *client* instructs you on additional aspects relating to the same matter), you are not required to confirm again in writing acceptance of the instructions or the terms and/or basis upon which you will be acting. In these circumstances, you will be deemed to have accepted the instructions when you begin the work, on the same terms or basis as before, unless otherwise specified.

rC24

You must comply with the requirements set out in Rules rC22 and rC23 before doing the work unless that is not reasonably practicable, in which case you should do so as soon as reasonably practicable.

Guidance to Rules C22-C24 | Guidance |

gC75

Compliance with the requirement in Rule rC22 to set out the terms and/or basis upon which you will be acting may be achieved by including a reference or link to the relevant terms in your written communication of acceptance. You may, for example, refer the *client* or *professional client* (as the case may be) to the terms of service set out on your website or to standard terms of service set out on the *Bar Council's* website (in which regard, please also refer to the guidance on the use of the standard terms of service). Where you agree to do your work on terms and conditions that have been proposed to you by the *client* or by the *professional client*, you should confirm in writing that that is the basis on which your work is done. Where there are competing sets of terms and conditions, which terms have been agreed and are the basis of your retainer will be a matter to be determined in accordance with the law of contract.

gC76

Your obligation under Rule rC23 is to ensure that the basis on which you act has been defined, which does not necessarily mean governed by your own contractual terms. In circumstances where Rule rC23 applies, you should take particular care to ensure that the *client* is clear about the basis for charging for any variation to the work where it may be unclear. You must also ensure that you comply with the requirements of the Provision of Services Regulations 2009. See, further Rule rC19 (not misleading *clients* or prospective *clients*) and the guidance to that rule at gC52 to gC62.

gC77

If you are a *self-employed barrister* a clerk may confirm on your behalf your acceptance of *instructions* in accordance with Rules rC22 and rC23 above.

gC78

When accepting instructions, you must also ensure that you comply with the complaints handling rules set out in Section 2.D.

gC79

When accepting instructions in accordance with Rule rC22, confirmation by email will satisfy any requirement for written acceptance.

gC80

You may have been instructed in relation to a discrete and finite task, such as to provide an opinion on a particular issue, or to provide ongoing services, for example, to conduct particular litigation. Your confirmation of acceptance of instructions under Rule rC22 should make clear the scope of the *instructions* you are accepting, whether by cross-referring to the *instructions*, where these are in writing or by summarising your understanding of the scope of work you are instructed to undertake.

gC81

Disputes about costs are one of the most frequent *complaints*. The provision of clear information before work starts is the best way of avoiding such *complaints*. The *Legal Ombudsman* has produced a useful guide "An Ombudsman's view of good costs service" which can be found on its website.

BSB Handbook   The BSB Handbook - Version 4.6

gC82

Where the *instructions* relate to public access or licensed access work and you are a *self-employed barrister*, you will also need to have regard to the relevant rules at 2.D2. If you are a *BSB entity*, you should have regard to the guidance to Rule S28.

Rules C25-C26 - Returning instructions | Rules |

rC25

Where you have accepted *instructions* to act but one or more of the circumstances set out in Rules rC21.1 to rC21.10 above then arises, you must cease to act and return your *instructions* promptly. In addition, you must cease to act and return your *instructions* if:

.1 in a case funded by the *Legal Aid Agency* as part of Criminal Legal Aid or Civil Legal Aid it has become apparent to you that this funding has been wrongly obtained by false or inaccurate information and action to remedy the situation is not immediately taken by your *client*; or

.2 the *client* refuses to authorise you to make some disclosure to the *court* which your duty to the *court* requires you to make; or

.3 you become aware during the course of a case of the existence of a document which should have been but has not been disclosed, and the *client* fails to disclose it or fails to permit you to disclose it, contrary to your advice.

rC26

You may cease to act on a matter on which you are instructed and return your *instructions* if:

.1 your professional conduct is being called into question; or

.2 the *client* consents; or

.3 you are a *self-employed barrister* and:

.a despite all reasonable efforts to prevent it, a hearing becomes fixed for a date on which you have already entered in your professional diary that you will not be available; or

.b illness, injury, pregnancy, childbirth, a bereavement or a similar matter makes you unable reasonably to perform the services required in the *instructions*; or

.c you are unavoidably required to attend on jury service;

.4 you are a *BSB entity* and the only appropriate *authorised individual(s)* are unable to continue acting on the particular matter due to one or more of the grounds referred to at Rules rC26.3.a to rC26.3.c above occurring;

.5 you do not receive payment when due in accordance with terms agreed, subject to Rule rC26.7 (if you are conducting litigation) and in any other case subject to your giving reasonable notice requiring the non-payment to be remedied and making it clear to the *client* in that notice that failure to remedy the non-payment may result in you ceasing to act and returning your *instructions* in respect of the particular matter; or

.6 you become aware of confidential or privileged information or documents of another person which relate to the matter on which you are instructed; or

.7 if you are conducting litigation, and your *client* does not consent to your ceasing to act, your application to come off the record has been granted; or

.8 there is some other substantial reason for doing so (subject to Rules rC27 to rC29 below).

Guidance to Rule C26 | Guidance |

gC83

In deciding whether to cease to act and to return existing instructions in accordance with Rule rC26, you should, where possible and subject to your overriding duty to the *court*, ensure that the *client* is not adversely affected because there is not enough time to engage other adequate legal assistance.

BSB Handbook

gC84

If you are working on a referral basis and your *professional client* withdraws, you are no longer instructed and cannot continue to act unless appointed by the *court*, or you otherwise receive new instructions. You will not be bound by the cab rank rule if appointed by the court. For these purposes working on a "referral basis" means where a *professional client* instructs a *BSB authorised individual* to provide *legal services* on behalf of one of that *professional client's* own clients

gC85

You should not rely on Rule rC26.3 to break an engagement to supply legal services so that you can attend or fulfil a non-professional engagement of any kind other than those indicated in Rule rC26.3.

gC86

When considering whether or not you are required to return instructions in accordance with Rule rC26.6 you should have regard to relevant case law including: English & American Insurance Co Ltd & Others -v- Herbert Smith; ChD 1987; (1987) NLJ 148 and Ablitt -v- Mills & Reeve (A Firm) and Another; ChD (Times, 24-Oct-1995).

gC87

If a fundamental change is made to the basis of your remuneration, you should treat such a change as though your original instructions have been withdrawn by the *client* and replaced by an offer of new *instructions* on different terms. Accordingly:

.1 you must decide whether you are obliged by Rule rC29 to accept the new *instructions*;

.2 if you are obliged under Rule rC29 to accept the new *instructions*, you must do so;

.3 if you are not obliged to accept the new *instructions*, you may decline them;

.4 if you decline to accept the new *instructions* in such circumstances, you are not to be regarded as returning your *instructions*, nor as withdrawing from the matter, nor as ceasing to act, for the purposes of Rules rC25 to rC26, because the previous *instructions* have been withdrawn by the *client*.

Rule C27 Rules

rC27

Notwithstanding the provisions of Rules rC25 and rC26, you must not:

.1 cease to act or return *instructions* without either:

.a obtaining your *client's* consent; or

.b clearly explaining to your *client* or your *professional client* the reasons for doing so; or

.2 return instructions to another person without the consent of your *client* or your *professional client*.

Rule C28 - Requirement not to discriminate Rules

rC28

You must not withhold your services or permit your services to be withheld:

.1 on the ground that the nature of the case is objectionable to you or to any section of the public;

.2 on the ground that the conduct, opinions or beliefs of the prospective client are unacceptable to you or to any section of the public;

.3 on any ground relating to the source of any financial support which may properly be given to the prospective *client* for the proceedings in question.

BSB Handbook

Guidance to Rule C28 [Guidance]

gC88

As a matter of general law you have an obligation not to discriminate unlawfully as to those to whom you make your services available on any of the statutorily prohibited grounds such as gender or race. See the Equality Rules in the BSB Handbook and the BSB's website for guidance as to your obligations in respect of equality and diversity. This rule of conduct is concerned with a broader obligation not to withhold your services on grounds that are inherently inconsistent with your role in upholding access to justice and the rule of law and therefore in this rule "discriminate" is used in this broader sense. This obligation applies whether or not the *client* is a member of any protected group for the purposes of the Equality Act 2010. For example, you must not withhold services on the ground that any financial support which may properly be given to the prospective *client* for the proceedings in question will be available as part of Criminal Legal Aid and Civil Legal Aid.

Rules C29-C30 - The cab rank rule [Rules]

rC29

If you receive *instructions* from a *professional client*, and you are:

.1 a *self-employed barrister* instructed by a *professional client*; or

.2 an *authorised individual* working within a *BSB entity*; or

.3 a *BSB entity* and the *instructions* seek the services of a named *authorised individual* working for you,

and the *instructions* are appropriate taking into account the experience, seniority and/or field of practice of yourself or (as appropriate) of the named *authorised individual* you must, subject to Rule rC30 below, accept the *instructions* addressed specifically to you, irrespective of:

.a the identity of the *client*;

.b the nature of the case to which the *instructions* relate;

.c whether the *client* is paying privately or is publicly funded; and

.d any belief or opinion which you may have formed as to the character, reputation, cause, conduct, guilt or innocence of the *client*.

rC30

The cab rank Rule rC29 does not apply if:

.1 you are required to refuse to accept the *instructions* pursuant to Rule rC21; or

.2 accepting the *instructions* would require you or the named *authorised individual* to do something other than in the course of their ordinary working time or to cancel a commitment already in their diary; or

.3 the potential liability for professional negligence in respect of the particular matter could exceed the level of professional indemnity insurance which is reasonably available and likely to be available in the market for you to accept; or

.4 you are a Queen's Counsel, and the acceptance of the *instructions* would require you to act without a junior in circumstances where you reasonably consider that the interests of the *client* require that a junior should also be instructed; or

.5 accepting the *instructions* would require you to do any *foreign work*; or

.6 accepting the *instructions* would require you to act for a *foreign lawyer* (other than a *European lawyer*, a lawyer from a country that is a member of EFTA, a *solicitor* or *barrister* of Northern Ireland or a *solicitor* or advocate under the law of Scotland); or

.7 the *professional client*:

.a is not accepting liability for your fees; or

.b represents, in your reasonable opinion, an unacceptable credit risk; or

BSB Handbook

.c is instructing you as a lay *client* and not in their capacity as a *professional client*; or

.8 you have not been offered a proper fee for your services (except that you shall not be entitled to refuse to accept *instructions* on this ground if you have not made or responded to any fee proposal within a reasonable time after receiving the *instructions*); or

.9 except where you are to be paid directly by (i) the *Legal Aid Agency* as part of the Community Legal Service or the Criminal Defence Service or (ii) the Crown Prosecution Service:

.a your fees have not been agreed (except that you shall not be entitled to refuse to accept *instructions* on this ground if you have not taken reasonable steps to agree fees within a reasonable time after receiving the *instructions*);

.b having required your fees to be paid before you accept the *instructions*, those fees have not been paid;

.c accepting the *instructions* would require you to act other than on (A) the Standard Contractual Terms for the Supply of Legal Services by Barristers to Authorised Persons 2020 as published on the *Bar Council's* website; or (B) if you publish standard terms of work, on those standard terms of work.

Guidance to Rules C29-C30 | Guidance |

---

gC89

Rule rC30 means that you would not be required to accept *instructions* to, for example, *conduct litigation* or attend a police station in circumstances where you do not normally undertake such work or, in the case of litigation, are not authorised to undertake such work.

gC90

In determining whether or not a fee is proper for the purposes of Rule C30.8, regard shall be had to the following:

.1 the complexity length and difficulty of the case;

.2 your ability, experience and seniority; and

.3 the expenses which you will incur.

gC91

Further, you may refuse to accept instructions on the basis that the fee is not proper if the instructions are on the basis that you will do the work under a *conditional fee agreement* or damages based agreement.

gC91A

Examples of when you might reasonably conclude (subject to the following paragraph) that a *professional client* represents an unacceptable credit risk for the purposes of Rule C30.7.b include:

.1 Where they are included on the *Bar Council's* List of Defaulting Solicitors;

.2 Where to your knowledge a *barrister* has obtained a judgment against a *professional client*, which remains unpaid;

.3 Where a firm or sole practitioner is subject to insolvency proceedings, an individual voluntary arrangement or partnership voluntary arrangement; or

.4 Where there is evidence of other unsatisfied judgments that reasonably call into question the *professional client's* ability to pay your fees.

Even where you consider that there is a serious credit risk, you should not conclude that the *professional client* represents an unacceptable credit risk without first considering alternatives. This will include considering whether the credit risk could be mitigated in other ways, for example by seeking payment of the fee in advance or payment into a third party payment service as permitted by rC74, rC75 and associated guidance.

gC91B

The standard terms referred to in Rule C30.9.c may be drafted as if the *professional client* were an *authorised person* regulated by the Solicitors Regulation Authority (SRA). However, the cab rank rule applies (subject to the various exceptions in Rule C30) to instructions from any *professional client*, therefore you may be instructed under the cab rank rule by *authorised persons* who are

BSB Handbook

regulated by another *approved regulator*.

The BSB expects all *authorised persons* to be able to access the cab rank rule on behalf of their *clients* in the same way. Therefore, if you are instructed by an *authorised person* who is not regulated by the SRA, you are obliged to act on the same terms. You should therefore apply the standard terms referred to in Rule C30.9.c as if (i) the definition of *professional client* includes that *authorised person*, and (ii) any references to the SRA or its regulatory arrangements are references to that person's *approved regulator* and its regulatory arrangements.

Rules C31-C63   Rules

Removed.

Part 2 - C4. You and your regulator   Rules

Outcomes C21-C23   Outcomes

oC21

BSB regulated persons are effectively regulated.

oC22

The public have confidence in the proper regulation of *persons* regulated by the *Bar Standards Board*.

oC23

The *Bar Standards Board* has the information that it needs in order to be able to assess risks and regulate effectively and in accordance with the *regulatory objectives*.

Rule C64 - Provision of information to the Bar Standards Board   Rules

rC64

You must:

.1 promptly provide all such information to the *Bar Standards Board* as it may, for the purpose of its regulatory functions, from time to time require of you, and notify it of any material changes to that information;

.2 comply in due time with any decision or sentence imposed by the *Bar Standards Board*, a *Disciplinary Tribunal*, the High Court, the *First Tier Tribunal*, an *interim panel*, a *review panel*, an *appeal panel*, an *Independent Decision-Making Panel* or a *Fitness to Practise Panel*;

.3 if you are a *BSB entity* or an *owner* or *manager* of a *BSB entity* and the conditions outlined in rS113.5 apply, give the *Bar Standards Board* whatever co-operation is necessary:

.4 comply with any notice sent by the *Bar Standards Board* or its agent; and

.5 register within 28 days if you undertake work in the Youth Court if you did not register when applying for a practising certificate.

Guidance to Rule C64   Guidance

BSB Handbook

gC92

Your obligations under Rule rC64 include, for example, responding promptly to any request from the *Bar Standards Board* for comments or information relating to any matter whether or not the matter relates to you, or to another *BSB regulated person* or *unregistered barrister*.

gC92A

A notice under rC64.4 refers to a notice under any part of the Legal Services Act 2007, or the Legal Services Act 2007 (General Council of the Bar) (Modification of Functions) Order 2018.

gC93

The documents that you are required to disclose pursuant to Rule C64 may include client information that is subject to legal professional privilege. Pursuant to R (Morgan Grenfell & Co Ltd) v Special Commissioner [2003] 1 A.C. 563, referred to in R (Lumsdon) v Legal Services Board [2014] EWHC 28 (Admin) at [73], the BSB is entitled to serve you with a notice for production of those documents.

Where you are being required to report serious misconduct by others and legal professional privilege applies, this will override the requirement to report serious misconduct by another. However, the BSB may subsequently serve you with a notice for production of documents in which case the same principles set out above apply.

For the avoidance of doubt, none of this casts any doubt on your entitlement to withhold from the BSB any material that is subject to your own legal privilege (such as legal advice given to you about your own position during a BSB investigation).

Rule C65 - Duty to report certain matters to the Bar Standards Board   `Rules`

rC65

You must report promptly to the *Bar Standards Board* if:

.1 you are charged with an *indictable offence*; in the jurisdiction of England and Wales or with a *criminal offence* of comparable seriousness in any other jurisdiction;

.2 subject to the Rehabilitation of Offenders Act 1974 (as amended) you are convicted of, or accept a caution, for any *criminal offence*, in any jurisdiction, other than a *minor criminal offence*;

.3 you (or an entity of which you are a *manager*) to your knowledge are the subject of any disciplinary or other regulatory or enforcement action by another *Approved Regulator* or other regulator, including being the subject of disciplinary proceedings;

.4 you are a *manager* of a *regulated entity* (other than a *BSB entity*) which is the subject of an intervention by the *approved regulator* of that body;

.5 you are a *registered European lawyer* and:

.a to your knowledge any investigation into your conduct is commenced by your home regulator; or

.b any finding of professional misconduct is made by your home regulator; or

.c your authorisation in your *home state* to pursue professional activities under your *home professional title* is withdrawn or *suspended*; or

.d you are charged with a disciplinary offence.

.6 any of the following occur:

.a bankruptcy proceedings are initiated in respect of or against you;

.b *director's disqualification* proceedings are initiated against you;

.c a *bankruptcy order* or *director's disqualification order* is made against you;

.d you have made a composition or arrangement with, or granted a trust deed for, your creditors;

.e winding up proceedings are initiated in respect of or against you;

.f you have had an administrator, administrative receiver, receiver or liquidator appointed in respect of you;

.g administration proceedings are initiated in respect of or against you;

.7 you have committed serious misconduct;

.8 you become authorised to *practise* by another *approved regulator*.

Guidance to Rule C65 | Guidance |

---

gC94

In circumstances where you have committed serious misconduct you should take all reasonable steps to mitigate the effects of such serious misconduct.

gC94.1

For the avoidance of doubt rC65.2 does not oblige you to disclose cautions or criminal convictions that are "spent" under the Rehabilitation of Offenders Act 1974 unless the Rehabilitation of Offenders Act 1974 (Exceptions) Order 1975 (SI 1975/1023) applies. However, unless the caution or conviction is immediately spent, you must notify the BSB before it becomes spent.

Rules C66-C69 - Reporting serious misconduct by others | Rules |

---

rC66

Subject to your duty to keep the affairs of each *client* confidential and subject also to Rules rC67 and rC68, you must report to the *Bar Standards Board* if you have reasonable grounds to believe that there has been serious misconduct by a *barrister* or a *registered European lawyer*, a *BSB entity*, *manager* of a *BSB entity* or an *authorised (non-BSB) individual* who is working as a *manager* or an employee of a *BSB entity*.

rC67

You must never make, or threaten to make, a report under Rule rC66 without a genuine and reasonably held belief that Rule rC66 applies.

rC68

You are not under a duty to report serious misconduct by others if:

.1 you become aware of the facts giving rise to the belief that there has serious misconduct from matters that are in the public domain and the circumstances are such that you reasonably consider it likely that the facts will have come to the attention of the *Bar Standards Board*; or

.2 you are aware that the person that committed the serious misconduct has already reported the serious misconduct to the Bar Standards Board; or

.3 the information or documents which led to you becoming aware of that other person's serious misconduct are subject to legal professional privilege; or

.4 you become aware of such serious misconduct as a result of your work on a *Bar Council* advice line.

rC69

You must not victimise anyone for making in good faith a report under Rule C66.

Guidance to Rules C65.7-C68 | Guidance |

---

gC95

It is in the public interest that the *Bar Standards Board*, as an *Approved Regulator*, is made aware of, and is able to investigate, potential instances of serious misconduct. The purpose of Rules rC65.7 to rC69, therefore, is to assist the *Bar Standards Board* in undertaking this regulatory function.

gC96

Serious misconduct includes, without being limited to:

.1 dishonesty (CD3);

.2 assault or harassment (CD3 and/or CD5 and/or CD8);

.3 seeking to gain access without consent to *instructions* or other confidential information relating to the opposing party's case (CD3 and/or CD5); or

.4 seeking to gain access without consent to confidential information relating to another member of *chambers*, member of staff or *pupil* (CD3 and/or CD5);

.5 encouraging a witness to give evidence which is untruthful or misleading (CD1 and/or CD3);

.6 knowingly or recklessly misleading, or attempting to mislead, the *court* or an opponent (CD1 and/ or CD3); or

.7 being drunk or under the influence of drugs in *court* (CD2 and/or CD7); or

.8 failure to report promptly to the *Bar Standards Board* pursuant to rC65.1-rC65.5 and/or rC66 above or if;

• *director's disqualification* proceedings are initiated against you;

• a *director's disqualification* order is made against you;

• winding up proceedings are initiated in respect of or against you;

• you have had an administrator, administrative receiver, receiver or liquidator appointed in respect of you;

• administration proceedings are initiated in respect of or against you;

.9 a breach of rC67 above; for example, reporting, or threatening to report, another *person* as a litigation tactic or otherwise abusively; or merely to please a *client* or any other *person* or otherwise for an improper motive;

.10 conduct that poses a serious risk to the public.

gC97

If you believe (or suspect) that there has been serious misconduct, then the first step is to carefully consider all of the circumstances. The circumstances include:

.1 whether that person's *instructions* or other confidential matters might have a bearing on the assessment of their conduct;

.2 whether that person has been offered an opportunity to explain their conduct, and if not, why not;

.3 any explanation which has been or could be offered for that person's conduct;

.4 whether the matter has been raised, or will be raised, in the litigation in which it occurred, and if not, why not.

gC98

Having considered all of the circumstances, the duty to report arises if you have reasonable grounds to believe there has been serious misconduct. This will be so where, having given due consideration to the circumstances, including the matters identified at Guidance gC97, you have material before you which as it stands establishes a reasonably credible case of serious misconduct. Your duty under Rule rC66 is then to report the potential instance of serious misconduct so that the *Bar Standards Board* can investigate whether or not there has in fact been misconduct.

gC99

Circumstances which may give rise to the exception from the general requirement to report serious misconduct set out in Rule rC68.1 include for example where misconduct has been widely reported in the national media. In these circumstances it would not be in the public interest for every *BSB regulated person* and *unregistered barrister* to have an obligation to report such serious misconduct.

gC100

In Rule rC68.4 "work on the *Bar Council* advice line" means:

.1 dealing with queries from *BSB regulated persons* and *unregistered barristers* who contact an advice line operated by the *Bar Council* for the purposes of providing advice to those persons; and

.2 either providing advice to *BSB regulated persons* and *unregistered barristers* in the course of working for an advice line or to any individual working for an advice line where (i) you are identified on the list of *BSB regulated persons* maintained by the *Bar Council* as being permitted to provide such advice (the "approved list"); and (ii) the advice which you are being asked to provide to the individual working for an advice line arises from a query which originated from their work for that service; and

.3 providing advice to *BSB regulated persons* and *unregistered barristers* where any individual working for an advice line arranges for you to give such advice and you are on the approved list.

.4 for the purposes of Rule C68, the relevant advice lines are:

– the Ethical Queries Helpline;

– the Equality and Diversity Helpline;

– the Remuneration Helpline; and

– the Pupillage Helpline.

gC101

Rule rC68.4 has been carved out of the general requirement to report serious misconduct of others because it is not in the public interest that the duty to report misconduct should constrain *BSB regulated persons* or *unregistered barristers* appointed by or on behalf of the *Bar Council* to offer ethical advice to others from doing so or inhibit *BSB regulated persons* or *unregistered barristers* needing advice from seeking it. Consequently, *BSB regulated persons* or *unregistered barristers* appointed by or on behalf of the *Bar Council* to offer ethical advice to *BSB regulated persons* or *unregistered barristers* through a specified advice service will not be under a duty to report information received by them in confidence from persons seeking such advice, subject only to the requirements of the general law. However, in circumstances where Rule C68.4 applies, the relevant *BSB regulated person* or *unregistered barrister* will still be expected to encourage the relevant *BSB regulated person* or *unregistered barrister* who has committed serious misconduct to disclose such serious misconduct to the *Bar Standards Board* in accordance with Rule C65.7.

gC102

Misconduct which falls short of serious misconduct should, where applicable, be reported to your HOLP so that they can keep a record of non-compliance in accordance with Rule rC96.4.

Rule C70 - Access to premises | Rules |

rC70

You must permit the *Bar Standards Board*, or any person appointed by them, reasonable access, on request, to inspect:

.1 any premises from which you provide, or are believed to provide, *legal services*; and

.2 any documents or records relating to those premises and your *practice*, or *BSB entity*, and the *Bar Standards Board*, or any person appointed by them, shall be entitled to take copies of such documents or records as may be required by them for the purposes of their functions.

Rule C71 - Co-operation with the Legal Ombudsman | Rules |

rC71

You must give the *Legal Ombudsman* all reasonable assistance requested of you, in connection with the investigation, consideration, and determination, of *complaints* made under the Ombudsman scheme.

BSB Handbook

Rule C72 - Ceasing to practise   Rules

rC72

Once you are aware that you (if you are a *self-employed barrister* or a *BSB entity*) or the *BSB entity* within which you work (if you are an authorised individual or *manager* of such *BSB entity*) will cease to practise, you shall effect the orderly wind-down of activities, including:

.1 informing the *Bar Standards Board* and providing them with a contact address;

.2 notifying those *clients* for whom you have current matters and liaising with them in respect of the arrangements that they would like to be put in place in respect of those matters;

.3 providing such information to the *Bar Standards Board* in respect of your practice and your proposed arrangements in respect of the winding down of your activities as the *Bar Standards Board* may require.

Part 2 - C5. You and your practice   Rules

Outcomes C24-C25   Outcomes

oC24

Your *practice* is run competently in a way that achieves compliance with the Core Duties and your other obligations under this *Handbook*. Your employees, *pupils* and trainees understand, and do, what is required of them in order that you meet your obligations under this *Handbook*.

oC25

Clients are clear about the extent to which your services are regulated and by whom, and who is responsible for providing those services.

Rules C73-C75 - Client money   Rules

rC73

Except where you are acting in your capacity as a *manager* or employee of an *authorised (non-BSB) body*, you must not receive, control or handle *client money* apart from what the client pays you for your services.

rC74

If you make use of a third party payment service for making payments to or from or on behalf of your *client* you must:

.1 Ensure that the service you use will not result in your receiving, controlling or handling *client money*; and

.2 Only use the service for payments to or from or on behalf of your *client* that are made in respect of legal services, such as fees, disbursements or settlement monies; and

.3 Take reasonable steps to check that making use of the service is consistent with your duty to act competently and in your *client's* best interests.

rC75

The *Bar Standards Board* may give notice under this rule that (effective from the date of that notice) you may only use third party payment services approved by the *Bar Standards Board* or which satisfy criteria set by the *Bar Standards Board*

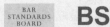 **BSB Handbook**   The BSB Handbook - Version 4.6

Guidance to Rules C73-C74   Guidance

gC103

The prohibition in Rule rC73 applies to you and to anyone acting on your behalf, including any "ProcureCo" being a company established as a vehicle to enable the provision of *legal services* but does not in itself supply or provide those *legal services*. Rule rC73 prohibits you from holding *client money* or other *client* assets yourself, or through any agent, third party or nominee.

gC104

Receiving, controlling or handling *client money* includes entering into any arrangement which gives you de facto control over the use and/or destination of funds provided by or for the benefit of your *client* or intended by another party to be transmitted to your *client*, whether or not those funds are beneficially owned by your client and whether or not held in an account of yours.

gC105

The circumstances in which you will have de facto control within the meaning of Rule rC73 include when you can cause money to be transferred from a balance standing to the credit of your *client* without that *client's* consent to such a withdrawal. For large withdrawals, explicit consent should usually be required. However, the *client's* consent may be deemed to be given if:

.1 the *client* has given informed consent to an arrangement which enables withdrawals to be made after the *client* has received an invoice; and

.2 the *client* has not objected to the withdrawal within a pre-agreed reasonable period (which should not normally be less than one week from receipt of the invoice).

gC106

A fixed fee paid in advance is not *client money* for the purposes of Rule rC73.

gC107

If you have decided in principle to take a particular case you may request an 'upfront' fixed fee from your prospective *client* before finally agreeing to work on their behalf. This should only be done having regard to the following principles:

• You should take care to estimate accurately the likely time commitment and only take payment when you are satisfied that:

– it is a reasonable payment for the work being done; and

– in the case of public access work, that it is suitable for you to undertake.

• If the amount of work required is unclear, you should consider staged payments rather than a fixed fee in advance.

• You should never accept an upfront fee in advance of considering whether it is appropriate for you to take the case and considering whether you will be able to undertake the work within a reasonable timescale.

• If the *client* can reasonably be expected to understand such an arrangement, you may agree that when the work has been done, you will pay the *client* any difference between that fixed fee and (if lower) the fee which has actually been earned based on the time spent, provided that it is clear that you will not hold the difference between the fixed fee and the fee which has been earned on trust for the *client*. That difference will not be *client money* if you can demonstrate that this was expressly agreed in writing, on clear terms understood by the *client*, and before payment of the fixed fee. You should also consider carefully whether such an arrangement is in the *client's* interest, taking into account the nature of the instructions, the *client* and whether the *client* fully understands the implications. Any abuse of an agreement to pay a fixed fee subject to reimbursement, the effect of which is that you receive more money than is reasonable for the case at the outset, will be considered to be holding *client money* and a breach of rC73. For this reason, you should take extreme care if contracting with a *client* in this way.

• In any case, rC22 requires you to confirm in writing the acceptance of any instructions and the terms or basis on which you are acting, including the basis of charging.

gC108

Acting in the following ways may demonstrate compliance with Rules rC73, rC74 and rC75:

BSB Handbook

gC109

Checking that any third party payment service you may use is not structured in such a way that the service provider is holding, as your agent, money to which the *client* is beneficially entitled. If this is so you will be in breach of Rule rC73.

gC110

Considering whether your *client* will be safe in using the third party payment service as a means of transmitting or receiving funds. The steps you should take in order to satisfy yourself will depend on what would be expected in all the circumstances of a reasonably competent legal adviser acting in their *client's* best interests. However, you are unlikely to demonstrate that you have acted competently and in your *client's* best interests if you have not:

.1 ensured that the payment service is authorised or regulated as a payment service by the Financial Conduct Authority (FCA) and taken reasonable steps to satisfy yourself that it is in good standing with the FCA;

.2 if the payment service is classified as a small payment institution, ensured that it has arrangements to safeguard *clients'* funds or adequate insurance arrangements;

.3 ensured that the payment service segregates *client money* from its own funds;

.4 satisfied yourself that the terms of the service are such as to ensure that any money paid in by or on behalf of the *client* can only be paid out with the *client's* consent;

.5 informed your *client* that moneys held by the payment service provider are not covered by the Financial Services Compensation Scheme.

gC111

Unless you are reasonably satisfied that it is safe for your client to use the third party payment service (see rC74.3, gC109 and gC110 above), advising your *client* against using the third party payment service and not making use of it yourself.

gC112

The *Bar Standards Board* has not yet given notice under rule rC75.

Rules C76-C78 - Insurance   `Rules`

rC76

You must:

.1 ensure that you have adequate insurance (taking into account the nature of your practice) which covers all the *legal services* you supply to the public; and

.2 if you are a *BSB authorised person* or a *manager* of a *BSB entity* then in the event that the *Bar Standards Board*, by any notice it may from time to time issue under this Rule C76, stipulates a minimum level of insurance and/or minimum terms for the insurance which must be taken out by *BSB authorised persons*, you must ensure that you have or put in place within the time specified in such notice, insurance meeting such requirements as apply to you.

rC77

Where you are acting as a *self-employed barrister*, you must be a member of *BMIF*, unless:

.1 you are a *pupil* who is covered by your *pupil supervisor's* insurance; or

.2 you were called to the *Bar* under Rule Q25, in which case you must either be insured with *BMIF* or be covered by insurance against claims for professional negligence arising out of the supply of your services in England and Wales in such amount and on such terms as are currently required by the *Bar Standards Board*, and have delivered to the *Bar Standards Board* a copy of the current insurance policy, or the current certificate of insurance, issued by the insurer.

rC78

If you are a member of *BMIF*, you must:

.1 pay promptly the insurance premium required by *BMIF*; and

BSB Handbook

.2 supply promptly such information as *BMIF* may from time to time require pursuant to its rules.

Guidance to Rules C76-C78 | Guidance |

gC113

Where you are working in a *BSB entity*, you will satisfy the requirements of Rule rC76.1 so long as the *BSB entity* has taken out insurance, which covers your activities. A *BSB entity* will have to confirm each year that it has reviewed the adequacy of its insurance cover on the basis of a risk analysis and that they have complied with this rule.

gC114

Any notice issued under Rule rC76 will be posted on the *Bar Standards Board's* website and may also be publicised by such other means as the *Bar Standards Board* may judge appropriate. Notices issued under Rule C76, which stipulate minimum terms of cover for *self-employed barristers* and *BSB entities*, are currently in force and available on the *Bar Standards Board's* website.

The *Bar Standards Board's* requirements in respect of professional indemnity insurance, including the minimum terms, are concerned with ensuring consumer protection, specifically that there is adequate cover for liabilities which *BSB regulated persons* may incur to their *clients* or other parties to whom they may owe duties when performing their *legal services*. This includes claims for contribution which third parties, such as instructing *solicitors*, may make on the basis that the *BSB regulated person* has such a liability to a mutual *client*. However, Rule C76.1 of the *Handbook* does not require *BSB regulated persons* to carry insurance for other types of liability, which do not relate to their liabilities towards consumers, such as a contractual liability to instructing *solicitors* in respect of losses incurred by the *solicitor* that are not based on any liability the *solicitor* has in turn incurred to the *client*. Nor are the minimum terms concerned with the latter type of liability and whether and on what terms to seek to insure against such exposure is a commercial judgment for *BSB regulated persons* to make. You should however ensure that you are aware of and comply with any general legal requirements for you to carry other types of insurance than professional indemnity cover.

BSB regulated persons considering excluding or limiting liability should consider carefully the ramifications of the Unfair Contract Terms Act 1977 and other legislation and case law. If a *BSB regulated person* is found by the court to have limited liability in a way which is in breach of the Unfair Contract Terms Act, that might amount to professional misconduct.

BSB regulated persons should regularly review the amount of their professional indemnity insurance cover, taking into account the type of work which they undertake and the likely liability for negligence. They should be aware that claims can arise many years after the work was undertaken and that they would be prudent to maintain adequate insurance cover for that time since cover operates on a "claims made" basis and as such it is the policy and the limits in force at the time a claim is made that are relevant, not the policy and limits in force when the work was undertaken. They should also bear in mind the need to arrange run-off cover if they cease practice.

gC115

Where you are working in an *authorised (non-BSB) body*, the rules of the *approved regulator* of that body will determine what insurance the *authorised (non-BSB) body* must have.

gC116

Where you are working as an *employed barrister (non-authorised body)*, the rule does not require you to have your own insurance if you provide *legal services* only to your *employer*. If you supply *legal services* to other people (to the extent permitted by the Scope of Practice and Authorisation, and Licensing Rules set out at Section S.B you should consider whether you need insurance yourself having regard to the arrangements made by your *employer* for insuring against claims made in respect of your services. If your *employer* already has adequate insurance for this purpose, you need not take out any insurance of your own. You should ensure that your *employer's* policy covers you, for example, for any pro-bono work you may do.

gC117

Where you are a *registered European lawyer*, the rule does not require you to have your own insurance if:

.1 you provide to the *Bar Standards Board* evidence to show that you are covered by insurance taken out or a guarantee provided in accordance with the rules of your *home State*; and

.2 the *Bar Standards Board* is satisfied that such insurance or guarantee is fully equivalent in terms of conditions and extent of cover to the cover required pursuant to Rule rC76. However, where the *Bar Standards Board* is satisfied that the equivalence is only partial, the *Bar Standards Board* may require you to arrange additional insurance or an additional guarantee to cover the elements which are

BSB Handbook

not already covered by the insurance or guarantee contracted by you in accordance with the rules of your *home state*

Rules C79-C85 - Associations with others   `Rules`

rC79

You may not do anything, practising in *an association*, which you are otherwise prohibited from doing.

rC80

Where you are in *an association* on more than a one-off basis, you must notify the *Bar Standards Board* that you are in *an association*, and provide such details of that association as are required by the *Bar Standards Board*.

rC81

If you have a material commercial interest in an organisation to which you plan to refer a *client*, you must:

.1 tell the *client* in writing about your interest in that organisation before you refer the *client*; and

.2 keep a record of your referrals to any such organisation for review by the *Bar Standards Board* on request.

rC82

If you have a material commercial interest in an organisation which is proposing to refer a matter to you, you must:

.1 tell the *client* in writing about your interest in that organisation before you accept such *instructions*;

.2 make a clear agreement with that organisation or other public statement about how relevant issues, such as conflicts of interest, will be dealt with; and

.3 keep a record of referrals received from any such organisation for review by the *Bar Standards Board* on reasonable request.

rC83

If you refer a *client* to a third party which is not a *BSB authorised person* or an *authorised (non-BSB) person*, you must take reasonable steps to ensure that the *client* is not wrongly led to believe that the third party is subject to regulation by the *Bar Standards Board* or by another *approved regulator*.

rC84

You must not have a material commercial interest in any organisation which gives the impression of being, or may be reasonably perceived as being, subject to the regulation of the *Bar Standards Board* or of another *approved regulator*, in circumstances where it is not so regulated.

rC85

A material commercial interest for the purposes of Rules rC78 to rC84 is an interest which an objective observer with knowledge of the salient facts would reasonably consider might potentially influence your judgment.

rC85A

You must not act as a supervisor of an immigration adviser for the purposes of section 84(2) of the Immigration and Asylum Act 1999 (as amended) (IAA 1999) where the Office of the Immigration Services Commissioner has refused or cancelled the adviser's registration, or where the adviser is:

1. disqualified in accordance with paragraph 4 of Schedule 6 to the IAA 1999; or

2. prohibited or suspended by the First-tier Tribunal (Immigration Services); or

3. permanently prohibited from practising by an *approved regulator*, or a designated professional body under the IAA 1999, pursuant to its powers as such, and removed from the relevant register; or

4. currently suspended from practising by an *approved regulator*, or a designated professional body under the IAA 1999, pursuant to its powers as such.

BSB Handbook

Guidance to Rules C79-C85 (and CD5)   Guidance

gC118

You may not use an association with the purpose of, or in order to evade rules which would otherwise apply to you. You may not do anything, practising in *an association*, which you are individually prohibited from doing.

gC119

You will bring yourself and your profession into disrepute (CD5) if you are personally involved in arrangements which breach the restrictions imposed by the Legal Services Act 2007 on those who can provide reserved legal activities. For example, you must not remain a member of any "ProcureCo" arrangement where you know or are reckless as to whether the ProcureCo is itself carrying on reserved legal activities without a licence or where you have failed to take reasonable steps to ensure this is not so before joining or continuing your involvement with the Procureco.

gC120

The purpose of Rules rC79 to rC85 is to ensure that *clients* and members of the public are not confused by any such association. In particular, the public should be clear who is responsible for doing work, and about the extent to which that person is regulated in doing it: see Rules rC79-85.

gC121

This *Handbook* applies in full whether or not you are practising in an association. You are particularly reminded of the need to ensure that, notwithstanding any such association, you continue to comply with Rules C8, C9, C10, C12, C15, C19, C20, C28, C73, C75, C79, C82 and C86 (and, where relevant C80, C81, C83, C74 and C110).

gC122

References to "organisation" in Rules rC81 and C82 include   *BSB entities* and *authorised (non-BSB) bodies*, as well as non-authorised bodies. So, if you have an interest, as owner, or manager, in any such body, your relationship with any such organisation is caught by these rules.

gC123

These rules do not permit you to accept *instructions* from a third party in any case where that would give rise to a potential conflict of interest contrary to CD2 or any relevant part of Rule rC21.

gC124

You should only refer a *client* to an organisation in which you have a material commercial interest if it is in the *client's* best interest to be referred to that organisation. This is one aspect of what is required of you by CD2. Your obligations of honesty and integrity, in CD3, require you to be open with *clients* about any interest you have in, or arrangement you have with, any organisation to which you properly refer the *client*, or from which the *client* is referred to you. It is inherently unlikely that a general referral arrangement obliging you (whether or not you have an interest in such organisation) to refer to that organisation, without the option to refer elsewhere if the *client's* circumstances make that more appropriate, could be justified as being in the best interests of each individual *client* (CD2) and it may well also be contrary to your obligations of honesty and integrity (CD3) and compromise your independence (CD4).

gC125

The *Bar Standards Board* may require you to provide copies of any protocols that you may have in order to ensure compliance with these rules.

gC126

Your obligations under CD5 require you not to act in *an association* with a person where, merely by being associated with such person, you may reasonably be considered as bringing the profession into disrepute or otherwise diminishing the trust that the public places in you and your profession.

Rule C86 - Outsourcing   Rules

BSB Handbook

rC86

Where you outsource to a third party any support services that are critical to the delivery of any *legal services* in respect of which you are instructed:

.1 any outsourcing does not alter your obligations to your *client*;

.2 you remain responsible for compliance with your obligations under this *Handbook* in respect of the *legal services*;

.3 you must ensure that such outsourcing is subject to contractual arrangements which ensure that such third party:

.a is subject to confidentiality obligations similar to the confidentiality obligations placed on you in accordance with this *Handbook*;

.b complies with any other obligations set out in this Code of Conduct which may be relevant to or affected by such outsourcing;

.c processes any personal data in accordance with your *instructions*;

.d is required to allow the *Bar Standards Board* or its agent to obtain information from, inspect the records (including electronic records) of, or enter the premises of such third party in relation to the outsourced activities or functions, and;

.e processes any personal data in accordance with those arrangements, and for the avoidance of doubt, those arrangements are compliant with any relevant data protection laws.

Guidance to Rule C86   Guidance

gC127

Rule C86 applies to the outsourcing of clerking services.

gC128

Rule C86 does not apply where the *client* enters into a separate agreement with the third party for the services in question.

gC129

Rule C86 does not apply where you are instructing a *pupil* or a *devil* to undertake work on your behalf. Instead rC15 will apply in those circumstances.

gC130

Removed from 11 June 2018.

Rules C87-C88 - Administration and conduct of self-employed practice   Rules

rC87

You must take reasonable steps to ensure that:

.1 your practice is efficiently and properly administered having regard to the nature of your practice; and

.2 proper records of your practice are kept.

When deciding how long records need to be kept, you will need to take into consideration various requirements, such as those of this *Handbook* (see, for example, Rules C108, C129 and C141), any relevant data protection law and HM Revenue and Customs. You may want to consider drawing up a Records Keeping policy to ensure that you have identified the specific compliance and other needs of your *practice*.

rC88

You must:

.1 ensure that adequate records supporting the fees charged or claimed in a case are kept at least until the later of the following:

.a your fees have been paid; and

.b any determination or assessment of costs in the case has been completed and the time for lodging an appeal against that assessment or determination has expired without any such appeal being lodged, or any such appeal has been finally determined;

.2 provide your *client* with such records or details of the work you have done as may reasonably be required for the purposes of verifying your charges.

Rules C89-C90 - Administration of chambers   Rules

rC89

Taking into account the provisions of Rule rC90, you must take reasonable steps to ensure that:

.1 your *chambers* is administered competently and efficiently;

.2 your *chambers* has appointed an individual or individuals to liaise with the *Bar Standards Board* in respect of any regulatory requirements and has notified the *Bar Standards Board*;

.3 *barristers* in your *chambers* do not employ any person who has been disqualified from being employed by an authorised person (i) by the *Bar Standards Board* and included on the *Bar Standards Board's* list of disqualified persons, or (ii) by another approved regulator or *licensing authority* pursuant to its powers as such, and such disqualification is continuing in force. This shall not apply where the *barrister* obtains the express written consent of the *Bar Standards Board* to the appointment of a person who has been disqualified before they are appointed;

.4 proper arrangements are made in your *chambers* for dealing with *pupils* and pupillage;

.5 proper arrangements are made in *chambers* for the management of conflicts of interest and for ensuring the confidentiality of *clients'* affairs;

.6 all non-authorised persons working in your *chambers* (irrespective of the identity of their *employer*):

.a are competent to carry out their duties;

.b carry out their duties in a correct and efficient manner;

.c are made clearly aware of such provisions of this *Handbook* as may affect or be relevant to the performance of their duties;

.d do nothing which causes or substantially contributes to a breach of this *Handbook* by any *BSB authorised individual* or *authorised (non-BSB) individual* within *chambers*,

and all *complaints* against them are dealt with in accordance with the complaints rules;

.7 all *registered European lawyers* and all *foreign lawyers* in your *chambers* comply with this *Handbook* insofar as applicable to them;

.8 appropriate risk management procedures are in place and are being complied with; and

.9 there are systems in place to check that:

.a all persons practising from your *chambers* whether they are members of the *chambers* or not have insurance in place in accordance with Rules rC75 to rC77 above (other than any *pupil* who is covered under their *pupil supervisor's* insurance); and

.b every *BSB authorised individual* practising from your *chambers* has a current *practising certificate* and every other *authorised (non-BSB) individual* providing *reserved legal activities* is currently authorised by their *Approved Regulator*.

rC90

For the purposes of Rule rC89 the steps which it is reasonable for you to take will depend on all the circumstances, which include, but are not limited to:

.1 the arrangements in place in your *chambers* for the management of *chambers*;

.2 any role which you play in those arrangements; and

.3 the independence of individual members of *chambers* from one another.

BSB Handbook

Guidance to Rules C89-C90   Guidance

gC131

Members of *chambers* are not in partnership but are independent of one another and are not responsible for the conduct of other members. However, each individual member of *chambers* is responsible for their own conduct and the constitution of *chambers* enables, or should enable, each individual member of *chambers* to take steps to terminate another person's membership in specified circumstances. Rule C89 does not require you to sever connection with a member of *chambers* solely because to your knowledge they are found to breach this *Handbook*, provided that they are not disbarred and comply with such sanctions as may be imposed for such breach; however, your chambers *constitution* should be drafted so as to allow you to exclude from chambers a member whose conduct is reasonably considered such as to diminish the trust the public places in you and your profession and you should take such steps as are reasonably available to you under your constitution to exclude any such member.

gC132

The *Supervision Team* of the *Bar Standards Board* reviews the key controls that are in place in *chambers* and *BSB entities* to manage the risks in relation to key processes. These key processes are shown in guidance that is published on the Supervision section of the *Bar Standards Board's* website. You should retain relevant policies, procedures, monitoring reports and other records of your practice so that they are available to view if a Supervision visit is arranged.

gC133

Your duty under Rule rC89.4 to have proper arrangements in place for dealing with pupils includes ensuring:

.1 that all *pupillage* vacancies are advertised in the manner set out in the Bar Qualification Manual;

.2 that arrangements are made for the funding of *pupils* by *chambers* which comply with the Pupillage Funding Rules (rC113 to rC118); and

.3 the chambers meets the mandatory requirements set out in the *Authorisation Framework* and complies with conditions imposed upon its authorisation as an *Authorised Education and Training Organisation (AETO)*.

gC134

Your duty under Rule rC89.5 to have proper arrangements in place for ensuring the confidentiality of each *client's* affairs includes:

.1 putting in place and enforcing adequate procedures for the purpose of protecting confidential information;

.2 complying with data protection obligations imposed by law;

.3 taking reasonable steps to ensure that anyone who has access to such information or data in the course of their work for you complies with these obligations; and .4 taking into account any further guidance on confidentiality which is available on the Bar Standards Board's website.

gC135

In order to ensure compliance with Rule rC89.6.d, you may want to consider incorporating an obligation along these lines in all new employment contracts entered into after the date of this *Handbook*.

gC136

For further guidance on what may constitute appropriate risk management procedures in accordance with Rule rC89.8 please refer to the further guidance published by the *Bar Standards Board* which can be accessed on the Supervision section of its website.

gC137

Rule rC90.3 means that you should consider, in particular, the obligation of each individual members of *chambers* to act in the best interests of their own *client* (CD2) and to preserve the confidentiality of their own *client's* affairs (CD6), in circumstances where other members of *chambers* are free (and, indeed, may be obliged by the cab rank rule (rC29) to act for *clients* with conflicting interests.

Rules C91-C95 - Administration of BSB entities   Rules

Duties of the BSB entity, authorised (non-BSB) individuals and managers of BSB entities

rC91

If you are a *BSB entity*, you must ensure that (or, if you are a *BSB regulated individual* working within such *BSB entity* you must use reasonable endeavours (taking into account the provisions of Rule rC95) to procure that the *BSB entity* ensures that):

.1 the *BSB entity* has at all times a person appointed by it to act as its *HOLP*, who shall be a *manager*;

.2 the *BSB entity* has at all times a person appointed by it to act as its *HOFA*; and

.3 subject to rC92, the *BSB entity* does not appoint any individual to act as a *HOLP* or a *HOFA*, or to be a *manager* or employee of that *BSB entity*, in circumstances where that individual has been disqualified from being appointed to act as a *HOLP* or a *HOFA* or from being a *manager* or employed by an *authorised person* (as appropriate) (i) by the *Bar Standards Board* and included on the *Bar Standards Board's* list of disqualified persons, or (ii) by another *Approved Regulator* or *licensing authority* pursuant to its powers as such and such disqualification is continuing in force.

rC92

Rule rC91.3 shall not apply where the *BSB entity* obtains the express written consent of the *Bar Standards Board* to the appointment of a person who has been disqualified before they are appointed.

rC93

If you are a *manager* or employee, you must not do anything to cause (or substantially to contribute to) a breach by the *BSB entity* or by any *BSB authorised individual* in it of their duties under this *Handbook*.

rC94

If you are a *BSB entity*, you must at all times have (or, if you are a *BSB regulated individual* working in such *BSB entity* you must use reasonable endeavours (taking into account the provisions of Rule rC95 to procure that the *BSB entity* shall have) suitable arrangements to ensure that:

.1 the *managers* and other *BSB regulated individuals* working as employees of the *BSB entity* comply with the *Bar Standards Board's* regulatory arrangements as they apply to them, as required under section 176 of the LSA;

.2 all employees:

.a are competent to carry out their duties;

.b carry out their duties in a correct and efficient manner;

.c are made clearly aware of such provisions of this *Handbook* as may affect or be relevant to the performance of their duties;

.d do nothing which causes or substantially contributes to, a breach of this *Handbook* by the *BSB entity* or any of the *BSB regulated individuals* employed by it; and

.e co-operate with the *Bar Standards Board* in the exercise of its regulatory functions, in particular in relation to any notice under rC64 or any request under rC70;

.3 the *BSB entity* is administered in a correct and efficient manner, is properly staffed and keeps proper records of its practice;

.4 *pupils* and *pupillages* are dealt with properly;

.5 conflicts of interest are managed appropriately and that the confidentiality of *clients'* affairs is maintained at all times;

.6 all *registered European lawyers* and all *foreign lawyers* employed by or working for you comply with this *Handbook* insofar as it applies to them;

.7 every *BSB authorised individual* employed by, or working for, the *BSB entity* has a current *practising certificate* (and where a *barrister* is working as an *unregistered barrister*, there must be appropriate systems to ensure that they are complying with the provisions of this *Handbook* which apply to *unregistered barristers*) and every other *authorised (non-BSB) individual* providing *reserved legal activities* is currently authorised by their *Approved Regulator*; and

BSB Handbook

.8 adequate records supporting the fees charged or claimed in a case are kept at least until the later of the following:

.a your fees have been paid; and

.b any determination or assessment of costs in the case has been completed and the time for lodging an appeal against that assessment or determination has expired without any such appeal being lodged, or any such appeal has been finally determined;

.9 your *client* is provided with such records or details of the work you have done as may reasonably be required for the purpose of verifying your charges;

.10 appropriate procedures are in place requiring all *managers* and employees to work with the *HOLP* with a view to ensuring that the *HOLP* is able to comply with their obligations under Rule rC96;

.11 appropriate risk management procedures are in place and are being complied with; and

.12 appropriate financial management procedures are in place and are being complied with.

rC95

For the purposes of Rule rC91 and rC94 the steps which it is reasonable for you to take will depend on all the circumstances, which include, but are not limited to:

.1 the arrangements in place in your *BSB entity* for the management of it; and

.2 any role which you play in those arrangements.

Gudiance to Rule C94   Guidance

gC138

Section 90 of the *LSA* places obligations on *non-authorised individuals* who are employees and *managers* of *licensed bodies*, as well as on *non-authorised individuals* who hold an ownership interest in such a *licensed body* (whether by means of a shareholding or voting powers in respect of the same) to do nothing which causes, or substantially contributes to a breach by the *licensed body* or by its employees or *managers*, of this *Handbook*. Rule C94 extends this obligation to *BSB entities* other than *licensed bodies*.

gC139

Your duty under Rule rC94.4 to have proper arrangements for dealing with pupils includes ensuring:

.1 that all *pupillage* vacancies are advertised in the manner manner set out in the Bar Qualification Manual;

.2 that arrangements are made for the funding of *pupils* by the *BSB entity* which comply with the Pupillage Funding Rules (rC113 to rC118); and

.3 the *BSB entity* meets the mandatory requirements set out in the *Authorisation Framework* and complies with conditions imposed upon its authorisation as an *Authorised Education and Training Organisation (AETO)*.

Rules C96-C97 - Duties of the HOLP and HOFA   Rules

rC96

If you are a *HOLP*, in addition to complying with the more general duties placed on the *BSB entity* and on the *BSB regulated individuals* employed by it, you must:

.1 take all reasonable steps to ensure compliance with the terms of your *BSB entity's* authorisation;

.2 take all reasonable steps to ensure that the *BSB entity* and its employees and *managers* comply with the duties imposed by section 176 of the LSA;

.3 take all reasonable steps to ensure that *non-authorised individuals* subject to the duty imposed by section 90 of the LSA comply with that duty;

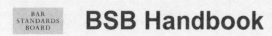

.4 keep a record of all incidents of non-compliance with the Core Duties and this *Handbook* of which you become aware and to report such incidents to the *Bar Standards Board* as soon as reasonably practicable (where such failures are material in nature) or otherwise on request by the *Bar Standards Board* or during the next monitoring visit or review by the *Bar Standards Board*.

rC97

If you are a *HOFA*, in addition to complying with the more general duties placed on the *BSB entity* and its *BSB regulated individuals*, you must ensure compliance with Rules rC73 and rC74.

Rule C98 - New managers, HOLPs and HOFAs   Rules

rC98

A *BSB entity* must not take on a new *manager*, *HOLP* or *HOFA* without first submitting an application to the *Bar Standards Board* for approval in accordance with the requirements of Section S.D.

Part 2 - D. Rules Applying to Particular Groups of Regulated Persons   Rules

Part 2 - D1. Self-employed barristers, chambers and BSB entities   Rules

Outcomes C26-C29   Outcomes

oC26

Clients are provided with appropriate information about redress, know that they can make a *complaint* if dissatisfied, and know how to do so.

oC27

Complaints are dealt with promptly and the *client* is kept informed about the process.

oC28

Self-employed barristers, *chambers* and *BSB entities* run their practices without *discrimination*.

oC29

Pupils are treated fairly and paid in accordance with the Pupillage Funding Rules.

Rules C99-C109 - Complaints rules   Rules

Provision of information

rC99

You must notify *clients* in writing when you are *instructed*, or, if that is if not practicable, at the next appropriate opportunity:

.1 of their right to make a *complaint*, including their right to complain to the *Legal Ombudsman* (if they have such a right), how, and to whom, they can complain, and of any time limits for making a *complaint*;

.2 if you are doing referral work, that the lay *client* may complain directly to *chambers* or the *BSB entity* without going through *solicitors*.

BSB Handbook

rC100

If you are doing public access, or licensed access work using an *intermediary*, the *intermediary* must similarly be informed.

rC101

If you are doing referral work, you do not need to give a *professional client* the information set out in Rules rC99.1 and rC99.2, in a separate, specific letter. It is enough to provide it in the ordinary terms of reference letter (or equivalent letter) which you send when you accept *instructions* in accordance with Rule rC21.

rC102

If you do not send a letter of engagement to a lay *client* in which this information can be included, a specific letter must be sent to them giving them the information set out at Rules rC99.1 and rC99.2.

rC103

Each website of *self-employed barristers*, *chambers* and *BSB entities* must display:

.1 on the homepage, the text "regulated by the Bar Standards Board" (for sole practitioners) or "barristers regulated by the Bar Standards Board" (for *chambers*) or "authorised and regulated by the Bar Standards Board" (for *BSB entities*); and

.2 in a sufficiently accessible and prominent place:

.a information about their complaints procedure, any right to complain to the Legal Ombudsman, how to complain to the Legal Ombudsman and any time limits for making a complaint;

.b a link to the decision data on the Legal Ombudsman's website; and

.c a link to the Barristers' Register on the BSB's website.

.3 All e-mail and letterheads from *self-employed barristers* and *BSB entities*, their *managers* and employees must state "regulated by the Bar Standards Board" (for *self-employed barristers*) or "authorised and regulated by the Bar Standards Board" (for *BSB entities*).

.4 *Self-employed barristers*, *chambers* and *BSB entities* must have regard to guidance published from time to time by the *Bar Standards Board* in relation to redress transparency.

Response to complaints

rC104

All *complaints* must be acknowledged promptly. When you acknowledge a *complaint*, you must give the complainant:

.1 the name of the person who will deal with the *complaint* and a description of that person's role in *chambers* or in the *BSB entity* (as appropriate);

.2 a copy of the *chambers'* complaints procedure or the *BSB entity's* Complaints Procedure (as appropriate);

.3 the date by which the complainant will next hear from *chambers* or the *BSB entity* (as appropriate).

rC105

When *chambers* or a *BSB entity* (as appropriate) has dealt with the *complaint*, complainants must be told in writing of their right to complain to the *Legal Ombudsman* (where applicable), of the time limit for doing so, and how to contact them.

Documents and record keeping

rC106

All communications and documents relating to complaints must be kept confidential. They must be disclosed only so far as is necessary for:

.1 the investigation and resolution of the *complaint*;

.2 internal review in order to improve *chambers'* or the *BSB entity's* (as appropriate) handling of complaints;

.3 complying with requests from the *Bar Standards Board* in the exercise of its monitoring and/or auditing functions.

BSB Handbook

rC107

The disclosure to the *Bar Standards Board* of internal documents relating to the handling of the *complaint* (such as the minutes of any meeting held to discuss a particular *complaint*) for the further resolution or investigation of the *complaint* is not required.

rC108

A record must be kept of each *complaint*, of all steps taken in response to it, and of the outcome of the *complaint*. Copies of all correspondence, including electronic mail, and all other documents generated in response to the *complaint* must also be kept. The records and copies should be kept for 6 years from resolution of the *complaint*.

rC109

The person responsible for the administration of the procedure must report at least annually to either:

.1 the *HOLP*; or

.2 the appropriate member/committee of *chambers*,

on the number of *complaints* received, on the subject areas of the *complaints* and on the outcomes. The *complaints* should be reviewed for trends and possible training issues.

Rules C110-C112 - Equality and diversity   Rules

rC110

You must take reasonable steps to ensure that in relation to your *chambers* or *BSB entity*:

.1 there is in force a written statement of policy on equality and diversity; and

.2 there is in force a written plan implementing that policy;

.3 the following requirements are complied with:

Equality and Diversity Officer

.a *chambers* or *BSB entity* has at least one *Equality and Diversity Officer*;

Training

.b removed.

.c save in exceptional circumstances, every member of all selection panels must be trained in fair recruitment and selection processes;

Fair and objective criteria

.d recruitment and selection processes use objective and fair criteria;

Equality monitoring

.e your *chambers* or *BSB entity*:

.i conducts a regular review of its policy on equality and diversity and of its implementation in order to ensure that it complies with the requirements of this Rule rC110; and

.ii takes any appropriate remedial action identified in the light of that review;

.f subject to Rule rC110.3.h *chambers* or *BSB entity* regularly reviews:

.i the number and percentages of its *workforce* from different groups; and

.ii applications to become a member of its *workforce*; and

.iii in the case of *chambers*, the *allocation of unassigned work*,

.g the reviews referred to in Rule rC110.3.f above include:

.i collecting and analysing data broken down by race, disability and gender;

.ii investigating the reasons for any disparities in that data; and

.iii taking appropriate remedial action;

.h the requirement to collect the information referred to in Rule C110.3.g does not apply to the extent that the people referred to in Rule rC110.3.f.i and Rule rC110.3.f.ii refuse to disclose it.

Fair access to work

.i if you are a *self-employed barrister*, the affairs of your *chambers* are conducted in a manner which is fair and equitable for all members of *chambers*, *pupils* and/or employees (as appropriate). This includes, but is not limited to, the fair distribution of work opportunities among *pupils* and members of *chambers*;

Harassment

.j *chambers* or *BSB entity* has a written anti-*harassment* policy which, as a minimum:

.i states that *harassment* will not be tolerated or condoned and that *managers*, employees, members of *chambers*, *pupils* and others temporarily in your *chambers* or *BSB entity* such as mini-pupils have a right to complain if it occurs;

.ii sets out how the policy will be communicated;

.iii sets out the procedure for dealing with *complaints* of *harassment*;

Parental leave

.k *chambers* has a *parental leave* policy which must cover as a minimum:

.i the right of a member of *chambers* to take *parental leave*;

.ii the right of a member of *chambers* to return to *chambers* after a specified period, or number of separate periods, of *parental leave*, provided the total leave taken does not exceed a specified maximum duration (which must be at least one year);

.iii a provision that enables *parental leave* to be taken flexibly and allows the member of *chambers* to maintain their *practice* while on *parental leave*, including the ability to carry out fee earning work while on *parental leave* without giving up other *parental leave* rights;

.iv the extent to which a member of chambers is or is not required to contribute to chambers' rent and expenses during parental leave;

.v the method of calculation of any waiver, reduction or reimbursement of *chambers'* rent and expenses during *parental leave*;

.vi where any element of rent is paid on a flat rate basis, the *chambers'* policy must as a minimum provide that *chambers* will offer members taking a period of *parental leave* a minimum of 6 months free of *chambers'* rent;

.vii the procedure for dealing with grievances under the policy;

.viii *chambers'* commitment to regularly review the effectiveness of the policy;

Flexible working

.l *chambers* or *BSB entity* has a flexible working policy which covers the right of a member of *chambers*, *manager* or employee (as the case may be) to take a career break, to work part-time, to work flexible hours, or to work from home, so as to enable them to manage their family responsibilities or disability without giving up work;

Reasonable adjustments policy

.m *chambers* or *BSB entity* has a reasonable adjustments policy aimed at supporting disabled *clients*, its *workforce* and others including temporary visitors;

Appointment of Diversity Data Officer

.n *chambers* or *BSB entity* has a Diversity Data Officer;

.o *chambers* or *BSB entity* must provide the name and contact details of the Diversity Data Officer to the *Bar Standards Board* and must notify the *Bar Standards Board* of any change to the identity of the Diversity Data Officer, as soon as reasonably practicable;

Responsibilities of Diversity Data Officer

.p The Diversity Data Officer shall comply with the requirements in relation to the collection, processing and publication of *diversity data* set out in the paragraphs rC110.3.q to .t below;

BSB Handbook

Collection and publication of diversity data

.q The Diversity Data Officer shall invite members of the *workforce* to provide *diversity data* in respect of themselves to the Diversity Data Officer using the model questionnaire in Section 7 of the BSB's Supporting Information on the BSB Handbook Equality Rules, which is available on the BSB's website;

.r The Diversity Data Officer shall ensure that such data is anonymised and that an accurate and updated summary of it is published on *chambers'* or *BSB entity's* website every three years. If *chambers* or the *BSB entity* does not have a website, the Diversity Data Officer shall make such data available to the public on request;

.s The published summary of anonymised data shall:

.i removed;

.ii exclude diversity data in relation to any characteristic where there is a real risk that individuals could be identified, unless all affected individuals consent; and

.iii subject to the foregoing, include anonymised data in relation to each characteristic, categorised by reference to the job title and seniority of the *workforce*.

.t The Diversity Data Officer shall:

.i ensure that *chambers* or *BSB entity* has in place a written policy statement on the collection, publication, retention and destruction of *diversity data* which shall include an explanation that the provision of *diversity data* is voluntary;

.ii notify the *workforce* of the contents of the written policy statement; and

.iii ask for explicit consent from the *workforce* to the provision and processing of their *diversity data* in accordance with the written policy statement and these rules, in advance of collecting their *diversity data*.

rC111

For the purposes of Rule rC110 above, the steps which it is reasonable for you to take will depend on all the circumstances, which include, but are not limited to:

.1 the arrangements in place in your *chambers* or *BSB entity* for the management of *chambers* or the *BSB entity*; and

.2 any role which you play in those arrangements.

rC112

For the purposes Rule rC110 above "allocation of unassigned work" includes, but is not limited to work allocated to:

.1 *pupils*;

.2 *barristers* of fewer than four *years' standing* ; and

.3 *barristers* returning from *parental leave*;

Guidance to Rules C110-C112   Guidance

gC140

Rule rC110 places a personal obligation on all *self-employed barristers*, however they practise, and on the *managers* of *BSB entities*, as well as on the entity itself, to take reasonable steps to ensure that they have appropriate policies which are enforced.

gC141

In relation to Rule rC110, if you are a Head of *chambers* or a *HOLP* it is likely to be reasonable for you to ensure that you have the policies required by Rule rC110, that an *Equality and Diversity Officer* is appointed to monitor compliance, and that any breaches are appropriately punished. If you are a member of a *chambers* you are expected to use the means available to you under your constitution to take reasonable steps to ensure there are policies and that they are enforced. If you are a *manager* of a *BSB entity*, you are expected to take reasonable steps to ensure that there are policies and that they are enforced.

---

gC142

For the purpose of Rule rC110 training means any course of study covering all the following areas:

a) Fair and effective selection & avoiding unconscious bias

b) Attraction and advertising

c) Application processes

d) Shortlisting skills

e) Interviewing skills

f) Assessment and making a selection decision

g) Monitoring and evaluation

gC143

Training should ideally be undertaken via classroom sessions. However, it is also permissible for training to be undertaken in the following ways: online sessions, private study of relevant materials such as the Bar Council's Fair Recruitment Guide and completion of CPD covering fair recruitment and selection processes.

gC144

The purpose of Rule rC110.3.d is to ensure that applicants with relevant characteristics are not refused employment because of such characteristics. In order to ensure compliance with this rule, therefore, it is anticipated that the *Equality and Diversity Officer* will compile and retain data about the relevant characteristics of all applicants for the purposes of reviewing the data in order to see whether there are any apparent disparities in recruitment.

gC145

For the purpose of Rule rC110 "regular review", means as often as is necessary in order to ensure effective monitoring and review takes place. In respect of data on pupils it is likely to be considered reasonable that "regularly" should mean annually. In respect of managers of a *BSB entity* or tenants, it is likely to be considered reasonable that "regularly" should mean every three years unless the numbers change to such a degree as to make more frequent monitoring appropriate.

gC146

For the purposes of Rule rC110, "remedial action" means any action aimed at removing or reducing the disadvantage experienced by particular relevant groups. Remedial action cannot, however, include positive discrimination in favour of members of relevant groups.

gC147

Rule rC110.3.f.iii places an obligation on *practices* to take reasonable steps to ensure the work opportunities are shared fairly among its *workforce*. In the case of *chambers*, this obligation includes work which has not been allocated by the solicitor to a named *barrister*. It includes fairness in presenting to solicitors names for consideration and fairness in opportunities to attract future named work (for example, fairness in arrangements for marketing). These obligations apply even if individual members of *chambers* incorporate their practices, or use a "ProcureCo" to obtain or distribute work, as long as their relationship between each other remains one of independent service providers competing for the same work while sharing clerking arrangements and costs.

gC148

a) Rule rC110.3.k applies to all members of *chambers*, irrespective of whether their partner or spouse takes *parental leave*.

b) A flexible policy might include for example: keeping in touch (KIT) days; returns to practice in between periods of *parental leave*; or allowing a carer to practise part time.

c) Any periods of leave/return should be arranged between *chambers* and members taking *parental leave* in a way that is mutually convenient.

gC149

Rule rC110.3.k.vi sets out the minimum requirements which must be included in a *parental leave* policy if any element of rent is paid on a flat rate. If rent is paid on any other basis, then the policy should be drafted so as not to put any *self-employed barrister* in a worse position than they would have been in if any element of the rent were paid on a flat rate.

gC150

For the purposes of Rule rC110 above investigation means, considering the reasons for disparities in data such as:

.1 Under or overrepresentation of particular groups e.g. men, women, different ethnic groups or disabled people

.2 Absence of particular groups e.g. men, women, different ethnic groups or disabled people

.3 Success rates of particular groups

.4 In the case of *chambers*, over or under allocation of unassigned work to particular groups

gC151

These rules are supplemented by the BSB's Supporting Information on the BSB Handbook Equality Rules ("the Supporting Information") which is available on the BSB's website. These describe the legal and regulatory requirements relating to equality and diversity and provide guidance on how they should be applied in *chambers* and in *BSB entities*. If you are a *self-employed barrister*, a *BSB entity*, or a *manager* of a *BSB entity*, you should seek to comply with the Supporting Information as well as with the rules as set out above.

gC152

The Supporting Information is also relevant to all *pupil supervisors* and *AETOs*. *AETOs* will be expected to show how they comply with the Supporting Information as a condition of authorisation.

gC153

Although the Supporting Information does not apply directly to *BSB authorised persons* working as *employed barristers (non-authorised bodies)* or *employed barristers (authorised non-BSB body)*, they provide helpful guidance which you are encouraged to take into account in your practice.

Rules C113-C118 - Pupillage funding   Rules

Funding

rC113

The members of a set of *chambers* or the *BSB entity* must pay to each non-practising *pupil* (as appropriate), by the end of each month of the non-practising period of their *pupillage* no less than:

.1 the *specified amount*; and

.2 such further sum as may be necessary to reimburse expenses reasonably incurred by the *pupil* on:

.3 travel for the purposes of their *pupillage* during that month; and

.4 attendance during that month at courses which they are required to attend as part of their *pupillage*.

rC114

The members of a set of *chambers*, or the *BSB entity*, must pay to each practising *pupil* by the end of each month of the practising period of their *pupillage* no less than:

.1 the *specified amount*; plus

.2 such further sum as may be necessary to reimburse expenses reasonably incurred by the *pupil* on:

.a travel for the purposes of their *pupillage* during that month; and

.b attendance during that month at courses which they are required to attend as part of their *pupillage*; less

.c such amount, if any, as the *pupil* may receive during that month from their *practice* as a *barrister*; and less

.d such amounts, if any, as the *pupil* may have received during the preceding months of their practising *pupillage* from their *practice* as a *barrister*, save to the extent that the amount paid to the *pupil* in respect of any such month was less than the total of the sums provided for in

sub-paragraphs rC114.2.a and .b above.

rC115

The members of a set of *chambers*, or the *BSB entity*, may not seek or accept repayment from a *chambers pupil* or an entity *pupil* of any of the sums required to be paid under Rules rC113 and rC114 above, whether before or after they cease to be a chambers pupil or an entity *pupil*, save in the case of misconduct on their part.

rC116

If you are a *self-employed barrister*, you must pay any *chambers pupil* for any work done for you which because of its value to you warrants payment, unless the *pupil* is receiving an award or remuneration which is paid on terms that it is in lieu of payment for any individual item of work.

Application

rC117

Removed.

rC118

For the purposes of these requirements:

.1 " *chambers pupil*" means, in respect of any set of *chambers*, a *pupil* doing the non-practising or practising period of *pupillage* with a *pupil supervisor*, or *pupil supervisors*, who is or are a member, or members, of that set of *chambers*;

.2 "entity *pupil*" means, in respect of a *BSB entity* a *pupil* doing the non-practising or practising period of *pupillage* with a *pupil supervisor* or *pupil supervisors* who are *managers* or employees of such *BSB entity*;

.3 "non-practising *pupil*" means a *chambers pupil* or an entity *pupil* doing the non-practising period of *pupillage*;

.4 "practising *pupil*" means a *chambers pupil* or an entity *pupil* doing the practising period of *pupillage*;

.5 "month" means calendar month starting on the same day of the month as that on which the *pupil* began the non-practising, or practising, period *pupillage*, as the case may be;

.6 any payment made to a *pupil* by a *barrister* pursuant to Rule rC115 above shall constitute an amount received by the *pupil* from their *practice* as a *barrister*; and

.7 the following travel by a *pupil* shall not constitute travel for the purposes of their *pupillage*:

.a travel between their home and *chambers* or, for an entity *pupil*, their place of work; and

.b travel for the purposes of their *practice* as a *barrister*.

Part 2 - D2. Barristers undertaking public access and licensed access work   `Rules`

Outcomes C30-C32   `Outcomes`

oC30

Barristers undertaking public access or licensed access work have the necessary skills and experience required to do work on that basis.

oC31

Barristers undertaking public access or licensed access work maintain appropriate records in respect of such work.

oC32

Clients only instruct via public access when it is in their interests to do so and they fully understand what is expected of them.

BSB Handbook

Rules C119-C131 - Public access rules   Rules

rC119

These rules apply to *barristers* instructed by or on behalf of a lay *client* (other than a *licensed access client*) who has not also instructed a *solicitor* or other *professional client* (public access clients). Guidance on public access rules is available on the *Bar Standards Board* website.

rC120

Before accepting any *public access instructions* from or on behalf of a *public access client*, you must:

.1 be properly qualified by having been issued with a full *practising certificate*, by having satisfactorily completed the appropriate public access training, and by registering with the *Bar Standards Board* as a public access practitioner;

.2 Removed from 1 February 2018.

.3 take such steps as are reasonably necessary to ensure that the *client* is able to make an informed decision about whether to apply for legal aid or whether to proceed with public access.

rC121

As a barrister with less than three *years' standing* who has completed the necessary training you must have a *barrister* who is a qualified person within Rule S22 and has registered with the *Bar Standards Board* as a public access practitioner readily available to provide guidance to you.

rC122

You may not accept *instructions* from or on behalf of a public access *client* if in all the circumstances, it would be in the best interests of the public access *client* or in the interests of justice for the public access *client* to instruct a *solicitor* or other *professional client*.

rC123

In any case where you are not prohibited from accepting *instructions*, you must at all times consider the developing circumstances of the case, and whether at any stage it is in the best interests of the public access *client* or in the interests of justice for the public access *client* to instruct a *solicitor* or other *professional client*. If, after accepting *instructions* from a public access *client* you form the view that circumstances are such that it would be in the best interests of the public access *client*, or in the interests of justice for the public access *client* to instruct a *solicitor* or other *professional client* you must:

.1 inform the public access *client* of your view; and

.2 withdraw from the case in accordance with the provisions of Rules rC25 and rC26 and associated guidance unless the *client* instructs a *solicitor* or other *professional client* to act in the case.

rC124

You must have regard to guidance published from time to time by the *Bar Standards Board* in considering whether to accept and in carrying out any public access *instructions*.

rC125

Having accepted *public access instructions*, you must forthwith notify your public access *client* in writing, and in clear and readily understandable terms, of:

.1 the work which you have agreed to perform;

.2 the fact that in performing your work you will be subject to the requirements of Parts 2 and 3 of this *Handbook* and, in particular, Rules rC25 and rC26;

.3 unless authorised to *conduct litigation* by the *Bar Standards Board*, the fact that you cannot be expected to perform the functions of a *solicitor* or other *person* who is authorised to *conduct litigation* and in particular to fulfil obligations arising out of or related to the *conduct of litigation*;

.4 the fact that you are self-employed, are not employed by a *regulated entity* and (subject to Rule S26) do not undertake the management, administration or general conduct of a client's affairs;

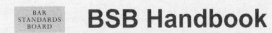

.5 in any case where you have been instructed by an *intermediary*:

.a the fact that you are independent of and have no liability for the *intermediary*; and

.b the fact that the *intermediary* is the agent of the lay *client* and not your agent;

.6 the fact that you may be prevented from completing the work by reason of your professional duties or conflicting professional obligations, and what the *client* can expect of you in such a situation;

.7 the fees which you propose to charge for that work, or the basis on which your fee will be calculated;

.8 your contact arrangements; and

.9 the information about your complaints procedure required by D1.1 of this Part 2.

rC126

Save in exceptional circumstances, you will have complied with Rule rC125 above if you have written promptly to the public access *client* in the terms of the model letter provided on the *Bar Standards Board* website.

rC127

In any case where you have been instructed by an *intermediary*, you must give the notice required by Rule C125 above both:

.1 directly to the public access *client*; and

.2 to the *intermediary*.

rC128

Having accepted *public access instructions*, you must keep a case record which sets out:

.1 the date of receipt of the *instructions*, the name of the lay *client*, the name of the case, and any requirements of the *client* as to time limits;

.2 the date on which the *instructions* were accepted;

.3 the dates of subsequent *instructions*, of the despatch of advices and other written work, of conferences and of telephone conversations; and

.4 when agreed, the fee.

rC129

Having accepted *public access instructions*, you must either yourself retain or take reasonable steps to ensure that the lay *client* will retain for at least seven years after the date of the last item of work done:

.1 copies of all *instructions* (including supplemental *instructions*);

.2 copies of all advices given and documents drafted or approved;

.3 the originals, copies or a list of all documents enclosed with any *instructions*; and

.4 notes of all conferences and of all advice given on the telephone.

rC130

Removed from 1 February 2018.

rC131

Save where otherwise agreed:

.1 you shall be entitled to copy all documents received from your lay *client*, and to retain such copies;

.2 you shall return all documents received from your lay *client* on demand, whether or not you have been paid for any work done for the lay *client*; and

.3 you shall not be required to deliver to your lay *client* any documents drafted by you in advance of receiving payment from the lay *client* for all work done for that *client*.

.4 Removed from 1 February 2018.

Rules C132-C141 - Licensed access rules   Rules

rC132

Subject to these rules and to compliance with the Code of Conduct (and to the *Scope of Practice, Authorisation and Licensing Rules*) a barrister in self-employed practice may accept *instructions* from a *licensed access client* in circumstances authorised in relation to that *client* by the Licensed Access Recognition Regulations (which are available on the BSB's website) whether that *client* is acting for themselves or another.

rC133

These rules apply to every matter in which a *barrister* in self-employed *practice* is instructed by a *licensed access client* save that Rules rC134.2 and rC139 do not apply to any matter in which a *licensed access client* is deemed to be a *licensed access client* by reason only of paragraph 7 or paragraph 8 of the Licensed Access Recognition Regulations (which are available on the BSB's website).

rC134

You are only entitled to accept *instructions* from a *licensed access client* if at the time of giving instructions the *licensed access client*:

.1 is identified; and

.2 you ensure that the *licensed access client* holds a valid Licence issued by the *Bar Standards Board* (either by requiring the *licensed access client* to send you a copy of the Licence, or referring to the list of *licensed access clients* published on the *Bar Standards Board* website).

rC135

You must not accept any *instructions* from a *licensed access client*:

.1 unless you are able to provide the services required of you by that *licensed access client*;

.2 if you consider it in the interests of the lay *client* or the interests of justice that a *solicitor* or other *person* who is authorised to *conduct litigation* or some other appropriate *intermediary* (as the case may be) be instructed either together with you or in your place.

rC136

If you agree standard terms with a *licensed access client*, you must keep a copy of the agreement in writing with the *licensed access client* setting out the terms upon which you have agreed and the basis upon which you are to be paid.

rC137

Having accepted *instructions* from a *licensed access client*, you must promptly send the *licensed access client*:

.1 a statement in writing that the *instructions* have been accepted (as the case may be) on the standard terms previously agreed in writing with that *licensed access client*; or

.2 if you have accepted *instructions* otherwise than on such standard terms, a copy of the agreement in writing with the *licensed access client* setting out the terms upon which you have agreed to do the work and the basis upon which you are to be paid; and

.3 unless you have accepted *instructions* on standard terms which incorporate the following particulars must at the same time advise the *licensed access client* in writing of:

.a the effect of rC21 as it relevantly applies in the circumstances;

.b unless authorised by the *Bar Standards Board* to *conduct litigation*, the fact that you cannot be expected to perform the functions of a *solicitor* or other *person* who is authorised to *conduct litigation* and in particular to fulfil obligations arising out of or related to the conduct of litigation; and

.c the fact that circumstances may require the *client* to retain a *solicitor* or other *person* who is authorised to *conduct litigation* at short notice and possibly during the case.

rC138

If at any stage you, being instructed by a *licensed access client*, consider it in the interests of the lay *client* or the interests of justice that a *solicitor* or other *person* who is authorised to *conduct litigation* or some other appropriate *intermediary* (as the case may be) be instructed

BSB Handbook   The BSB Handbook - Version 4.6

either together with you or in your place:

.1 you must forthwith advise the *licensed access client* in writing to instruct a *solicitor* or other *person* who is authorised to *conduct litigation* or other appropriate *intermediary* (as the case may be); and

.2 unless a *solicitor* or other *person* who is authorised to *conduct litigation* or other appropriate *intermediary* (as the case may be) is instructed as soon as reasonably practicable thereafter you must cease to act and must return any *instructions*.

rC139

If at any stage you, being instructed by a *licensed access client*, consider that there are substantial grounds for believing that the *licensed access client* has in some significant respect failed to comply with the terms of the Licence granted by the *Bar Standards Board* you must forthwith report the facts to the *Bar Standards Board*.

rC140

Having accepted *instructions* from a *licensed access client*, you must keep a case record which sets out:

.1 the date of receipt of the *instructions*, the name of the *licensed access client*, the name of the case, and any requirements of the *licensed access client* as to time limits;

.2 the date on which the *instructions* were accepted;

.3 the dates of subsequent *instructions*, of the despatch of advices and other written work, of conferences and of telephone conversations; and

.4 when agreed, the fee.

rC141

Having accepted *instructions* from a *licensed access client*, you must either yourself retain or take reasonable steps to ensure that the *licensed access client* will retain for seven years after the date of the last item of work done:

.1 copies of *instructions* (including supplemental *instructions*);

.2 copies of all advices given and documents drafted or approved;

.3 a list of all documents enclosed with any *instructions*; and

.4 notes of all conferences and of all advice given on the telephone.

Part 2 - D3. Registered European lawyers | Rules |

Outcome C33 | Outcomes |

---

oC33

Clients are not confused about the qualifications and status of *registered European lawyers*.

Rules C142-C143 | Rules |

---

rC142

If you are a *registered European lawyer* and not a *barrister*, you must not hold yourself out to be a *barrister*.

rC143

You must in connection with all professional work undertaken in England and Wales as a *registered European lawyer*.

BSB Handbook   The BSB Handbook - Version 4.6

.1 use your *home professional title*;

.2 indicate the name of your *home professional body* or the *court* before which you are entitled to practise in that *Member State*; and

.3 indicate that you are registered with the *Bar Standards Board* as a *European lawyer*.

Part 2 - D4. Unregistered barristers   Rules

Outcome C34   Outcomes

oC34

Clients who receive *legal services* from *unregistered barristers* are aware that such *unregistered barristers* are not subject to the same regulatory safeguards that would apply if they instructed a *practising barrister*.

Rule C144   Rules

rC144

If you are an *unregistered barrister* and you supply *legal services* (other than as provided for in Rule rC145) to any inexperienced *client* then, before supplying such services:

.1 you must explain to the *client* that:

.a (unless you are supplying *legal services* pursuant to Rule S12) you are not acting as a *barrister*;

.b you are not subject to those parts of the Code of Conduct and other provisions of this *Handbook* which apply only to *BSB authorised persons*;

.c the *Bar Standards Board* will only consider *reports* about you which concern the Core Duties or those parts of the Code of Conduct and other provisions of this *Handbook* which apply to you;

.d (unless you are covered by professional indemnity insurance) you are not covered by professional indemnity insurance;

.e they have the right to make a *complaint*, how they can complain, to whom, of any time limits for making a *complaint* but that they have no right to complain to the *Legal Ombudsman* about the services you supply; and

.f in respect of any legal advice you provide, there is a substantial risk that they will not be able to rely on legal professional privilege.

.2 you must get written confirmation from the *client* that you have given this explanation.

For the purposes of this Rule rC144, an inexperienced *client* includes any individual or other person who would, if you were a *BSB authorised person*, have a right to bring a complaint pursuant to the *Legal Ombudsman* Scheme Rules.

Gudiance to Rule C144   Guidance

gC154

For the purposes of determining whether Rule rC144 applies, the people who would be entitled to complain to the *Legal Ombudsman* if you were a *BSB authorised person* are:

.1 an individual; or

.2 a business or enterprise that was a micro-enterprise within the meaning of Article 1 and Article 2(1) and (3) of the Annex to

BSB Handbook

Commission Recommendation 2003/361/EC (broadly a business or enterprise with fewer than 10 employees and turnover or assets not exceeding €2 million), when it referred the *complaint* to you; or

.3 a charity with an annual income net of tax of less than £1 million at the time at which the complainant refers the *complaint* to you; or

.4 a club, association or organisation, the affairs of which are managed by its members or a committee of its members, with an annual income net of tax of less than £1 million at the time at which the complainant refers the *complaint* to you; or

.5 a trustee of a trust with an asset value of less than £1 million at the time at which the complainant refers the *complaint* to you; or

.6 a personal representative or beneficiary of the estate of a person who, before they died, had not referred the complaint to the *Legal Ombudsman*.

Rule C145   Rules

rC145

rC144 does not apply to you if you supply *legal services*:

.1 as an employee or *manager* of a *regulated entity*;

.2 as an employee or *manager* of a body subject to regulation by a professional body or regulator;

.3 as provided for in Section S.B9 (*Legal Advice Centres*);

.4 pursuant to an authorisation that you have obtained from another *approved regulator*; or

.5 in accordance with Rules S13 and S14.

Guidance to Rule C145   Guidance

gC155

Guidance on the disclosures which unregistered barristers should consider making to *clients* covered by Rule rC145, and other *clients* who are not inexperienced *clients*, to ensure that they comply with Rule rC19 and do not mislead those *clients* is available on BSB website.

Part 2 - D5. Cross-border activities between CCBE States   Rules

Outcome C35   Outcomes

oC35

BSB regulated persons who undertake *cross-border activities* comply with the terms of the *Code of Conduct for European Lawyers*.

Rule C146   Rules

rC146

If you are a *BSB regulated person* undertaking *cross-border activities* then, in addition to complying with the other provisions of this *Handbook*

BSB Handbook

which apply to you, you must also comply with Rules rC147 to rC158 below.

Guidance to Rule C146 | Guidance |

gC156

Where the *cross-border activities* constitute *foreign work* (in other words, limb (a) of the definition of *cross-border activities*), you should note, in particular, Rules rC13 and rC14 and the associated guidance.

gC157

The purpose of this section D5 is to implement those provisions of the *Code of Conduct for European Lawyers* which are not otherwise covered by the *Handbook*. If a provision of the *Code of Conduct for European Lawyers* has not been included here then the equivalent provisions of *Handbook* need to be complied with in respect of all *cross-border activities* (including where they place a higher burden on the *BSB regulated person* than the *Code of Conduct for European Lawyers* itself which is the case, for example, in respect of the handling of *client money* (Rule rC73 and rC74)).

Rules C147-C158 | Rules |

Incompatible occupations

rC147

If you act in legal proceedings or proceedings before public authorities in a *CCBE State* other than the *UK*, you must, in that *CCBE State*, observe the Rules regarding incompatible occupations as they are applied to lawyers of that *CCBE State*.

rC148

If you are established in a *CCBE State* other than the *UK* and you wish to participate directly in commercial or other activities not connected with the practice of the law in that *CCBE State*, you must respect the Rules regarding forbidden or incompatible occupations as they are applied to lawyers of that *CCBE State*.

Fee sharing with non-lawyers

rC149

You must not share your fees with a person situated in a *CCBE State* other than the *UK* who is not a lawyer except where otherwise permitted by the terms of this *Handbook* or Rule rC150 below.

rC150

Rule rC149 shall not preclude you from paying a fee, commission or other compensation to a deceased lawyer's heirs or to a retired lawyer in respect of taking over the deceased or retired lawyer's practice.

Co-operation among lawyers of different member states

rC151

If you are approached by a lawyer of a *CCBE State* other than the UK to undertake work which you are not competent to undertake, you must assist that lawyer to obtain the information necessary to find and instruct a lawyer capable of providing the service asked for.

rC152

When co-operating with a lawyer of a *CCBE State* other than the UK you must take into account the differences which may exist between your respective legal systems and the professional organisations, competencies and obligations of lawyers in your respective states.

Correspondence between lawyers in different CCBE states

rC153

If you want to send to a lawyer in a *CCBE State* other than the UK a communication which you wish to remain "confidential" or "without

BSB Handbook

prejudice", you must, before sending the communication, clearly express your intention in order to avoid misunderstanding, and ask if the lawyer is able to accept the communication on that basis.

rC154

If you are the intended recipient of a communication from a lawyer in another *CCBE State* which is stated to be "confidential" or "without prejudice", but which you are unable to accept on the basis intended by that lawyer, you must inform that lawyer accordingly without delay.

Responsibility for fees

rC155

If in the course of practice you instruct a lawyer of a *CCBE State* other than the UK to provide *legal services* on your behalf, you must pay the fees, costs and outlays which are properly incurred by that lawyer (even where the *client* is insolvent) unless:

.1 you were simply introducing the *client* to them and the lawyer of the *CCBE State* other than the UK has since had a direct contractual relationship with the *client*; or

.2 you have expressly disclaimed that responsibility at the outset, or at a later date you have expressly disclaimed responsibility for any fees incurred after that date; or the lawyer of the *CCBE State* other than the UK is, in the particular matter, practising as a lawyer in England or Wales (whether authorised by the *BSB* or any other *Approved Regulator*).

Disputes amongst lawyers in different member states

rC156

If you consider that a lawyer in a *CCBE State* other than the UK has acted in breach of a rule of professional conduct you must draw the breach to the other lawyer's attention.

rC157

If any personal dispute of a professional nature arises between you and a lawyer in a *CCBE State* other than the UK you must first try to settle it in a friendly way.

rC158

You must not commence any form of proceedings against a lawyer in a *CCBE State* other than the UK on matters referred to in Rules rC156 or rC157 without first informing the *Bar Council* and the other lawyer's bar or law society in order to allow them an opportunity to assist in resolving the matter.

Part 2 - D6. Price and service transparency rules for self-employed barristers, chambers and BSB entities | Rules |

Outcome C36 | Outcomes |

---

oC36

Clients are provided with appropriate information to help them make informed choices and understand the price and service they will receive.

Rules C159-C163 - Self-employed barristers, chambers and BSB entities | Rules |

Publication of information

rC159

Each website of *self-employed barristers*, *chambers* and *BSB entities* must, in a sufficiently accessible and prominent place:

.1 state that professional, licensed access and/or lay clients (as appropriate) may contact the *barrister*, *chambers* or *BSB entity* to obtain a

BSB Handbook

quotation for *legal services* and provide contact details. Quotations must be provided if sufficient information has been provided by the *client*, and the *barrister*, *barristers* in *chambers* or *BSB entity* would be willing to provide the legal services. Quotations must be provided within a reasonable time period, and in clear and readily understandable terms;

.2 state their most commonly used pricing models for *legal services*, such as fixed fee or hourly rate. Where different models are typically used for different *legal services*, this must be explained;

.3 state the areas of law in which they most commonly provide *legal services*, and state and describe the *legal services* which they most commonly provide, in a way which enables clients to sufficiently understand the expertise of the *barrister*, *chambers* or *BSB entity*; and

.4 provide information about the factors which might influence the timescales of their most commonly provided *legal services*.

rC160

All *self-employed barristers*, *chambers* and *BSB entities* must review their website content at least annually to ensure that it is accurate and complies with the transparency requirements referred to in Rules C103, C159 and where applicable, Rules C164 – C168.

rC161

Self-employed barristers, *chambers* and *BSB entities* must comply with the transparency requirements referred to in Rules C103, C159 and where applicable, Rules C164 – C168 by ensuring the required information is readily available in alternative format. This must be provided on request (for example, if they do not operate a website, or a *client* or prospective *client* does not have Internet access).

Provision of information to the Bar Standards Board

rC162

All *self-employed barristers*, *chambers* and *BSB entities* must notify the *Bar Standards Board* of their website address(es) offering *legal services*, and any changes to their website address(es), within 28 days of the creation or change of the same.

Bar Standards Board guidance

rC163

When offering their services to *clients* and prospective *clients*, all *self-employed barristers*, *chambers* and *BSB entities* must have regard to guidance published from time to time by the *Bar Standards Board* in relation to price and service transparency.

Rules C164-C169 - Self-employed barristers undertaking public access work and BSB entities supplying legal services directly to the public

Rules

Public Access Guidance for Lay Clients

rC164

Each website of *self-employed barristers* undertaking public access work and/or their chambers, and *BSB entities* supplying *legal services* directly to the public, must in a sufficiently accessible and prominent place display a link to the Public Access Guidance for Lay Clients on the BSB's website.

Price transparency policy statement

rC165

Self-employed barristers undertaking public access work and/or their *chambers*, and *BSB entities* supplying *legal services* directly to the public, must comply with the *Bar Standards Board's* price transparency policy statement insofar as it applies to them.

Publication of information

rC166

Self-employed barristers undertaking public access work and/or their *chambers*, and *BSB entities* supplying *legal services* directly to the public, are required by the *Bar Standards Board's* price transparency policy statement to provide price information in relation to certain *legal services* in certain circumstances. In relation to those *legal services* and in those circumstances, each website of *self-employed barristers* undertaking public access work and/or their *chambers*, and *BSB entities* supplying *legal services* directly to the public, must in a sufficiently

BSB Handbook

accessible and prominent place:

.1 state their pricing model(s), such as fixed fee or hourly rate;

.2 state their indicative fees and the circumstances in which they may vary. For example, a fixed fee and the circumstances in which additional fees may be charged, or an hourly rate by seniority of *barrister*;

.3 state whether their fees include VAT (where applicable); and

.4 state likely additional costs, what they cover and either the cost or, if this can only be estimated, the typical range of costs.

rC167

In compliance with the requirements of Rule C166 above:

.1 a sole practitioner must provide price information in relation to them as an individual *barrister*;

.2 a *BSB entity* must provide price information in relation to the entity; and

.3 a *chambers* may provide price information either in relation to (1) individual *barristers*, or (2) *barristers* in *chambers* in the form of ranges or average fees.

rC168

Self-employed barristers undertaking public access work and/or their *chambers*, and *BSB entities* supplying *legal services* directly to the public, are required by the *Bar Standards Board's* price transparency policy statement to provide service information in relation to certain *legal services* in certain circumstances. In relation to those legal services and in those circumstances, each website of *self-employed barristers* undertaking public access work and/or their *chambers*, and *BSB entities* supplying *legal services* directly to the public, must in a sufficiently accessible and prominent place:

.1 state and describe the *legal services*, including a concise statement of the key stages, in a way which enables *clients* to sufficiently understand the service of the sole practitioner, *barristers* in chambers or *BSB entity*; and

.2 provide an indicative timescale for the key stages of the *legal services*.

rC169

Self-employed barristers undertaking public access work, and BSB entities supplying *legal services* directly to the public, may be asked to accept instructions to provide the *legal services* listed in the *Bar Standards Board's* price transparency policy statement at short notice. In these circumstances, you are not required to comply with Rules C166 – C168 above before accepting the *instructions*. However, you must do so as soon as reasonably practicable after accepting the *instructions*.

Part 3

Scope of Practice, Authorisation and Licensing Rules

BSB Handbook   The BSB Handbook - Version 4.6

Part 3: Scope of Practice, Authorisation and Licensing Rules

Part 3 - A. Application   Rules

rS1

Section 3.B applies to all *BSB regulated persons* and *unregistered barristers* and "You" and "Your" should be construed accordingly. It provides that you must not carry on any *reserved legal activity* or practise as a *barrister* unless you are authorised to do so, and explains the different capacities within which you may work if you are so authorised and any limitations on the scope of your *practice*. It also explains the further requirements which you must follow if you intend to work in more than one capacity.

rS2

Section 3.C applies to *barristers* and *registered European lawyers* and sets out the basis on which they may apply for a *practising certificate* which will entitle them to practise within England and Wales.

rS3

Section 3.D applies to *European lawyers* and provides details about how to apply to become a *registered European lawyer* in England and Wales, thus entitling them to apply for a *practising certificate* in accordance with the provisions of 3.C.

rS4

Section 3.E applies to all entities wishing to be regulated by the BSB and sets out the basis upon which entities may be:

.1 authorised to practise as a *BSB authorised body*; or

.2 licensed to practise as a *BSB licensed body*.

rS5

Section 3.F applies to all *BSB entities*. It contains the continuing compliance requirements which apply to them.

Part 3 - B. Scope of Practice   Rules

Part 3 - B1. No practice without authorisation (Rule S6)   Rules

rS6

You must not carry on any *reserved legal activity* unless you are entitled to do so under the *LSA*.

Guidance to Rule S6   Guidance

gS1

You are not entitled to carry on any *reserved legal activity*, whether on your own behalf or acting as a *manager* or employee, unless you are either authorised or exempt in respect of that *reserved legal activity*. Where you are a *manager* or employee of a *person* who, as part of their *practice*, supplies services to *the public* or to a section of *the public* (with or without a view to profit), which consist of, or include, the carrying on of *reserved legal activities*, that *person* must also be entitled to carry on that *reserved legal activity* under the LSA. Authorisation in accordance with this Part 3 permits you to carry on the *reserved legal activities* specified in your authorisation.

Part 3 - B1. No practice without authorisation (Rules S7-S15) | Rules |

rS7

You must not permit any third party who is not authorised to provide *reserved legal activities* to provide such *reserved legal activities* on your behalf.

rS8

If:

.1 you are an individual and do not have a *practising certificate*; or

.2 you are an entity and you have not been authorised or licensed to provide *reserved legal activities* in accordance with Section 3.E, then:

.a you may not practise as a *barrister* or a *registered European lawyer* or as a *BSB entity* (as appropriate); and

.b you are not authorised by the *Bar Standards Board* to carry on any *reserved legal activity*.

rS9

For the purposes of this *Handbook*, you practise as a *barrister* or a *registered European lawyer*, or a *BSB entity* if you are supplying *legal services* and:

.1 you are an individual and you hold a *practising certificate*; or

.2 you hold yourself out as a *barrister* or a *registered European lawyer* (as appropriate) or

.3 you are an entity and you have been authorised or licensed to provide *reserved legal activities* in accordance with Section 3.E; or

.4 you act as a *manager* of, or have an ownership interest in, an *authorised (non-BSB) body* and as such you are required by the rules of that body's *Approved Regulator* to hold a *practising certificate* issued by the *Bar Standards Board* (as the case may be).

rS10

For the purposes of this Section 3.B1 any reference to the supply of *legal services* includes an offer to supply such services.

rS11

Rule rS9.1 above does not apply to you if you are a *pupil* without a provisional practising certificate if and insofar as you accept a noting brief with the permission of your *pupil supervisor* or head of *chambers* or *HOLP*.

rS12

If you are an *unregistered barrister* or *registered European lawyer* but do not hold a *practising certificate* and you supply *legal services* in the manner provided for in Rules rS13, rS14 and rS15 below, then you shall not, by reason of supplying those services:

.1 be treated for the purposes of this Section B of Part 3 as *practising barrister* or a *registered European lawyer*; or

.2 be subject to the rules in Part 2 of this *Handbook* or the rules in this Section 3.B which apply to *practising barristers*.

rS13

Rule rS12 applies to you if and insofar as:

.1 you are practising as a *foreign lawyer*; and

.2 you do not:

(a) give advice on *English Law*; or

(b) supply *legal services* in connection with any proceedings or contemplated proceedings in England and Wales (other than as an expert witness on foreign law).

rS14

Rule rS12 applies to you if:

.1 you are authorised and currently permitted to carry on reserved legal activities by another *Approved Regulator*; and

BSB Handbook

.2 you hold yourself out as a *barrister* or a *registered European lawyer* (as appropriate) other than as a *manager* or employee of a *BSB entity*; and

.3 when supplying *legal services* to any *person* or *employer* for the first time, you inform them clearly in writing at the earliest opportunity that you are not practising as a *barrister* or a *registered European lawyer*.

rS15

Rule rS12 applies to you provided that:

.1 you supplied *legal services* prior to 31 March 2012 pursuant to paragraph 206.1 or 206.2 of the 8th Edition of the Code; and

.2 if you supply any *legal services* in England and Wales, you were called to the *Bar* before 31 July 2000; and

.3 before 31 March in each year, and promptly after any change in the details previously supplied to the *Bar Standards Board*, you provide in writing to the *Bar Standards Board*, details of the current address(es) with telephone number(s) of the office or premises from which you do so, and:

(a) if you are employed, the name, address, telephone number and nature of the *practice* of your *employer*; or

(b) if you are an employee or *manager* of, or you have an ownership interest in, a *regulated entity*, the name, address, email address, telephone number and the name of the *regulated entity* and its *Approved Regulator*; and

.4 unless you only offer services to your *employer* or to the *regulated entity* of which you are a *manager* or an employee or which you have an ownership interest in, you are (or, if you are supplying *legal services* to *clients* of your *employer* or *regulated entity* of which you are an *owner, manager* or an employee, your *employer* or such body is) currently insured in accordance with the requirements of Rule C76r and you comply with the requirements of Section 2.D4.

Part 3 - B2. Provision of reserved legal activities and of legal services | Rules |

rS16

You may only carry on *reserved legal activities* or supply other *legal services* in the following capacities:

.1 as a *self-employed barrister*, subject to the limitations imposed by Section 3.B3;

.2 as a *BSB entity* subject to the limitations imposed by Section 3.B4;

.3 as a *manager* of a *BSB entity* or as an *employed barrister (BSB entity)*, subject to the limitations imposed by Section 3.B5;

.4 as a *manager* of an *authorised (non-BSB) body* or as an *employed barrister (authorised non-BSB body)*, subject to the limitations imposed by Section 3.B6;

.5 as an *employed barrister (non authorised body)*, subject to the limitations imposed by Section 3.B7; or

.6 as a *registered European lawyer* in any of the above capacities, in which case the equivalent limitations that would have applied if you were practising as a *barrister* shall apply to your *practice* as a *registered European lawyer*.

rS17

Where you carry on *reserved legal activities* in one of the capacities set out at Rule rS16, so as to be subject to regulation by the *Bar Standards Board* in respect of those *reserved legal activities*, any other *legal services* you may supply in that same capacity will also be subject to regulation by the *Bar Standards Board*, even if unreserved.

rS18

You may only *practise* or be involved with the supply of *legal services* (whether *reserved legal activities* or otherwise) in more than one of the capacities listed in Rule rS16 after:

.1 having obtained an amended *practising certificate* from the *Bar Standards Board* which recognises the capacities in respect of which you are intending to practise; and

.2 having agreed with each *employer* or *regulated entity* with which you are involved a protocol that enables you to avoid or resolve any conflict of interests or duties arising from your *practice* and/or involvement in those capacities,

and provided always that you do not work in more than one capacity in relation to the same case or issue for the same *client*, at the same time.

rS19

If you are a *pupil* with a provisional practising certificate, you may only supply *legal services* to *the public* or exercise any right which you have by reason of being a *barrister*, if you have the permission of your *pupil supervisor*, or head of *chambers* or *HOLP* (as appropriate).

rS20

Subject to Rule rS21, if you are a *barrister* of less than three *years' standing* , you may:

.1 only supply *legal services* to the public or exercise any *right of audience* by virtue of authorisation by the *Bar Standards Board*; or

.2 only *conduct litigation* by virtue of authorisation by the *Bar Standards Board*,

if your principal place of *practice* (or if you are *practising* in a dual capacity, each of your principal places of *practice*) is either:

.a a *chambers* or an annex of *chambers* which is also the principal place of *practice* of a relevant qualified *person* who is readily available to provide guidance to you; or

.b an office of an organisation of which an employee, *partner*, *manager* or *director* is a relevant qualified *person* who is readily available to provide guidance to you.

rS21

If you are an *employed barrister (non-authorised body)* and you are only exercising a *right of audience* or conducting litigation for those *persons* listed at Rule rS39.1 to rS39.6, then the place of *practice* from which you perform such duties is only required to be an office of an organisation of which an employee, *partner*, *manager* or *director* is a relevant qualified *person* who is readily available to provide guidance to you if you are of less than one year's standing.

rS22

In Rule rS20 and Rule rS21 above, the references to "qualified *person*" mean the following:

Supply of legal services to the public – qualified person

.1 Where you are a *barrister* intending to supply *legal services* to *the public*, a *person* shall be a qualified *person* for the purpose of Rule rS20 if they:

.a have been entitled to *practise* and have *practised* as a *barrister* (other than as a *pupil* who has not completed *pupillage* in accordance with the Bar Qualification Rules) or as a *person* authorised by another *Approved Regulator* for a period (which need not have been as a *person* authorised by the same *Approved Regulator*) for at least six years in the previous eight years; and

.b for the previous two years have made such *practice* their primary occupation; and

.c are not acting as a qualified *person* in relation to more than two other people; and

.d has not been designated by the *Bar Standards Board* as unsuitable to be a qualified *person*.

The exercise of a right of audience – qualified person

.2 Where:

.a you are a *barrister* exercising a *right of audience* in England and Wales, a *person* is a qualified *person* for the purpose of Rule rS20 if they:

.i have been entitled to *practise* and have *practised* as a *barrister* (other than as a *pupil* who has not completed *pupillage* in accordance with the *Bar Qualification Rules*) or as a *person* authorised by another *Approved Regulator* for a period (which need not have been as a *person* authorised by the same *Approved Regulator*) for at least six years in the previous eight years; and

.ii for the previous two years:

(1) have made such *practice* their primary occupation; and

(2) have been entitled to exercise a *right of audience* before every *court* in relation to all proceedings; and

.iii are not acting as a qualified *person* in relation to more than two other people; and

.iv have not been designated by the *Bar Standards Board* as unsuitable to be a qualified *person*.

The exercise of a right to conduct litigation – qualified person

.3 Where:

BSB Handbook   The BSB Handbook - Version 4.6

.a you are a *barrister* exercising a *right to conduct litigation* in England and Wales, a *person* is a qualified *person* for the purpose of Rule rS20 if they:

.i have been entitled to *practise* and have *practised* as a *barrister* (other than as a *pupil* who has not completed *pupillage* in accordance with the Bar Qualification Rules) or as a *person* authorised by another *Approved Regulator* for a period (which need not have been as a *person* authorised by the same *Approved Regulator*) for at least six years in the previous eight years; and

.ii for the previous two years have made such *practice* their primary occupation; and

.iii are entitled to *conduct litigation* before every *court* in relation to all proceedings; and

.iv are not acting as a qualified *person* in relation to more than two other people; and

.v have not been designated by the *Bar Standards Board* as unsuitable to be a qualified *person*.

Guidance to Rules S20-S22 | Guidance |

gS2

If you are a *practising barrister* of less than three *years' standing* and you are authorised to *conduct litigation*, you will need to work with a qualified *person* who is authorised to do litigation as well as with someone who meets the criteria for being a qualified *person* for the purpose of providing services to *the public* and exercising *rights of audience*. This may be, but is not necessarily, the same *person*.

Part 3 - B3. Scope of practice as a self-employed barrister (Rules S23-S24) | Rules |

rS23

Rules rS24 and rS25 below apply to you where you are acting in your capacity as a *self-employed barrister*, whether or not you are acting for a fee.

rS24

You may only supply *legal services* if you are appointed or instructed by the *court* or instructed:

.1 by a *professional client* (who may be an employee of the *client*); or

.2 by a *licensed access client*, in which case you must comply with the *licensed access rules*; or

.3 by or on behalf of any other *client*, provided that:

.a the matter is *public access instructions* and:

.i you are entitled to provide public access work and the *instructions* are relevant to such entitlement; and

.ii you have notified the *Bar Standards Board* that you are willing to accept *instructions* from lay *clients*; and

.iii you comply with the *public access rules*; or

.b the matter relates to the *conduct of litigation* and

.i you have a litigation extension to your *practising certificate*; and

.ii you have notified the *Bar Standards Board* that you are willing to accept *instructions* from lay *clients*.

Guidance to Rule S24 | Guidance |

gS3

References to professional *client* in Rule rS24.1 include *foreign lawyers* and references to *client* in Rule rS24.3 include *foreign clients*.

BSB Handbook

gS4

If you are instructed by a *foreign lawyer* to provide advocacy services in relation to *court* proceedings in England and Wales, you should advise the *foreign lawyer* of any limitation on the services you can provide. In particular, if *conduct of litigation* will be required, and you are not authorised to *conduct litigation* or have not been instructed to do so, you should advise the *foreign lawyer* to take appropriate steps to instruct a *person* authorised to *conduct litigation* and, if requested, assist the *foreign lawyer* to do so. If it appears to you that the *foreign lawyer* is not taking reasonable steps to instruct someone authorised to *conduct litigation*, then you should consider whether to return your *instructions* under rules C25 and C26.

Part 3 - B3. Scope of practice as a self-employed barrister (Rules S25-S26) [Rules]

rS25

Subject to Rule rS26, you must not in the course of your *practice* undertake the management, administration or general conduct of a *client's* affairs.

rS26

Nothing in Rule rS25 prevents you from undertaking the management, administration or general conduct of a client's affairs where such work is *foreign work* performed by you at or from an office outside England and Wales which you have established or joined primarily for the purposes of carrying out that particular *foreign work* or *foreign work* in general.

Part 3 - B4. Scope of practice as a BSB entity (Rules S27-S28) [Rules]

rS27

Rules rS28 and rS29 apply to you where you are acting in your capacity as a *BSB entity*.

rS28

You may only supply *legal services* if you are appointed or instructed by the *court* or instructed:

.1 by a professional *client* (who may be an employee of the *client*);

.2 by a *licensed access client*, in which case you must comply with the *licensed access rules*; or

.3 by or on behalf of any other *client*, provided that:

.a at least one manager or employee is suitably qualified and experienced to undertake public access work; and

.b you have notified the *Bar Standards Board* that you are willing to accept *instructions* from *lay clients*.

Guidance to Rule S28 [Guidance]

gS5

References to professional client in Rule rS28.1 include foreign lawyers and references to client in Rule rS28.3 include foreign clients.

gS6

If you are instructed to provide advocacy services in relation to *court* proceedings in England and Wales by a *foreign lawyer* or other professional *client* who does not have a *right to conduct litigation* pursuant to Rule rS28.1 and you are not authorised to *conduct litigation* yourself or you are otherwise not instructed to conduct the litigation in the particular matter, then you must:

.1 advise the *foreign lawyer* to take appropriate steps to instruct a *solicitor* or other authorised litigator to conduct the litigation and, if requested, take reasonable steps to assist the *foreign lawyer* to do so;

.2 cease to act and return your *instructions* if it appears to you that the *foreign lawyer* is not taking reasonable steps to instruct a *solicitor* or other authorised litigator to conduct the litigation; and

BSB Handbook

.3 not appear in *court* unless a *solicitor* or other authorised litigator has been instructed to conduct the litigation.

gS7

The public access and licensed access rules do not apply to *BSB entities* as their circumstances will vary considerably. Nevertheless those rules provide guidance on best practice. In the case of a barrister, "suitably qualified and experienced to undertake public access work" will mean successful completion of the public access training required by the BSB or an exemption for the requirement to do the training. If you are a *BSB entity*, you will also need to have regard to relevant provisions in the Code of Conduct (Part 2 of this Handbook), especially C17, C21.7, C21.8 and C22. You will therefore need to consider whether:

.1 You have the necessary skills and experience to do the work, including, where relevant, the ability to work with a vulnerable client;

.2 The employees who will be dealing with the *client* are either authorised to *conduct litigation* or entitled to do public access work or have had other relevant training and experience;

.3 it would be in the best interests of the client or of the interests of justice for the client to instruct a solicitor or other professional client if you are not able to provide such services;

.4 If the matter involves the *conduct of litigation* and you are not able or instructed to *conduct litigation*, whether the client will be able to undertake the tasks that you cannot perform for them;

.5 The *client* is clear about the services which you will and will not provide and any limitations on what you can do, and what will be expected of them;

.6 If you are not able to act in legal aid cases, the *client* is in a position to take an informed decision as to whether to seek legal aid or proceed with public access.

gS8

You will also need to ensure that you keep proper records.

Part 3 - B4. Scope of practice as a BSB entity (Rules S29-S30)   `Rules`

rS29

Subject to Rule rS30, you must not in the course of your *practice* undertake the management, administration or general conduct of a *client's* affairs.

rS30

Nothing in Rule rS29 prevents you from undertaking the management, administration or general conduct of a client's affairs where such work is foreign work performed by you at or from an office outside England and Wales which you have established or joined primarily for the purposes of carrying out that particular foreign work or foreign work in general.

Part 3 - B5. Scope of practice as a manager of a BSB entity or as an employed barrister (BSB entity)   `Rules`

rS31

Rules rS32 and rS33 below apply to you where you are acting in your capacity as a *manager* of a *BSB entity* or as an *employed barrister (BSB entity)*.

rS32

You may only supply *legal services* to the following *persons*:

.1 the *BSB entity*; or

.2 any employee, *director*, or company secretary of the *BSB entity* in a matter arising out of or relating to that *person's* employment;

.3 any *client* of the *BSB entity*;

.4 if you supply *legal services* at a *Legal Advice Centre*, clients of the *Legal Advice Centre*; or

.5 if you supply *legal services* free of charge, members of the public.

rS33

Subject to Rule rS34, you must not in the course of your practice undertake the management, administration or general conduct of a *client's* affairs.

rS34

Nothing in Rule rS33 prevents you from undertaking the management, administration or general conduct of a client's affairs where such work is foreign work performed by you at or from an office outside England and Wales which you have established or joined primarily for the purposes of carrying out that particular foreign work or foreign work in general.

Part 3 - B6. Scope of practice as a manager of an authorised (non-BSB) body or as an employed barrister (authorised non-BSB body)
Rules

rS35

Rules rS36 and rS37 apply to you where you are acting in your capacity as a *manager* of an *authorised (non-BSB) body* or as an *employed barrister (authorised non-BSB body)*.

rS36

You may only supply legal services to the following persons:

.1 the *authorised (non-BSB) body*;

.2 any employee, *director* or company secretary of the *authorised (non-BSB) body* in a matter arising out of or relating to that *person's* employment;

.3 any *client* of the *authorised (non-BSB) body*;

.4 if you provide *legal services* at a *Legal Advice Centre*, *clients* of the *Legal Advice Centre*; or

.5 if you supply *legal services* free of charge, members of the public.

rS37

You must comply with the rules of the *Approved Regulator* or *licensing authority* of the *authorised (non-BSB) body*.

Part 3 - B7. Scope of practice as an employed barrister (non authorised body)   Rules

rS38

Rule rS39 applies to you where you are acting in your capacity as an *employed barrister (non authorised body)*.

rS39

Subject to s. 15(4) of the Legal Services Act 2007, you may only supply *legal services* to the following *persons*:

.1 your *employer*;

.2 any employee, *director* or company secretary of your *employer* in a matter arising out of or relating to that *person's* employment;

.3 if your *employer* is a public authority (including the Crown or a Government department or agency or a local authority), another public authority on behalf of which your *employer* has made arrangements under statute or otherwise to supply any *legal services* or to perform any of that other public authority's functions as agent or otherwise;

.4 if you are employed by or in a Government department or agency, any Minister or Officer of the Crown;

.5 if you are employed by a *trade association*, any individual member of the association;

.6 if you are, or are performing the functions of, a *Justices' clerk* , the Justices whom you serve;

BSB Handbook

.7 if you are employed by the *Legal Aid Agency*, members of the public;

.8 if you are employed by or at a *Legal Advice Centre*, *clients* of the *Legal Advice Centre*;

.9 if you supply *legal services* free of charge, members of the public; or

.10 if your *employer* is a *foreign lawyer* and the *legal services* consist of foreign work, any *client* of your *employer*.

Guidance to Rule S39   Guidance

gS8A

If you provide services through a *non-authorised body* (A) whose purpose is to facilitate the provision by you of in-house *legal services* to another *non-authorised body* (B) then for the purposes of rS39 you will be treated as if you are employed by B and you should comply with your duties under this *Handbook* as if you are employed by B.

gS8B

If you provide services through a *non-authorised body* (C) whose purpose is to facilitate the provision by you of *legal services* to an authorised body (D) or clients of D (where those services are provided by D and regulated by D's *Approved Regulator*) then you will be treated as if you are employed by D and you should comply with your duties under this *Handbook* as if you are employed by D.

gS8C

Reserved legal activities may only be provided in a way that is permitted by s15 of the *Legal Services Act 2007*. S15 details when an employer needs to be authorised to carry on *reserved legal activities* and prevents those activities from being provided to the public, or a section of the public, by a *non-authorised body*.

Part 3 - B8. Scope of practice of a barrister called to undertake a particular case   Rules

rS40

If you are called to the *Bar* under rQ25 (temporary call of QFLs), you may not *practise* as a *barrister* other than to conduct the case or cases specified in the certificate referred to in rQ26.

Part 3 - B9. Legal Advice Centres   Rules

rS41

You may supply *legal services* at a *Legal Advice Centre* on a voluntary or part time basis and, if you do so, you will be treated for the purposes of this *Handbook* as if you were employed by the *Legal Advice Centre*.

rS42

If you supply legal services at a *Legal Advice Centre* to clients of a *Legal Advice Centre* in accordance with Rule rS41:

.1 you must not in any circumstances receive either directly or indirectly any fee or reward for the supply of any *legal services* to any *client* of the *Legal Advice Centre* other than a salary paid by the *Legal Advice Centre*;

.2 you must ensure that any fees in respect of *legal services* supplied by you to any *client* of the *Legal Advice Centre* accrue and are paid to the *Legal Advice Centre*, or to the Access to Justice Foundation or other such charity as prescribed by order made by the Lord Chancellor under s.194(8) of the Legal Services Act 2007; and

.3 you must not have any financial interest in the *Legal Advice Centre*.

BSB Handbook

Guidance to Rules S41-S42   Guidance

gS9

You may provide *legal services* at a *Legal Advice Centre* on an unpaid basis irrespective of the capacity in which you normally work.

gS10

If you are a *self-employed barrister*, you do not need to inform the Bar Standards Board that you are also working for a *Legal Advice Centre*.

gS11

Transitional arrangements under the LSA allow *Legal Advice Centres* to provide *reserved legal activities* without being authorised. When this transitional period comes to an end, the Rules relating to providing services at *Legal Advice Centres* will be reviewed.

Part 3 - B10. Barristers authorised by other approved regulators   Rules

rS43

If you are authorised by another *Approved Regulator* to carry on a *reserved legal activity* and currently permitted to *practise* by that *Approved Regulator*, you must not *practise* as a *barrister* and you are not eligible for a *practising certificate*.

Part 3 - C. Practising Certificate Rules   Rules

Part 3 - C1. Eligibility for practising certificates and litigation extensions   Rules

rS44

In this Section 3.C, references to "you" and "your" are references to   *barristers* and *registered European lawyers* who are intending to apply for authorisation to *practise* as a *barrister* or a *registered European lawyer* (as the case may be) or who are otherwise intending to apply for a *litigation extension* to their existing *practising certificate*.

rS45

You are eligible for a *practising certificate* if:

.1 you are a *barrister* or *registered European lawyer* and you are not currently *suspended* from *practice* and have not been disbarred; and

.2 you meet the requirements of Rules rS46.1, rS46.2, rS46.3 or rS46.4; and

.3 either:

.a within the last 5 years either (i) you have held a *practising certificate*; or (ii) you have satisfactorily completed (or have been exempted from the requirement to complete) the pupillage component of training; or

.b if not, you have complied with such training requirements as may be imposed by the *Bar Standards Board*.

rS46

You are eligible for:

.1 a *full practising certificate* if either:

.a you have satisfactorily completed *pupillage*; or

.b you have been exempted from the requirement to complete pupillage; or

BSB Handbook

.c on 30 July 2000, you were entitled to exercise full *rights of audience* by reason of being a *barrister*; or

.d you were called to the *Bar* before 1 January 2002 and:

.i you notified the *Bar Council* that you wished to exercise a *right of audience* before every *court* and in relation to all proceedings; and

.ii you have complied with such training requirements as the *Bar Council* or the *Bar Standards Board* may require or you have been informed by the *Bar Council* or the *Bar Standards Board* that you do not need to comply with any such further requirements;

in each case, before 31 March 2012;

.2 a *provisional practising certificate* if you have satisfactorily completed (or have been exempted from the requirement to complete) a period of pupillage satisfactory to the *BSB* for the purposes of Rule Q4 and at the time when you apply for a *practising certificate* you are registered as a *Pupil*;

.3 a *limited practising certificate* if you were called to the *Bar* before 1 January 2002 but you are not otherwise eligible for a *full practising certificate* in accordance with Rule rS46.1 above; or

.4 a *registered European lawyer's practising certificate* if you are a *registered European lawyer*.

rS47

You are eligible for a litigation extension:

.1 where you have or are due to be granted a *practising certificate* (other than a *provisional practising certificate*); and

.2 where you are:

.a more than three *years' standing* ; or

.b less than three *years' standing* , but your principal place of *practice* (or if you are *practising* in a dual capacity, each of your principal places of *practice*) is either:

.i a *chambers* or an annex of *chambers* which is also the principal place of *practice* of a qualified *person* (as that term is defined in Rule rS22.3) who is readily available to provide guidance to you; or

.ii an office of an organisation of which an employee, *partner*, *manager* or *director* is a qualified *person* (as that term is defined in Rule rS22.3) who is readily available to provide guidance to you;

.3 you have the relevant administrative systems in place to be able to provide *legal services* direct to *clients* and to administer the conduct of litigation; and

.4 you have the procedural knowledge to enable you to *conduct litigation* competently.

Guidance to Rule S47.3 | Guidance |

gS12

You should refer to the more detailed guidance published by the *Bar Standards Board* from time to time which can be found on its website. This provides more information about the evidence you may be asked for to show that you have procedural knowledge to enable you to *conduct litigation* competently

Part 3 - C2. Applications for practising certificates and litigation extensions by barristers and registered European lawyers

| Rules |

rS48

You may apply for a *practising certificate* by:

.1 completing the relevant application form (in such form as may be designated by the *Bar Standards Board*) and submitting it to the *Bar Standards Board*; and

.2 submitting such information in support of the application as may be prescribed by the *Bar Standards Board*; and

.3 paying (or undertaking to pay in a manner determined by the *Bar Council*) the appropriate *practising certificate fee* to the *Bar Council* in the amount determined in accordance with Rule rS50 (subject to any reduction pursuant to Rule rS53).

rS49

You may apply for a litigation extension to a *practising certificate* (other than a *provisional practising certificate*) by:

.1 completing the relevant application form supplied by the *Bar Standards Board* and submitting it to the *Bar Standards Board*; and

.2 confirming that you meet the relevant requirements of Rule rS47.1;

.3 paying (or undertaking to pay in a manner determined by the *Bar Standards Board*) the *application fee* (if any) and the *litigation extension fee* (if any) to the *Bar Standards Board*;

.4 confirming, in such form as the *Bar Standards Board* may require from time to time, that you have the relevant administrative systems in place to be able to provide *legal services* direct to *clients* and to administer the *conduct of litigation* in accordance with Rule rS47.3; and

.5 confirming, in such form as the *Bar Standards Board* may require from time to time, that you have the procedural knowledge to enable you to *conduct litigation* competently in accordance with Rule rS47.4.

rS50

An application will only have been made under either Rule rS48 or rS49 once the *Bar Standards Board* has received, in respect of the relevant application, the application form in full, together with the *application fee*, the *litigation extension fee* (if any, or an undertaking to pay such a fee in a manner determined by the *Bar Standards Board*), all the information required in support of the application, confirmation from you, in the form of a declaration, that the information contained in, or submitted in support of, the application is full and accurate, and (in the case of Rule S48) once the *Bar Council* has received the *practising certificate fee* (if any, or an undertaking to pay such a fee in a manner determined by the *Bar Council*).

rS51

On receipt of the application, the *Bar Standards Board* may require, from you or a third party (including, for the avoidance of doubt, any *BSB entity*), such additional information, documents or references as it considers appropriate to the consideration of your application.

rS52

You are personally responsible for the contents of your application and any information submitted to the *Bar Standards Board* by you or on your behalf and you must not submit (or cause or permit to be submitted on your behalf) information to the *Bar Standards Board* which you do not believe is full and accurate.

rS53

When applying for a *practising certificate* you may apply to the *Bar Standards Board* for a reduction in the *practising certificate fee* payable by you if your gross fee income or salary is less than such amount as the *Bar Council* may decide from time to time. Such an application must be submitted by completing the form supplied for that purpose by the *Bar Standards Board*.

Part 3 - C3. Practising certificate fees and litigation extension fees | Rules |

rS54

The *practising certificate fee* shall be the amount or amounts prescribed in the Schedule of *Practising Certificate Fees* issued by the *Bar Council* from time to time, and any reference in these Rules to the "appropriate *practising certificate fee*" or the " *practising certificate fee* payable by you" refers to the *practising certificate fee* payable by you pursuant to that Schedule, having regard, amongst other things, to:

.1 the different annual *practising certificate fees* which may be prescribed by the *Bar Council* for different categories of *barristers*, e.g. for Queen's Counsel and junior counsel, for *barristers* of different levels of seniority, and/or for *barristers practising* in different capacities and/or according to different levels of income (i.e. *self-employed barristers, employed barristers, managers* or employees of *BSB entities* or *barristers practising* with dual capacity);

.2 any reductions in the annual *practising certificate fees* which may be permitted by the *Bar Council* in the case of *practising certificates* which are valid for only part of a *practising certificate year*;

BSB Handbook

.3 any discounts from the annual *practising certificate fee* which may be permitted by the *Bar Council* in the event of payment by specified methods;

.4 any reduction in, or rebate from, the annual *practising certificate fee* which may be permitted by the *Bar Council* on the grounds of low income, change of category or otherwise; and

.5 any surcharge or surcharges to the annual *practising certificate fee* which may be prescribed by the Bar Council in the event of an application for renewal of a *practising certificate* being made after the end of the *practising certificate year*.

rS55

The *litigation extension fee* shall be the amount or amounts prescribed by the *Bar Standards Board* from time to time, and in these Rules the "appropriate *litigation extension fee*" or the " *litigation extension fee* payable by you" is the *litigation extension fee* payable by you having regard to, among other things:

.1 any reductions in the annual *litigation extension fees* which may be permitted by the *Bar Standards Board* in the case of *litigation extensions* which are valid for only part of a *practising certificate year*;

.2 any discounts from the annual *litigation extension fee* which may be permitted by the *Bar Standards Board* in the event of payment by specified methods;

.3 any reduction in, or rebate from, the annual *litigation extension fee* which may be permitted by the *Bar Standards Board* on the grounds of low income, change of category, or otherwise; and

.4 any surcharge or surcharges to the annual *litigation extension fee* which may be prescribed by the *Bar Standards Board* in the event of an application for a *litigation extension* being made at a time different from the time of your application for a *practising certificate*.

rS56

If you have given an undertaking to pay the *practising certificate fee* to the *Bar Council* or the *litigation extension fee* to the *Bar Standards Board*, you must comply with that undertaking in accordance with its terms.

Part 3 - C4. Issue of practising certificates and litigation extensions   `Rules`

---

rS57

The *Bar Standards Board* shall not issue a *practising certificate* to a *barrister* or *registered European lawyer*:

.1 who is not eligible for a *practising certificate*, or for a *practising certificate* of the relevant type; or

.2 who has not applied for a *practising certificate*; or

.3 who has not paid or not otherwise undertaken to pay in a manner determined by the *Bar Council*, the appropriate *practising certificate fee*; or

.4 who is not insured against claims for professional negligence as provided for in Rule C76.

rS58

The *Bar Standards Board* shall not grant a *litigation extension* to a *barrister* or *registered European lawyer*:

.1 in circumstances where the *Bar Standards Board* is not satisfied that the requirements of *litigation extension* are met; or

.2 who has not applied for a *litigation extension*; or

.3 who has not paid or not otherwise undertaken to pay in a manner determined by the *Bar Standards Board*, the appropriate *application fee* (if any) and the *litigation extension fee* (if any).

rS59

The *Bar Standards Board* may refuse to issue a *practising certificate* or to grant a *litigation extension*, or may revoke a *practising certificate* or a *litigation extension* in accordance with Section 3.C5, if it is satisfied that the information submitted in support of the application for the *practising certificate* or *litigation extension* (as the case may be) is (or was when submitted) incomplete, inaccurate or incapable of verification, or that the relevant *barrister* or *registered European lawyer*:

.1 does not hold adequate insurance in accordance with Rule C76;

.2 has failed and continues to fail to pay the appropriate *practising certificate fee* to the *Bar Council* or *litigation extension fee* to the *Bar Standards Board* when due;

.3 would be, or is, *practising* in breach of the provisions of Section 3.B;

.4 has not complied with any of the requirements of the Continuing Professional Development Regulations applicable to them;

.5 has not declared information on type and area of practice in a form determined by the BSB;

.6 has not made the declarations required by the BSB in relation to Youth Court work;

.7 has not made the declarations required by the BSB in relation to the Money Laundering, Terrorist Financing and Transfer of Funds (Information on the Payer) Regulations 2017;

.8 has not provided the BSB with a unique email address.

rS60

When the *Bar Standards Board* issues a *practising certificate* or a *litigation extension*, it shall:

.1 inform the relevant *barrister* or *registered European lawyer* of that fact; and

.2 in the case of a *practising certificate*, publish that fact, together with the name and *practising address* of the *barrister* and *registered European lawyer* and the other details specified in Rule rS61 in the register on the *Bar Standards Board's* website; or

.3 in the case of a litigation extension:

.a issue a revised and updated *practising certificate* to incorporate an express reference to such litigation extension in accordance with Rule rS66; and

.b amend the register maintained on the Bar Standards Board's website to show that the relevant *barrister* or *registered European lawyer* (as the case may be) is now authorised to *conduct litigation*.

rS61

A *practising certificate* must state:

.1 the name of the *barrister* or *registered European lawyer* (as the case may be);

.2 the period for which the *practising certificate* is valid;

.3 the *reserved legal activities* which the *barrister* or *registered European lawyer* (as the case may be) to whom it is issued is thereby authorised to carry on;

.4 the capacity (or capacities) in which the *barrister* or *registered European lawyer* (as the case may be) practises; and

.5 whether the *barrister* or *registered European lawyer* (as the case may be) is registered with the *Bar Standards Board* as a *Public Access* practitioner.

rS62

A *practising certificate* may be valid for a *practising certificate year* or part thereof and for one month after the end of the *practising certificate year*.

rS63

A *full practising certificate* shall authorise a *barrister* to exercise a *right of audience* before every *court* in relation to all proceedings.

rS64

A *provisional practising certificate* shall authorise a *pupil* to exercise a *right of audience* before every *court* in relation to all proceedings.

rS65

A *limited practising certificate* shall not authorise a *barrister* to exercise a *right of audience*, save that it shall authorise a *barrister* to exercise any *right of audience* which they had by reason of being a *barrister* and was entitled to exercise on 30 July 2000.

rS66

A *practising certificate* shall authorise a *barrister* to *conduct litigation* in relation to every *court* and all proceedings if the *practising certificate* specifies a litigation extension.

rS67

BSB Handbook

Every *practising certificate* issued to a *barrister* shall authorise the *barrister*:

.1 to undertake:

.a *reserved instrument activities*;

.b *probate activities*;

.c *the administration of oaths*; and

.d *immigration work*.

rS68

A *registered European lawyer's practising certificate* shall authorise a *registered European lawyer* to carry on the same *reserved legal activities* as a *full practising certificate* issued to a *barrister*, save that:

.1 a *registered European lawyer* is only authorised to exercise a *right of audience* or *conduct litigation* in proceedings which can lawfully only be provided by a *solicitor*, *barrister* or other qualified *person*, if they act in conjunction with a *solicitor* or *barrister* authorised to *practise* before the *court*, tribunal or public authority concerned and who could lawfully exercise that right; and

.2 a *registered European lawyer* is not authorised to prepare for remuneration any instrument creating or transferring an interest in land unless they have a *home professional title* obtained in Denmark, the Republic of Ireland, Finland, Sweden, Iceland, Liechtenstein, Norway, the Czech Republic, Cyprus, Hungary or Slovakia.

Part 3 - C5. Amendment and revocation of practising certificates and litigation extensions   Rules

rS69

You must inform the *Bar Standards Board* as soon as reasonably practicable, and in any event within 28 days, if any of the information submitted in support of your *practising certificate* application form or *litigation extension* application form:

.1 was incomplete or inaccurate when the application form was submitted; or

.2 changes before the expiry of your *practising certificate*.

rS70

If you wish to:

.1 change the capacity in which you *practise* (e.g. if you change from being an *employed barrister* or a *manager* or employee of a *BSB entity* or an *authorised (non-BSB) body* to a *self-employed barrister*, or vice versa, or if you commence or cease *practice* in a dual capacity); or

.2 cease to be authorised to *conduct litigation*,

before the expiry of your *practising certificate*, you must:

.a notify the *Bar Standards Board* of such requested amendment to your *practising certificate*; and

.b submit to the *Bar Standards Board* such further information as the *Bar Standards Board* may reasonably require in order for them to be able to determine whether or not to grant such proposed amendment to your *practising certificate*; and

.c within 14 days of demand by the *Bar Council* pay to the *Bar Council* the amount (if any) by which the annual *practising certificate fee* which would apply to you in respect of your amended *practising certificate* exceeds the annual *practising certificate fee* which you have already paid (or undertaken to pay) to the *Bar Council*. In the event that the revised annual *practising certificate fee* is less than the amount originally paid to the *Bar Council* or in circumstances where you wish to cease to be authorised to *conduct litigation*, the *Bar Council* is not under any obligation to refund any part of the annual *practising certificate fee* already paid although it may in its absolute discretion elect to do so in the circumstances contemplated by the Schedule of *Practising Certificate* Fees issued by the *Bar Council* from time to time. In circumstances where you wish to cease to be authorised to *conduct litigation*, the *Bar Standards Board* is not under any obligation to refund any part of the *litigation extension fee* already paid although it may in its absolute discretion elect to do so.

rS71

The *Bar Standards Board* may amend a *practising certificate* if it is satisfied that any of the information contained in the relevant application form was

inaccurate or incomplete or has changed, but may not amend a *practising certificate* (except in response to a request from the *barrister* or a *registered European lawyer*) without first:

.1 giving written notice to the *barrister* or *registered European lawyer* of the grounds on which the *practising certificate* may be amended; and

.2 giving the *barrister* or *registered European lawyer* a reasonable opportunity to make representations.

rS72

The *Bar Standards Board* shall endorse a *practising certificate* to reflect any qualification restriction or condition imposed on the *barrister* or *registered European lawyer* by the *Bar Standards Board* or by a *Disciplinary Tribunal, Interim Suspension or Disqualification Panel, Fitness to Practise Panel* or the High Court.

rS73

The *Bar Standards Board*:

.1 shall revoke a *practising certificate*:

.a if the *barrister* becomes authorised to practise by another *approved regulator*;

.b if the *barrister* or *registered European lawyer* is disbarred or *suspended* from *practice* as a *barrister* or *registered European lawyer* whether on an interim basis under section D of Part 5 or otherwise under section B of Part 5;

.c if the *barrister* or *registered European lawyer* has notified the *Bar Standards Board* that they no longer wish to have a *practising certificate*;

.d in the case of a *Registered European Lawyer*, where the individual no longer meets the eligibility requirements; and

.2 may revoke a *practising certificate*:

.a in the circumstances set out in Rule rS59; or

.b if the *barrister* or *registered European lawyer* has given an undertaking to pay the appropriate *practising certificate fee* and fails to comply with that undertaking in accordance with its terms, but in either case only after:

(i) giving written notice to the relevant *barrister* or *registered European lawyer* of the grounds on which the *practising certificate* may be revoked; and

(ii) giving the relevant *barrister* or *registered European lawyer* a reasonable opportunity to make representations.

rS74

The *Bar Standards Board*:

.1 shall revoke a *litigation extension* if the *barrister* or *registered European lawyer* has notified the *Bar Standards Board* that they no longer wish to have the *litigation extension*; and

.2 may revoke a *litigation extension*:

.a in the circumstances set out in Rule rS59; or

.b if the *barrister* or *registered European lawyer* has given an undertaking to pay the appropriate *litigation extension fee* and fails to comply with that undertaking in accordance with its terms, but in either case only after:

(i) giving written notice to the relevant *barrister* or *registered European lawyer* of the grounds on which the *litigation extension* may be revoked; and

(ii) giving the relevant *barrister* or *registered European lawyer* a reasonable opportunity to make representations.

Part 3 - C6. Applications for review Rules

rS75

If you contend that the *Bar Standards Board* has:

.1 wrongly failed or refused to issue or amend a *practising certificate*; or

.2 wrongly amended or revoked a *practising certificate*; or

BSB Handbook

.3 wrongly failed or refused to issue a *litigation extension*; or

.4 wrongly revoked a *litigation extension*,

in each case in accordance with this Section 3.C, then you may lodge an application for review using the form supplied for that purpose by the *Bar Standards Board* which can be found on its website. For the avoidance of doubt, this Section 3.C6 does not apply to any amendment or revocation of a *practising certificate* or *litigation extension* made by order of a *Disciplinary Tribunal, Interim Suspension* or *Disqualification Panel, Fitness to Practise Panel* or the High Court.

rS76

The decision of the *Bar Standards Board* shall take effect notwithstanding any application for review being submitted in accordance with Rule S75. However, the *Bar Standards Board* may, in its absolute discretion, issue a temporary *practising certificate* or *litigation extension* to a *barrister* or *registered European lawyer* who has lodged an application for review.

rS77

If the review finds that the *Bar Standards Board*:

.1 has wrongly failed or refused to issue a *practising certificate*, then the *Bar Standards Board* must issue such *practising certificate* as ought to have been issued; or

.2 has wrongly failed or refused to amend a *practising certificate*, then the *Bar Standards Board* must make such amendment to the *practising certificate* as ought to have been made; or

.3 has wrongly amended a *practising certificate*, then the *Bar Standards Board* must cancel the amendment; or

.4 has wrongly revoked a *practising certificate*, then the *Bar Standards Board* must re-issue the *practising certificate*; or

.5 has wrongly failed or refused to grant a *litigation extension*, then the *Bar Standards Board* must grant such *litigation extension* as ought to have been granted; or

.6 has wrongly revoked a *litigation extension*, then the *Bar Standards Board* must re-grant the *litigation extension*.

Part 3 - D. The Registration of European Lawyers Rules   Rules

rS78

If you are a *Qualified Swiss lawyer* and wish to *practise* in England and Wales under a *home professional title*, you may apply to the *Bar Standards Board* to be registered as a *registered European lawyer*. Such an application will be valid if it was made before 1 January 2025 and in accordance with the *Swiss Citizens' Rights Agreement*.

rS79

An application for registration must be made before 1 January 2025 in such form as may be prescribed by the *Bar Standards Board* and be accompanied by:

.1 a certificate, not more than three months old at the date of receipt of the application by the *Bar Standards Board*, that you are registered with the Competent Authority in Switzerland as a lawyer qualified to *practise* in that *Member State* under a relevant Swiss professional title;

.2 a declaration that:

.a you have not on the grounds of misconduct or of the commission of a *criminal offence* been prohibited from practising in Switzerland and are not currently *suspended* from so practising;

.b no *bankruptcy order* or *directors disqualification order* has been made against you and you have not entered into an individual voluntary arrangement with your creditors;

.c you are not aware of any other circumstances relevant to your fitness to *practise* under your *home professional title* in England and Wales; and

.d you are not registered with the Law Society of England and Wales, of Scotland or of Northern Ireland; and

.3 the prescribed fee.

BSB Handbook

rS80

Provided that it is satisfied that the application complies with the requirements of Rule rS79, the *Bar Standards Board* will:

.1 register you as a *registered European lawyer*; and

.2 so inform you and the competent authority in your *Member State* which has issued the certificate referred to in Rule rS79.1.

rS81

The *Bar Standards Board* will:

.1 remove a *registered European lawyer* from the register:

.a pursuant to a sentence of a *Disciplinary Tribunal*; or

.b if the *registered European lawyer* ceases to be a *European lawyer*;

.2 suspend a *registered European lawyer* from the register:

.a pursuant to a sentence of either a *Disciplinary Tribunal* or an *Interim Suspension Panel*; or

.b if the *registered European lawyer's* authorisation in their *home State* to pursue professional activities under their *home professional title* is *suspended*;

and in each case, notify the *European lawyer's home professional body* :

.c of their removal or suspension from the register; and

.d of any criminal conviction or *bankruptcy order* of which it becomes aware against a *registered European lawyer*.

Part 3 - E. Entity Application and Authorisation   Rules

Part 3 - E1. Eligibility for authorisation to practise as a BSB entity   Rules

rS82

In this Section 3.E, "you" and "your" refer to the   *partnership*, *LLP* or *company* which is applying for, or has applied for (in accordance with this Section 3.E) authorisation or (if a licensable body) a licence to practise as a *BSB entity*, and references in these Rules to "authorisation to practise" mean the grant by the *Bar Standards Board* of an authorisation or a licence (as the case may be) under this Section 3.E (distinguishing between the two only where the context so requires).

rS83

To be eligible for authorisation to *practise* as a *BSB entity*, you:

.1 must have arrangements in place designed to ensure at all times that any obligations imposed from time to time on the *BSB entity*, its *managers*, *owners* or employees by or under the *Bar Standards Board's* regulatory arrangements, including its rules and disciplinary arrangements, are complied with and confirm that the *BSB entity* and all *owners* and *managers* expressly consent to be bound by the *Bar Standards Board's* regulatory arrangements (including disciplinary arrangements);

.2 must have arrangements in place designed to ensure at all times that any other statutory obligations imposed on the *BSB entity*, its *managers*, *owners* or employees, in relation to the activities it carries on, are complied with;

.3 must confirm that, subject to the provisions of rS131, you will have in place, at all times, individuals appointed to act as a *HOLP* (who must also be a *manager*) and a *HOFA* of the *BSB entity*;

.4 must confirm that you have or will have appropriate insurance arrangements in place at all times in accordance with Rule C76 and you must be able to provide evidence of those insurance arrangements if required to do so by the *Bar Standards Board*;

.5 must confirm that, in connection with your proposed *practice*, you will not directly or indirectly hold *client money* in accordance with Rule C73 or have someone else hold *client money* on your behalf other than in those circumstances permitted by Rule C74;

.6 must confirm that no individual that has been appointed or will be appointed as a *HOLP*, *HOFA*, *manager* or employee of the *BSB entity* is

BSB Handbook

disqualified from acting as such by the *Bar Standards Board* or any *Approved Regulator* pursuant to section 99 of the *LSA* or otherwise as a result of its regulatory arrangements;

.7 must confirm that you will at all times have a *practising address* in England or Wales;

.8 must confirm that:

.a if you are an *LLP*, you are incorporated and registered in England and Wales, Scotland or Northern Ireland under the Limited Liability Partnerships Act 2000;

.b if you are a *Company*, you are:

.i incorporated and registered in England and Wales, Scotland or Northern Ireland under Parts 1 and 2 of the Companies Act 2006;

.9 must confirm that at least one *manager* or employee is an *authorised individual* in respect of each *reserved legal activity* which you wish to provide;

.10 must confirm that you will pay annual fees as and when they become due.

rS84

In addition to the requirements set out at Rule rS83:

.1 to be eligible for authorisation to *practise* as a *BSB entity*:

.a all of the *managers* of the *partnership*, *LLP* or *company* (as the case may be) must be *BSB authorised individuals* or *authorised (non-BSB) individuals*; and

.b all of the owners (whether or not the ownership interest is material) of the *partnership*, *LLP* or *company* (as the case may be) must be *BSB authorised individuals* or *authorised (non-BSB) individuals*;

.2 to be licensed to *practise* as a *BSB licensed body*:

.a the body must be a *licensable body*, as defined by section 72 of the *LSA* but must also meet the eligibility requirements set out at Rule rS83; and

.b all of the non-authorised owners in the *partnership*, *LLP* or *company* (as the case may be) must be approved by the *Bar Standards Board* as being able to hold such interest taking into account the relevant *suitability criteria*.

rS85

In the event that you meet the eligibility criteria set out in Rule rS83, you may submit an application in accordance with Section 3.E2 and the *Bar Standards Board* will review that application in accordance with Section 3.E3 and 3.E4 to determine whether or not to authorise you or to grant you a licence (as appropriate) to *practise* as a *BSB entity*. In the event that the *Bar Standards Board* determines that you should be authorised or licensed (as appropriate) to practise as a *BSB entity* then it may either:

rS86

Authorise you to *practise* as a *BSB entity* in the event that you also meet the eligibility criteria set out in Rule rS84.1 and you have applied to be authorised as such in your relevant application form; or

.1 license you to *practise* as a *BSB licensed body*, in the event that you also meet the eligibility criteria set out in Rule rS84.2 and you have applied to be authorised as such in your relevant application form.

rS87

Such authorisation or licence (as appropriate) will entitle you to:

.1 to exercise a *right of audience* before every *court* in relation to all proceedings;

.2 to carry on:

.a *reserved instrument activities*;

.b *probate activities*;

.c the *administration of oaths*;

.3 to do *immigration work*; and

.4 if you have been granted a *litigation extension*, to *conduct litigation*.

Guidance to Rules S82-S85 | Guidance |

gS13

Single person entities are permitted under these arrangements. Therefore, a *BSB entity* may (subject to any structural requirements imposed by general law for the particular type of entity) comprise just one barrister who is both the owner and manager of that entity.

gS14

These are mandatory eligibility requirements. The *Bar Standards Board* has a discretion to take other factors into account in deciding whether an *applicant body* is one which it would be appropriate for it to regulate (see Section 3.E3 and 3.E4 below).

Part 3 - E2. Applications for authorisation (Rules S88-S89) | Rules |

Application to be authorised or licensed as a BSB entity

rS88

To apply for authorisation to *practise* as a *BSB entity* you must:

.1 complete the application form supplied by the *Bar Standards Board* and submit it to the *Bar Standards Board*; and

.2 submit such other information, documents and references in support of the application as may be required by the application form or by the *Bar Standards Board* from time to time; and

.3 pay the *application fee* in the amount determined in accordance with Rule rS94 and the *authorisation or licence fee* for the first year.

Application for a litigation extension

rS89

To apply for a *litigation extension* you must:

.1 make this clear on your application form submitted in accordance with rS88 (where appropriate) or otherwise submit the relevant application form made available by the *Bar Standards Board* on its website for this purpose; and

.2 pay (or undertake to pay in a manner prescribed by the Bar Standards Board) the *application fee* (if any) and the relevant *litigation extension fee* (if any) in the amount determined in accordance with Rule rS94; and

.3 provide such other information to the *Bar Standards Board* as it may require in order to satisfy itself that:

.a you have the relevant administrative systems in place to be able to provide *legal services* direct to *clients* and to administer the *conduct of litigation*; and

.b you have a sufficient number of *persons* who are authorised to *conduct litigation* and to provide guidance to any *managers* or employees that may be involved in assisting in the *conduct of litigation* who are not themselves authorised and that you have an adequate number of qualified *persons* to provide guidance to any persons authorised to *conduct litigation* who are of less than three years' standing.

Guidance to Rules S88-S89 | Guidance |

---

gS15

In the event that your application is rejected, the *authorisation fee* and/or *litigation fee* (as appropriate) will be reimbursed to you but the *application fee(s)* shall be retained by the Bar Standards Board.

gS16

A qualified *person* referred to in Rule rS89.3 shall be defined in accordance with Rule S22.3.

BSB Handbook

Part 3 - E2. Applications for authorisation (Rules S90-S94)   Rules

Approval applications for any new HOLPs, HOFAs, owners and/or managers

rS90

If, following authorisation or the grant of a licence (as appropriate), a *BSB entity* wishes to appoint a new *HOLP, HOFA, owner* or *manager*, the *BSB entity* must:

.1 notify the *Bar Standards Board* of such a proposed appointment before it is made; and

.2 make an application to the *Bar Standards Board* for approval of the new *HOLP, HOFA, owner* or *manager* (as appropriate); and

.3 ensure that the new *HOLP, HOFA, owner* or *manager* (as appropriate) has expressly consented to be bound by the *Bar Standards Board's* regulatory arrangements (including disciplinary arrangements); and

.4 pay any fees set by the *Bar Standards Board* in respect of such approval applications.

Application Process

rS91

An application for authorisation and/or a *litigation extension* is only made once the *Bar Standards Board* has received the application form in full, together with the appropriate fees, all the information required in support of the application and confirmation from you in the form of a declaration that the information contained in, or submitted in support of, the application is full and accurate.

rS92

On receipt of the application, the *Bar Standards Board* may require, from you or from a third party, such additional information, documents or references as it considers appropriate to the consideration of your application.

rS93

You are responsible for the contents of your application and any information submitted to the *Bar Standards Board* by you, or on your behalf, and you must not submit (or cause or permit to be submitted on your behalf) information to the *Bar Standards Board* which you do not believe is full and accurate.

rS94

The *application fee* and the *litigation extension fee* shall be the amount or amounts prescribed by the *Bar Standards Board* from time to time. The *authorisation fee* and *litigation fee* shall also be payable and shall be the amount or amounts prescribed by the *Bar Standards Board* from time to time.

Guidance to Rules S91-S93   Guidance

gS17

Application forms and guidance notes for completion can be found on the *Bar Standard Board's* website.

gS18

Once you have submitted an application, if you fail to disclose to the *Bar Standards Board* any information of which you later become aware and which you would have been required to supply if it had been known by you at the time of the original application the Bar Standards Board may refuse your application in accordance with rS101.5.

gS19

Details of the relevant *application fee, litigation extension fee, authorisation fee, licence fee* and *litigation fee* can be found on the *Bar Standards Board's* website.

BSB Handbook

Part 3 - E3. Decision process   Rules

rS95

Subject to Rules rS96 and rS97, the *Bar Standards Board* must make a decision in respect of each valid and complete application within the *decision period*.

rS96

In the event that the *Bar Standards Board* is not able to reach a decision within the *decision period*, it must notify you and must confirm to you the latest date by which you will have received a response to your application from the *Bar Standards Board*.

rS97

The *Bar Standards Board* may issue more than one notice to extend the *decision period* except that:

.1 any notice to extend must always be issued before the decision period expires on the first occasion, and before any such extended *decision period* expires on any second and subsequent occasions; and

.2 no notice to extend can result in the total *decision period* exceeding more than 9 months.

rS98

During its consideration of your application form, the *Bar Standards Board* may identify further information or documentation which it needs in order to be able to reach its decision. If this is the case, you must provide such additional information or documentation as soon as possible after you receive the relevant request from the *Bar Standards Board*. Any delay in providing this information shall further entitle the *Bar Standards Board* to issue an extension notice in accordance with Rule rS96 and rS97 (as the case may be) or to treat the application as having been withdrawn.

Part 3 - E4. Issues to be considered by the Bar Standards Board (Rules S99-S100)   Rules

Applications for authorisation or the grant of a licence

rS99

In circumstances where the mandatory conditions in Rules rS83 and rS84 have been met, the *Bar Standards Board* must then consider whether to exercise its discretion to grant the authorisation or licence (as appropriate). In exercising this discretion, the *Bar Standards Board* will consider whether the entity is one which it would be appropriate for the *Bar Standards Board* to regulate, taking into account its analysis of the risks posed by you, the *regulatory objectives* of the *LSA* and the Entity Regulation Policy Statement of the *Bar Standards Board* as published from time to time.

rS100

In circumstances where the mandatory conditions set out at Rules S83 and S84 have not been met, the *Bar Standards Board* must refuse to grant the authorisation or licence (as appropriate).

Guidance to Rules S99-S100   Guidance

gS20

In exercising its discretion whether to grant the authorisation or licence the *Bar Standards Board* will have regard to its current Entity Regulation Policy Statement.

Part 3 - E4. Issues to be considered by the Bar Standards Board (Rule S101)   Rules

BSB Handbook

rS101

Where the *Bar Standards Board* concludes that you are an entity which it is appropriate for it to regulate the *Bar Standards Board* may nonetheless in its discretion refuse your application for authorisation if:

.1 it is not satisfied that your *managers* and *owners* are suitable as a group to operate or control a *practice* providing services regulated by the *Bar Standards Board*;

.2 if it is not satisfied that your proposed *HOLP* and *HOFA* meet the relevant *suitability criteria*;

.3 it is not satisfied that your management or governance arrangements are adequate to safeguard the *regulatory objectives* of the *LSA* or the policy objectives of the *Bar Standards Board* as set out in the Entity Regulation Policy Statement;

.4 it is not satisfied that, if the authorisation is granted, you will comply with the *Bar Standards Board's* regulatory arrangements including this *Handbook* and any conditions imposed on the authorisation;

.5 you have provided inaccurate or misleading information in your application or in response to any requests by the *Bar Standards Board* for information;

.6 you have failed to notify the *Bar Standards Board* of any changes in the information provided in the application;

.7 removed;

.8 for any other reason, the *Bar Standards Board* considers that it would be inappropriate for the *Bar Standards Board* to grant authorisation to you, having regard to its analysis of the risk posed by you, the regulatory objectives of the *LSA* or the Entity Regulation Policy Statement of the Bar Standards Board.

Guidance to Rule S101 | Guidance |

gS21

In circumstances where the *Bar Standards Board* rejects your application on the basis of Rule rS101, you will have the opportunity to make the necessary adjustments to your composition and to re-apply to become a *BSB entity*.

Part 3 - E4. Issues to be considered by the Bar Standards Board (Rules S102-S103) | Rules |

Applications for authorisation to conduct litigation

rS102

If the *Bar Standards Board* is unable to satisfy itself that the *BSB entity* meets the requirements set out in Rule rS89, it can refuse to grant the litigation extension.

Approval applications for any new HOLPs, HOFAs, owners and/or managers

rS103

The *Bar Standards Board* must consider any approval applications for any new *HOLPs, HOFAs, owners* and/or *managers* made in accordance with Rule rS90 and must determine any application by deciding whether the relevant individual meets the *suitability criteria* which apply relevant to such a proposed appointment.

Part 3 - E5. Suitability criteria in respect of HOLPs, HOFAs, owners and managers | Rules |

rS104

The *Bar Standards Board* must conclude that an individual does not meet the suitability criteria to undertake the role of a *HOLP* if:

.1 they are not an *authorised individual*;

.2 they are disqualified from acting as a *HOLP* by the *Bar Standards Board* or an *Approved Regulator* or *licensing authority* pursuant to section 99 of the *LSA* or otherwise as a result of its regulatory arrangements; or

.3 It determines that the individual is not able effectively to carry out the duties imposed on a HOLP by section 91 of the LSA.

rS105

The *Bar Standards Board* may conclude that an individual does not meet the suitability criteria to undertake the role of a *HOLP* if any of the circumstances listed in Rule rS110 apply to the individual designated as the *HOLP*.

rS106

The *Bar Standards Board* must conclude that an individual does not meet the suitability criteria for acting as a *HOFA* if:

.1 they are disqualified from acting as a *HOFA* by the *Bar Standards Board* or by an *Approved Regulator* or *licensing authority* pursuant to section 99 of the *LSA* or otherwise as a result of its regulatory arrangements; or

.2 the *Bar Standards Board* determines that they are not able effectively to carry out the duties imposed on a *HOFA* by section 92 of the *LSA*.

rS107

The *Bar Standards Board* may conclude that an individual does not meet the suitability criteria for acting as a *HOFA* if any of the circumstances listed in Rule rS110 apply to them.

rS108

If an *owner* is also a *non-authorised individual*, the *Bar Standards Board* must approve them as an *owner*. The *Bar Standards Board* shall approve a *non-authorised individual* to be an *owner* of a *BSB licensed body* if:

.1 their holding of an ownership interest does not compromise the *regulatory objectives*; and

.2 their holding of an ownership interest does not compromise compliance with the duties imposed pursuant to section 176 of the *LSA* by the *licensed body* or by any authorised individuals who are to be employees or *managers* of that *licensed body*; and

.3 they otherwise meet the *suitability criteria* to hold that ownership interest taking into account:

(a) their probity and financial position;

(b) whether they are disqualified pursuant to section 100(1) of *LSA* or included in the list maintained by the *Legal Services Board* pursuant to paragraph 51 of Schedule 13 of the *LSA*; and

(c) their *associates*; and

(d) the *suitability criteria* in Rule rS110 which apply to *managers* and employees.

rS109

If a *manager* is a *non-authorised individual*, the *Bar Standards Board* must approve them as a *manager*. The *Bar Standards Board* must approve a *non-authorised individual* to be a *manager* of a *BSB licensed body* if they meet the *suitability criteria* to hold that interest taking into account:

.1 their probity;

.2 whether they are disqualified pursuant to section 100(1) of the *LSA* or included in the list maintained by the *Legal Services Board* pursuant to paragraph 51 of Schedule 13 of the *LSA*; and

.3 the *suitability criteria* in Rule rS110 which apply to *managers* and employees.

rS110

The *Bar Standards Board* may reject an application if it is not satisfied that:

.1 an individual identified in an application for authorisation or the grant of a licence as a proposed *owner, manager, HOLP or HOFA* of the relevant *applicant body*; or

.2 any individual identified as a replacement owner, manager, *HOLP* or *HOFA*,

meets the *suitability criteria* to act as an *owner, manager, HOLP* or *HOFA* of a *BSB entity*. Reasons why the *Bar Standards Board* may conclude that an individual does not meet the *suitability criteria* include where an individual:

BSB Handbook

.3 has been committed to prison in civil or criminal proceedings (unless the Rehabilitation of Offenders Act 1974 (Exceptions) Order 1975 (SI 1975/1023) applies, this is subject to any conviction being unspent under the Rehabilitation of Offenders Act 1974 (as amended));

.4 has been disqualified from being a *director*;

.5 has been removed from the office of charity trustee or trustee for a charity by an order under section 72(1)(d) of the Charities Act 1993;

.6 is an undischarged bankrupt;

.7 has been adjudged bankrupt and discharged;

.8 has entered into an individual voluntary arrangement or a *partnership* voluntary arrangement under the Insolvency Act 1986;

.9 has been a *manager* of a *regulated entity* or a *BSB entity* which has entered into a voluntary arrangement under the Insolvency Act 1986;

.10 has been a *director* of a *company* or a *member* of an *LLP* (as defined by section 4 of the Limited Liability Partnerships Act 2000) which has been the subject of a winding up order, an administration order or administrative receivership; or has entered into a voluntary arrangement under the Insolvency Act 1986; or has been otherwise wound up or put into administration in circumstances of insolvency;

.11 lacks capacity (within the meaning of the Mental Capacity Act 2005) and powers under sections 15 to 20 or section 48 of that Act are exercisable in relation to that individual;

.12 is the subject of an outstanding judgment or judgments involving the payment of money;

.13 is currently charged with an *indictable offence*, or has been convicted of an *indictable offence*, any offence of dishonesty, or any offence under the Financial Services and Markets Act 2000, the Immigration and Asylum Act 1999 or the Compensation Act 2006 (unless the Rehabilitation of Offenders Act 1974 (Exceptions) Order 1975 (SI 1975/1023) applies, this is subject to the Rehabilitation of Offenders Act 1974 (as amended));

.14 has been disqualified from being appointed to act as a *HOLP* or a *HOFA* or from being a *manager* or employed by an *authorised or licensed body* (as appropriate) by the *Bar Standards Board* or another *Approved Regulator* or *licensing authority* pursuant to its or their powers under section 99 of the *LSA* or otherwise as a result of its regulatory arrangements;

.15 has been the subject in another jurisdiction of circumstances equivalent to those listed in Rules rS110.1 to rS110.14;

.16 has an investigation or disciplinary proceedings pending against them and/or has professional conduct findings against them either under the disciplinary scheme for *barristers* or otherwise; or

.17 has been involved in other conduct which calls into question their honesty, integrity, or respect for the law;

.18 has not consented to be bound by the regulatory arrangements (including disciplinary arrangements) of the *Bar Standards Board*.

Guidance to Rule S110   `Guidance`

gS21.1

For the avoidance of doubt rS110 does not oblige you to disclose cautions or criminal convictions that are "spent" under the Rehabilitation of Offenders Act 1974 unless the Rehabilitation of Offenders Act 1974 (Exceptions) Order 1975 (SI 1975/1023) applies. The latter entitles the BSB to ask for disclosure of unprotected cautions or criminal convictions that are "spent" in relation to   *HOLPs* and *HOFAs* of *licensed bodies* when seeking authorisation and owners who require approval under Schedule 13 to the LSA.

Part 3 - E6. Notification of the authorisation decision   `Rules`

rS111

The *Bar Standards Board* will notify you of its decision in writing within the *decision period* or by such later date as may have been notified to the *applicant body* in accordance with Rules rS96 or rS97. In the event that the *Bar Standards Board* decides to refuse to grant the application, it must give the reasons for such refusal.

Part 3 - E7. Terms of authorisation   Rules

rS112

Any authorisation given by the *Bar Standards Board* to a *BSB entity*, and the terms of any licence granted by the *Bar Standards Board* to a *BSB licensed body* in accordance with this Section 3.E must specify:

.1 the activities which are *reserved legal activities* and which the *BSB entity* is authorised to carry on by virtue of the authorisation or the licence (as the case may be); and

.2 any conditions subject to which the authorisation or the licence (as the case may be) is given (which may include those in Rule rS114).

rS113

Authorisations and licences must, in all cases, be given on the conditions that:

.1 any obligation which may from time to time be imposed on you (or your *managers*, employees, or *owners*) by the *Bar Standards Board* is complied with; and

.2 any other obligation imposed on you (or your *managers*, employees or *owners*) by or under the *LSA* or any other enactment is complied with.

.3 you (and your *managers*, employees, and *owners*) consent to be bound by the regulatory arrangements (including the disciplinary arrangements) of the *Bar Standards Board*; and

.4 if the conditions outlined at rS113.5 apply, the *Bar Standards Board* may without notice:

.a modify an authorisation granted under rS116;

.b revoke an authorisation under rS117;

.c require specific co-operation with the *Bar Standards Board* as provided for in rC64 and rC70;

.d take such action as may be necessary in the public or *clients'* interests and in the interests of the regulatory objectives; and

.e recover from the *BSB entity* any reasonable costs that were necessarily incurred in the exercise of its regulatory functions.

.5 The conditions referred to in rS113.4 are that:

.a one or more of the terms of the *BSB entity's* authorisation have not been complied with;

.b a person has been appointed receiver or manager of the property of the *BSB entity*;

.c a relevant insolvency event has occurred in relation to the *BSB entity*;

.d the *Bar Standards Board* has reason to suspect dishonesty on the part of any *manager* or employee of the *BSB entity* in connection with either that *BSB entity's* business or the business of another body of which the person was a manager or employee, or the *practice* or former *practice* of the *manager* or employee;

.e the *Bar Standards Board* is satisfied that it is necessary to exercise any of the powers listed in rS113.4 in relation to the *BSB entity* to protect the interests of *clients* (or former or potential *clients*) of the *BSB entity*.

rS114

In addition to the provisions in Rule rS113, an authorisation or a licence may be given subject to such other terms as the *Bar Standards Board* considers appropriate including terms as to:

.1 the *non-reserved activities* which you may or may not carry on; and/or

.2 in the case of *licensed bodies*:

(a) the nature of any interest held by a non-authorised *owner* provided always that the *Bar Standards Board* complies with its obligations under paragraph 17 of Schedule 13 to the *LSA*; and/or

(b) any limitations on the shareholdings or voting controls which may be held by non-authorised *owners* in accordance with paragraph 33 of Schedule 13 to the *LSA*.

BSB Handbook

Part 3 - E8. Duration of the authorisation/licence granted | Rules |

rS115

Except where indicated otherwise in the authorisation or licence, any authorisation or licence granted in accordance with this Section 3.E will be of unlimited duration except that the authorisation or licence:

.1 the authorisation or licence shall cease to have effect on the occurrence of any of the following:

(a) if you have your authorisation/licence withdrawn in accordance with Rule rS117; or

(b) if you obtain authorisation/licence from an *Approved Regulator* or *licensing authority*;

.2 the authorisation or licence may cease to have effect on the occurrence of any of the following:

(a) if you fail to provide the relevant monitoring information or fail to pay any relevant fees in circumstances where the *Bar Standards Board* has notified you (i) that such information or payment is required within a particular time; and (ii) that failure to provide such information or payment within that time may result in the withdrawal of your authorisation or licence in accordance with this Rule rS115; or

(b) if you fail to replace your *HOLP/HOFA* in accordance with the requirements of this *Handbook*.

.3 The licence of a partnership or other unincorporated body ("the existing body") may continue where the existing body ceases to exist and another body succeeds to the whole or substantially the whole of its business subject to the following in rS115.3(a)-(b):

(a) you have notified the *Bar Standards Board* of such a change within 28 days;

(b) if there is no remaining *partner* who was a *partner* before the existing body ceased to exist the licence shall cease to have effect from the date the existing body ceased to exist.

Part 3 - E9. Modification of an authorisation/licence | Rules |

rS116

In addition to any powers which the *Bar Standards Board* may have in accordance with Part 5, the *Bar Standards Board* may modify the terms of an authorisation or licence granted by it:

.1 if you apply to the *Bar Standards Board* for the terms of such authorisation or licence (as the case may be) to be modified; or

.2 if it is satisfied that any of the information contained in the relevant application form was inaccurate or incomplete or has changed; or

.3 if such modification is required in accordance with the provisions of this *Handbook*; or

.4 where the *Bar Standards Board* reasonably considers that such modification is appropriate and in accordance with the *regulatory objectives* under the *LSA* or the policy objectives of the *Bar Standards Board*; or

.5 where the conditions in rS113.5 are met,

but, in the circumstances set out in Rules rS116.2 to rS116.4 above, shall only be entitled to do so after:

.a giving notice to you in writing of the modifications which the *Bar Standards Board* is intending to make to your authorisation or licence (as the case may be); and

.b giving you a reasonable opportunity to make representations about such proposed modifications.

Part 3 - E10. Revocation or suspension of an authorisation/licence | Rules |

rS117

In addition to any powers which the Bar Standards Board may have in accordance with Part 5, the *Bar Standards Board* may:

BSB Handbook

.1 revoke an authorisation or licence granted by it:

(a) subject to Section 3.F, in the event that you no longer comply with the mandatory requirements set out in Rules rS83 and rS84; or

(b) if your circumstances have changed in relation to the issues considered by the *Bar Standards Board* in Section 3.E4; or

(c) if revocation otherwise appears appropriate taking into account the *regulatory objectives* of the *Bar Standards Board*; or

(d) where the conditions in rS113.5 are met.

.2 suspend an authorisation or licence granted by it to give it an opportunity to investigate whether or not your authorisation or licence should be revoked in accordance with Rule rS117 (for the avoidance of doubt a *BSB entity* whose authorisation has been suspended remains a *BSB regulated person*),

but (except for when the conditions in rS113.5 are met) in either case only after:

(i) giving written notice to the relevant *BSB entity* of the grounds on which the authorisation or licence may be revoked; and

(ii) giving the relevant *BSB entity* a reasonable opportunity to make representations.

Part 3 - E11. Applications for review `Rules`

rS118

If you consider that the *Bar Standards Board* has (other than pursuant to [Section 5]):

.1 wrongly refused an application for authorisation or licence; or

.2 wrongly imposed a term or condition on an authorisation or licence; or

.3 wrongly modified the terms of your authorisation or licence; or

.4 wrongly refused to modify the terms of your authorisation or licence; or

.5 wrongly revoked or *suspended* your authorisation or licence; or

.6 wrongly done any of these things in relation to a litigation extension to your authorisation or licence; or

.7 failed to provide to you notice of a decision in accordance with this Section 3.E, then you may lodge an application for review of that decision using the form supplied for that purpose by the *Bar Standards Board*. Such application for review will only have been made once the *Bar Standards Board* has received the relevant fee in respect of such application for review.

rS119

Any individual:

.1 designated to act as a *HOLP* or a *HOFA*; or

.2 identified as a non-authorised *owner* or *manager* of the *applicant body*,

who considers that the *Bar Standards Board* has wrongly concluded that they do not meet the *suitability criteria* which apply to their proposed position in the entity, may lodge an application for a review of that decision using the form supplied for that purpose by the *Bar Standards Board*. Alternatively, you may lodge an application for review on their behalf whether or not they have asked you to. In either case, such an application for a review will only have been made once the *Bar Standards Board* has received the relevant fee for it.

rS120

Any application for a review of the decision must be made within 28 days from the date when the decision is notified to you.

rS121

The decision of the *Bar Standards Board* will take effect notwithstanding the making of any application for a review in accordance with Rule rS118 or rS119. However, the *Bar Standards Board* may, in its absolute discretion, issue a temporary authorisation, licence or litigation extension to a *BSB entity* which has lodged an application for a review in accordance with this Section 3.E11.

BSB Handbook   The BSB Handbook - Version 4.6

rS122

If the review finds that the *Bar Standards Board*:

.1 has wrongly failed or refused to grant an authorisation or licence; or

.2 has wrongly imposed a term or condition on an authorisation or licence;

then in each case the *Bar Standards Board* must issue such authorisation or licence as ought to have been issued.

rS123

If the review finds that the *Bar Standards Board*:

.1 finds that the *Bar Standards Board* has wrongly modified an authorisation or licence; or

.2 finds that the *Bar Standards Board* has wrongly refused to modify an authorisation or licence,

then in each case the Bar Standards Board shall make such modification to the authorisation or licence as ought to have been made.

rS124

If the review finds that the *Bar Standards Board* has wrongly revoked or *suspended* an authorisation or licence, then the *Bar Standards Board* shall re-issue such authorisation or licence.

.1 If the review finds that the *Bar Standards Board* has wrongly done any of the things described in rS122 or–rS123 in relation to your *litigation extension*, then the *Bar Standards Board* shall grant such *litigation extension* as ought to have been granted.

rS125

If the review finds that the *Bar Standards Board* has wrongly concluded that an individual does not meet the *suitability criteria* relevant to their proposed position, the *Bar Standards Board* shall amend its decision and confirm that they do meet the suitability criteria which apply to their proposed position.

rS126

If, after such a review, you or the relevant individual(s) (as the case may be) do not agree with the decision you or the relevant individual(s) may appeal to the *First Tier Tribunal* against the decision.

rS127

Any appeal to the *First Tier Tribunal* against a decision of the BSB must be lodged within 28 days from the date that the decision is notified to you.

rS127A

Where a BSB decision is appealed to the *First Tier Tribunal*, the *First Tier Tribunal* may suspend the effect of that decision until the conclusion of the appeal.

Part 3 - E12. Register   Rules

---

rS128

The *Bar Standards Board* must keep a public register containing the names and places of practice of all *BSB entities* (together with details of the *reserved legal activities* which such *BSB entities* are able to undertake) as well as details of any bodies which have in the past been granted authorisation or obtained a licence from the *Bar Standards Board* but where such licence and/or authorisation is no longer current.

rS129

If an authorisation or licence is, at any time, suspended or made subject to conditions, this must be noted on the register of *BSB entities* by the Bar Standards Board.

BSB Handbook

Part 3 - F. Continuing Compliance with the Authorisation and Licensing Requirements | Rules |

Part 3 - F1. Non-compliance with the mandatory conditions | Rules |

rS130

If, at any time, and for whatever reason, you fail to meet the mandatory conditions in Rules rS83 and rS84 which apply to the type of *BSB entity* which you are, then you must notify the *Bar Standards Board* of your failure to comply with the mandatory conditions within seven days of your failure to comply and, at the same time, you must submit your proposals for rectifying that non-compliance which, for the avoidance of doubt, must include your proposed timetable for rectifying them. If the *Bar Standards Board* considers that your proposals for rectifying them are not sufficient, the *Bar Standards Board* may issue a notice suspending or revoking your authorisation or licence (as appropriate) in accordance with Section 3.E10.

Guidance to Rule S130 | Guidance |

gS22

Examples of non-compliance include:

.1 where your last remaining *authorised person*:

.a dies; or

.b abandons, retires or resigns from the *practice*; or

.2 where you are a *BSB entity* (other than a BSB licensed body) a *non-authorised individual* is appointed as a *manager* of or otherwise acquires an ownership interest in such a practice;

.3 where you cease to have available at least one employee who is authorised to carry on a particular reserved activity which you are authorised to provide. Examples of situations where an individual should be considered to be unavailable to a *BSB entity* include where:

.a they are committed to prison;

.b they are unable to attend to the *practice* because of incapacity caused by illness, accident or age;

.c they become and continue to lack capacity under Part 1 of the Mental Capacity Act 2005;

.d they are made subject to a condition on their *practising certificate* or registration which would be breached if they continue to be an *owner* and/or *manager* of the body; or

.e they are no longer authorised to perform the particular *reserved legal activity*.

.4 you cease to have a *HOLP* or a *HOFA* appointed;

.5 your *HOLP*, *HOFA*, any *manager* or *owner* ceases to meet the relevant *suitability criteria*; or

.6 where you are a *licensed body*, your last remaining *owner* and/or *manager* who is a *non-authorised individual* dies or otherwise leaves the *practice*.

gS23

Examples of proposals that you may submit in order to rectify such non-compliance include:

.1 In the case of Guidance gS22.1, that you are seeking to appoint a different *authorised person* to be an *owner* and/or a *manager* of a *BSB entity*;

.2 In the case of Guidance gS22.2, confirmation that you will take the necessary steps to rectify your status, whether by submitting an application to the *Bar Standards Board* for authorisation to *practise* as a *licensed body* and/or for approval of the *non-authorised individual* as a *manager* or by ensuring that the *non-authorised person* divest themselves of their interest as soon as is reasonably practicable, or by seeking a licence from another *licensing authority*, as the case may be [but note Guidance gS24];

.3 in the case of Guidance gS22.4, that you are seeking to appoint a replacement *HOLP* or *HOFA* (as appropriate) in accordance with the relevant procedure in Rule sS90;

BSB Handbook

.4 in the case of Guidance gS22.5, that you are taking the necessary steps to exclude the relevant individual from the *practice* and, where necessary, you are taking steps to replace them; and

.5 in the case of Guidance gS22.6, you confirm whether or not you are likely to appoint a replacement *non-authorised individual* or, if not, whether you will be seeking authorisation from the *Bar Standards Board* to practise as a *BSB authorised body*.

gS24

In respect of Guidance gS23.2, it may be the case that a *non-authorised individual* obtains an ownership interest in a *BSB entity* following the death of a *barrister* or a *non-authorised person*. Similarly, a *non-authorised person* who has not been approved pursuant to the *suitability criteria* may acquire an ownership interest in a *licensed body*. In these cases, it may be that the *BSB entity* will not need to apply for authorisation to *practise* as a *licensed body* or for approval of such *non-authorised individual* (as appropriate) if the *BSB entity* instead satisfies the *Bar Standards Board* that it is taking steps to ensure that such *non-authorised individual* divest themselves of their interest as soon as is reasonably practicable (for example, on completion of the relevant probate).

Part 3 - F2. Temporary emergency approvals for HOLPs and HOFAs 〔 Rules 〕

rS131

If a *BSB entity* ceases to have a *HOLP* or *HOFA* whose designation has been approved by the *Bar Standards Board*, the *BSB entity* must immediately and in any event within seven days:

.1 notify the *Bar Standards Board*;

.2 designate another *manager* or employee to replace its previous *HOLP* or *HOFA*, as appropriate; and

.3 make an application to the *Bar Standards Board* for temporary approval of the new *HOLP* or *HOFA*, as appropriate.

rS132

The *Bar Standards Board* may grant a temporary approval under this Section 3.F2 if on the face of the application and any other information immediately before the *Bar Standards Board*, there is no evidence suggesting that the new *HOLP* or *HOFA* is not suitable to carry out the duties imposed on them under this *Handbook*.

rS133

If granted temporary approval under Rule rS132 for its designation of a new *HOLP* or *HOFA*, the *BSB entity* must:

.1 designate a permanent *HOLP* or *HOFA*, as appropriate; and

.2 submit a substantive application for approval of that designation in accordance with Rule rS90,

before the expiry of the temporary approval or any extension of that approval by the *Bar Standards Board*, otherwise the *Bar Standards Board* may be entitled to suspend or revoke the authorisation or licence in accordance with Section 3.E10.

Part 4

Qualification Rules

BSB Handbook

Part 4: Qualification Rules

Part 4 - A. Application   Rules

rQ1

Section 4.B applies to all individuals who wish to be called to the *Bar* and to become qualified to practise as a *barrister* and to *Authorised Education and Training Organisations (AETOs)*. Until 1 January 2020, for the purposes of any proceedings of the Inns Conduct Committee, Part 4 applies as if version 3.5 of the BSB Handbook were in force.

rQ2

Section 4.C applies to all *practising barristers*.

Part 4 - B. Bar Qualification Rules   Rules

Part 4 - B1. Purpose of the Bar Qualification Rules   Outcomes

oC1

To provide routes for the qualification of *barristers* that enable them to meet the Professional Statement and to provide for the regulation of AETOs.

Part 4 - B2. Routes to Qualification as a barrister and authorised person   Rules

rQ3

To be called to the *Bar* by an *Inn* an individual must have successfully completed the following:

.1 academic legal training;

.2 vocational training;

.3 the number of qualifying sessions as a student member of an *Inn* as prescribed from time to time by the *BSB*; and

.4 pay such fee or fees as may be prescribed.

rQ4

To obtain a *provisional practising certificate* a *barrister* must:

.1 have successfully completed a period of *pupillage* satisfactory to the *BSB*;

.2 pay such fee or fees as may be prescribed.

rQ5

To obtain a *full practising certificate* a *barrister* must:

.1 have successfully completed a further period of *pupillage* satisfactory to the *BSB*;

.2 pay such fee or fees as may be prescribed.

rQ6

The BSB shall set out in writing:

.1 the requirements to be met by an *Inn* in admitting student members and calling individuals to the *Bar*;

.2 the manner in which an *Inn* shall assess whether such individuals are fit and proper; and

.3 the minimum requirements for the delivery of qualifying sessions by an *Inn*.

rQ6A

Where it is alleged that the *call declaration* made by a *barrister* on *call* was false in any material respect or that the *barrister* has engaged before *call* in conduct which is dishonest or otherwise discreditable to a *barrister* and which was not, before *call*, fairly disclosed in writing to the *Inn* calling them or where any undertaking given by a *barrister* on *call* to the *Bar* is breached in any material respect that shall be treated as an allegation of a breach of this *Handbook* and will be subject to the provisions of Part 5.

Exemptions   Rules

rQ7

The *BSB* may grant exemptions from all or part of the requirements set out in rQ3 to rQ5 above.

rQ8

In deciding whether to grant an exemption from part or all of any component of training, the *BSB* will determine whether the relevant knowledge and experience of the applicant make it unnecessary for further training to be required.

rQ9

An exemption from part or all components of training may be granted unconditionally or subject to conditions, which may include in an appropriate case:

.1 a requirement to do training instead of the training prescribed by this Section; and/or

.2 a condition that the applicant must pass a *Bar Transfer Test*.

rQ10

Where the BSB exempts an individual pursuant to rQ7 above, it may also:

.1 grant exemption in whole or in part from the requirement to attend *qualifying sessions*; and

.2 specify the period within which any requirement to attend *qualifying sessions* must be fulfilled, which may be a period ending after the individual concerned has been called to the *Bar*.

rQ11

An application for exemption under this Section must be in such form as may be prescribed by the *BSB* and contain or be accompanied by the following:

.1 details of the applicant's educational and professional qualifications and experience that meets the standards required of candidates;

.2 evidence (where applicable) that the applicant is or has been entitled to exercise rights of audience before any court, specifying the rights concerned and the basis of the applicant's entitlement to exercise such rights;

.3 any other representations or evidence on which the applicant wishes to rely in support of the application;

.4 verified English translations of every document relied on which is not in the English language; and

.5 payment of such fee or fees as may be prescribed.

rQ12

Before deciding whether to grant any exemption under this Section, the *BSB* may make any further enquiries or require the applicant to provide any further information that it considers relevant.

BSB Handbook

Full exemption   Rules

rQ13

If the *BSB* is satisfied that an applicant falls within Rule Q14, the *BSB* will:

.1 exempt the applicant from any component of training prescribed by this Section which the applicant has not fulfilled; and

.2 authorise the applicant to practise as a *barrister* on their being admitted to an Inn and called to the *Bar* subject to complying with the Handbook.

rQ14

The following categories of individual fall within this Rule:

.1 an individual who has been granted rights of audience by an *approved regulator* and who is entitled to exercise those rights in relation to all proceedings in all courts of England and Wales;

.2 subject to Rule Q15, an individual who has been granted rights of audience by an *approved regulator* and who is entitled to exercise those rights in relation to either all proceedings in the High Court or all proceedings in the Crown Court of England and Wales (but not both);

.3 a *barrister* of Northern Ireland who has successfully completed pupillage in accordance with the rules of the Bar of Northern Ireland;

.4 subject to Rule Q16, a *Qualified Swiss Lawyer.*

rQ15

The *BSB* may exceptionally require an applicant who falls within Rule Q14.2 to do part of *pupillage* if it considers this necessary having regard particularly to the knowledge, professional experience and intended future *practice* of the applicant.

rQ16

Subject to Rules Q18 to Q20, the *BSB* may require a *Qualified Swiss Lawyer* to pass a *Bar Transfer Test* if the *BSB* determines that:

.1 the matters covered by the education and training of the applicant differ substantially from those covered by the *academic legal training* and the *vocational training*; and

.2 the knowledge acquired by the applicant throughout their professional experience does not fully cover this substantial difference.

Registered European Lawyers   Rules

rQ17

The Rules governing registration as a *Registered European Lawyer* are in Section 3.D of this *Handbook*.

rQ18

To the extent provided in the *Swiss Citizens' Rights Agreement* , the BSB may not require an applicant who is a *Registered European Lawyer* and who falls within Rule Q20 or Q21 to pass a *Bar Transfer Test* unless it considers that the applicant is unfit to practise as a *barrister.*

rQ19

In considering whether to require an applicant who falls within Rule Q21 to pass a *Bar Transfer Test*, the *BSB* must:

.1 take into account the professional activities the applicant has pursued while a *Registered European Lawyer* and any knowledge and professional experience gained of, and any training received in, the law of any part of the United Kingdom and of the rules of professional conduct of the *Bar*; and

.2 assess and verify at an interview the applicant's effective and regular pursuit of professional activities and capacity to continue the activities pursued.

BSB Handbook The BSB Handbook - Version 4.6

rQ20

To fall within this Rule an applicant must have:

.1 for a period of at least three years been a *Registered European Lawyer*; and

.2 for a period of at least three years effectively and regularly pursued in England and Wales under a *Home Professional Title* professional activities in the law of England and Wales; and

.3 applied for admission to the *Bar* before 1 January 2025.

rQ21

To fall within this Rule an applicant must have:

.1 for a period of at least three years been a *Registered European Lawyer*; and

.2 for a period of at least three years effectively and regularly pursued in England and Wales professional activities under a *Home Professional Title*; and

.3 for a period of less than three years effectively and regularly pursued in England and Wales under a *Home Professional Title* professional activities in the law of England and Wales; and

.4 applied for admission to the *Bar* before 1 January 2025.

rQ22

For the purpose of this Section, activities are to be regarded as effectively and regularly pursued if they are actually exercised without any interruptions other than those resulting from the events of everyday life such as absence through illness or bereavement, customary annual leave or parental leave.

Partial exemption Rules

rQ23

If the *BSB* is satisfied that an applicant falls within Rule Q24, the *BSB* will exempt the applicant from the *academic legal training* and the *vocational training* and, if the *BSB* thinks fit, from part or all of *pupillage*.

rQ24

If the *BSB* is satisfied that an applicant falls within Rule Q24, the *BSB* will exempt the applicant from the *academic legal training* and the *vocational training* and, if the *BSB* thinks fit, from part or all of *pupillage*. The following categories of individual fall within this Rule:

.1 an individual who has been granted rights of audience by another *Approved Regulator* and is entitled to exercise those rights in relation to any class of proceedings in any of the Senior Courts or all proceedings in county courts or magistrates' courts in England and Wales;

.2 a *Qualified Foreign Lawyer* who has for a period of at least three years regularly exercised full rights of audience in courts which administer law substantially similar to the common law of England and Wales;

.3 a teacher of the law of England and Wales of experience and academic distinction.

Temporary call to the Bar of Qualified Foreign Lawyers Rules

rQ25

A *Qualified Foreign Lawyer* ("the applicant") who falls within Rule Q24.2 may apply to be called to the *Bar* by an *Inn* on a temporary basis for the purpose of appearing as counsel in a particular case before a *court* of England and Wales without being required to satisfy any other requirements of this Section if the applicant has:

.1 obtained from the *BSB* and submitted to an *Inn* a *Temporary Qualification Certificate* specifying the case for the purposes of which the applicant is authorised to be called to the *Bar*;

.2 duly completed and signed a *call declaration* in the form prescribed by the *BSB* from time to time; and

BSB Handbook

.3 paid such fee or fees as may be prescribed.

rQ26

The *BSB* will issue a *Temporary Qualification Certificate* if the applicant submits to the *BSB*:

.1 evidence which establishes that the applicant is a *Qualified Swiss Lawyer* or falls within Rule Q24.2;

.2 a *certificate of good standing*; and

.3 evidence which establishes that a *professional client* wishes to instruct the applicant to appear as counsel in the case or cases for the purposes of which the applicant seeks temporary *call* to the *Bar*.

rQ27

Admission to an *Inn* and *call* to the *Bar* under Rule Q25 take effect when the applicant is given notice in writing by the *Inn* that the applicant has been admitted to the *Inn* and called to the *Bar* under Rule Q26 and automatically cease to have effect on conclusion of the case or cases specified in the applicant's *Temporary Qualification Certificate*.

rQ28

Where an individual is dissatisfied with a decision by either the *BSB* or an *Inn* in relation to rQ3 to rQ5 and rQ7 to rQ26 above they may apply to the *BSB* for a review.

Part 4 - B3. Authorised Education and Training Organisations | Rules |

rQ29

Providers of *vocational training* and *pupillage* must be authorised by the *BSB* as an *AETO*.

rQ30

An application to become an *AETO* must be made in such form and be accompanied by payment of such fee or fees as may be prescribed by the *BSB*.

rQ31

In determining an application from an applicant to become an *AETO*, the *BSB* will have regard to the *Authorisation Framework* and in particular the mandatory criteria. The BSB will not approve an application to become an *AETO* unless it is satisfied that it is:

.1 able to meet the mandatory criteria set out in the *Authorisation Framework* relevant to the application; and

.2 a suitable provider for the purposes of the *Authorisation Framework*.

rQ32

The *BSB* may grant authorisation to an *AETO* on such terms and conditions as it considers appropriate including the period of authorisation.

rQ33

The BSB may vary, amend, suspend or withdraw authorisation of an *AETO* in the following circumstances:

.1 the *AETO* has applied for such variation, amendment, suspension or withdrawal;

.2 the *AETO* ceases to exist, becomes insolvent or merges;

.3 the *AETO* fails to comply with conditions imposed upon its authorisation;

.4 the *BSB* is of the view that the *AETO* has failed or will fail to fulfil the mandatory requirements set out in the *Authorisation Framework*;

.5 the *BSB* is of the view that the *AETO* is not providing the training for which it was authorised to an adequate standard or there has been a material change in the training provided; or

.6 the *BSB* is of the view that the continued authorisation of the *AETO* would inhibit the *Regulatory Objectives*.

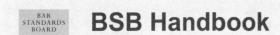

BSB Handbook

rQ34

An *AETO* which is dissatisfied by a decision in relation to rQ31 – rQ33 above may apply to the *BSB* for a review.

Part 4 - B4. Review and Appeals   Rules

rQ35

Where provision is made under this Section for a review by the *BSB* of a decision, any request for such a review must be accompanied by:

.1 a copy of any notice of the decision and the reasons for it received by the person requesting the review ("the applicant");

.2 where the decision is a decision of an *Inn* or the *ICC*, copies of all documents submitted or received by the applicant which were before the *Inn* or the *ICC*;

.3 any further representations and evidence which the applicant wishes the *BSB* to take into account; and

.4 payment of such fee or fees as may be prescribed.

rQ36

Where the decision under review is a decision of an *Inn*, the *BSB* will invite the *Inn* to comment on any further representations and evidence which the applicant submits under Rule Q35.3.

rQ37

On a review under this Section the *BSB*:

.1 may affirm the decision under review or substitute any other decision which could have been made on the original application;

.2 may in an appropriate case reimburse the fee paid under Rule Q35.4; and

.3 will inform the applicant and any other interested *person* of its decision and the reasons for it.

rQ38

Where provision is made under this Section for a review of a decision by the *BSB*, this review may be delegated to an *Independent Decision-Making Panel*, where specified by the *BSB*.

rQ39

Where under this Section provision is made for a review by the *BSB* of a decision, no appeal may be made to the High Court unless such a review has taken place.

rQ40

An individual who is adversely affected by a decision of the *BSB* under Section B.2 may appeal to the High Court against the decision.

rQ41-rQ129

Removed.

Part 4 - C. The CPD Rules   Rules

The mandatory continuing professional development requirements (Rules Q130-Q131)   Rules

rQ130

For the purpose of this Section 4.C:

.1 "calendar year" means a period of one year starting on 1 January in the year in question;

BSB Handbook

.2 "continuing professional development" ("CPD") means work undertaken over and above the normal commitments of a *barrister* and is work undertaken with a view to developing the *barrister's* skills, knowledge and professional standards in areas relevant to their present or proposed area of practice in order to keep the *barrister* up to date and maintain the highest standards of professional practice.

.3 "CPD Guidance" means guidance issued by the Bar Standards Board from time to time which sets out the CPD structure with which an EPP *barrister* should have regard to.

.4 "EPP" means the Established Practitioners Programme which requires *barristers*, once they have completed the NPP, to undertake CPD during each calendar year in accordance with these Rules.

.5 the "mandatory requirements" are those in Rules Q131 to Q138 below.

.6 "NPP" means the New Practitioner Programme which requires *barristers* to complete CPD in their first three calendar years of practice in accordance with these rules.

.7 a " *pupillage* year" is any calendar year in which a *barrister* is at any time a *pupil*.

.8 a " learning objective" is a statement of what a *barrister* intends to achieve through their CPD activities for that calendar year with reference to a specific aim and one or more outcomes.

rQ131

Any practising *barrister* who, as at 1 October 2001, had started but not completed the period of three years referred to in the Continuing Education Scheme Rules at Annex Q to the Sixth Edition of the Code of Conduct must complete a minimum of 42 hours of CPD during their first three years of *practice*.

Guidance to Rule Q131   Guidance

gQ1

Rule rQ131 is intended to apply only in those limited circumstances where a *barrister* started *practice* before 1 October 2001 but after the NPP first came into force, left *practice* before completing the NPP, but has since returned. Rule rQ131 requires them to finish their NPP during whatever is left of their first three years of *practice*.

The mandatory continuing professional development requirements (Rule Q132)   Rules

rQ132

Any practising NPP *barrister* who starts *practice* on or after 1 October 2001 must during the first three calendar years in which the *barrister* holds a *practising certificate* after any *pupillage* year complete a minimum of 45 hours of CPD.

Guidance to Rule Q132   Guidance

gQ2

NPP *barristers* should have regard to rQ137 and the NPP guidance which will note the details of any compulsory courses the NPP *barristers* must complete. It also provides guidance as to the types of activities that count towards CPD.

The mandatory continuing professional development requirements (Rules Q133-Q134)   Rules

rQ133

Subject to Rule Q136, any EPP *barrister* who holds a *practising certificate* or certificates during a calendar year must undertake CPD.

rQ134

An EPP *barrister* who is required to undertake CPD must:

1. prepare a written CPD Plan setting out the *barrister's* learning objectives and the types of CPD activities they propose to undertake during the calendar year

2. keep a written record of the CPD activities the *barrister* has undertaken in the calendar year

3. keep a written record in the CPD Plan for each calendar year of:

a. the *barrister's* reflection on the CPD they have undertaken;

b. any variation in the *barrister's* planned CPD activities; and

c. the *barrister's* assessment of their future learning objectives.

4. Retain a record of the CPD Plan and completed CPD activities for three years.

5. submit to the Bar Standards Board an annual declaration of completion of CPD in the form specified by the BSB.

Guidance to Rules Q133-Q134 | Guidance |

---

gQ3

EPP *barristers* who are required by these Rules to undertake CPD should refer to the CPD Guidance. The CPD Guidance provides further detailed information which EPP *barristers* should have regard to when planning, undertaking and recording their CPD. The CPD Guidance is not prescriptive. Its purpose is to provide a structure that would represent good practice for most *barristers* when considering their CPD requirements.

gQ4

The CPD Guidance explains that these Rules do not specify a minimum number of CPD hours which an EPP *barrister* must undertake in a calendar year: it is the responsibility of the individual *barrister* to determine the CPD activities they will undertake in order meet the requirements of CPD. The Bar Standards Board will assess and monitor *barristers'* compliance with CPD.

gQ5

The underlying principle behind the requirement to plan CPD and set learning objectives is that *barristers* consider their own circumstances and development needs when they complete CPD activities. This best ensures that activities completed contribute to the development of the barrister's practice.

The mandatory continuing professional development requirements (Rules Q135-Q138) | Rules |

---

rQ135

Upon the request of the Bar Standards Board, a *barrister* must produce their CPD Plan and record of CPD activities for assessment.

rQ136

Rule Q133 does not apply:

.1 in the case of a *barrister* to whom Rule Q131 applies, to any calendar year forming or containing part of the period of 3 years referred to in Rule Q131; or

.2 in the case of a *barrister* to whom Rule Q132 applies, during any *pupillage* year or during the first three calendar years in which the *barrister* holds a *practising certificate*.

BSB Handbook

rQ137

The *Bar Standards Board* may, by resolution, specify the nature, content and format of courses and other activities which may be undertaken by *barristers* (or by any category of *barristers*) in order to satisfy the mandatory requirements.

rQ138

The *Bar Standards Board* may, by resolution and after consultation with the Inns, Circuits and other providers as appropriate, vary the minimum number of hours of CPD which must be completed by an NPP *barrister* in order to satisfy any of the mandatory requirements.

APPENDIX 2
Excerpts from the Bar Standards Board Code Guidance

Unregistered Barristers Guidance

1. Introduction

The BSB Handbook defines a practising barrister as a barrister who is supplying legal services and holds a practising certificate. There are many barristers who do not have a practising certificate either by choice or because they do not qualify for a practising certificate.

Such barristers are now called "unregistered barristers" because they are not on the public register of barristers who have practising certificates. It is important to note that the term "non-practising barrister" which has been used in the past should no longer be used as it can cause confusion since some barristers without practising certificates do provide legal services and are, in effect, practising as lawyers.

Many unregistered barristers will have chosen careers other than the law or may be retired and are therefore not covered by this guidance unless they provide any legal services.

Even though the rules which apply only to practising barristers do not apply to them, all unregistered barristers remain members of the profession and are expected to conduct themselves in an appropriate manner. In this context, they remain subject to certain Core Duties and Conduct Rules at all times. If they provide legal services, they must comply with all the Core Duties and they have a responsibility not to mislead anyone about their status. This guidance will assist those barristers to comply with these obligations in the BSB Handbook.

2. Who is this guidance for?

This guidance relates to 'unregistered barristers', or barristers without practising certificates, who wish to provide legal services to employers or to the public, whether such barristers are employed or self-employed. It also addresses restrictions on 'holding out' as a barrister in connection with the supply of legal services.

It is a criminal offence for a barrister without a practising certificate to provide legal services which are reserved legal activities under the Legal Services Act 2007. This guidance provides advice on what legal services may be provided by a barrister without a practising certificate and on the rules which must be followed when doing so.

Core Duties 5 and 9 of the BSB Handbook apply to unregistered barristers at all times. The other Core Duties apply when supplying legal services, as do certain other rules (see below).

The main outcome this guidance relates to is Outcome C34 in the BSB Handbook:

> Clients who receive legal services from unregistered barristers are aware that such unregistered barristers are not subject to the same regulatory safeguards that would apply if they instructed a practising barrister.

3. What are legal services and reserved legal activities?

You must not carry on any reserved legal activity unless you are entitled to do so under the Legal Services Act.

Under the Legal Services Act certain legal services are reserved to those who are authorised to provide them. For barristers, only those who have practising certificates are

authorised persons. Such services are known as 'reserved legal activities'[1] which are as follows:

- the exercise of a right of audience;
- the conduct of litigation;
- reserved instrument activities;
- probate activities;
- notarial activities[2] and
- the administration of oaths.

As it is a criminal offence to carry out a reserved legal activity without a practising certificate, it is important that unregistered barristers are clear that they are not permitted to carry out these services. However, advocacy is not a reserved legal activity unless it involves the exercise of a right of audience. Thus, advocacy before an arbitrator or other tribunal where rights of audience are not required is not a reserved legal activity.

If you are also a solicitor, or regulated by another approved regulator, you may be authorised to carry out reserved legal activities in that capacity. Guidance for those barristers who are dual qualified can be found at paragraph 8.6 below.

As an unregistered barrister, you can provide any legal services that are not reserved legal activities. However, there are some important rules in the BSB Handbook which you need to follow in doing so.

Legal services are defined in the definitions section of the Handbook as follows:

---

[1] Section 12 of the Legal Services Act 2007
[2] The Bar Council does not authorise any barrister whether practising or not to perform notarial activities.

3

[Legal services] includes legal advice, representation and drafting or settling any statement of case, witness statement, affidavit or other legal document but does not include:

a) *sitting as a judge or arbitrator or acting as a mediator, early neutral evaluation, expert determination and adjudications;*

b) *lecturing in or teaching law or writing or editing law books articles or reports;*

c) *examining newspapers, periodicals, books, scripts and other publications for libel, breach of copyright, contempt of court and the like;*

d) *communicating to or in the press or other media;*

e) *giving advice on legal matters free to a friend or relative or acting as unpaid or honorary legal adviser to any charitable benevolent or philanthropic institution;*

f) *in relation to a barrister who is a non-executive director of a company or a trustee or governor of a charitable benevolent or philanthropic institution or a trustee of any private trust, giving to the other directors trustees or governors the benefit of his learning and experience on matters of general legal principle applicable to the affairs of the company institution or trust;*

g) *early neutral evaluation, expert determination and adjudications.*

In addition to not providing reserved legal services, you must not provide immigration advice and services unless authorised to do so by the Office of the Immigration Services Commissioner (OISC). Immigration work is not a reserved legal activity under the Legal Services Act 2007, but it is regulated under another statute. Barristers with a practising certificate are entitled to do immigration work but unregistered barristers are not, unless authorised by OISC.

4. Holding out as a barrister

Rule S8 provides that you must not practise as a barrister unless you have a practising certificate, and Rule S9 defines practising as a barrister as including holding yourself out as a barrister while providing legal services. The restriction on 'holding out' prevents barristers

who do not have a practising certificate but who are supplying or offering to supply legal services from using the title 'barrister' or otherwise conveying the impression that they are practising as barristers. It is not possible to provide a comprehensive list of the circumstances which might amount to holding out, but it is hoped that the following examples will give an idea of what is prohibited.

- Describing oneself as a barrister in any printed material used in connection with the provision of legal services: in particular in advertising or publicity, on a card or letterhead, or on premises

- Describing oneself as a barrister to clients or prospective clients

- Describing oneself to clients or prospective clients as a non-practising barrister or barrister-at-law (titles which have been allowed in the past but not in recent years)

- Indicating to opposing parties or their representatives (e.g. in correspondence) that one is a barrister

- Describing oneself as a barrister or (when supplying services to the public) as "counsel", wearing robes, or sitting in a place reserved for counsel, in court

- Using other descriptions in connection with supplying, or offering to supply, legal services which imply that the individual is a barrister (e.g. membership of an Inn of Court)

(These examples are not exhaustive).

The restriction on holding out only applies in the context of legal services. If you have been called to the Bar, there is no restriction on referring to yourself as a barrister if it is not in connection with the supply of legal services.

It should also be noted that for a BVC or BPTC graduate to mention that he/she is a holder of this qualification, is not considered as holding out as a barrister.

5. **What job title can I hold; what can I/my employer put on a business card/letterhead/website etc.?**

The fundamental principle is that you must not mislead or allow anyone else to mislead any person to whom you or your employer supply or offer to supply *legal services*.

You can use the title "barrister" when **not** providing *legal services*. See paragraph 3 for activities which are not regarded as *legal services* ("non-legal" services). However, you must be careful not to mislead third parties as to your status as a barrister. This would apply particularly if you were also providing *legal services* to the same people to whom you provide "non-legal" services.

It is important that you/your employer do not use the title barrister, unregistered barrister or non-practising barrister on business cards, promotional material, letterheads, and business names. If you are employed whether by a regulated or unregulated firm, you should make sure that your employer does not use any of these titles in connection with you in its printed material or on its website.

You can use the titles "lawyer" or "legal adviser". If you are self-employed, or work for an unregulated employer, you should not use the title "counsel". However, if you provide legal services only to your employer you may use titles commonly used in companies, such as legal counsel, general counsel, corporate counsel. You may also use the description "of Counsel" if you work for an employer which is an authorised person under the Legal Services Act.

In a curriculum vitae, you can state that you qualified as a barrister.

You can refer to yourself as a BVC/BPTC graduate.

If you are a QC but do not have a practising certificate, you may continue to use the title but if you are providing *legal services* you must explain that you are not practising as a barrister.

6. Why do special rules apply to unregistered barristers who supply legal services?

Legal services, other than reserved legal activities, can be supplied by anyone and are not subject to any special statutory regulation. It would therefore be disproportionate to impose regulatory requirements on unregistered barristers who supply such services just because they are barristers, except where there would otherwise be a clear risk to their potential clients. The risk that needs to be managed is that most potential clients are not aware of the different categories of barrister and will tend to assume that the same regulatory requirements and protections apply to all barristers. Barristers with practising certificates are subject to important requirements, such as having insurance and keeping their professional knowledge up-to-date, which do not apply to unregistered barristers. Some of their clients also have the right to complain to the Legal Ombudsman. These are important safeguards for clients, who may assume that they will apply whenever they seek legal services from someone they know or believe to be a barrister. The rules discussed below are intended to manage this risk while still allowing unregistered barristers to provide unreserved legal services.

7. What Rules and Duties apply to you as an unregistered barrister providing legal services?

When you are providing legal services all the Core Duties in the BSB Handbook apply to you (see Rules C1.2 and C2.1-2.2). The Core Duties are:

> *CD1 – You must observe your duty to the court in the administration of justice*

The Bar Standards Board
Handbook

CD2 – You must act in the best interests of each client

CD3 – You must act with honesty and integrity

CD4 – You must maintain your independence

CD5 – You must not behave in a way which is likely to diminish the trust and confidence which the public places in you or in the profession

CD6 – You must keep the affairs of each client confidential

CD7 – You must provide a competent standard of work and service to each client

CD8 – You must not discriminate unlawfully against any person

CD9 – You must be open and co-operative with your regulators

CD10 – You must take reasonable steps to manage your practice, or carry out your role within your practice, competently and in such a way as to achieve compliance with your legal and regulatory obligations

Even when you are not providing legal services, Core Duties 5 and 9 apply to you.

The Conduct Rules (and associated guidance) which apply to unregistered barristers at all times are as follows:

- Rule C8 – Your duty not to do anything which could be seen to undermine your honesty, integrity and independence
- Rule C16 – Your duty to your client is subject to your duty to the court, and your obligations to act with honesty and integrity, and to maintain your independence.
- Rules C64-70 – Duties in relation to provision of information to the BSB and co-operation with the BSB. These duties include the duty to report serious misconduct by other barristers (see separate guidance).

In addition, the following Conduct Rules and associated guidance apply when providing legal services:

- Rules C4 and C5 – your duty to your client is subject to your duty to the court , and your duty to the court does not require you to breach your duty to keep the affairs of your client confidential
- Rule C19 – not misleading clients
- Rules C144 and 145 – rules relating to information which unregistered barristers must give to inexperienced clients

Rule C19 is a rule which applies to all barristers. It provides that **you must not mislead** anyone to whom you supply or offer to supply *legal services*. For unregistered barristers this means:

- You must not use the title "barrister" in connection with the supply of or offer to supply *legal services*. This is known as "holding out" and is explained further in section 4. Similarly, you should not use the description "unregistered barrister" when supplying or offering to supply *legal services* except to the very limited extent discussed in paragraph 8 below and subject to explaining what the term means. Barristers registered under Rule S15 may continue to use the title "barrister", but must comply with the terms of the rule.

- You must not mislead clients or employers about:
    - your status;
    - the extent to which you are regulated;
    - the services you can supply; and
    - your insurance cover.

In order to comply with the obligation not to mislead clients or employers, you will need to consider what information you should give them about your status as discussed further in paragraph 8 below. In certain circumstances, the Handbook prescribes the information you must give (see below).

Rules C144-145 set out the information which must be provided by unregistered barristers when providing legal services to an inexperienced client (see paragraph 8.4 below).

8. Information to be given by unregistered barristers to employers, clients or prospective clients

This section describes what information you may, or in some cases **must**, give to those with whom you deal. Keep in mind the purpose of giving the information as discussed in paragraph 6 above. Check which of the following applies to you. When you provide the explanation required by Rule C144 or suggested by this guidance, the BSB would not normally consider this as constituting holding yourself out as a barrister.

8.1 I provide *legal services* only to my employer

You may describe yourself orally as an unregistered barrister or a barrister without a practising certificate, to your employer, colleagues and any third parties with whom you deal and you should explain what this means if there is any risk of anyone being misled. You may also state on a CV that you have been called to the Bar.

8.2 I work for a regulated professional body and provide services to clients

This applies to unregistered barristers working for solicitors' firms, other bodies which are authorised under the Legal Services Act such as licensed conveyancers, or other regulated professional firms such as accountants or patent agents.

You may describe yourself to your employer and colleagues as an unregistered barrister or a barrister without a practising certificate and you should explain what this means if there is any risk of anyone being misled. You should **not** describe yourself as a barrister or unregistered barrister to clients of your employer but if you are asked whether you are a barrister or if it becomes known that you are, you may

say that you are an unregistered barrister and explain what this means. You should seek to ensure that any publicity put out by your employer does not describe you as a barrister. You must also comply with any regulatory requirements of the professional body which regulates your employer.

8.3 I am self-employed and I provide unreserved *legal services* to experienced business clients

This applies to those barristers dealing with larger businesses or firms which can be expected to make informed judgments about sourcing legal services.

You may not advertise or refer to yourself as a barrister but in tendering for work you may state to a prospective client that you are an unregistered barrister provided that you explain to the client what this means. If you are in any doubt, a written statement should be provided along the same lines as that detailed in paragraph 8.4 below. Whilst we strongly advise all barristers providing legal services to carry professional indemnity insurance, if you decide not to insure then you should so advise clients or prospective clients.

You must also explain to clients that in respect of any legal advice you provide, there is a substantial risk that they will not be able to rely on legal advice privilege.

8.4 I am self-employed and supply unreserved *legal services* to inexperienced clients, such as individuals, small companies and charities.

If you supply legal services to inexperienced clients, Rule C144 applies to you. Inexperienced clients are defined as including individuals and small organisations which would be entitled under the Legal Ombudsman Scheme Rules to make a

complaint to the Legal Ombudsman if you were a practising barrister.[3] As you are not practising as a barrister your clients have no redress under this scheme, so you are required to make your status very clear to them. But other clients, for example slightly larger organisations which only occasionally require legal services, may also be inexperienced. If you are in any doubt as to whether your client has sufficient experience to understand the implications of instructing an unregistered barrister instead of a practising barrister, then you should give them the written statement detailed in this paragraph.

Where Rule C144 applies, you **must** explain to your client:

- that you are not acting as a barrister
- that you are not subject to certain Conduct Rules applying to practising barristers and the Bar Standards Board cannot consider complaints against you in relation to these rules but only in relation to the rules which do apply to you
- if you are not covered by professional indemnity insurance you must say so
- that your client has no right to complain to the Legal Ombudsman

Your client must also confirm in writing that they have received this explanation.

A suggested form of statement is contained in Annex 1.

These requirements do not apply to legal services provided when working for a Legal Advice Centre[4] as defined in the Handbook, or if you are authorised to provide reserved legal activities by another approved regulator[5] (see paragraph 8.6 below).

---

[3] They provide that complaints may be made by micro enterprises (headcount below 10 and turnover or balance sheet total of 2 million euros or less), charities with an income of £1million or less and clubs and other organisations with a turnover of £1 million or less). See http://www.legalombudsman.org.uk/.
[4] Rule c145.3 and section S B9.
[5] Rule c145.4

They do however apply if you are registered under Rule S15. You may also wish to refer to the definition of legal services in paragraph 3 above in deciding whether you are providing legal services.

8.5 I am employed by an unregulated organisation which provides unreserved *legal services* to the public

The same requirements apply as if you were self-employed depending on whether the client is an experienced large business or an inexperienced client such as an individual or small business. You should follow the guidance in paragraph 8.3 or 8.4 above as appropriate. It is your responsibility, and not your employer's, to see that the relevant information is given and you should advise your employer of the rules so that they do not hold you out as a barrister.

Barristers who do not hold practising certificates (including pupils in their non-practising period) are permitted to provide free legal advice to clients of a Legal Advice Centre, providing they do not hold themselves out as barristers and do not undertake or offer to undertake any reserved legal services.

8.6 I am authorised to carry out legal services by another Approved Regulator

Under the LSA, only approved regulators can authorise the carrying out of reserved legal activities (see above). The following approved regulators can currently authorise the conduct of litigation and/or exercise of rights of audience: the Solicitors Regulation Authority, CILEx Regulation, the Intellectual Property Regulation Board and the Costs Lawyer Standards Board.

Rule S43 states that, if you are authorised by another approved regulator to carry on a reserved legal activity and currently permitted to practise by that approved

regulator, you must not practise as a barrister and you are not eligible for a practising certificate (although you may apply to the BSB for a waiver from this rule, which may be granted subject to conditions to ensure that clients understand the capacity in which you are acting and the regulatory regime that applies in each case). If you are practising as a person authorised by one of the other approved regulators, you may hold yourself out as a barrister in addition to your other qualification, provided that you comply with Rule S14. This rule states that if you hold yourself out as a barrister or a registered European lawyer then, when supplying legal services to any person or employer for the first time, you must inform them clearly in writing at the earliest opportunity that you are not practising as a barrister or a registered European lawyer.

9. What are the rules for pupils?

In your non-practising period, as you do not have a practising certificate, you cannot supply legal services as a practising barrister but you can accept a noting brief with permission of your pupil supervisor or head of Chambers. You may describe yourself as a pupil barrister in that capacity. If you provide unreserved legal services in any other capacity, for example if providing pro bono advice, you should not describe yourself as a barrister or a pupil barrister and should follow the rules and guidance for unregistered barristers.

In your practising period, when you have a provisional practising certificate, you may provide legal services in accordance with Rule S19. You may describe yourself as a pupil barrister and you should ensure that the client understands your status.

10. Further Help and Advice

It is recognised that the rules are complex. The Bar Council Ethical Queries helpline (020 7611 1307) is available for questions on professional issues.

The Bar Standards Board
Handbook

October 2019

Bar Standards Board

Annex 1 – Explanation to clients

Suggested statement to be given in accordance with Rule C144

This statement, or an explanation containing the same information on the points shown in bold, must be given to any inexperienced client to whom you offer to provide <u>legal services</u> and you must receive written confirmation that they have received it before providing any such services.

Your name: **Date:**

This statement is to explain my status in offering to provide you with legal services.

Although I am qualified as a barrister, **I am not entitled to practise as a barrister**. **I do not have a practising certificate** and am not on the register of practising barristers.

Therefore, in providing any legal services to you I am not acting as a barrister and **I am not subject to many of the rules which regulate practising barristers.**

This limits the services I can provide to you. I can provide you with legal advice and represent you before certain Tribunals, but **I cannot exercise rights of audience in Court**.

I aim to provide you with a good service and if you have any concerns about what I do for you, please let me know and I will try to resolve the problem. But you should know that **you would have only limited rights to complain about me to anyone else.**

The Legal Ombudsman, which can adjudicate on complaints about poor service by practising barristers, cannot consider any complaint against me.

If I cannot resolve your concerns, **you can complain to the Bar Standards Board** and it will investigate whether I have failed to comply with any of the rules which apply to me, but it cannot investigate possible breaches of rules which apply only to practising barristers

I am [am not] covered by professional indemnity insurance.

In respect of any legal advice I provide, there is a substantial risk that you will not be able to rely on legal advice privilege.

Signed: Date:

I confirm that I have received the above statement from [   ].

Signed: Date:

Confidentiality Guidance

Maintaining confidentiality

The Bar Standards Board (BSB) would like to remind barristers that all client communications are privileged and that such communications, client information and Chambers confidential data (financial or otherwise) must be stored, handled and disposed of securely.

Attention in particular is drawn to Core Duty 6, Rule C5 and Rule C15.5 of the BSB Handbook, which require barristers to preserve the confidentiality of their client's affairs. Any barrister who does not adhere to this by, for example, allowing other people to see confidential material, losing portable devices on which unprotected information is stored, or not disposing of client papers securely could face disciplinary action by the BSB.

Barristers are data controllers under the Data Protection Act 2018, must comply with the requirements of the Act in handling data to which that Act applies, and must also comply with the General Data Protection Regulation (GDPR). A breach of the Act or the GDPR is likely to constitute a breach of Core Duty 10 of the BSB Handbook, which states that "you must take reasonable steps to manage your practice, or carry out your role within your practice, competently and in such a way as to achieve compliance with your *legal* and regulatory *obligations*" (emphasis added). A breach of the Act and/or the GDPR may also constitute a breach of Core Duty 5 of the BSB Handbook, which states that "you must not behave in a way which is likely to diminish the trust and confidence which the public places in you or in the profession".

Barristers are responsible for the conduct of those who undertake work on their behalf and are advised to ensure that clerks and other chambers' staff are aware of the need to handle and dispose of confidential material securely. Chambers must have appropriate systems for looking after confidential information.

In making arrangements to look after the information entrusted to them, barristers should seek to reduce the risk of casual or deliberate unauthorised access to it. Consideration needs to be given to information kept in electronic form as well as on paper. The arrangements should cover:

- The handling and storage of confidential information. Papers should not be left where others can read them, and computers should be placed so that they cannot be overlooked, especially when working in public places. When not being used, papers should be stored in a way which minimises the risk of unauthorised access. Computers should be password protected.
- Suitable arrangements should be made for distributing papers and sending faxes and emails.
- Particular care should be taken when using removable devices such as laptops, removable discs, CDs, USB memory sticks and PDAs. Such devices should be used to store only information needed for immediate business purposes, not for permanent storage. Information on them should be at least password protected and preferably encrypted. Great care should be taken in looking after the devices themselves to ensure that they are not lost or stolen.
- When no longer required, all confidential material must be disposed of securely, for example by returning it to the client or professional client, shredding paper, permanently erasing information no longer required and securely disposing of any electronic devices which hold confidential information.

Additional safeguards will need to be put in place for particularly sensitive information, or for cases in which barristers from the same chambers are appearing on opposing sides.

Bar Standards Board
October 2019

Reporting Serious Misconduct of Others Guidance

Introduction

1. This guidance provides further explanation about your duty to report the serious misconduct of other barristers or registered European lawyers. You should read it in conjunction with Rules C66 to C69 and Guidance C95 to C101 in the BSB Handbook.

2. Rule C66 states that, subject to your duty to keep the affairs of each client confidential and subject also to Rules C67 and C68, you must report to the Bar Standards Board if you have reasonable grounds to believe that there has been serious misconduct by a barrister or a registered European lawyer.

3. The BSB intends this rule to achieve the following outcomes:

   - Outcome C2:1 BSB regulated persons are effectively regulated;
   - Outcome C22: The public have confidence in the proper regulation of persons regulated by the BSB;
   - Outcome C23: The BSB has the information that it needs in order to be able to assess risks and regulate effectively and in accordance with the regulatory objectives.

4. It is strongly in the public interest that the BSB is made aware of any serious misconduct. The duty to report serious misconduct is also consistent with parallel obligations for professionals in other sectors.

5. The BSB recognises that the application of this rule may be particularly difficult in some circumstances. If you require further guidance you may wish to contact the Bar Council's Ethical Queries Helpline on 020 7611 1307, or at http://www.barcouncil.org.uk/for-the-

bar/introduction-to-member-services/ethical-enquiries-line/. This service is confidential and is provided by individuals on an approved list who are not subject to the duty to report serious misconduct of which they become aware as a result of dealing with enquiries on the helpline.

What should you report?

6. You are obliged to report to the BSB instances of serious misconduct by other barristers or registered European lawyers. Whether or not misconduct is *serious* misconduct is a matter of judgement, which will depend on the particular circumstances. It will ultimately be for the BSB to decide whether enforcement or other regulatory action is necessary in the public interest. If, having considered the factors and circumstances discussed below, you remain unsure whether or not the behaviour in question amounts to serious misconduct, you should err on the side of caution and make a report to the BSB.

7. You should refer to the list at Guidance C96 for examples of serious misconduct; however, you should be aware that this is not a closed list and that breaches of other provisions may also amount to serious misconduct. Whether serious misconduct has occurred may be a question of the degree to which one or more of the obligations in the Handbook has been breached. Guidance C96 lists the following examples of serious misconduct:

    1. dishonesty (CD3);
    2. assault or harassment (CD3 and/or CD5 and/or CD8);
    3. seeking to gain access without consent to instructions or other confidential information relating to the opposing party's case (CD3 and/or CD5);
    4. seeking to gain access without consent to confidential information relating to another member of chambers, member of staff or pupil (CD3 and/or CD5);
    5. encouraging a witness to give evidence which is untruthful or misleading (CD1 and/or CD3);

6. knowingly or recklessly misleading, or attempting to mislead, the court or an opponent (CD1 and/or CD3);

7. being drunk or under the influence of drugs in court (CD2 and/or CD7);

8. failure by a barrister to report promptly to the Bar Standards Board pursuant to rC65.1-rC65.5 (duty to report criminal charges, cautions and convictions, and disciplinary action by other regulators) and/or rC66 (duty to report serious misconduct by others);

9. a breach by a barrister of rC67 (for example, reporting, or threatening to report, another person as a litigation tactic or otherwise abusively; or merely to please a client or any other person or otherwise for an improper motive);

10. conduct that poses a serious risk to the public.

When discrimination becomes serious misconduct

8. Discrimination can constitute serious misconduct. You should be aware of the seven different types of discrimination under the Equality Act 2010.

9. These are:

    •   Direct discrimination – where someone is treated less favourably than another person because of a protected characteristic[1].

    •   Associative discrimination – this is direct discrimination against someone because they are associated with another person who possesses a protected characteristic.

    •   Discrimination by perception – this is direct discrimination against someone because others think that they possess a particular protected characteristic. They do not necessarily have to possess the characteristic.

---

[1] The Equality Act 2010 introduced the term 'protected characteristics' to refer to groups that are protected under the Act. These are: age, disability, gender reassignment, marriage and civil partnership, pregnancy and maternity, race, religion and belief, sex, and sexual orientation.

- Indirect discrimination – this can occur when a rule or policy that applies to everyone disadvantages a person with a particular protected characteristic.
- Harassment – this is behaviour that is deemed to be offensive by the recipient. Recipients can now complain about behaviour that they find offensive even if it is not directed at them.
- Victimisation – this occurs when someone is treated badly because they have made or supported a complaint or grievance under this legislation.

Harassment and victimisation

10. The Bar functions on a system based on trust and confidence between colleagues, and individual barristers depend to a large extent on the reputation they hold amongst their colleagues. In this context it is understandable that some barristers may be concerned about the personal impact of reporting serious misconduct. This is especially the case where the nature of the misconduct itself relates to harassment or victimisation.

11. Harassment is defined in the Equality Act 2010 as:

- Unwanted conduct that has the purpose or effect of creating an intimidating, hostile, degrading, humiliating or offensive environment for the complainant, or violating the complainant's dignity.
- Unwanted conduct of a sexual nature (sexual harassment).
- Treating a person less favourably than another person because they have either submitted to, or did not submit to, sexual harassment or harassment related to sex or gender reassignment.

12. Rule C69 creates an obligation on all barristers not to victimise anyone for making in good faith a report of serious misconduct. This means that barristers must not treat any individual less favourably because they have made such a report to the BSB. This rule is intended to expressly protect you where you make a report of serious misconduct. It is

of vital importance to the intended outcomes of Rule C66, discussed above, that individuals are not discouraged from reporting serious misconduct by the risk of suffering victimisation as a result of doing so.

13. You should also take account of the fact that pupil barristers and barristers of fewer years' standing may be particularly vulnerable due to their relatively junior status and their relative dependence on more senior barristers for work, guidance and support. Pupils or new entrants to the profession may worry that by reporting to the BSB they will subsequently be treated less favourably or otherwise subjected to unwanted conduct, or that their career may be impacted negatively (whether or not such concerns are well founded in particular instances).

14. If you are a pupil barrister, or relatively new entrant to the profession, who has become aware of behaviour potentially amounting to serious misconduct, you may wish first to discuss your concerns with relevant colleagues, with your supervisor, the head of chambers or head of legal practice. You may wish to establish whether any other person is aware of the misconduct in question and/or whether that individual is willing to report the misconduct, or has already done so. You do not need to make a report yourself if you reasonably believe that another person has already done so. You can also contact the Bar Council's Ethical Enquiries Helpline for further assistance.

15. If the matter relates to conduct which affects you personally, you still remain under an obligation to report serious misconduct to the BSB. However, the BSB will treat any report of discrimination, harassment (whether of a sexual nature or otherwise), or victimisation as sensitively as possible and will not act without first consulting the person who has been affected. Given the sensitivity of this issue, the BSB has a policy of not taking enforcement action for failing to comply with the duty to report if you may have been the subject of these types of misconduct. Nevertheless, we would encourage you to report matters to the BSB and we will always treat such reports sensitively.

16. In addition to this guidance, barristers should take full account of the Equality Rules in the Handbook and should refer to the Supporting Information on the Equality Rules wherever relevant.

17. If you are in doubt as to whether or not particular behaviour amounts to serious misconduct you should consider discussing this with the Bar Council's Ethical Enquiries Helpline (see above). It is important to be aware that by reporting what you believe may be serious misconduct simply puts the BSB in a position to decide what action, if any, to take by making a fair assessment as to whether or not serious misconduct (or any misconduct) has in fact occurred. Action will only be taken in relation to the barrister or lawyer concerned where this is appropriate, proportionate and in accordance with the BSB's policies.

How should you report?

18. You should report serious misconduct to the BSB's Contact and Assessment Team by completing the online form on the 'reporting concerns' section of the BSB's website – there is an option on the online form for reports of serious misconduct.

19. Using the online form is the best way to report your concerns. However, if you do not wish to report using the online form, you have any access requirements or you would first like advice on the reporting process, please contact our Information Line on 020 7611 1445.

20. You should make a report to the BSB as soon as reasonably practicable. You will receive an acknowledgement of receipt of the report, including an explanation of how the BSB will handle the information we receive. Our Contact and Assessment Team will assess the report you have made and decide what the initial regulatory response should be. This may include sending for enforcement action, or passing the information to our Supervision Team.

21. Please note that, while the BSB would not normally stay in contact with you once you have made a report and it has been acknowledged, the BSB may request your assistance in supplying further information if it is necessary to carry out a proper assessment of the information or an investigation. All reports made to the BSB will be treated sensitively. If you wish to provide information confidentially, we may be able to take reasonable steps to protect your identity. However, depending on the facts of the case, it may be difficult to take enforcement action without identifying you.

When should you report?

22. Your duty to report serious misconduct is intended to help ensure that the BSB has the information that it needs in order to be able to assess risks and regulate effectively and in accordance with the regulatory objectives. With this practical purpose in mind, you are not expected to report unnecessarily or simply as a matter of form. Rule C68 removes the duty to report where:

   - the relevant facts are already in the public domain; and/or
   - you reasonably consider that those facts will have come to the BSB's attention; and/or
   - the relevant person has already reported the misconduct to the BSB.

23. Rule C68 exempts you from the duty to report if you are aware that the relevant person who committed the serious misconduct has already reported it to the BSB. In other cases, if you are aware that another relevant person, such as the head of chambers, head of legal practice, or a person or committee within a practice which has responsibility for the administration of that practice or for investigating the matter in the first instance, has made a report, then you do not need to do so yourself. However, if you are aware for any reason that the relevant person or committee has failed to report the matter to the BSB, or if there is another reason for not doing so, you should be

prepared to report the matter yourself. Guidance C96 lists failure by a barrister to report such matters promptly to the BSB as an example of potential serious misconduct.

24. You should also apply your professional judgement to whether there has been serious misconduct. Guidance C97 sets out some matters you should consider before reporting. These are:

- whether the individual's instructions or other confidential matters might have a bearing on the assessment of their conduct;
- whether the person concerned has been offered an opportunity to explain their conduct, and if not, why not;
- any explanation which has been or could be offered for that person's conduct;
- whether the matter has been raised, or will be raised, in the litigation in which it occurred, and if not, why not.

25. Depending on the nature of the misconduct, you may also wish to take further circumstances into account. In particular, you should consider whether there is a risk that the misconduct will continue or be repeated if no action is taken. For example, if the individual's behaviour relates to discrimination, harassment, victimisation, there may be a further risk of discrimination, harassment or victimisation occurring in the future (see below).

26. Having taken into account these and any other relevant circumstances, you should then go on to consider whether you have reasonable grounds to believe the individual has committed serious misconduct. You should report misconduct where you have material before you which as it stands establishes a reasonably credible instance of serious misconduct. Issues of competence will not normally constitute serious misconduct unless so serious that it poses a serious risk to the public or would diminish the trust and confidence which the public places in the profession.

27. Rule C67 states that you must never make, or threaten to make, a report of serious misconduct without a genuine and reasonably held belief that the obligation to report applies. For example, you should not report serious misconduct merely speculatively, out of malice, or to use the reporting of misconduct, or the threat of it, as a 'litigation tactic'. You should only make a report with regard to the outcomes which the rule is intended to achieve, described above.

Barristers acting in a judicial capacity

28. Serious misconduct before the court will usually be apparent to the judge, and in such cases, the judge hearing the matter may bring the serious misconduct in question to the attention of the BSB. If you are a barrister acting in a judicial capacity, your conduct duties as a judge take precedence over your professional duties as a barrister. The BSB would not expect to take enforcement action against a barrister acting in a judicial capacity. Whilst the obligation to report does not impact on a barrister sitting in a judicial capacity, nothing in this guidance should be taken as preventing barristers from reporting to the regulator serious misconduct observed by a barrister, when sitting, in the normal way.

29. Rules E23 – E24 cover the BSB approach to concerns raised about a regulated person acting in judicial or quasi-judicial capacity, and preclude the BSB from exercising enforcement powers in respect of such a regulated person. Any concerns raised with the BSB about the conduct of a barrister acting in a judicial capacity will be referred to the Judicial Conduct Investigations Office (http://judicialconduct.judiciary.gov.uk/).

October 2019
Bar Standards Board

Conducting Litigation Guidance

Introduction

1. This guidance document is for barristers, users of barristers' services and others who wish to understand:

   - the BSB's view on the activities that amount to the reserved legal activity of 'conduct of litigation';

   - how barristers can become authorised to conduct litigation; and

   - how to determine whether a barrister is authorised to conduct litigation.

2. The conduct of litigation is a reserved legal activity under the Legal Services Act 2007 (LSA). Barristers do not have the right to conduct litigation unless they are authorised by the BSB to do so, or are otherwise entitled to conduct litigation by virtue of other legislation. If a barrister conducts litigation without authorisation they are not only breaching the BSB Handbook, but also committing a criminal offence under the Legal Services Act 2007.

Section 1: What activities amount to 'conducting litigation'?

3. The LSA defines the conduct of litigation as:

   a. the issuing of proceedings before any court in England and Wales[1];

   b. the commencement, prosecution and defence of such proceedings; and

---

[1] The LSA defines 'court' in s207(1) as including some tribunals:
http://www.legislation.gov.uk/ukpga/2007/29/section/207

c.   the performance of any ancillary functions in relation to such proceedings (such as entering appearances to actions).

4.   The term 'ancillary functions' has been defined further in relation to civil litigation by *Agassi v Robinson* [2005] EWCA Civ 1507. The definition of ancillary functions is construed narrowly and limited to the formal steps required in the conduct of litigation.

5.   The BSB's view is that the following fall within the definition of the conduct of litigation, and therefore **a barrister should refuse to do them if they are not authorised to conduct litigation**:

- issuing proceedings or applications (beginning court proceedings by filing details of the claim, such as the Claim Form and Particulars of Claim, at court, or making an application for a court order);

- filing an acknowledgement of proceedings;

- giving their address as the address for service of documents;

- filing documents at court or serving documents on another party;

- issuing notices of appeal (informing the court and the other side that the unsuccessful party seeks a review of the case);

- signing off on a list of disclosure (so that all parties know of all documents which have a bearing on the case); and

BAR STANDARDS BOARD

REGULATING BARRISTERS

- laying of an information in a Magistrates' court.[2]

6. This list is not exhaustive. Given that the interpretation of 'ancillary functions' in the case law is somewhat of a grey area, the boundaries of what does and does not fall within 'conducting litigation' are somewhat unclear. Barristers should therefore carefully consider this guidance and relevant authorities before determining whether an activity constitutes the conduct of litigation. For example, the right to conduct litigation can only be delegated to an agent who has been properly authorised (*Gregory v Turner* [2003] EWCA Civ 183). Therefore litigants in person cannot conduct their litigation through an agent other than an authorised legal representative, such as a barrister authorised to conduct litigation.

7. If a barrister is authorised to conduct litigation:

- They must within an agreed timescale, or within a reasonable period of time, comply with any undertaking they give in the course of conducting litigation (Rule C11 in the BSB Handbook);

- This does not affect the prohibition on receiving or handling clients' money, except as payment for fees (Rule C73 – C75). The prohibition means that a barrister cannot make disbursements on behalf of a client; for example, by paying court fees or witnesses' expenses;

- They must, if they are of less than three years' standing, have a 'qualified person' for conducting litigation at their principal place of practice or, if they are practising in a dual capacity, at each of their principal places of practice (Rule S20.2). However, if an employed barrister in a non-authorised body is only conducting litigation for their employer, they only need to have a 'qualified

---

[2] *Media Protection Services Ltd v Crawford* [2012] EWHC 2373 (Admin)

3

person' for conducting litigation if they are of less than one year's standing. The purpose of a 'qualified person' is to be readily available to provide guidance to the barrister. The definition of a 'qualified person' for conducting litigation can be found at Rule S22.3;

- This does not affect the prohibition on undertaking the general management, administration or conduct of a client's affairs (Rule S25); and

- They may act as a 'professional client' i.e. instruct another barrister on behalf of a client. The definition of 'professional client' in the BSB Handbook states that 'any BSB authorised person who is authorised to conduct litigation' may give instructions to a barrister.

Section 2: What is not 'conducting litigation'?

8.   Certain activities look like they might fall within the definition of conducting litigation, but in fact do not. This is generally because it is work that barristers have traditionally done when instructed by solicitors. The BSB's view is that the following activities are therefore **permissible if a barrister is not authorised to conduct litigation**:

- *conducting correspondence on behalf of clients*. Barristers may send letters on their chambers' letterhead or faxes or e-mails. However, they must only conduct correspondence if they are satisfied it is in their client's best interests to do so, and they have adequate systems, experience and resources for managing the correspondence. They must also have adequate insurance in place which covers, amongst other things, any loss suffered by the client as a result of conducting correspondence. Finally, where the other side is legally represented and barristers are conducting correspondence in respect of the particular matter, they

are expected to correspond at all times with that other party's legal representative;

- *lodging documents for hearings.* It is proper for barristers or clerks to lodge certain types of document for hearings, provided that they are secondary to the barrister's role as an advocate. Barristers often draft the case summary, chronology, list of issues or position statement. There is nothing wrong with barristers or clerks lodging these sorts of document;

- *skeleton arguments.* Exchanging skeletons with an opponent or sending skeletons and bundles of authorities to the court is allowed. In a criminal case, defence barristers often hand a defence case statement to the Crown or the court;

- *covering applications to fix trial dates.* Clerks regularly fix trial dates to ensure that the date is convenient for the barrister instructed. It is also permissible for clerks to make representations to the Masters in relation to hearing dates;

- *court orders.* Liaising with the other side or the court over the preparation of an order is something barristers often do and is allowed. Clerks regularly deal with the sealing of court orders and so this, too, is permitted;

- *discharging a duty or a courtesy to the court.* For example, a letter or e-mail to a judge explaining an absence from court, or providing dates to avoid or corrections to a draft judgment;

- *signing a statement of truth.* A statement of truth may be signed by a legal representative, which is defined as including a barrister (Civil Procedure Rules Part 2.3). Therefore a barrister may sign a statement of truth on behalf of their client (*O'Connor v BSB* (2012)). However, a barrister should ensure that the

provisions of the Civil Procedure Rules are complied with before they do so, in particular Part 22 PD paragraph 3.8; and

- *instructing expert witnesses on behalf of a lay client*. While the instruction of an expert does not fall within the definition of the conduct of litigation, the filing of an expert report and serving the report on another party does fall within the definition. Part 35 of the Civil Procedure Rules also places duties on experts.

Section 3: Authorisation to conduct litigation

9.   There are three ways in which barristers are able to conduct litigation:

- self-employed and employed barristers can apply to the BSB for an extension to their practising certificate, authorising them to conduct litigation;

- employed barristers previously authorised to conduct litigation under Annex I of the Bar Code of Conduct (8th Edn.) will retain their authorisation, provided that they remain in employed practice. If they enter self-employed or dual capacity practice, they will need to apply to the BSB for authorisation to conduct litigation; or

- by being entitled to conduct litigation under primary legislation.

Authorisation to conduct litigation by the BSB

10.   Barristers who apply for authorisation to conduct litigation will need to satisfy the BSB that they have:

- appropriate systems in their place of practice to enable them to conduct litigation;

- the requisite skills and knowledge of litigation procedure to enable them to provide a competent service to clients; and

- adequate insurance. Members of the Bar Mutual Indemnity Fund are covered.

11.   More information on the application process for authorisation to conduct litigation can be found on the BSB's website.

12.   In addition, the LSA states that in order for reserved legal activities (including the conduct of litigation) to be delivered through an entity, both the entity and the individuals providing services must be authorised to do so. Employed barristers in entities who are conducting litigation must therefore ensure that the entity in which they are working is also authorised to conduct litigation.

13.   BSB regulated entities which apply for authorisation to conduct litigation will need to satisfy the BSB that they have at least one employee who is authorised to conduct litigation, and the necessary systems in place to be able to manage cases appropriately.

14.   More information on the application process for entity authorisation can be found on the BSB's website.

Entitlement to conduct litigation under primary legislation

15.   Barristers employed in central government roles (including Crown Prosecutors) may be entitled to conduct litigation without the need for authorisation from the BSB. The exemption from the requirement to seek authorisation from the BSB is by virtue of primary legislation.

16.   All barristers employed by the Crown Prosecution Service (CPS) who have been appointed as Crown Prosecutors do not need further authorisation from the BSB to conduct litigation within that role. The exemption applies because barristers employed in this capacity act under the authority of the Director of Public Prosecutions in accordance with the Prosecution of Offences Act 1985. Crown Prosecutors are not entitled to conduct litigation outside of their role with the CPS without first securing BSB authorisation to do so.

17.   Employed government barristers also have a right to conduct litigation as part of their employment by Treasury Solicitors, any government department, or any public body which performs functions on behalf of the Crown. This exemption applies because of historical and current legislation.

18.   It is important to note that the right to conduct litigation, unless otherwise specified by primary legislation, is restricted to the barrister's employment. Therefore:

   - if an employed barrister wishes to conduct litigation outside of their employment (for example, on a pro bono basis or for a law centre) they must seek authorisation from the BSB to do so;

   - if an employed barrister leaves their post, their entitlement to conduct litigation will cease; and

   - if an employed barrister changes their post and wishes to continue conducting litigation, they must either ensure that they are still entitled to do so, or seek authorisation from the BSB.

Section 4: Determining whether a barrister is authorised to conduct litigation

19. If a barrister is authorised by the BSB to conduct litigation, this will be listed on their entry on the BSB's Barristers' Register. The Barristers' Register can be found on the BSB's website.

20. Employed barristers in entities who are conducting litigation must ensure that the entity in which they are working is also authorised to conduct litigation. If a BSB regulated entity is authorised by the BSB to conduct litigation, this will be listed on its entry on the BSB's Entities' Register. The Entities' Register can also be found on the BSB's website.

21. If a barrister is entitled to conduct litigation under primary legislation, this will not be listed on their entry on the BSB's Barristers' Register. This is because their right to conduct litigation is by virtue of primary legislation, and not authorisation from the BSB (see the 'Entitlement to conduct litigation under primary legislation' section above).

October 2019
Bar Standards Board

Public Access Guidance for Barristers

Contents

Scope of this guidance

1. A barrister may accept instructions directly from or on behalf of a member of public, also known as a lay client (the "client") (rS24 of the Scope of Practice section of the BSB Handbook). This is known as Public Access. In carrying out Public Access work a barrister must comply with the BSB Handbook and in particular the Public Access Rules which are at rC119-rC131 of the Code of Conduct section.

2. This document gives guidance on the interpretation of the Handbook and good practice. You should have regard to it in considering whether to accept and in carrying out Public Access instructions in accordance with the rules set out in the Handbook.

Qualification requirements

3. Before you may accept Public Access instructions, you must:

    (1) Hold a full practising certificate. If you have less than three years' standing you must have a qualified person readily available to you to provide guidance, if necessary (see paragraph 4 below);

    (2) Have undertaken and satisfactorily completed a Bar Standards Board approved training course. Details of such courses can be obtained from the BSB's website;

    (3) Notify the Bar Council (acting by the BSB) of your intention to undertake such work; and

    (4) Have insurance cover as required by the Handbook. BMIF cover satisfies this requirement.

Additional requirements for barristers with less than three years' standing

4.   If you are less than three years' standing and undertaking Public Access work, you must have a qualified person available to provide guidance. A person shall be a "qualified person" for these purposes if they are Public Access registered and have[1]:

(a) been entitled to practise and have practised as a barrister or have been authorised to practise by another approved regulator for a period (which need not have been as a person authorised by the same approved regulator) of at least six years in the previous eight years;

(b) made such practice their primary occupation for the previous two years; and

(c) been entitled to exercise a right of audience before every court in relation to all proceedings.

Nature and scope of Public Access work

5.   A barrister may accept Public Access instructions in any area of practice. You are reminded that rC21.8 of the Handbook prohibits you from accepting instructions if you lack sufficient experience or competence to handle the matter. In a Public Access case you should remember that dealing directly with a client may be more difficult or demanding than acting for a professional client and you must be able to handle those demands.

6.   Public Access does not widen the types of work a barrister may do. You are performing the same functions as you would if you were instructed by a solicitor. Examples of the type of work you may do for a Public Access client are:

---

[1] rS22, BSB Handbook

- advocacy;

- drafting documents;

- advising in writing or in conference;

- representation in alternative dispute resolution (ADR) such as mediation or arbitration;

- Negotiating on behalf of your client;

- Investigating and collecting evidence. **You should however have regard to the guidance on investigating or collecting evidence and taking witness statements which is published on the BSB's website.** In particular, you must not conduct a case in court if you have previously investigated or collected evidence in the case unless you reasonably believe that the investigation and collection of that evidence is unlikely to be challenged;

- Corresponding on behalf of your client. You may send letters on your chambers' letterhead or faxes or emails. However, you must only conduct correspondence if you are satisfied it is in your client's best interests to do so and you have adequate systems, experience and resources for managing the correspondence (see relevant guidance at gC24 and gC71). Bear in mind that solicitors' offices have systems for logging incoming and outgoing correspondence and dealing with urgent letters in the absence of the fee earner which your chambers may not be able to offer.

4

General restrictions

(A) Restriction on conducting litigation without authorisation

7.   Public Access does not put barristers on a par with solicitors. A key difference is
     that solicitors may conduct litigation on behalf of their client. A barrister in
     independent practice does not have the right to conduct litigation unless authorised
     by the BSB to do so. If you conduct litigation without authorisation you are not only
     breaching the Handbook but also committing a criminal offence under the Legal
     Services Act 2007.

8.   The Legal Services Act 2007 defines the conduct of litigation as:

     a.   the issuing of proceedings before any court in England and Wales;

     b.   the commencement, prosecution and defence of such proceedings; and

     c.   the performance of any ancillary functions in relation to such proceedings
          (such as entering appearances to actions).

9.   The BSB takes the view that the following fall within this definition and therefore
     you should refuse to do them if you are not authorised to conduct litigation:

     •   issuing proceedings or applications;

     •   acknowledging service of proceedings;

     •   giving your address as the address for service;

- filing documents at court or serving documents on another party; and

- issuing notices of appeal.

10. You may advise your client on how to take any of these steps. For example, you may advise on the procedure for lodging an appeal and you may of course draft the grounds of appeal. However, the steps in question must be taken by the client as a litigant in person if you are not authorised to do them. Normally Public Access clients who are litigants in person will be expected to be able to perform the activities usually undertaken by an authorised litigator with little or no prompting. If this is not the case, you must consider whether it is proper to act on a Public Access basis (see paragraphs 18 to 22 below). This consideration is particularly relevant when dealing with vulnerable clients. 'Vulnerable clients' is interpreted widely and may include clients who have English as a second language, who have mental or physical impairments or who are otherwise vulnerable e.g. because of their age, caring responsibilities or immigration status.

11. Certain activities at first blush look like they might fall within the definition of conducting litigation but in fact do not. This is generally because it is work that barristers have traditionally done when instructed by solicitors. The following are therefore **permissible if you are not authorised to conduct litigation**:

- Lodging documents for hearings. It is proper for you or your clerk to lodge certain types of documents for hearings, provided that they are ancillary to your role as an advocate. Barristers often draft the case summary, chronology, list of issues or position statement. There is nothing wrong with clerks or barristers lodging this sort of documents.

- Skeleton arguments. Exchanging skeletons with an opponent or sending skeletons and bundles of authorities to the court is allowed. In a criminal

case, defence barristers often hand a defence case statement to the Crown or the court and this would also be permitted if instructed directly.

- Covering applications to fix trial dates. Clerks regularly fix trial dates to ensure that the date is convenient for counsel instructed. This is permissible whether instructed by a solicitor and therefore also when instructed directly. Clerks making representations to the Masters in relation to hearing dates is permissible for the same reasons.

- Court orders. Liaising with the other side or the court over the preparation of an order is something barristers often do and is allowed. Clerks regularly deal with the sealing of court orders and so this, too, is permitted.

- Discharging a duty or a courtesy to the court. For example, a letter or e-mail to a judge explaining an absence from court or providing dates to avoid or corrections to a draft judgment.

- Signing a statement of truth. A statement of truth may be signed by a legal representative, which is defined as including a barrister (Civil Procedure Rules Part 2.3). Therefore you may sign a statement of truth on behalf of your client (*O'Connor v BSB* (2012) Visitors to the Inns of Court, August 17, unrep.). However, you should ensure that the provisions of the Civil Procedure Rules are complied with before you do so, in particular Part 22 PD paragraph 3.8.

For further information on the restriction on conducting litigation without authorisation, you should refer to the BSB's 'Conducting Litigation Guidance', which is published on the BSB's website.

(B) Code of Conduct restrictions

12.   The following are expressly prohibited by the Code of Conduct:

- Receiving or handling clients' money, except as payment for fees. The prohibition against holding clients' money means that a barrister cannot make disbursements on behalf of a client, for example by paying court fees or witnesses' expenses (rC73-rC75, BSB Handbook).

- Undertaking the general management, administration or conduct of a client's affairs (rS25, BSB Handbook).

Public funding (legal aid)

13.   In each case, before a barrister accepts a Public Access instruction, it is a Code of Conduct requirement to:

> 'Take such steps as are reasonably necessary to ensure that the client is able to make an informed decision about whether to apply for legal aid or whether to proceed with Public Access.' (rC120.4, BSB Handbook)

14.   If a client qualifies for legal aid it may be, and often will be, in their best interests to instruct a solicitor on a public funding basis. There may however be some situations where the client will prefer to instruct a barrister on Public Access – for example if their legal aid contributions would be higher than instructing a barrister without a solicitor, or they want to instruct a more senior barrister, such as a QC, than they would be entitled to on legal aid.

15.   It is important that the client makes an informed choice about public funding. In many cases it will be obvious from the nature of the case, or the nature of the client,

that public funding is unlikely to be available. However, in other cases you may take the view that it would be in the best interests of the client to explore their eligibility for legal aid. In those cases, you are likely to want to discuss this with them when you first meet and draw their attention to where they can find out more about legal aid and get help to assess their eligibility. Before accepting an instruction, you will want to discuss this matter with the client to ensure that they understand the position regarding legal aid, have made an informed decision and that proceeding on a Public Access basis will be in their best interests.

16.   **Information for clients about public funding is available in the guidance for lay clients, which is available on the BSB's website.**

17.   The model client care letter (see paragraph 30 below) explains that a barrister cannot be instructed directly on a legal aid basis, gives details of how the client can find out if they are eligible for public funding and the basis on which you can advise and represent them. Writing to your client in the terms set out in the model client care letter can therefore help to demonstrate that you have covered this matter with them.

Interests of the client and interests of justice

18.   You cannot accept Public Access instructions if you form the view that it is either in the best interests of your client or in the interests of justice for the client to instruct a solicitor or other professional client (rC120.3, BSB Handbook). This is a continuing duty which you must keep under review during the course of a case.

19.   This decision is likely to depend both on the complexity of the case, the capability of the client and whether you are authorised to conduct litigation e.g. a well-resourced client, such as a large corporation, may be able to handle very complex litigation.

20.   In making this assessment you are likely to reach one of three views:

- The level of the case and the likely work involved is within the client's capabilities and there is no obvious reason why a solicitor or other professional client should be instructed.

- The case is of such complexity or has reached a stage that it is not in the client's interests or the interests of justice to instruct a barrister without a solicitor or other professional client. Having reached such a view, you can no longer act on a Public Access basis. You would be able to act if instructed by a solicitor (or other professional client) and you can make recommendations as to who could act.

- The case may well become complex and may involve work which the client cannot do, but you do not consider that a solicitor or other professional client needs to be instructed yet.

21.   In every case you must make your client aware at the outset that there may be circumstances in which you will have to recommend that a solicitor (or other professional client) is instructed, and that you will have to withdraw if that advice is not heeded. There is a paragraph in the model client care letter (see paragraph 30 below) setting this out.

22.   It is essential that barristers should consider at every point at which they are instructed whether a client needs to instruct a solicitor and to advise as soon as it becomes clear that this is the case. This is of particular importance where limitation periods are involved or where hearings are imminent. Barristers failing to do this may find themselves at risk of actions in negligence, findings of inadequate professional service by the Legal Ombudsman, or professional misconduct charges by the BSB.

REGULATING BARRISTERS

Relationship with client

(A) Initial contact

23. It is likely that initial contact will be by a telephone call or email between the client and yourself or your clerk, or the receipt of written instructions in chambers. You are required to keep a record of the date that instructions were received, the name of the client, the name of the case and any requirement of the client as to time limits (rC128). As you will also need to send a client care letter you will need the client's address.

24. You may take the view that a preliminary meeting is required. This may be necessary to comply with the requirements of the Money Laundering Regulations (see paragraphs 74 to 77 below). If so, you should write to the client summarising those regulations and setting out what is required in order to satisfy the identification requirements. A preliminary meeting may be helpful to decide whether you will accept the instructions. It is open to you to accept instructions for the limited purpose of reading papers and advising whether you are able to perform substantive professional work; in such a situation it is open to you to make an arrangement that you are paid a fee for doing so. If you decide to charge for the preliminary meeting, a client care letter should be sent to the client in the usual way, setting out the charge for the advice and any other work done and making it clear that you do not agree to do more in the first instance than assess whether or not you can assist the client. In many cases, you may consider that it is good client care not to charge for a preliminary meeting.

11

(B) Identifying and representing vulnerable clients

25. There are a number of factors which may make a client vulnerable and which may have implications for how you manage their case. Some of these factors may be obvious, for example a client may be very young or may not be able to speak English. Issues related to the protected characteristics listed in the Equality Act 2010 which may make a client vulnerable include:

Race

- Clients with English as a second, third or non-existent language.
- Asylum seeking or refugee clients who may have mental health issues such as post-traumatic stress conditions related to treatment (e.g. torture or persecution) in their home country.
- Immigration clients who may have been separated from their families or who are new to the UK, may be unfamiliar with the UK legal system and who may have difficulties carrying out litigation work.

Gender

- Clients with caring responsibilities for young or disabled children, particularly lone parents who may have difficulties in undertaking tasks such as serving documentation at court.
- Clients with caring responsibilities for older dependents, in particular lone carers.
- Lone parents who may have access to less financial resources than other clients.
- Sensitivity of men or women in relation to one to one meetings with the opposite sex – if this is necessary or in relation to questioning/discussion of intimate subjects.

<u>Disability</u>

- Clients with physical impairments which may impact upon their ability to undertake physical aspects of litigation.
- Clients with physical or mental health issues which may impact upon their ability to undertake litigation activities.
- Clients with learning disabilities.
- Clients who are heavily reliant on carers to manage their day to day activities.

<u>Age</u>

- Very young clients.
- Clients who for reasons relating to their age (particularly older clients) may find the physical aspects of litigation difficult.
- Clients who for reasons relating to their age have difficulties associated with memory loss and/or confusion.

<u>Pregnancy/maternity</u>

- Heavily pregnant or new mothers who may find the physical aspects of conducting litigation difficult.
- New mothers with post-natal health issues affecting physical mobility or mental health (e.g. post-natal depression).

<u>Gender re-assignment</u>

- Clients undergoing transition (which may involve frequent visits to hospital or other medical appointments).

<u>Religion or belief</u>

- Clients whose religious beliefs make it difficult for them to undertake litigation activities on particular days or at particular times.

26.   Other relevant factors to consider in relation to the vulnerability of a client include:

- Limited access to financial resources to pay for the cost of litigation activities or additional unforeseen costs.
- Illiteracy or low levels of literacy.
- Vulnerability or trauma arising from the matter at issue (e.g. the matter involves a serious crime such as serious assaults or sexual offences perpetrated against the client).
- Homelessness.
- Drug or alcohol dependency or other addiction issues.

27.   The term 'vulnerable client' should be interpreted widely. You will need to identify any factors that may make a client vulnerable when considering whether or not to take on their case. Having identified any such factors, you will need to consider what additional measures, if any, are necessary to ensure that the client is supported properly and understands fully any information which you communicate to them, so that you may act in their best interests. This may involve ensuring that documentation provided to your client is translated into another language or into plain English. You should also consider whether you can direct the client to any external resources or agencies for further advice and support.

(C) The basis of the agreement and the client care letter

28.   The agreement between barrister and client is contractual. This means that:

- the barrister is bound by the agreement and may be liable in contract for failure to perform;
- it should be clear what is to be done under the contract, the charging rate and any other special terms that may be agreed (note your general duties under rC22 in addition to the Public Access Rules); and

- the barrister will be able to sue for fees.

29.   There are a number of things a barrister must inform his client about at the outset of the agreement. These are set out in rC125. They include warning a client that you are an independent practitioner and there may be occasions where a clash of professional commitments prevents you from carrying out an instruction.

30.   **A model client care letter is on the BSB's website.** Provided you have promptly written to your client in the terms of the model letter you will have complied with the notification requirements in rC125. Where the client has previously instructed you in respect of the same matter it may well be unnecessary for you to provide a full client care letter in respect of every new instruction received. Barristers must still ensure that the fundamentals of the client care letter are set out in respect of each new instruction i.e. the work that is to be undertaken, the cost and the payment mechanism. Other matters which you are required to inform your client about, such as the barrister's limitations (if any) with respect to litigation, how to complain and the fact the barrister may have to withdraw can be covered by referring the client to the original client care letter.

31.   It may also be possible in limited circumstances for you to enter into a retainer or novel fee arrangement with a Public Access client. However, care should be taken to ensure you continue to observe your general Handbook duties around independence and conflict of interest.

(D) Non-discrimination rules

32.   In deciding not to accept an instruction, you should be mindful of rC28 of the Handbook. This states that you must not withhold your services or permit your services to be withheld:

    a.   on the ground that the nature of the case is objectionable to you or to any section of the public;

    b.   on the ground that the conduct, opinions or beliefs of the prospective client are unacceptable to you or to any section of the public; or

    c.   on any ground relating to the source of any financial support which may properly be given to the prospective client for the proceedings in question.

33.   rC12 states that a barrister must not discriminate unlawfully against, victimise or harass any other person on the grounds of race, colour, ethnic or national origin, nationality, citizenship, sex, gender re-assignment, sexual orientation, marital or civil partnership status, disability, age, religion or belief or pregnancy and maternity.

34.   The effect of these rules is that, whilst the 'cab rank' rule does not apply to Public Access cases, you must not discriminate in the way you accept, refuse or carry out Public Access instructions. Potential clients may feel aggrieved if a barrister refuses to take on a case and may allege that they did so for improper reasons. It would be prudent for a barrister refusing a case to make a brief note of the reasons for so doing in case this is questioned in future.

(E) Withdrawal from a case

35.   rC25 to rC27 of the Handbook highlight the scenarios where a barrister must or may cease to act and return instructions.

36.   In addition to the usual reasons for withdrawal from a case, barristers are required to cease to act in a Public Access case where they have formed the view (for instance, as a result of receiving further information about the case) that it is in the

interests of the client or in the interests of justice for the client to instruct a solicitor or other professional client.

37.   If, as a result of being told that you cannot continue to act without a solicitor or professional client being instructed, the client instructs a solicitor or other professional client, then you will be able to continue to act. It is open to you, therefore, to give the client the opportunity to instruct a solicitor or other professional client before you finally withdraw from the case.

38.   In a Public Access case, the issue of withdrawing from a case will only arise once you have accepted the instruction. That will usually be when the client care letter is sent. You will need to take care in deciding whether to withdraw not only because you owe a duty under the Handbook to act in the best interests of your client, but also because you may owe them contractual duties. Unless your decision to withdraw is justified by your obligations under the Handbook you are likely to place yourself in breach of your contract with the client.

39.   It will therefore very rarely be appropriate for you to withdraw where there is simply a difference of opinion between yourself and the client. In particular, the fact that a client legitimately rejects your advice on tactics or a settlement will not in itself justify you in withdrawing from the case; nor does the fact that a client may raise a minor complaint or question about the service provided by you. Where such disagreements arise, however, you would be prudent to make full attendance notes of the discussion and have them agreed by the client.

40.   A barrister acting for a client who is a party to proceedings must bear in mind the particular difficulties which the client might encounter if the barrister withdraws. A hearing may be imminent, or the client may experience real difficulty in finding a solicitor willing to take on the case. Where there is doubt, or a difference of opinion as to whether you should withdraw, and withdrawal would or might cause

difficulties for the client, it would be prudent for a barrister to contact the Bar Council's Ethical Enquiries Service: https://www.barcouncil.org.uk/supporting-the-bar/ethical-enquiries-service/

41.   Where you consider that you are required to withdraw and it appears that, by reason of the proximity of a hearing, a client may have difficulty finding another lawyer to take on the case in the time available, you should provide such assistance as is proper to protect the client's position. This can include:

    a.   applying to the court for an adjournment if it is necessary to withdraw during the course of the hearing;

    b.   drafting letters for the client to send to the court and the other side seeking an adjournment;

    c.   providing supporting letters for the client explaining that, for professional reasons, you have had to withdraw and, so far as this is possible without breaching confidentiality or prejudicing the client's position, explaining the reasons;

    d.   where the matter is urgent or it is otherwise appropriate, contacting solicitors or other suitable intermediaries who may be willing to take on the client's case.

(F) Complaints

42.   The Handbook requires barristers to have in-house procedures for dealing with complaints (rC99-rC109). Such procedures can be a useful source of feedback to chambers and also a way of retaining client goodwill when mistakes occur. Public Access work may result in chambers receiving a substantially greater number of

complaints from clients, which may or may not be legitimate. However, all such complaints should be addressed and acted upon within an appropriate timescale.

43.   **You should have regard to the BSB's guidance on first tier complaints handling, which is available on the BSB's website.** In particular, you must:

   a.   ensure that the client is told about the procedure in the client care letter;

   b.   deal with complaints promptly and according to that procedure as they arise;

   c.   inform the client that, if they are dissatisfied with the way in which the complaint has been handled, they may refer it to the Legal Ombudsman.

Fees

(A) Notifying the client

44.   If you accept Public Access instructions you must forthwith notify your client in clear and readily understandable terms of the work you have agreed to perform and the fees which you propose to charge or the basis on which your fee will be calculated. You should therefore complete those parts of the model client care letter which deals with these matters.

45.   rC22 and rC88 require barristers to keep adequate records to support fees charged, and to provide such records or details to clients on request. Such records should contain separate items for each piece of paperwork and, where substantial telephone advice is provided, separate items for each piece of such advice. If the client requires further detail and, notably, the exact work done and the cost of it in respect of each item involved this should be provided.

(B) Payment in advance

46.   rC73 prohibits a barrister from handling client money. The associated guidance
       (gC106-gC107) clarifies that a fixed fee paid in advance is not client money for the
       purposes of rC73. If you agree with a client, who can reasonably be expected to
       understand the implications of such an agreement, that (1) your fee for any work
       will be charged according to the time spent on it, but (2) you will be paid a fixed fee
       in advance for it, and (3), when the work has been done, you will pay the client any
       difference between that fixed fee and the fee which has actually been earned, and
       (4) you will not hold the difference between the fixed fee and the fee which has
       been earned on trust for the client, that difference will not be client money. Such
       fees may be considered as client money if you cannot demonstrate that the
       agreement was made in advance and on clear terms. You should also consider
       carefully whether such an arrangement is in the client's interest and that the client
       fully understands the implications.

(C) Withholding paperwork until paid

47.   Barristers may withhold paperwork until fees have been received. However, it
       should be made clear to the client at the time of instruction that this will be the
       arrangement. It should be expressly stated in the client care letter. Barristers
       should note that while they are permitted to withhold the work they have done, they
       may not be permitted to withhold the client's papers.

(D) Lien

48.   We are not aware of any authority by which barristers gain a general lien on
       documents belonging to the client until the fees are paid, although there seems to
       be nothing in the law to invalidate an express agreement made between a barrister
       and a client permitting the barrister to exercise such a lien. In the absence of a

contractually enforceable lien you should return the papers to your client on request, but first ensure that you have complied with your record keeping obligations (see paragraphs 69 to 73 below).

(E) Disbursements

49.   You may agree with your client that you are entitled to charge disbursements, such as travel and accommodation expenses and photocopying. This can include charging for the work of a clerk, administrative assistant or paralegal. This must be agreed in advance and therefore should be included in the client care letter.

(F) Overcharging and disputes

50.   It is likely that clients will, on occasion, seek to dispute the amount that is charged by a barrister or to claim that they have been overcharged. The scope for such disputes is obviously greatly reduced if there is clarity about the charging arrangements beforehand.

51.   It is obviously appropriate for you to seek to resolve the dispute informally if this is possible. Otherwise two options exist:

a.   the client can refuse to pay and the dispute may have to be resolved by litigation;

b.   the client can complain to the Legal Ombudsman (LeO) if they consider that you have provided inadequate professional services. In appropriate cases LeO has the power to fine you and/or order that fees be repaid. LeO may also refer information to the Bar Standards Board where the alleged conduct may amount to a breach of the Handbook.

(G) Conditional Fee Agreements (CFA) and Damages-based Agreements

52.   While in principle there is nothing to prevent barristers undertaking Public Access work on a Conditional Fee Agreement or a Damages-based Agreement, particular care should be taken with such arrangements. You should consider the level of risk and the likelihood of recovering base costs and the success fee in the case of a Conditional Fee Agreement and the likelihood of recovering the percentage of the claimant's damages in the case of a Damages-based Agreement.

53.   You should also consider the question of payment. Payment in advance or on completion of a particular piece of work would not be possible since, by definition, no fee is payable until success had been achieved. Generally, any money paid in advance would be considered client money and barristers are not permitted to hold this (see paragraph 46 above for circumstances when payment in advance may be possible). If you require further advice please contact the Bar Council's Ethical Enquiries Service: https://www.barcouncil.org.uk/supporting-the-bar/ethical-enquiries-service/

Intermediaries

54.   You may find yourself asked to perform legal services by a person or organisation that is an intermediary, for the benefit of a named client. For example, an independent financial adviser may wish to take advice for a client, or arrange to have a document drafted. A son or daughter may want to instruct you on behalf of an elderly parent. A sponsor in this country may wish you to act in an immigration matter for a person who is out of the country. There is no objection in principle to a barrister accepting instructions from such an intermediary, but care must be taken in respect of a number of matters.

55.   You must ensure that the intermediary is not acting, or proposing to act, as a 'litigator'. It is a criminal offence under the Legal Services Act 2007 for an unauthorised person to act as a litigator, and a barrister who facilitated such activity might also be criminally liable.

56.   When specifically providing services to an immigration adviser who is acting as an intermediary, barristers should satisfy themselves that they are not engaging with anyone who is acting outside of the Immigration and Asylum Act 1999 (IAA 1999), as anyone acting in this way would be committing a criminal offence and be liable to face prosecution. Barristers who accept work which is within the scope of the IAA 1999 and do so from an OISC regulated advisor should take steps to ensure they are aware of what that advisor is entitled to do.

57.   You must ensure that both intermediary and client understand the true nature of the arrangement. To this end, you should send a client care letter to both the intermediary and the client. It is assumed that the intermediary will undertake contractual responsibility for your fees. If the intermediary does not wish to do so, you would be entitled to enquire why you should deal with the intermediary at all, rather than directly with the client. **Model letters to both intermediary and client are available on the BSB's website.**

58.   You should bear in mind the possibility that the intermediary may have negotiated a contingent fee arrangement with the client and the potential conflict of interest which could thus arise between the intermediary and the client. Barristers are already familiar with the risks of potential conflicts of interest between solicitors and clients where conditional fee agreements have been made. However, in the case of unregulated intermediaries you may feel that there is an even greater need to be alert to the risk that the manner in which information is transmitted to you may have been coloured by the intermediary's own commercial interests.

23

59.   If you form the view that there is a conflict of interest between client and intermediary, for example, because the intermediary has been negligent, Core Duty 2, rules such as rC15 and rC17 and related guidance require you to consider whether it would be in the client's interest to instruct another professional, and, if you consider it would be, you must both so advise and take steps to ensure that such advice reaches the client. However, it is not your duty to police the relationship between intermediary and client, which is a matter private to them.

60.   Where the intermediary instructs you to perform advocacy services, for example, before a domestic tribunal or in an arbitration, you must take such steps as appear appropriate to ensure that the client does, in fact, wish you to appear for them. In many cases this will involve having a conference with the client. A barrister performing advocacy services should inform the tribunal that they are acting for their client. You have the same obligation to a tribunal to which you send a skeleton argument.

61.   You must have regard to the relevant provisions of the Money Laundering Regulations (see paragraphs 74 to 77 below). Where instructed by an intermediary, you must normally follow the identification procedures in respect of the client. The only exception will be where the intermediary is a regulated professional and informs you by letter or certificate that they are a professional within the regulated sector as defined in Proceeds of Crime Act (POCA) and the Money Laundering Regulations and have carried out identification procedures.

62.   If you are approached by an intermediary you remain under the same obligation to satisfy yourself before accepting the case that it is appropriate to do so without a solicitor or other professional client as you would be under if you were approached by the client direct. If you are familiar with the intermediary and the way in which the intermediary operates then this will be a relevant factor, but will not obviate the

need for you, in respect of each prospective case, to satisfy yourself that no solicitor is required.

63. The client care letter to the client should be sent to the client's home or, as appropriate, business address and not to the intermediary's address. The client's address will therefore be one of the pieces of information which you will need before accepting instructions through an intermediary.

64. It is prohibited for you to pay or receive a referral fee to or from an intermediary, or to any other person for introducing a client or providing you with work. **Full guidance on referral fees can be found on the BSB's website.**

Advertising and referrals

65. It is common, particularly in Public Access, for barristers to use advertising and marketing services, barrister owned referral companies and third party introducers to obtain work. For example:

    1) Barristers may appoint a marketing or advertising business to promote their services;

    2) Barristers may establish, own and manage a limited company in order to advertise and market their services more effectively; and

    3) Third parties may set up services (which are often web-based platforms) to introduce Public Access clients to barristers. If you are obtaining work from a third party, you are practising in an association and must comply with the Associations with Others Rules in the BSB Handbook (Rules C79 – C85). In particular, you must complete the Associations Notification Form and return it to the BSB's Supervision

Department (Supervision@BarStandardsBoard.org.uk). The Associations Notification Form is available on the BSB's website.

66. In using these three models to obtain work, barristers must ensure that they do not breach the prohibition on paying or receiving referral fees (Rule C10 in the BSB Handbook and associated guidance). **Further guidance on using these models and not breaching the referral fees prohibition can be found in the BSB's 'Referral Fees Guidance', which is available on the BSB's website.**

67. In using these models to obtain work, barristers must also take steps to ensure that:

   o They do not enter into terms which interfere with their duties to act independently and in their clients' best interests (Core Duties 2 and 4 in the BSB Handbook);

   o In accordance with Rule C73 in the BSB Handbook, they do not handle client money (this also applies to anyone acting on a barrister's behalf). If a barrister decides in principle to take a case, they may request an 'upfront' fixed fee from a potential client before finally agreeing to the work. This should only be done having regard to Guidance C107 of the BSB Handbook, or there may be a breach of Rule C73. In particular, a barrister should never accept an upfront fee before considering whether it is appropriate for them to take the case, and considering whether they will be able to undertake the work in a reasonable time;

   o If they make use of third party payment services, they must comply with Rule C74 in the BSB Handbook and note the associated guidance;

- o   Companies which are not authorised by a legal regulator are not providing reserved legal activities (in breach of the Legal Services Act 2007);

- o   In accordance with Rule C19 in the BSB Handbook (not misleading clients and potential clients), any advertising and marketing material is accurate, clear and not likely to mislead;

- o   Clients are not confused about who is responsible for the service provided, and the service operates as described;

- o   Clients are not confused about the extent to which activity is regulated by the BSB, or by another regulator; and

- o   Clients are not confused about what redress they have (and against whom) if things go wrong. In accordance with Rule C99 in the BSB Handbook, clients must be notified in writing about their right to complain to the barrister/chambers, right to complain to the Legal Ombudsman (if any) and right to complain to any third party. Clients must also be notified in writing about how to complain and, in accordance with Rule C103 in the BSB Handbook, chambers' websites must display information about the complaints procedure. Clients should be clear about when they are complaining to a barrister/chambers and when they are complaining to a third party.

68.   Finally, barristers are reminded that their obligations under Core Duty 5 in the BSB Handbook require them not to act in an association with a person where, merely by being associated with such a person, they may reasonably be considered as bringing the profession into disrepute. Barristers are encouraged to undertake appropriate due diligence on third parties and how their services operate before agreeing to use them.

Administration and record keeping

69.   When taking on Public Access work, chambers need to be aware that the expectations of clients are likely to be very different from those of solicitors. They will not necessarily understand that barristers work on a different basis from solicitors and that it will not always be possible to speak directly to the barrister and that there are limits to what can and cannot be done by barristers. This should be made clear at an early stage and may be something that you would want to discuss with a client at a preliminary meeting. Barristers and clerks may need to adopt a flexible approach to dealing directly with the public and keep under review whether chambers' administration should be adjusted accordingly.

70.   In the absence of a solicitor it will be crucial for you to maintain records about your role in providing advice to the client in case questions or complaints arise afterwards. In particular, if it is not clear from other documentation, you should maintain a record of:

    a.   the initial contact with the client;

    b.   the work you have been asked to do;

    c.   the dates of conferences and notes of advice given;

    d.   records of telephone conversations and advice given;

    e.   significant changes to instructions; and

    f.   hearings attended and advice given.

These records should be retained for at least seven years.

71.   It is likely that clients will provide you with original documents. It is for each barrister to decide, in consultation with the client, whether they wish to retain those documents or work from copies. It is perfectly appropriate to charge for photocopying the documents but you should make it clear in your client care letter

The Bar Standards Board
Handbook

what the charge will be. You may also be asked to store the original documents on behalf of the client, but barristers are strongly discouraged from agreeing to do so unless retention by you is required in order to undertake litigation on behalf of the client (if you have been authorised to do so). The following matters should be kept in mind:

a. the original documents belong to the client and, unless otherwise agreed (for example because a lien has been agreed), must be returned to the client on demand at any stage;

b. if you agree to store original documents for the client you must keep the documents in a secure place and may be liable in negligence for failing to do so;

c. it will almost always be impractical for you to store original documents for long periods of time unless your chambers is prepared to guarantee such a service even after you have left chambers or ceased to practise. If originals are retained, you should specify to the client a date by which they must be collected or will be returned.

72. In any case it is prudent to keep papers following the conclusion of the case because there might be an appeal, a complaint or an action for professional negligence. If a solicitor is instructed that obligation generally falls on the solicitor. In a Public Access case the obligation falls on the barrister. You must keep for a period of seven years the originals, copies or a list of all documents you have received or take reasonable steps to ensure that the client will do so.

73. Electronic storage is permissible if appropriate – you may wish to consult the Bar Council for further information and guidance on Information Security.

Money laundering and proceeds of crime

74.   If you undertake work that falls within the Money Laundering and Terrorist Financing and Transfer of Funds (Information on the Payer) Regulations 2017 ("Regulations") then you have specific obligations under the Regulations. The BSB along with other legal regulators has produced detailed guidance on the Regulations and AML compliance ("Guidance"). **The Guidance can be accessed on the BSB's website.**

   The Bar Council has also produced an additional document with some case studies to further assist barristers, chambers and BSB entities in deciding whether the work that they do falls within the scope of the Regulations. The document can be accessed on the Bar Council's website.

75.   Barristers and BSB entities are most likely to undertake work within the ambit of the Regulations in the following circumstances:

   o   As tax advisers in accordance with 11(d) of the Regulations;
   o   Participating in a financial or real property transaction by assisting a client in the planning or execution of a transaction involving the buying and selling of real property or business entities, or in relation to the creation, operation or management of companies or trusts or similar structures; and
   o   Acting as a trust or company service provider in accordance with 12(2) of the Regulations.

76.   Regulation 19 requires barristers, chambers and BSB entities who conduct work within the Regulations to have written policies, controls and procedures (PCPs) in place to mitigate and manage money laundering risks identified in their risk assessment. Detailed information is contained in the Guidance but in summary the PCPs must address the following:

- Customer due diligence (see regulations 27 to 38);
- Record keeping procedures (see regulations 39 to 40);
- Risk management practices;
- Internal controls (see regulations 21 to 24);
- Disclosures to the National Crime Agency; and
- The monitoring and management of compliance with the PCPs.

77. Under the Proceeds of Crime Act 2002, it is an offence to enter into or become concerned in an arrangement which you know or suspect facilitates (by whatever means) the acquisition, retention, use or control of criminal property by or on behalf of another person.

Solicitors and professional clients

78. Two main issues arise in respect of solicitors and other professional clients in relation to Public Access work:

   a.   acceptance of work where there is already a solicitor or professional client advising the client; and

   b.   the recommendation of solicitors to Public Access clients.

79. There is no objection to you accepting instructions from a client where a solicitor is currently instructed in the matter, if the solicitor is aware that the client is doing so. There is no obligation on the solicitor to instruct you directly and, in some cases, solicitors having done the necessary preparatory work will be content for the client then to brief you directly. In such circumstances, however, it is important that you should:

a.   consider whether there is any reason why the solicitor needs to instruct you directly (for example, because the matter is complex or the client cannot properly undertake the litigation component of the case, if you are not authorised to do so);

b.   be satisfied that the solicitor is aware that the client is instructing you.

If you are satisfied that the client does not require a solicitor's involvement, then you may accept the case.

80.   A more difficult question arises where the solicitor does not know that the client is coming to you for advice. In some cases, the client will be seeking advice on the conduct of the solicitor or for a second opinion. Here there is no reason why you should not provide advice. You should not inform the solicitor of this without the client's consent. Where a case is litigious it is advisable for you, if client gives their consent, to liaise with the solicitor as necessary

81.   It is possible that clients will wish to seek a barrister's advice directly in respect of matters for which a public funding certificate is already in existence and where the certificate does not extend to a barrister's advice. You should be alert to guard against any breach of the rules against "topping up". Where the client has indicated that they already have a solicitor, you should seek to establish whether or not a certificate is in existence in respect of such work.

82.   If you decide that a client should instruct a solicitor or professional client, the client may well ask you to recommend a particular individual. You may properly do this (and, if prudent, may well suggest suitable names) provided that:

a.   you have reasonable grounds to believe that the solicitor or professional client is competent to do the work; and

b.   you receive no payment for the referral; and

c.   the solicitor is free to instruct another barrister.

Transparency rules

83.   The BSB has introduced mandatory rules on price, service and redress
transparency for all self-employed barristers, chambers and BSB entities. The
information provided will help consumers understand the price and service they will
receive, what redress is available, and the regulatory status of their provider.

84.   There are also additional transparency rules for those undertaking Public Access
work. This includes self-employed barristers undertaking Public Access work, and
BSB entities supplying legal services directly to the public. **In particular, if you
provide the Public Access services listed in the current version of the BSB's
price transparency policy statement (which is available on the BSB's website),
you must comply with additional price transparency rules in relation to those
legal services.**

85.   **Full details of the transparency rules and supporting guidance is available on
the BSB's website.** This guidance aims to support you in complying with the
mandatory rules and encourage you to go beyond the mandatory rules (the
guidance includes additional best practice on transparency to help you to do so).
The guidance also provides checklists to help you comply with the transparency
rules, and information about the BSB's supervision and enforcement strategy.

Bar Standards Board
October 2019

Social Media Guidance

1.   We recognise that you are likely to want to use social media for a variety of private and professional reasons. We have written this guidance to help you understand your duties under the BSB Handbook as they apply to your use of social media. This applies to you in both a professional and personal capacity, since the inherently public nature of the Internet means that anything you publish online may be read by anyone and could be linked back to your status as a barrister.

2.   **Remember that you are bound by Core Duty 5 not to behave in a way which is likely to diminish the trust and confidence which the public places in you or the profession <u>at all times</u>.** Unregistered barristers should also bear this guidance in mind when using social media; as members of the profession, they are expected to conduct themselves in an appropriate manner and are also subject to certain Core Duties and other rules. Social media use includes posting material online, sharing content, promoting your business as a barrister or networking. This might be on sites such as Twitter, content communities such as YouTube, social networking sites like Facebook or LinkedIn and Internet forums.

3.   Comments designed to demean or insult are likely to diminish public trust and confidence in the profession (CD5). It is also advisable to avoid getting drawn into heated debates or arguments. Such behaviour could compromise the requirements for barristers to act with **honesty and integrity** (CD3) and **not to unlawfully discriminate against any person** (CD8). You should always take care to consider the content and tone of what you are posting or sharing. Comments that you reasonably consider to be in good taste may be considered distasteful or offensive by others.

4.   You should also bear in mind your **duty to keep your client's affairs confidential** (CD6). It is inadvisable to send confidential communications to your client over social

media. You should not do so unless your client has agreed and you are satisfied that your client's confidentiality will not be at risk. If your client does wish to be contacted in this way, you will need to consider not only the security of the system that you are using, but also its privacy policy. Some host sites allow the host to access otherwise private information, despite it not being posted to the client's public facing "wall" or "blog".

5.   You may also want to consider less obvious risks; for example, by advertising the fact that you are in a particular location at a particular time (perhaps via a "geotagged" status update), you may risk inadvertently revealing that you act for a particular client.

6.   When you are using social media, you should bear this guidance in mind at all times. This guidance will be considered by the BSB in any action it takes over concerns about social media use. If you are the subject of a complaint concerning your use of social media, we will investigate the matter carefully and in line with the process explained on our website.

October 2019
Bar Standards Board

Clash of Hearing Dates Guidance

Introduction

1. This guidance provides further explanation of the application of the BSB Handbook in the event that you have a clash of hearing dates (listings).

2. Rule C18 in the BSB Handbook states that your duty to provide a competent standard of work and service to each client (CD7) includes a duty to inform your professional client, or your client if instructed directly by a lay client, as far as reasonably possible in sufficient time to enable appropriate steps to be taken to protect the client's interests, if:

    - it becomes apparent to you that you will not be able to carry out the instructions within the time requested, or within a reasonable time after receipt of instructions; or there is an appreciable risk that you may not be able to undertake the instructions.

3. Rule C26 states that you may cease to act on a matter on which you are instructed and return your instructions if you are a self-employed barrister and despite all reasonable efforts to prevent it, a hearing becomes fixed for a date on which you have already entered in your professional diary that you will not be available. This may include a prior arranged hearing relating to another case.

Preventing clashes

4. You should make all reasonable efforts to prevent a clash of dates. This involves communicating effectively with the Court and managing and diarising your cases effectively.

What to do if there is a clash

5. In some instances, it may be impossible to prevent a clash of hearing dates. Where there is a clash, you must exercise your professional judgement in deciding which hearing is most important to attend.

6. In addition, particular types of hearings may have to take precedence as a matter of law or procedure. You should take direction from the Court and have regard to any relevant case management rules.

7. Where an order of precedence is not clear, you should consider your duty to act in the best interests of each of your clients and, in particular, which of your clients is likely to be most prejudiced by alternative representation being arranged at short notice. You should take particular care to consider the needs of vulnerable clients and the impact of your decision on access to justice.

8. You should consider all the relevant circumstances relating to each case including the following issues:

   - the length of time that you have been instructed on each case;
   - the complexity and difficulty of each case;
   - the amount of work you have already done on the case;
   - relevant access to justice considerations and the likely impact on your client.

What to do in respect of the missed hearing

9. You should at all times take reasonable steps to keep all parties concerned informed of any clash of hearing dates. In particular you should ensure that your clients are informed of any clash as soon as possible.

10. You should take all reasonable steps to assist clients to find alternative representation where you are unable to attend a hearing date.

Bar Standards Board
October 2019

Investigating and Collecting Evidence and Taking Witness Statements Guidance

1. There is no longer a rule which prohibits a self-employed barrister from investigating or collecting evidence generally or therefore from taking statements from potential witnesses (which is treated for these purposes as investigating or collecting evidence). In this context, taking witness statements means interviewing the potential witness with a view to preparing a statement or taking a proof of evidence. A barrister has always been entitled to settle a witness statement taken by another person, and this is not investigating or collecting evidence. However, Rule C21.10 of the BSB Handbook states 'you must not accept instructions to act in a particular matter if there is a real prospect that you are not going to be able to maintain your independence'. Guidance C73 then states that the rule 'is an aspect of your broader obligation to maintain your independence (Core Duty 4). Your ability to perform your duty to the court (Core Duty 1) and act in the best interests of your client (Core Duty 2) may be put at risk if you act in circumstances where your independence is compromised. Examples of when you may not be able to maintain your independence include appearing as an advocate in a matter in which you are likely to be called as a witness (unless the matter on which you are likely to be called as a witness is peripheral or minor in the context of the litigation as a whole and is unlikely to lead to your involvement in the matter being challenged at a later date)'.

2. It follows that if the nature of the evidence or the circumstances in which it was investigated or collected are such that there is likely to be an issue about that in court, where the barrister might be needed to give evidence, the barrister can properly be involved in the preparations for a case but cannot accept a brief to conduct the case in court, even as the junior member of a team of barristers. Only if the barrister reasonably believes that the investigation and collection of that evidence (as distinct from the evidence itself) is unlikely to be challenged can the barrister properly conduct the case in court. (The above is intended to apply to the case where a barrister properly accepts a brief and then, as part of his conduct of the case at court, has urgently to take a statement from his client or a

potential witness. It applies where a barrister has investigated or collected evidence before arriving at court at the start of the case).

3. The Bar Standards Board considers that it is a key function of a junior member of a team of barristers that they should be in a position to conduct the case in court if and when required, and that it is unacceptable to have briefed as a junior barrister in a case someone who may not be in a position to take on the full advocacy role in that case should it become necessary. The risks to the client's interests and to the due administration of justice generally are too great to allow a barrister to conduct a case in court, even as a junior in a team of barristers, if there is a real risk that the circumstances of the taking of the evidence that barrister has collected will be challenged in the case. If a junior member of the team is called upon to conduct the case and the circumstances of their investigation and collection of evidence is an issue in the case, the barrister might have to stand down, damaging the client's interests (the client having then been deprived of each member of their chosen team) and the due administration of justice (through the inconvenience and delay in the conduct of the case).

4. When investigating or collecting evidence, barristers should bear carefully in mind the dangers of unconsciously affecting or contaminating the evidence that a witness is able to give. Barristers should also be aware of the risks as a result of becoming involved in investigating or collecting evidence, and take these risks into account when deciding:

a. whether to undertake such work in the first place; and
b. if they have done, whether or not they can properly accept a brief at a subsequent trial.

5. The BSB Handbook places the onus squarely on the barrister who has investigated or collected evidence prior to accepting a brief to consider and reach a reasonable conclusion whether or not his/her involvement is likely to be challenged.

6. In assessing whether to accept a brief in these circumstances, the barrister should be mindful of the risk where they have been involved in the collection or investigation of evidence. The barrister's duty is to reach a reasonable decision on the risk involved before accepting a brief. The brief can only properly be accepted if it is reasonable for the barrister to conclude that the circumstances of his investigation or collection of evidence are unlikely to be challenged. If the barrister's decision is not a reasonable one, and the trial is subsequently adjourned as a result of the barrister withdrawing from the case, the barrister risks being exposed to an order for wasted costs as well as enforcement action being taken against them for a breach of the BSB Handbook.

7. Even where a brief is properly accepted, the question of whether the barrister should continue to act is a matter that they must keep under review during the case in light of any later developments. Guidance C73 states that 'if it appears that you are likely to be a witness on a material question of fact, and therefore must withdraw from a case as there is a real prospect that you are not going to be able to maintain your independence (Rules C21.10 and C25), you must also comply with Rule C27'.

Bar Standards Board
September 2020

First Tier Complaints Handling Guidance

1. This guidance supplements Section D1.1 of the Code of Conduct in the BSB Handbook. It covers three areas:

   a. the scope of chambers complaints handling

   b. the obligation to notify clients of their right to complain

   c. guidance to chambers in developing chambers complaints procedures

2. The key outcomes of Section D1.1 of the Code of Conduct in the BSB Handbook are (1) clients are provided with appropriate information about redress, should know that they can make a complaint if dissatisfied, and know how to do so, and (2) complaints should be dealt with promptly and the client kept informed about the process. References to "client" in the BSB Handbook and this guidance are to the lay client.

A. Scope of chambers complaints handling

3. Complaints are expressions of dissatisfaction by clients. This guidance draws a distinction between complaints that relate to service, professional negligence and misconduct. A single complaint may have elements of all three and the obligations on chambers are different for each aspect.

Service complaints

4. The requirements set out in Section D1.1 of the Code of Conduct relate to the handling of service complaints which are within the jurisdiction of the Legal Ombudsman.

5. Chapter 2 of the Legal Ombudsman's scheme rules set out the types of complaint that are within its jurisdiction. These are complaints that relate to an act or omission by an authorised person in relation to services provided to the complainant (directly or indirectly).

6. In addition, the Legal Ombudsman's website sets out a list of the categories of complaint which it investigates. These include the following categories (some of which may also include aspects of negligence or misconduct):

- Costs excessive
- Costs information deficient
- Data protection/breach of confidentiality
- Delay/failure to progress
- Discrimination
- Failure to advise
- Failure to follow instructions
- Failure to investigate complaint internally
- Failure to keep complainant informed of progress
- Failure to keep papers safe

Misconduct and professional negligence

7. Chambers may not be best placed to seek to resolve or provide redress for complaints which relate to misconduct or professional negligence, and there is no positive obligation to investigate matters of misconduct.

8. However, it is likely that in many cases a complaint which raises issues relating to professional misconduct or professional negligence will also amount to an accusation of the provision of poor service or will include a service element. Where this is the case, the service issues should be dealt with in accordance with Section D1.1 of the Code of Conduct. It is not acceptable for chambers not to investigate elements of a complaint which relate to service because the complaint also amounts to, or includes elements which relate to, misconduct or could potentially give rise to a negligence claim.

9. Complainants should be informed in writing if any aspects of their complaint are deemed to be outside of chambers complaints handling procedures. This should include information on how to complain to the Legal Ombudsman.

Barristers are also reminded that they must report promptly to the BSB if they have committed serious misconduct. In addition, subject to their duty to keep the affairs of each client confidential, barristers must report to the BSB if they have reasonable grounds to believe that there has been serious misconduct by another barrister. The relevant provisions of the BSB Handbook are Rules C65 – C69 and Guidance C95 – C102. Guidance C96 in particular provides examples of what serious misconduct includes without being exhaustive. Further guidance on reporting serious misconduct of others is also available on the BSB's website.

Bar Mutual Indemnity Fund

10. Where a complaint raises an allegation of negligence it may be appropriate to inform BMIF and to consult them before any proposals for resolution are made to the client.

Non-client complaints

11. The Legal Ombudsman will only deal with complaints from consumers of lawyers' services. This means that only complaints from the barrister's clients fall within the Ombudsman's jurisdiction. This does not mean that non-client complaints should not be investigated by chambers. Some non-client complaints, such as discourtesy, may be capable of resolution by chambers. However, the BSB recognises that chambers' ability to resolve many kinds of non-client complaints is limited and that they are more suited to consideration under the disciplinary processes of the BSB. Accordingly, if chambers feel that the issues raised by non-clients cannot be satisfactorily resolved through the chambers complaints process they should refer the complainant to the BSB.

B. Notifying the client of the right to complain

11. Barristers must notify clients in writing at the time of engagement or if not practicable at the next appropriate opportunity:

> (a) Of their right to make a complaint, how and to whom this can be done, including their right to complain to the Legal Ombudsman at the conclusion of the complaints process, the timeframe for doing so and the full details of how to contact the Legal Ombudsman;

> (b) That the lay client may complain directly to chambers without going through solicitors; and

> (c) Of the name and web address of an approved alternative dispute resolution (ADR) body which can deal with any complaint in the event that: the barrister is unable to resolve the complaint through their complaints process, *and* both the barrister and the client agree to use the scheme. The barrister is therefore not required to use ADR, and is only required to inform the client of the option. This is a requirement under the Alternative Dispute Resolution for Consumer Disputes (Amendment) Regulations 2015.

12. At the conclusion of the complaints process, complainants must be informed in writing of their right to complain to the Legal Ombudsman (which has responsibility for dealing with all service complaints against legal professionals), the timeframe for doing so and the full details of how to contact them.

13. The barrister must also notify the client in the same letter of the name and web address of an ADR body which would be competent to deal with the complaint. However, it should be noted that neither the barrister nor the client is required to use ADR. The only

requirement is for the barrister to inform the client of the option, and the client retains their right to complain to the Legal Ombudsman provided they fall within their jurisdiction.

14. The Chartered Trading Standards Institute (CTSI) approves ADR entities which are able to provide mediation services. At the time of writing, barristers can use ProMediate or Small Claims Mediation, and they should consider which provider may be the most appropriate for them and the client. Barristers should also be aware that the time limit for contacting an ADR approved body will likely be different to the time limit for contacting the Legal Ombudsman, and they should make the client aware of the time limit in the letter. If the barrister and the client use mediation, neither party is required to accept the proposed resolution. If mediation does not resolve the complaint, the client may still make a complaint to the Legal Ombudsman (provided they fall within their jurisdiction and they do so within the time limit).

At the time of writing the CTSI has not approved any ADR entities which are able to provide arbitration services. If the barrister and the client use a separate arbitration scheme, the outcome will be legally binding and the parties will need to agree to this. In itself, this does not prevent the client from then making a complaint to the Legal Ombudsman. However, the Legal Ombudsman reserves the right to dismiss any complaint if it feels that a comparable independent complaints (or costs-assessment) scheme has already dealt with the same issue satisfactorily.

Complaints to chambers

15. The Legal Services Board (LSB) have specified a requirement to which the BSB is obliged to give effect under s112(2) of the Legal Services Act 2007. The requirement relates to "first-tier" complaints which, so far as self-employed barristers are concerned, relate to the procedure whereby a client makes a complaint to chambers in the first instance.

16. The LSB seeks to ensure consumers have confidence that:

(a) complaints handling procedures provide effective safeguards for them; and

(b) complaints will be dealt with comprehensively and swiftly, with appropriate redress where necessary.

17. Chambers complaint handling processes must be convenient and easy to use (in particular for those that are vulnerable or have disabilities). They should make provision for complaints to be made by any reasonable means. The way in which complaints are dealt with must be transparent and clear in relation to process, well publicised and free. The process itself should be prompt and fair, with decisions based on a sufficient investigation of the circumstances. Where appropriate, there should be an offer of a suitable remedy.

18. Most consumers will be able to make a complaint to the Legal Ombudsman about the services they received after the chambers complaints processes has concluded. Sufficient information must be provided to all clients to identify whether they do have a right to take their complaint to the Legal Ombudsman, and to contact the Legal Ombudsman direct to clarify whether they can (clients will also need to be informed about ADR – see paragraph 13 above).

19. Please note that the Legal Ombudsman, the independent complaints body for service complaints about lawyers, has time limits in which a complaint must be raised with them. The time limits are:

a) The act or omission, or when the complainant should reasonably have known there was cause for complaint, must have been after 5 October 2010; and

b) The complainant must refer the complaint to the Legal Ombudsman no later than six years from the act/omission, or three years from when the complainant should reasonably have known there was cause for complaint.

BAR
STANDARDS
BOARD

REGULATING BARRISTERS

c) The complainant must also refer the complaint to the Legal Ombudsman within six months of the complaint receiving a final response from their lawyer, if that response complies with the requirements in rule 4.4 of the Scheme Rules (which requires the response to include prominently an explanation that the Legal Ombudsman was available if the complainant remained dissatisfied, and the provision of full contact details for the Ombudsman and a warning that the complaint must be referred to them within six months).

20. Chambers must have regard to that timeframe when deciding whether they are able to investigate a complaint. Chambers will not therefore usually deal with complaints that fall outside of the Legal Ombudsman's time limits. The Ombudsman can extend the time limit in exceptional circumstances.

21. Clients who have, or may have, a right to complain to the Legal Ombudsman[1] must at the conclusion of the complaint process be informed of their right to complain to the Legal Ombudsman, the timeframe for doing so and full details of how to contact the Legal Ombudsman (clients will also need to be informed about ADR – see paragraph 13 above).

22. Where a barrister accepts instructions from a new client, or instructions on a new matter from an existing client, the client must be notified of the right to make a complaint, how and to whom this can be done. It is essential that systems be set up by chambers to ensure that these requirements are properly complied with. This will be straightforward for Public

---

[1] Those clients who are able to complain to the Legal Ombudsman are as follows:
a) Individuals;
b) Businesses or enterprises that are micro-enterprises within the meaning of Article 1 and Article 2(1) and (3) of the Annex to Commission Recommendation 2003/361/EC (broadly businesses or enterprises with fewer than 10 employees and turnover or assets not exceeding €2 million);
c) Charities with an annual income net of tax of less than £1 million;
d) Clubs, associations or organisations, the affairs of which are managed by its members or a committee of its members, with an annual income net of tax of less than £1 million;
e) Trustees of trusts with an asset value of less than £1 million; and
f) Personal representatives or beneficiaries of the estates of persons who, before they died, had not referred the complaint to the Legal Ombudsman.

Access clients, but because self-employed barristers will usually be instructed by a solicitor or other professional client on behalf of the client, procedures must be put in place for notifying other clients.

Compliance with requirements to notify clients

23. The LSB has specified a requirement that the BSB must require all individuals and entities they regulate to notify all clients in writing at the time of engagement, or existing clients at the next appropriate opportunity, of their right to make a complaint, how and to whom this can be done (including their right to complain to the Legal Ombudsman at the conclusion of the complaint process, the timeframe for doing so and full details of how to contact the Legal Ombudsman). Clients will also need to be informed about ADR – see paragraph 11c) above.

24. The BSB is required to enforce the LSB requirement and compliance by chambers. The BSB will, as part of its supervision processes, monitor chambers to ensure that the requirement is being complied with.

25. The guidance below is set out to assist barristers and Chambers in setting up systems to effect compliance with the requirement of the LSB in a way that is neither disproportionate nor onerous.

26. Where the barrister is aware of the contact details for the client, the obligation can be satisfied by a letter or e-mail sent directly to the client (which may be sent by someone else on the barrister's behalf) providing the required information.

27. If the information has not been provided beforehand in writing, it may be provided on the first occasion that the barrister meets the client at court, or in conference.

28. Subject to the points made below, it is not acceptable for barristers simply to make the information available to solicitors. Nor is it sufficient that the information is available on chambers' website. There is a positive obligation on the barrister to provide it to the client.

29. An unequivocal agreement by the professional client to pass on chambers' complaint information to the client, either in a particular case, or in relation to each case in which a member of chambers is instructed by that professional client, will serve to discharge the obligation to provide the client with the information. However, there must be a positive agreement on the part of the professional client: silence is not sufficient. Where chambers receive high volume instructions from a particular professional client it will not be necessary to obtain written confirmation in relation to each instruction. In those circumstances, positive written confirmation should be obtained at regular and reasonable intervals from the professional client that complaints information continues to be passed on to lay clients.

Client information sheets

30. Some barristers may be unhappy at the prospect that the first thing they do when they meet the client is to advise the client how to make a complaint. A "client information sheet" is one way in which the information may be communicated to the client. The information sheet giving details about the barrister as well as information on how to complain could be given to the client by the barrister. Whilst the information sheet carries the necessary information, it also carries helpful information for the client about the barrister and should not give rise to any negative impression. The client information sheet may be sent or handed out to the client; it may also be provided by the clerk or receptionist when the client arrives for a conference.

Compliance

31. It is recognised that there will be circumstances in which, in individual cases, it is impractical to comply strictly with the requirements. What is important is that chambers set

up systems, and establish procedures, to effect compliance with these requirements consistent with this guidance. The precise solutions will differ according to different fields of practice. If this has been done responsibly, then as part of its supervision processes the BSB will regard sympathetically particular difficulties which occur, or are likely to occur, in individual cases.

Cases where the procedure cannot be followed

32. Where the barrister has the contact details of the client, or when the barrister meets the client in the course of the matter, compliance should not in general present a problem.

33. However, there will be areas of practice, and particular cases, where it is not possible or practical for the barrister to satisfy the notification requirement in this way. For example, the barrister may not have the contact details of the client, cannot readily obtain them, and does not anticipate meeting the client in the course of being instructed or at least not for some time.

34. Some common sense is required in setting up procedures so as to fulfil the notification requirements. For example, where a barrister acts for government departments or public bodies it should be possible to agree a standing arrangement with Treasury Solicitors or other in-house lawyers whereby details of the complaints system is provided to the professional client to be passed on to the client body. Most barristers will be able to think of examples within their own field of practice where procedures can be responsibly adopted so as to fulfil the notification requirement.

35. In some cases there will be no realistic alternative to compliance by providing the requisite information to the solicitor or other professional client with instructions to provide that information to the client on behalf of the barrister, even when the solicitor has not expressly agreed to do so. But this course should only be adopted when other better means of compliance are not practical.

C. Chambers complaints procedure: guidance

36. This guidance is provided to chambers to assist them to develop a complaints procedure which is compliant with the mandatory requirements set out at Section D1.1 of the Code of Conduct in the BSB Handbook. Chambers are not obliged to follow the guidance absolutely. If chambers decide not to adopt the model procedure provided at Appendix 1 below, they should have regard to this guidance when devising their own complaints handling arrangements.

37. All barristers must be familiar with the requirements of Section D1.1 of the Code of Conduct in the BSB Handbook, and the requirements of the Alternative Dispute Resolution for Consumer Disputes (Amendment) Regulations 2015 in respect of informing clients about ADR (see paragraphs 11(c) and 13 above).

38. Those barristers who are responsible for dealing with complaints should ensure that they and any staff who deal with complaints are adequately trained. The BSB will monitor chambers complaints handling, including the sufficiency of training, as part of its supervision processes.

39. This annex sets out the contents of an effective procedure. Model complaints procedures are at Appendix 1 (multi member sets of Chambers) and Appendix 2 (sole practitioners). Chambers must ensure that their website and brochure carries information about the chambers complaints procedure.

40. Chambers are not obliged to adopt the model complaints procedures provided below. The model procedures set out good practice arrangements for handling complaints, but the BSB is aware that there are alternative methods which may be just as effective. Chambers have discretion to either devise their own procedure, or to amend the model procedure to best fit their own administrative arrangements or the particular circumstances of a complaint. The only requirements are that Chambers adopts a complaints procedure that

includes the mandatory requirements set out at Section D1.1 of the Code of Conduct in the BSB Handbook, and the requirements of the Alternative Dispute Resolution for Consumer Disputes (Amendment) Regulations 2015 in respect of informing clients about ADR (see paragraphs 11(c) and 13 above)

41. Possible alternatives to the arrangements in the model procedure have been provided where appropriate. These alternatives are not exhaustive but are used to highlight that other procedures may be more suitable for chambers depending on their size, practice type or administrative set up.

Chambers complaints procedure: first stage

42. Where a client is dissatisfied with some aspect of the service provided by a barrister or by chambers they should be invited to telephone an individual nominated under the chambers complaints procedure to deal with complaints; for example, the Chambers Director, Practice Manager or Head of Chambers. In order to ensure consistency of approach, this individual should be the first point of contact for all complaints. The client should also be told that if they prefer they may make the complaint in writing, and the chambers complaints procedure should be sent to them unless it has already been provided.

43. Where a complaint is made by telephone, a note of the complaint should be made. It should record:

- The name and address of the complainant;
- The date of the complaint;
- Against whom the complaint is made;
- The detail of the complaint; and
- What the complainant believes should be done about the complaint.

44. In many cases the complaint will be resolved over the telephone during the first call. When that occurs, the individual nominated to deal with complaints should record the outcome on the note of complaint. The client should be asked whether they are content with the outcome and informed of the Legal Ombudsman's complaints procedure. If they are, that fact will be recorded. The complaints procedure should suggest that the client may wish to make their own note. If the client is not content they should be invited to put the complaint in writing so that it may be investigated formally. At that stage they should be sent a copy of the chambers complaints procedure unless it has already been provided. The client should also be informed of the Legal Ombudsman's complaints procedure.

Chambers complaints procedure: second stage

45. It is recommended that chambers set up a complaints panel made up of experienced practitioners from different practice areas and a senior member of staff. A head of panel should be appointed. There should be a nominated deputy. All complaints (other than those resolved at stage one) should be put before the head of the panel or, in their absence, the deputy. The role of the panel is to appoint from its members an independent person to investigate a complaint and to ensure that all complaints are handled consistently and in accordance with the chambers complaints procedure.

46. It may not be appropriate or possible for a small set of chambers to convene a complaints panel. Chambers are encouraged to set up a complaints panel where possible or otherwise nominate an individual or individuals to investigate the complaint.

47. Sole practitioners may not feel able to investigate independently a complaint raised against them and, if a complaint remains unresolved, should therefore offer for an independent person (for example, a barrister in another chambers) to investigate the complaint. A suggested approach to this is set out in the model procedure for sole practitioners at Appendix 2 below.

The Bar Standards Board
Handbook

48. A complaint received in writing should, where possible, be acknowledged within two days of receipt and, in any event, promptly. Within 14 days of that acknowledgment the head of the panel (where one has been set up) or their deputy should appoint a member of the panel to investigate the complaint. Where the complaint is against a member of staff the person appointed will normally be the senior staff member. Where the complaint is against the senior staff member the head of the panel should appoint another member of the panel to investigate. Where the complaint is against the head of the panel, the Head of Chambers should investigate or, in their discretion, appoint a member of the panel to investigate. Where the Head of Chambers is the head of the panel, the deputy head of the panel should be the appointed person. No barrister should investigate a complaint of which they are the subject. Where no panel has been established, chambers should ensure that the individual or individuals nominated to investigate the complaint are impartial.

49. The appointed person/nominated individual should write to the client as soon as they are appointed. They should inform the client that they are to investigate the complaint and that they will report back to the client within 14 days. If it becomes plain that a response cannot be sent within 14 days a realistic timeframe should be set and the client informed accordingly.

50. The appointed person/nominated individual should investigate the complaint. They should speak to the barrister/member of staff complained against, and any other people they identify as having something to contribute. They should review all relevant documents. If necessary, they should revert to the client for further information and clarification.

51. The appointed person/nominated individual should prepare a report to the client (with a copy to the barrister/member of staff complained against). The report should set out all the matters referred to at paragraph 43 above, the nature and scope of the investigations carried out in respect of each complaint, their conclusions and the basis for their conclusions. The report should be drafted using clear and concise language. Where a

complaint is found to be justified, the report should provide proposals for resolution (e.g. reduction in fees, apology, compensation, etc.).

52. The report should be sent to the client within 14 days of the appointed person's appointment, or such longer period as has been communicated to the client in advance (see paragraph 49). Note that the client will be entitled to take their complaint to the Legal Ombudsman if they do not receive a final response from you within eight weeks of their initial complaint. A copy of the report should also be provided to the barrister/member of staff complained against.

The Legal Ombudsman's website has a number of helpful resources for legal professionals, including how to signpost clients to the Legal Ombudsman, good practice in handling complaints and use of language when responding to complaints:
http://www.legalombudsman.org.uk/

Charging for complaints

53. Chambers should not charge clients for dealing with their complaint or using mediation services. To do so brings the Bar into disrepute and could amount to professional misconduct.

Confidentiality

54. All conversations and documents shall be confidential and disclosed only to the extent necessary. They may be disclosed only to the client, the person complained about, the Head of Chambers, the head of the complaints panel or relevant senior member of the panel, the nominated individual, the management committee (for carrying out the task at paragraph 51) and any other individual with whom enquiries need to be made for the purpose of the investigation.

Record keeping

55. Where the procedure ends after the first stage, the person responsible for recording the outcome on the note of complaint should ensure that the note of complaint is placed on the chambers complaints file.

56. Where the procedure ends after the second stage, the head of the panel/nominated individual should ensure that the following documents are placed on the chambers complaints file:

- Note/letter of complaint (see paragraph 43); and
- Appointed person's/nominated individual's report (see paragraph 51).

Review and monitoring

57. The chambers complaints file should be inspected regularly by the management committee. Papers should be anonymised where necessary. The person responsible for the administration of the system should report at least annually to such appropriate committee of chambers on the number of complaints received and the subject area of the complaints. In such a report all the details should be anonymised, but should be reviewed for trends and possible training issues.

58. As part of its supervision processes the BSB will monitor chambers complaints handling including, where appropriate, the sufficiency of training. All barristers must comply promptly with requests for information from the BSB.

October 2019
Bar Standards Board

Appendix 1

The model procedures for chambers and for sole practitioners are based on the suggested arrangements for handling complaints set out in the above guidance. Chambers or sole practitioners may decide to adopt the model procedure but are free to develop their own procedure or set of rules for dealing with complaints. Chambers must ensure that any procedure they develop is compliant with the mandatory requirements set out at Section D1.1 of the Code of Conduct in the BSB Handbook, and the requirements of the Alternative Dispute Resolution for Consumer Disputes (Amendment) Regulations 2015 in respect of informing clients about ADR.

Model chambers complaints procedure for multi-member sets

1. Our aim is to give you a good service at all times. However, if you have a complaint you are invited to let us know as soon as possible. It is not necessary to involve solicitors in order to make your complaint, but you are free to do so should you wish.

2. Please note that the Legal Ombudsman, the independent complaints body for service complaints about lawyers, has time limits in which a complaint must be raised with them. The time limits are:

   a) The act or omission, or when the complainant should reasonably have known there was cause for complaint, must have been after 5 October 2010; and

   b) The complainant must refer the complaint to the Legal Ombudsman no later than six years from the act/omission, or three years from when the complainant should reasonably have known there was cause for complaint.

   c) The complainant must also refer the complaint to the Legal Ombudsman within six months of the complaint receiving a final response from their lawyer, if that response

complies with the requirements in rule 4.4 of the Scheme Rules (which requires the response to include prominently an explanation that the Legal Ombudsman was available if the complainant remained dissatisfied, and the provision of full contact details for the Ombudsman and a warning that the complaint must be referred to them within six months).

3. Chambers must have regard to that timeframe when deciding whether they are able to investigate your complaint. Chambers will not therefore usually deal with complaints that fall outside of the Legal Ombudsman's time limits. The Ombudsman can extend the time limit in exceptional circumstances.

4. The Ombudsman will also only deal with complaints from consumers. This means that only complaints from the barrister's client are within their jurisdiction. Non-clients who are not satisfied with the outcome of the Chambers' investigation should contact the BSB rather than the Legal Ombudsman.

5. It should be noted that it may not always be possible to investigate a complaint brought by a non-client. This is because the ability of chambers to satisfactorily investigate and resolve such matters is limited and complaints of this nature are often better suited to the disciplinary processes maintained by the BSB. Therefore, chambers will make an initial assessment of the complaint and if they feel that the issues raised cannot be satisfactorily resolved through the chambers complaints process they will refer you to the BSB.

Complaints made by telephone

6. You may wish to make a complaint in writing and, if so, please follow the procedure in paragraph 8 below. However, if you would rather speak on the telephone about your complaint, then please telephone the individual nominated under the chambers complaints procedure to deal with complaints [NAME] or (if the complaint is about a member of staff) the [senior member of staff - NAME]. If the complaint is about the [senior member of staff]

telephone [the Head of Chambers - NAME or other member of Chambers appointed by head]. The person you contact will make a note of the details of your complaint and what you would like to have done about it. They will discuss your concerns with you and aim to resolve them. If the matter is resolved they will record the outcome, check that you are satisfied with the outcome and record that you are satisfied. You may also wish to record the outcome of the telephone discussion in writing.

7. If your complaint is not resolved on the telephone you will be invited to write to us about it, so it can be investigated formally.

Complaints Made in Writing

8. Please give the following details:

   • Your name and address;
   • Which member(s) of chambers you are complaining about;
   • The detail of the complaint; and
   • What you would like done about it.

9. Please address your letter to [name of preferred recipient and chambers' address]. We will, where possible, acknowledge receipt of your complaint within two days and provide you with details of how your complaint will be dealt with.

10. Our chambers has a panel headed by [name] and made up of experienced members of chambers and a senior member of staff, which considers any written complaint. Within 14 days of your letter being received the head of the panel (or their deputy in their absence) will appoint a member of the panel to investigate it. If your complaint is against the head of the panel, the next most senior member of the panel will investigate it. In any case, the person appointed will be someone other than the person you are complaining about.

11. The person appointed to investigate will write to you as soon as possible to let you know they have been appointed and that they will reply to your complaint within 14 days. If they find later that they are not going to be able to reply within 14 days they will set a new date for their reply and inform you. Their reply will set out:

- The nature and scope of their investigation;
- Their conclusion on each complaint and the basis for their conclusion; and
- If they find that you are justified in your complaint, their proposals for resolving the complaint.

Confidentiality

12. All conversations and documents relating to the complaint will be treated as confidential and will be disclosed only to the extent that is necessary. Disclosure will be to the Head of Chambers, members of our management committee and to anyone involved in the complaint and its investigation. Such people will include the barrister member or staff who you have complained about, the head or relevant senior member of the panel and the person who investigates the complaint. The BSB is entitled to inspect the documents and seek information about the complaint when discharging its monitoring functions.

Our policy

13. As part of our commitment to client care we make a written record of any complaint and retain all documents and correspondence generated by the complaint for a period of six years. Our management committee inspects an anonymised record regularly with a view to improving services.

REGULATING BARRISTERS

Complaints to the Legal Ombudsman/alternative dispute resolution

14. If you are unhappy with the outcome of our investigation and you fall within their jurisdiction you may take up your complaint with the Legal Ombudsman, the independent complaints body for complaints about lawyers, at the conclusion of our consideration of your complaint. The Ombudsman is not able to consider your complaint until it has first been investigated by chambers. Please note the timeframe for referral of complaints to the Ombudsman as set out at paragraph 2 above. Those clients who are able to complain to the Legal Ombudsman are as follows:

a) Individuals;

b) Businesses or enterprises that are micro-enterprises within the meaning of Article 1 and Article 2(1) and (3) of the Annex to Commission Recommendation 2003/361/EC (broadly businesses or enterprises with fewer than 10 employees and turnover or assets not exceeding €2 million);

c) Charities with an annual income net of tax of less than £1 million;

d) Clubs, associations or organisations, the affairs of which are managed by its members or a committee of its members, with an annual income net of tax of less than £1 million;

e) Trustees of trusts with an asset value of less than £1 million; and

f) Personal representatives or beneficiaries of the estates of persons who, before they died, had not referred the complaint to the Legal Ombudsman.

You can write to the Legal Ombudsman at:

Legal Ombudsman
PO Box 6806,
Wolverhampton
WV1 9WJ

Telephone number: 0300 555 0333

Email: enquiries@legalombudsman.org.uk

More information about the Legal Ombudsman is available on their website:
http://www.legalombudsman.org.uk/

If you are unhappy with the outcome of the investigation, alternative complaints bodies
(such as [include one of the following: ProMediate and Small Claims Mediation and the
website]) also exist which are competent to deal with complaints about legal services,
should you and the barrister both wish to use such a scheme. If you wish to use [include
one of the above], please contact us to discuss this. Please also note that: (1) the time limit
for contacting [include one of the above] is [insert time limit], and (2) if mediation is used,
neither you nor the barrister is required to accept the proposed resolution. If mediation does
not resolve the complaint, you may still make a complaint to the Legal Ombudsman
(provided you fall within their jurisdiction and you do so within the time limit).

15. If you are not the barrister's client and are unhappy with the outcome of our investigation
then please contact the Bar Standards Board at:

Bar Standards Board
Contact and Assessment Team
289-293 High Holborn
London
WC1V 7JZ

Telephone number: 0207 6111 444
Website: www.barstandardsboard.org.uk

Appendix 2

Model complaints procedure - sole practitioners

1. My aim is to give all my clients a good service at all times. However, if you have a complaint please let me know as soon as possible, by telephone or in writing. I will treat your complaint as confidential although I may discuss it with other barristers or officials from the Bar Standards Board as part of their monitoring functions. I will not reveal your name to others unless I appoint an independent person to investigate a complaint or set up mediation. I will deal with your complaint promptly.

2. Please note that the Legal Ombudsman, the independent complaints body for service complaints about lawyers, has time limits in which a complaint must be raised with them. The time limits are:

   a) The act or omission, or when the complainant should reasonably have known there was cause for complaint, must have been after 5 October 2010; and
   b) The complainant must refer the complaint to the Legal Ombudsman no later than six years from the act/omission, or three years from when the complainant should reasonably have known there was cause for complaint.
   c) The complainant must also refer the complaint to the Legal Ombudsman within six months of the complaint receiving a final response from their lawyer, if that response complies with the requirements in rule 4.4 of the Scheme Rules (which requires the response to include prominently an explanation that the Legal Ombudsman was available if the complainant remained dissatisfied, and the provision of full contact details for the Ombudsman and a warning that the complaint must be referred to them within six months).

3. Chambers must have regard to that timeframe when deciding whether they are able to investigate your complaint. Chambers will not therefore usually deal with complaints that fall

outside of the Legal Ombudsman's time limits. The Ombudsman can extend the time limit in exceptional circumstances.

4. The Ombudsman will also only deal with complaints from consumers. This means that only complaints from the barrister's client are within their jurisdiction. Non-clients who are not satisfied with the outcome of the investigation should contact the Bar Standards Board rather than the Legal Ombudsman.

5. It should be noted that it may not always be possible to investigate a complaint brought by a non-client. This is because my ability to satisfactorily investigate and resolve such matters is limited and complaints of this nature are often better suited to the disciplinary processes maintained by the Bar Standards Board. Therefore, I will make an initial assessment of the complaint and if I feel that the issues raised cannot be satisfactorily resolved through my complaints process I will refer you to the Bar Standards Board.

Complaints made by telephone

6. If you wish to make a complaint by telephone, I will make a note of the details of your complaint and what you would like done about it. I will endeavour to resolve matters with you on the telephone. If after discussion you are satisfied with the outcome I will make a note of the outcome and the fact that you are satisfied. If you are not satisfied you may wish to make a written complaint.

Complaints made in writing

7. If you wish to make a written complaint please give me the following details:

- Your name, telephone number and address;
- The detail of your complaint; and
- What you would like done about it.

Procedure for dealing with your complaint

8. There are a number of ways in which your complaint may be dealt with:

    (a) Discussion over the telephone;

    (b) Dealt with by correspondence;

    (c) Discussion at a meeting between us;

    (d) The appointment of an independent person to investigate the complaint.

9. If we decide to appoint an independent person to investigate the complaint (for example, a barrister in another chambers), we both would need to agree who to appoint. An independent person who has considerable experience in the area that is the subject matter of the dispute should be chosen.

10. Upon receipt of a written complaint I will:

    (a) Reply in writing, normally within 48 hours, to acknowledge the complaint and inform you how I shall be dealing with it.

    (b) Reply within 14 days responding in full to your complaint. I will offer you the opportunity to meet with you if that is appropriate. If I find later that I am not going to be able to reply within 14 days I will set a new date for my reply and inform you. My reply will set out:

        • The nature and scope of my investigation;

        • My conclusion on each complaint and the basis for my conclusion; and

        • If I find that you are justified in your complaint, my proposals for resolving the complaint.

11. If you are not happy with my final written response and you fall within their jurisdiction, you may make a formal complaint to the Legal Ombudsman, the independent complaints handling body for complaints about lawyers. Please note the timeframe for referral of complaints to the Ombudsman as set out at paragraph 2 above. Those clients who are able to complain to the Legal Ombudsman are as follows:

a) Individuals;

b) Businesses or enterprises that are micro-enterprises within the meaning of Article 1 and Article 2(1) and (3) of the Annex to Commission Recommendation 2003/361/EC (broadly businesses or enterprises with fewer than 10 employees and turnover or assets not exceeding €2 million);

c) Charities with an annual income net of tax of less than £1 million;

d) Clubs, associations or organisations, the affairs of which are managed by its members or a committee of its members, with an annual income net of tax of less than £1 million;

e) Trustees of trusts with an asset value of less than £1 million; and

f) Personal representatives or beneficiaries of the estates of persons who, before they died, had not referred the complaint to the Legal Ombudsman.

You can write to the Legal Ombudsman at:

Legal Ombudsman

PO Box 6806,

Wolverhampton

WV1 9WJ

Telephone number: 0300 555 0333

Email: enquiries@legalombudsman.org.uk

More information about the Legal Ombudsman is available on their website:

http://www.legalombudsman.org.uk/

If you are unhappy with my final written response, alternative complaints bodies (such as [include one of the following: ProMediate and Small Claims Mediation and the website]) also exist which are competent to deal with complaints about legal services, should we both wish to use such a scheme. If you wish to use [include one of the above], please contact me to discuss this. Please also note that: (1) the time limit for contacting [include one of the above] is [insert time limit], and (2) if we use mediation, neither you nor I am required to accept the proposed resolution. If mediation does not resolve the complaint, you may still make a complaint to the Legal Ombudsman (provided you fall within their jurisdiction and you do so within the time limit).

12. If you are not my client and are unhappy with the outcome of our investigation then please contact the Bar Standards Board at:

Bar Standards Board
Contact and Assessment Team
289-293 High Holborn
London
WC1V 7JZ

Telephone number: 0207 6111 444
Website: www.barstandardsboard.org.uk

13. I will maintain confidentiality at all times and discuss your complaint only to the extent that is necessary for its resolution and to comply with requests for information from the Bar Standards Board discharging its monitoring functions.

14. I will retain all correspondence and other documents generated in the course of your complaint for a period of six years and I will review complaints at least once a year to ensure that I maintain good standards of service.

Barristers Supervising Immigration Advisers Guidance

Contents

Introduction

1. Self-employed barristers, BSB entities and employed barristers in authorised non-BSB bodies are able to act as supervisors for the purposes of immigration advice and services, as this is permitted by section 84(2)(e) of the Immigration and Asylum Act 1999 (IAA 1999) (as amended).

2. This guidance sets out what the Bar Standards Board (BSB) expects of you when acting as a supervisor in accordance with the IAA 1999.

The legislative position

3. The IAA 1999 provides that no person may provide immigration advice and services unless they are a qualified person. As the Bar Council is a designated qualifying regulator for the purposes of the IAA 1999, an authorised barrister or BSB entity is a qualified person for the purposes of the Act.

4. A person[1] is also a qualified person if they are acting on behalf of, and under the supervision of, a person within paragraph three above and providing advice and services within England and Wales. It is the view of the BSB that this creates a link between the lay client and the barrister, irrespective of whether the service is being provided by the barrister or the immigration adviser. You must therefore comply with your regulatory obligations to clients as if the adviser's client were your client. If you are acting as a self-employed barrister, the relevant Public Access requirements apply.

The BSB position

5. Barristers supervising an immigration adviser under the IAA 1999 must only do so in instances where it would be appropriate and in the client's best interests (Core Duty 2).

---

[1] This can include both corporate and unincorporated persons.

To determine what is 'appropriate', the BSB has consulted with the Office of the Immigration Services Commissioner (OISC). They regulate immigration advisers, ensuring they are fit and competent and act in the best interests of their clients. To ensure they do so effectively, they have a number of powers and sanctions they can impose against immigration advisers and organisations they regulate where they (the immigration adviser or organisation) have failed to meet their standards[2].

6. Rule C85A of the <u>BSB Handbook</u> prohibits you from acting as a supervisor of an immigration adviser in certain circumstances. This is to ensure:

- The BSB's regulatory regime is consistent with, and does not undermine, OISC's regime or those of other approved regulators;

- There is a consistent and robust level of consumer protection; and

- You comply with the Associations rules and Core Duty 5. Guidance C126 states that your obligations under Core Duty 5 require you not to act in an association with a person where, merely by being associated with such person, you may reasonably be considered as bringing the profession into disrepute[3] or otherwise diminishing the trust that the public places in you and the profession.

Rule C85A provides that:

You must not act as a supervisor of an immigration adviser for the purposes of section 84(2) of the Immigration and Asylum Act 1999 (as amended) (IAA 1999)

---

[2] The OISC were set up under the <u>Immigration and Asylum Act 1999</u>. They derive their powers from this Act, the <u>Nationality, Immigration and Asylum Act 2002</u> and the <u>Immigration Act 2014</u>.
[3] gC126 of the BSB Handbook

where the Office of the Immigration Services Commissioner has refused or cancelled the adviser's registration, or where the adviser is:

1. *disqualified in accordance with paragraph 4 of Schedule 6 to the IAA 1999; or*

2. *prohibited or suspended by the First-tier Tribunal (Immigration Services); or*

3. *permanently prohibited from practising by an approved regulator, or a designated professional body under the IAA 1999, pursuant to its powers as such, and removed from the relevant register; or*

4. *currently suspended from practising by an approved regulator, or a designated professional body under the IAA 1999, pursuant to its powers as such.*

7. In relation to rC85A.1, an adviser may be disqualified from registration or continued registration as a qualified person[4] if they have been convicted of an offence under the Immigration Act 1971 (1971 Act) of facilitating illegal entry, altering immigration documents or obstructing an immigration officer or other person acting in the execution of the 1971 Act[5].

8. In relation to rC85A.2, the First-tier Tribunal (Immigration Services) may suspend registration with OISC if the individual has been charged with an offence involving dishonesty or deception, or those listed within sections 25 or 26(1)(d) or (g) of the 1971 Act.

---

[4] s84(2) of the IAA 1999 Act
[5] http://www.legislation.gov.uk/ukpga/1999/33/notes/division/5/11

4

9. In relation to rC85A.3-.4, approved regulator has the same meaning as in the BSB Handbook and the Legal Services Act 2007. The relevant regulatory bodies are:

- The Solicitors Regulation Authority;

- The Bar Standards Board;

- The Chartered Institute of Legal Executives;

- The Council for Licensed Conveyancers;

- Intellectual Property Regulation Board;

- Costs Lawyers Standards Board;

- Master of the Faculties; and

- Institute of Chartered Accountants in England and Wales.

10. In relation to rC85A.3-.4, the designated professional bodies under the IAA 1999[6] regulate lawyers outside of England and Wales. The relevant designated professional bodies are:

- The Law Society of Scotland;

- The Law Society of Northern Ireland;

- The Faculty of Advocates; and

---

[6] s86 of the IAA 1999 Act

- The General Council of the Bar of Northern Ireland.

Before starting a supervision arrangement

11. Before entering into a supervision arrangement, you must hold a practising certificate, or be authorised as a BSB entity, and should read this guidance in full to ensure you understand your obligations.

12. **Before beginning any supervision of an immigration adviser, you must notify the BSB that you intend to supervise in accordance with Rule C80. Self-employed barristers should do this via your MyBar account. After this declaration, you will need to complete the Immigration Advisers Associations Form on the** BSB website **and submit this to** supervision@barstandardsboard.org.uk.

13. **If you are supervising via a BSB entity, you will need to complete the Immigration Advisers Associations Form on the** BSB website **and submit this to** entityregulation@barstandardsboard.org.uk.

14. Within the Immigration Advisers Associations Form, you should provide details of your proposed supervision arrangements and the due diligence undertaken. As a minimum, to comply with Rule C85A, we would expect you to establish if the immigration adviser has ever been registered with OISC, an approved regulator or a designated professional body under the IAA 1999. If they have ever been subject to one of the sanctions listed in Rule C85A, you should contact the relevant organisation for verification. Full details of how to do this are set out in Annex A.

15. Your notification form should set out any further checks you have undertaken, including identification documents and how you have assured yourself the

immigration adviser is professionally competent. This can include reviewing their training record, including any specific training undertaken in relation to vulnerability and how much experience they have.

16. If you are supervising an immigration adviser, they should have either a written contract of employment with you, or they should be under a written contract for services with you which is for a determinate period (subject to any provision for earlier termination on notice). Note that the rules on outsourcing also apply (Rule C86).

17. You must comply with the rules on insurance within the BSB Handbook (Rule C76) and ensure adequate insurance cover is in place for the work undertaken by the immigration adviser. You should inform your professional indemnity insurer of the proposed supervision arrangement.

Your obligations and the BSB Handbook

18. The BSB takes the view that you are <u>personally responsible</u> for any immigration work undertaken by the immigration adviser (Rule C20 and Guidance C65) and that this amounts to Public Access work. You should refer to the Public Access Guidance for Barristers and pay particular attention to the section on intermediaries. The guidance can be found on the BSB's <u>website</u>. You should also ensure you comply with the relevant transparency rules. Guidance on compliance can be found on the BSB's <u>website</u>. Where you are working via a BSB entity, the entity will be responsible for the work of the adviser.

19. A lay client receiving legal advice or other legal services from an immigration adviser working on your behalf, and under your supervision, relies on that relationship to ensure that:

- The advice given is correct,

- The services provided are to a competent standard, and

- The services are provided by a person that is fit to provide them.

20. You must comply with all the relevant provisions of the Code of Conduct, including the Core Duties, and should not act as a supervisor in relation to any matter for which you do not have the necessary relevant experience (Rule C21.8).

21. You should pay particular attention to Rule C22.1 and associated guidance when engaging with clients in relation to immigration advice and services. The rule requires that the terms and/or basis on which instructions have been accepted should be set out in writing to the client. You should provide details of the supervision arrangements in this documentation to your client, to ensure they are fully informed. You should not mislead or allow your client to be misled about the status of an immigration adviser, nor the arrangements for supervision.

22. You must ensure that you comply with the rules in the Handbook relating to client complaints (Rules C99-C109), so clients can raise any concerns they have with you or the entity. You should also have regard to the BSB's Guidance on First Tier Complaints Handling[7]. If the work has been undertaken on a Public Access basis, the Public Access Model Client Care Letter to the Client in an Intermediary Case sets out avenues for redress and should be appropriately adapted and provided to the lay client[8].

---

[7] https://www.barstandardsboard.org.uk/for-barristers/bsb-handbook-and-code-guidance/code.html
[8] https://www.barstandardsboard.org.uk/resources/resource-library/public-access-model-client-care-letter-to-the-client-in-an-intermediary-case-doc.html

23. You should have regard to the rules and guidance relating to intermediaries in Public Access cases and:

- Consider whether you have the necessary skills and experience to do the work, including, where relevant, the ability to work with a vulnerable client;

- If the immigration adviser has limited experience, you should consider the amount of direct contact they should have with clients and in any event, assure yourself that your policies and processes have been complied with;

- Consider whether it would be in the best interests of the client or of the interests of justice for the client to instruct a solicitor or other professional client;

- If the matter involves the conduct of litigation and you are not able or instructed to conduct litigation, consider whether the client will be able to undertake the tasks that you cannot perform for them;

- Consider whether the client is clear about the services which you will and will not provide and any limitations on what you can do, and what will be expected of them; and

- If you are not able to act in legal aid cases, consider if the client is in a position to make an informed decision as to whether to seek legal aid or proceed with Public Access.

24. When entering into an arrangement with an immigration adviser, you should remind yourself of the BSB Handbook rules regarding the prohibition on paying or receiving referral fees (Rule C10) and entering into associations with non-BSB regulated persons (Rule C79-C85A).

25. If you are outsourcing work, this does not alter your obligations to your client. You must comply with the outsourcing rules (Rule C86) and you remain personally responsible for the work (Guidance C65).

Accepting instructions

<u>Self-employed barristers</u>

26. If you are supervising an immigration adviser as a self-employed barrister, you must be Public Access registered and comply with Rules S24 and C87-90, as they relate to the administration of your practice. In particular, you must ensure that all non-authorised persons working in your chambers, including immigration advisers, are competent and do nothing which causes, or substantially contributes to, a breach of the BSB Handbook (Rule C89.6.d).

<u>BSB entities</u>

27. If you are supervising an immigration adviser via a BSB entity, you must comply with the rules relating to BSB entities. In particular, you must ensure that all employees and immigration advisers are competent and do nothing which causes, or substantially contributes to, a breach of the BSB Handbook (Rule C94.2.d). You should have regard to Guidance S7 in the Handbook and the relevant provisions in the Code of Conduct, especially Rules C17, C21.7, C21.8 and C22.

<u>Employed in an authorised (non-BSB) body</u>

28. If you are supervising an immigration adviser in your capacity as an employed barrister of an authorised (non-BSB) body, you must comply with the rules of the approved regulator that regulates the authorised non-BSB body (Rules I8 and S36). If you are employed by an authorised non-BSB body but the supervision

arrangements <u>do not</u> constitute part of the organisation's work, you will need a dual capacity practising certificate (employed and self-employed). This will enable you to provide supervision as a self-employed barrister, provided that you comply with all relevant rules for self-employed practice and have regard to this guidance.

What does a suitable supervision arrangement look like?

29. The BSB takes the view that the following factors are likely to be present as part of any effective supervision arrangements:

- The immigration adviser is genuinely acting on your behalf and under your supervision and you are readily available to provide guidance and supervision to the immigration adviser;

- The arrangements are discussed between you and the immigration adviser before you begin to supervise and documented in a protocol, which is included within their contract (of either employment or services). This will be in place for each immigration adviser you propose to supervise and include the terms of engagement with clients and any financial and insurance arrangements. This will help ensure that you: have undertaken due diligence; can manage your own workload; understand the level of supervision which is required and act appropriately; and set clear expectations governing your relationship with the immigration adviser. The BSB may ask to see a copy of this protocol (Guidance C125);

- You regularly supervise in person so you can have proper oversight of the work. Whilst this may need to be provided remotely from time to time, you need to assure yourself that all processes are being followed correctly; and

- You have frequent documented contact with the immigration adviser so that you have full up to date knowledge and understanding of all the casework the immigration adviser is undertaking in your name.

Examples of good practice
<ul><li>Completing a risk assessment of the case to ensure the supervised immigration adviser is competent to deal with all the relevant issues that may arise;</li><li>Weekly contact and oversight of case progress;</li><li>Daily availability so the immigration adviser can contact you if there is an urgent matter;</li><li>Assigning appropriate cover if you are taking holiday;</li><li>The use of training logs, checklists and regular feedback to monitor the ability and professional development of the immigration adviser, to ensure competence;</li><li>Limiting direct client contact by the immigration adviser unless and until certain internal quality standards have been demonstrated to have been met; and</li><li>Ensuring that tasks on a case are appropriately delegated and no immigration adviser is asked to complete a task that is beyond their competence.</li></ul>

Examples of high risk practices
• The barrister has no experience of supervising others' work and has undertaken no training to develop their skills in this area;
• More than three immigration advisers being supervised by one barrister;
• A lack of training for the immigration adviser or barrister on the case management systems used as this could increase the risk of errors and/or result in insufficient oversight; and
• The barrister has not carried out an assessment of the immigration adviser's advocacy skills to ensure that the adviser is competent to attend Tribunal hearings on the barrister's behalf (where relevant).

BSB concerns about supervision arrangements

30. The BSB will not formally approve the supervision arrangement. However, if there are concerns about your compliance with Rules C80 and C85A, the BSB will consider the extent to which you can demonstrate your compliance with this guidance when determining what regulatory action, if any, to take in relation to an alleged breach of Rule C85A.

Further advice

31. If you would like to discuss your duties and responsibilities when supervising an immigration adviser, contact the Bar Council's Ethical Enquiries Service: https://www.barcouncil.org.uk/supporting-the-bar/ethical-enquiries-service/

February 2020

Bar Standards Board

Annex A – How to check if an immigration adviser has been sanctioned

OISC

Sanction	Where to check
Prohibited from practice or currently suspended	On their website
Whether the adviser, or their organisation, has had their registration refused or cancelled	Email foi-dpa@oisc.gov.uk. Note that this can take up to 20 working days

Approved regulators

Sanction	Where to check
Bar Standards Board	
Past disciplinary findings, including disbarments and current suspensions	On the 'Past disciplinary findings' page of our website
Current suspensions pending a disciplinary hearing	On the 'Interim suspended barristers' page of our website
Solicitors Regulation Authority	On their website Any further queries can be submitted to the Contact Centre

The Bar Standards Board
Handbook

Chartered Institute of Legal Executives	On their website

Designated professional bodies under the IAA 1999

Sanction	Where to check
The Law Society of Scotland	The Scottish Solicitors' Discipline Tribunal's website
The Law Society of Northern Ireland	Email enquiry@lawsoc-ni.org
The Faculty of Advocates	Email the Dean's Secretariat deans.secretariat@advocates.org.uk
The General Council of the Bar of Northern Ireland	Submit a letter to the Chief Executive of the Bar Council of Northern Ireland stating the purpose for which you require the information. Send this to: The Bar Library 91 Chichester Street Belfast BT1 3JQ Northern Ireland

Transparency Standards Guidance – Introduction

Contents

<u>**Purpose of the guidance**</u>

There are four main sections to this guidance:

- **Section 1: mandatory rules on price, service and redress transparency for everyone (all self-employed barristers, chambers and BSB entities, but not employed barristers);**
- **Section 2: additional transparency rules for those undertaking Public Access work (self-employed barristers undertaking Public Access work, and BSB entities supplying legal services directly to the public);**
- **Section 3: additional best practice on transparency for everyone (which goes beyond the mandatory rules); and**
- **Section 4: checklists to help you comply with the transparency rules, and information about the BSB's supervision and enforcement strategy.**

The Competition and Markets Authority (CMA) has recommended that all legal regulators **deliver a step change in standards of transparency for consumers.**[1]

The CMA described this as the information needed to help consumers understand the price and service they will receive, what redress is available, and the regulatory status of their provider.

The Bar Standards Board (BSB) has therefore introduced mandatory rules on price, service and redress transparency for everyone. By "everyone", we mean all self-employed barristers, chambers and BSB entities, but not employed barristers.

---

[1] https://assets.publishing.service.gov.uk/media/5887374d40f0b6593700001a/legal-services-market-study-final-report.pdf

There are also additional transparency rules for those undertaking Public Access work. This includes self-employed barristers undertaking Public Access work, and BSB entities supplying legal services directly to the public. In particular, if you provide the Public Access services listed in the current version of the BSB's price transparency policy statement (Annex B), you must comply with additional price transparency rules in relation to those legal services.

You must comply with these transparency rules from **July 2019**.

This guidance aims to:

- Support you in complying with the mandatory rules from July 2019 (sections 1 – 2); and
- Encourage you to go beyond the mandatory rules. The guidance includes additional best practice on transparency to help you to do so (section 3).

We have also provided checklists to help you comply with the transparency rules, and information about the BSB's supervision and enforcement strategy (section 4).

In complying with the transparency rules, you must have regard to the current version of this guidance.

To whom the rules apply

The mandatory rules on price, service and redress transparency only apply to self-employed barristers, chambers and BSB entities.

If you work for an entity which is authorised by another legal regulator (for example, a law firm authorised by the Solicitors Regulation Authority (SRA)), then you may find this

guidance useful as best practice, but you must comply with the transparency rules of the other regulator.

If you work in-house for an employer which is not authorised by a legal regulator (for example, a Government Department or financial institution), then you will not need to comply with the transparency rules.

How to comply with the rules

Everyone must comply with the transparency rules by providing information about price, service and redress on their websites.

Multiple websites

If you operate multiple websites as part of your practice, you must comply with the transparency rules on each website offering legal services, as appropriate. For example:

> *Barrister A is self-employed and practises from chambers. The chambers' website complies with the transparency rules. Barrister A also operates a separate website for their Public Access practice. There are additional transparency rules for those undertaking Public Access work, so their separate website must also comply with these additional rules.*

> *Barrister B is self-employed and practises as a sole practitioner. Their website complies with the transparency rules. Barrister B also works for a BSB entity. The BSB entity's website must also comply with the transparency rules.*

> *Barrister C is self-employed and practises from chambers. The chambers' website complies with the transparency rules. Barrister C also operates a separate website for their work acting as a mediator. Acting as a mediator is not included in the*

definition of 'legal services' in the BSB Handbook, so their separate website does not need to comply with the transparency rules.

A chambers in London operates a website for their members' work in England and Wales. The chambers' website complies with the transparency rules. The chambers also operates a separate website for their members' work from an annex of chambers, which is located abroad. This separate website must also comply with the transparency rules.

BSB entities as members of chambers

You may be a barrister practising through a BSB entity as a member of a chambers, and not operating multiple websites. In this case, you will not need to provide additional information on your chambers' website beyond that which the other (self-employed) members provide. However, your chambers' website must display the following text <u>on the homepage</u>: *"barristers regulated by the Bar Standards Board"*. This must be accompanied by a statement that the BSB entity is *"authorised and regulated by the Bar Standards Board"* – see the mandatory rules on redress transparency in section 1.

Providing information in alternative format on request

You must also comply with the transparency rules by ensuring the required information is readily available in alternative format. This must be provided on request. For example:

Barrister A's website complies with the transparency rules, but they are contacted by a prospective client who does not have Internet access. The prospective client requests price, service and redress information in alternative format. Barrister A's clerk sends the prospective client the information in alternative format.

Barrister B does not have a website. They are contacted by a prospective client who requests price, service and redress information in alternative format. Barrister B's clerk sends the prospective client the information in alternative format.

You can provide information in alternative format in the form of a 'fact sheet'. You should not charge a fee for this. An example of a fact sheet can be found at Annex A.

Responsibility for compliance

Sole practitioners are responsible for complying with the transparency rules.

The BSB Handbook requires all self-employed barristers to take reasonable steps to ensure that their chambers are administered competently and efficiently – this includes ensuring compliance with the transparency rules. In practice, compliance with the transparency rules will in most cases be a matter for the management of chambers. However, individual self-employed barristers in chambers are still required to take reasonable steps to ensure compliance with the transparency rules.

BSB entities are responsible for complying with the transparency rules. The BSB Handbook also requires those working in entities to take reasonable steps to ensure that they are administered competently and efficiently – this includes ensuring the transparency rules are complied with. In practice, compliance with the transparency rules will in most cases be a matter for the management of entities. However, individuals working in entities are still required to take reasonable steps to ensure compliance with the transparency rules.

Plain English

All information provided should be in plain English so that it can be easily understood by consumers. The Plain English Campaign's website has a number of free guides that you may find useful.

CURRENT GUIDANCE

Transparency Standards Guidance – Section 1

Mandatory rules on price, service and redress transparency for everyone

By "everyone", we mean all self-employed barristers, chambers and BSB entities, but not employed barristers.

Contents

Summary

All websites must:

- State that professional, licensed access, and/or lay clients (as appropriate) may contact the barrister, chambers or BSB entity to obtain a quotation for legal services;
- Provide contact details;
- State the barrister, chambers or BSB entity's most commonly used pricing models for legal services, such as fixed fee or hourly rate;
- State the areas of practice in which the barrister, chambers or BSB entity most commonly provides legal services;
- State and provide a description of the barrister's, chambers' or BSB entity's most commonly provided legal services;
- Provide information about the factors which might influence the timescales of the barrister's, chambers' or BSB entity's most commonly provided legal services;
- Display the appropriate *"regulated by the Bar Standards Board"* text <u>on the homepage</u>;
- Display information about their complaints procedure, any right to complain to the Legal Ombudsman (LeO), how to complain to LeO, and any time limits for making a complaint;
- Link to the <u>decision data</u> on LeO's website; and
- Link to the <u>Barristers' Register page</u> on the BSB's website.

The required information must be sufficiently accessible and prominent on websites, accurate and up to date and readily available in alternative format (an example can be found at Annex A). All professional e-mail and letterheads must also display the appropriate *"regulated by the Bar Standards Board"* text.

Price transparency – mandatory rules for everyone

1) Websites must state that professional, licensed access, and/or lay clients (as appropriate) may contact the barrister, chambers, or BSB entity to obtain a quotation for legal services, and provide contact details. Quotations must be provided if sufficient information has been provided by the client, and the barrister, barristers in chambers, or BSB entity would be willing to provide the legal services. Quotations must also be provided within a reasonable time period, and in clear and readily understandable terms.

This will ensure consumers are aware that they can contact you to obtain quotations, and know how to do so.

Professional clients include solicitors and other practising lawyers who are able to instruct barristers.

Licensed access clients are able to instruct barristers either because they hold a licence issued by the BSB, or are a member of a professional body which has been recognised by the BSB. For more information, see the BSB's Licensed Access Recognition Regulations.

Your chambers may not have any self-employed barristers undertaking Public Access work, or you may be a BSB entity which does not supply legal services directly to the public. In this case, it is best practice to state that lay clients may not contact you directly to obtain quotations as solicitors will do this.

Quotations must be provided if sufficient information has been provided by the client, and the barrister, barristers in chambers or BSB entity would be willing to provide the legal services. Quotations must also be provided within a reasonable time period, and in clear and readily understandable terms.

The test for "sufficient information being provided" is whether the consumer has provided sufficient information such that you can quote a meaningful range for the legal services in question. If you are able to quote a meaningful range, you must do so within a reasonable time period and not incur unnecessary delay by asking to read further papers – the aim is to help consumers to "shop around" for legal services. A "reasonable time period" will normally mean within 14 days, although depending on consumer need/urgency quotations may need to be provided sooner.

It is acceptable for clerks to provide quotations on behalf of barristers (although under the BSB Handbook, you are responsible for the service provided by your clerks). If your input is needed to provide a quotation, but you have urgent work commitments, it is acceptable to take longer than 14 days provided the consumer's expectations are managed.

You should not charge for providing quotations and, when quoting a meaningful range, you can state that you would need to read further papers to quote a more precise figure and advise whether you would be able (or willing, subject to the cab-rank rule) to provide the legal services in question. It is open to you to accept instructions and charge a fee for reading further papers and advising whether you can act, but in many cases it is best practice not to do so (for example, if the consumer is not requesting that you quote a more precise figure).

While quotations will be binding, you can state that if the scope of the legal services changes then the quotation will not be binding. When providing a quotation, you should also make it clear to the consumer that this does not amount to the acceptance of instructions. If once you have provided a quotation the consumer decides to instruct you, you must comply with Rule C22.1 of the BSB Handbook by confirming in writing acceptance of the instructions and the terms and/or basis on which you will be acting, including the basis of charging. If you are acting on a Public or Licensed Access basis, you must also comply with Rule C125 or Rule C127 of the BSB Handbook (as appropriate).

If you are not able (or willing, subject to the cab-rank rule) to provide the legal services in question, you will need to explain this clearly to the consumer within a reasonable time period. It is also best practice to then refer such consumers to directories of legal services providers such as <u>Chambers and Partners</u>, the <u>Legal 500</u>, <u>Juriosity</u> and the Bar Council's <u>Direct Access Portal</u>.

In addition, you must keep consumers' data safe and secure, and handle it according to the General Data Protection Regulation (GDPR). The Bar Council's GDPR Toolkit is available on their website: <u>https://www.barcouncil.org.uk/supporting-the-bar/bar-council-training-courses/gdpr-toolkit/</u>.

2) Websites must state the barrister, chambers or BSB entity's most commonly used pricing models for legal services. Where different models are typically used for different legal services, this must be explained.

This will ensure consumers are aware of the different pricing models that are available, and in what circumstances (it will be acceptable to state that pricing models are only available in certain circumstances). Commonly used pricing models include brief fees and refreshers, fixed fees and hourly rates. However, the BSB takes no view on the most appropriate pricing models for different legal services.

If your clients are less experienced and less expert consumers, and/or instruct you on a Public Access basis, it may be particularly useful for you to explain the pricing models you commonly use. A list of commonly used pricing models, along with an explanation for each one, can be found at Annex K.

If you are also open to using other types of pricing models, you can state this. For example:

"Barristers in chambers also accept instructions under conditional fee agreements ("no win, no fee" agreements) in certain circumstances. For more information, please contact the clerks on XX (or e-mail XX)."

The mandatory rules on price transparency are a minimum standard which everyone must meet. However, we encourage you to go beyond this – see the additional best practice on price transparency in section 3.

Service transparency – mandatory rules for everyone

1) Websites must state the areas of practice in which the barrister, chambers or BSB entity most commonly provides legal services, in a way which enables consumers to sufficiently understand their expertise.

This should enable consumers to understand the areas of practice in which you specialise at a glance. For example:

"Barristers in chambers practise in criminal, immigration and licensing law."

Chambers, sole practitioners and BSB entities must provide this level of practice area information as a minimum. Chambers can also provide practice area information for each individual self-employed barrister, as many do already.

Barristers will already declare their areas of practice when applying to the Bar Mutual Indemnity Fund (BMIF) for professional indemnity insurance. You can use the same terminology that BMIF use for areas of practice. This can be found on their website: https://www.barmutual.co.uk/downloads/.

2) Websites must state and provide a description of the barrister, chambers or BSB entity's most commonly provided legal services, in a way which enables consumers to sufficiently understand their expertise.

This will ensure consumers have a basic knowledge of your most commonly provided legal services, and sufficiently understand your expertise. For example:

> *"Barristers in chambers specialise in criminal work. Our barristers advise and represent clients facing criminal charges in the Magistrates' or Crown Courts. Our barristers also act for clients in the High Court and Court of Appeal, and for the Crown Prosecution Service."*

Chambers, sole practitioners and BSB entities must provide this level of information as a minimum. Chambers can also provide information for each individual self-employed barrister, as many do already.

3) Websites must provide information about the factors which might influence the timescales of the barrister, chambers or BSB entity's most commonly provided legal services.

For example, you can include generic information about how the following might influence the timescales:

- Your availability;
- The availability of the client or relevant third parties;
- The complexity of the case;
- The amount of papers you need to review;
- The need for additional information or documents;
- The approach taken by the other side;
- Third parties intervening in the case; and

- Court waiting times.

This will help consumers to understand what they can expect from a case and from you, and manage those expectations. The information will be particularly useful if your clients are less experienced and less expert consumers, and/or instruct you on a Public Access basis.

However, we recognise that the information will be indicative only and, in many cases, specific to your practice area. We are therefore not prescribing that websites must provide standardised information about the factors which might influence the timescales of your most commonly provided legal services. Instead, you will need to provide this information in a way which is relevant to your practice.

We appreciate that the Bar will already be providing much of this information about their services on their websites. The mandatory rules on service transparency are a minimum standard which everyone must meet. However, we encourage you to go beyond this – see the additional best practice on service transparency in section 3.

Redress transparency – mandatory rules for everyone

1) Websites must display the following text <u>on the homepage</u>:

- **For sole practitioners, *"regulated by the Bar Standards Board"***
- **For chambers, *"barristers regulated by the Bar Standards Board"***
- **For BSB entities, *"authorised and regulated by the Bar Standards Board"***

This will ensure consumers are aware that you are regulated by the BSB. They will have confidence that the Bar is a properly regulated profession.

This text must be displayed on the homepage of your website as a minimum. However, it is best practice to display this text on all pages of your website.

2) Websites must display information about your complaints procedure, any right to complain to the Legal Ombudsman (LeO), how to complain to LeO, and any time limits for making a complaint.

The BSB Handbook already requires you to display information about your complaints procedure on your website. You now must also display information about any right to complain to LeO, how to complain to LeO and any time limits for making a complaint. This will ensure consumers know about LeO and how to complain to them.

You must state on your website that:

- Clients can complain to LeO if they are unhappy with the final response to their complaint, or if their complaint has not been dealt with in eight weeks; and
- Clients who have a right to complain to LeO are individuals and, broadly speaking, small businesses and charities.

The full list of who has a right to complain to LeO is available on their website: http://www.legalombudsman.org.uk/?faqs=who-can-use-our-service. You can provide this link on your website for reference.

You must also display information on your website about how to complain to LeO. You should summarise the key information, rather than simply providing a link to LeO's website. For example:

"You can write to the Legal Ombudsman at:

Legal Ombudsman
PO Box 6806,
Wolverhampton.
WV1 9WJ.

Telephone number: 0300 555 0333.

Email: enquiries@legalombudsman.org.uk.

More information about the Legal Ombudsman is available on their website:
http://www.legalombudsman.org.uk/."

Finally, you must display information on your website about any time limits for making a complaint to LeO. For example:

> *"You must complain to the Legal Ombudsman **either** within six years of your barrister's actions/failure to act, **or** no later than three years after you should reasonably have known there were grounds to complain.*
>
> *You must also complain to the Legal Ombudsman within six months of receiving your barrister's final response to your complaint."*

3) Websites must link to the decision data on LeO's website.

The link to the decision data on LeO's website is http://www.legalombudsman.org.uk/raising-standards/data-and-decisions/#ombudsman-decision-data.

You should explain that the decision data on LeO's website shows providers which received an ombudsman's decision in the previous 12 months. In each case, the data shows whether LeO required the provider to give the consumer a remedy.

Linking to this page will allow consumers to see whether a barrister was required to provide any remedies in the previous 12 months. This will help consumers to make informed decisions about whom to instruct.

4) Websites must link to the Barristers' Register page on the BSB's website.

The link to the Barristers' Register page on the BSB's website is
https://www.barstandardsboard.org.uk/regulatory-requirements/the-barristers'-register/.

You should explain that the BSB's Barristers' Register shows (1) who has a current practising certificate, and (2) whether a barrister has any disciplinary findings, which are published on the Barristers' Register in accordance with our policy.

The Barristers' Register page also links to the BSB's Entities' Register. If you are a BSB entity, you should explain that the BSB's Entities' Register shows which entities are currently authorised by the BSB.

Linking to this page will help consumers to make informed decisions about whom to instruct.

The mandatory rules on redress transparency are a minimum standard which everyone must meet. However, we encourage you to go beyond this – see the additional best practice on redress transparency in section 3.

Further mandatory rules for everyone

1) All professional e-mail and letterheads must state:

- For self-employed barristers, *"regulated by the Bar Standards Board"*
- For BSB entities, their managers and employees, *"authorised and regulated by the Bar Standards Board"*

This will ensure consumers, professional clients and others are aware that you are regulated by the BSB. Consumers will have confidence that the Bar is a properly regulated

profession. Professional clients and others will also be able to find information about the BSB and our regulatory standards.

"Professional e-mail and letterheads" includes fee notes and invoices.

2) You must tell us your website address(es).

Self-employed barristers must tell us their chambers' website address(es) during the Authorisation to Practise process, which takes place in February – March each year. The process is completed using the MyBar portal.

You may operate multiple websites as part of your practice. For example, you may operate a separate website for your Public Access practice. In this case, you must tell us each website address via MyBar.

BSB entities must also tell us their website addresses during the entity renewal process, which takes place in February – March each year.

We will then verify your website address(es).

3) You must tell us about changes to your website address(es) within 28 days.

Self-employed barristers must do this using the MyBar portal.

You may operate multiple websites as part of your practice. For example, you may operate a separate website for your Public Access practice. In this case, you must still tell us about website address changes via MyBar.

BSB entities must tell us about website address changes by contacting the Entity Authorisation Team.

We will then verify your new website address(es).

4) To comply with the transparency rules, you must ensure the required information is sufficiently accessible and prominent on your website.

This means that in most cases the required information should either be on the homepage or one or two clicks away from the homepage (one way to achieve this is to have a 'quick links' page). The information should also be in a font size that enables it to be easily read.

In some cases, you may take the view that it is appropriate for the required information to be further away from the homepage. However, you will need to be able to justify this.

You should also consider whether the required information is accessible for people with disabilities – see the additional best practice on website accessibility in section 3.

The appropriate "regulated by the Bar Standards Board" text must also be displayed <u>on the homepage</u> – see the mandatory rules on redress transparency above.

5) To comply with the transparency rules, you must ensure your website content is not misleading to clients and prospective clients. You must also review your website content at least annually to ensure it is accurate and complies with the transparency rules.

You must of course ensure your website content is not misleading to clients and prospective clients. For example, stating a price which you would not charge in any circumstances would clearly be misleading and would breach the BSB Handbook.

Reviewing your website content at least annually to ensure it is accurate and complies with the transparency rules will allow you to update price, service and redress information if

necessary. You can review your website content more often than this, but it must be done at least annually. Checklists to help you with this can be found in section 4.

It is recommended that you keep copies of checklists. This will allow you to demonstrate to the BSB that you have done these reviews.

In addition, it is recommended that website pages state the date on which they were last reviewed.

You may use analytics software to help you with reviewing your website content. This will allow you to monitor traffic to each of your website pages to see what is attracting interest, and help you to see where you may wish to make changes (while still complying with the transparency rules).

If you use analytics software, you must seek your website users' consent to monitor which website pages they are visiting. This is part of your obligation to handle consumers' data consistently with the General Data Protection Regulation (GDPR). The Bar Council's GDPR Toolkit is available on their website: https://www.barcouncil.org.uk/supporting-the-bar/bar-council-training-courses/gdpr-toolkit/.

Transparency Standards Guidance – Section 2

Additional transparency rules for those undertaking Public Access work

This includes self-employed barristers undertaking Public Access work, and BSB entities supplying legal services directly to the public.

Contents

Summary

If some or all of the barristers practising from a chambers are undertaking Public Access work, or if a BSB entity is supplying legal services directly to the public, websites must link to the Public Access Guidance for Lay Clients page on the BSB's website.

If the Public Access services listed in the BSB's price transparency policy statement (Annex B) are being provided, websites must:

- State which pricing model(s) are used, such as fixed fee or hourly rate;
- State indicative fees and the circumstances in which they may vary;
- State whether fees include VAT (where applicable);
- State likely additional costs, what they cover, and either the cost or, if this can only be estimated, the typical range of costs; and
- State and provide a description of the relevant Public Access services, including a concise statement of the key stages and an indicative timescale for the key stages.

The required information must be sufficiently accessible and prominent on websites, accurate and up to date, and readily available in alternative format.

Price transparency – mandatory rules for those undertaking Public Access work

1) If you provide the Public Access services listed in the current version of the BSB's price transparency policy statement (Annex B), your website must also state the following in relation to those legal services:

- **Your pricing model(s), such as fixed fee or hourly rate;**

2

The Bar Standards Board

Handbook

REGULATING BARRISTERS

- **Your indicative fees and the circumstances in which they may vary. For example, a fixed fee and the circumstances in which additional fees may be charged, or an hourly rate by seniority of barrister;**
- **Whether your fees include VAT (where applicable); and**
- **Likely additional costs, what they cover and either the cost or, if this can only be estimated, the typical range of costs.**

If you provide the Public Access services listed in the current version of the BSB's price transparency policy statement (Annex B), you must comply with additional price transparency rules in relation to those legal services.

In this case, your website must state your pricing model(s) in relation to those legal services; for example, fixed fee, hourly rate, etc. This will ensure consumers are aware of the pricing model(s) that you use for the service in question (it will be acceptable to state that pricing models are only available in certain circumstances). It may be useful for you to explain the pricing model(s). A list of commonly used pricing models, along with an explanation for each one, can be found at Annex K.

You must also state your indicative fees for the service in question and the circumstances in which they may vary. For example, a fixed fee and the circumstances in which additional fees may be charged, or an hourly rate by seniority of barrister. Fees may also vary depending on where barristers are located (say, a regional annex of chambers), or the client's needs – fees may be higher if the client has a more complex case and/or needs a more experienced barrister. This information will help consumers to "shop around" for the service. We recognise that fees will be indicative only, and this should be stated on your website. For example:

"All information is correct as of X, but fees are estimates only. For a quotation, please contact the clerks on XX (or e-mail XX)."

③

You must also state whether your fees include VAT (where applicable).

Finally, you must state likely additional costs (for example, court fees), what they cover and either the cost or, if this can only be estimated, the typical range of costs. Where appropriate, you can link to external websites (for example, the court and tribunal fees section of gov.uk).

For each Public Access service listed in the current version of the BSB's price transparency policy statement (Annex B), the specific circumstances in which price transparency requirements apply and an example of the required price and service transparency can be found at Annexes C – J.

You may also find the Legal Ombudsman's (LeO's) view of good costs service useful in stating your pricing model(s) and your indicative fees and the circumstances in which they may vary. Disputes about costs are one of the most frequent areas of complaint. The provision of clear information is the best way of avoiding such complaints.

2) You must state your pricing model(s), your indicative fees and the circumstances in which they may vary, whether your fees include VAT (where applicable), and likely additional costs, as follows:

- **If asked to accept instructions at short notice, as soon as reasonably practicable after accepting instructions;**
- **For a sole practitioner, in relation to you as an individual barrister;**
- **For a BSB entity, in relation to the entity; and**
- **For a chambers, either in relation to (1) individual barristers, or (2) barristers in chambers in the form of ranges or average fees.**

We recognise that you may not currently be providing the Public Access services listed in the current version of the BSB's price transparency policy statement (Annex B), but may be

asked to accept instructions to do so at short notice. In this case, you will not need to comply with additional price transparency rules before accepting instructions. However, you must do so as soon as reasonably practicable after accepting instructions.

How you comply with additional price transparency rules will also depend on whether you are a self-employed barrister in chambers, sole practitioner or BSB entity. Sole practitioners and BSB entities are what is known as 'single economic units'. This means that you contract with clients, and set fees as a standard offering. A sole practitioner will do this individually, and a BSB entity will do this for the whole entity. If you are a BSB entity, it may also be useful for you to state whether the Public Access service in question would normally be provided by a more senior or junior member of staff.

However, unlike sole practitioners and BSB entities, chambers are not single economic units as they are made up of a number of self-employed barristers. This means that chambers do not contract with clients, and cannot set fees as a standard offering. It also means that self-employed barristers in chambers have the option of providing:

- Price information for each individual barrister (option one); or
- Price information in the form of ranges or average fees for barristers in chambers (option two).

Providing price information for each individual barrister (option one) may not help consumers to "shop around" for legal services. The larger your chambers, the more appropriate it will be for you to provide price information in the form of ranges or average fees for barristers in chambers (option two). It will be easier for consumers to understand, and easier for you to administer and keep updated.

If you use option two, you should state the basis on which you are providing price information for barristers in chambers – either ranges or average fees. These indicative fees must be accompanied with the circumstances in which they may vary. For example, fees for

barristers in chambers may vary depending on the client's needs – fees may be higher if the client has a more complex case and/or needs a more experienced barrister. Fees for barristers in chambers may also vary depending on the seniority of barrister, or where barristers are located (say, a regional annex of chambers). If you use option two, you can provide price information for barristers in chambers (either ranges or average fees):

- On the basis of all barristers in chambers;
- By seniority of barrister; or
- By location/annex of chambers.

You should consider which type of price information would be most useful for your clients.

Whether you use option one or two, you must ensure that self-employed barristers in chambers remain able to compete with each other. This means that chambers must not set fees as a standard offering, and barristers must not co-ordinate with each other to keep prices at a certain level, agree to charge the same prices, or put mechanisms in place for setting prices. Doing so could risk breaching competition law. The CMA has produced guidance on complying with competition law, and a four-step competition law compliance process. You should have regard to these documents.

It is also important to ensure that barristers do not risk breaching competition law where they practise from different chambers and BSB entities, or operate multiple websites as part of their practice (for example, a barrister may operate a separate website for some Public Access work). Again in these circumstances, barristers must not co-ordinate with each other to keep prices at a certain level, agree to charge the same prices, or put mechanisms in place for setting prices.

If you are involved in setting prices for a BSB entity and also practise as a self-employed barrister (either as a sole practitioner or from chambers), you may be competing directly with the BSB entity and/or its partners and employees (if they also practise in a self-

employed capacity). In this case, you should consider seeking specialist advice to ensure that you do not risk breaching competition law. You may be advised to establish internal rules on who is allowed to set the BSB entity's prices where they relate to offering similar services to the same set of customers in the same geographic market. To comply with competition law, you will need to prevent the exchange of commercially sensitive price information between competitors.

The mandatory rules on price transparency are a minimum standard which must be met. However, we encourage you to go beyond this – see the additional best practice on price transparency in section 3.

Service transparency – mandatory rules for those undertaking Public Access work

1) Websites must link to the Public Access Guidance for Lay Clients page on the BSB's website.

This is only required if some or all of the barristers practising from a chambers are undertaking Public Access work, or if a BSB entity is supplying legal services directly to the public. It will help members of the public to understand how the Public Access scheme works, and explain how they can use it to instruct barristers directly.

The link to the Public Access Guidance for Lay Clients page on the BSB's website is https://www.barstandardsboard.org.uk/for-the-public/finding-and-using-a-barrister/how-to-instruct-a-barrister/public-access-guidance-for-lay-clients.html.

2) If you provide the Public Access services listed in the current version of the BSB's price transparency policy statement (Annex B), your website must also state and provide a description of those legal services. The description must include a concise statement of the key stages and an indicative timescale for the key stages. This must be done in a way which ensures consumers sufficiently understand the service.

If you provide the Public Access services listed in the current version of the BSB's price transparency policy statement (Annex B), you must comply with additional price transparency rules in relation to those legal services. See the mandatory rules on price transparency in section 1.

In this case, your website must also state and provide a description of those legal services. The description must include a concise statement of the key stages to ensure that consumers sufficiently understand the service you are providing.

If it would not be obvious to a lay client what a stage of the service is, provide a short explanation. This will ensure consumers have a basic knowledge of the legal services, and may help them to assess how feasible 'unbundling' would be – assuming responsibility for some aspects of the case themselves, if they are able to do so.

The description must also include an indicative timescale for the key stages of the service. This will help consumers to understand what they can expect from the case and from you, and manage those expectations. However, we recognise that timescales will be indicative only and so we only require a concise statement which assists clients in making informed choices, rather than detailed information about timescales. It will also be useful for you to state whether indicative timescales include possible appeals. For example:

> "*As a guide, court hearings for an order tend to take six to twelve months. This does not include possible appeals.*"

Finally, it will be useful for you to explain any limitations of the service you are able to offer. For example, if you/barristers in chambers are not authorised to conduct litigation and if relevant to the legal service in question, it will be useful for you to explain that Public Access clients will need to issue proceedings, file documents at court, and serve documents on other parties themselves. The BSB's Guidance on Conducting Litigation will help you to explain this where relevant.

The Bar Standards Board
Handbook

For each Public Access service listed in the current version of the BSB's price transparency policy statement (Annex B), the specific circumstances in which price transparency requirements apply and an example of the required price and service transparency can be found at Annexes C – J.

The mandatory rules on service transparency are a minimum standard which must be met. However, we encourage you to go beyond this – see the additional best practice on service transparency in section 3.

REGULATING BARRISTERS

CURRENT GUIDANCE

Transparency Standards Guidance – Section 3

Additional best practice on transparency for everyone

By "everyone", we mean all self-employed barristers, chambers and BSB entities, but not employed barristers. The additional best practice in this section encourages you to go beyond the mandatory rules.

In considering whether to adopt these best practice suggestions, remember that price transparency in particular can be a good way to encourage consumers to seek the services of fully qualified and regulated practitioners (rather than seeking the services of Mackenzie friends, or not seeking legal advice and representation). However, if you do decide to adopt some of these best practice suggestions, you should think about whether providing the information would actually improve consumer understanding, and therefore help consumers to make informed decisions about their case.

Contents

Summary

If you would like to go beyond the mandatory rules on price transparency, your website can also:

- State your indicative fees for your most commonly provided legal services, the circumstances in which they may vary, whether your fees include VAT (where applicable), and likely additional costs;
- Include information about the typical range of costs for different stages of cases (where appropriate);
- Include information about how to avoid/manage the risk of costs increasing significantly, and any price flexibility;
- Include information about legal insurance;
- Include information about legal aid eligibility;
- Include information about any third party payment services you use; and
- State that you, barristers in chambers or the BSB entity is registered for VAT, and that you can provide your VAT number(s) on request.

If you would like to go beyond the mandatory rules on service transparency, your website can also:

- As part of the (mandatory) description of your most commonly provided legal services, include a concise statement of the key stages and an indicative timescale for the key stages;
- Explain the nature of your business e.g. chambers, or BSB entity (company, partnership or LLP);
- State the mix of people commonly involved in providing services;
- Include information about you and your practice, and how to instruct you;

(2)

- Include information for people with disabilities and language requirements on how to access your services and request reasonable adjustments;
- Include information about the Legal Choices website; and
- Include information about further sources of support and advice.

If you would like to go beyond the mandatory rules on redress transparency, your website can also:

- State that you have professional indemnity insurance cover for all the legal services you supply to the public;
- Include information about any alternative dispute resolution (ADR) services you use;
- State that you, barristers in chambers, or the BSB entity is registered with the Information Commissioner's Office (ICO); and
- Display the BSB's logo.

You should ensure that the information is sufficiently accessible and prominent on websites, accurate and up to date and readily available in alternative format.

Price transparency – best practice

If you would like to go beyond the mandatory rules on price transparency, your website can also state:

1) Your indicative fees for your most commonly provided legal services, the circumstances in which they may vary, whether your fees include VAT (where applicable), and likely additional costs.

You must state your most commonly used pricing models for legal services – see the mandatory rules on price transparency in section 1. You can go beyond this by stating your indicative fees for your most commonly provided legal services, and the circumstances in

which they may vary. For example, a fixed fee and the circumstances in which additional fees may be charged, or an hourly rate by seniority of barrister. If you state your indicative fees, you should also state whether they include VAT (where applicable). You can also state likely additional costs (for example, court fees), what they cover and either the cost or, if this can only be estimated, the typical range of costs.

This is mandatory for those who must comply with additional price transparency rules in relation to Public Access services (the specific circumstances in which price transparency requirements apply in relation to Public Access services can be found at Annexes C – J). It is not mandatory for others, but the price information will be particularly useful if your clients are less experienced and less expert consumers, and/or instruct you on a Public Access basis. This will help consumers to "shop around" for legal services. If you are undertaking referral work, you may take the view that it would be more appropriate for your client's solicitors to provide information about likely additional costs (given barristers are not permitted to hold client money, and therefore solicitors normally pay disbursements). However, you can still state that while likely additional costs such as court fees are not included in your indicative fees, they could be a key factor which determines price, and therefore clients should discuss them with their solicitor.

If you state your fees for your most commonly provided legal services on your website, you should state that they are indicative only. You should also give careful consideration to how your state your indicative fees, depending on whether you are a self-employed barrister in chambers, sole practitioner or BSB entity, and taking into account the need to avoid breaching competition law. For guidance on this, see the mandatory rules on price transparency in section 2.

2) Information about the typical range of costs for different stages of cases (where appropriate).

If you provide the Public Access services listed in the current version of the BSB's price transparency policy statement (Annex B), your website must also state and provide a description of those legal services. The description must include a concise statement of the key stages – see the mandatory rules on service transparency in section 2. It is not mandatory for others to provide a statement of the key stages of services.

However, if you do provide a statement of the key stages of services (either by choice or because this is mandatory), it may be useful for you to provide information about the typical range of costs for these stages. By helping consumers to understand how much the different stages of the case may cost, you may help them to budget. Nonetheless, the typical range of costs for different stages of the case may be very wide (for example, in complex contested disputes). In these cases, you should consider whether providing this information would in fact improve consumer understanding.

3) Information about how to avoid/manage the risk of costs increasing significantly, and any price flexibility.

If your clients are less experienced and less expert consumers, and/or instruct you on a Public Access basis, it may be particularly useful for you to provide information about how to avoid/manage the risk of costs increasing significantly. In many cases, this information will be specific to the service in question. However, it will help to manage consumers' anxiety about the cost associated with obtaining legal advice and representation.

If your clients are less experienced and less expert consumers, and/or instruct you on a Public Access basis, it may also be particularly useful for you to highlight any potential price flexibility. For example:

"Unless our barristers are charging fixed fees or a fixed hourly rate, you are invited to discuss the level of your fees with us in terms of your particular case and personal circumstances. For more information, please contact the clerks."

If this potential price flexibility is not referred to on websites, some consumers may wrongly assume that they cannot afford legal advice or representation. You can also include information about whether you are willing to offer innovative pricing structures. For example, an initial meeting to discuss a case either for free or a fixed fee, or staged payment plans.

4) Information about legal insurance.

If your clients are less experienced and less expert consumers, and/or instruct you on a Public Access basis, it may be particularly useful for you to include information about legal insurance. For example, some clients:

- May not know the difference between before the event insurance and after the event insurance;
- May not realise that they already have before the event insurance; for example, through membership of a trade union, or as part of a financial product they have purchased;
- May not know that after the event insurance might be appropriate; for example, if they are instructing you on a Public Access basis under a conditional fee agreement (a "no win, no fee" agreement). For more information, see the BSB's Guidance on After the Event Insurance.

You can either cover these points on your website or you can link to the legal insurance page on the Legal Choices website: https://www.legalchoices.org.uk/legal-choices/money-talks/after-the-event-insurance/. The website is run by the legal regulators and makes information available to assist consumers.

Which? also has a guide on legal insurance on its website, which you can link to: https://www.which.co.uk/money/insurance/legal-expenses-insurance/guides.

5) Information about legal aid eligibility.

If you practise in an area in which clients may be eligible for legal aid, it may be useful for you to link to the legal aid eligibility calculator on the gov.uk website: https://www.gov.uk/check-legal-aid. This will help prospective clients to understand whether they may be eligible for legal aid. However, if you do so, you should explain that barristers cannot do legal aid work unless they have been instructed by a solicitor.

If your clients instruct you on a Public Access basis, each client will need to make an informed decision about whether to apply for legal aid, or proceed with Public Access (Rule C120.3 in the BSB Handbook). It will therefore be particularly useful for you to link to the legal aid eligibility calculator above.

6) Information about any third party payment services you use.

Barristers and BSB entities are not permitted to hold client money (apart from the money clients pay them for their services). Some barristers and BSB entities therefore use third party payment services for making payments to, from, or on behalf of clients.

If you use a third party payment service, it may be useful for you to explain:

- How it works – the service will receive money from clients for legal services. This could include legal fees, alternative dispute resolution (ADR) costs, settlement money and disbursements (money lawyers spend on behalf of clients, such as fees for expert witnesses); The service holds the money separately from their own money; Any money paid in by a client can only be paid out with their consent;
- The fees for using the service;

- The service is insured. You can state by whom;
- The service is authorised/regulated by or registered with the Financial Conduct Authority (FCA). You can also provide the FCA reference number; and
- Clients can complain to the Financial Ombudsman Service.

7) You, barristers in chambers or the BSB entity is registered for VAT, and you can provide your VAT number(s) on request.

This may be useful to professional clients such as solicitors.

<u>**Service transparency – best practice**</u>

If you would like to go beyond the mandatory rules on service transparency, your website can also state:

1) As part of the description of your most commonly provided legal services, a concise statement of the key stages and an indicative timescale for the key stages.

You must state and provide a description of your most commonly provided legal services – see the mandatory rules on service transparency in section 1. The description can also include a concise statement of the key stages and an indicative timescale for the key stages.

This is mandatory for those who must comply with additional price transparency rules in relation to Public Access services (the specific circumstances in which price transparency requirements apply in relation to Public Access services can be found at Annexes C – J). It is not mandatory for others, but the information will be particularly useful if your clients are less experienced and less expert consumers, and/or instruct you on a Public Access basis.

A concise statement of the key stages will ensure consumers have a basic knowledge of the legal services, and may help them to assess how feasible 'unbundling' would be – assuming

The Bar Standards Board
Handbook

responsibility for some aspects of the case themselves, if they are able to do so. If it would not always be obvious to a client what a stage of the service is, provide a short explanation. This will ensure consumers sufficiently understand the service you are providing.

An indicative timescale for the key stages will also help consumers to understand what they can expect from a case and from you, and manage those expectations. However, we recognise that timescales will be indicative only and so we recommend a concise statement which assists clients in making informed choices, rather than detailed information about timescales. It will also be useful for you to state whether indicative timescales include possible appeals.

Finally, it will be useful for you to explain any limitations of the service you are able to offer. For example, if you/barristers in chambers are not authorised to conduct litigation and if relevant to the legal service in question, it will be useful for you to explain that Public Access clients will need to issue proceedings, file documents at court and serve documents on other parties themselves. The BSB's Guidance on Conducting Litigation will help you to explain this where relevant.

2) The nature of your business.

If your clients are less experienced and less expert consumers, and/or instruct you on a Public Access basis, it may be particularly useful for you to explain that self-employed barristers in chambers are separate and independent from one another, and not responsible for one another's work.

Similarly, if you are a BSB entity it may be useful for you to explain the nature of your business: a company, partnership or limited liability partnership (LLP). Websites should not create the impression of a chambers with self-employed barristers. If the entity is a company or LLP, you can also include your registered name (if different from your trading name) and number.

3) The mix of people commonly involved in providing services.

Self-employed barristers can outsource work to pupils, other barristers in the same chambers, and other third parties, subject to rules on confidentiality and outsourcing. However, the barrister remains responsible to the client for the work. (Barristers must also ensure consumers' data is kept safe and secure, and handled according to the General Data Protection Regulation [GDPR]).

If you are a sole practitioner or chambers, you may therefore decide it is not necessary for your website to state the 'mix' of people commonly involved in providing legal services. Nevertheless, if your clients are less experienced and less expert consumers, and/or instruct you on a Public Access basis, it may be useful for you to explain that members of chambers can work together on the same case, but they remain separate and independent from one another. It may also be useful for you to explain the role of your clerks and what clients can expect from them.

BSB entities are more likely to operate similarly to law firms authorised by the SRA, with a mix of staff providing services. If you are a BSB entity with a mix of staff providing services, it may be particularly useful for your website to state this. For example:

> *"Our team is led by Barrister A and your case will be assigned to either Barrister B or Solicitor C. D (a paralegal) may also contact you about your case."*

This will help consumers to understand how your business operates, and what they can expect from your staff.

4) Information about you and your practice, and how to instruct you.

The Bar already provides a significant amount of information about its practices on chambers' and barristers' websites. If you do not do so already, you can consider including:

- Details of cases you have undertaken (subject to rules on confidentiality);
- Your directory recommendations, such as those in <u>Chambers and Partners</u> and the <u>Legal 500</u>;
- The advantages of instructing you, such as a particular expertise or the benefits of early legal advice;
- Quality indicators such as accreditation schemes or quality marks;
- Links to practice related publications; and
- The terms on which you undertake work, such as the Bar Council's <u>standard contractual terms</u> or the standard terms of a Specialist Bar Association (SBA). It may be useful to provide a plain English summary of the terms where appropriate.

Providing this additional service information (particularly alongside price information) will help clients to decide whether to instruct you. If your clients instruct you on a Public Access basis, it may be particularly useful for you to set out how to do so. For example:

"Try to clarify the nature of your problem and what it is that you want one of our barristers to do. Please contact the clerks and tell them that you wish to instruct a barrister directly. They will be happy to help."

5) Information for people with disabilities and language requirements on how to access your services, and request reasonable adjustments.

For example, you can include the following information about your premises: the number of steps, width of doorways, parking facilities, toilet facilities, hearing loops, etc. This will mean those affected will not need to contact you before coming to your premises. You can also include information about translation services (and the cost of those services) where that may be beneficial to meeting consumer need.

In addition, it may be useful for you to provide a copy of your reasonable adjustments policy on your website. You are required to have a policy under the Equality Rules in the BSB Handbook.

For more information and a model policy, see the BSB's Supporting Guidance on the Equality Rules. The guidance states "chambers should state on its website and in any publicity material that reasonable adjustments will be made and should identify the person or persons to whom requests should be made".

6) Information about the Legal Choices website.

This is run by the legal regulators and provides help with choosing a provider, information about costs, how to complain about a provider and more. The link is https://www.legalchoices.org.uk/.

7) Information about further sources of support and advice.

For example, you can link to and provide contact telephone numbers for:

Advice UK: a network of advice centres across the country.
Advocate: free advice and representation on legal matters (applications-based). Contact: 020 7092 3960.
Citizens Advice: free, independent and impartial advice on a range of issues and rights. Advice Line: 03444 111 444 (England); 03444 77 20 20 (Wales).
Law Centres Network: search for local law centres in England.
Law Works: connects people in need of legal advice with lawyers who are able to help for free. Searchable directory of local legal advice clinics in England and Wales.
Personal Support Unit: provides advice, information and support for litigants in person (those representing themselves in court). Telephone: 020 7073 4760.

Samaritans: helpline support for anyone who wants to talk to someone about the problems they are facing in their life. Helpline: 116 123.

The Money Advice Service: free, confidential advice about managing finances and dealing with debts. Advice line: 0800 138 7777.

You can also consider including information about further sources of support and advice which are specific to your practice area.

Redress transparency – best practice

If you would like to go beyond the mandatory rules on redress transparency, your website can also state:

1) You have professional indemnity insurance cover for all the legal services you supply to the public.

Self-employed barristers must be members of the BMIF and take out at least the minimum level of cover, which is £500,000. BMIF's maximum limit of cover is £2.5 million. Self-employed barristers must also have insurance which covers all the legal services they supply to the public. Some must therefore take out additional cover with other insurers.

BSB entities must also have insurance which covers all the legal services they supply to the public.

In addition to stating that you have cover for all the legal services you supply to the public, your website can also state:

- The name of your insurer(s);
- Their contact details; and

- The territorial coverage of the insurance. For example, some coverage is worldwide subject to certain exclusions.

If your clients are less experienced and less expert consumers, and/or instruct you on a Public Access basis, it may be particularly useful for you to explain that professional indemnity insurance covers you if you make a mistake which causes a client to lose money. This will assure clients that they will not lose out financially.

2) Information about any alternative dispute resolution (ADR) services you use.

When clients instruct you, you must notify them in writing of an ADR provider which can deal with any complaint if you are unable to resolve the complaint through your complaints process, *and* both you and the client agree to use the scheme. You are therefore not required to use ADR, and must only inform the client of the option (under the Alternative Dispute Resolution for Consumer Disputes (Amendment) Regulations 2015). The client is also still entitled to complain to LeO.

You can also include this information on your website. The Chartered Trading Standards Institute (CTSI) approves ADR entities which are able to provide mediation services. At the time of writing, you can use ProMediate or Small Claims Mediation. You should consider which provider may be the most appropriate for you and your clients.

If mediation does not resolve the complaint, the client may still complain to LeO. For more information, see the BSB's Guidance on First Tier Complaints Handling.

3) You, barristers in chambers or the BSB entity is registered with the Information Commissioner's Office (ICO).

Under the General Data Protection Regulation (GDPR), self-employed barristers must be registered with the ICO individually. BSB entities must also be registered with the ICO.

Stating that you are registered with the ICO and providing your registration number will assure consumers their data will be kept safe and secure, and handled according to the legislation. You can include these details in your privacy notice, which you are required to have under the legislation.

4) Websites can also display the BSB's logo.

This will help to give consumers assurance that you are regulated by the BSB. If you do display the BSB's logo, it is important that you ensure you are using the current version. E-mail ContactUs@BarStandardsBoard.org.uk for a file of the current version of the logo – once we have verified your website address(es), we will send this to you.

<u>**Providing information – best practice**</u>

The legal regulators commissioned research into client care letters to find out how they can be most useful to clients. While the research focused on client care letters, the principles identified are applicable to all written communications, including websites.

Considering the principles will help you to comply with the transparency rules in the most effective way. The principles are:

- **Show a clear purpose** – what is the information about? Why is it important?
- **Keep it concise** – is it too long? Is the structure clear?
- **Put it in plain English** – is there any jargon? Are sentence structures short and simple? The Plain English Campaign's website has a number of free guides that you may find useful.
- **Prioritise information** – focus on information that is most relevant to clients and prospective clients. Put key information at the beginning.
- **Personalise information** – use personal pronouns (I, you, etc.) and specifics about you and your practice (where this is relevant).

- **Make it easy to read** – is it too text-heavy? Should you use bullet points, tables or headings? Use appropriate spacing.
- **Highlight key information** – use visual tools. For example, bold text, summary boxes and highlighting to draw attention.
- **Consider additional opportunities to engage clients and prospective clients** – for example, is some information better provided in another format, such as audio visual content or a fact sheet? Is some information better provided at a later stage, such as when first meeting a client?

Website accessibility – best practice

For many consumers, a website can be an important source of information and is often the first contact they will have with you. You should seek to remove barriers that prevent interaction with or access to your website, particularly for people with disabilities and language requirements.

If your website is not easy to read or navigate, or content is difficult to understand, it could deter clients from seeking your services. For example, consider whether consumers would struggle with small font sizes, colours, jargon they cannot be expected to understand or, if accessing your website via a mobile device, small buttons. You can also consider providing website content in different languages where that may be beneficial to meeting consumer need. Remote access via video calling may be an option for clients who, due to location, would otherwise not be able to access your services.

The Web Content Accessibility Guidelines (WCAG) are an internationally recognised set of recommendations for improving web accessibility. For tips on getting started with web accessibility, visit the Web Accessibility Initiative's website: https://www.w3.org/WAI/gettingstarted/. It explains how to make digital services accessible to everyone. You can also consider installing software to ensure website accessibility.

Transparency of third party providers – best practice

It is common, particularly in Public Access, for barristers to appoint marketing or advertising businesses to promote their services.

Third parties may also set up services (which are often web-based platforms) to introduce Public Access clients to barristers. If you are obtaining work from a third party introducer, you are practising in 'an association' and must notify the BSB's Supervision Department (Supervision@BarStandardsBoard.org.uk).

The BSB's transparency rules do not apply to non-regulated, third party providers. However, barristers who have appointed marketing or advertising businesses and/or obtain work from third party introducers may wish to consider their arrangements with such providers in light of their own transparency obligations. For example, barristers may wish to only enter into arrangements with providers which comply with the spirit of the BSB's transparency rules.

In any event, barristers are encouraged to undertake appropriate due diligence on third parties and how their services operate before agreeing to use them. This includes considering whether practices lack transparency for clients and are potentially anti-competitive. Barristers must also take steps to ensure that:

- They do not breach the prohibition on paying or receiving referral fees. The BSB has published Guidance on Referral and Marketing Arrangements;
- They do not enter into terms which interfere with their duties to act independently and in their clients' best interests (Core Duties 2 and 4 of the BSB Handbook);
- Any advertising and marketing material is accurate, clear and not likely to mislead;
- Clients are not confused about who is responsible for providing legal services, and are clear about both the third party's fees, and the barrister's fees for legal services; and

The Bar Standards Board
Handbook

- Clients are not confused about which services are regulated by the BSB, or about what redress they have (and against whom) if things go wrong. Under Rule C99 in the BSB Handbook, clients must be notified in writing about their right to complain to the barrister/chambers, right to complain to LeO (if any) and right to complain to any third party.

Anti-Money Laundering (AML) Guidance

New Anti-Money Laundering (AML) guidance in 2021

The Legal Sector Anti-Money Laundering (AML) Group (comprising legal sector regulators and representative bodies) has completed an extensive review of the guidance that we published after the implementation of **The Money Laundering, Terrorist Financing and Transfer of Funds (Information on the Payer) Regulations 2017**.

The updated version builds upon the guidance previously published and incorporates amendments implemented via **The Money Laundering and Terrorist Financing (Amendment) Regulations 2019** and **The Money Laundering and Terrorist Financing (Amendment) (EU Exit) Regulations 2020**.

Status of the guidance

The new guidance replaces the previous version and has been published in draft form, pending approval by HM Treasury.

You are not required to follow this guidance but doing so will make it easier to account to regulators and others for your actions.

We will consider whether a barrister or BSB entity has complied with this guidance when undertaking our role as a supervisory authority for the purposes of the Regulations. You may be asked to justify a decision to deviate from this guidance.

This guidance has been submitted to HM Treasury for approval. In accordance with the Proceeds of Crime Act 2002 and Regulation 86(2)(b) of the Money Laundering Regulations, once approved, the court is required to consider compliance with this guidance in assessing whether a person committed an offence or took all reasonable steps and exercised all due diligence to avoid committing the offence.

This status is explained more fully in the introduction to the guidance.

How to use the guidance

The guidance is in two parts:

Part 1 **Guidance for the legal sector**

Part 2 Sector specific guidance:

- **Guidance for Barristers and BSB Entities**
- **Guidance for Trust or Company Service Providers**

Self-employed barristers and BSB entities who engage in work that is within scope of the Money Laundering Regulations should read the sector specific guidance in Part 2 in the first instance. It has been written specifically to reflect the type of work that barristers typically engage in and it contains a number of useful FAQs and case studies to assist interpretation. If you require further detail (for example in the area of conducting due diligence and in relation to Legal Professional Privilege) you should refer to Part 1.

The Legal Sector AML Group has also **published guidance** to manage risks arising from the Covid-19 pandemic.

Please contact us at **aml@barstandardsboard.org.uk** if you need this guidance to be made available in an alternative format.

Guidance for Employed barristers

Barristers who work in organisations such as financial institutions or law firms that are regulated by other supervisors under the Money Laundering Regulations (such as the Financial Conduct Authority or the Solicitors Regulation Authority) should refer to guidance published by the relevant regulator.

Further assistance in interpreting your obligations

The Bar Council provides a confidential **Ethical Enquiries Service** for the benefit and assistance of barristers and staff to assist them to identify, interpret and comply with their professional obligations.

For more information on our respective roles, please see our **Protocol for Anti-Money Laundering and Counter-Terrorist Financing with the Bar Council.**

BSB Anti-Money Laundering and Counter Terrorist Financing Annual Report for 2020-21

Last updated 06 Dec 2021

In this section

Declaration at Authorisation to Practise and obtaining a criminal records check

Money laundering risk assessment

Anti-Money Laundering (AML) Guidance

Bar Standards Board
289-293 High Holborn
London
WC1V 7HZ

About us
Equality and diversity
Working with others
Working for the BSB

Contact Us

© 2022 Bar Standards Board. All rights reserved.   Design & Development by **Pixl8**

INDEX

Tom Cla

Life, Liberty, Revolution

About the author

Originally from Lurgan, County Armagh, Gerard MacAtasney holds a PhD from the University of Liverpool. He lives and works in Belfast.

Tom Clarke

Life, Liberty, Revolution

Gerard MacAtasney

MERRION

First published in 2013 by Merrion
an imprint of Irish Academic Press

8 Chapel Lane
Sallins
Co. Kildare, Ireland

920 NE 58th Avenue, Suite 300
Portland, Oregon,
97213–3786, USA

© 2013 Gerard MacAtasney

British Library Cataloguing-in-Publication Data
An entry can be found on request

978-1-908928-06-1 (cloth)
978-1-908928-07-8 (paper)
978-1-908928-18-4 (Ebook)

Library of Congress Cataloging in Publication Data
An entry can be found on request

Clarke, Thomas James, 1858-1916.
Tom Clarke : life, liberty, revolution.
1. Clarke, Thomas James, 1858-1916--Correspondence.
2. Irish Republican Brotherhood--Sources.
3. Revolutionaries--Ireland--Correspondence.
I. Title II. MacAtasney, Gerard.
941.5'082'092-dc23

ISBN-13: 9781908928061

Typeset by FiSH Books Ltd, Enfield, London
Printed and bound by CPI Group (UK) Ltd, Croydon, CR0 4YY

For my great friend Ben Fearon, Mulladry,
Portadown, County Armagh

Ní bheidh a leithéid arís ann

Poem written by Tom Clarke in the late 1880s while in Chatham Prison
(courtesy of Cardinal Ó Fiaich Library and Archive, Armagh)

Contents

Acknowledgements

I wish to thank the following individuals and institutions for their help in researching this book: Ken Bergin and the staff of the Archives Department of the University of Limerick; Sandra Heise, Lar Joye and Finbarr Connolly, National Museum, Dublin; Anne-Marie Ryan, Kilmainham Gaol Archives; Frances Clarke and Colette O'Daly, National Library, Dublin; Maria O'Shea, National Photographic Archive, Dublin; Neil Cobbett, English National Archives, Kew, London; Roddy Hegarty, Ó Fiaich Library and Archive, Armagh; Mary Conefrey, Leitrim County Library. I am grateful to the *Irish Times* for publishing a letter seeking assistance from its readers and I wish to acknowledge those who took the time to contact me: Frank Bouchier-Hayes; Paddy Fawl; J.P. Lane; Art Kelly and Peter O'Curry. Thanks also for information received from Helen Litton, Patrick Bermingham, Michael Whelan, Sister Ann Taylor and Mike McCormack. I am grateful to my sister, Mary Kellegher, for carrying out research in Leitrim County Library. I conducted two interviews as part of my research and I am indebted to Bertie Foley and the late Sister Mary Benignus for meeting me in Dungannon and Mairead and Nora de Hóir for sparing the time to talk to me in Limerick. I am thankful to my readers for taking the time to critically examine drafts – Fearghal McGarry, Dept. History at Queen's University, Belfast and Eoghan Fearon. I wish to offer my sincere thanks to Fonsie and George Mealy of Mealy's Auctions, County Kilkenny and to Gerry Kavanagh of the National Library. Without them this book would never have come to fruition. Finally, I am grateful to Irish Academic Press for agreeing to accept my proposal for a book on Tom Clarke; special thanks go to Lisa Hyde who guided the project from start to finish.

Chronology

May 1857	Marriage of James Clarke and Mary Palmer.
March 1858	Birth of Thomas James Clarke.
April 1859	Clarke family moves to British Army garrison in South Africa.
March 1865	Family returns to Ireland and settles in Dungannon, County Tyrone.
August 1880	Tom Clarke involved in IRB ambush on police in Dungannon. Shortly afterwards he emigrates to America.
April 1883	Clarke is sent on a bombing mission to England. He is arrested and sentenced to penal servitude for life.
September 1898	Clarke is released from Portland Prison on licence.
November 1899	Clarke emigrates to America.
July 1901	Marriage of Tom Clarke and Kathleen Daly in New York.
December 1907	Clarke family returns to Ireland and opens a tobacconist's shop in Dublin.
March 1909	Clarke is elected president of local branch of Sinn Féin.
July 1915	Clarke organises the funeral of Jeremiah O'Donovan Rossa.
September 1915	Clarke is co-opted onto the military council of the IRB organising the rising.
April 1916	Clarke takes part in the Easter Rising.
May 1916	Clarke is executed in Kilmainham Gaol.

List of Illustrations

Preface

Recent years have witnessed the publication of a plethora of books on the Irish revolutionary period. Research has been aided to a great degree by the release of the records of the Bureau of Military History containing hundreds of interviews with those who participated in the events of the early twentieth century. Against this background it is difficult to understand how such a pivotal figure as Thomas J. Clarke has been almost ignored by historians. However, the fact remains that, outside the figures of Patrick Pearse and James Connolly, little is known about the leaders of the 1916 Rising. Indeed, it wasn't until 2004 that Seán MacDiarmada was the subject of a biography, while the life of Eamonn Ceannt was the focus of a similar work in 2005.

Tom Clarke joined the IRB in Dungannon, fled to America as a result of an attack on the police in that town, was sent to London on a bombing mission and spent almost sixteen years in prison. On his release he married the niece of prominent Fenian John Daly, worked with John Devoy on the *Gaelic American* and was pre-eminent amongst those who sought to initiate a military rising against British rule in Ireland, culminating in the Easter Rising. Yet, to date, he has been the subject of only one biography – that penned by Breton author Louis Le Roux in 1936. The latter had earlier published a biography of Patrick Pearse (1932) and was probably seen by the Clarke family as a 'safe pair of hands'. Evidence that his work on Clarke was facilitated by Kathleen Clarke and Madge Daly, who allowed him access to the family papers, is suggested by the fact that at times his writing tends to be more hagiography than biography and is as interesting for what it excludes as much as for the information it contains.

This book, therefore, is the first to be written about Tom Clarke in seventy-five years and the intention is to attempt to understand the man as he was – his personal life as well as his role in revolutionary affairs. It is in two sections: the first is a brief biography which is intended as an overview to contextualise the second section – his letters. When researching a biography of Seán MacDiarmada I was struck by the way in which that individual's personality emerged on a reading of his letters. However, these had to be paraphrased and while this is essential in the writing of a major biography, something of the essence of the person is lost in such an academic exercise. Therefore, I wished to adopt a different approach when examining the life of Clarke. Of course, one of the inherent difficulties in such a method is to write a short biography without reference to the wealth of material in his correspondence. I hope for the most part I have managed to achieve this, thus leaving the life of Tom Clarke to be understood – in his own words.

PART ONE

Chapter one

Early Days

James Clarke was born in the townland of Errew in the parish of Carrigallen, County Leitrim in 1830. There his father, James, shared a small four-acre farm with his brother Owen. Locally the family were also known by the name Clerkin and were members of the Established Church.[1] After leaving school, James became a groom and on 4 December 1847, in the midst of Black '47, the worst year of the Great Famine, he enlisted in the British Army at Ballyshannon, County Donegal. Clarke subsequently saw service in one of the most significant conflicts of the nineteenth century when Britain joined forces with the French, Ottomans and the Kingdom of Sardinia against the Russians in the Crimean War – a struggle that lasted from 1853–6. He spent just over two years in Crimea and saw a considerable amount of action, being awarded a medal for his efforts along with clasps for fighting in the battles of Alma (20 September 1854), Balaklava (25 October 1854), Inkerman (5 November 1854) and the siege of Sebastopol (25 September 1854 – 8 September 1855). On 1 October 1856 he was promoted to the rank of Bombardier.[2]

While in garrison at Clonmel, County Tipperary, Clarke had met Mary Palmer of Clogheen. The couple eventually married and although Mary was a Catholic the wedding took place in Shanrahan Church of Ireland on 31 May 1857.[3] Within a year of the marriage a child was born, the family bible recording 'Thomas James Clarke born 11th of March 1858 at Hurst Castle, Hampshire, England'. Despite his father being a Protestant, Thomas was baptised a Catholic.[4] A couple of weeks later, on 1 April, Clarke was promoted to Corporal and on 9

April 1859 he was drafted to South Africa. The family narrowly escaped drowning during the voyage when their ship became involved in a serious collision.[5] On 23 December 1859 Maria Jane was born at Natal, and Thomas attended school in the district. The family lived for more than five years in South Africa in various garrisons until 15 March 1865 when they returned to Ireland.[6]

Having attained the rank of Battery Sergeant, Clarke was appointed Sergeant of the Ulster Militia which had its headquarters at Charlemont Castle, County Armagh. He was then transferred to Dungannon, County Tyrone. Given that there was little in the way of adequate provisions for a family in the Dungannon militia barracks, the family lived initially in a rented house in Ann Street in the town before moving to a residence in Northland Row opposite St Patrick's Catholic Church. It was here that another two children were born, Hanna Palmer on 24 August 1868 and Alfred Edward on 24 May 1870.[7] Mary gave birth to eight children in total but the remainder all died as infants.[8]

On 26 December 1868, at the age of thirty-nine, James Clarke claimed his discharge from the 12th Brigade, Royal Regiment of Artillery, at Gosport. This was confirmed on 12 January 1869 when he was admitted an out-pensioner of the Royal Hospital at Chelsea on a pension of 1/11 per day.[9]

In the meantime the family's eldest son, Thomas, had been attending St Patrick's National School in Dungannon. His first teacher was Francis Daly who was succeeded by Cornelius Collins; the latter subsequently engaged Tom as an assistant teacher until the school closed as a consequence of a declining roll in 1881.[10] While at school Tom had taken a great interest in Irish history despite the fact that his father had tried to discourage him, maintaining that Ireland could never become independent due to the power of the British Empire.[11]

However his interest was further stirred by the arrival of a veteran of the 1867 Fenian Rising, John Daly of Limerick. Daly had led an unsuccessful Fenian attack on a police barracks in Kilmallock, County Limerick and in the aftermath had been forced to flee to England and then America. He returned to Ireland in 1869 and eventually worked as a full-time organiser for the Irish Republican Brotherhood (IRB).[12] It was in this role that he addressed a meeting on Drumcoo Hill, just outside Dungannon, in 1878. During the late 1870s and early 1880s the 'new departure' dominated Irish political and social life and the IRB became an important force within the Land League whilst maintaining a close association with the Irish Parliamentary Party and its leader Charles Stewart Parnell. It was under these circumstances that the organisation enjoyed the most successful period in its history with almost 40,000 members and 10,000 firearms.[13] It seems that this context proved crucial in influencing young men such as Clarke, Billy Kelly and Louis McMullen in believing that insurrection was the only viable means of achieving Irish independence.[14]

Billy Kelly remembered that there was a dramatic club in Dungannon in which Tom Clarke and he were associated and in 1880 they both travelled on an excursion organised by the club to Dublin. While there they were introduced to Michael Davitt by John Daly and according to Kelly part of the discussion centred on the possibility of organising an IRB circle in Dungannon. A short time afterwards a circle was formed in the town and Tom Clarke was appointed as the centre, in charge of twenty-three men, including Kelly. Daly later visited Dungannon to address the members, focusing on 'the intensive organisation of the IRB with the object of taking military action against the RIC – the drilling, training and arming of the members of our organisation for that objective'.[15]

Like most towns in the north Dungannon suffered from sectarian animosity and on 15 August it was the scene of a 'dreadful and fatal conflict between the authorities and the people'.[16] That day was known as Lady Day, when Catholics celebrated the Feast of the Assumption, and on this occasion participants in a parade were attacked by a crowd of Protestants. A riot ensued in which stones were thrown at the police who read the Riot Act and then opened fire on the crowd with live ammunition. One man, 51 year-old William O'Rourke, died and a further twenty-seven were injured, including Billy Kelly's brother Patrick. Only one casualty was reported on the side of the police.[17]

At the subsequent coroner's inquest a member of the constabulary maintained that he had been in Belfast, Lurgan, Lisburn and Scarva during riots and had never seen anything to equal the 'violence and intemperance and determination displayed on that day'.[18] However, what was not reported in the press was that on the night following the riots the IRB, including Clarke and Kelly, ambushed eleven RIC men in Irish Street in the town. Kelly recalled how 'we opened fire on the police and they escaped into a public house in Anne Street. Reinforcements of police arrived on the scene and we had to retreat'.[19]

1. Tom Clarke, 1881
(courtesy of the National Library of Ireland).

A couple of weeks later, on 29 August, Clarke, Kelly and a few others left Dungannon and boarded a ship for America. Clarke's decision probably had more to do with the recent events than the fact that he had become unemployed. Previous to leaving they obtained a transfer from the Dungannon circle of the IRB to Camp No. 1 in New York.[20]

The party arrived in New York in October 1880 and immediately made their way to the house of Tyrone Clan na Gael member Patrick O'Connor. Shortly after admission to that organisation Clarke was appointed as its recording secretary and found employment in O'Connor's shoe shop. In spring of the following year both Clarke and Kelly went to work in the Mansion House Hotel in Brooklyn, New York – Kelly as a boilerman and Clarke as a night porter.[21]

That summer they joined the Napper Tandy Club which was run by Dr. Thomas Gallagher. According to Kelly 'the purpose of this club was the instruction of its members in the use of explosives'.[22] However, shortly after joining, Kelly had to move to Garden City as his employer had opened a new hotel. Nevertheless, he 'maintained contact with Clarke and he told me of the continuation of his lessons on explosives under Gallagher'.[23] Part of these lessons included trips to Staten Island to experiment on rocks with nitroglycerine.

Gallagher's classes were part of a long-term strategy then being adopted by Clan na Gael, the centrepiece of which was a sustained bombing campaign in Britain. However, the organisation's plans were disrupted by the initiative of veteran Fenian, Jeremiah O'Donovan Rossa, now resident in America. Through letters in the *Irish World* newspaper Rossa had succeeded in obtaining funds to send a series of bombers to Britain and between January 1881 and March 1883, on his instructions, bombs were detonated in Salford (killing a young boy), Glasgow, Liverpool and London.[24]

Rossa's actions, described by one historian as representing a 'one-man terrorist directorate'[25] were denounced by his erstwhile Fenian colleagues. John O'Leary referred to the scheme as 'insane' while Captain William Mackey Lomasney – one of the leaders of the proposed Clan campaign – referred to Rossa as 'imbecilic and farcical'.[26] Indeed, so opposed were the Clan to Rossa's methods that one of their leading members in London became an informer in order to prevent any further explosions.[27] As far as the Clan was concerned Rossa's campaign simply alienated people from any actions in support of Irish independence. At the same time they ensured that the British authorities remained on high alert throughout these years, thereby jeopardising their own campaign. It was in this environment that Clarke's life was to change forever.

2. Tom Clarke, 1883
(courtesy of the National Library of Ireland).

Early in 1883 Clarke was due to take up a new post as manager of the Brighton Beach Hotel when, in March, Timothy O'Riordan, secretary of Camp No 1, ordered him to prepare with the utmost secrecy for an early voyage.[28] O'Riordan gave Clarke money and instructions to sail to England where, on landing, he was to go to a shop owned by James Murphy (alias Alfred Whitehead) in Birmingham. Clarke travelled via Boston but his ship struck an iceberg and sank shortly after sailing. He lost his luggage but was picked up by a passing vessel and landed in Newfoundland where he gave his name as Henry Hammond Wilson, an Englishman returning home. He was given new clothes and £5 and eventually landed in Liverpool.[29]

In England Clarke worked mainly in conjunction with Thomas Gallagher and Whitehead in the procurement and manufacture of explosives. The Clan favoured this strategy rather than the alternative of smuggling them into Britain. However, bulk purchases of chemicals necessary to make nitroglycerine carried a risk of generating suspicion and potential exposure. He rented a room on the third floor at 17 Nelson Square, Blackfriars Road, London on Saturday 31 March 1883, informing his landlady that he was staying there as he was studying 'for the medical' and had a tutor at Charing Cross.[30] On 2 April he planned to see Whitehead in Birmingham and wrote to him 'Dear friend, if you are not otherwise engaged I would like the pleasure of your company at one of the theatres this evening. I will be at the place decided upon to meet on any such occasion at 6.30'.[31] However, the police had intercepted and copied this and all other letters and telegrams despatched by Clarke and his fellow conspirators.[32] As soon as the police were satisfied that each of the men had sufficient evidence in his possession they made simultaneous swoops in Birmingham and London. Whitehead was arrested in his shop in Birmingham on 4 April. Clarke, together with Gallagher, was arrested at his lodgings the following day in London. Although he had no incriminating documents in his possession Clarke's portmanteau was found to contain an India rubber stocking full of a liquid stated to be a dangerous explosive.[33]

Clarke, under the pseudonym Henry Hammond Wilson, appeared at the Central Criminal Court, Old Bailey, London on 28 May 1883 with co-accused Thomas Gallagher, Alfred Whitehead, William Ansburgh, John Curtin and Bernard Gallagher. Clarke and Ansburgh chose to defend themselves while the others had legal representation. The men were charged with levying war, conspiring to 'destroy and damage by nitro-glycerine and other explosive substances' and conspiracy to murder. They were tried under the Treason-Felony Act of 1848 which had been passed in the aftermath of the Young Ireland rising of that year. All the prisoners pleaded 'not guilty'. Clarke's defence was that he had not actually committed any such acts as those alleged, that commission of no such overt acts was proven against him, and that intention to commit a crime did not in itself constitute a crime.[34]

The main prosecution witness was a former member of Clan na Gael, Joseph William Lynch alias William J Norman, who, on being arrested, turned state's evidence against his comrades. The fact that he had done so was seized upon by Clarke in his own cross-examination of the witness. Although we do not have Clarke's questions we can infer from Lynch's answer that he doubted how a man who could break an oath he took to the Clan could be trusted to tell the truth in court. Lynch replied: 'I consider the oath which I took then as binding as the oath I have taken today. It was that I would stand by the watch-word and preserve the funds of the brotherhood. I suppose "stand by the watchword" meant to go anywhere. The secret of the society was to keep all the transactions. I have not kept them secret. I have broken my oath if it was an oath. I do not consider that I committed perjury. I cannot answer you what the difference is; I won't answer it.'[35]

However, Clarke was also identified by two salesmen who worked for the company of Cow, Hill and Co., Cheapside, London. One remembered selling him two India rubber bags on 4 April remarking how 'we do not often sell two at a time'. Another sold him, on the following day, three air pillows.[36] The fact that Clarke was forced to travel around with a heavy case of explosive material was noted by those with whom he had come into contact. Thus, a cab driver and a platform attendant both remembered seeing him and the latter, under cross-examination by Clarke, stated: 'I am prepared to identify you – I could not swear to or identify every one for whom I carry luggage – I can swear to you, because from the weight of the portmanteau I took notice of you'.[37]

When Clarke was cross-examined he made a crucial mistake when he inadvertently corrected the prosecution on the composition of explosive found in his portmanteau. The counsel commented 'so, you know all about it'.[38] Before the trial ended both Whitehead and Ansburgh made statements of innocence to the jury; however, Clarke simply remarked that he would let his case 'go to the jury as it stands'.[39]

On Thursday 14 June the jury, after deliberating for slightly more than one hour, acquitted Ansburgh and Bernard Gallagher but found Thomas Gallager, Whitehead, Curtin and Clarke 'guilty'. The judge then sentenced these four men to penal servitude for life. Clarke immediately rose to address the court but was removed from the dock before doing so.[40]

In *Glimpses of an Irish Felon's Prison Life* Clarke described the events after sentencing: 'Immediately the Lord Chief Justice passed the sentence we were hustled out of the dock into the prison van, surrounded by a troop of mounted police and driven away at a furious pace through the howling mobs that thronged the streets from the Courthouse to Millbank prison'.[41]

Once inside the latter, with his head close-cropped, Clarke was read the prison rules and two regulations immediately struck him. He was made aware of the fact that as a life-sentence prisoner he had no hope of release until he had completed at least twenty years in prison. Second, he was informed that strict silence would have to be observed at all times as 'under no circumstances must one prisoner speak to another'.[42]

Looking back on his time in Millbank, Clarke remembered it as 'a dreary time of solitary confinement in the cold, white-washed cell, with a short daily exercise varying the monotony. Day after day all alike, no change, maddening silence, sitting hopeless, friendless and alone with nothing in this world to look forward to but the occasional note coming from some one or other of my comrades, Gallagher, Whitehead, and Curtin, who were in the same plight as myself'.[43]

Clarke was experiencing what had become known as the 'separate system' and the founding fathers of it, Whitworth Russell and William Crawford, justified it as follows:

> In short, upon the offender in his separate cell all the moral machinery of the system is brought to bear with as much force and effect as if the prison contained no other culprit but himself. His submission then must be immediate and complete: he will be calm, for there is nothing to ruffle or discompose him; he will be disposed to self communion, for he has no companion but his own thoughts; he will be led to listen with attention and respect to the instruction, reproof or consolation, of his keepers and instructors, for almost the only accents of friendly intercourse are those which issue from their lips; and he will apply himself with ardour to the labour of his hands as a relief from the 'insufferable burden and idleness and ennui'.[44]

However, some prisoners described actual stages of deterioration in separation from initial intense yearning for familiar parts of life, such as family or home, giving way to a hardening of emotions and diminution of sensitivity towards the suffering of others – what one referred to as 'the death of the soul'.[45] A woman ex-prisoner wrote as follows in 1884: 'cold, darkness, silence and solitude ...are not curative or reformatory or humanising influences. They disease the body and depress, stupefy and debase the mind. Their tendency is to fill it with gloom, hatred and desperation'.[46]

Nevertheless, despite the silence and isolation, Clarke found that in his five months in Millbank 'when the feeling against us was at fever heat outside the walls' he 'never experienced a single annoyance ... we were treated just as the ordinary prisoners ... no special line of treatment was planned for us'.[47] This situation was soon to change as in December 1883 Clarke and the other three prisoners were moved to

Chatham prison where they were joined by various groups of Irish prisoners who had been sentenced for similar sentences. Here he became prisoner J 464, with his height recorded as 5ft 8ins (exactly the same as his father) and his weight as 133lbs.[48] The prisoners were sent to the penal cells and it was in one of these, measuring 10ft 6ins by 6ft 6ins by 8ft 6 ins (580 cubic feet) that Clarke was to spend the next six years.[49]

In early 1884 to his 'grief and surprise'[50] Clarke recognised two new Irish prisoners – John Daly and James Egan. Daly had of course initiated him into the IRB in Dungannon and he had met up with him again in America. In Chatham the treason–felony prisoners were known as the 'special men' and were kept in the penal (punishment) cells, 'so that we would be the more conveniently persecuted, for the authorities aimed at making life unbearable for us'. Clarke described his experience as follows:

> This was a scientific system of perpetual and persistent harassing, which gave the officers in charge of us a free hand to persecute us just as they pleased. It was made part of their duty to worry and harass us all the time. Harassing morning, noon and night and on through the night, harassing always and at all times, harassing with bread and water punishments and other punishments, with 'no sleep' torture and other tortures. This system was applied to the Irish prisoners and to them only and was specially devised to destroy us mentally and physically – to kill or drive insane. It worked to its utmost against us for six or seven years, and it was during that time that all the men who succumbed went mad.[51]

It would take all Clarke's ingenuity to ensure that he would not become one of those men.

Notes

1.	Michael Whelan, 'Clarke's Leitrim Background', *The Leitrim Guardian*, 1969 (2), pp.65–70; Francis McKiernan, 'Carrigallen Parish in 1821', *Breifne Journal*, 1962, vol. ii, no 5, p.125.
2.	National Archives, Kew, London, (hereafter NAUK), War Office Papers (WO) 97/1313.
3.	National Library of Ireland, (hereafter NLI), Thomas Clarke Papers, ACC 6410, Box 3, IV; Louis Le Roux, *Tom Clarke and the Irish Freedom Movement* (Dublin, The Talbot Press, 1936), p.8.
4.	NLI, Thomas Clarke Papers, ACC 6410, Box 3, IV. In a letter to the author (25 October 2011) J.P. Lane pointed out that Hurst Castle is not on the Isle of Wight, as often stated in relation to Clarke's birthplace, but is on the opposite side of the Solent at the end of a long promontory of shingle and marshland stretching out from the Hampshire coastline.
5.	Le Roux, *Tom Clarke and the Irish Freedom Movement*, p.8.
6.	Ibid., pp.8–9.
7.	Ibid., p.9.
8.	1911 Census of Ireland.
9.	NAUK, WO 97/1313 and Le Roux, *Tom Clarke and the Irish Freedom Movement*, pp.7–9.
10.	Le Roux, *Tom Clarke and the Irish Freedom Movement*, p.10.
11.	Leitrim County Library, Local Studies Collection, File 1598, Kathleen Clarke to Michael Whelan, 5 June 1966.
12.	Ciarán Ó Gríofa, 'John Daly The Fenian Mayor of Limerick', in David Lee (ed.), *Remembering Limerick: Historical Essays Celebrating the 800th Anniversary of Limerick's First Charter Produced in 1197* (Limerick: Limerick Civil Trust, 1997), p.198.
13.	Owen McGee, 'Who Were the "Fenian dead"?: The IRB and the background to the 1916 Rising', in Gabriel Doherty and Dermot Keogh (eds), *1916: The Long Revolution* (Dublin: Mercier Press, 2008), p.104.
14.	O'Fiaich Library and Archive, Armagh (hereafter OFLA), Papers of Father Louis O'Kane, including statement of William Kelly senior.
15.	Ibid.
16.	*Belfast Morning News*, 18 August 1880.
17.	Ibid.
18.	Ibid., 19 August 1880.
19.	OFLA, Statement of William Kelly senior.
20.	Ibid.
21.	Le Roux, *Tom Clarke and the Irish Freedom Movement*, p.18.
22.	OFLA, Statement of William Kelly senior.
23.	Ibid.
24.	Seán McConville, *Irish Political Prisoners, 1848–1922 – Theatres of War* (London, Routledge, 2003), pp.332, 342–7.
25.	Ibid., p.348.
26.	Ibid., pp.340, 345.
27.	McGee, Owen, *The IRB – The Irish Republican Brotherhood From The Land League To Sinn Féin* (Dublin: Four Courts Press, 2005), p.83.
28.	Le Roux, *Tom Clarke and the Irish Freedom Movement*, p.24.
29.	Ibid., pp.24–5.
30.	www.oldbaileyonline.org (accessed 27 July 2011).
31.	Le Roux, *Tom Clarke and the Irish Freedom Movement*, p.28.
32.	Ibid., p.29.
33.	Ibid., p.31.
34.	Ibid., pp.31, 33.

35. www.oldbaileyonline.org (accessed 27 July 2011).

36. Ibid.

37. Ibid.

38. Le Roux, *Tom Clarke and the Irish Freedom Movement*, p.34.

39. Ibid.

40. Ibid., p.35.

41. Thomas J. Clarke, *Glimpses of an Irish Felon's Prison Life. With an introduction by P.S. O'Hegarty* (Dublin: Maunsel and Roberts, 1922, 1970), p.11. This book was originally written as a series of articles for *Irish Freedom*, beginning in January 1912. A recent analysis of Fenian prison writing suggests that Clarke's memoirs, together with other such works, were an attempt by a young generation of writers such as Bulmer Hobson and Pat McCartan to 'assert their ownership of the Fenian heritage'. It also claims that the work 'had an important impact upon the small cohort of IRB sympathisers who would be among the first to go to prison during the revolutionary period'. See William Murphy, 'Narratives of Confinement: Fenians, Prisons and Writing, 1867–1916', in F. McGarry and J. McConnel (eds), *The Black Hand of Republicanism: Fenianism in Modern Ireland* (Dublin, Irish Academic Press, 2009), p.171.

42. Clarke, *Glimpses of an Irish Felon's Prison Life*, p.12.

43. Ibid., pp.12–13.

44. Bill Forsythe 'Loneliness and Cellular confinement in English Prisons 1878–1921', *British Journal of Criminology* (2004), 44 (5), 7 May 2004, p.760.

45. Ibid., pp.763–4.

46. Ibid., p.764.

47. *Minutes of Evidence taken before the visitors of her Majesty's Convict Prison at Chatham as to the Treatment of certain prisoners convicted of Treason Felony, H.C., 1890, xxxii.* (hereafter, *Chatham Report*), Appendix Paper E, Statement handed in by Convict Henry H. Wilson and read March 8, 1890.

48. Ibid., *Appendix Paper F, Report of Medical Officer of Chatham Prison (Dr Walker) on health of Treason Felony Prisoners, February 20, 1889.*

49. Ibid., *Appendix Paper W, Particulars as to cubical contents and temperature of cells of Chatham Convict Prison.*

50. Clarke, *Glimpses of an Irish Felon's Prison Life*, p.13.

51. Ibid., pp.13–14.

Chapter two

A Living Tomb

Due to the fact that he had travelled to England under the pseudonym Henry Hammond Wilson, none of Clarke's family was aware of his trial, conviction and imprisonment. Even his close friend Billy Kelly was unaware of the events but as soon as he heard the news he travelled to Clonakilty, County Cork, to relate the story to Clarke's sister, Maria.[1] Consequently, Clarke did not receive his first prison visit until 2 October 1885 when, after a wait of nine months, Kelly was allowed to see him.[2] His next visit was almost eighteen months later, on 14 February 1887, when the visitor was once again Kelly, who subsequently revealed how he had obtained the visits by posing as Clarke's next of kin. Only after he had spent almost six years in prison did Clarke receive his first visit from a family member. Thus, on 5 February 1889, his sister Hannah saw her brother for the first time in nine years. This was followed by another visit to him on 1 August in the same year.[3]

In his prison memoirs Clarke related how he, together with Daly and Egan, attempted to circumvent the strict policy of non-communication between prisoners:

> Daly, Egan and myself right along were in constant communication with each other. We had our code of signals for communicating to each other by sight – these we owed to Egan; we had our post office, authorised, not by the Postmaster-General, but by John Daly. Through our post office thousands of notes passed. We had our telephones and our cell telegraph, which latter was introduced by myself very early in our imprisonment.[4]

Tapping system

Clarke explained how, shortly after arriving at Chatham Prison he established a method of communication with his fellow prisoners:

> All that I could remember about the subject was that the Morse system was based upon two sounds – which were represented on paper by a dot and a dash. The problem was to produce two different kinds of knocks on the wall of the cell and to combine the two sounds into a workable alphabet. After trying different kinds of knocks on my cell table I was satisfied that the dull knock made by the knuckles could not be mistaken for the sharp knock made by a button or slate pencil. I got my slate and soon had an alphabet worked out.[5]

However, Clarke's ingenious attempts to maintain contact with his comrades came at a price and he was regularly severely reprimanded when apprehended. On such occasions he was sentenced to a period of solitary confinement on a bread and water diet. The following table notes his offences and numbers of days spent on the punishment diet:

RECORD OF PRISON OFFENCES OF J464 HENRY HAMMOND WILSON[6]

Date	Offence	No. Days
04/12/83	Signalling to the man in the next cell	2
26/12/83	Signalling to other prisoners by tapping the wall of his cell after a caution	3
17/03/84	Talking when marching to chapel	2
21/06/84	*ditto*	2
13/09/84	Communicating with his fellow prisoners by knocking at his cell wall	2
14/01/85	Having a piece of newspaper in his possession and dropping it in the passage leading to the RC chapel	23
28/03/85	Having a piece of lead secreted in his cell broom	13

26/06/85	Talking when marching to labour	2
10/07/85	Talking when at work in the bath house	3
16/07/86	Talking when parading for labour	2
16/11/86	Writing a clandestine letter on waste paper (addressed to another prisoner) and dropping it close to the door of the penal cells	13
21/07/87	Talking on parade on return from labour	2
04/07/88	Striking another prisoner when employed in the foundry	2
08/10/89	Refusing to do part of his orderly work in penal cells	1

The convictions of John Daly and James Egan had always been clouded in uncertainty as many people felt that both men had been the objects of an agent provocateur working on behalf of the Birmingham police department. However, the poisoning of Daly with belladonna in 1889 (accidentally or otherwise) only served to highlight the harsh conditions being endured by Irish prisoners, and the following year saw the establishment of an official enquiry into conditions in Chatham. Thus, prisoners were enabled to voice grievances about maltreatment by warders including sleep deprivation, inadequate diet and lack of essential medical treatment. Clarke was one of the few prisoners to actually write his comments in a detailed report which offered an insight into his prison experience. One of his main complaints related to medical provision for Irish prisoners. He reported how one man, Denis Deasy, who died in 1884, was constantly treated in his cell while he was ill and according to Clarke, 'it struck me at the time that it was rather brutal to oblige a dying man to get up out of bed and come to his door to take in his food'.[7] He had experienced similar treatment himself especially while undergoing medication for a heart complaint and found the most annoying thing to be 'the continual banging of the gates and doors and the running up and down stairs'.[8] In contrast, he claimed that other prisoners, once requiring medical treatment, were immediately removed to the infirmary. On a number of occasions, when feeling unwell, he had asked to see the doctor but claimed his requests had been ignored. After eventually visiting him, he reported this and was subsequently placed on a punishment diet of bread and water for three days. Similarly, if normal prisoners were feeling unwell they were excused labour but the Irish prisoners, if remaining in their cell due to ill-health, received punishment.[9]

Clarke also alleged that instead of being allocated one hour's exercise each day he and his colleagues were put to work 'ramming gravel in the yard'. He maintained this was a 'special get up for ourselves'.[10] The pettiness of some of the officers was reflected in the fact that they ordered the Irish inmates to walk slowly in the winter, thereby preventing them from keeping warm, and fast in the summer, making them sweat.

When taking their weekly bath Clarke stated how the Irish prisoners were given the 'punishment bath' each time. Thus, they had to strip off in their cell and march to the bathroom 'where a very cold bath would be ready'. While in the bath he was watched by one officer at each end 'both with clubs drawn'. The bath only lasted about a minute and then they were ordered to get out. He contrasted this treatment with that of the prisoners in the 'divisions' where each was marched from their cells fully clothed and then changed in the bath room in a private compartment. In addition they were able to bathe in water of a comfortable temperature.[11]

Another grievance was the lack of intellectual stimulus, or rather the attempts to frustrate such. Prisoners were allowed two educational books and could exchange them for others once every twelve months.[12] On his arrival in Chatham Clarke had requested a Latin Grammar and Dictionary. However, he was told he had to choose from the list on the library card and that he could then exchange those books for the ones he originally requested. He complied with the rules but was then informed, after months of waiting, that he could not have the Latin books, but could have a French Grammar and Dictionary instead. But when he agreed to this he was told, after more delay, that they were only for use by foreigners. Thus, from the time he entered Chatham in December 1883 the only book in his possession was 'English Dictionary and Mensuration'. In 1885 he received another on Euclid and Algebra and read nothing else until April 1889.[13] A further aggravation was that any study was severely restricted by two aspects of his cell. The stools in the penal cells were the same as those allocated to men undergoing punishment (logs fastened to the floor) and these could not be moved to enable the prisoner to sit in a comfortable position. In addition:

> In my cell, reading at night is almost out of the question – indeed at times it is quite impossible – there are only two such cells in the place; between them I have spent three winters and my weakened eyes let me know it. In no other part of this prison, or for the matter of that, in no other part of any prison in the country would such a blinding arrangement be tolerated, unless by way of punishment – at least so I believe.[14]

Finally, Clarke complained that letters sent to him had been delayed, thereby resulting in him missing visits and being unable to return letters. He gave one example of being handed a letter from his sister dated 28 August 1889 which he only received by the middle of the following February. The letter contained a new address for his sister but since it had never been passed on to him he had written to her at her previous address. Doubtless, this would have been obvious to the ever vigilant eyes of those who heavily censored all letters in and out of the prison.[15] In conclusion, Clarke maintained:

> The bitter hatred of the average Chatham officer for the Irish Fenian that makes itself felt in a thousand ways has to be taken into account, and it is the fostering of this spirit of hatred by the authorities that I loudly complain of. We are treated by the lower officer in this or that way, only because he knows he can do so with impunity.[16]

As far as Clarke was concerned the only effective way to deal with these issues was by removal to another prison. Anything else, he stated, would be 'worse than useless'.[17] However, he noted that things had actually improved within the past two years or so but put this down to 'the Authorities expecting an enquiry of some sort'.[18]

Another aspect of the prison regime which caused annoyance was an apparent attempt to manipulate Irish prisoners by asking them to give evidence as part of a special commission examining links between Charles Stewart Parnell and political violence. In March 1887 *The Times* published a series of articles entitled 'Parnellism and Crime' in which Home Rule League leaders had been accused of consorting with members of the IRB. Central to the case was a number of letters purportedly written by Parnell implicating him in such acts. The government eventually set up a commission to investigate the charges and this sat between September 1888 and November 1889. Eight prisoners were visited, including Daly and Clarke, the former receiving three visits as part of the special commission while Clarke was visited on 19 February 1889 by Chief Inspector Littlechild. He was allowed a visit 'unrestricted as to time' to discuss 'the dynamite and other conspiracies' under the instructions of the Secretary of State.[19] Clarke recalled the meeting as follows:

> Presently came my turn, and I was marched away and ushered into a cosy little room, where I found Mr Littlechild sitting at a table in front of the fire. He and I were old acquaintances. He was in charge of the party of Scotland Yard officers who arrested Dr. Gallagher and myself in London; it was he who had charge of working up the case to convict us.[20]

Littlechild then informed him of the work of the commission 'to investigate certain allegations that have been made against the Irish Parliamentary Party'. He told Clarke there were allegations that the IPP was in cahoots with the 'Irish Revolutionary Party' in America. Given that Clarke had travelled from America it was felt that he could offer

Political prisoners being used as objects of political disputes

valuable evidence to the commission. Clarke remembered the next part of the conversation as follows:

> 'Now', said he, dipping his pen in the ink, "I am ready to take down anything you'd wish to say". My answer was brief and to the point. 'Look here, Mr. Inspector, if a single word of information would get me out of here tomorrow, sooner than give it to you, I'd prefer to remain here till the day of judgment. Please take that as final'.[21]

Thus, despite being offered his release and a job in the Civil Service, Clarke refused to give evidence that could have been used against Parnell. Daly also refused and claimed to have been offered his liberty together with a 'certificate of indemnity' by Richard Pigott. The latter eventually admitted to forging the letters and fled to Madrid where he committed suicide. Parnell was exonerated and after bringing a libel action against *The Times*, received a large compensation fee.

The fact that Irish prisoners were seen to be suffering in an English prison was the catalyst for an amnesty campaign and in 1890 the Amnesty Association, originally formed in 1869, was revived, with branches being established in towns throughout Ireland and in several cities in Britain.[22] The campaign was pursued on a number of fronts. Within the political establishment Irish MPs constantly raised the issue in the British House of Commons while on the streets momentum was sustained by a series of public rallies and petitions in Ireland and abroad. One of the earliest public gatherings took place in Tipperary in September 1890 to protest against the treatment 'which Mr John Daly and his fellow-prisoners have been subjected to in Chatham Prison'.[23] In addition, pamphlets were occasionally published such as *The Inhuman Treatment of John Daly and Other Political Prisoners in English Jails* (1890) and *The Case For Amnesty*, the latter penned by John Redmond MP in 1893.[24]

Speaking in the House of Commons on 11 February 1892 John O'Connor, MP for Tipperary, quoted Clarke's assertion about the antipathy of the Chatham prison officers and maintained that 'Daly and his associates were tried in passion, convicted in passion and they are to be retained in passion by an appeal to the passions of the people of this country and to the passions of some honourable members of this House'.[25]

One of the most prominent and diligent advocates of the amnesty movement was John Redmond, the MP for Waterford. His father, William, had played a key role in calling for the release of those imprisoned after the Fenian rising of 1867 and a quarter of a century later his son was involved in a similar campaign.[26] In Parliament, he demanded the 'speedy release' of the men, asserting they were 'political prisoners' by virtue of the fact they had been tried under the Treason-Felony Act and not under any explosives acts. While reassuring the House that he had 'no desire to palliate offences known as dynamite outrages', which were 'not only stupid but … intensely criminal' he maintained that any further detention of the prisoners would 'amount to vindictiveness and cruelty'.[27] However, he was rather more forthright in his opinions some weeks later when speaking on a public platform in Waterford. Talking of the Irish men 'eating their hearts out' in English convict cells, he maintained, 'They are our kith and kin. They are men who sacrificed everything that was most dear to them in an effort to benefit Ireland. What do we care whether their effort was a wise one or not, whether a mistaken one or not?'[28] However, the British government dismissed such claims and the Secretary of State for the Home Department maintained instead that John Daly was 'a fanatic – a dangerous fanatic'.

While the prisoners' grievances were being aired at the highest levels of the political establishment Clarke's case was taken up by some citizens of his home town of Dungannon. In the early months of 1892 a petition to Queen Victoria was presented to T. O'Neill Russell, MP for South Tyrone, the occasion being marked by the lighting of a bonfire in the Square in Dungannon.[29] The document was signed by Viscount Avonmore and included the names of a cross-section of public representatives in the Dungannon area, including 11 magistrates, 16 resident gentry, 9 'professional men', 13 Dungannon Town Commissioners, 27 'leading merchants' of the town, 5 poor law guardians and 7 clergymen of various Protestant denominations. In addition, three officers of the Mid Ulster Artillery, in which James Clarke had served, also added their names.[30]

The petition included a large number of Protestants, much to the annoyance of the Unionist weekly, the *Tyrone Courier*, which remarked how 'the Orangemen of Dungannon and neighbourhood are now beginning to lose caste. Some of their leaders (?) are busy forging a band of sympathy with Fenians and secret-societymen in a very practical way indeed'.[31] The paper accused them of signing a petition 'pledging their sympathy with and affection for the dynamiters'.[32] It was further enraged by the news that the Cookstown Board of Guardians had passed a resolution supporting the release of political prisoners.[33] However, the paper, in maintaining that 'some sort of excuse' could be found for the decision of the Cookstown board (thought it did not specify what that was), continued its tirade against the Dungannon petitioners and their 'infamous petition'[34]:

> ...but what sort of excuse can be found for the Dungannon Orangemen who, scorning the idea of a motion only being put on public books, prepared and signed a petition, canvassed for signatures to it and ultimately had it presented to Her Most Gracious Majesty, the Queen for the release of these men. Orangemen and Churchmen who wear the colours, and pretend to worship at the shrine of the Glorious, Pious, and Immortal William III, did this in Dungannon, the town of the Volunteers. 'Political and religious Hypocrites' we call them. 'Whited sepulchres' who rant in Church pulpits, Pretenders who roar and fume on political platforms, making motions and amendments having for their aim and object the libelling, and slandering of their political opponents, while secretly sympathising with them, and their ends, we unhesitatingly dub them.[35]

The Dungannon petitioners sought to 'humbley crave'[36] the queen to remit Clarke's sentence for a number of reasons and cited both the service given by his father in the British Army as well as his own good behaviour while in prison. However, their main contention was that Clarke had committed the offences for which he was imprisoned while still a young man. They maintained that while in New York 'he unfortunately became acquainted with certain men ... and they persuaded him to join a secret organisation representing to him that it had for its object the destruction of public buildings in England without causing loss of life'.[37]

However, when the document was presented to the Duke of Abercorn for his signature he refused to sign it given the 'enormity of the crime'.[38] While the petition was similar to many others organised for various prisoners it seems that the Parnellite nationalists of Tyrone believed there was a distinct electoral advantage to be gained by supporting calls for the release of Clarke. The following memo, written by Louis McMullan, reflected their thinking:

> In working up the matter I am acting with the leading Nationalists or Parnellites as we are called in this district and we have no desire to be again misrepresented by the little man who now sits for East Tyrone. I have little doubt if you were successful in obtaining Clarke's release we would get the extreme men in the constituency to support a third candidate at the next election which would of course result in relieving Mr Reynolds of going to London to take part in the sole division he turns up for each year. By no other means can the friends of Mr Corbett hope for his return.[39]

The MP for East Tyrone since 1885 had been James Reynolds (the 'little man' referred to) and he was a representative of the anti-Parnellite faction of the Irish Parliamentary Party. McMullan's thinking seemed to reflect the opinion of others that the release of Clarke would see a resurgence of support for a Parnellite candidate in the constituency, if for no other reason than to split the vote and remove Reynolds. The *Tyrone Courier* reported how a gentleman by the name of Oldham, a Protestant Home Ruler, had been selected for this purpose. However, when it came to submitting papers only two candidates contested the election – the sitting MP and the Unionist T.L. Corbett. Reynolds won the subsequent contest.[40]

Further pressure on the government resulted from reports that some of the Irish prisoners had shown signs of insanity. In February 1893 William Redmond, MP for East Clare, quoted a report from the recently-released prisoner Thomas Callan and informed the House of Commons that Thomas Gallagher was insane.[41] Secretary of State Herbert Asquith stated in reply that he had read the same report and assured the House that such claims were 'totally without foundation'. He also confirmed that he had made 'careful enquiries respecting the medical condition of Gallagher with the result that I have come to the conclusion that he is perfectly sane'.[42]

However, agitation on behalf of Gallagher was not restricted to Ireland and Irish parliamentarians. Gallagher was an United States citizen and throughout 1892 a campaign was initiated in American political circles to have him and his fellow prisoners released. In October of that year the Legation of the United States in London reported how the 'unhappy fate' of the men had 'aroused much sympathy' throughout the United States.[43] The House of Representatives, 'in response to numerous petitions on behalf of Dr. Gallagher from all parts of the country' had passed a resolution requesting the Department of State to examine into the case. It was also revealed that the various representations had 'aroused the President's sympathetic interest'. The Legation concluded by requesting that the prisoners be released as soon as possible – a request that was refused.[44]

The plight of the prisoners led to regular visits both from members of the Amnesty Association and Irish politicians. One of the most high-profile campaigners was Maud Gonne, political activist, actress and love interest of poet W.B. Yeats. She immersed herself in the work of the amnesty movement, sometimes spending up to eight hours a day corresponding on various aspects of the cause.[45] She used her conversations with prisoners to highlight their plight to the outside world and on 22

May 1893 *Figaro*, a French newspaper, published an article under the headline 'Atrocités Anglaises' and, quoting Gonne, claimed that five prisoners had gone mad.[46] The article incensed both the prison authorities and the Home Office which claimed that 'this lady appears to have violated the understanding which she gave when she was allowed to visit the prisons. She must not do so again'.[47] In their opinion Gonne had given 'currency to malicious false charges' which 'do much harm'.[48] Hence, from 17 June 1893, under instruction from Asquith, Maud Gonne was banned from any future visits to Irish prisoners.[49]

Despite such knee-jerk reactions the British Home Office and prison authorities sought to allay concerns in both Irish and American political circles about the condition of Thomas Gallagher and Alfred Whitehead and from 1889 onwards regular medical examinations were made of all the prisoners.

By early 1890 Clarke had been admitted into the prison hospital at Chatham four times: on 8 June 1888, he burned his right foot and remained under treatment for three weeks. On 5 April 1889 he reported having palpitations. The medical officer diagnosed the problem as 'a bruit audible over cardiac area, believed to be pulmonary and not due to organic disease'. He was discharged after three days with the condition stated to be 'much relieved'. However, after just three days the condition recurred and this time Clarke remained under treatment for nineteen days. Upon recovery he was excused any further heavy work. Finally, on 3 January 1890 he suffered influenza and was discharged cured after five days' treatment. On each of the above occasions Clarke was treated in his cell, not in the prison hospital.[50]

From February 1886 until March 1889 Clarke had worked as a moulder in the iron foundry on heavy castings.[51] He described this job as 'the most laborious work in the prison' and it appears that this occupation may have had a detrimental impact on his heart.[52] Prior to this he had been a cleaner for three years and from March 1889 onwards he was variously employed as a darner (until April 1889), a stereotyper in the print shop (until 20 January 1891) and then as a tailor until 4 March 1892.[53]

Despite his removal to lighter employment Clarke's heart condition meant that from 1893 onwards he received regular medical examinations at the hands of a variety of doctors. On 21 October 1893 the prison medical officer, Lilley, stated that although 'this prisoner's heart's action is weak' he was otherwise well and his mind was sound.[54] On 8 November 1895 the same gentleman declared that after examining him he found Clarke to be of sound mind, 'in good bodily health' and added that imprisonment had not had a deteriorating effect upon him.[55] Six weeks later a further examination elicited similar comments with the addition that 'he has indigestion at times but states he had better health at Portland than at Chatham'.[56]

However, in light of the constant reassuring tone of reports on the health of prisoners who were subsequently proven to have been suffering greatly, these comments need to be treated with a certain amount of circumspection.

Indeed, due to the statements made by visitors such as Maud Gonne and John Redmond, regular medical reports were issued in relation to two men in particular: Thomas Gallagher and Alfred Whitehead. In October 1893 Dr Lilley stated that Whitehead's mind was 'sound'.[57] On 23 December 1895 he was reported as being 'not mentally strong ... but not insane' with Drs Maudsley and Nicolson commenting how 'he seems to have enough cunning in his disposition to make him feign insanity as he is reported to have done'.[58] Similarly, the same men declared Gallagher to be sane and proffered the opinion that his condition 'exhibits nothing more than the natural effects of imprisonment upon a man of his education and temperament'.[59] Having examined all the men Maudsley and Nicolson declared that 'none of the prisoners have suffered injuriously or unduly in mental or bodily health. There are no grounds for any special medical treatment and we desire to testify to the skill and discretion with which these difficult cases appear to have been dealt with by the medical officers of the prison'.[60]

However, there was strong anecdotal evidence that Gallagher and Whitehead were indeed insane. In June 1895 Clarke had written to John Redmond informing him that he had found Albert Whitehead eating glass in the carpenter's shop.[61] This letter was censored but it appears that Redmond was able to receive information through his visits to prisoners such as Clarke and Daly as their 'legal advisor'. In this capacity he was allowed to conduct interviews with prisoners within view, but out of earshot, of prison officers. Consequently, the governor of the prison, Harris, complained that as it appeared the details emerged as a result of Redmond's visits, such were 'being used for a purpose which surely was not intended'.[62] An incident in 1894 involving Clarke also suggested that Gallagher had lost his mind. On 12 February of that year Harris made the following report of a disturbance to the prison's visiting director:

> Sir, the noises which disturbed the congregation on the occasion referred to were intended to represent the grunting of a pig and appeared to be an allusion to the facial development of a prisoner named Wilson (J464) whom he had previously assaulted on 30 October 1893. The prisoner Wilson has abnormally large ears and it is supposed that this feature was turned into ridicule by Gallagher to insult him.[63]

Harris revealed that in the earlier attack Whitehead had assaulted Clarke 'with his fist'.[64]

Thus, despite the reassuring tone of various medical reports, John Redmond stated that he was 'not convinced' as he had 'for years been hearing it persistently asserted that certain of the prisoners are insane'.[65] Redmond's doubt as to the veracity of these reports led him to suggest that rather than the men being merely examined they should instead be observed over a period of time without their knowledge. He also asserted that Dr Nicolson, being head of Broadmoor Criminal Asylum was effectively a government appointee and could not be regarded as an independent examiner.[66]

Nevertheless, what appeared obvious to Redmond and prisoners such as Clarke was not admitted by medical staff until mid-1896. On 29 July Drs Buzzard and Maudsley stated how 'we cannot say that at the present time he (Gallagher) is otherwise than sane'. Consequently they recommended his release on medical grounds. The same opinion was also made in relation to Whitehead and these men, together with John Daly, were released in August 1896.[67] Within months the British Foreign Office in New York informed the Home Office that both men had been admitted as inmates of the Amityville Asylum on Long Island.[68]

The release of Gallagher and Whitehead witnessed an explosion of anger against the British government in the Irish-American press. The *New York Press* ran a story on the prisoners under the headline 'Monstrous Cruelty in British Prisons – Punishment more terrible than Siberian Banishment'.[69] For its part *The World* focused on Gallagher with the headline 'Driven insane in prison – inside story of the treatment that made maniacs of several of the Irish-American convicts in English cells'.[70] The paper reported how the arrival of Gallagher as a 'drivelling idiot' had caused a 'shock of indignation throughout the country'.[71] Further to this, an article by Irish MP Bernard Molloy was published in the *Progressive Review* of November 1896. Entitled 'Insanity in Prisons' it caused much anger among the prison authorities and civil servants in the Home Office.

In order to avoid the same fate Clarke remembered resorting to what he realised were 'many and strange expedients':'It was ever present before me that were I to "let go" of myself madness was inevitable. It required, at all times, all the effort I was capable of making to enable me to choke off the despondency and wrench the mind away from dwelling upon the miseries of such a life.'[72] Hence, he related how he had spent hours and hours attempting various calculations:

> I [have] counted every brick in my cell and every bolt that studded the ironclad doors, and every perforation in the iron ventilators in that cell, and calculated the weight of the bricks used in building it, and also worked out the number of bricks used in building the entire prison and figured out the total weight.[73]

Similarly, he claimed he could calculate the total number of buttons on the clothing of the entire population of the prison while, by keeping cuttings from his trips to the prison barber, he estimated that after thirteen years imprisonment more than six feet of hair had been cut from his head.[74] Clarke also mastered shorthand, using a book called *Cassell's Popular Educator* and several times translated the Bible from beginning to end into that medium.[75] Nevertheless, he admitted that, due to the 'increasing tension on my nerves previous to my release' he too would have been 'driven mad' if he had been forced to remain much longer in prison.[76]

The evident unease resulting from the controversy over Gallagher and Whitehead was reflected in the number of medical reports sought in relation to the remaining prisoners. On 20 July 1896, some weeks prior to their release, Dr. Lilley had stated that while 'some slight deterioration of health' had taken place during Clarke's imprisonment 'his life and sanity' were not endangered.[77] However, just two days later the prison authorities asserted that the 'most unsatisfactory' cases had appeared to be those of Gallagher, Whitehead and Clarke and requested a 'special report' from another medic. However, Dr. Gover stated that Clarke was in good health and 'no special comment' was necessary.[78] Similarly Drs Maudsley and Buzzard (on 29 July) simply noted that Clarke had a murmur at the base of the heart and was employed in holding tools at wood-turning. Nevertheless, the Secretary of State at the Home Office, on hearing how Clarke's health was 'continually breaking down', demanded a further report on his condition.[79] The assistant surgeon in charge therefore examined Clarke on 26 December 1896 and declared that although he had a weak heart and was anaemic he was in good mental health. He did admit that his 'bodily health' had deteriorated slightly since his conviction and subsequent imprisonment as there had been no sign of a heart problem at the time of his conviction. He was adamant, however, that such deterioration was not due to imprisonment although he admitted that this conclusion would be 'contested by his (Clarke's) friends'. Consequently it was decided that further imprisonment would not endanger him.[80]

While John Redmond pursued the release of prisoners on medical grounds his colleagues in the British Parliament tried alternative means. It was pointed out in 1893 that while the Irish prisoners had been sentenced to penal servitude for life a group such as the Walsall Anarchists, who had been convicted of similar dynamite offences, were sentenced to a maximum of ten years' imprisonment.[81] Similarly a question was put to Home Secretary Asquith on August 1893 as to how a man convicted of the murder of a policeman and soldier during rioting in Belfast, although sentenced to twenty years' penal servitude, had been released after just seven.[82] On such occasions Asquith's mantra was 'every case must of course be judged upon its own merits'.[83]

Irish Parliamentarians also used the approach of Queen Victoria's diamond jubilee in 1897 as an opportunity to appeal for the release of prisoners. For example, on 5 February 1897, John G. Swift Mac Neill, MP for South Donegal asked if the queen would enable the prisoners to be released 'by a liberal exercise of prerogative of pardon'.[84] The answer given by government ministers on all such occasions was in the negative.

While Irish petitions to parliament had, by the mid-1890s, become commonplace there was evidence that the appeal to release the prisoners had reached a wider audience. In 1896 John Redmond noted how the Upper Chamber of the South African Cape Colony had adopted a resolution calling on the government of the Colony to approach the British Government to ask them to extend to the Irish prisoners a clemency similar to that extended by President Kruger to the reform leaders.[85] A few months later a petition was signed by 9,000 citizens of Johannesburg urging the release of those prisoners still in Portland while it emerged that a similar appeal had been signed by the mayor, sheriff, thirty justices of the peace and forty town councillors of Newcastle-upon-Tyne.[86]

The release of close friend John Daly on medical grounds was to prove of huge significance to Clarke. While Daly initially recuperated in Paris he thereafter immersed himself in the work of the Amnesty Association and spoke at meetings all over the country, demanding the release of his comrades, especially Clarke.

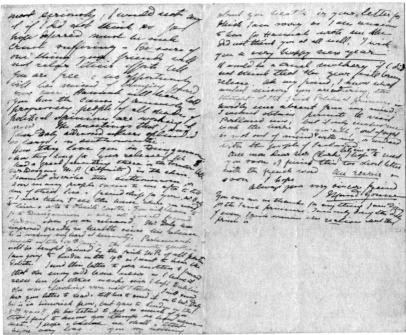

3. Letter from Maud Gonne to Tom Clarke, 29 December 1896.

(courtesy of Archives Dept., Limerick University)

His case was also championed by Maud Gonne who, despite not having direct access to the prisoners, maintained her efforts on their behalf. In the summer of 1896 she coordinated a campaign to petition for the release of Clarke and sought a number of testimonials as to his good character when living in Dungannon. By November 1896 she was able to send them to members of the British parliament and they were subsequently referenced by E.J.C. Morton, MP for Devonport, in a speech on 11 February 1897 in the House of Commons, in which he called for the immediate release of Irish prisoners. Clarke's medical condition was also mentioned by the MP for Louth West, T.M. Healy, who reported how, due to his bad heart, he had been removed from stone-breaking.[87]

Essentially, these documents sought to portray Clarke as a conscientious young individual who had been exploited by more experienced men.

Hence, in confirming that Clarke had been his assistant in the Dungannon Male National School, Cornelius Collins stated how he had 'always found him a quiet, harmless, good boy, regular in his attendance to school duty, and respectful and attentive in the discharge of the work laid off for him by me'.[88]

Parish Priest, Fr P.J. Byrne, corroborated this statement and added his opinion that Clarke was 'a very young man when he engaged in his criminal folly and also the dupe of older and more cunning conspirators'.[89] A further testimonial was offered by James Kelly in his role as president of the Dungannon branch of the Total Abstinence Society. Describing Clarke as being a 'useful, vigilant and attentive teacher of its night school' he continued:

> I assert that … I have met no young man of his time of life more worthy, more straightforward, better conducted in every way or more calculated to adorn society, than Tommie Clarke. This was my opinion often expressed before I ever thought that I would have to write of him under such distressing circumstances … If necessary hundreds in this town in the highest positions will endorse what I have said.[90]

In sending these testimonials Maud Gonne also revealed that when Clarke's mother heard of her son's imprisonment 'this news so affected her that she lost her reason and had to be confined in a lunatic asylum'.

Despite the fact she had been allowed to return home 'her health is broken and she cannot work or be left alone'.[91] The family had been dealt a huge blow by the death of their father from pneumonia at the age of sixty-four in 1894.[92] Aside from the personal tragedy for all concerned his death saw the termination of his British Army pension and left the remaining family members financially stricken. The difficult situation in which Mrs Clarke now found herself, her thanks to Gonne for all her efforts, and her desire to see her son once again were all encapsulated in a letter she wrote on 5 November 1895:

> Dear Miss Gonne,
> Thank you so much for your kind letter to me not only that but all the cheques you have sent me. When I wanted money most May God bless and protect you is all I can say I could not express all the gratitude I feel to you. Dear Miss Gonne God will bless you for holding out hope to me that you think the poor prisoners may soon be released. What a blessing to me it would be for me. I pray God every day that my poor boy will be home with me for Christmas, the first for 14 years. It is so lonely since the death of my dear husband. We have all ready for him when he comes. I have his own cup and teapot waiting for him and his room prepared. God will bless you for all you are doing for the poor prisoners and their families. I have waited so long but I can't help it. Oh dear Miss Gonne do say it might be true. I remain dear Miss Gonne your very grateful, Mary Clarke.[93]

Gonne and John Daly combined their efforts by organising an Amnesty meeting in Dungannon on 17 December 1896. This gathering was held in the Foresters Hall and chaired by Patrick Doogan the anti-Parnellite MP for East Tyrone. A number of resolutions were proposed by Clarke's close friend Billy Kelly condemning the 'inhuman treatment to which the political prisoners are subjected and which in many cases leaves them only fit for a lunatic asylum when released' and calling for the release of the remaining political prisoners.[94]

The chief speakers were Gonne and Daly with the former being introduced as someone who had been 'engaged in the cause of amnesty for years and had addressed meetings in France, Holland and Belgium'.

In her speech she maintained that while the English referred to the prisoners as 'dynamitards' 'she [England] might well be ashamed to use the word when in Matabeleland she was using dynamite cartridges against the helpless blacks who were not provided with modern weapons of warfare'. Referring to meetings held in France in support of the same cause she asserted that they 'had the sympathy of the whole civilized world in their struggle for freedom' while 'England by her treatment of the Irish political prisoners lost her right for ever to speak in the name of civilization'. Meanwhile, Daly demanded the release of Clarke on the 'admitted fact' that he was suffering from heart disease.[95]

Some days later Daly wrote to Hannah Clarke commenting 'Oh my dear girl had you or your dear mother been in Dungannon the night of the meeting and had you seen the houses illuminated and the kind, loving manner that every one spoke of Tom you would indeed feel very proud of your dear brother'.[96] He also expressed the hope that this would be the last Christmas behind bars for the 'bravest and the most loyal comrade a man ever had in suffering'.[97] Similar sentiments were expressed by Maud Gonne in a letter to Clarke on 29 December. Also referring to the 'great meeting' in Dungannon she expressed her disappointment at his not being released but added 'I have great hopes that you will be released before long. I say this most seriously. I would not say it if I did not think so for hope deferred must be such cruel suffering'.[98] Within a few months Gonne further highlighted the amnesty case to an international audience by publishing a monthly paper entitled *l'Irlande Libre* which, while covering stories on various aspects of Irish politics, included articles on the activities of the Amnesty Association.[99] Her commitment to this cause was indefatigable and during a six-month period beginning in April 1897 she spoke several times in Paris, four times in Dublin and at least once in London, York, Glasgow, Manchester, and Cork.[100]

However, while those outside prison fought to attain his freedom it was evident that Clarke, without the company of Daly and others who had been released, was feeling the effects of his long years of incarceration.

On 20 December 1896 Hannah Clarke wrote to Michael Lambert, President of the Amnesty Association. She had just returned from a visit to her brother and her impressions of him made for grim reading:

> I could hardly tell you how deeply grieved and shocked I was to find such a terrible alteration for the worse in his appearance and health, since I saw him last. He is now little short of being a complete wreck – pale, emaciated, and generally broken down – and I feel perfectly certain he cannot long endure the treatment to which he is subjected in Portland Prison. Of late his health has almost entirely failed him, and although the excitement of my visit helped to sustain him while speaking to me, yet I could not fail to notice the many evidences of deep suffering which his hollow cheeks and glistening eyes only too truly betrayed. The fact that he has taken, as he told me, much more medicines within the past few months than during the period of his entire fourteen years' imprisonment is a further evidence, if such were needed, of his failing condition.[101]

A further medical examination by Dr Lilley on 30 January 1897 revealed that Clarke's heart condition persisted while it was also noted that he complained of 'giddiness' at times. While this cardiac weakness was deemed as being 'not at present of a serious nature' prison officials regarded Clarke, together with Harry Burton, as the 'most delicate' prisoners.[102] Thus, on 24 May Drs Hubert and Smalley examined all the men 'giving special attention to Henry Hammond Wilson [Clarke] and Harry Burton'. Clarke was described as being in 'fair general health' and although he suffered an 'irritable heart' they reported that the deputy medical officer of the prison was 'fully alive' as to his state of health, keeping him under 'close supervision'. While Clarke was said to be 'fidgety' they were confident that he showed no sign of insanity.[103]

Hannah Clarke's letter to Lambert reflected the fact that the Amnesty Association was one of the few means by which relatives could obtain support for imprisoned family members. However, correspondence between John Daly and herself, only a few months after her letter to the Association, suggests that this body was not fulfilling its obligations. On 11 June 1897 Daly sent Hannah £3/10 and expressed his annoyance at not being informed 'as to what the Dublin Amnesty people may have done or may not have done in the way of interfering with people whom I expected assistance from'.[104] A couple of weeks later he again wrote on the same matter:

> Now on the subject of the house what I propose to do is this. To send a copy of Mr Kelly's [Honorary Secretary] letter to the Amnesty Association of London and ask them to write to the York St [Dublin Amnesty headquarters] people for an explanation of why they refused your mother assistance in the matter and to ask them to forward whatever money she may require for the house you say Alf was looking at in Ballsbridge.
>
> So my Dear girl don't let your mother or yourself be in any way put out by Mr Kelly's letter as I am quite sure the London Amnesty Assoc. will stand by Tom's mother if the Dublin people will not.
>
> Tell Alf to secure the house if he can't get a better one and let me know at once what money you will require to get you into it ... if you want money to get into the house, let me know at once.[105]

In a communication with Michael Lambert Daly referred to Mrs Clarke's application to that body for assistance and informed him that 'she is about to be thrown out of her home'. He revealed how he had given her £10/10 but advised her to tell the association she had only received £2 as he feared her son Alf 'might be wanting money from her if she said she got more'. Daly stated that he could not afford to do much but that he, together with James Egan, 'would not be a party to refusing the mother of Tom Clarke a paltry sum of money when you have it to give' insisting that 'Clarke would not be either pleased or thankful for a visit from the Association that could not afford to help his mother out of the difficulty she finds herself in now'. He maintained, further, that 'if Tom Clarke were released tomorrow nothing but necessity would compel him to accept money from men who could not see their way to stand by his mother at a time when a few pounds may mean so much to her'.[106]

Meanwhile, Clarke had completed fifteen years of incarceration and Irish politicians railed against the policy which ensured he remained confined.

On 28 June 1898 in a speech in the House of Commons, the MP for South Mayo, Michael Davitt, accused the British government of treating the prisoners 'with a spirit of vindictiveness and retaliation unparalleled in any country with which I am acquainted'.[107] He was supported in this assertion by the member for Newington West, Captain Norton, who proffered the opinion that 'there is a prejudice against political prisoners in this country simply because the prisoners are, in nine cases out of ten, Irishmen'.[108] Meanwhile, in reiteration of a point made many times in the previous few years, William Redmond, MP for East Clare, argued that the men still imprisoned would have been released if they had been tried under the Dynamite Act.[109]

The pressure mounted by various individuals and groups eventually told and on 15 June 1898 it was reported in the press that John Redmond had been informed that Clarke's sentence was now to be treated as one of twenty years instead of life and with a five-year deduction for good behaviour he would be released shortly.[110] It was initially argued by the Home Office that as Clarke had accumulated 199 marks for bad behaviour and would not reap the maximum benefit of the government decision he would not be released until 3 December.

However, it was subsequently ascertained that all misconduct and forfeiture of marks had occurred in the early part of his prison term in Chatham and that he was now categorised as a 'first class' prisoner, being 'clear of report' for four years. In addition, officials contended that it would be better to predicate their decision on the fact that he had served fifteen years rather than make reference to his marks.[111] Therefore the Home Office agreed to release him on licence on 14 September 1898. His co-prisoners, Pat Flanagan and Tim Featherstone, were also beneficiaries of this change of policy but the administration stipulated that the prisoners were to be released at intervals of a week or so and not together.[112]

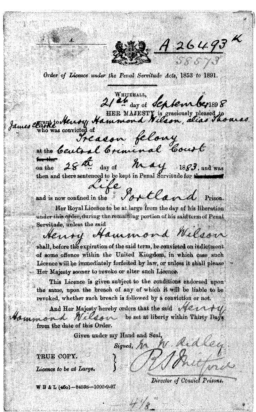

4. Tom Clarke's 'ticket-of-leave', 21 September 1898.

(courtesy of the National Museum of Ireland).

On 11 August 1898 Clarke was examined by the prison doctor for the last time, being deemed to be in 'fair good health'.[113] On 20 September he left Portland and travelled to Pentonville Prison. The following day Home Secretary Sir Matthew Ridley issued the royal licence which allowed him 'to be at large from the day of his liberation' but stipulated that if he was further convicted of any offence the licence would be revoked, resulting in his immediate re-imprisonment.[114]

On 30 September the *Irish Daily Independent* carried a detailed report on the release of Clarke. On walking from Pentonville he was met by his brother Alfred and John Daly. They then went to the residence of Clarke's friend and Tyrone native Joseph Hart before travelling in the evening to Euston railway station to meet James Egan. On the platform they were greeted by members of the London Amnesty Association including Dr Mark Ryan while also in the party was Solomon Gillingham from Pretoria who greeted Clarke as 'a fellow South African'.[115]

Upon seeing Clarke for the first time the reporter described him as 'a man of medium height and intelligent aspect. The face and body are emaciated from cruel years of hardship and deprivation while the long-enduring penal labour has left its mark in a slight stoop of the shoulders'.[116] He also noted how he had become 'somewhat browned' due to the fact he had been allocated work outside the prison walls in his last few months of incarceration. Noting that Clarke was dressed 'in a smart blue serge suit and a fashionable soft hat', he asked him if the prison had supplied the clothes. Clarke replied:

> No, I refused to take anything away from the English jail but myself. I had earned as a prisoner £6, or rather £3, the other came from the Prisoners' Aid Society which I had refused to join. When the money was offered me I declined it and said I only wanted my old letters. These clothes were kindly brought to me by Mrs Hart. The only thing I took from the prison was my old letters and they are very dear to me.[117]

5. Group portrait taken on the occasion of Clarke's return to Dungannon, October 1898. Left to right: James Egan; Terence Cullen; Tom Clarke; Joseph Hart; Ferdinand Morrison.

(photo courtesy of Archives Dept., Limerick University; names courtesy of Bertie Foley, Dungannon, County Tyrone).

He revealed how, in the months before his release, the prison doctor had been 'trying to fatten me up for public view' by 'plying' him three times a day with doses of cod liver oil and malt.[118] The reporter unsuccessfully attempted to engage Clarke in a detailed interview about his time in prison but he said he was too tired to do so. However, he expressed his anger at the length of time he had served and revealed he had known between sixty and seventy English life prisoners who had served a maximum of twelve years, the majority being released after ten. He also disclosed that he had been visited by John Redmond eight or nine times and stated that his efforts 'meant a great deal to us', remarking, 'as far as I am concerned I felt the good effects of his visits for a week afterwards and sometimes for a fortnight. A visit of this kind is good and I shall always feel thankful to Mr Redmond for his visits'.[119]

Clarke savoured his initial period of freedom by staying with friends in London. A few days later he returned home to Ireland to meet his mother for the first time in eighteen years.

Notes

1.   O' Fiaich Library and Archive (hereafter, OFLA), Papers of Father Louis O'Kane, includ-
      ing statement of William Kelly senior.
2.   Ibid.
3.   National Archives, Kew, London, (hereafter, NAUK), Home Office Papers (hereafter, HO)
      144/925/A46664C.
4.   Thomas J. Clarke, *Glimpses of an Irish Felon's Prison Life. With an introduction by P.S.
      O'Hegarty* (Dublin: Maunsel and Roberts, 1922, 1970), p.15.
5.   Ibid.
6.   NAUK, HO 144/925/A46664/32-4.
7.   *Minutes of Evidence taken before the visitors of her Majesty's Convict Prison at Chatham as to the
      Treatment of certain prisoners convicted of Treason Felony, H.C., 1890, xxxii.* (hereafter, *Chatham
      Report*), *Appendix Paper E, Statement handed in by Convict Henry H. Wilson and read March
      8th, 1890.*
8.   Ibid.
9.   Ibid.
10.   Ibid.
11.   Ibid.
12.   Ibid.
13.   Ibid.
14.   Ibid.
15.   Ibid.
16.   Ibid.
17.   Ibid.
18.   Ibid.
19.   NAUK, HO 144/925/A46664.
20.   Clarke, *Glimpses of an Irish Felon's Prison Life*, p.24.
21.   Ibid., p.25.
22.   Seán McConville, *Irish Political Prisoners, 1848–1922 – Theatres of War* (London, Routledge,
      2003), pp.381–2.
23.   *Freeman's Journal*, 22 September 1890.
24.   NAUK, HO 144/195/A46664C (101-393).
25.   Hansard Parliamentary Debates (hereafter, Hansard), vol. I, 11 February 1892, cols. 259;
      264-6.
26.   Dermot Meleady, *Redmond: The Parnellite* (Cork: Cork University Press, 2007), p.17.
27.   Hansard, vol. I, 11 February 1892, cols. 237-8 and 249.
28.   Meleady, *Redmond: The Parnellite*, p.21.
29.   *Tyrone Courier*, 26 March 1892.
30.   National Library of Ireland (hereafter, NLI), Thomas Clarke Papers, Acc 6410, Box 3, V.ii.
31.   *Tyrone Courier*, 10 March 1892.

32. Ibid., 2 April 1892.
33. Ibid., 10 March 1892.
34. Ibid., 2 April 1892.
35. Ibid. In its edition of 27 July 1895 the paper noted how local Fenian leaders had canvassed for Corbett in the general election of that year.
36. NLI, Thomas Clarke Papers, ACC 6410, Box 3, V.ii.
37. Ibid.
38. Ibid., Box 3, V.i., Duke of Abercorn to P. Jordan, 11 January 1892.
39. Ibid., Box 3, V.ii.
40. *Tyrone Courier*, 30 June 1892.
41. Hansard, vol. VIII, 3 February 1893, col. 393.
42. Ibid.
43. NAUK, HO 144/116/A26493.
44. Ibid.
45. Margaret Ward, *Maud Gonne: Ireland's Joan of Arc* (London: Pandora, 1990), p.37.
46. NAUK, HO 144/195/46664C (101-393).
47. Ibid.
48. Ibid.
49. Ibid.
50. *Chatham Report, Appendix paper G, Report of Medical Inspector of Convict Prisons (Dr Gover) on Health of Treason Felony Prisoners in Chatham Prison, seen by him on 14th February 1890.*
51. NAUK, HO 144/194/A46664C (1-100).
52. Clarke, *Glimpses of an Irish Felon's Prison Life*, p.14.
53. NAUK, HO 144/194/A46664C (1-100).
54. Ibid., HO 144/195/A46664C (101-393).
55. Ibid., HO 144/195/A46664D.
56. Ibid., HO 144/925/A46664.
57. Ibid., HO 144/195/A46664C (101-393).
58. Ibid.
59. Ibid.
60. Ibid.
61. Clarke, *Glimpses of an Irish Felon's Prison Life*, p.17.
62. NAUK, HO 144/195/A46664C (101-393).
63. Ibid.
64. Ibid.
65. Ibid.
66. Ibid.
67. Ibid., 29 July 1896.
68. Ibid., HO 144/195/A46664D, 8 January 1897, Francies Bertie to Under Sec. Home Office.
69. Ibid., HO 144/195/A46664C (101-393), *New York Press* (4 October 1896).
70. Ibid., *The World* (4 October 1896).
71. Ibid.
72. Clarke, *Glimpses of an Irish Felon's Prison Life*, p.45.
73. Ibid.
74. Ibid.
75. Ibid.
76. Ibid., p.58.
77. NAUK, HO 144/195/A46664D, 20 July 1896.
78. Ibid.
79. Ibid.

80. Ibid.
81. Hansard, vol. XVI, 25 August 1893, col. 1106.
82. Ibid., 29 August 1893, col. 1357.
83. Ibid.
84. Ibid., vol. XLV, 5 February 1897, col. 1435.
85. Ibid., vol. XLII, 29 June 1896, col. 270.
86. Ibid., vol. XLVI, 25 February 1897, col. 1138 and vol. L, 1 July 1897, col. 871.
87. Ibid., vol. LIII, 11 February 1898, cols. 448-450 and col. 455.
88. NAUK, HO 144/194/A46664C (1-100).
89. Ibid.
90. Ibid.
91. Ibid.
92. General Registrar's Office, Deaths registered in the district of No 1 East in the union of north Dublin in the County of City of Dublin, no. 167.
93. NAUK, HO 144/194/A46664C (1-100).
94. *Tyrone Courier*, 19 Dec 1896.
95. Ibid.
96. University of Limerick Archives (hereafter, ULA), Daly Papers, Mealy's 2006 auction, accession lot 371, John Daly to Hannah Clarke, 23 December 1896.
97. Ibid.
98. Ibid., Daly Papers, Box 2, Folder 69, Maud Gonne to Tom Clarke, 29 December 1896.
99. Samuel Levenson, *Maud Gonne* (London: Cassell & Co., 1977), pp.115–16.
100. Ibid., p.116.
101. *Freeman's Journal*, 23 December 1896.
102. NAUK, HO 144/195/A46664D.
103. Ibid., HO 144/194/A46664C (1-100).
104. ULA, Daly Papers, Box 2, Folder 61, John Daly to Michael Lambert, 24 July 1897.
105. Ibid., Mealy's 2006 auction, accession lot 371, John Daly to Dora (Hannah) Clarke, 24 June 1897.
106. Ibid., Daly Papers, Box 2, Folder 61, John Daly to Michael Lambert, 24 July 1897.
107. Hansard, vol. LX, 28 June 1898, col. 436.
108. Ibid.
109. Ibid., vol. LIII, 11 February 1898, col. 441.
110. NAUK, HO 144/195/A46664D.
111. Ibid.
112. Ibid.
113. Ibid.
114. National Museum of Ireland (hereafter, NMIHE), EW.437.
115. *Irish Daily Independent*, 30 September 1898.
116. Ibid.
117. Ibid.
118. Ibid.
119. Ibid.

Chapter three

America and Back

On 8 October 1898 the press reported on the return of Tom Clarke to the North Wall in Dublin aboard the *SS Banshee*. He had been accompanied on the journey by his former prison comrades James Egan and Henry Dalton. On their arrival they were greeted by a number of friends including both Michael Lambert and James Bermingham of the Amnesty Association.[1]

After spending a couple of weeks with his mother and sister at 5 St Anthony's Road, Kilmainham, Dublin, Clarke, together with Tim Featherstone and Dalton, was publicly acknowledged at an Amnesty demonstration at the Rotunda in the city.[2] At the end of October he joined Egan and John Daly on a journey to Dungannon where they were met by a deputation from the local Amnesty Association. An address of welcome was read by Hugh Birney, a member of the Irish National Foresters, who offered Clarke congratulations on his 'survival and deliverance from a living tomb after undergoing nearly 16 years['] imprisonment for a crime of which we still believe and know you were not guilty'.[3] Clarke then proceeded to make his first ever public speech:

> Mr Chairman and friends of the old bye-gone days – friends of my boyhood and early manhood – I cannot find words warm enough to thank you for the magnificent reception you have given to me and to the comrades who spent so many years by my side in the dungeons of England. I shall never forget this welcome which Dungannon has given us. Right well do I know why you welcome us, thus suffering as we did for the Old Land. We have

been felons for Ireland's sake. The head and front of our sin has been honest-souled service for Ireland, and honest hatred for her enemies. (Applause) Our crime has been the same for which so many sons of old Ireland, generation after generation, trod the dark path or mounted the scaffold or filled the felon's grave. Bad and dark though the pages of Irish history may be – and dark and black many are – bright and glorious stories they tell. They speak of the illustrious felons of old, who so nobly dared and died for the old land. (Cheers) From my earliest years I have been a reader of Irish history and oft have I looked up to the illustrious men with the deepest reverence and love and it is proud I am that one of the rank and file of Irishmen should have been able to walk for even a small distance along the path of the suffering for the Old Land – the path they trod – that path that bears such foot-prints. No need here to trace back or wade through our history. No need to rehearse the doings of those Irishmen – Wolfe Tone, the Sheares brothers and other martyred heroes.

'They rose in dark and evil days,
To free their native land.'

Those men keep alive the loving flame that glows in Irish hearts. Right well do they deserve to be honoured; right well do we know the spirit which they in their day helped to keep alive and to hand down. How would it be to-day with Ireland but for such men? Those men go down to posterity, differently to the sringing whining people who lived in their day. Confidently did they look to the time when Irishmen would be free to live at home in the Old Land, enjoying their rights as men. In your address allusion has been made to the treatment in prison and to English dungeons … As far as savage treatment is concerned, better fall into the hands of the American Red Indian or the African Ashantee, than to be dealt with as we were in the pris-ons of England. The Red man or the Black man's treatment of his prisoner, horrible as it is, falls far short of the diabolical scientific barbarity with which England tortures her prisoners. Sooner than go through a tenth part of the horrible sufferings in English jails, better submit to the worst form of death conceivable; better to be blown from the muzzle of the canon – one of England's nineteenth-century methods. Once more I return you my sincere thanks. I cannot express how deeply I feel this evening's welcome.[4]

Having been presented with a purse of sovereigns Clarke and the deputation then marched through the town, led by a variety of bands, to a dinner in the Forester's Hall.[5] On 23 November another reception, this time given by the Ulstermen's (Dublin) '98 Club, was held in his honour at the Verdon Hotel in the capital.[6]

News of Clarke's release was also met with celebrations in Limerick where local bands marched through the city followed by 'immense crowds'.[7] Nowhere was the excitement more palpable than in the Daly household, as evidenced by a letter from John Daly to Clarke in which he remarked, 'and as sure as the Lord made little apples you'll be marked black and blew [sic] as soon as my girls lay hands on your poor bones'.[8] Since his release from prison Daly had established a successful bakery business in William Street in Limerick. In addition, he had been elected Mayor of the city as a result of the recently-enacted Local Government (Ireland) Act of 1898. This measure effectively ended landlord control of local government in Ireland and allowed people to take decisions affecting themselves. The County and the sub-county District Councils thus created a political platform for proponents of Home Rule displacing Unionist influence in many areas. Such was the case in Limerick and Daly endeavored to use this office to honour his close friend by resolving to offer Clarke the freedom of the city.

However, it appears that Clarke was reluctant to accept the tribute bestowed by his colleague. On 9 February 1899 Daly informed him that 'I read carefully all you had to say on the freedom question, consulted my friends on the subject and arrived at the conclusion that there was nothing in it beyond your own natural modesty'.[9] He then advised Clarke to 'come down here and accept it, and without more ado put it in your britches pocket, where Dannell [*sic*] put the repeal'.[10]

Clarke's delay in travelling to Limerick was also perhaps the consequence of the fact that he had to slowly acclimatise to being a free man. While he occasionally gave lectures on his prison experience to interested parties, he generally remained with his mother and sister while they nursed him back to something like full health throughout the first few months of 1899.[11] However, on 2 March 1899 Clarke travelled to Limerick and was bestowed with the Freedom of the city. Speaking at the ceremony Daly noted how in previous years the honour had been 'at one time reserved for those who came to us as friends of the invader or the foreigner'.[12] However, on this occasion it was made to Tom Clarke 'in recognition of his heroic sacrifices in the cause of Ireland and of the sufferings he endured in British prisons for 15½ years'.[13] In his acceptance speech Clarke constantly referred to his friendship with Daly and the sacrifices they had both made:

> This Corporation of your city of Limerick for the first time in its existence as a city, represents the people of the city, truly representing the democracy of the city, and when you confer its freedom upon me, as you, Mr Mayor, have already remarked, it is the people of the city who really confer it (hear, hear). And why? Because you believe me to be an Irish Nationalist of the stamp of John Daly (hear, hear). Because like him I have worn the felon's fetters through many dark and dreary years for Ireland's sake, for the self-same cause for which he himself has suffered, and because you believe that I am, like John Daly, a man who will always stand by the cause and never flinch from doing my duty by it. It is true I was fired in my early boyhood by what I knew of the past of my country, and what I could see of the misgovernment that was going on through the country around me. It is true the history of our country in the past is the history of the struggles of the victim enveloped in the folds of the boa-

constrictor – the victim too strong to be crushed outright, but not strong enough to free itself from the reptile's clutches – a victim who receives no relaxation from the reptile's clutches, unless when that reptile is afraid to do so, when danger threatens in the distance. Truly it has been said 'the reptile's difficulty is Ireland's opportunity' (hear, hear). Now, Mr Mayor, you confer this freedom upon me, but after listening to the eulogistic way you have spoken of me, I find that it is simply impossible to concentrate my thoughts sufficiently to make a coherent speech here tonight. I feel quite knocked out over it, but I will say this, that after the honour you have paid to me, I will strive through my future life in connection with the old cause to prove worthy of the honour (applause).[14]

Clarke then spent a couple of weeks with the Daly family and it must have been a busy household as John Daly lived with his elderly mother, sister, sister-in-law and eight nieces and one nephew.[15]

While such events may have proven uncomfortable to a quiet and somewhat introverted person such as Clarke, they were meant to raise his spirits and illustrate that his years in prison had been recognised by people in his own country. However, what he needed as soon as possible was employment and in May 1899 the Amnesty Association sent an application in his name for the vacant post of clerk of the Rathdown Poor Law Union in County Wicklow. Michael Lambert and Thomas Kelly explained to the Board of Guardians that part of their remit was to attempt to secure jobs for released political prisoners. In doing so they maintained that Clarke was 'not a dynamitard' basing this upon the fact that he had been tried under the Treason-Felony statute and was therefore '*de jure* a Political Prisoner'. In addition, they argued that he had been sentenced as a result of 'perjured evidence'.[16]

Revealing that Clarke had refused to cooperate with the Parnell Commission, despite the offer of release and employment, the representatives of the Association suggested that 'surely a Nationalist who resisted so terrible a temptation, refused so great a bribe and preferred to patiently endure such long and savage punishment, ought to be eligible for office in a Union that Irish Nationalists control'.[17]

In addition, they pointed out that Clarke was presently unemployed and was 'in urgent need of ... suitable and permanent position'. Given that the other candidates for the post were already employed the Association asked them to withdraw in favour of Clarke. Finally they asserted that as Clarke was an 'Amnesty Candidate' this changed the election from being a 'local affair' to a 'public event'.[18]

Indeed, Clarke's candidature was supported by a wide variety of colleagues and public representatives. In a letter to the chairman of the board of guardians, James Egan, now Dublin City Sword Bearer, vouched that Clarke would bring to the service of the board 'ability, integrity and an earnest honesty in the performance of his work'.[19] Cordier Marmion, a J.P. from Dungannon, recommended him 'with confidence'[20] while John Redmond in stating that he had had 'many opportunities' to judge his 'character and abilities' during the 'distressing period' of his imprisonment revealed how he subsequently formed for Clarke 'feelings of the greatest respect and goodwill'.[21] Another MP, John Dillon, told Clarke he would make a 'thoroughly competent official' and expressed the hope that 'it will be recognised by any Irish Board controlled by Nationalists that your claim to their consideration is stronger than any other who is likely to come before them'.[22]

A similar political argument was articulated by Canon J.J. McCartan, parish priest of Donaghmore, near Dungannon. He had known Clarke as a member of the teaching staff in Dungannon National School and believed him to be 'as good and as promising a young man as could be found in this neighbourhood'.[23] Suggesting that for 'honour and integrity and honesty he cannot be surpassed' he concluded with the following plea to the guardians: 'It would be a most graceful and patriotic act on the part of the Rathdown Guardians to elect Mr. Clarke if only as a protest against the exceptional brutality and, I might say, the vengeance with which England treats all Irish political prisoners'.[24] However, these testimonials proved to be in vain as the post was subsequently allocated to another candidate.

With little prospect of a job in Ireland Clarke wrote to John Devoy, the prominent Fenian leader in America, to ask him to organise a lecture tour. In later years John Daly stated how 'to Devoy I owe all... he helped me to build up a home for my darlings, a real happy old home'.[25] Upon his release Daly had travelled to America and, thanks to the efforts of Devoy, had enjoyed a very successful lecture tour during which he had outlined his experiences in prison. This had furnished him with enough money to start his bakery business in Limerick.[26] Clarke hoped for a similar response from the American side to his request. However, he was to be grievously disappointed as Devoy refused to help him. While Clarke was deflated by the news, Daly was incensed, remarking, 'It's about as cold-blooded an epistle as ever I read, but keep it to yourself for the present. ... All I can, or will say now Tom is never say die. We lived through a bloody sight worse than the cold indifference of Mr. Devoy and his friends'.[27]

From a modern perspective it is difficult to understand why Devoy should have refused a man who had just served almost half his life behind prison bars. One would presume that Clarke would have been lauded by Fenians throughout the world and had all his needs catered for. However, it is important to examine the question in its contemporary context. Almost from the time of his incarceration Daly had been a *cause célèbre* in Irish political circles and had a pedigree which included involvement in the last rebellion in the country – the Fenian rising of 1867. Further to this he had been arrested in 1876 after a Home Rule meeting in support of Isaac Butt.[28] In 1895, while still in prison and running as a Parnellite candidate, he was elected unopposed as MP for Limerick. Added to this was the fact that Daly was a larger-than-life individual who was not afraid to make his feelings clear, regardless of the company. The 1890 Chatham Visitors' report is dominated by testimony from Daly, largely due to the almost fatal dose of belladonna he had received. Similarly, the Home Office papers in the National Archives, Kew, contain more information about Daly than any other prisoner. When IPP members complained in the House of Commons of maltreatment of Irish prisoners, they invariably focused on the case of Daly. Hence, when he was released he was regarded as a hero by those in Fenian circles.

By contrast, Tom Clarke was just one of the twenty-one Irish prisoners who languished in Chatham and Portland prisons in the 1880s and 1890s. Demands for his release did not become significant until the mid-1890s when most of the other prisoners had secured freedom. He had entered prison as a relatively young man and would have been regarded by those in the IRB and Clan na Gael as just another 'foot soldier'. In other words, Tom Clarke meant much less to John Devoy than did John Daly and while the latter may have vouched for him, this seems to have made little impact on the old Fenian.

However, while he faced difficulty in trying to obtain a job, another aspect of his life was bringing him much happiness. In Louis Le Roux's rather hagiographical account he states that 'even before she met him, Kathleen Daly…had regarded Tom with romantic admiration'.[29] However, the reality was revealed by Kathleen in her memoirs some years later when she remembered how, initially, 'I was keenly disappointed. His appearance gave no indication of the kingly, heroic qualities which Uncle John had told us about; there was none of the conquering hero which I had visioned. He was emaciated and stooped from the long imprisonment and hardship'.[30]

Nevertheless, during his stay in Daly's home when he was being awarded the Freedom of Limerick, 'his appearance receded into the background and the man Uncle John had portrayed was revealed'.[31] Several times each year the Dalys rented a holiday lodge in Kilkee, County Clare and in the summer of 1899 Clarke spent a month with the family. It was during this period that Kathleen and he became romantically involved. In fact, they agreed to become engaged. The immediate impact Tom had made on Kathleen was evident from her letters to him after this period; for example on 4 August she confided how 'the morning you left I felt as if I'd like to run after the train and bring you back'.

However, the match did not meet with the approbation of her family, including Clarke's great friend, John Daly. Kathleen told him

6. Tom Clarke, September 1899.
(courtesy of the National Library of Ireland)

that 'Uncle John and herself [Madge] give me a hot five minutes now and then. The worst of his attacks, though short, is that they are so unexpected you never know when the sword, as it were, will fall upon you'.[32]

A couple of weeks later she still faced strident opposition to their romance and commented how 'To tell you the truth I get such a hot time of it when I mention your name – either to ask a question or anything else – that I stay as clear of doing so as I possibly can. I tried to pluck up my courage a few times to do so but failed'.[33]

Kathleen stated that the opposition stemmed mainly from her mother and aunt who opposed Clarke on the grounds that he had no job or obvious career prospects.[34] However, her correspondence with Tom suggests that her entire family circle, (whom she referred to as 'the criticizing crowd here')[35] vehemently opposed the romance. Of course the situation was not helped by Clarke's employment difficulties and, determined to carve a new life for himself with Kathleen, he took the decision to emigrate to America in the hope that, when he obtained a steady job, she would follow later.

Acquaintances later noted that Clarke was so disenchanted with his life at this point that he seriously contemplated going to fight with the Boers in South Africa.[36]

However, he determined instead to attempt to start afresh and so in early October 1899 Clarke sailed to America with his sister Maria aboard the SS *Severin*. Before he left Kathleen was depressed, telling him 'I hate to think of you going to America, it seems so far away'.[37]

Tom and Maria Clarke settled in New York and Tom was soon employed as a pattern-maker in the Cameron Pump works on 23rd East Street at a wage of thirty-five dollars a week. In the evenings he worked as a night clerk at the Clan na Gael headquarters for a further fifteen dollars a week.[38] Despite the fact he had been forced to leave Ireland his friends continued to seek employment for him and in August 1900 the Amnesty Association put his name forward for another position – this time the post of Superintendent of the Dublin Abattoirs, with a starting salary of £150 a year and a house. Having just established himself in New York, Clarke hesitated to return home but between 13 and 17 September he received four telegrams from the Association urging him to return at once as he was certain to get the job.[39] He therefore made the long journey home and stayed with his mother and sister Hannah at 5, Blessington Place in Dublin where his mother ran a small lodging house.[40] However, in spite of the hopes of his colleagues and the support of those such as John Dillon MP, who argued that 'the claim of Mr Clarke on Irish Nationalists is extremely strong'[41] he was once again to be disappointed. The confident boast of

**7. Letter from Tom Clarke to Jim Bermingham,
4 October 1899, on his way to America.**

(courtesy of Archives Dept., University of Limerick)

James Egan that he would win 'hands down'[42] soon dissipated when it became clear that a proposed open vote would instead become a secret ballot. Under these circumstances Clarke was once more unsuccessful.[43]

So Clarke returned to America and waited impatiently for his sweetheart to arrive. However, her family refused to allow her to travel by herself and she informed Tom that 'Uncle John and mama won't consent to my going out to you so soon. I can hardly believe it'.[44] Kathleen also remarked on her sister Madge's curiosity at how she could be 'willing to leave everyone I ever knew for what she calls almost a stranger. I told her you were no stranger to me'.[45] Another major obstacle was placed in their way when, on an outing in Dublin, Kathleen witnessed an accident involving a van owned by the *Freeman's Journal* newspaper and James Egan's wife. As principal witness she had to postpone any thoughts of making a journey to America, much to Tom's chagrin.[46] Eventually, after a delay of seven months, Kathleen, accompanied by the Egans, travelled to New York in July 1901 where they were met by Tom and Maria. Together at last they were immediately married in St Augustine's Catholic Church on 16 July, the witnesses being Major John MacBride and Catherine McFadden.[47] Two months later, on 15 September, they were present at a similar ceremony in the Bronx when Maria Clarke married Edward Fleming.[48]

The Clarkes settled in Greenpoint, Brooklyn and Tom was elected president of the local Clan na Gael club where he heavily promoted Irish music, language and dancing.[49] Kathleen later recalled his efforts:

> He published a journal under the auspices of the Celtic Club called *The Clansman*, and it was a real propagandist Irish-Ireland publication. One article he wrote for it that I remember was on the Irish language, in which he said that a free Ireland without its language was inconceivable, and that the Gaelic League was doing invaluable work for Ireland in reviving the language, and deserved the support of every Irish man and woman.[50]

Further to this Clarke was an eager participant in the activities of the Brooklyn Gaelic Society where, as a member of the lectures committee, he helped arrange talks for members on a variety of topics relevant to Irish culture. In 1902 Kathleen gave birth to their first son, Daly, named after John Daly.[51] However, a short time later Tom lost his job at the Cameron Pump Works and was reduced to his earnings of fifteen dollars with the Clan. To supplement this meagre income Kathleen bought an ice-cream and sweet shop in Greenpoint, Brooklyn. Desperate to obtain money Clarke even applied to become a road sweeper with the New York City Cleansing Department, but was refused.[52]

Tom's main duties at Clan headquarters were to act as private secretary to John Devoy and it appears that, despite the latter's previous unhelpful attitude, he had developed a good relationship with the veteran IRB man. Devoy was a notoriously prickly individual but his respect for Clarke was reflected in the fact that he asked him to oversee the establishment of a journal which would represent the voice of the IRB. In this he proved successful and in September 1903 the *Gaelic American* was launched with Devoy as editor and Clarke as his assistant.[53]

**8. Tom Clarke's certificate of membership of the
Clan Na Gael Irish Volunteers, 1 January 1906.**

(courtesy of the National Museum of Ireland)

Clarke's immersion in Clan activities was highlighted by his membership of its military wing, the Irish Volunteers and on 1 January 1906 he was appointed to the rank of Regimental Adjutant in the Second Infantry.[54] In that year he also joined the Irish-American Athletic Club, based in Celtic Park, New York.[55] His respect for previous generations who had risen in arms against British rule in Ireland was reflected by initiatives both in America and, later, in Ireland. For example, in seeking to revitalise an inactive IRB veterans' association in New York, he instigated a search for the graves of Fenians in the city. When approximately forty previously forgotten and neglected sites had been located he ensured they were looked after by the veterans. Thus, on the annual American Decoration Day, they laid wreaths on each grave.[56] Another commemoration introduced by Clarke was the yearly pilgrimage to the grave of Matilda Tone (wife of Wolfe Tone) at Greenwood Cemetery, held as near as possible to the pilgrimage in Ireland to the grave of her husband at Bodenstown.[57]

From 1903 onwards the Clarkes lived at 1551 Fulton Street, Brooklyn but it appears that from this period onwards Kathleen began to suffer regular bouts of ill-health.[58] For example, in June and July 1904 she spent a couple of weeks at St Michael's Villa in Englewood, New Jersey. This establishment was run by the Sisters of St Joseph of Peace and offered vacation opportunities to Irish girls working in the locality. It may have been felt that Kathleen, together with her son Daly, would have benefited from some time outside the city.[59]

The following year their young son was diagnosed with diphtheria, thus necessitating a six-week period of quarantine for mother and child.[60] Indeed in August 1905, Kathleen and Daly travelled to spend a few months with her family in Limerick. Obviously the holiday had the desired effect and on 4 October Kathleen informed Tom that 'Kilkee did both myself and Daly a world of good … and every one says that both him and myself look different creatures altogether to what we were when we came over. I'm sure you will see a wonderful change in us'.[61]

While his wife and son were recuperating in Ireland Clarke received

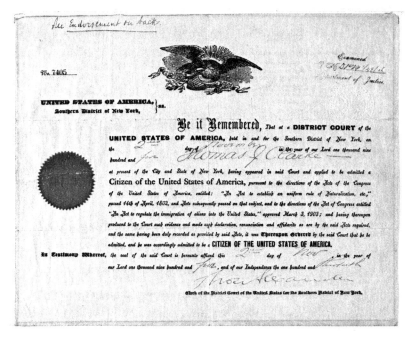

9. **Tom Clarke's certificate of American citizenship,**
2 November 1905.

(courtesy of the National Museum of Ireland)

the news that he had become an American citizen, being awarded his
certificate on 2 November 1905.[62] However, within a few months of
returning to America Kathleen's health again faltered and she was
advised by a doctor to permanently move outside New York to the
country. Thus, the Clarkes bought a small market garden farm, Manor
Culverton, in Manorville, Long Island, a purchase facilitated by the
Daly family in Limerick, and Tom was forced to resign his position on
the *Gaelic American*.[63] In her memoirs Kathleen commented how she
'loved the land and growing things and the joy of being together all the
time'.[64] However, she claimed that by 1907 'Tom was hinting that he
would like to go back to Ireland and get things moving'.[65] Despite her
initial opposition she eventually relented and the family decided to
return home. This explanation seems plausible enough given that

Clarke may have been influenced by his experience of a young breed
of Irish republicanism while in New York. In 1905 the Dungannon
Clubs of Belfast had been established by Denis McCullough and
Lisburn Quaker Bulmer Hobson. This group sought to articulate an
argument in favour of the total separation of Ireland and Britain and
eschewed any notion of participation in parliamentary politics. Hobson
toured America in early 1907 and Clarke had undertaken all the
arrangements for the visit which included lectures in New York,
Brooklyn, Philadelphia, Cleveland, Indianapolis, Chicago, St Louis and
Boston.[66] Hobson was an accomplished speaker and Clarke could not
have failed to have been impressed by him. For Clarke, and others,
Hobson was representative of a new, vibrant Fenianism and there is no
doubt that this experience made an impact on him.

Thus, the Clarkes returned to Ireland in November 1907, being met
at Queenstown by John and Madge Daly. Their appearance was noted
by the British authorities who reported the arrival of Thomas J. Clarke
'ex-convict and dynamiter'.[67] The family stayed in Limerick for a few
weeks but within days Tom travelled to Dublin to meet with leading
republicans such as P.T. Daly, Boer War veteran Major John MacBride[68],
Fred Allan, Jack O'Hanlon and old prison friend James Egan. He subsequently journeyed to Derry where he met members of Sinn Féin. His
reflections of the visit were penned in a letter to James Reidy when he
commented: 'The young fellows I met there and in Dublin who take
the lead in the Sinn Féin movement impressed me very much by their
earnestness and ability. I am delighted to find them away above what I
had expected'.[69] Unable to catch a train to a Sinn Féin meeting in
Castlebar he stayed a couple of days with Billy Kelly in Dungannon.

The haste with which Clarke sought out fellow republicans would
appear to support the contention that he returned to Ireland for political reasons. However, in the same letter his own words seem to pour
cold water on this notion:

> I have made up my mind to stay on this side if I can possibly do
> so; in any case I would not think of returning till middle of

240.—Contract for Property.

John Polhemus Printing Company, Printers and Mf'g Stationers, 101 Fulton St., New York.

Agreement made the 1st day of November in

the year one thousand nine hundred and six.

Between HENRY W. WATERLING of the town of Brookhaven,

County of Suffolk, and State of New York, party

of the first part, and THOMAS J. CLARKE of the Borough of Brooklyn,

City and State of New York, party

of the second part, in manner following : The said part y of the first part, in consideration of the sum of Three thousand six hundred ($3,600) dollars

to be fully paid as hereinafter mentioned, hereby agrees to sell unto the said part y of
the second part,

ALL that lot, piece or parcel of land with the buildings and
improvements thereon, together with all crops whether of annual
cultivation or otherwise, now lying, being and situate in the
town of Brookhaven, County of Suffolk and State of New York, at
Manor, and bounded on the north by land of Hallock; east by the
Highway (road to Moriches so called); south by land of Mrs.
Graber formerly lands of Henry Corwin, Mrs. Graber, W. Benjamin
and the Gerry property, and west by land of Charles Bowers, containing thirty (30) acres, to be the same more or less.

And the said party of the second part hereby agree s to purchase said prem-

ises at the said consideration of Three thousand six hundred ($3,600)
Dollars, and to pay the same as follows :

One hundred dollars on the signing of this contract, the receipt whereof is hereby acknowledged;	$100.00
Nine hundred dollars in cash at the time hereinafter fixed for the delivery of the deed, hereinafter pro-vided for;	900.00
Two thousand six hundred dollars thereof by the party of the second part executing to the party of the first part his Bond conditioned for the payment of said sum of Two thousand six hundred dollars to bear interest at the rate of five per centum per an-num, payable semi-annually, the principal of said Bond to be paid in installments within three years, as hereafter provided for, and as security a purchase money mortgage conveying the above described premises The principal of said Bond shall be payable as follows: Eight hundred and sixty-seven dollars at the end of one year after the delivery of said deed; Eight hundred and sixty-six dollars at the end of two years after delivery of said deed; Eight hundred and sixty-six dollars at the end of three years after delivery of said deed. The interest on the Bond, as aforesaid,	2,600.00

County of _____ ss :

On this _____ day of _____ one thousand nine hundred

before me personally came

to me known, and known to me to be the individual described in and who executed
the foregoing instrument, and he thereupon duly acknowledged to me that he had
executed the same.

10. Agreement for purchase of land between Tom Clarke and Henry Waterling in Brookhaven, Suffolk County, New York, 21 November 1906.

(courtesy of Archives Dept., University of Limerick)

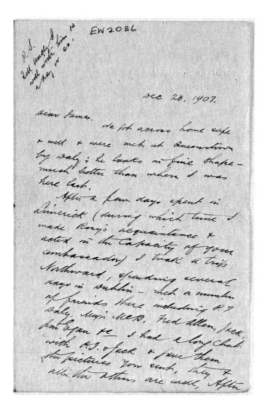

**11. Letter from Tom Clarke to James Reidy,
28 December 1907, announcing his return to Ireland.**

(courtesy of the National Museum of Ireland)

summer as Katty tells me there will be a visit from the stork in March – so there you are – there's what living the simple life – 'close to nature' – brings on a fellow.[70]

Hence, Clarke had certainly not determined to stay in Ireland and had not ruled out the possibility of returning to America. Kathleen Clarke's narrative, written many years after the events, may have been an attempt to portray the family's return as one motivated solely by political considerations, in order to elevate the post-Rising status of her husband. She was adamant until the day she died that her husband, and not Patrick Pearse, would have been president of any future republic, maintaining that Pearse was 'very ambitious and as vain as a peacock'.[71] Portraying a situation where she reluctantly returned home in order to allow Tom to focus on work for a rising would only have assisted in enhancing such a belief.

However, the reality was somewhat different and it is likely that two key factors must have heavily influenced the decision to return to Ireland. As has been noted, Kathleen Clarke regularly suffered from ill-health. Whether this was a consequence of complications arising from the birth of her first child cannot be ascertained. But there is no doubt that from 1903 onwards she required regular medical treatment for a range of ailments, such as neuralgia. She was also very close to her family and this may well have played a part in any decision. However, the major factor was the family's inability to make a decent living in America. Although Kathleen claimed to have loved her life on the farm, there is little doubt that for someone like Clarke, with no experience of rural life and suffering from a heart condition, it would have proven difficult to make a viable commercial undertaking from the land. Although nothing was directly said about the latter Kathleen gave a glimpse of a possible financial motive when writing to Tom about his efforts to find a suitable site for a shop in Dublin asking, 'Have you told her [Hannah] anything about our reason for coming home, how we are fixed at present or anything concerning us other than the fact that you wish to get into business?'[72] Strong evidence of financial difficulty was revealed in another letter from Kathleen when she asked him 'did you ever write to Jones about the Long Island lots after. It always strikes me as queer how we were talked out of them and our money'.[73] Indeed, Clarke himself lamented that they had arrived home with 'a load of debt that has to be cleared off.'[74]

In later years she confided in family members and told them that they had been forced to return home due to lack of money. While in America they had been financially supported by the Daly family. Although the money was always believed to have come from John Daly, it was from his niece, Madge, who ran a very successful bakery enterprise in Limerick. While John had initially established the William Street business, he had proved ineffective as a businessman and Madge, who had previously worked as a milliner, decided to step in before the bakery floundered. With a natural flair for business she was so successful that another, much bigger, property was later purchased at 15 Barrington Street. Madge subsequently bought many investment properties in the city and also proved successful in stocks and shares. Her nieces recall how she was extremely generous to all family members and ensured they were all financially independent. Such was the success of her venture that the family could afford to employ two maids and a gardener.[75] It was this money which enabled her sister Kathleen to purchase the sweet shop in New York. Similarly, the farms on Long Island were bought by the Dalys and while initially registered in the name of Tom Clarke, they were almost immediately transferred to that of John Daly.[76] Thus, Madge Daly offered to set her sister and brother-in-law up in business if they returned to Ireland.

With this financial backing, Tom Clarke walked the streets of Dublin in the early days of January 1908 trying to locate the best site for a tobacconist/newsagent shop. His sister Hannah had been in that line of business at 176 Great Britain Street since 1904[77] and was the sole distributor of the *Gaelic American* in Dublin.[78] Apparently much to his surprise she assisted him in every way possible. The unexpected nature of her interest was reflected in a letter from Kathleen on 6 January 1908:

> I told Uncle John and Madge what you told me about business in your last letter. U. J. says he thinks with Hannah that there is no small business pays as well as the tobacco and cigars. I am quite surprised and really pleased that Hannah has shown herself so friendly to you. Blood is thicker than water after all. She must be one of the class whose bark is worse than their bite.[79]

Certainly it appeared that, in the past, there had been bad blood between Clarke's sister and his wife as Kathleen commented how 'your report of Hannah's opinion of the store is very encouraging and I'll not think any more harsh thoughts of her for the way she has acted towards you right through this affair'.[80] Indeed, family tradition maintains that Kathleen did not enjoy a friendly relationship with any members of Tom's family.[81] Clarke eventually located a shop at 55 Amiens Street and opened for business on 14 February 1908.[82] The purchase of the shop, the redecorating costs and the buying of stock were all facilitated by the Daly family. Madge Daly also encouraged the idea of the Clarkes opening a barber's shop in the capital, but this was strenuously opposed by Tom on the basis that it would be too much pressure too soon.[83]

Louis Le Roux has noted how 'his shop became the rendezvous of IRB leaders from all parts of Ireland'.[84] However, Kathleen warned Tom against restricting his range of customers:

> Jack Byrnes was speaking to Madge recently about you and the shop and said that he'd consider you'd make a big mistake to get your shop known as belonging to any clique, Sinn Féin, Gaelic League, or any other, as those cliques will support you only for a time and then they get tired of it, or for some reason or other drop off – meanwhile they probably have antagonised other people who would have supported you. Of course I would not accept as gospel all people will say but I think there is enough in his talk to make you be very careful in your dealings with all classes who come in and above all keep a close mouth. Our endeavour should now be to make ourselves independent. When that is accomplished we can be anything we like.[85]

While Tom was establishing their business in Dublin Kathleen remained with her family in Limerick while she prepared for the birth of their second child. During these months they corresponded regularly and she was aware of the emotional and physical strain he was under as he struggled to cope with the demands of their new venture. Her sympathy for him, and her fear that perhaps they had left behind a difficult life for an even more precarious one, was reflected in her comment in March 1908 that 'I wonder when easy times for you will arrive. They look as far away as ever. Sometimes I wonder were we wise to come home'.[86] The pressure eventually told on Clarke and he succumbed to typhoid fever in July and was incapacitated for much of the rest of that year.[87]

12. Tom Clarke standing outside his shop at 75A Parnell Street, Dublin, c. 1912.

(courtesy of the National Library of Ireland)

However, their venture proved to be a success and in the following year they rented another shop at 75a Parnell Street.[88] In 1910 they vacated the property at 55 Amiens Street and moved a few doors up to number 77 to a shop with a house overhead.[89] The success of his business was evident in that the family could afford to rent a house in the affluent St Patrick's Road, Drumcondra in 1911.[90] Apart from his sister Maria, who was still in America, Tom lived close to his mother and other siblings. Hannah resided with her mother at 176 Great Britain Street while Alfred had come home after spending a few years in London. He returned with a wife (Emily) and three children – James, John and Nora. The family lived in St Michaels Hill in the Merchant's Quay area.[91]

While his successful business occupied much of his time Clarke made sure to involve himself in political affairs and the advice and experience he could impart proved invaluable to the rising generation he had first witnessed in New York.

Notes

1. *Southern Star*, 8 October 1898. I am grateful to Pat Bermingham for this reference.
2. *Freeman's Journal*, 22 October 1898. I am grateful to Pat Bermingham for this reference.
3. *Tyrone Courier*, 27 October 1898.
4. Ibid.
5. Ibid.
6. National Library of Ireland (hereafter, NLI), Thomas Clarke Papers, ACC 6410, Box 3, V.iii.
7. *Irish Daily Independent*, 30 September 1898.
8. University of Limerick Archives (hereafter, ULA), Daly Papers, Mealy's 2006 auction, accession lot 371, John Daly to Tom Clarke, 2 November 1898.
9. Ibid., 9 February 1899.
10. Ibid.
11. I am grateful to Paddy Fawl, Leixslip, County Kildare for this information.
12. *Limerick Leader*, 3 March 1899.
13. Ibid.
14. Ibid.
15. 1901 Census of Ireland.
16. ULA, Daly Papers, Box 2, Folder 51.
17. Ibid.
18. Ibid.
19. NLI, Thomas Clarke Papers, ACC 6410, Box 3, V.vi., James Egan to Wm. Reynolds, 29 May 1899.
20. Ibid., Statement, 26 May 1899.
21. Ibid., John Redmond to Tom Clarke, 26 May 1899.
22. Ibid., John Dillon to Tom Clarke, 29 May 1899.
23. Ibid., J.J. McCartan (Canon) P.P., to Mr McMullan, 30 May 1899.
24. Ibid.
25. ULA, Daly Papers, Mealy's 2006 auction, accession lot 371.

26. Helen Litton (ed.), *Kathleen Clarke, Revolutionary Woman, An Autobiography* (Dublin: The O'Brien Press, 1991), p.22.

27. ULA, Daly papers, Mealy's 2006 auction, accession lot 371.

28. Ciarán Ó Gríofa 'John Daly The Fenian Mayor of Limerick', David Lee (ed.), *Remembering Limerick: Historical Essays Celebrating the 800th Anniversary of Limerick's First Charter Produced in 1197* (Limerick: Limerick Civil Trust, 1997), p.199.

29. Louis Le Roux, *Tom Clarke and the Irish Freedom Movement* (Dublin: The Talbot Press, 1936), p.56.

30. Ibid., pp.24–5.

31. Ibid., p.25.

32. NLI, Thomas Clarke Papers, ACC 6410, Box 1, I.i.2, Kathleen Daly to Tom Clarke, 15 August 1899.

33. Ibid., Box 1, I.i.3, 2 September 1899.

34. Litton (ed.), *Kathleen Clarke*, p.25.

35. NLI, Thomas Clarke Papers, Box 1, I.i.3, Kathleen Daly to Tom Clarke, 21 September 1899.

36. Bureau of Military History (hereafter, BMH), Witness Statement (hereafter, WS) 368, Sean McGarry.

37. NLI, Thomas Clarke Papers, ACC 6410, Box 1, I.i.3, Kathleen Daly to Tom Clarke, 24 August 1899.

38. Le Roux, *Tom Clarke and the Irish Freedom Movement*, p.58.

39. NLI, Thomas Clarke Papers, ACC 6410, Box 3, V.vi.

40. 1901 Census of Ireland.

41. NLI, Thomas Clarke Papers, ACC 6410, Box 3, V.vi.

42. Ibid., Jim Egan to John Daly, 9 August 1900.

43. Le Roux, *Tom Clarke and the Irish Freedom Movement*, pp.58–9.

44. NLI, Thomas Clarke Papers, ACC 6410, Box 1, I.i.6, Kathleen Daly to Tom Clarke, 10 April 1900.

45. Ibid.

46. See Tom Clarke's letters from 1899 to 1901 in next section.

47. Le Roux, *Tom Clarke and the Irish Freedom Movement*, p.60.

48. See www.ancestry.com (accessed 10 September 2011).

49. Litton (ed.), *Kathleen Clarke*, p.30.

50. Ibid.

51. Le Roux, *Tom Clarke and the Irish Freedom Movement*, pp.67–8.

52. Ibid., p.62.

53. Ibid., p.63.

54. Ibid., pp.68–9.

55. Mealy's Auction, April 2006, accession lot 46.

56. Le Roux, *Tom Clarke and the Irish Freedom Movement*, p.71.

57. Ibid., p.72.

58. Ibid., p.70.

59. Information contained in email sent from Sister Ann Taylor to author, 4 October 2011.

60. Litton (ed.), *Kathleen Clarke*, p.33.

61. NLI, Thomas Clarke Papers, ACC 6410, Box 1, I.i.12, Kathleen Clarke to Tom Clarke, 4 October 1905.

62. National Museum of Ireland (hereafter, NMIHE), EW. 375.

63. Litton (ed.), *Kathleen Clarke*, p.33.

64. Ibid.

65. Ibid., p.35.

66. Marnie Hay, *Bulmer Hobson and the Nationalist Movement in Twentieth-Century Ireland*,

(Manchester: Manchester University Press, 2009), pp.67–71; Le Roux, *Tom Clarke and the Irish Freedom Movement*, p.80.

67. National Archives, Kew, London, (hereafter, NAUK), Colonial Office Papers (CO) 904/117.

68. John MacBride (1865–1916) was born in Westport, County Mayo on 7 May 1865. He emigrated to South Africa in 1896 and became chief organiser, and Major, of the first Irish Brigade in the Boer War. He returned to Ireland in 1905 and was made Water Bailiff under Dublin Corporation. A member of the IRB, he was executed for his participation in the 1916 Rising as one of Commandant Thomas MacDonagh's principal officers (5 May 1916).

69. NMIHE, EW. 2086, Tom Clarke to James Reidy, 28 December 1907.

70. Ibid.

71. NLI, P.T. Madden Papers, Ms 31,696, Kathleen Clarke to P.T. Madden, 5 June 1961.

72. NLI, Thomas Clarke Papers, ACC 6410, Box 1, I.i.14, Kathleen Clarke to Tom Clarke, 6 January 1908.

73. Ibid., Box 1, I.i.18, Kathleen Clarke to Tom Clarke, 8 May 1908.

74. Ibid., Box 1, I.ii.12, Tom Clarke to Kathleen Clarke, 31 March 1908.

75. Interview with Mairead and Nora de Hóir on 29 November 2011.

76. ULA, Daly Papers, Box 2, Folder 47, Tom Clarke to John Daly, 28 June 1907.

77. *Thom's Official Directory of the United Kingdom of Great Britain and Ireland for the year 1904*, p.1832.

78. Owen McGee, *The IRB – The Irish Republican Brotherhood From The Land League To Sinn Féin* (Dublin: Four Courts Press, 2005), p.350.

79. NLI, Thomas Clarke Papers, ACC 6410, Box 1, I.i.14, Kathleen Clarke to Tom Clarke, 6 January 1908.

80. Ibid., Kathleen Clarke to Tom Clarke, 16 January 1908.

81. Interview with Mairead and Nora de Hóir on 29 November 2011.

82. NLI, Thomas Clarke Papers, ACC 6410, Box 1, I.i.10, Tom Clarke to Kathleen Clarke, 14 February 1908.

83. Ibid., Box 1, I.ii.9, Tom Clarke to Kathleen Clarke, letter marked 'Monday evening', January 1908.

84. Le Roux, *Tom Clarke and the Irish Freedom Movement*, p.82.

85. NLI, Thomas Clarke Papers, Box 1, I.i.15, Kathleen Clarke to Tom Clarke, 10 February 1908.

86. Ibid., Box 1, I.i.16, Kathleen Clarke to Tom Clarke, 30 March 1908.

87. Litton (ed.), *Kathleen Clarke*, p.38. During that summer Kathleen's sister, Annie, had died from the same ailment.

88. Le Roux, *Tom Clarke and the Irish Freedom Movement*, pp.81–2.

89. Ibid.

90. 1911 Census of Ireland

91. Ibid.

Chapter four

Pulling the Strings

On his return to Ireland Tom Clarke had been co-opted as a member of the supreme council of the IRB.[1] At this stage the policy of that organisation was to gradually gain an influence in all aspects of Irish life and hence Clarke, together with others, immersed himself in various cultural and political organisations. He became president of the pipers' club affiliated to the Laurence O'Toole Gaelic Football Club based in the North Wall area and was also voted president of the North Dock Ward Branch of Sinn Féin.[2] His influence was immediately evident in a resolution proposed by him and passed at a meeting in April 1909. At that time trade unionist Jim Larkin was advocating closer ties between Irish and British trade union bodies. However, Clarke found this anathema and, in describing English trade unionism as 'the enemy of commercial Ireland' proposed that, 'We heartily approve of the movement now on foot amongst Trades Bodies in Ireland to break all connection with the English Trade Unions and we consider it our duty… to strengthen the aim of those who aim at effecting a federation of trades bodies in Ireland that will be absolutely independent of English control'.[3]

Despite his willingness to propose this motion two factors ensured that he could never become a prominent public face in republican manoeuvrings: first, he had been released 'on licence', and faced the possibility of being returned to prison if suspected of subversive activities; second, as he revealed in letters to James Reidy, his hectic business and personal life ensured, or as he alluded to, gave him the excuse, not to become involved with too many organisations. Indeed, one of

13. Group portrait of bandsmen from St Laurence O'Toole Papers' Band featuring Tom Clarke (marked with x), c. 1913.
(courtesy of the National Library of Ireland)

Clarke's major concerns after returning, and for a couple of years thereafter, was his financial difficulties in America. He left control of all such matters to Reidy and their correspondence throughout this period demonstrates the anxiety he felt over the Long Island farms and the trouble he had in attempting to sell them without losing money.

Politically, Clarke was surrounded by many young men who represented the new generation of Irish republicanism. In 1908 both Bulmer Hobson and Seán MacDiarmada moved from Belfast to Dublin. The latter had previously been organiser for the Dungannon Clubs and election agent for Sinn Féin candidate Charles J. Dolan in the recent North Leitrim by-election.[4] Indicative of the successful IRB infiltration policy was the fact that future prominent individuals such as Thomas Ashe, Con Collins, Con Keating and Gearoid O'Sullivan, along with MacDiarmada, were members of the Keating branch of the Gaelic League in the city.[5]

In October 1910 Clarke had an opportunity to meet up with old friends when 'well-known members'[6] of Clan na Gael – James Reidy, James Mark Sullivan and J.J. Teevans all travelled to Ireland and stayed with John Daly in Limerick.[7] While they no doubt discussed many aspects of the current political situation it is likely that their journey was made to oversee the launch of *Irish Freedom*, a new monthly paper espousing IRB opinion.

Clarke played a leading role in initially advocating the establishment of such an organ and ensuring it received financial backing (via the Daly family). His years working as assistant editor on the *Gaelic American* had demonstrated the potential of reaching a wide audience through a newspaper. In addition, those former members of the Dungannon Clubs with whom he was in regular contact such as Hobson and Denis McCullough had, in 1906, established the *Republic*, a Belfast-based journal with an out-and-out Fenian philosophy.[8] Hence, support amongst young men from these quarters was guaranteed.

An editorial committee was established with Clarke as chairman while other members included Hobson, Pat McCartan, Piaras Beaslai, Sean McGarry and Seán MacDiarmada as treasurer and secretary.[9] The first issue of the paper appeared on 15 November 1910 and its philosophy, and that of the IRB, was encapsulated in its editorial:

> We stand not for an Irish party but for national tradition – the tradition of Wolfe Tone and Robert Emmet, of John Mitchel and John O'Leary. We stand for the complete and total separation of Ireland from England and the establishment of an Irish Government untrammelled and uncontrolled by any other government in the world.[10]

From the republican perspective the appearance of *Irish Freedom* was timely as Irish politics was entering a period which would totally change the face of the country.

The November 1910 British general election left the Irish Parliamentary Party (IPP), under John Redmond, holding the balance of power in the House of Commons. The 'People's Budget' of 1909, which sought to introduce new taxes on the wealthy, had failed to pass through the House of Lords. In response, the Liberals brought forward the Parliament Bill, a measure which aimed at limiting the veto previously enjoyed by the upper chamber. In order to gain the support of Redmond for their proposed budget the Liberals also agreed to meet the IPP demand for a Home Rule Bill. However, previous Liberal governments had brought forward such bills in 1886 and 1893 and while they had passed the House of Commons they had foundered in the unionist-dominated House of Lords. However, the Parliament Bill eventually became law in 1911 thereby allowing the possibility of a successful passage of a bill supporting Home Rule for Ireland for the first time.[11]

In the midst of such events the spring of 1911 witnessed a visit by King George V to Ireland. The supreme council of the IRB decided to forbid any resolutions relating to the visit and these stipulations applied to a Robert Emmet Commemoration Concert to be held in March.[12] Clarke, as he had done in America, played a major role in events commemorating those who had taken up arms in previous generations. Obviously he believed this to be one method by which the interest of the youth could be stimulated. Thus, he was heavily involved in the Emmet event as well as in the annual pilgrimage to the grave of Wolfe Tone at Bodenstown. He also coordinated the establishment of a series of committees throughout the country to contribute to the support of the elderly parents of William Philip Allen, one of the 'Manchester Martyrs', executed in 1867.[13]

On the night of the Emmet concert, Patrick Pearse made a fiery speech and as soon as he finished Pat McCartan mounted the platform and proposed a resolution opposing loyal addresses to the King. This was immediately seconded by Tom Clarke and carried by the audience.[14] These actions, in direct contravention of their orders, enraged the members of the supreme council and they sought to exact vengeance by removing McCartan from his position as editor of *Irish Freedom*. Consequently, December saw the production of rival issues of the paper and McCartan and Clarke were summoned to appear before an IRB court-martial.[15] Significantly, Clarke had, by his actions, aligned himself with the younger men in the organisation while, in contrast, Fred Allan, in his official capacity as secretary to the Lord Mayor of Dublin, had accompanied the latter in paying his respects to the King.[16] The difference in outlook and mentality could not have been greater. P.S. O'Hegarty recalled that at the subsequent proceedings 'there was some brilliant dialective [sic] by Hobson, some very clever leading questions by Clarke and some very clever answers by MacDermott'.[17] In consequence the old guard, Fred Allan and Jack O'Hanlon, agreed to 'whitewash everybody concerned on the grounds that the whole business was a misunderstanding'.[18] Shortly afterwards, both men resigned their positions on the supreme council, with Allan's post being taken by Seán MacDiarmada. Such machinations, supported totally by Clarke, now ensured that the IRB was 'practically entirely in the hands of the younger men'.[19]

Indeed, Clarke's attitude to the royal visit was made very visible by the fact that he displayed a poster outside his shop taken from an *Irish Freedom* headline entitled 'Your concessions be damned! England!! We want our country'. Kathleen Clarke recalled being alone in the shop when a number of English sailors spat at, kicked and finally threw the poster back inside. She promptly returned it to its original position outside.[20]

Nevertheless, it is important not to overstate the importance of events within the IRB vis-à-vis wider Irish society. As Owen McGee has noted, by April 1912, 'the IRB in Ireland was essentially nothing more than the *Irish Freedom* newspaper, three small circles led by Denis McCullough in Belfast and Hobson's following'.[21] Hence, the important events were taking place in the British parliament.

With the emasculation of the House of Lords the safe passage of the Home Rule Bill through parliament was assured. In response the Ulster Unionists declared that not only would they refuse to pay taxes but they would establish their own government defended by an armed force of volunteers. By July 1914 they had remained true to their word, having formed both a provisional government alongside an armed organisation – the Ulster Volunteer Force (UVF).[22]

This set an example to others on the island who favoured the use of arms to obtain their goals. Thus, on 25 November 1913 the Irish Volunteers were established and in the words of Kathleen Clarke 'gave the IRB the chance they had been looking for'.[23] One historian offered the following analysis of the situation:

> By 1913 ... the IRB had little or no organisation left ... its experienced leadership had resigned and it had no initiatives except for keeping *Irish Freedom* in print, and this was achieving very little. Consequently, once the Irish Volunteers were formed, an excited Clarke and MacDermott decided to bank all their hopes for the future upon the volunteer movement. Their goal was to build up new IRB circles within the volunteers and to make these new circles alone the future of the 'organisation'; a task in which they were remarkably successful.[24]

A vital element in this strategy was to ensure that surveillance by the authorities was kept to a minimum; hence, the IRB stipulated that no members were to assume positions of seniority in the new organisation.[25] Nevertheless, Bulmer Hobson accepted the role of secretary, arguing that 'the measure of control I secured was intended only to prevent the Volunteers from being captured ... and diverted from its publicly declared aims and used for partisan ends by any other parties'.[26] He later claimed that both Clarke and MacDiarmada wished to establish an 'IRB caucus' within the Volunteers which would act as they desired. In his opinion this had to be avoided as others may have wished to do likewise and it would then have proven impossible to maintain a united organisation. Despite the justification of his actions Hobson had, for the first time in the political sphere, taken a position contrary to that of Clarke. According to Kathleen this had come as a 'complete surprise' to Tom and 'shook the complete faith he had in Hobson'.[27]

Perhaps Clarke was surprised because he had the utmost respect for the political *nous* of Hobson and this move appeared to suggest a somewhat naïve understanding of what was happening. Of the thirty members who constituted the new provisional committee of the volunteers, twelve were members of the IRB, while three others, Patrick Pearse, Joseph Plunkett and Thomas McDonagh, soon joined that body.[28] Indicative of this influence was the unconfined joy at events represented in the pages of *Irish Freedom*. The paper noted with satisfaction how the new movement represented 'the rebirth of manhood unto this nation, the flow of energy and buoyancy and self-reliance into veins that were to all outward seeming wasted unto nothingness'.[29]

Initially the Irish Parliamentary Party wanted nothing to do with the volunteers and members were deterred from joining. However, the Party had underestimated the appeal of the new phenomenon and watched aghast as the organisation increased from 3,000 members in November 1913 to 129,000 in May 1914.[30] Unwilling to further ignore the emergence of such a potentially significant force John Redmond published an ultimatum to the leaders of the volunteers which stipulated that unless they acceded to a demand to co-opt twenty-five of his nominees onto the provisional committee he would establish a rival volunteer movement to be run by the IPP.[31] After discussions, Bulmer Hobson, Roger Casement and Eoin MacNeil decided that, in order to avoid a split in the movement, they would agree to Redmond's ultimatum. Hobson felt that this would ensure the IRB would not 'remain forever a small organisation of little clubs meeting in back rooms' and argued that its power could only be enhanced by 'linking up with and permeating much larger organisations which had a wider national appeal'.[32] However, Clarke maintained a completely contrary position and had, together with Seán MacDiarmada, appealed to Hobson, Casement and MacNeil, to instead fight Redmond reasoning that if a split were to come it should be at the present time rather than at a later period. Kathleen Clarke remembered the consequences of the decision:

> Sean MacDermott told me that Bulmer Hobson used all his influence and worked very hard to get Redmond's demand agreed to. Tom was deeply disturbed by Hobson's action as he

had idealised him. It was through Tom that Hobson had been
invited to the United States by Clan na Gael during the time we
lived there. I had warned him more than once that he was ideal-
ising the man too much though I liked Hobson. It took
Hobson's own action to destroy the complete faith and trust
Tom had in him; after that he dropped all association with him.[33]

Sean McGarry related how Clarke regarded Hobson's actions as 'cold-
blooded and contemplated treachery likely to bring about the
destruction of the only movement in a century which brought fulfil-
ment of all his hopes'.[34] Madge Daly recalled how both Hobson and
Casement came to see John Daly who was then holidaying at Glasthule
just outside Dublin. The three men were joined by Clarke.

> In all my life I never experienced such a tense atmosphere as in
> that little sitting by the sea. It was electric and I was thoroughly
> miserable. During the discussion my uncle got very excited and
> shouted to Bulmer Hobson 'Do you know Hobson what I
> would do to you if you were on trial before me for your actions
> yesterday? I would hang you from the nearest gas lamp'.[35]

Similarly, after being summoned to an executive meeting of the IRB
in Clarke's house, Hobson faced the wrath of Clarke, MacDiarmada
and P.S. O'Hegarty, commenting:

> I had expected disapproval of the action I had taken but I was
> completely taken by surprise when I was met with a storm of
> hysterical abuse and accusations of having betrayed the move-
> ment. When asked (by Clarke) how much I had been paid I was
> shocked to find that men so sincere and devoted had such paltry
> minds.[36]

Hobson immediately resigned his position as editor of *Irish Freedom* and
announced his intention to withdraw from the supreme council of the

IRB. Consequently, he never met Clarke again and his position as Irish correspondent for the *Gaelic American* was terminated by John Devoy, on the advice of Clarke.[37]

Hobson's anger at this turn of events burned within him for the rest of his life and many years later he penned the following analysis of events:

> I had been aware for some time of an increasingly critical attitude on the part of Clarke and MacDermott. They were both deeply sincere men, completely devoted to the national cause; but were both narrow partisans, inclined to distrust anybody who was not a member of our small organisation. They were very suspicious of my co-operation with men like MacNeill and Casement who belonged intellectually and socially to a different world. Clarke told me about that time that he was sure Casement was a British spy.[38]

While he may or may not have 'belonged … to a different world', Eoin MacNeil also faced censure for voting to accept Redmond's nominees. In a meeting in Clarke's shop he explained how he had been under the impression that Hobson had been acting with the support of the IRB in adopting his position and therefore voted accordingly. Despite this, Clarke informed him he would not, as had been previously agreed, be making the speech at the Wolfe Tone Commemoration at Bodenstown.[39] Thus, Clarke decided to make a rare public appearance and give the speech himself, which according to Kathleen was 'a thing he disliked, for he said he was no orator'.[40] In a short address Clarke outlined what he believed the volunteers would bring to the Irish political scene:

> The spirit of Wolfe Tone still lives. That spirit is moving through the length and breadth of the land today. The tramp of marching men eager to grasp the rifle is evidence of that spirit. We are here to honour the memory and principles of Wolfe Tone. We have with us Irishmen of different religious beliefs – a symbol of that

union of all Irishmen for which Wolfe Tone worked. With the new spirit abroad we hope there will come the realisation of our ideal. We know what Wolfe Tone's name stands for amongst Irishmen, not only in Ireland but wherever the sons of the Gael are to be found; and today thousands of eyes are turning to this sacred spot, looking for signs that Wolfe Tone's principles are still a vital force in our country. We are here to honour Wolfe Tone's memory, and no one, I am sure, has come to the graveside but with feelings of reverence. The time of speech-making is rapidly passing (cheers). The drilling and arming of the people of Ireland is what is going to count and what is going to be the determining factor as to just how our national ambition is going to be fulfilled.[41]

14. Tom Clarke and Dermot Lynch at the Wolfe Tone Commemoration, Bodenstown, 1915.

(courtesy of the National Library of Ireland)

While the Irish Volunteers had been torn by faction-fighting their counterparts in Ulster directed their energies towards the logical development of their own volunteer movement by arming their recruits. Hence, on 24 April 1914 35, 000 rifles and almost 3,500,000 rounds of ammunition were landed at the ports of Larne, Bangor, Donaghadee and Ballywalter.[42] By contrast the Irish Volunteers had little or no armaments but after much secret planning they successfully landed 900 guns and 26,000 rounds of ammunition at Howth on 26 July.[43] As with so much of volunteer actions, IRB members maintained a low profile and on the day of the landings Clarke remained in his house in Amiens Street. There, along with Seán MacDiarmada, he was kept in touch with events by couriers sent by Cathal Brugha and Eamonn Ceannt. However, as the day wore on and they noticed a number of trams filled with British military personnel heading towards Howth they hired a taxi and on reaching the port loaded several rifles into the vehicle. They decided to make the same journey a number of times, each time ferrying back rifles and ammunition.[44] Clarke sent a telegram to the *Gaelic American* announcing that 2,000 rifles had been landed.[45] Given that this was more than twice the actual figure it may well have represented his excitement at how events were moving. Ever mindful of his IRB colleagues in Dungannon he ordered that thirty of the rifles be sent to Billy Kelly.[46] However, his joy was to be short-lived.

On 28 July 1914 the First World War started and less than two months later on 20 September John Redmond made a seminal speech at Woodenbridge, County Wicklow in which he maintained that the Irish Volunteers should join the war on behalf of Britain.[47] Despite Clarke's confident reassurances to John Devoy and Joseph McGarrity the overwhelming majority of members sided with Redmond and a split occurred within the ranks of the movement which, from a republican perspective, decimated the organisation. Indicative of such was the reaction in Sandymount, County Dublin where, out of an enrolment of 800, only eleven men did not side with the Redmondites.[48] Hence, two new organisations emerged – the Irish National Volunteers under the auspices of the IPP and the Irish Volunteers under the titular leadership of Eoin MacNeill.

In the aftermath, Joe McGarrity reflected the position of Clan na Gael by praising MacNeill and his committee for ridding itself of what he termed the 'corrupting influences'[49] of Redmond. However, these developments must have been devastating for Clarke. He had carefully fostered and supported a young generation of Irish republicans and perhaps never in his wildest dreams did he anticipate having any influence over an organisation as large as the Irish Volunteers. It is possible that, given the huge numbers enrolling, he foresaw a situation where the volunteers could engage British troops in a manner similar to that adopted by the Boers in South Africa a few years earlier. However, that dream was now dashed as the Irish Volunteers were reduced to, at most, a few thousand men.

At a meeting on 10 October 1914 the constitution of the Irish Volunteers was adopted it was at this stage that large amounts of money were sent from America to the new group. On 20 October Eoin MacNeill received $10,000 while on 14 November he was mailed a further $15,000. Indeed, by 14 August 1915 more than $136,000 had been lodged in the name of the Irish Volunteer Fund in the Irish National Bank, New York.[50]

The onset of war allowed for even greater scrutiny of those regarded as posing a threat to British security and as a consequence Clarke found himself at the top of a 'Special War B List' – a compilation of names of those deemed subversive. According to the compilers of this list one of Clark's distinguishing features was his 'dazed look'.[51] In conjunction with this classification was the censoring of all letters of individuals such as Clarke, John Daly and Seán MacDiarmada from November 1914. However, given that all concerned had been well aware of close surveillance for years it is no surprise that such censorship was quickly terminated by January 1915 the authorities admitting 'these persons receive their correspondence other than through the general post'.[52]

Such was the level of surveillance on Clarke that the Dublin Metropolitan Police rented a room opposite his shop to enable them to watch his every move. Similarly, in Limerick a policeman was posted at the wall of the Daly household and recorded every person who entered and left the residence.

This new year was to prove one of the busiest of Tom Clarke's life. In May his eldest son, Daly, moved to St Enda's School which was run by Patrick Pearse. On 11 May he had been visited by both his parents and, although only there for three weeks, Pearse informed his aunt Madge that he was 'getting on splendidly'.[53] In the following month Clarke's close friend Seán MacDiarmada was arrested for making a speech in Tuam which was deemed to be in contravention of the Defence of the Realm Act. He was sentenced to six months' imprisonment during which time he was aided by the Clarkes and visited by Tom.[54] However, Clarke was busy in various other fields. Following the seizure of *Irish Freedom* on 3 December 1913 attempts had been made with varying success to propagate the voice of republicanism. Thus, *Éire* was launched on 26 October 1914 and *Scissors and Paste* on 12 December. Clarke supported both publications through funds provided by John Daly.[55] On June 26 1915 *Nationality*, a weekly republican paper in the mould of *Irish Freedom* and likewise representing the IRB, was launched with Arthur Griffith as editor, despite the intense opposition of Seán MacDiarmada.[56] Once again this venture was supported by the Daly family.

Three days later, on 29 June, veteran Fenian Jeremiah O'Donovan Rossa died in America. The Revolutionary Directory of Clan na Gael immediately sent a cable to Clarke enquiring whether the IRB was prepared to receive the body. He replied that it should be sent over immediately and indicated that he intended to give Rossa a national funeral. This reply was communicated to Rossa's widow and on John Devoy's advice she acceded to Clarke's wishes and authorised him to take charge of the matter. Thus Clarke, under the auspices of the Wolfe Tone Memorial Association, a cover for the IRB, became president of the O'Donovan Rossa Funeral Committee. He subsequently established fifteen sub-committees which met daily and reported twice each week.[57] The work of each was strictly marked out so that there would

**15. Group portrait taken on occasion of the funeral of
Jeremiah O'Donovan Rossa, July 1915.
Left to right: Mrs O'Donovan Rossa, Fr Michael O'Flanagan,
Eileen O'Donovan Rossa, Tom Clarke.**

(courtesy of the National Library of Ireland)

be no overlap. The marshalling arrangements for the funeral were
undertaken by the Irish Volunteers and this allowed Clarke to work for
the first time in conjunction with Thomas McDonagh.[58]

Mrs O'Donovan Rossa and her daughter Eileen landed at Liverpool
on 18 July and were met by Kathleen Clarke and Sean McGarry (both
of whom had stated their nationality as 'British' when asked, in order

to avoid any difficulties).[59] The following day the party arrived in Kingstown where they were greeted by Tom Clarke and members of the executive of the funeral committee.[60]

After considerable negotiation the Archbishop of Dublin, Rev. Dr William Walsh, eventually agreed to allow the remains to lie in state in the Pro-Cathedral from the afternoon of 27 July until the following day when they were removed to the City Hall escorted by a guard of honour drawn from the ranks of the Irish Volunteers and the Citizen Army.[61] The casket was placed on a bier and Clarke draped it with the Tricolour of the Irish Republic.[62] During the lying in state more than 100,000 people passed before the body. Louis Le Roux commented how, 'at Clarke's suggestion, Patrick Pearse was asked to deliver the graveside oration'. While he was preparing the draft of his speech during the week, Pearse sent a note to Clarke asking how far he could go. 'As far as you can', he replied. 'Make it as hot as hell, throw all discretion to the winds'.[63]

The timing of the O'Donovan Rossa funeral could not have been better as far as the IRB was concerned. Pearse's famous oration represented the highlight of a meticulously stage-managed event designed to illustrate to the widest possible audience that a young, vibrant, Fenian organisation had re-emerged, carefully nurtured, in the main, by Tom Clarke. One observer instantly recognised the significance of the event. Father Michael Curran, secretary to Archbishop Walsh, remembered it as 'the date that publicly revealed that a new political era had begun'. As far he was concerned 'the supremely impressive moment was the triple volley fired by the volunteers'. This represented 'more than a farewell to an old Fenian – it was a defiance to England by a new generation in Ireland'.[64]

There is little doubt that the advent of the First World War, and more particularly Britain's dominant role in the conflict, acted as a catalyst for those keen to advance plans for a rising. It appears that Clarke had been haunted by the failure of any attempt to exploit Britain's war with the Boers at the start of the century. Sean McGarry commented:

I might here say that one of his greatest disappointments after his release was that there was no thought of a rising during the Boer War. He never understood it and never gave up thinking of it. The old feeling of humiliation at the failure of his generation (as he called it) during the Boer War was still with him and he wanted to do all that one man could to assure that should another war come, it would be proved to the world that there were still in Ireland men who were willing to fight and die for Irish freedom.[65]

Thus, in the background plans were carefully being laid for a rising. On 4 August 1914 Britain entered the First World War and by September the supreme council of the IRB had resolved to start a rebellion before the end of the conflict.[66] P.S. O'Hegarty remembered how at a meeting of the supreme council in early 1915 a military committee was appointed to consider such plans.[67] However, during discussions it emerged that Joseph Plunkett had been working on a military strategy for a number of years and when put to the council it was accepted without alteration. The rather ambitious plan revolved around an uprising in Dublin supported by military reinforcements from Germany. Plunkett originally envisaged that 12,000 German troops would land at Limerick bringing with them 40,000 rifles for distribution to the Volunteers in Munster and Connacht. This force, led by German officers, would then move eastwards to Dublin in support of the ongoing insurrection there.[68] Thus, by May 1915, a small military committee, consisting of Patrick Pearse, Plunkett and Eamonn Ceannt, was endeavouring to formulate a detailed plan of insurrection while Seán T. O'Kelly had been given an oral message, outlined to him by Clarke and Seán MacDiarmada, which informed John Devoy and his American associates of ongoing developments.[69]

After the release of Seán MacDiarmada from Mountjoy Gaol in September 1915, both Clarke, and he were co-opted onto the military council (previously the military committee) of the IRB. At a significant meeting held in Clontarf to vote in a new executive of the IRB supreme council Clarke and MacDiarmada gained control by engineering the election of Denis McCullough as chairman. Of course McCullough argued that his residence in Belfast rendered him incapable of carrying out the functions of the position but this was exactly why Clarke and MacDiarmada voted for him. In their positions as secretary and treasurer respectively, they effectively controlled the supreme council and could therefore direct policy for the entire organisation.[70] Thus, when Pat McCartan objected to organising a rising at a meeting in January 1916, MacDiarmada countered by proposing that 'we fight at the earliest opportunity';[71] while Richard Connolly, another member of the supreme council, remembered how Clarke was so determined to initiate a rising that he stated he would organise one without the support of his colleagues.[72]

After much discussion a compromise was reached whereby it was agreed that a rising should take place in the event of either an attempt at a general arrest of the Volunteers; an effort to enforce conscription; or the likelihood of an early termination of the war. At the end of that month various IRB circles in Scotland and the north of England were informed of an intended rising to take place in the very near future. In anticipation of such, Clarke and MacDiarmada made arrangements to organise transport and accommodation for those who wished to come to Ireland.[73]

In the meantime, another development witnessed an attempt by Roger Casement to participate in the plans. Casement had been knighted by the British administration for his work in exposing the human rights abuses in Africa and South America. He had been active in organising the Volunteers but his acceptance of Redmond's nominees led to him being viewed with deep suspicion by men such as Tom Clarke.

In the summer of 1914 Casement had travelled to Germany via America with the intention of recruiting Irish prisoners-of-war for an Irish brigade to fight in the proposed rising. Although highly sceptical at first, Clarke eventually approved the sanction by the Revolutionary Directory in America to Casement's efforts.[74] While this scheme proved unsuccessful Casement did manage to reach an agreement with the Germans to send arms to Ireland. Hence, on 9 April 1916 the *Libau*, now renamed the *Aud*, set sail for Ireland posing as a neutral Norwegian vessel, with a cargo of 20,000 rifles, ten machine guns and one million rounds of ammunition. However, due to communication problems the ship did not land. It also failed to reconnoitre as planned with a submarine carrying Casement. Hence, on the morning of Good Friday Casement was set ashore together in County Kerry with some colleagues. Within a few hours he was arrested.[75]

When reports of this event reached Eoin MacNeill he, without consulting the members of the military council, immediately decided to send out orders countermanding mobilisation of the volunteers on Easter Sunday. Crucially, to ensure that this message reached as many volunteers as possible, MacNeill placed an advert in the *Sunday Independent* to the same effect. Clarke maintained that MacNeill, on hearing of the capture of Casement, should have told the members of the council, withdrawn from any further participation if he so wished and left the decision on any subsequent action to them. He believed that secretly sending out countermanding orders was 'despicable and to my mind, dishonourable'.[76] The consequent effect on one of the Rising's main architects was devastating, as noted by Sean McGarry:

> I found Tom Clarke afterwards and for the first time since I knew him he seemed crushed. He was weary and crestfallen. The shock of the morning's blow had been terrific. I accompanied him home that evening. He was very silent. After a while he recovered and discussed the affair. He regarded McNeill's action as one of the blackest and greatest treachery.[77]

In later years Kathleen Clarke commented that the countermanding order was something Clarke and the other leaders had 'never envisioned' and proved a 'death-blow to their hopes'.[78]

However, the counter-argument from those opposed to the rising was that Clarke and MacDiarmada had been equally duplicitous in their determination to make the rising a reality. Indeed, it could be argued that both men rode roughshod over their opponents and ignored the rules of the organisation to which they pledged loyalty. In 1873 the IRB adopted a new constitution resolving to 'await the decision of the Irish nation, as expressed by a majority of the Irish people, as to the fit hour of inaugurating a war against England'.[79] This was the basis on which Hobson, McCartan and McCullough – all members of the IRB – opposed the plans. At a concert on Palm Sunday Hobson publicly rebuked those intent on military action, arguing that the time was not yet right. A few days later, on the orders of MacDiarmada, he was kidnapped and held at gunpoint until the rising had commenced.[80] McCullough was president of the supreme council of the IRB, but his election, engineered by Clarke and MacDiarmada, ensured he was sidelined from any decision-making. Hence, he only became aware of the plans when informed by a fellow member of the IRB in Belfast. He immediately travelled to Dublin to confront MacDiarmada and it was only after many fruitless hours that he eventually located him. Even then, he had to lock the door of MacDiarmada's office to force him to reveal the plans.[81]

Obliged to go on the run during the rising Pat McCartan left Joesph McGarrity in no doubt as the extent to which he had been mislaid:

> They provided for no system of communication so that we are isolated. I expected to know when the trouble was coming but I believe it was deliberately kept from myself and Denis (McCullagh) [sic]. I know they also kept it from two other members of the Council, so that as far as the Council was concerned it was completely ignored. That of course, I wouldn't mind except that I was mislaid by being on it and thinking to know it all. The whole business was like a thunderbolt to me and I blame Tom (Clarke) and MacDermott entirely, and especially Tom for I trusted so much to him … Though I know they acted for the best, but just the same I'm done with them for ever, no matter what turn events may take.[82]

It was somewhat ironic, then, and perhaps inevitable that the very methods resorted to by Clarke and MacDiarmada – obfuscation and duplicity – proved their undoing.

By this stage all plans were in disarray and on Easter Sunday the military committee met throughout the day to discuss how to salvage the Rising. Clarke fervently argued that they should maintain their strategy and strike as planned. Others countered that a new order could be sent out telling men not to demobilise and to carry on as agreed. Clarke contended that if they adhered to the original strategy news of the rising would reach the rest of the country faster than couriers. In the event of any postponement he believed that the British would be enabled to prevent a further mobilisation. Finally, he feared they would all be arrested that night and their plans would never come to fruition. However, his pleas fell on deaf ears and the rest of the body, MacDiarmada included, voted to postpone the Rising until the following day.[83]

Clarke, probably because of his age, was not asked to march from Liberty Hall on Easter Monday, 24 April 1916, with the contingent of Irish Volunteers and Irish Citizen Army who were to take over the General Post Office (GPO). Instead, he walked ahead with Seán MacDiarmada. It is difficult to imagine two more unlikely revolutionaries – MacDiarmada limping along with the aid of a walking stick and Clarke with his right arm in a sling as a result of being accidentally shot by Sean McGarry some months earlier.[84]

Both men were in O'Connell Street when the main garrison arrived at noon, entered the GPO with the others after James Connolly's order to occupy it, and took their places beside their comrades. Clarke was at Pearse's side when, at 12.45pm, the latter read the Proclamation of the Irish Republic outside the GPO.[85] His satisfaction with the way events had progressed was noted by Diarmuid Lynch who recalled seeing him sitting on the edge of the mails platform, together with MacDiarmada, 'beaming satisfaction and expressing congratulations'.[86]

Clarke was a member of B Company, 1st Battalion, of the Dublin Brigade of the Volunteers together with MacDiarmada, Major John

MacBride, Sean T. O'Kelly and Dr. Jim Ryan and although he held no formal military rank he was recognised by the garrison as one of the commanders, along with MacDiarmada and Connolly. Indeed as the week progressed the influence of Clarke on events became evident, as noted by historians Barton and Foy:

> Although both Clarke and MacDermott were in civilian cloth-ing their increasingly open authority was accepted without question by the garrison. Those Volunteers who were members of the IRB knew the importance of the pair, an importance now publicly proclaimed by their membership of the Provisional Government and the respect and deference displayed to them in the GPO by Pearse, Connolly and Plunkett.[87]

Throughout that week intense fighting was witnessed in various parts of the city: Michael Mallin, accompanied by Countess Markievicz and a battalion of the Citizen Army, occupied Stephen's Green. A group under the command of Thomas McDonagh, aided by Major John McBride, gained control of Jacob's biscuit factory in Bishop Street. Other manoeu-vres saw the 3rd Battalion under Eamonn de Valera occupy Boland's Mill while the Mendicity Institution was garrisoned by a dozen men led by Seán Heuston and Clarke's brother-in-law, Ned Daly.[88]

One observer has described the actions of the rebels as 'flawed' and representing 'an unhappy cross between guerrilla and conventional warfare':

> They divided up their forces in Dublin and seized and held a number of public buildings with the intention of forming a defensive ring against Crown forces, to buy time for a general rising of their own units and militant sections of the general population ... The plan failed to address realities and contingen-cies, and assumed the availability of a far greater force than was actually deployed. The depleted ranks ensured little communica-tion between the units and, with no mobility or ability to take

the initiative, it was only a matter of time before superior British forces, fully armed and supplied and backed with machine guns and artillery, blasted and burned them out.[89]

Hence, the British military establishment, initially taken by surprise, soon began to mobilise reinforcements. Having made arrangements for the transfer of 10,000 troops from camps in England, Brigadier – General Lowe arrived in Dublin on Tuesday morning with a further 1,000 men.

By that evening the first garrison had surrendered when the men in the Mendicity Institution were forced to capitulate. On the following day the British moved a naval vessel, the *Helga*, up the River Liffey and commenced firing on Liberty Hall.[90]

On Friday the GPO came under sustained and heavy bombardment both from the *Helga* and heavy guns placed in the immediate vicinity. After a meeting involving Clarke, Connolly, Plunkett, Pearse and MacDiarmada, it was decided to evacuate the building in consequence of the constant barrage. On evacuation, the leaders made their way into Moore Lane and then the adjacent Moore Street where they were joined by Sean McLoughlin, who now took control of military affairs, Julia Grennan, a member of Cumann na mBan and Elizabeth Farrell, a nurse. Having seen the carnage in that part of the city and unwilling to cause further deaths, the leaders decided to surrender, doing so against the wishes of Clarke.[91] Indeed, on the Tuesday in the GPO, he had exhorted his colleagues to 'die fighting as they would in any case be executed if they surrendered' while on the Saturday he, alone of the leaders, insisted that they should fight on till death.[92] One of the volunteers in the party, Joe Good, remembered how after the decision to surrender had been taken the other leaders sat quietly talking amongst themselves while Clarke 'stood near a window, silent and alone'.[93] Julia Grennan noted that when the surrender order came some members of the garrison were reluctant to yield and spoke to Clarke. She remembered how he outlined his own personal struggle for freedom and maintained that as he was now satisfied with the achievement of Easter

Week, they should feel equally buoyant. However, Joe Good, for one, stated that while Clarke had spoken with 'great force and sincerity' he 'failed to convince me'.[94] It is likely that he did not manage to even convince himself and when Elizabeth Farrell was leaving with the white flag of surrender in her hands 'Clarke turned his face to the wall and broke down, sobbing'.[95]

That evening the Volunteers formed up outside, marched into Sackville Street and, on orders from a British officer, laid down their arms and equipment on the pavement outside the Gresham Hotel.[96] They were then marched to a grassy area in front of the Rotunda Hospital and 400 prisoners were herded into an area capable of accommodating only 150 and held there overnight.[97] One observer commented that the conduct of many of the British officers was 'savage and brutal'. Indeed, many eyewitnesses remarked on the fact that Clarke and some other prisoners were stripped naked while he also had his injured arm pulled out of its sling.[98]

In a memo sent from General Sir John Maxwell to Prime Minister Herbert Asquith, he justified the court martial of Clarke on the following grounds:

> This man was a signatory to the declaration of Irish Independence already adverted to. He was one of the most prominent leaders in the Sinn Féin movement in Dublin. He was present with the rebels in the G. Post Office, Sackville Street, where some of the heaviest fighting took place and was proved to have been in a position of authority there.
>
> On the 28th May 1883, under the name of Henry H. Wilson, he was sentenced in London to Penal Servitude for life for treason-felony, and was released on licence on the 20th September 1898.
>
> He exercised a great influence over the younger members of the organization with which he was connected.[99]

Clarke's court-martial on the afternoon of 2 May was a brief affair, lasting no more then fifteen minutes. The prosecution called only one witness, Lieutenant S.L. King of the Enniskillen Fusiliers. He recalled being taken prisoner on the morning of Tuesday 25 April and, while in custody, claimed he often saw Clarke who 'appeared to be a person in authority although he was not in uniform. Some of the men obtained a key from him at different times and some wore uniform. I have no doubt that he was one of the Rebels.'[100] Under cross-examination by Clarke the soldier admitted that 'whilst in the Post Office I was very well treated'. After this brief exchange the court martial appeared to end with the words, 'the prosecution closed. The accused does not call any witnesses and makes no statement'.[101] Years later the prosecution counsel, William Wylie, could 'remember distinctly' Tom Clarke: 'He was the oldest of them and had been a Fenian and a member of the IRB all his life … He did not defend himself either and was perfectly calm and brave throughout the proceedings. He struck me as a particularly kindly man, who could not injure anyone'.[102]

Having been sentenced to 'death, by being shot', Clarke requested a visit from his wife Kathleen who was then a prisoner in Dublin Castle, having been arrested after a raid on her house. In the early hours of 3 May she was brought under military escort to Kilmainham Gaol to pay a farewell visit to her husband. When she arrived she was met by a 'brown-habited' priest who asked her to allow him to see her husband. She replied, 'I have never interfered with my husband in anything he thinks right, and I am not going to begin now. If he will not see you, he has his reasons'.[103]

She spent an hour with her husband in a cell illuminated only by the light of a candle held by a soldier.[104] While chatting to Tom she asked what had happened between the priest and himself:

> He told me that the priest had wanted him to say he was sorry for what he had done; 'unless I did he could not give me absolution. I told him to clear out of my cell quickly. I was not sorry for what I had done. I gloried in it and the men who had been with me. To say I was sorry would be a lie, and I was not going to face my God with a lie on my tongue.'[105]

Clarke described his court martial as a 'farce' and indicated that he had made 'no speech from the dock or anything like that'.[106] He told her there were two things he wanted her to do; firstly, to dispel any notion that the Germans had failed to follow through on their promises. He insisted that 'the Germans carried out their promise to us to the last letter – they never promised men, we did not ask for men. They could promise only a small cargo of arms'.[107] Secondly, he asked her to publicise the role that Eoin MacNeill had played during the events of that week:

> I want you to see to it that our people know of his treachery to us. He must never be allowed back into the National life of the country, for so sure as he is, so sure will he act treacherously in a crisis. He is a weak man, but I know every effort will be made to whitewash him.[108]

The short visit over, Clarke was attended by Father Columbus and Father Tom Ryan of Inchicore. He was then marched out to the stone-breaker's yard at Kilmainham where he was executed along with Patrick Pearse and Thomas McDonagh 'by 4.15 a. m.' on 3 May 1916.[109]

The following day Kathleen Clarke's brother, Ned Daly, was also executed and on 30 June her uncle, John, finally succumbed to motor neurone disease, being unable to speak for the last few weeks of his life.[110] At the time of the Rising Kathleen was pregnant with the couple's fourth child but she never informed Tom of this. She suffered a miscarriage shortly after the events of Easter 1916.[111]

In March 1917 Kathleen Clarke received the items which had been in Tom's possession at the time of his death – a spectacle case, a knife and a stamp book containing seven stamps. She was also forwarded a £1 note taken from him by two members of the Dublin Metropolitan Police at the Rotunda on 30 April.[112]

Notes

1. Bureau of Military History (hereafter, BMH), Witness Statement (hereafter, WS) 841, P.S. O'Hegarty.
2. Jimmy Wren, *St Laurence O'Toole G. A. C. Centenary History* (Dublin, 2001), p.9.
3. National Library of Ireland (hereafter, NLI), Thomas Clarke Papers, ACC 6410, Box 2, I.ii.6.
4. Marnie Hay, *Bulmer Hobson and the Nationalist Movement in Twentieth-Century Ireland,* (Manchester: Manchester University Press, 2009), p.94.
5. BMH, WS, 593, Bean Mhicil Uí Fhoghludha.
6. National Archives, Kew, London, (hereafter, NAUK), Colonial Office Papers (hereafter, CO) 904/12, October 1910.
7. Ibid.
8. Marnie Hay, *Bulmer Hobson*, pp.53–5.
9. Ibid.
10. *Irish Freedom*, November 1910.
11. Gerard MacAtasney, *Seán MacDiarmada, The Mind of the Revolution* (Leitrim: Drumlin Publications, 2004), p.49.
12. NLI, Pat McCartan Papers, Ms 17,666, Statement made by Pat McCartan, 2 November 1938.
13. The Dungannon Committee of the 'Allen Testimonial' consisted of John Hayburn (Donaghmore Road), John Brannigan (Ann Street), Patrick Cassidy (Scotch Street) and Peter Donnelly (Irish Street). Donnelly was the grand uncle of Peter O'Curry and I am grateful to the latter for allowing me to use this document.
14. NLI, Pat McCartan Papers, Ms 17,666, Statement made by Pat McCartan, 2 November 1938.
15. NLI, Joseph McGarrity Papers, Ms 17,550, Statement made by Joe McGarrity on 11 January 1912.
16. BMH, WS, 1,022, Seán Matthews.
17. Ibid., WS, 26, P.S. O'Hegarty.
18. Ibid.
19. Ibid.
20. Louis Le Roux, *Tom Clarke and the Irish Freedom Movement* (Dublin: The Talbot Press, 1936), pp.97–8.
21. Owen McGee, *The IRB – The Irish Republican Brotherhood From The Land League To Sinn Féin* (Dublin: Four Courts Press, 2005), p.353.
22. Patrick Buckland, *Irish Unionism 1885–1922: A Documentary History* (London: Historical Association, 1973), pp.207–8.
23. Helen Litton (ed.), *Kathleen Clarke, Revolutionary Woman, An Autobiography* (Dublin: The O'Brien Press, 1991), p.64.
24. McGee, *The IRB – The Irish Republican Brotherhood From The Land League To Sinn Féin*, p.355.
25. MacAtasney, *Seán MacDiarmada*, p.64.
26. Bulmer Hobson, *Ireland Yesterday and Tomorrow* (Tralee: Anvil Books, 1968), p.46.
27. Litton, *Kathleen Clarke*, p.44.
28. F.X. Martin, *The Irish Volunteers 1913–1915: Recollections and Documents* (Dublin: J. Duffy, 1963), pp.30–1.
29. *Irish Freedom*, January 1914.
30. F.X. Martin, *The Easter Rising and University College Dublin* (Dublin: Browne and Nolan, 1966), p.18.

31. Martin, *The Irish Volunteers 1913–1915*, p.45.
32. NLI, Bulmer Hobson Papers, Ms 13,171, Statement given to Joe McGarrity at his request by Bulmer Hobson, undated.
33. Litton (ed.), *Kathleen Clarke*, p.46.
34. Hobson, *Ireland Yesterday and Tomorrow*, pp.52–3.
35. University of Limerick Archives (hereafter, ULA), Daly Papers, Box 3/4, no. 80.
36. Hobson, *Ireland Yesterday and Tomorrow*, pp.52–3.
37. Ibid., p.53.
38. Ibid., p.52.
39. Litton (ed.), *Kathleen Clarke*, p.46.
40. Ibid.
41. *Irish Freedom*, July 1914.
42. *Irish Volunteer*, 9 May 1914.
43. MacAtasney, *Seán MacDiarmada*, p.71.
44. Le Roux, *Tom Clarke and the Irish Freedom Movement*, pp.140–1.
45. NLI, John Devoy Papers, Ms 18,137 (4), Special Cable to the *Gaelic American*, 27 July 1914.
46. Le Roux, *Tom Clarke and the Irish Freedom Movement*, p.142; O'Fiaich Library and Archive, Armagh (hereafter, OFLA), Papers of Father Louis O'Kane, including statement of William Kelly senior.
47. Martin, *The Irish Volunteers 1913–1915*, p.148.
48. BMH, WS, 251 Richard Balfe.
49. NLI, Joseph McGarrity Papers, Ms 17,504 (3), Joe McGarrity to Eoin MacNeill, 17 December 1914.
50. Ibid., Ms 17,647 (4), Note on the finances of the Irish Volunteers.
51. Archives of University College Dublin, P/59/2, Irish Volunteers.
52. NAUK, CO 904/164, January 1915.
53. ULA, Daly Papers, Box 1, Folder 29, Patrick Pearse to Madge Daly, 19 April 1915 and 11 May 1915.
54. National Archives Dublin, General Prison Board Hunger Strikes 1912-18, Box 1, No. 3,748, 1 July 1915.
55. Le Roux, *Tom Clarke and the Irish Freedom Movement*, pp.152–3.
56. Ibid., p.156.
57. Ibid., p.164.
58. Litton (ed.), *Kathleen Clarke*, p.56.
59. Ibid., p.57.
60. Ibid.
61. Ibid.
62. Le Roux, *Tom Clarke and the Irish Freedom Movement*, p.167.
63. Ibid., p.168.
64. Fearghal McGarry, *Rebels: Voices from the Easter Rising* (London: Penguin Publishing Ltd, 2011), p.116.
65. BMH, WS, 368, Sean McGarry.
66. Fearghal McGarry, *The Rising, Ireland: Easter 1916* (Oxford University Press: Oxford, 2011), p.84.
67. BMH, WS, 841, P. S. O'Hegarty.
68. Brian Barton, *From Behind a Closed Door, Secret Court Martial Records of the 1916 Rising* (Belfast: Blackstaff Press, 2002), p.303.
69. *Irish Press*, 10 July 1961, memoirs of Seán T. O'Kelly.
70. BMH, WS, 915, Denis McCullough.
71. Ibid., WS, 4, Diarmuid Lynch.
72. Ibid., WS, 523, Richard Connolly.

73. Ibid., WS, 367, Joseph Gleeson.
74. Ibid., WS, 368, Sean McGarry.
75. Tim Pat Coogan, *1916: The Easter Rising* (London: Cassell & Co., 2002), pp.77–81.
76. Litton (ed.), *Kathleen Clarke*, p.76.
77. BMH, WS, 368, Sean McGarry.
78. Litton (ed.), *Kathleen Clarke*, p.74.
79. Fearghal McGarry, *The Rising, Ireland: Easter 1916*, p.19.
80. MacAtasney, *Seán MacDiarmada*, p.108.
81. Ibid., p.127.
82. Ibid., pp.161–2.
83. Le Roux, *Tom Clarke and the Irish Freedom Movement*, p.208.
84. Litton (ed.), *Kathleen Clarke*, p.65.
85. MacAtasney, *Seán MacDiarmada*, p.117.
86. Brian Barton, *From Behind a Closed Door*, p.303.
87. Brian Barton and Michael Foy, *The Easter Rising* (Stroud: Sutton Publishing, 1999), p.141.
88. MacAtasney, *Seán MacDiarmada*, p.118.
89. Seán McConville, *Irish Political Prisoners, 1848–1922 – Theatres of War* (London: Routledge, 2003), p.424.
90. MacAtasney, *Seán MacDiarmada*, p.119.
91. Brian Barton, *From Behind a Closed Door*, p.140.
92. Ibid.
93. Ibid.
94. Ibid., p.141.
95. Ibid., p.140.
96. Ibid., p.306.
97. *Catholic Bulletin*, April 1917.
98. Coogan, *1916: The Easter Rising*, pp.133–5.
99. Barton, *From Behind a Closed Door*, p.133.
100. NAUK, War Office Papers (WO) 71/347.
101. Ibid.
102. Barton, *From Behind a Closed Door*, p.143.
103. Litton (ed.), *Kathleen Clarke*, p.92.
104. Barton, *From Behind a Closed Door*, p.143.
105. Litton, (ed.), *Kathleen Clarke*, p.93.
106. Barton, *From Behind a Closed Door*, p.144.
107. Litton (ed.), *Kathleen Clarke*, p.94.
108. Ibid., p.99.
109. Barton, *From Behind a Closed Door*, p.144.
110. Interview with Mairead and Nora de Hóir on 29 November 2011.
111. Litton, (ed.), *Kathleen Clarke*, pp.95–6. In his will John Daly left the sum of £2,390 to his niece, Madge.
112. Le Roux, *Tom Clarke and the Irish Freedom Movement*, p.238.

Conclusion

On his release from prison Tom Clarke did not show any obvious signs of having being unduly affected by his ordeal. Indeed, one of the first things he did was to request a visit with his comrade Harry Burton in Portland Prison.[1] Forced to emigrate to America due to lack of employment opportunities he was disgusted by what he witnessed within republican circles: individuals jockeying for position, others trying to exploit him and the majority quite content to talk about taking action against Britain but making no effort to do so. However, Clarke remained a man of action and wanted to organise an effective challenge to British rule in Ireland. Hence, when he returned home in 1907 one of the first things he did was to visit members of the IRB and Sinn Féin throughout the country in order to assess the level of support for the Fenian policy of insurrection. However, as been noted, his main motivation for returning was financial – not political.

In a study such as this, which necessarily focuses on the main play-ers in Irish Republicanism, it is easy to overstate the influence of the IRB in early twentieth-century Ireland and to magnify the importance of individuals such as Clarke, McCullough, Hobson, MacDiarmada, etc., in wider society. However the reality and relevance of their posi-tion was evident to Pat McCartan during the 1908 by-election:

> I had a very interesting experience in North Leitrim. It had a tendency to cool my ardour about Republicanism. The National spirit is completely killed by poverty in some places and the idea of doing anything against the Government is out of the ques-

tion. They would ask you what would the poor people do only for the government and so on.[2]

Indicative of the fact that the republican voice was very much a minority one was the inability to establish and support a viable newspaper. The *Gaelic American* had been a huge success in America but republicans in Ireland witnessed the launch and demise of a series of journals such as *The Republic, Sinn Féin, Irish Freedom* and *Nationality*. This was due to the fact that people were not prepared to accept the radical philosophy of an independent Irish Republic as espoused by such journals. Indeed, some of these only lasted as long as they did due to the willingness of Clan na Gael, and the Daly family, to maintain financial support.

This lack of a firm support base was reflected in the membership of the IRB. Between 1908 and 1914 P.S. O'Hegarty estimated the number in Dublin at between 700 to 1,000; that in London around 100; while the figure for Glasgow was in the region of 150. He also stated that it was 'alive but not very vigorous' in Belfast, Cork, Limerick, Wexford, Liverpool and Manchester.[3] Obviously Tom Clarke was aware of such factors and thus attempted to increase the influence of the organisation by a policy of infiltration of members into various cultural and sporting organisations. In addition, he sought to inspire people with the examples of nationalist heroes such as Wolfe Tone and Robert Emmet with concerts and pilgrimages held in their memory. This was a policy he had also successfully adopted whilst in America.

However, what changed the political situation completely was, ironically, the success of the despised (by republicans) Irish Parliamentary Party at Westminster under John Redmond. This had resulted in the policy of Home Rule being actively advocated by the Liberal government of the day, a policy which saw Ulster Unionists establish their own army. This, in turn, was the catalyst for the formation of the Irish Volunteers and the creation of a provisional committee, a significant number of whom were members of the IRB. It was at this stage that a rising became a possibility and with the entry of Britain into the First World War this then became a probability.

For men such as Clarke who had lamented that no effort was made by the IRB during the Boer War this represented an opportunity that had to be grasped. His enthusiastic endorsement of the volunteers during the early months of 1914 is palpable in his letters and consequently his devastation at the subsequent split was great. Nevertheless, the new scenario ensured that Clarke and the IRB now realised they had a hardcore prepared to take military action when called upon to do so. The death of O'Donovan Rossa occurred at an opportune time as far as Clarke was concerned and he stage-managed every aspect of the funeral to ensure that the Irish Volunteers took centre stage in a huge public demonstration of re-born Irish Republicanism.

Having seen the devastating effects of an informer at his own trial in 1883 it is perhaps no surprise that Clarke was highly secretive in planning for the Rising. Secrecy was the cement that held the IRB together. Of course this strategy ensured that while the British were not aware of what was happening, many of those who could have participated were also unaware of its advent due to Clarke's paranoia about secrecy. Thus, from a military perspective, the strength of the planning of the Rising represented its greatest weakness.

Why did Clarke support a Rising and what did he hope to achieve from it? Most men would have been content that having spent the best years of their lives in prison they had contributed significantly to the cause of Irish freedom. When Clarke was released he was publicly fêted on a number of occasions, but almost immediately was snubbed by John Devoy. However, Clarke considered the struggle for Irish independence to be above personal glory or petty politicking. One contemporary noted how, 'to fight England was to him the most natural thing in the world for an Irishman'.[4] Crucial to the timing of this fight were the political fortunes of Britain and consequently the First World War provided the catalyst the IRB needed to launch an insurrection. It has already been noted how Clarke bitterly regretted that no action had been taken during the Boer War and indeed Seán MacDiarmada commented that neither Clarke or himself wished to live 'if this thing passed off without making a fight'.[5] Thus, a stand had to be made – just as it had been in 1798, 1803, 1848 and 1867 – and it can be argued that the outcome, to men like Clarke, was irrelevant: the effort was necessary to ensure that the Fenian tradition remained strong. In the words of Denis McCullough:

> Frankly, I believe neither my colleagues nor myself were greatly troubled about ethical questions like 'moral insurrection'. To us the issue was a simple and straight one, viz: break England's grip on Ireland and to get rid of her occupation of all our territory. We were prepared to use every just means – men, movements or materials – that came to hand to achieve our purpose. We pledged our lives and those of our members to that purpose.[6]

During Easter week Min Ryan (Seán MacDiarmada's girlfriend) engaged Clarke in a long conversation in the GPO and heard him articulate his belief that a rising was essential in the current circumstances as the chance may not have presented itself again. He also maintained that such action was necessary in order to press Ireland's claims at any forthcoming post-war peace conference. Further, he explained that a republic had been proclaimed 'in order to appeal to the imagination of the world'.[7]

His joy at the path events were taking both before and during the Rising was noted by those whom he encountered. Annie MacSwiney, sent from Cork to Dublin on Spy Wednesday to assess the position in Dublin, recounted her meeting with Clarke:

> He was exhilarated. His whole spirit seemed to burn in his glowing eyes. He spoke with enthusiasm of help from Germany and said that John Devoy had a document, signed by the Kaiser, recognising the Republic of Ireland.[8]

When Patrick Rankin, an IRB man from Newry reached the GPO on Easter Wednesday he informed Clarke that he was unaware of any military activity in the north. However, he recalled that Clarke was not downhearted but instead 'he looked about thirty years younger and seemed so happy you would imagine you were talking to him in his old shop in Parnell Street'.[9] Clarke's philosophy was encapsulated in a speech made by Patrick Pearse in March 1914 when he outlined how the torch of separatism had been handed down to the present generation:

> If the men of '98 had not risen, if Emmet had not died, the men of '48 would not have risen, nor the men of '67. And if the men of '67 had not risen who in Ireland would be taking up the cause today. We have set our faces again towards the old paths, and we have taken up again the old work, and we hope to use the opportunities that the mercy of God has given.[10]

Thus, for Clarke, the Rising represented a continuation of his work in honouring the Fenian dead in New York cemeteries and acknowledging the role played by figures such as O'Donovan Rossa. In order for the present generation to produce its own Tone, Emmet, Mitchel and O'Leary a rising was necessary.

However, he did not subscribe to the notion of a blood sacrifice in terms articulated by Pearse. While Pearse may have attempted to equate his sacrifice on behalf of the Irish nation with that of Christ for the sins of man, Clarke was in no way religious. Denunciations by the Catholic hierarchy of membership of the IRB may have contributed to this but there is little doubt that his prison experiences were also a factor. When attempting to confide in the prison chaplain he found that the priest was a member of the establishment first and a Catholic second. The same experiences shaped the religious outlook of John Daly who then passed them onto his nieces, including Kathleen. Of course, it may be argued that their beliefs were simply those of an earlier Fenian generation and not shared by the other leaders of the rising. However, Seán MacDiarmada (25 years younger than Clarke) also resented the attitude of the hierarchy to the republican ideal and experienced much clerical opposition during his days as organiser for the Dungannon Clubs.

Consequently, he became a lapsed Catholic shortly afterwards. It is also interesting to note that Bulmer Hobson renounced his Quaker beliefs, finding them incompatible with his membership of the IRB and artic- ulation of the need for armed insurrection.

Although Clarke told Annie MacSwiney that 'victory was assured'[11], it is unlikely he meant a military victory would ensue. Indeed, after the arrest of Roger Casement he informed Pat McCartan on Holy Saturday, 'It is hopeless but we must go on'.[12] Instead, he opined that 'we in the front rank, of course, go down. We know that, but the repub- lic is safe, nothing can prevent that'.[13] In addition, he reassured Min Ryan that at all periods in the history of Ireland the shedding of blood had always succeeded in raising the spirit and morale of the people. Hence he predicted that 'of course, we [the leaders] shall be all wiped out'. She noted how 'he said this almost with gaiety. He had got into the one thing he had wanted to do during his whole lifetime'.[14]

Consequently, it appears that he was quite happy to sacrifice his own life in the belief that his actions, and those of his comrades, would result in a groundswell of opinion against British rule in Ireland, thereby creating the conditions for a country-wide insurrection.

In correspondence with John Daly and John Devoy in April and May 1914, Clarke's joy at the rapid development of the Irish Volunteers seemed to have blinded him to the threat to an Irish republic posed by the Ulster Volunteers. He enthusiastically related how, on information received from Pat McCartan, it appeared that the 'Carsonites' had a 'somewhat friendly face for the Irish Volunteers'.[15] Indeed, there was a genuine belief among some of the volunteers, endorsed by Clarke, that 'if it comes to a scrap between them (Carsonites) and the English they know that the Irish Volunteers would fight with them and not against them'.[16] Clarke hailed this as 'an extraordinary change in the attitude of the one-time Orangeman, when he even allows himself to entertain the thought of himself and the papists fighting together in any circum- stances'.[17] Such comments reflect an incredible naivety on Clarke's part and are all the more surprising given that he, more than any of the other leaders, should have been aware of the strength of feeling which had manifested itself in events such as the signing of the Ulster Covenant by almost 500,000 Unionists and the formation and arming of the Ulster Volunteer Force. He had lived in Dungannon since the age of seven until he left in his early twenties, the catalyst for his departure being an attack by Orange supporters on a Catholic parade. Hence, Dungannon was his home town – a fact reflected in the petition of 1892 and his triumphant return six years later – and he would therefore also have been cognisant of the bitterness which characterised party politics in his native east Tyrone. Although he lived in Dublin he was familiar with the unionist perspective on political developments. While it has often been noted that his shops became a focal point for republicans, there were others who frequented his premises to engage in political dialogue. Amongst these was Bertie Smyllie, editor of the *Irish Times* in the 1940s, and in an article written in July 1943 he recalled his student days at Trinity College, Dublin during the period 1912–13. Due to a business arrangement organised by his father Smyllie had reason to regularly visit Clarke 'who was of rather a dour disposition, or so it seemed to me, but occasionally used to unbend, particularly when I was exceedingly hard-up and tried to cajole him'.[18] Significantly, both men engaged in political debate and Smyllie recalled how, 'I was a violent Carsonite in those far-off days, and often used to argue the Unionist toss with Tom Clarke when the two of us were alone in the shop'.[19] Hence, Clarke would have been very aware of the Unionist opposition to any form of Home Rule and the fact that the Ulster Volunteers represented the violent incarnation of that opposition. Thus, it can be argued that little thought had been given by republicans to the reality and extent of unionist opposition to Home Rule.

In this sense it appears that the 1916 Proclamation accurately reflected the fact that the leaders had not seriously considered the political landscape of any new country that might emerge after Easter week. It simply stated that the provisional government would 'administer the civil and military affairs of the Republic in trust for the people, pending the election of a permanent National Government'.[20] Thus, for Clarke, an independent Irish Republic – free to choose its own government and make its own laws – was the goal of Irish republicans. In essence his political philosophy boiled down to the Fenian creed of separatism.

Clarke's influence on Irish history, representing what has been referred to as 'the apostolic link with an earlier generation of Fenians',[21] was encapsulated by Denis McCullough as follows:

> Tom Clarke's reputation enabled the younger men, Seán MacDiarmada, Bulmer Hobson, Diarmuid Lynch, P.S. O'Hegarty, etc, to move forward with his backing in organising, preaching and teaching the value and necessity of a physical force movement. It protected them from the usual charges of youthful over-enthusiasm and of insincerity. I say with every confidence that Tom Clarke's person and Seán MacDiarmada's energy and organising ability were the principal factors in creating and guiding events to make the Rising possible.[22]

Notes

1.   National Library of Ireland (hereafter, NLI), Thomas Clarke Papers, Box 3, V.i. Clarke's request was refused.
2.   NLI, Joseph McGarrity Papers, Ms 17,617, Pat McCartan to Joe McGarrity, 24 July 1907.
3.   Bureau of Military History, Witness Statement 841, P.S. O'Hegarty.
4.   Fearghal McGarry, *The Rising, Ireland: Easter 1916* (Oxford: Oxford University Press, 2011), p.103.
5.   Ibid., p.98.
6.   Archives of the University College, Dublin, P/120/14, McCullough Papers.
7.   McGarry, *The Rising, Ireland: Easter 1916*, p.154.
8.   Ibid., p.112.
9.   Seán McConville, *Irish Political Prisoners, 1848–1922 – Theatres of War* (London: Routledge, 2003), p.419.
10. Ibid., p.448.
11. McGarry, *The Rising, Ireland: Easter 1916*, p.112.
12. Ibid., p.221.
13. Ibid., p.112.
14. Ibid., p.154.
15. See letters no. 161 (29 April 1914) and 162 (14 May 1914).
16. Ibid.
17. Ibid.
18. *Irish Times*, 19 July 1943. I am grateful to Frank Bouchier-Hayes for this reference.

19.   Ibid.
20.   McGarry, *The Rising, Ireland: Easter 1916*, p.134.
21.   McConville, *Irish Political Prisoners, 1848–1922 – Theatres of War*, p.414.
22.   NLI, Denis McCullough Papers, Ms 31,653.

PART TWO

Introduction to Letters

This collection of letters has been sourced from a number of archives in Ireland and Britain. By far the largest group consists of private letters from Tom Clarke to his wife Kathleen, held in the National Library, Dublin. These were purchased at auction in April 2006 and contain over 300 letters between the couple. Prior to this they had been in the ownership of Clarke's youngest son, Emmet. Another important repository is the Archives Department of the University of Limerick which houses the papers of the Daly family. Correspondence has also been included from a variety of public and private collections. It has been made known to the author that a small number of letters remains in private hands. Despite attempts to access some of these the owners refused to consent to their being used in this publication. Nevertheless, the letters included here account for the vast majority of those extant. The correspondence has, as far as possible, been grouped thematically and within each theme, chronologically.

The collection opens with Clarke's earliest letters when writing under his prison pseudonym of Henry Hammond Wilson. Letters to and from him were routed through his sisters and then copied by them for wider circulation. Prison regulations stipulated that inmates were permitted to write one letter every three months. However, in his *Glimpses of an Irish Felon's Prison Life* Clarke regularly commented on the fact that many of the letters he wrote were suppressed 'and never got farther than the Governor of the prison'.[1] He noted that dozens of his letters were in the 'English Home Office' and preserved there together with his prison record. However, an exhaustive search of all the various relevant records in England has produced only a couple of these letters while it was noted by Home Office civil servants that his personal file – A26493K/18-23 – had been destroyed. Thus, this rather small collection includes some letters already quoted in Clarke's *Glimpses*.

The second section contains Clarke's private correspondence to loved ones, the majority to his wife Kathleen. The information we obtain about the couple from 1899 onwards is necessarily circum-scribed by those periods when they were apart and had to write in order to maintain contact. Thus, there are many letters from 1899 until July 1901, during which time Tom was in America. Obviously due to their living together in New York there was no correspondence in 1902/3. Problems with Kathleen's health resulted in a significant number of letters being written in 1904/5, especially as she spent several months in Limerick in the latter year. The next significant batch runs from 1907 until the following year, charting the family's return to Ireland and the opening of their shop in Amiens Street, Dublin. An interesting anomaly appears in Clarke's letters written in January 1908 as on all his correspondence for that month he wrote the date as 1907. This was only clarified after cross-referencing his writing for this period with the replies penned by Kathleen. Thereafter, this section contains sporadic correspondence written when the couple were parted for short periods.

The final part contains Clarke's political correspondence written to a variety of individuals and covering the period 1899 to 1916. How-ever, while there is much of interest, particularly from 1913 onwards, it is important to note that the really significant information being imparted in the years leading to the Rising was communicated orally and never written down.

It appears John Daly found the office of Mayor of Limerick an extremely burdensome occupation. Indeed, he commented to Clarke, 'Do you know old man I sometimes think there are worse places in this world than Chatham and Portland'.[2] Consequently, in order to main-tain regular contact with his friend he asked Kathleen to write to

Clarke informing him of all the happenings in Limerick. Hence, on 30 March 1899 he wrote, 'I hear Katty and you are going to do the correspondence now or until I get my room'.[3] Thus, it was John Daly's hectic schedule which necessitated that written contact be established between his niece and Clarke. Kathleen's first letter to him on 1 March 1899 began and ended very formally, 'Dear Mr. Clarke … I remain your very sincere friend, Kathleen'.[4] His first reply on 26 March 1899 was similarly formal in tone, 'Dear Kattie … Your very sincere friend, Thos. J. Clarke'.[5] As far as John Daly was concerned the correspondence saved him having to write lengthy letters to Tom and in September 1899 he jokingly enquired 'are you not ashamed of yourself knowing that that poor soft-hearted little girl of mine is writing pen black and blew by the way keeping you posted on all my doings'.[6]

However, an initial friendship, which had developed between Kathleen and Tom while he stayed in Limerick to receive the Freedom of the city, developed into romance when he holidayed with the family in Kilkee, County Clare, during July 1899. The last time Kathleen began a letter with the phrase 'Dear Mr. Clarke' was on 26 June.[7] Her first letter to him after the holiday was on 1 August and began 'Dear Tom' and ended 'With best wishes for your mother and sisters and best love to yourself. I remain yours ever, Kathleen'.[8] In this same letter she acknowledged the importance of events in Kilkee and how it had changed their relationship in commenting 'It does seem very strange to be addressing you in this way'.[9] The subsequent letters reveal the extent to which the relationship was objected to by Kathleen's family and how, in order to avoid prying eyes in Kilkee, they used to rise early each morning and go on long walks together. By September Kathleen was able to write 'I dream of you nearly every night though if I told Uncle John that he'd say I was suffering from indigestion'.[10]

John Daly did not openly criticise Clarke in any of his correspondence but made reference to the fact that he was aware a relationship had developed and gently mocked his friend. On 16 November 1900 he commented 'yours of the 6th arrived while I was in Dublin where Kattie is at present, as perhaps you know'.[11] In a similar tone he wrote a few weeks later that 'Kattie will explain all to you, between billing and cooing, etc, etc, etc'.[12] Daly also indulged in teasing Clarke and in one letter revealed that he had visited the latter's mother and sister, adding, 'Kattie goes there regular and Alf [Clarke's brother] sees her back. What do you think of that now?'[13]

A number of interesting perspectives about Tom Clarke emerge from a reading of this correspondence. His letters to Kathleen, both before and during their marriage, reveal the very deep love he had for his fiancé/wife and the affectionate terms by which he addressed her in 1899 were retained until the time of his death. Similarly, we witness an emotional man who broke into tears when informed by telegram of the birth of his second son and cried at a concert of Irish music in Dublin. The letters written both in America and Ireland also reveal the extent to which Kathleen suffered from health problems, often necessitating long periods of recuperation, usually in Limerick. Meanwhile, amongst those penned in 1905 were two which reveal that the Dalys were keen for Ned to live with the Clarkes for a year in New York and to attend school there. Consequently, a small piece of Irish history could have been changed because if Ned Daly had gone to the United States he might have remained there and not been executed for his part in the Rising.

In explaining his reasons for moving to another part of New York Clarke told Kathleen that the present area contained too many 'niggers' and maintained that Irish people had no time for 'those absurd people'. Kathleen replied in similar terms. The point can be made that this terminology was generally used at that time when reference was being made to black people. For example, John Daly informed Clarke that his nieces were 'working like niggers'. However, Clarke's terminology may well have been framed by a childhood spent in a British Army garrison in South Africa. The family lived in various parts of that country for six years and it is very likely that Tom as a young boy growing up in an environment where the black people were subservient in all aspects of life would have been very familiar with such derogatory language. Indeed, in his speech in Dungannon, in trying to contextualise his prison experience, he remarked that it was even worse than the 'savage treatment' of the 'American Red Indian or African Ashantee'.

Clarke's letters to Kathleen and John Daly are littered with humour, much of it self-deprecating and suggest he was a person with a very positive outlook on life. He is also revealed as speaking with an American 'twang' and indeed some of his spellings betray an adoption of the syntax of that country.

While all books dealing with this period simply note that Clarke opened a tobacconist's shop his letters to Kathleen tell us the extent of his efforts in doing so. As she was living with her family in Limerick from December 1907 to June 1908 (expecting their second child) he felt the need to explain in great detail every aspect of the business – the location and its benefits, the costs of renovating it, even the colour of the wallpaper he intended using. In this way we are made to feel almost as if we are standing in the shop in Amiens Street. For months after-wards Clarke kept Kathleen up to date with every facet of his new trade – the takings for each day, how that compared with the previous day, the comparative takings for each month and so on. He also informed her of local shops, presumably 'rivals', which had closed since he commenced business.

Clarke relied totally on his wife to maintain his clothes and when she was in Limerick she regularly had to send him clean shirts and ties. While his mother and sister, Hannah, lived in Dublin, his relationship with both was not good. Although Hannah helped greatly in develop-ing his business his surprise at this was evident in his letters to Kathleen. Indeed, in one letter he described her as 'an unbearable thing'. Similarly, he remarked that his mother could be very moody and made it obvious when she did not like somebody. His brother Alfred rarely features in his correspondence and here again the relationship does not appear to have been close. The fact that John Daly had to be circumspect when giving money to Mary Clarke in 1897 for fear that Alfred would take it from her suggests that this individual would not have been tolerated by his brother. However, Tom was close to Maria and they lived together in New York for eighteen months until Kathleen arrived. As has been noted Maria was married shortly after her brother but the letters reveal that the marriage to Edward Fleming was beset by problems from an early stage due to his problems with alcohol. They also demonstrate Clarke's love for this sister and his willingness to do all he could to assist her, while at the same time illustrating his detestation for her husband.

When writing his biography in 1936 Louis Le Roux stated that Clarke 'had always been a devout son of the Catholic Church'.[14] However, the evidence of his correspondence suggests this was far from the case. Given that Le Roux had access to this material it demonstrates how contemporary moral and ethical values can be made to dictate the content of historical research. Maria Clarke expressed the hope that Kathleen's imminent arrival in the summer of 1901 would make her brother a 'better Catholic'. However, Kathleen's letters illustrate that this was never likely. Her uncle, a strong influence on her and her siblings, had had several stormy interviews with a priest while in prison. When his sister Ellen visited him in February 1890 he told her that 'I believe in a God but I will not be led by what any man says'.[15] A letter written by Kathleen to Tom in the aftermath of the birth of their second son demonstrates her indifference to the Catholic faith and the fact that her children would not be raised in a religious household:

> ... tomorrow I go to be churched, if the weather permits ... I am of course thankful to God for covering over my time so well but how going down to the church, bringing a candle and having it lighted for a second could make my thanks more acceptable in his eyes is more than I can understand. I must go through it however or I'd have all the friends and acquaintances' hair standing on end in holy horror. Uncle John has a good laugh now and then at Daly when he betrays how very ignorant in the Catholic line he is. Today Ag took him into a church and on going in sprinkled herself with holy water. The first question

he put to her on coming out was why she wet her face before going in. She told him it was holy water so he asked her what was that … While I was sick he saw Laura kneeling down and praying on her beads and asked her what she was doing.[16]

While this group of letters has been designated 'personal' they do contain some references to contemporary political matters and so the designation is not strict. For example, Clarke could be talking about business matters to Kathleen and then inform her that a certain individual had called into the shop to talk about politics and then proceed to inform her of what had been said. Indeed, he was often so busy that he would sometimes begin a letter and write it over a number of days.

Similarly, some of the 'political' letters contain references to business or personal matters. This last group contains the most diverse number of recipients, all of whom were key figures in the IRB; hence, Clarke writes regularly to Major John MacBride, John Devoy, James Reidy, Joseph McGarrity and John Daly. On reading such the reader can almost feel the momentum increasing in the three years before the Rising. Clarke talks at length about the emergence of the Volunteers and his pleasure at such is obvious. However, his assessment of matters immediately prior to the split is completely awry and in a letter to Devoy he seriously underestimates the ability of the Redmondites to secure the adherence of a large percentage of the volunteers. In fact, this letter suggests that he was perhaps somewhat carried away by his enthusiasm for the organisation. Consequently, in another letter his unforgiving attitude towards Bulmer Hobson is very evident.

A feature of some of this correspondence is an attempt to write in 'code' and John Devoy recalled how Clarke liked to portray his letters as being to his 'uncle' in America and merely representing the comments of an interested spectator. He even wrote one in which he portrayed himself as an Orangeman. To today's eyes such efforts appear amateurish but as mentioned earlier it is important to remember that vital communication from Ireland to America was carried orally, not trusted to paper.

The letters end with a note handed by Clarke to his wife hours before his execution with the request that it be made available to the people of Ireland. It is in this sphere, as one of the seven signatories to the Proclamation and one of the leaders executed for his part in the Rising, that he has until now been almost totally associated. What these letters reveal is Tom Clarke, the man – as prisoner, friend, brother, lover, husband, father, businessman and revolutionary.

Note on grammar, punctuation, dates, etc.:

The letters have been edited so as to enable the reader to grasp the important aspects of each; hence, mundane matters such as discussions about the weather or social events involving the Daly sisters have been omitted. Otherwise, they have been transcribed exactly as they were written by Clarke. The influence of his time in America is evident in some of his spellings. Occasional grammatical errors have not been corrected but square brackets have been added to clarify locations and persons mentioned in the text.

Notes

1. Thomas J. Clarke, *Glimpses of an Irish Felon's Prison Life. With an introduction by P.S. O'Hegarty* (Dublin: Maunsel and Roberts, 1922, 1970), p. 16.
2. University of Limerick Archives, (hereafter, ULA), Daly Papers, Mealy's 2006 auction, accession lot 371, John Daly to Tom Clarke, 2 January 1901.
3. Ibid., John Daly to Tom Clarke to same, 30 March 1899.
4. National Library of Ireland (hereafter, NLI), Thomas Clarke Papers, ACC 6410, Box 1, I.i.1, Kathleen Daly to Tom Clarke, 1 March 1899.
5. Ibid., Box 1, I.ii.1, Tom Clarke to Kathleen Daly, 26 March 1899.
6. ULA, Daly Papers, Mealy's 2006 auction, accession lot 371, John Daly to Tom Clarke, 3 September 1899.
7. NLI, Thomas Clarke Papers, ACC 6410, Box 1, I.i.1, Kathleen Daly to Tom Clarke, 26 June 1899.
8. Ibid., Box 1, I.i.2, Kathleen Daly to Tom Clarke, 1 August 1899.
9. Ibid.
10. Ibid., Box 1, I.i.3, Kathleen Daly to Tom Clarke, 17 September 1899.
11. ULA, Daly Papers, Mealy's 2006 auction, accession lot 371, John Daly to Tom Clarke, 16 November 1900.
12. Ibid., John Daly to Tom Clarke, 2 January 1901.
13. Ibid., 16 November 1900.

14. Louis Le Roux, *Tom Clarke and the Irish Freedom Movement* (Dublin: The Talbot Press, 1936), p.48.
15. National Archives, Kew, London, (hereafter, NAUK), Home Office Papers (HO) 144/195/A46664C (101-393).
16. NLI, Thomas Clarke Papers, ACC 6410, Box 1, I.i.16, Kathleen Clarke to Tom Clarke, 3 March 1908.

Letters

Prison

1

Mr. Patrick Jordan,
Strabane,
Co. Tyrone
Portland Prison,   January 17th 1893

My Dear Paddy,

I received Maria's batch of letters – yours among the number – all
right, on Christmas Eve. I had just commenced dinner, with the
appetite a hard-labour convict has, when they were put into my hand.
That dinner had no further interest for me; it had to give place to my
letters and the reading of those gave me far greater enjoyment than I
could get from eating the best dinner ever cooked. Nowhere in the
world is a friend's letter so fully appreciated as in a convict prison, and
in here we know of no other pleasure save an occasional visit from the
friends we love. I am glad you got back safe after the visit and thankful for the trouble and bother you took. It is always good news for me
to hear that the Dear friends at home are enjoying good health. Long
may it be told to me. The Dublin news was especially interesting. It is
indeed gratifying to know "the Capital" is what it ought to be – first.
When I wrote last I was hopefully expecting that any day might see me
released. All I had heard for some months previous went to show that
my friends – each and all – were quite confident that we would be
released this winter. But the news to hand since then has knocked that
on the head. Still I wasn't as much disappointed as you might think, for
disappointment and I have so often, during the past couple of years,
shook hands on the same question of speedy release that I have come
to see the wisdom of always leaving room for him…in an appearance.
Yes, Paddy, have had it brought home to me, pretty forcibly, what is
meant by that little sentence: "Hope deferred maketh the heart sick".
But, after all, things are not looking <u>bad</u>. Our old friends – you of the
Amnesty Ass. – who have been working right along for us, are still

working as earnestly and as energetically as ever, and I have no doubt will continue to do so until you free us. And I may remark here I am well pleased you <u>are</u> working so energetically for I hold with you, Paddy, our release will be hastened just in proportion to the amount of pressure our friends can bring to bear. As for those others you speak of who call themselves the real friends of the prisoners but who would make our release entirely a matter of English generosity, well I daresay there are some – perhaps many – among them who wish us well and would be glad to think they had done something towards enabling the Irish Felons to know again what it is to breathe God's free fresh air. But there are, I am convinced, others…bitter enemies – people who if they came out honestly and spoke their mind would tell you "Hell is not hot enough nor eternity long enough to punish us". These know what they are about in passing as our "Real Friends" – they know right well what a mighty poor chance of release we should have if our Friends would only take their advice and give up doing anything for us. But sure it is no new thing – especially in Dublin – for those who oppose Amnesty and wish to bring things to a standstill to mix with the friends of Amnesty and when a favourable opportunity presents itself slip out a sly knife and cut the traces.

Concerning what you told me about the U. S. Consul having received directions from Washington to visit the Irish-American prisoners. He has not yet been here, and, to tell the truth I hardly expect he will come. After I saw you I remembered the Presidential Election was due in November; so I put this and that together and derived my own conclusions therefrom. However, it would be satisfactory to know just what the thing amounts to. So you or Maria might drop a note to Mr. Wm. M. Brown of New York (c/o Mr. F. G. Morrison will reach him) asking him kindly to give me all the particulars of this affair and anything else from his side of the water that is likely to be interesting. Tell him to send his letter to Maria for me.

Well, old friend, here we are in 1893 and with the first half of January gone by. Time goes rapidly enough for you, I daresay. For me it creeps slowly enough, Dear knows. By the 3rd of April I shall have been in prison ten years – almost a third of my lifetime. Can you realise what that means? Ah! no, Paddy, you cannot. No one can understand all the hardship and misery it means but myself. But you can realise that I <u>do</u> know that, notwithstanding it all, I am – from the heart's core to the finger tip – <u>Irish</u> still…proudly Irish as in the old days. That, though my clothing from the top of my cap to the bottom of my boots be plentifully marked with the Government "Broad Arrow", what does it matter when I can say within myself, "Thank God! There is no Broad Arrow – no, not a suspicion of a Broad Arrow stamp on this Celtic heart of mine". I intended to crush a note for my sister into this sheet but I have written at such length to you that I have left myself no paper. I have nothing in particular to say to her except that Mr. John Redmond, Q. C., M. P., can, I believe, get an order any time now to see me. I made my application to the Secretary of State on December 7th. I know Maria is as pleased to get a letter from me as I am to get one from her, so I have set her down first on the list for next writing time. And a thought just strikes me: Why not let Joe send this letter to her; she will send it on to you. That will be like killing two, or rather three, birds with the one stone. Best love to all at home, my Father, Mother, etc, ditto to yourself, your wife and to Joe and Mrs. Hart and loving remembrance to all Friends in the North. Send reply as usual to Maria – <u>she won't delay longer than 2 weeks</u>.

Afftly.

H. H. W.

———————————————

2

Portland Convict Prison,
England,
14th November 1893

My Dear Friend[1],

Since writing to you last I have heard several interesting items from your side of the water. It was like music to my ears to be told that at last you over there have taken off your coats and set yourselves to work in earnest to help on Amnesty. More power to you. If thanks of mine be of any value I from the bottom of my heart thank each and every one of our friends who are lending a helping hand. Now as regards another matter. Let me put it like this: – Suppose some U. S. citizens living abroad in a foreign land had been accused of a crime there and at their trial glaring violence was done to the law in order to bring about their conviction, and upon the conviction thus obtained they were flung into Prison for life. In such a case could any good reason be given why Republican America in justice to those citizens of hers should not interfere (to some purpose) on their behalf? Would year after year be allowed to go by and that case be for intents and purposes ignored by the U. S. authorities? Think you, would those unfortunate men for ten or eleven years be allowed to cry in vain from behind their prison bars "Why has our Government not seen justice done to us? Why?" Imagine all that my friend and it will bring home to you the case of the Citizens convicted with myself. Whether the questions I put are answered or not the fact remains that now at this late day I – for one – don't beguile myself with any hopes of being benefited by "American interference". But it may serve some good purpose – perhaps be useful to the friends who are working for us if I make that point clear where I speak of "glaring violence having been done to the law in order to bring about our conviction". You are aware I daresay that it is a principle (should I say a fundamental principle?) of the English Law that the word of one witness alone is not sufficient to convict a person. I don't know what law books have to say about it. I never opened one. But I do know that History bears witness that in Political cases here (other than the Irish) where that principle was involved the story because uncorroborated was considered worthless. While in our case the newspapers of the day can bear witness that we were convicted of Treason Felony on the uncorroborated story of one person (Norman). Here is his story in its chief points. He was a coach-maker by trade, working in his native city, Brooklyn. He was duped into joining the Emerald Club of New York. This club was a branch of a Society which had for its object the establishing of a Republic in

Ireland. He attended a number of meetings of the club. The chairman's name he heard was Sullivan. This Sullivan – with whom he had no acquaintance – gave him a letter to take to Dr Thomas Gallagher, Greenpoint Brooklyn. He took it and brought it to Gallagher. That was the first time he saw Gallagher, never had heard of him before that. After getting the letter Gallagher directed him to go over to England, he gave no reason for this astonishing order and Norman without any question or hesitation came as he was bid. After he had been some time in London he met Gallagher and in the course of some conversation they had he gathered his object over here was to blow down public buildings. Of the prisoners in the dock he never saw any of them before excepting Gallagher and Whitehead and his acquaintance with Whitehead only extended to a few hours before his arrest. That was Norman's tale. It doesn't require me to point out its absurdity, for the absurdity is quite palpable and is I think its most striking characteristic. There was no corroboration of it as I have said and yet upon it in defiance to what the law requires we were convicted. This fact becomes plain if for a moment no notice is taken of Norman and his story. What then did the other evidence of our trial amount to? Virtually this:-"two of those men in the dock were each in possession of explosives but there is nothing to lay to the charge of the others". That was the sum total of what all the other witnesses put together had to say against us and upon that surely a Treason Felony conviction was out of the question unless indeed the mere forms and appearances of justice were flung to the winds along with Justice itself. You will perhaps be asking how it was possible for Norman's story to convict myself and Curtin whom he said he never saw before. That's another of the "funny" points I should like to enlarge upon. I can only say now that the thing was done in "The-House-that-Jack-built" style. There's the Fenian Club that Norman joined – there's the letter that Norman took from the club to Gallagher –there's Curtin and Wilson (other witnesses say) were familiar with Gallagher. Therefore they are connected with that club or society. The reasoning there was pretty elastic wasn't it? And now old Friend Good Bye. I often think of you. My best wishes are yours.

Regards to all old Friends. Hoping they like yourself are well and doing well. I am as usual and ever yours, H. H. Wilson

PS Dear Hart I was much grieved to hear from Maria that Mrs H was so very ill. I hope she is quite recovered. Concerning your question about visiting me. Can you come in the New Year?

3

Portland Prison,
Dec 18th 1894

My Dear Maria,

I hope you got back safe and well after the visit. One thing you hadn't such a rough passage on the return as you had coming – that is if it will do to judge by the weather on this rock. I am just as you left me, in good health and feeling ever so much easier after hearing how nicely things are at home. You could hardly have brought better news than that. Yes I enjoyed the visit very much indeed. And by the way the same is to be said of the letters that were sent. Alf's in particular pleased me, though it was all too brief. So be sure you gave him my message. Jordan's Amnesty details were very interesting – as indeed were both your own and Dora's. When you write Jordan let him know I intend sending him my next letter and Yes tell him I am "A1" – he "kind of growls" (as they say "Out West") that you didn't say last time how I was getting on. Give him my love, he is a good fellow. That rumour you mentioned about release in Feby. I suppose means at bottom nothing more than that an Amnesty motion will be brought up in Parliament then and possible lead to release. Speaking of release reminds me of your alluding – during the visit – to what the Home Secretary has said thereon and you seemed somewhat disappointed when you heard me explain that my case from the point of view of ordinary remission was not just what you had been led to believe. Had there been time I would have compensated in a sort of way by showing you the matter in a more satisfactory light. But I can do that now as I have nothing else of any great importance to talk about. First of all let me repeat a life sentence does not mean 20 years with $^1/_4$ of that time knocked off. It is true prisoners who are sentenced to a given number of years – say 10 or 16 – may earn a remission of $^1/_4$ of that. For instance a man with a 16 years sentence who earns the full remission is released on completing 12 years. But as to life sentences. This is the rule word-for-word as well as I remember. "A prisoner sentenced to Penal Servitude for life must not – unless special instructions are given – entertain any expectation of release until he has completed 20 years". And with that I think I have said enough to set you right and to enable you to form a fair idea of the theory on remission and how it affects me. Now to come to that other view of the matter to which I have made allusions. You must understand what I give above – concerning remissions – are by no means hard and fast rules. Indeed no. The exceptions are numerous. Speaking on the strength of my own observations, which by the way extend no further than to that class of men who like myself were never previously in prison. Well a good percentage of this "Star Class" – as it is called – get a special reduction of sentence. And where this is given at all it is given with no stinted hand, for instance in some cases the sentence reduced by more than a half (the reduced sentence then subject to a further reduction of the ordinary $^1/_4$) – in other cases "lifers" whom a reprieve saved from execution liberated before they had been in prison as long as I have, etc, etc. Very well. In the face of this you will see that the Home Sec's' statement in that Amnesty debate may not by any means be what you and others of my friends understand it. If we Irish Political Prisoners are in point of fact to be dealt with – as far as release is concerned – just as other prisoners then according to my very lowest calculations release for us must surely be close at hand. Just look at it in this way and you will see it as it appears to me. Take things as they are. Take my case as it stands – without going back to protest against conviction or anything else, or without at all taking into a/c the significant bearing the Amnesty Movement has upon it. Simply take the case as it stands rendered on the Prison Books today and as it were, put it (or what amounts to the same thing in the case of the Irish Political Prisoners generally) on the one side and on the other put that of any other class of prisoners – let us say reprieved murderers – commonly considered the most hopeless case of any. Looking first at the one and then at the other – while at the same time remembering those "special reductions" – I can't for my life see how it is possible to make out that a case such as mine, on the one hand, has not at least as much claim to have the sentence chopped down a bit as any on the other hand. "Facts speak for themselves". And what more eloquent fact could there be to give emphasis to all this and to bring out clearly the force of what I say than that Birmingham affair which Alf mentioned to me. You know it I daresay. Two men a couple of years ago were arrested in possession of explosives – tried and convicted. But unlike me they were Englishmen and one of them was sentenced to 10 years, the other to 7 and – I now have done (reckoning full ordinary remission) almost those two sentences combined. So you see that if for a certainty we are to be dealt with on a par with the other prisoners, then for a certainty the time cannot be far off when our prison doors shall be thrown open for us. Dearest love to my mother. I trust she still keeps well and strong. This will be a lonely Christmas for her with the loss of father. I know you'll all feel it especially hard now and I judge by myself. Christmas time always makes me think a great deal of home and old times and the contrast it forces makes it the hardest wretchedest time in the whole year. This year father's death makes it worse. Love to Dora and Alf, ditto to my good friends Mr and Mrs Hart. I meant to write them occasionally. A big share of love to yourself, affect brother, H. H. Wilson

(PS Have I addressed this letter correctly? H. H. W.)

4

Letter to John E Redmond
Portland Prison
June 18th 1895

…It is nothing directly concerning myself or my case that causes me to take the unusual course of sending you a letter. What I wish to bring under your notice has reference to one of my fellow-prisoners here, J463, Albert Whitehead…Whitehead is, as you are doubtless aware, one of the unfortunate Irish prisoners whose mind has been shattered by the villainous treatment to which we have been subject. It is now some seven or eight years since he first broke down, and at no time since has he recovered…His fellow-prisoners – or those of them that are not so far gone as himself – are to a man convinced of his insanity, convinced many times over, and you will find all the lately-released Irish prisoners, without a single exception, are of the same opinion…It is true he is not what is called outrageous – the nearest approach to that are the times when he has kept us awake all night raving at the top of his voice. But although for so far not dangerous to others, he certainly is dangerous to himself, and it is upon this point what I am about to narrate bears.

One day, a couple of weeks ago, while at work in the carpenter's shop, where he and I are employed, happening to glance round in his direction (the officer was away at the other end of the shop) I saw Whitehead kneeling on the floor gathering something like salt off a board and putting the stuff into his mouth. The stuff was crushed glass. I went over to him, and dropping on my knees beside him caught him by the shoulder and asked him what he was eating glass for. He looked at me with the pitiful, dazed stare that is habitual to him now, and said, 'What, what!' I picked up some of the fragments that he had dropped, and again asked him, 'What do you mean by eating this glass; don't you know it will kill you?'. He replied in a dull, listless way, 'A pound of it would do you no harm', and then kept repeating in answer to all my questions, 'A pound of it would do you no harm.' With my handkerchief I dusted away the fragments before him and searched round his bench for more glass. Finding some more I threw it out of the window. All this only occupied a few minutes and, luckily for me, my 'flagrant violation of the prison rules' was unobserved by the officer. Had I been seen I would have been visited with a term of bread and water punishment. Just think of it – a whispered word of sympathy to this poor fellow – a single word spoken with a view to prevent him killing himself, and I would receive as severe a punishment as the authorities here inflict on habitual criminals for thieving. And yet here in England they go into hysterics over the horrors and brutality of Siberia and ring the changes on the humanity of the English prison system... The truth is that as far as a refined system of cruelty is concerned there is nothing on God's earth to-day to compare with the treatment which we Irish prisoners have been receiving at the hands of the English Government.

... Yours, H. H. Wilson

5

Mr. Patrick Jordan,
Strabane,
Co. Tyrone
Portland Prison,   December 21st 1897

My Dear Paddy,
... Yes, fifteen years is a dreadful long time sure enough, but the slow going days and hours of it never seemed to drag along as slowly as now. How I am longing for it to end! Longing – longing. Counting every moment and hour of the time as it passes – all the while longing and wishing May [the proposed date of his release] were here...

Afftly.

H. H. W.

6

Letter to Alfred Clarke, 1898

... I had a letter from Mrs. –, and was a good deal amused with her idea that the life I was living in here was something like that of a Carthusian saint or a 'Rapt Culdee'. Bless the woman's soul! That would never do at all. When a mortal man feels in all his bitterness what it is to have the delicate curves and tender angles of his human nature rubbed up and currycombed against the grain, then is not the time to 'rub salt in' from within by interior nig-nag and self-inflicted worry. Why, man alive, had I set to work on those lines, endeavouring to cultivate a lackadaisical tone of mind, my wits would have been gone years and years ago. No. Clinch your teeth hard and never say die.

Keep your thoughts off yourself all you can.

No mooning or brown studies.

Guard your self-respect (if you lost that you'd lose the backbone of your manhood).

Keep your eyes wide open and don't bang your head against the wall.

These and a few others, which the deferential regard my prison pen has for The Rules prevent me from mentioning here, are 'The Golden Rules of Life for a Long Sentence Prisoner,' that might be found hung up in my cell had I any say in the furnishing of it.

…Yours, H. H. W.

Personal

i 1899-1901

7

5 St Anthony's Road,
Kilmainham,
Dublin,
26 March '99

Dear Kattie,

I haven't heard a single word from Limerick since I left and of course I am wishing to hear, but Uncle John being too busy as he is and above all not having that great office yet ready in the town hall (where he promises to do extraordinary things in the letter-writing line) has a good excuse for not writing to me and so I – if I wanted to make an excuse for writing to you – have one to hand in this without any hunting around for it. Well now. Will you tell me how you all are – how Uncle John is getting on and what was the result of his letter about the Bishop and the St John's Hospital and how the St Patrick's Ball came off and how you and Madge and Eileen enjoyed it. The walks you take out the Mechanic's Institute way – or rather "ways" – for I really believe there most be more than one way of reaching that place. If Ag gives tea – or rather knows how to make tea – to Uncle John with the Variations? Lollie was very ill when I left and I hope she has got all right again. Will you tell her and Gran and your mother that I ask to be remembered to them in the warmest way? Also to Carrie and Laura, Annie and Nora and Ned. To every one of your happy family. You can have no idea how delightfully pleasant my last visit in particular was. Indeed I didn't quite realize that myself till it drew to an end. After coming to Dublin I left for England and spent some days with some old and very particular friends of mine – whom John also knows. It was a pleasant enough time but not at all to be compared to my experience with you in Limerick, Upon my word I felt just as much at home in your home as I do here in our own.

I got Dalton [O'Connor's] photo from himself – and nothing but the photo – this morning. He appears to have got very fat. I forgot to mention to John when I was writing yesterday that Burton is coming to Dublin tomorrow. I have asked him to stay with us. He only intends remaining in Dublin for a week and will go to the West then after which he says he will go back to America.

I wonder do you like short letters or long-winded ones. When I get started in a letter I – like the part in "Brook" – or rather like the Brook itself – I am apt to "go on forever". You may perhaps not like that sort of letter so I had better conclude. Hoping you keep well and feel stronger. Believe me Dear Kattie,

Your Very Sincere Friend,

Thos. J. Clarke

P. S. I have stupidly forgot to say I only returned from London yesterday and I am – like all at home here – quite well.

8

5 St Anthony's Road,
Kilmainham,
Dublin,
10th April '99

Dear Katty,

I am going to give a lecture here in a couple of weeks on "Prison Life"- 'tis to be hoped I wont make as sad a mess of it as I did when I attempted to speak that night in Limerick[2].

Thos. J. Clarke

9

5 St Anthony's Road,
Kilmainham,
Dublin,
26th April '99

Dear Katty,

The lecture came off all right and was a most decided success. Some of my own particular friends who were present and whose opinion on the matter I could rely upon as worth something were hardly more delighted than amazed at the story. My great trouble in putting it together was what to omit for I had such a stock of material to work out of that had it been required I might, since I got started, "go on forever". Ever since I got your letter I was hard at work on the thing and you must pardon my delay in not answering till now.

    Your very sincere friend, T. J. Clarke

10

5 St Anthony's Road,
Kilmainham,
Dublin,
4th May '99

Dear Katty,

I find myself with a spare half hour just now and must write or Heaven only knows when I would have another such chance. I am out every day now "on the warpath" after that clerkship – flying hither and thither through the South Co. Dublin attending to everything that must be attended to and on the whole I think myself and friends have been fairly successful. Popular opinion is strong – very strong for me, but these so-called Nationalists on the Board of Guardians are, for the most part, unprincipled, I am afraid and need to be very carefully looked after or they'll play the "duck" on me. Recognising this I am bound to work for all I am worth now that I am once into the thing. Uncle John's Resolution from the Limerick Corporation was a grand hit for me and I am not going to say how thankful I am to him for it. But enough of all that bothersome business...

    Your sincere friend,
    Thos. J. Clarke

11

5 St Anthony's Road,
Kilmainham,
Dublin,
21st May, '99

Dear Kattie,

I won't go into a long rigmarole to excuse myself for not being more punctual for the truth is I find the days now not half long enough to do the work I must do if I am to be successful in this fight I am making – for instance I left our house yesterday morning about nine and didn't get back till 3 this morning and I was up at 7 again and off at ten after reading up several acts of Parliament in the meantime. I am reading up everything bearing upon the duties of a clerk of the union so that if I do get the job I will be able to know my way about without depending on others – there now! Will you acquit me of neglect in not answering your letter sooner?

…The banks and the hedges and the country all round Limerick must surely be looking lovely just now – I wish I was there instead of flying round on the war path and reading ninety acts of Parliament. Thank Madge for me will you? Say I am quite flattered picturing her down on her knees praying to Heaven to put me in the Union. If I win – as there seems every prospect of – I'll always swear to the efficiency of Madge's prayers. But in the meantime convey my sincere thanks to her for the kind wishes…Oh yes I forgot when writing to Uncle J – to mention I am going to have a meeting in Dundrum on Sunday and another in Bray on the day following. The election comes off on Wednesday week – tell him will you?

I remain my Dear Kattie yours etc,

T. J. Clarke

12
5 St Anthony's Road,
Kilmainham,
Dublin,
5th June, '99

Dear Kattie,
It is surely time to acknowledge your last long "newsy" letter, but you know the circumstances that kept my hands full of work that I had to do unless I would have now to be upbraiding myself that I lost the fight through my own neglect. You know long before this that I lost. In fact I was badly beaten but as I have just said I have the satisfaction – such as it is – of knowing I did my level best to win and my friends did far more than I could expect to help me. The news in your last letter that John was coming up on Sunday was indeed a pleasant surprise. I knew what it meant and I wasn't disappointed. He made by far and away the best speech for me that was made during the campaign. When I set out to get the position I believed that if public opinion could be brought to bear upon the Guardians it would compel them to vote for me. This is where I was out in reckoning for we had public opinion right through the whole district running strong in my favour but the black-guards of Guardians quietly defied it. But they haven't heard the last of it. You'll be saying "Wish to goodness I had heard the last of the tiresome business". Well I am not going to say another word about it more.
    Your very sincere friend,
    T. J. Clarke

13

5 St Anthony's Road,
Kilmainham,
Dublin,
10th June, '99

Dear Kattie,

My mother was the least disappointed of any of us for we carefully kept all knowledge of the election from her til a few days after it was over. Our mother is as simple-minded and guileless as a child and as easy to deceive.

I am in first class health and now that I am free from that cursed election am able to indulge myself in long country walks and it is indeed glorious weather for strolling through the country. You must surely be looking forward with longing to Kilkee. If it lies in my power (I'll explain to John what I mean by that) I'll be there.

Your very sincere friend,

Thomas J. Clarke

14

5 St Anthony's Road,
Kilmainham,
Dublin,
31st July, '99

My Dear Kattie,

It is not much more than a week since I left Kilkee and the pleasure I had there but it seems months. Remembering my promise about writing I have been looking out all the time for this date – when you'd be back at home again – and I'd be getting a letter.

Now my dear girl how are you? Do you feel anything stronger than when you went down? You'll tell me all about yourself and how you got on after I left. Did you again try the bathing and if so with what result and be sure and tell me this also did you keep up your reputation as a good early riser – someway I'd like to think you didn't – since I wasn't there to share in the pleasures of the early morning walks. You won't have forgotten them, will you? or our cliff-climbing and hill-climbing… companionship? Kattie I can't. Often and often since returning home I have wished to be back in Kilkee and sure I might as well have been there the whole time since my London friends have not yet arrived and will not arrive till the end of this week…Of course you must affectionately remember me to Madge and to Eileen and Ag and our old friend the <u>detective</u>. You know who I mean. If she attempts quizzing you threaten her with that finger – she's very sensitive at being accused in that way. 'Twas a case of taking the bull by the horns and I must say was far more effective than I should have imagined.

…I am putting things in shape for my American trip – writing any amount of letters; that has kept me rather busy since I came home. My mother and sister are well and are now quite reconciled to my going over to America. I'll be writing to John again shortly. If he asks tell him I have not yet heard from Devoy.

With best wishes alone to my Dear Kattie, Believe me ever Yours, Tom

———————————

15
5 St Anthony's Road,
Kilmainham,
Dublin,
3rd August, '99

My Dear Kattie,
I only wish you could have heard all the nice things I whispered to myself about you when I opened and read your letter – and wrote it too so soon after your return. Of course you must know how delight-fully pleased you can make me now with such a letter. Why, I read and re-read it over and over again. It must I am sure seem strange to start addressing me by the "dear" name. To me it does seem strange <u>now</u> that it is you using it – but it <u>does</u> seem very pleasant.

So you felt lonesome too and lost your good reputation as an early riser! Do you know I am selfish enough to take considerable pleasure in the thought that it was so. Still Kattie I don't think you can feel as lonely and uneasy as I have.

I am pleased to hear from you that you are looking healthy after Kilkee – that's good. Mind, you must take as many walks in the open air these fine warm mornings as you can get. You are too much indoors and nothing I believe will strengthen you like the fresh air. I'm not near to hand to you or I would have added "especially the morning air" – that I know would do me good.

Do you know I am writing this and every one here is in bed hours ago – 'tis almost one o'clock. I have been pegging away with the pen all day writing over to America – tearing off letter after letter. I haven't yet heard from Devoy and I am feeling a bit anxious at the delay but have determined to write to the other people anyway.

About missing that mass I say I wish to God I had the same companion by my side out in a country road every Sunday in the summer and I'd let who liked to go to Church.

Every one here is well so I'll conclude with a "Good night" and love to my dear Kattie,

Ever yours, Tom

16
5 St Anthony's Road,
Kilmainham,
Saturday night,
August 1899

My Dear Kattie,
You have seen the letter I got from Devoy. I sent it to John and told him to slip it to you. Oh Kattie I never anticipated such a decision on the part of the "Bosses" on the other side. I was living in a fool's paradise all the while for I took it for granted those people would willingly, enthusiastically co-operate as they co-operated with John to make a lecturing tour

a success for me. I built everything upon that tour – hopes, plans and everything had that at the bottom of them – 'twas the groundwork for all – but alas hopes and plans and fairy castles and myself are knocked smash in a moment by that precious New York letter.

When I read that letter and analyzed what it meant – Kattie my first thought was about you and thank goodness I am strong enough to act fair and square with you no matter what the cost to myself may be. I have told your uncle just how things stand between you and I and told him I was going to write to you tonight and explain what that letter means for me.

I took it for granted I would go on a lecturing tour and that that tour would be successful. On the strength of that I built my hopes of having a home and the means that would gratify my going down to see you on my return and ask you to give me your hand and leave your own home. But now Kattie you must think over what I am going to say and decide for yourself and for me – no, no, only for yourself. That lecturing tour being knocked on the head my future is uncertain. I shall have to go to America and get employment of some sort – maybe I shall have to begin at the bottom rung of the ladder to knock out a living for myself and then depending upon me and God in Heaven only knows when I shall be able to get firmly upon my legs.

Recollect you have given me no promise; from my point of view you are now as free as if you had never seen me at all – free if you so wish it to stop writing to me even. But Kattie, my darling, I love you and I am cut to the heart and wretched[3].

Tom

17
Dublin,
8th August '99

My Dear Kattie,
God bless you for this brave loving letter – 'tis but a few moments ago that I got it – But I'm happy now. Fate may do its worst, my Kattie's

heart is safe in my own keeping for good and all now and I can feel the worst and feel confident that I'll succeed. After all, now that I think the prospect for me is not by any means so dark – oh yes I am happy and stronger.

You have no idea I think what it cost me to write that last letter to you – it wrung my heart lest you might misunderstand me or that understanding me you would do what I apparently wished you to do. But Kattie, I'll tell you now, I dreaded your answer – dreaded you would be wise but in my heart of hearts I had hopes you would do and say just what you have. God bless you for it my brave girl.

I'll be starting for America about the middle of the month. I haven't yet found the exact date – when I do you'll hear it at once and as I told you I'm not going to leave without seeing you again. You say you wish I was down there with you till you could talk to me about everything. Oh yes, I'll echo that wish, were I down there beside you or you here beside me now, time wouldn't hang heavily on my hands then.

My sisters and myself are going out tomorrow with them (the London friends). Yesterday we were all out at Howth –'Tis a fraud and not to be spoken of in the same voice as Kilkee but I'm thinking it might be a nice enough place if…Kattie was there with me.

My mother and sister know nothing about Devoy's letter yet. Only John and you were in the secret – but I will tell them now.

With fondest love to you my Darling, Believe me yours,

Tom

———————————

18
Dublin,
August 17th '99

My Dear Kattie,
…My dear girl I am very sorry and annoyed too that Miss Madge goes for you with her "chaff" and that Uncle J. helps her too. I wrote to him yesterday and reminded him he had given me a promise not to go at you in that way and was not to countenance any one else trying it. But

I suppose the pleasure was too much to resist the temptation. God knows Madge is a hard enough hitter and a biting tease when she sets herself out to give me "a bad quarter of an hour", without any assistance from that other master hand Uncle John. It isn't fair and it isn't right. So you think Ag knows more than we thought – Perhaps she does. Anyhow Ag is a good girl and I can't forget how considerate we found her at times. But as far as Ginger's head is concerned – No Kattie – that's your secret and mine. Anyhow as long as she doesn't tease you and I think poor Ag won't do that since it doesn't matter whether she knows or whether she doesn't. I am glad to hear such a good account of the detective. Has she got quite strong again? That's right about you doing all the bathing you can. Keep it up Kattie as often as you can and to the strolls out the country roads. Wouldn't I like to be there with you tho'. We had a nice day in Bray – took a waggonette and drove around some of the beauty places of Wicklow. Bray and district is ever so much a nicer place than Howth, but Kilkee for me and you know why. Yes I'll easily be ready for America by the middle of next month. Did I tell you my sister Maria was going out with me?

With love, your Tom

19

5 St Anthony's Road,
Kilmainham,
Dublin,
27th August, '99

My Dear Kattie,

I have purposely delayed this time – reason why, I got word on Friday that Egan wanted to see me very particularly over some situation that is about to become vacant under the Dublin Corporation. It wasn't till this morning that I was able to meet him and I learnt from him that he had been sent by John Clancy to ask me if I would accept the super-intendentship of the abattoir salary starting at £150 a year with free house, garden, coal and gas. If "yes" then he would make all the neces-

sary arrangements so that I would have nothing to do but step into it.
And the matter would be decided within a month.

I sent him back word that I was making arrangements to leave for
America by 21st Sept but had not yet taken the passage ticket and
would stay my hand sending for that for a couple of weeks and no
harm could come of it to me since I could then go on as I intended
on 21st if nothing came of that abattoir job.

Clancy has no doubt at all over my getting the job (he is chairman
of the committee) and neither has Egan and I know myself if it comes
to a question of voting in open council few of the corporation <u>dare</u> do
otherwise than vote for me – 'tis a different case here to what it was in
Rathdown, but unfortunately it isn't near as good a job. There now
that's what I wanted to have to tell you – what do you think? I am
delighted at the idea that I may not after all have to go to America, still
I am – and will keep myself – quite prepared to carry out my original
plan. There now! That's enough over that. Now to your own letter. I
am very glad Uncle J. the rogue didn't manage to make you admit
<u>anything</u> at all. He could then make it out you did wrong to complain
while now I can go at him and make him out wrong if he goes at you
again. If we could only keep him to order I fancy Madge would not
bother you much…Ludwig – of whom I heard a great deal in
Limerick – was in Dublin last week. I took my sisters to hear him and
we got a splendid treat. He deserves all that I had heard of his singing.
But he had poor houses. The Ancient Concert Room wasn't more than
half filled. If I were to pick out which of his songs and singing pleased
me best I would say "God save Ireland". Good lord how he did thunder that out and what feeling he threw into it. Since I was a schoolboy
I can only recollect tears flowing from me once – that was when I
heard of my father's death in Portland[4]. Ludwig dragged them out of
me once again in singing "General Monroe" – the pathos he put into
portions of that was marvellous. But 'tis disgraceful to find such a singer
and of such songs so badly patronised by Irishmen in Dublin.

With love, always yours, Tom.

20
Dublin,
1st Sept 1899

My Dear Kattie,
Very little has transpired in connection with that business since I wrote you last. But in next Monday's meeting of the Corporation there will be a motion to dismiss the present fellow (who has been guilty of swindling) brought in by Clancy who will hand in a report from the Markets committee that will pave the way for me. I am doing nothing at all in connection with the matter and I won't. These "friends" have the giving of the job and can give it to whom they chose. If they are really in earnest in their postulations and promises no need for me to run after the job. See Tuesday's papers they'll tell you what will really have been done over the matter.

I am engaged still, seeing to my arrangements for going to America so that even if this other Corporation job comes to nothing it will make very little difference to me. Perhaps there would be virtue in a four leaved shamrock just now. Still I must confess I'd rather be looking for it with you Kattie and see you find it for me than get it with the pope's blessing. That may perhaps sound a wee bit irreverent. I can't help it – 'tis time. Anyway I have your good wishes and I have more than that haven't I my girl? And 'tis more to me than all the four leaved shamrocks in creation. Don't you get worrying yourself by expressing anything you would be likely to say in your letters would make me hold back answering your letter – NO! Haven't I faith in you Kattie. Don't you know that. And don't I know you have faith in me. Can you realize all that means to me – the encouragement and strength it means to enable me to face with a light heart the new work that I may have to fall in struggling to get upon my legs. There now! That's in your own private ear as it were – so don't fear I am going to misunderstand my Kattie

Fondest love to yourself always,

Tom

21
Dublin,
Sept 5th 1899

My Dear Kattie,

I went out to Egan's yesterday to find out what had been done about that affair at Monday's meeting of the Corporation and it turns out that nothing was done and nothing was to be done – either I misunderstood Egan or he misunderstood Clancy for the affair was to be decided or rather is to be decided (that is the job to be vacant) at a Committee meeting of the whole house when Clancy will submit his report for adoption or rejection. This meeting to take place today or tomorrow, Egan not being sure which. But it comes off for certain this week – so he says – and if it does I shall then know definitely whether or no I leave for the States on the 21st.

The "Presentation Committee" I understand are quite satisfied they are going to have the thing a success. One of them was telling me yesterday that at last meeting of the Committee quite a number of young city lads who had got wind of the thing (you know of course it is private) came up to the room and asked to be allowed to show what they thought of so & so some throwing down a shilling some a half a crown and so on. I forgot to mention that to John when I was writing to him but I feel greatly pleased about the affair. It betokens a good spirit in some of the rising generation for these fellows are rebels. John will be greatly pleased over this too….

Does he or Madge ever "go" for you now Kattie? I hope not.

I am very glad you are doing a fair share of boating – that's right. Do you feel anything stronger after the summer sun and exercise you are giving yourself in the open? Of course you know the most interesting portions of your letters are those where you tell me of <u>yourself</u> and I fear you wouldn't believe me if I told you how much you are in my thoughts….

Of course soon as I ever hear anything definite about that superintendership you'll get the first word. I trust it may be right. If so, ah Kattie then…but let's wait.

Trusting you are in good health and wish love and best wishes to my dear girl from Tom

---

22
Dublin,
Sept 9th 1899

My Dear Kattie,
I have just been sorting out my letters and arranging my papers and I was quite astounded to find that I have such a big packet made up of letters that (after I had satisfied myself with reading when I got them) I marked with the word "Kathleen" on the cover of the envelope and put part under lock and key in the little cabinet where certain other treasures – of a different kind of course – are kept. Yes Kattie, they are all here from the first one to the last and I am getting them ready to take with me across the Atlantic. I wonder if you are able to realize just all that they mean to me. Yes, I think you can. Your womanly heart can picture it all… I shall start for Limerick on Monday by the mid-day train, but I'm thinking my sister ought to remain here till next day for if she were to go on Monday it might inconvenience the family to put us both up and of course I want to stop at 26 for if I had no other reason I want to see you as much as I can in the short time that I will be in Limerick. You see if my sister went down on Monday and had to put up at a hotel I would have to stop at the hotel too and that for me would never do at all. Now all this is between you and I and I want you to drop me a line soon as you get this telling me (in the same strict confidence) whether there is any room to spare for a second stranger (!). If not I can easily arrange for her to come down on the Tuesday so as to leave with me that night for Queenstown. I told you in my last that we sail on the 27th didn't I?

The presentation takes place on Saturday evening and there is to be a banquet and speechmaking (oh God, I can never forget the awful fish

I made of my Limerick speech at the presentation of the Freedom. Do you know I firmly believe you being there had something to do with that). I have no doubt but I shall be able to give a good account of myself at the Saturday night business. But somehow or another if you were there present I'd be almost certain to play the wooden-headed duffer again. My very anxiety <u>not</u> to make a "mug" of myself and my thoughts wondering off after where my heart had gone would end in the same disastrous way – as far as the speechmaking goes.

With fond love from Tom

23

Dublin,
Monday Morning

My Dear Kattie,

I am rather disquieted about that Clancy thing. I find now it wasn't to be discussed till last Saturday and up to the present I have not got the result. I made it a point to see Egan on Friday and it was then I got this last version. He himself was in town with Mrs Egan on Saturday but he didn't see me, but is to turn up this morning when I perhaps may get something definite that will enable me to say whether the thing is bogus or otherwise. You can understand how unsettled and anxious I feel over the thing seeing that it is drawing so near to the time that I have decided to start for America. Soon as I hear anything definite about the matter I'll let you know instantly.

I am in A1 and with my sister Maria spent a nice day out at James Stephens yesterday. This is Stephens the old Fenian Chief Centre[5]. We started out from Dublin two brakes full of friends to pick up Stephens and his family at Blackrock and go off pic-nicking but it kept steadily raining all morning and so we changed our plans and instead of getting ourselves completely drenched we all (upwards of twenty) remained for the greater part of the day, eating and singing and drinking and reciting during the remainder of the day. I enjoyed the singing and playing exceedingly but contributed nothing towards that part of the programme but did my own share of eating chicken and sandwiches and drinking all description of minerals. Of course we had a good number of ladies, old and young and midway but I didn't find any of them specially attractive and so whiled away a good portion of the time talking politics or rubbish to one or two old frail gents who interested or amused me. Faith, I'm thinking if you had been there Kattie (and I caught myself wishing that often enough yesterday) that wouldn't have been the story I would have to tell.

Best wishes to all and to yourself with fondest love my Kattie. Your Tom

---

24
5, St Anthony's Rd,
Kilmainham,
Dublin,
Sept 15th 1899

My Dear Kattie,

I got your letter this morning and of course felt the usual thrill of pleasure run through me when I recognised the handwriting on the envelope.

Answering your question about "that business" – 'tis settled for the time being. No action can be taken on the matter so the Town Clerk tells Clancy, till a couple of lawsuits that have a bearing upon the present suspended superintendent, are settled. So I am just after taking a passage ticket for myself and another for Maria to sail by the "Severin" of the Cunard line on 27th inst from Queenstown. But Clancy tells Egan and some of my other friends here that when that job becomes vacant, and he says it will for certain when the lawsuits are decided next month or the month after, it will be there for me if I will come back for it. But I won't depend too much upon that. I'll strike out when I get across to America just as if I was sure I hadn't a ghost of a chance of anything turning up for me here.

To my own Kathleen with fondest love from Tom

25

The Vanderbilt [Hotel],
New York,
7th Oct 1899,

My Dear Kattie,

Just one wee word to tell you I have arrived safe and well yesterday evening – Maria ditto and beyond that I have nothing in the shape of news except indeed I aim to go and tell you of the lively interest my sister Maria takes in a recent discovery she has made – sitting on deck with her the day after we left Queenstown she abruptly asks in the most unconcerned way "Will you settle down in Limerick, Tommy?". For the moment I didn't understand the drift of her question I replied "Why no – what makes you ask ?" "Why", said she, "aren't you in love with Kathleen?" "Yes and Kattie and I understand each other and the sooner I get straight and find us a home the sooner I'll have Kattie. But who told about me and Kattie?" "Och sure a fool could see it – but how peculiar it is – you who used to hate the girls – tell me how it came about? Was it at Kilkee?" and she wound up with "Well Kathleen is my favourite too" and then she went on to praise your good parts my lady and ended by declaring she admired your straight forwardness when she wanted you to go into the church and pray – you bluntly told her you couldn't do long prayers etc. I don't know what you'll think of all that but I felt like flinging my arms around Maria and hugging her.

I am going to write to Uncle J by this mail also but you come first. I wonder would he feel hurt to be put in the second place now? No. I'm not going to tell him of it.

…fondest love for yourself my Dear Kattie, Believe me Tom

26
109 West 94th Street,
New York City,
Monday Nov 5th 1899

My Dear Kattie,

I have delayed answering several days – Reason why:– I wanted to be able to give you something definite as to future prospects and held back writing from day to day hoping that I would by this time have been able to forecast the future with some degree of certainty. But up to the present I can't do so and so although I have but little news now that I couldn't have told you two or three days ago I have sat myself down to write knowing that, news or no news, my Kattie has a right to hear from me and now as to how I am getting on. I have taken a flat – people here in New York don't live in houses all by themselves – they live in <u>flats</u> – that is the houses are specifically built so as to have every accommodation for a family on each landing. Well, I have taken one of these and Maria has been in her glory going round getting in the things to furnish it.

…I find the lecturing tour that John had thought possible is just now out of the question. The Boer War is occupying every one's thoughts around here and even without that I don't know that a lecturing tour could have been managed[6]. I needn't go on and explain the reasons for thinking that – enough to state the fact.

There are several schemes on foot with a view to put me into suitable employment. The one that I regard with the most favour is this: Start a good shoe store in a good part of the city by means of a capital that will be raised by raising shares – these shares to be sold to members of the Irish Organization to which I belonged – that is sold to such of them as take an interest in me and wish to show it in a practical way. Well with money raised in that way the shoe store to be started and given into my charge to "run" it under such conditions that if the business turns out a success in my hands I will have the option of buying

back the shares from those who put money into it and so getting
ownership of the concern

I regard this scheme with favour because there is nothing of the
"begging hat" about it. The people who will put their two or five or
ten dollars (as the case may be) into it will get it back according as I
make the business pay. This scheme will take a couple of months to
work up and I see I have to calculate upon a certain amount of hostility on the quiet from "Friends" who are not satisfied unless I become
a "party man" and allow myself to be made a tool of by such "friends".

In the meantime I have been going around a great deal hunting up
folks who would have influence enough to make an opening for me
into some decent job. And I must say I have a good number of honest
well intentioned friends here who will stand by me till I am securely
fixed in some business or another – spite of the numbers of our politicians and party men.

…Now let me turn to your own letter. I won't attempt to tell you
what pleasure the reading and re-reading of this letter gives me. You'll
have to think of the happy hours I spent with you – the whispered
words in your ear that told you how much you are to me and you'll
know how much pleasure a letter of yours my girl is to me. Remember
too that I can't now think of the future in any shape or form but you
are in the picture. Just because it is so I feel uneasy and unsettled till I
can see just how things are going to shape themselves here for me till
I can, well have you with me…Never mind Uncle J's teasing of you –
that's a bad habit that he would do well to cure himself of, teasing
people. Just you tell him, if he talks in that way about you enjoying
yourself at dancing or other amusement simply because you have given
me your love and your promise.

I am glad indeed that you like the present. The chief fault I find to
it is that it is not half good enough for you. But wait – not for long I
hope – I hope to be able to satisfy myself when I shall be getting that
– ring. I'd like to see your face now after reading that. I know you have
that lovely blush I have seen at times on it. But Kattie don't forget
whenever you get your photo taken send me one. Maria has any

amount of photos of one kind or another hanging round the sitting room here or tricking out the mantle piece or shelves. Yours I don't want for that. When I am not here it would be locked up in my writing desk and only taken out when I'm alone.

Good Bye Dear Kattie with fondest love always,

Your Tom.

27

109 West 94th Street,
New York City,
Saturday 11th Nov '99,
12.15 p. m.

My Dear Kattie,

...I have been in real good humour all day since I got your unexpected letter – twas a delightful surprise and I have been telling myself at intervals ever since I received it that "Kattie's a brick" – not mind you that I required proof of that kind to assure me of the fact. But Kattie if you love me don't let this letter be the last of its kind to take me by surprise.

I didn't know Maria had told you <u>that.</u> But tis true. In a crude sort of a way didn't I tell you so. I never made the confession to any woman that I made to your ear – I couldn't.

You wonder how it came that I took to you. Oh I'll tell you that. I couldn't help it. Do you recollect the morning in the dining room I astonished you by tossing your hair. That was done on the impulse and my own astonishment was far greater than your own. Even yet when I think of it I can't understand how it came about. I couldn't help it. But I think it was that morning I got a clutch on hope. The hug and kiss was lost sight of in my lady's concern about her hair being tossed and that gave me heart and so I got yours and that's all I care about[7].

Now Kattie since I last wrote about a week ago things are brightening up for me and before very long I think I shall be opening a shoe business here in New York. I attend meetings in various parts of New York and Brooklyn almost every night and address those present. It rouses the greatest enthusiasm amongst the great majority of them and this is being felt by the folks who are blocking the way to anything being done that would be accepted by me – for some folks here would like to see me stranded so that they could step in and assist me on conditions of owning my soul and making a tool of me – but they'll never succeed in that.

Good night. Best love my darling. Believe me your Tom

───────────────

28
109 West 94th Street,
New York City,
28th Nov 1899

My Dear Kattie,

I got the photos. They are both good ones and I am delighted to have them. Somehow or another you seem close to me when I look at either of them and Kattie, I look at them often. They came yesterday morning as we were at breakfast (Dalton[8] who had been attending a meeting here in New York had stopped the night with us) so of course I wasn't going to "expose my hand" by opening the packet there and then. But the breakfast as far as I was concerned had no further attraction for me and after a few minutes I came through into the front room and carefully opened it had a good look and then locked them away. I had scarcely done so when Maria came in – "Tommy will you let me see the photo? Oh do!" She knew by the packet it was photos and she knows your handwriting and always laughs when she hands me your letters. Well, I showed her one, the front view one. She examined it and said "Its not a good one of her. Kathleen is better looking than the picture makes her". But as I have said I think they both are good pictures whether or not my imagination supplies what Maria misses is another thing. Anyhow I shall be quite satisfied with them till I get the reality. Well I left Dalton at the breakfast table and he came into the front room shortly after Maria and we got chatting over one or two things and he enquired when I had heard from Daly? I told him and his next question with a quizzical look on that old ecclesiastical face of his was "How is Kathleen?" Just fancy that wide awake old codger was taking notes and seeing things that evening he was in Limerick that I thought nobody had seen or could see. Upon my word I never remember being more surprised in my life than when he fired that question at me. But I pulled an innocent face and told him Katty and Madge and Eileen and the rest of the family were just as much when I last heard from Limerick. He knew better than push his nose further into my business.

…Since I started the preceding paragraph the night before last something has happened that I must tell you about. I have started work as a pattern maker in a Foundry. I got what I asked $2^1/2$ dollars a day or fifteen dollars (£3) a week. I wanted to get a foothold in the place and went in as an "improver" believing that before very long I shall be drawing full wages which will be 21 dollars a week. I was at work yesterday and got along all right. Today is a holiday here "Thanksgiving" so I was free and spent most of the day hunting round for some tools that I must have – very small. I am at present also getting another 15 dollars a week for clerical work keeping books etc that I am able to do after hours. This means one hour or two extra work every night. So this means that I have made a start. At the present time I am earning the equivalent of £6 English money per week.

Very well. I have sent for my brother as I am fearful he may be dragged off by the English to fight against the Boers. In a few weeks more I'll send for my mother and other sister and in the course of a few months hope to be in a position to start my sisters in some kind of business. My brother of course will be able to strike out for himself almost as soon as he lands but in any case I'll stand by him till he gets on his legs. If I only keep health and strength I now see a pretty clear way of getting along and feeling quite independent and I daresay you can understand how satisfied and pleased I feel about it.

…One of the days whilst I was at work Maria shifted down to a fresh house so as to be more convenient for my work. I work at 23rd St and we live now at 363 West 36 St so you will address your letters to that number now. I like the place ever so much better than the other house – 'tis more compact and homelike.

With love to yourself Kattie from Tom

29

363 West 36 St,
New York City,
Christmas Eve,
1899

My Dear Kattie,

…Now I am all right – quite myself again – but still busy, very busy, working for the past 9 or ten days from early morning (I get up at $^1/_2$ past five) until sometimes 2 in the morning. I have got to bed no night this week sooner than 1 o'clock.

…I'm sorry to hear you still are not feeling very well. If wishes had any virtue to make you quite well, quite well and happy, you would be Kattie for I often wish and hope regarding you. Perhaps this American climate will knock the trouble on the head and quite restore you. Some people who came out here – one to my own knowledge – as recognized invalids (which you are far from being) have got strong and healthy. I have great hopes that it will work in the same way in your case. This American climate suits some people – perhaps most people – better than the damp Irish climate. Tell me though are you familiarising yourself to the thought of being here in America? I see now I am going to make out all right here. And I see no reason why I shouldn't have a home and everything else ready for you by the middle of the year. But I'll leave this over till next letter and of course I will have to write to Uncle J and to your mother. But after all you are the all important one, mind you.

We have heard no news from home for the past month or so and we both are feeling very anxious. I sent my brother a passage ticket and some money and can't make out why the delay unless they have grabbed him up for the army. Well if they have and they send him to

Africa he will fight I know, but it <u>won't</u> be for the English.

 With fond love from Tom

30

363 West 36 St,

New York City,

January 9th 1900

My Dear Kattie,

…Well I had better start right here with myself. Here I am sitting here at my desk – tis about $\frac{1}{2}$ past ten – writing by the light of an incandescent gas lamp in the snug first room that Maria grandly calls the "Parlor". Right before me sitting against the pigeon holes of the desk and catching my eye every time I lift my head to a photo – the side face view – or rather three quarter. I never saw any other picture that pleased me as well, except the reality, as does this one of my "Guardian Angel" – my loving Irish girl.

 …well I have told you Katty although in a round about sort of way. Oh how I keep longing and wishing you were here with me! If you were here in New York tonight I'd be trying to induce you to come with me to the priest in the morning. But that opens up the question that I had intended to speak to you now. You are <u>not</u> in New York. At the present time and for perhaps a rather long time I can't – I must not throw up my jobs to go over to Ireland reason why I might – very likely would be – stranded on getting back again. That of course is what I should like to do – that is go over and fetch you back.

 Now there is an alternative. Kattie this <u>for the present </u>is between you and myself and I don't want you to consult any one till you tell me what you yourself think.

 From time to time there are always some friend or acquaintance coming from Ireland to America. Should John and your mother consent would you be equal to venturing yourself alone, so to speak, with some such friend. John would be sure at times to know of old friends coming – in the nice weather of course – say about July and of

course I'll insist – if you come at all in that way or your using whatever is required out of my purse – or should I say "Ours" for the
promise we made each other has fixed all that.

Now tell me what you think of such an idea and what you suppose
Uncle John and your mother will think of such an idea. Perhaps there
is a possibility that Uncle John himself might come over this summer
– he had been talking of coming some months ago, <u>that</u> would simplify
the whole thing for us.

Of course later on after hearing from you and finding you are willing to risk (if you consider it risk) coming alone. I'll broach the matter
to your uncle and mother. I'm laying the master plan before you and I
know you'll be just as frank. You are always frank to me Kattie and I'm
pleased indeed to know it.

After a delay of a couple of months we have heard from Dublin. My
brother won't come out now. He has a good job he says under the
Corporation and the scare about being drafted off to fight the Boers
has passed over and he appears to be no longer afraid.

…with fondest love for yourself,

From your Tom.

31
363 West 36 St,
New York City,
February 9th 1900

My Dear Kattie,
I am very much pleased with your last letter, quite jubilant over it. I am
quite satisfied everything is going to go right for us now that I am
certain you see no great difficulty in the way. I don't think there will
be any trouble with Uncle J and I certainly will make a supreme effort
to leave no room in his mind to doubt that what I am wanting no
rational person in this world could possibly disagree with. Since you say
it, I am hugging myself with the belief that your mother will be all
right. I really ought to have spoken to her myself before I left Ireland

but you see 'tis my first experience in that sort of thing and I really didn't know how to go about it. But at the same time I must candidly confess that on the whole I have succeeded remarkably well – that is of course as far as the important person is concerned.

The winter won't last too much longer and the spring will soon slip round and by July I hope to have you here. In the course of the next month I'll write to both your mother and Uncle John. That will allow plenty of time to every one there to reconcile themselves to the thought of parting with you.

…By the way did I mention to you that the Tyrone Ladies Assoc of New York made a great ado over me after I came here and presented me with a life-sized bust (in oil) of me as I was before going to prison. I believe some of the papers had a lengthy account of the affair but I didn't see them. But my own private opinion is that there's precious little resemblance to the original in that picture. All the same Maria has it here in the room. The most conspicuous thing in it perhaps, as it smiles from the easel.

Maud Gonne is here on a lecturing tour – the money she gets to aid the Boers' widows and orphans. She had a splendid meeting in New York and netted 900 dollars and so far as I can judge she is going to be fairly successful in the States altho' she is run by a few private persons, the chief of which is Rocky Mountain O'Brien. Tell John of this it will have some interest for him perhaps. I am sorry to hear he is not well. I hope he'll be all right by the time this reaches Limerick

Your Tom

32

New York City,
Feby 18th 1900

Dear Kattie
…This is Sunday night. Maria is out – away on important business she is. Some friends of hers induced her to join a lady's lodge of Forresters and then they honored (?) her by electing her the secretary – honorary

secretary of course and since then there has been such interminable writing of postal cards and minutes and what not, that poor Maria is as busy in her own way with her secretary's duties as I am with my writing. Oh yes, she's a very busy person indeed these times.

My brother has not returned me the ticket or money I sent him. He says he will hold it on lest things might take a turn to compel him to come out here. Later on – whether he comes or not – I will send for my mother and other sister but I first want you installed in my home. So it will very likely be autumn before I'll bring them on. By that time I may – if things go all right with me – be in a position to start Maria and the other sister in some business. In the meanwhile, of course, I send the people at home enough to ensure their not wanting for anything, besides having left something with them when I was leaving.

…We are going to have a big affair here on 4th March (Emmet Anniversary). Ludwig among others will sing. I am taking Maria and a couple of other friends to it and I am sure it will be thoroughly Irish and thoroughly enjoyable…

I haven't yet written to Uncle J. or your mother, but will very likely in the course of the ensuing week. Och! My good girl if some of my correspondents who expect letters from me and get none only knew that I found time to write punctually and lengthily too, to yourself wouldn't I (perhaps you too) come in for some tall swearing. But "where ignorance is bliss tis a folly to be wise" and certainly they'll remain ignorant as I haven't any particular hankering to enlighten them about the matter.

…With fondest love, best wishes my dear Kattie from your Tom

33
1750 Second Avenue,
New York City,
11th March 1900

My Dear Kattie,
…In a manner I am sorry that you should be feeling unhappy and

anxious over me, but at the same time I must confess to a feeling of pleasurable satisfaction to think I am so much in your thoughts – 'tis flattering and human nature loves flattery from loved ones and loves it all the more when no flattery is intended. Oh no I don't think you a goose for it but I tell myself you are a good warm-hearted and loyal Irish girl.

I'm delighted to know you are keeping so well and I don't by any means share your horror about getting fat – provided of course that you don't get so fat that I won't be able to get my arms around you.

I was off all morning looking at flats to find a more comfortable one than this which is I find in a rather bad neighbourhood. There are any amount of niggers living hereabouts and we Irish as a rule don't care for coming too much into contact with those absurd folks[9]. Maria had been house-hunting all the week and had a list of those that pleased her and ready for me to go and see today. One pleases me well and I'm sure you'll like it too – 'tis a newly-built home with all modern improvements except that the rooms are not steam heated. The locality is good and the station of the elevated railroad is almost at the door so I can be whipped down to my work in almost a $\frac{1}{4}$ of an hour – besides the electric surface runs past the door.

…And so Uncle J was up in Mayo working for John McBride – Bravo. But I'm sorry he wasn't successful. 'Tis disgusting to find how rotten the spirit of our people has become through the teaching of the Parliamentarian moral force man.

…Now my Dear Girl good bye with best wishes and fondest love to you – longing for the day when I can take you in my arms and call you my own Kathleen.

I remain, faithfully, Tom

34
1750 Second Avenue,
New York City,
March 25th 1900

My Dear Kattie,
Just a brief note now to yourself to tell you I have just finished writing to Uncle J and to your mother.

The gist of these letters is simply to ask their consent to your marrying me and to your coming out here to me. I give the reasons that forbid me doing what I'd like to do – that is to go over and fetch you myself. I haven't said I have yet asked your consent but the tone of my letters will give them to understand that I feel no misgivings on that score. So now my dear girl I trust everything will go all right and that you will be here in June or July. I may mention that I told your mother that if she or Uncle J saw no serious objection to your coming I would make the necessary arrangements with you to come about that time – which of course means I'll send you over the necessary cash.

…Of course I will be feeling uneasy and anxious till I hear what they have to say but I know my Dear girl will not delay in giving me word.

With fondest love believe me Dear Kattie, Your Tom.

35
1750 Second Avenue,
New York City,
April 20th 1900

My own Dear Kattie,
How I have longed for this letter expecting of course happier news – and how very disappointed I feel now that I get it and read what you tell me. You had seemed so near to me for the last month or so and now – twelve months quite horrifies me – horrifies me as the prospect of twelve months inside prison walls never did. But if that is the sentence

and the final one why I suppose you and I must try and reconcile ourselves to it. All the same I want to hear what Uncle John has to say; perhaps he is not reasonable, at any rate I'll plead the case earnestly with him and I know you'll do your part to try and get a mitigation of the sentence. You ask me to write you without delay. I am doing so instantly and would have done this even had you not made the request. You also ask me to tell you that I don't mind the delay! Good Lord my girl I can't and I won't tell you that. Not mind the delay! I feel savage and in such a mood that if I went out to attend a meeting that I intended to be at I would go "bald headed" for some of the tricksters likely to be there and so get rid of the wrath I feel. Of course I know I can't justify feeling in this savage mood by reasoning the whole matter out. I haven't tried. I only know that's how I feel and it's the result of the keen disappointment. But Kattie my girl don't for a moment suppose that I in any shape or form lay the least blame on you – quite the reverse. I told you before of the faith I have in you. You have my love and I am quite satisfied yours is mine and that you will be mine sooner or later and this thought comes every now and then to comfort me as I write this to you. Indeed you are wrong in thinking that it was your feeling so sure about them letting you come so soon that influenced me to write and ask them. No, my lady, it wasn't that so you mustn't be blaming yourself undeservedly but what did influence me to write to Uncle J and your mother and say what I have was that I had your assurance that you were willing. And if you can condemn me blaming you for <u>that</u> well wait till I get hold of you and I'll teach you differently.

Uncle John's reasons are flimsy and I'd love to tell him so and will if he gives me such reasons as "where's the need of such hurry?" The answer to that is "where's the need of delay?" and it carries more weight than his "You are young". Yes but you are a woman and not a slip of a schoolgirl. If so how can that tell for delay? No there is nothing in those reasons. Had he said I was objectionable (which I know he would not) <u>that</u> would be a good reason. Had he objected to your coming out alone, that from his point of view (had he taken it) would have some reason to it, but would be knocked on the head by the answer that I would be just as jealous of propriety in the woman I wished to be my wife as any one. But let me pass my soul in patience till I hear from himself.

Good night fond love Kattie, Tom

36

1750 Second Avenue,
New York City,
May 12th 1900

My Dear Kattie,

Your mother's letter and your own came together and I must tell you of this first so as to get it off my mind. My letter to her she says was a surprise in one way and not in another as she knew you and I corresponded and had some kind of an understanding between us and that on getting my letter she spoke to you about it and was considerably surprised to find you're indeed to marry me. She likes me she says but does not like your going to America so far away from her. Besides she wishes me to be more settled than I am (which I can exactly grasp the meaning of) and further stipulates that as she understands my mother and all my family are going to America I must try and get them settled first "and we will talk of Kattie after". That's the gist of the letter and I won't make a single remark on it to you Kattie further than to say it has considerably disappointed me especially in the latter portions of it. In her anxiety for your welfare she appears not to credit me with a sense of duty or honor. But God bless her 'tis anxiety for you that prompts her to say every word she does no matter how harsh it may be to me.

Your own loving letter pleases me tho', as your letters always do, and I know you must feel also disappointed at the turn things have taken. For my own part Kattie I am going to leave the matter to <u>you</u> and I want you to think the matter over and weigh everything your family says to you – letting none of them influence you reasoning that <u>you</u>

<u>yourself</u> cannot approve of and tell me when you will come to me. Your wish will be law to me for you are too dear to me to risk making you unhappy by influencing you to do anything you'd think was wrong. But understand Kattie my future will depend on how you decide. Even now I can fix my family in some little business here. If need be I'll do so right off and take myself off to make or mar another future for myself in the Transvaal. I've a strong hankering during the past month, since I found how your people felt, to go down there.

Uncle John is forgetting himself, or apparently forgetting one and some of my characteristics when he talks of my killing myself with hard work. No I won't. If there was danger of that I'm not such an absolute fool as to continue it. But I'm working as I'm doing because there is a pleasure to me in so doing and because I feel I have it in me to do so. And no matter where I may be or where I have been I must and have did the same. So don't you allow any one to work on your sympathy and generosity by taking the view that you would be in any way responsible for my killing myself with hard work.

…The Tyrone Men's Assoc are to have an excursion and see me up the river shortly and they have me on the arrangement committee which means more work as I believe I have to write up something about it for the papers and they have also appointed me a delegate to the New York "United Irish Societies' Committee". This is work that I could shirk if I felt inclined but I'm not going to and it shows you I won't believe it will kill me. All the same I know I work as hard and energetically as ever a man in New York but as I say it seems rational to me to do so and in a manner I can't help myself – that is my strong point just as "talking" is my weak one.

I'll be anxiously looking forward to hear how you decide Kattie but take time, turn everything over in your mind – that's if you haven't done so already and tell me just what you think and when you will come to me. But don't delay a letter for that. I'm all the time hungering to hear from you and all the time I may say, thinking of you and yearning for you.

With best wishes and love from Tom

37

New York City,
June 8th 1900

My Dear Kattie,

I am feeling a different sort of fellow altogether since I got your letter before the last. How I counted the days till that letter from you with maybe "good news" for me – maybe "bad news" – would be due here. And while waiting how uneasy and unsettled I felt! At times getting in that state that is rare to me…But the letter came and it had nothing but "good news" and I feel – well – I feel life is really worth living after all not only that but I'm thinking there are very few in this big city who feel as satisfied and content as myself for the last couple of days. If I read that letter once, I have read it over a score of times and find keen pleasure in it every time I do so. Just before starting this letter I read yours again and on finishing I said to myself "I only wish I could write Kattie a letter that would give her as much pleasure as this gives me". And when I recollected that you told me in one of your letters a short time ago how sorry you felt that you couldn't make your meaning so plain to me (as you thought) as I did in my letters to you. I had to smile at that. Your letters require no apology on that score. They are as plain and clear to me as any I ever read. And none I ever got, my lady, were anything like so interesting to me. And you know the reason why Kattie. But let me come to your last letter. It arrived the next day after the other and was a delightful surprise and I actually do <u>not</u> object to one extra letter or indeed to such a one seven times a week.

I am delighted to find you have decided for yourself and decided in the way you have – that to me is everything and I'll leave the matter completely in your own hand now and will only say that I'll approve of whatever you do and expect of course that if yielding on secondary points (where they are reasonable) would prevent unpleasantness of any kind that you will yield. For God knows the furthest wish from me is that you or any one of your family would be subject to unpleasantness or worry.

When I hear in your next as to when you expect to be leaving I'll send you a post office order for twenty pounds – or send it in any other way or shape you wish.

…Maria is all right. I haven't room here to tell you what she said when I gave love to her from you. She is A1 and I am in the seventh Heaven of delight,

Yours Tom.

38
1750 Second Avenue,
New York City,
Sunday,
July 22 1900

My Dear Kattie,
Your welcome letter came all right this week and removed the anxiety I had felt that you must surely be sick since I wasn't getting the accustomed letter – I am easy in that sense now – but still anxious in another direction about you. When I think – as I often do – how unsettled and worried you must be at finding yourself alone and opposed (so to speak) to all at home because of me. I can quite understand what an ordeal this means for you and I do not want you my dear girl to distress yourself still more by thinking I won't feel perfectly satisfied with anything you may do to try and get U. J. and the others reconciled to your coming over to me – since I too feel in sore straits over the view they all take of it. But all the same they are wrong in opposing <u>your</u> wish in such a matter. Believe me I am there with you in spirit and would much like to be there in person beside you and say my say with you to them.

…Maria and I did go to that excursion and met any amount of old Friends there – friends we knew in Tyrone – and spent a very pleasant time. We have also been to several other affairs… "The Irish Volunteers Pic Nic" which I didn't much care for, and a pic nic given by the Brooklyn Clan na Gael. This last I did enjoy as there too I dropped across any number of old Friends…

I'm not a bit thankful to miss Madge worrying you with arguefication – for that sort of thing must worry you. But no doubt she is right when she says she doesn't understand you – that to some extent excuses her.

Since writing last I have given up one of my jobs – the hardest one – and hold on in the other which is turning out to be a very good one since I have the opportunities for running some kind of a business on my own hook. The change for the better has taken place in the latter only recently and I can't yet tell exactly what way it will "pan out". But at all events I am assured of a living in it. Tell all the kids I send them my love and also to Ag – that is if you dare mention my name to her, for I suppose she feels angry with me for wanting to take you away from her…

I won't tell you how I am longing for you Kattie and how much of my thoughts are with you. Soon, I hope, I'll have you here and tell you all that and a lot more that I say nothing about in my letters. Goodbye my dear girl with fondest and best love from Tom.

39
1750 Second Avenue,
New York City,
Saturday 4th Aug 1900

My Dear Kattie,
…How I could hug you for that paragraph in your letter! I'll agree to share my trouble, the only trouble that I feel, let me whisper in your ear what it is: I want Kattie to come to me soon – to share everything with her.

Now my Darling you must not be worrying yourself imagining all sorts of things. Above all things don't be imagining that I feel or think about you otherwise than when we parted, or when we were together at Kilkee. Even if you try I question whether you could make me feel angry with you. So don't let the like of that enter your head again.

…Believe me yours for ever,
Tom

40
1750 Second Avenue,
New York City,
Saturday Aug 29th 1900

My Dear Kattie,
…As to Egan's suggestion contained in that letter you sent me. I quite
agree with you and John. It would be silly of me to go over there now
that I have been fairly fixed here on the off chance of getting something better there. I wouldn't for a moment entertain the thought. Of
course if they succeed in having me elected (which I doubt they will)
then of course without any hesitation I'd return to Ireland for such a
position would be better than anything I could hope for here for some
time. That disposes of that subject.
…Of course U. J. is right about waiting to see what the result of the
election will be. But if it goes against me, then Kattie he can't surely
put in any further delay if he is reasonable. The election I suppose will
be decided somewhere about the first of Sept so we don't have long to
wait for that. Anyway I feel very lonely at times in this big city and keep
longing to have you and the happiness it would mean to me were you
at my side. In truth I don't care to go on confessing how much I keep
thinking of you and longing to see you again. You are everything to me
and before everyone to me.
…with fondest love, Tom

41
New York,
Monday Sep 17th 1900

My Dear Kattie,
Just a few brief lines to say that owing to repeated cable-grams – the
last of these received this morning from Dublin – I have decided to sail
tomorrow morn for Ireland. I am not sure of the line but I think it will

be the Cunard that leaves here tomorrow. I'll go by way of Queens-town and go on direct to Dublin as the election for that position comes off on the 28th.

If I am elected, well and good you and I can in that case arrange certain things. If not elected I start back again here immediately and expect you will be ready to come too.

I am risking nothing in going across as I can have either of my old jobs back should I return.

…Fondest love to you,

Tom

42

5 Blessington Place,
Dublin,
Tuesday Morning

My Dear Kattie,

Its over and I feel easy once more and can sit myself down to write you. As I sent John the Telegraph of yesterday evening with result of the election I need say nothing further about it than that I wasn't very much surprised, neither am I much disappointed. Truth to tell I am very little disappointed.

Egan gave me your letter on Saturday but I wanted to see how things would go before I wrote.

I have bound myself to return to New York immediately the election was over should it turn out unfavourably in order to pick up my old job there, consequently I must start <u>not</u> <u>later</u> than Wednesday (of next week). How would that suit you? I'll be down with you on Saturday and can then arrange about everything that needs to be arranged which after all is very little I think now. I had at first thought it might be sensible to leave by Sunday's boat from Queenstown but I see that would not leave a sufficient margin for us. I am sure you have been just in as much suspense over this election business as myself. On the whole I think things have turned out for the best. I left New York with the greatest reluctance and only did so because I felt my friends here (who really have worked night and day) would be placed in a ridiculous position if I failed to be on the spot. I have since seen that I was not quite right in that view. Everything that had to be done could have been done without my presence being necessary. However, the trip across will be as good as a holiday for health sake and can't do harm. Besides, and this mind you was perhaps the strongest lever of all to move me across, it brings me to you and settles the difficulty about you going to America under proper escort.

I am going to hold over everything that I want to say and tell you about until I get beside you and can whisper it in your own ear – and I am longing for that.

...fondest love to yourself my Dear Kattie,

I remain faithfully Tom

43

1750 Second Avenue,

New York,

22nd Oct. 00

My Dear Kattie,

...Maria of course didn't expect me to come by way of Boston and so when I landed in here that morning she became for a moment almost paralysed with surprise. Her first question was "Where's Kathleen?" and she looked quite disappointed when I told her how matters stood. She had been getting everything ready for you since I had sent her word. I was not going to pull long faces and say how I felt about the disappointment. Every time I think of it I try to console myself with the thought "Well January won't be long till its here any way" and then you'll be here with me surely and no more disappointments.

Fondest and best love to yourself my Dear girl,

Love from Tom

44

New York City,
Nov 13th 1900

My Dear Kattie,

...I was of course much interested in hearing about your visit to my mother. I am not at all surprised about her being abrupt, especially over Uncle J. not calling lately when he had been in Dublin. I say I'm not surprised because she thinks a lot of him and gets on with him (she calls him Shaun) better than any one else I know and she was making great complaints to me when I was home over his not calling. But I am glad indeed that she and you got along so nicely. Dora[10] is a queer little woman and has been a perpetual struggle to me. She has a lot of clear good common sense with a mixture of ridiculous odd notions that has quite mystified me at times. She and Maria are very much unlike – Dora will "fight her corner" like a dogged politician while Maria is all for peace and quietness and never shows temper unless her corns are being trod on too heavily. She and I get along without the least jar and it always was the same. Alf is a good steady generous fellow but in some respects <u>very</u> thoughtless – just a lump of genuine Irish impulse.

...And that reminds me. I have written to U. J. and tried to explain exactly what the situation is here in view to his coming here to lecture. I fear such a lecture would not be a success unless he made the proper connection with some of his old friends here who were interested in his last lectures being a success and doesn't seem to quite realize how much irritated at his never sending them a single line since he saw them then.

...we are all "down in the dumps" over the result of the National Election here. But I know you are not much of a politician and so won't inflict a long winded explanation on you about the matter[11].

...with fondest love believe me your Tom

45

New York,
November 25th 1900

My Dear Kattie,

Your last letter has quite shattered me for I see there is earnestness in this talk of Egan going to claim heavy damages and the importance of yourself as a witness for him. It never entered my head till I read your last that the accident to Mrs Egan could possible throw any hitch into our arrangements and so I kept hugging myself with the belief that come what may you would be with me here in January. But now I don't feel so sure about that and can't for my life just see where this thing of Egan's case is going to end. Of course I sincerely hope Egan may win in the case and get all he claims and I certainly would not hesitate to make any reasonable sacrifice to help him out in that. But it would be asking too much off you and asking too much off me to expect us to break through our arrangements in order that you might be on hand as a witness for god only knows how long. For perhaps if he wins on the first count the case may be appealed and a couple of years elapse before it would be finally settled. Perhaps after all I am frightening myself with a bogey. You may not be needed in the case at all. There may be other eye witnesses who would be quite sufficient to prove everything for Egan. I fervently hope there may and that Egan's talk about you as a witness amounts to nothing more than chaff. And perhaps it doesn't amount to anything more serious as you appear to take it lightly and give no opinion one way or another about the thing. But all the same I feel very uneasy since I got your letter Kattie and will be on the strain till I get a letter from you making this matter clear and giving such points as will enable me to fully understand how long you would have to stay if you are absolutely necessary for the case and consent yourself to remain. Should your mind not be made up tell me exactly or as well as you can how you regard the matter and then I'll advise you and at the same time decide for myself what I shall say to

Egan. I wrote to him a couple of weeks ago but made no reference whatever in my letter to this what I am writing about for the reason that I have indicated. It never entered into my calculations one way or another that my girl would be mixed up in the law case. But I'll turn away to something else.

…My mother must certainly have taken to you (and nowadays she takes to very few people) for I know she would not have gone to Mrs Egan had you not asked her. And I'm delighted to think you both got along so well.

That must have been an interesting scene in the Dublin Council Chamber over Clancy's motion to present Freedom of City to Kruger. I see they are giving the old man a magnificent reception in France. I hope but no matter Johnny Bull may get enough before the Boer War is over yet. By the way we had ninety of the Boys from the Transvaal Irish Brigade in New York last week. And I spent some very pleasant hours among them listening to their tales of the war. They are a fine hardy lot of fellows and a credit to Ireland in every way. One young fellow, O'Reilly who left Dublin, got a French passport and got into the Transvaal after the war broke out and was in all the fights of the Brigade since – came up this day week and had tea with Maria another friend and myself and spent the evening telling us of life in the Transvaal. He remains here in New York and has already got employment. Miss Gonne knows him very well. In fact twas she managed to get him smuggled in to Africa.

…Until I got your letter I had intended to get in a new piano for you but I won't now till I feel certain that this case of Egan's is not going to knock our arrangements on the head. Maria can't play and it would be no use in the house now.

I also got a bad cold last Saturday – caught it coming home from Philadelphia where I had been on business but I am ok again. One of the nights which I had it I lay awake and could think of nothing else but you and this infernal law case of Egan's and it made me feel much worse than I really was.

…With fondest love, your Tom

46
1305 Brook Ave,
New York,
13th Dec 1900

My Dear Kattie,
…I have written twice to U. J. lately giving him points about how the situation is here in view of the likelihood of his lecturing. I don't know that he will be able to manage that. But in any case he promised faithfully, lecturing tour or not, that he would arrange for your coming out in February. That was the last word we had as I was leaving Limerick. Now I know there is every chance of Miss Gonne coming out here next month. I have told John about that and I hope he will arrange for you to come with her in the event of his not coming himself. My Dear Kattie if I only knew just how he feels about coming himself I would write to Miss Gonne myself and arrange the matter. But then again John might like to do that himself. In any case I'll write to Jim Egan next week when I hope to have the letter I am longing to get from you and will post Jim about arranging the matter with Miss Gonne, unless he hears from you that Uncle John is attending to the matter. So Kattie if writing to Egan is needful you needn't be afraid to speak plainly as I'll post him that he must consider my letter and yours on the subject as strictly confidential.
    …Fondest love your Tom

47
1305 Brook Ave,
New York,
Dec 15th 1900

My Dear Kattie,
…Now Kattie – about your coming out. I am just after having a talk with Major McBride and I can now say definitely that Miss Maud Gonne is coming out and coming out very soon.

…But let me go back to what I was saying about Miss Gonne. Bring round the subject with U. J. and tell him I can now speak positively about Miss Gonne coming out here after the holidays to lecture with Major McBride. It will save me writing another letter to him as I have nothing else to say in addition to what I have said in my two last to him.

…Fondest love to yourself from your Tom

48

1305 Brook Ave,
New York,
Dec 31st 1900

My Dear Kattie,

This letter and the news you give has sent me into the seventh Heaven. How I do hope you may be over along with Miss Gonne! But I am half afraid she will be starting much sooner than the 2nd of January. She has been cabled to but up to the present no reply has been received from her. But Major McBride, speaking for her, says she is sure to come and expects her here in about a fortnight's time. I have written to her myself in connection with the lecture, but at the same time told her about you and that you were coming out towards the end of the month and said I would much like that you were coming accompanied by her.

I got a letter from John by same mail as I got yours. He says he talked the matter over with you and (I'll quote directly) "have decided putting ourselves in communication with Miss Gonne and have Kattie go out with her, you don't object to that, do you?" he asks and underlines it as I have done and then drops the subject entirely. Kattie, by all means come with Miss Gonne if you can manage it. Don't trouble yourself with what Jim Egan may say. I told Jim Egan as positively and emphatically as I could tell that nothing would induce me to apply again for anything the Dublin Corporation may have to dispose of and didn't wish my friends there to think of me in connection with such positions. Of course it would quite another thing if they secured a position

– and one that would be worth accepting – for me and had it a sure thing to walk into. But I have very little hopes of that and trouble my head not one bit about Dublin Corporation jobs. U. J. said in his letter that Jim Egan left Limerick after his last visit in the belief that the Freeman people would settle the case for £2,000. I gather he expected the settlement very soon and if that is the case Egan's case wouldn't have to go to court at all – you would be free of it entirely. I know how disagreeable the thought of appearing in the witness box must be to you and for that reason alone, apart from the other one, I shall be heartily glad if the case can be settled outside the court. Any way you know how I am longing for you to be here with me and you know – but no never mind I'll tell you all that when I have you here. And when you will tell me what you promise including what that lady read from your palm. I'm a bit of a fortune teller too and I know part at least of what she told you is quite true and I am going to do my best to make it so. I'll bet that is proof that what she told you is almost true in every respect. Indeed I am very curious to hear just what it is tho'. But let me come to a more serious subject. Don't fail to let me know the <u>date</u> and the <u>ship</u> you are to sail in. I'll try to have things fixed here so that we can go off and see the priest that same day that you arrive or the next day. I know you are also in favour of a quiet wedding. The thought of anything else but that is a horror to me and altho' I didn't say much when you told me how you felt on the subject I was none the less delighted that on that also we were on the one mind. I hope we shall always be so on everything.

...I am going to write to Egan today or tomorrow. I see where a good thing can be done here in making money. There is no Irish Bog Oak goods sold in America at all and they'd sell like wild fire and the mystery to me is why no one has never started that line. I want to get from Egan all the information he can give me about that trade and also about other peculiarly Irish manufactures. He is working with others in Ireland to push Irish manufactures and so will be interested in the thing. I'd have to start in a small way at first if on my own hook. But perhaps if the Committee at home took the matter up the thing could be started in a big way, with myself as the American agent or manager of an Irish Manufacture concern located here in New York. I'm convinced there are sacks of money in the thing. Is U. J. on that Committee pushing Irish manufactures do you know?

…With fondest love wishing you many many happy new years and every other dearest wish from Tom

———————————

49
New York,
January 22 1901

My Dear Kattie,
I have had a letter from Miss Gonne (I told you about writing to her and what I said). It is mainly about her lecture tour but she also has a good deal to say about you. My news wasn't news at all for her – she says she knew all about it. Of course I wasn't surprised at that as I supposed she did. Well she says she will write to you about coming over with her and speaks of the pleasure etc it would be for her to have you along with her on the voyage. But she says it is always the French steamer she voyages in and that perhaps that would not be convenient for you. It never occurred to me that she would be coming otherwise than by one of the QTown or Southampton steamers. Why I don't know; however it was that idea in my head right along when I was considering the matter. I fear now that it may be decidedly awkward for you to have to go to Harve to take the steamer and I must confess it seems to me a case of choosing the lesser of two evils for coming alone on one of the Qtown vessels must be lonely and far from pleasant. However, it will be only for a few days Kattie and knowing you as I do I feel satisfied you can nerve yourself to endure even that.

…So U. J. hadn't written to Miss Gonne up to the time you wrote. No excuse he could give would justify his neglect in that since he led us both to believe he would attend to the matter at once. He ought to realize that although it may not be of any pressing importance to him it is of the greatest importance to you and I. Kattie I feel mad with him.

He ought to remember the centre of the universe is not at all times himself.

…With fondest love always, your

Tom

50

1305 Brook Ave,

New York,

Feb 27 1901

My Dear Kattie,

Your letter came only a day before John arrived. Up to that I was quite sure you would be with him and even after getting it I still had hopes that things might have turned out in such a way as would enable you to start with him. I was on the tip toe of expectation all day Saturday. One time reasoning it out with myself that "Kattie is coming sure enough" – other times reasoning it out with myself that I was an ass to think anything of the sort and so on back and forward went my hopes till John arrived. He tried to give me some small crumb of consolation by telling me you might perhaps be free to start early enough to arrive here before he returns. I fear not and here I am ever praying since for the Freeman's Journal Co and the English law and everything else that has kept you away from me. Oh I'd like to bundle them all up and send them to…well to Jerusalem or Jericho or further still. John has explained the whole matter to me the night he arrived and I see of course that it was simply impossible that you could leave yet, so that might mean the losing of the case for Jim Egan and I am bound to say that in looking at the whole matter from that point of view you have did quite right in not coming. But by heavens I have got to force myself to admit that Kattie. I am very glad to know John did what he could to keep his promise in regard to having you come the time he promised. I am satisfied he did. Bad luck to the law and bad luck to the Freeman's Journal Co. wagons, lawyers and all.

…He (John) was to come up and have dinner with us yesterday (we live about two miles away from the Vanderbilt – that will give you an idea of the extent of New York) but Mr St John Gaffney trotted him off to lunch at his place much to the disappointment of Maria who I suspect had made a somewhat elaborate dinner for yesterday. She is first class and feels disappointed at your not being here. 'Tis she who has given me the points about what must be done in connection with a marriage. She has great hopes that you will make me a kind of a saintly Holy Roman Catholic and influence me to be more regular at Mass than she can[12]. She doesn't know anything about that Sunday at Kilkee when Ag took us to task for losing her and ourselves out the Ennis Road. I remember all that – all the other incidents about Kilkee as vividly as if they had happened but yesterday.

...I saw her (Miss Gonne) the morning she arrived and of course knew the reason why you hadn't come. McBride and she are away lecturing thro the country and the tour is going to be a successful one unless Miss Gonne does something to upset the plans that have been made.

...Fondest to yourself my darling,

Good bye Tom.

51

New York,
April 15 1901

My Dear Kattie,

...I wanted to have definite information for Madge about what the Limerick Assn. are going to do to help the Daughters of Erin[13] in the scheme that Madge and the others have in hands. I made an appointment to go down to the Limerick men's meeting on Sunday and attend to the matter but just as I was about to start six or seven old Tyrone friends came in to see Maria and I and of course I couldn't break away. One of them is a very good violin player and he had his violin with him. Another of the party – a young lady – plays the piano very well and so they started into the music and there was some singing and I contributed my share to the evening's entertainment by performing long solos on my big crooked pipe and the performance gave considerable satisfaction (to myself). Well I had to write and apologise to the big man of the Limerick Assn. to which I got a reply asking to come down next Sunday, which I certainly will no matter what turns up. I got the newspapers and read them all with great interest. I seem now to take more interest in Limerick news than of any other place except Boerland.

...There now! That finishes the "business" portion of my letter. Now to the pleasant part. Kattie in my heart of hearts I feel very discontented over these disappointments. I say nothing to nobody but I tell myself all about it when alone. How unfortunate things have turned out. I had set my heart on having you back with me from Ireland. John reasoned me out of it and I reasoned you to wait till Feb when you would be coming for sure. Then I expected you with Miss Gonne and disappointed in that I had hopes you'd be with U. J. and the infernal law case done with and settled. Such a chapter of accidents[14]. And here we are still my dear girl nothing definite as to the time when you can come and then that infernal bostoon of a lawyer has the nerve to write to you in the strain that he does. I feel that I'd like to be able to make Mr. Buckley eat that letter. Bad as I feel over the disappointment I know full well circumstances make you feel it even worse. It's a case of making a virtue of necessity and keeping patience. May our unlucky month! That's all tosh. There's no luckier month in the year for me than May if it only brings you to me. I take no stock − not the least − in the old fashioned superstition. I am to that extent very un-Irish. Maria, like Eileen, sets some store on almost everything of that kind − goes to Gypsies and tells fortunes by cards and all that rot. I had to laugh at your description of Madge and Eileen eating U. J. Truth Kattie there's a hunger on myself too that I'd give much to satisfy. Oh wait! They had only six weeks to pull up for.

You ask what kind of a fellow is Major McBride − a small man, reddish hair, high forehead, light moustache, just the reverse in appearance as the "bon sabacus". His manner is not very taking but the more one knows him the better you like him. He is a first class fellow I find in every respect – I like him. All the fellows who served with him in Africa speak of him as having great pluck. I have had half a dozen of letters from him since he started on the lecture tour. The tour is not the success I anticipated. Up to the present it has only netted about $3,000 (that's dollars). I mentioned that lest U. J. may be enquiring about "what news?" and that sort of thing would interest him.

…I am very much pleased Kattie to find you have – like myself – reconciled yourself to the idea of waiting till Egan's case is decided finally. I read with satisfaction that you too, like myself, saw that there really was no other course, that wait we must. Speaking of this you say "Anyhow its coming off sooner than you think" and I see Buckley speaks of April. Does that mean that it really is going to be wound up then? Or is Buckley only giving a "bluff" – as the Americans here say. I earnestly hope that he speaks truly and that you'll be with me in the course of a few weeks from now.

I have just read the first page of this letter and I am reminded that I haven't yet mentioned that I got a pretty nice piano for you several months ago. I think you'll like it.

…Anyway I keep you in my heart with fondest love,

Ever Tom

52

New York,
May 6 1901

My Dear Kattie,

I am delighted to hear the good news that that long spun out unfortunate trial is at length ended and that you are now free. I just got the letter now and I fancy it has put new life into me. Someway I felt that after seeing how often and how many things had gone astray to thwart our intentions I felt that perhaps that was how things were going to go on to the end of the chapter and that good luck and you were not for me over here in America. But all those gloomy imaginings are banished by your last letter. And now the real question is when are you to be here? I hope the answer to that may be yourself. You can't come too soon for me and surely now after the awful delay there can't be anything else to prevent an early start. Kattie for God sake start as soon as ever you can, perhaps something else might crop up like the Egan case to keep you back were you to stay for any length of time. I won't be sure of you till I have you in my arms. That's how I feel, still as I say, I now, after the good news you send, have tangible hope that the waiting and waiting is over and it is only a question of a few weeks till you are here with me.

…Miss Gonne will be going home next week. I saw her a few days ago and she was enquiring all about you and the chances of your being here before she left. Maria and I will be going over to Brooklyn on Sunday to hear her and McB [John McBride].

…Hoping soon, soon to have you here, Believe me always your Tom

---

53
New York,
May 31 1901

My Dear Kattie,
I have just received your eagerly expected letter. How keenly I am disappointed with the latest turn things have taken. Sure after the previous letter I was away up to the height of certainty almost – thought the wearisome waiting and suspense was all over and had arrived at the point where everything was going to go smoothly for you and I. But now here we are back again at the tedious and tiresome waiting for the end that doesn't seem to be anywhere in sight yet. Egan has been doing, or rather he has <u>not</u> been doing, a great many things which he ought to have done and I'd like to kick the careless fellow. He ought to have answered you at once on the point about which you asked information. He ought if he appreciated the difference between a paltry half hour of his given to scribbling a few lines and the sacrifice that you have been making for him and Mrs. Egan. I feel mad with

him when I think of it. Of course your interpretation of his neglect to answer you is the correct one. He'd write without delay if he could give you good news. Because he can't give that he does not write.

…Miss Gonne left here a couple of weeks ago and said she was disappointed at not having the pleasure of being the bridesmaid. McBride is still here and he too does be quizzing me about it and I answer by promising to get him fixed up with a certain lady of his acquaintance. He too is leaving here for California next week but returns in a month or so after which he leaves America for France.

…I sometimes wonder if you know how often you are in my thoughts and how much I long to have you here. My first thoughts in the morning and the last thought at night are with you my darling. Good bye, may you soon be with me. Tom

---

54
New York,
June 28 1901

My Dear Kattie,
That newspaper cutting telling that Egan's law case had ended was the first thing that caught my eye on opening the bundle of newspapers you sent. Day by day ever since I have been on the eager look out for a letter telling me when you were going to start but I am now fearing that disappointment is in store and am screwing my courage up to the point that will enable me to hear without any great surprise that Egan's case is not ended yet – that something or another has happened about it that will still keep you from me. However, in spite of my reasoning on these lines I will still cling to the hope that your next letter will come as a forerunner of yourself and that all the weary longing and waiting has ended.

…Good bye – you have my heart and myself, Ever Tom

ii 1904–05

55

Shackamaxon Hotel,
Atlantic City, N. J.,
June 1904

Dear Katty,

I have just got your second letter and mailed you two to that St Joseph's Convent Coytesville address. You say none has yet reached you.

You have me all in a "tremor" at the thought of finding you suffering from a stroke of piety when you get home. The picture of my demure girl hands and fingers correctly folded up in front of your breast and the uplifted holy and nun-like eyes – with a heavenward gaze is the picture that has me sitting here in fear and trembling. However I'll wait till I see you and then I'll investigate for myself as to what manner of change has taken place.

Daly is a nice little fellow to strongly object to take his religion without gain or music. He is a chip off the old block I think in that respect. I am glad to hear such a good report about him but I would rather that tired feeling was absent in your own case.

…Good luck, Yours Tom

56

The Office of the *Gaelic American*,
New York,
August 26 1904

Dear Katty,

…I am glad to know you are feeling more at home up there than you did in the Blessed Convent and I hope it will put health and strength into you and enough of both that you will be able to give me a good wrestle when you get back.

…Good bye,

Thos. J.

57

The Office of the *Gaelic American*,
New York,
July 23 1905

Kattie,

…I won't feel easy till I hear from you my girl and hear how you stood the voyage. I am not a bit concerned about Daly. He will be a pretty good sailor after the first two days aboard but in the "run down" condition you were in I am worrying lest the voyage may take too much out of you.

…Do I feel lonely? Yes, but the predominant feeling in my mind is satisfaction and pleasure at your going away. It will be the means of returning you to health and strength and I am already picturing you coming back to me full of health with dancing eyes and rosy cheeks and ready to start out to enjoy life to the fullest. But you will need at least two months at "home" to do all that. We can't tell for sure when you can pay another visit and that being so a month would be all too short not only for yourself but for the "home circle". I know full well the pleasure it must give them all to have you back once more. Don't worry about me – "Cut that out" as Daly used to say. I'll look after myself and the pleasure it will give me to know that you and Daly are in clover and that U. J. and Madge and faithful Ag and your mother and all the other dear ones are happy at your being with them will be only second to the pleasure you are feeling at being in your Irish home with all the family (Gran excepted) still to the fore and in good health.

…I suppose Ned is grown quite a big fellow and I hope he takes after his father and Uncle John.

…may all happiness be yours my dear girl, Your Tom

58
[New York]
Friday Aug 4, 05

My Kattie
I am longing for that letter from you telling me how you stood the voyage across. It will I suspect be here tomorrow. If I don't get it then I will conclude you were so ill on the way across that you were unable to write the letter and have it ready to mail immediately you land.

I am lonely without you – very lonely sometimes. Last Sunday I felt quite blue and went and ransacked my desk for something and after a long search found it. I had quite a long talk with myself about my sweetheart…don't construe this against me in the direction that you should come home after a six paltry weeks stay at home and I don't think you will. Kattie the thought of the benefit it will do your health to stay for 6 or 8 weeks and the thought of the pleasure it will give to those at home amply compensates me for being separated for that time from you Kattie. And of course you will understand that I make it a point of honor to look after myself in the matter of feeding, etc, far better than if you were at home. I must only mention in corroboration of this that I spent all this week with Reidy in the country fishing and rowing and walking in the nicest country I know of. It is at City Island on Pelham Bay about four stations away on the suburban railway by which you and I travelled going to New Rochelle that Sunday.

It has been a very enjoyable time and my only regret is that I hadn't you and Daly with me – it would then be the utmost enjoyment. I have been already making arrangements in my own mind for a camping out expedition in the Bay of the whole family for several weeks next year. My hands and face are the colour of a boiled lobster and I have been eating as I haven't eat in years.

I have a thousand and one questions I'd like to ask about yourself and about Daly and about each one at home but will bide my time till I get you home.

Do they notice you much yankeefied? I daresay a good deal more than you expected.

Love to everyone. Kiss Daly. Good night Darling, Tom

59

[New York]

Friday August 11, 05

Dear Kattie

…But about that neuralgia that will handicap you badly in gaining health and strength if it remains. I trust it has only been brought on by the excitement of your thoughts at going home and will have worn off before this. Anyway, tell me whether it is or not as I will be feeling very uneasy over it.

…My thoughts are with you all the time Kattie and I had to sneak to my desk again the other evening to have a chat with that sweetheart of mine that I have there and I had to be satisfied with a kiss on the papers but how different it would be to have it from the original.

Time is up, Your Tom

60

[New York]

August 15 1905

Dear Kattie,

I got your letter of 5th August yesterday – the Etruria only arrived on Sunday and no mails were delivered till yesterday (Sunday). I am concerned about your face being still sore. You only make a slight reference to it but if you have neuralgia same as you used to get it here some short time ago then I am fearing you will not get a chance to benefit by the "home life".

… I am much pleased to know the two Johns take to each other so well and was much amused at the idea of John # 2 ordering John # 1 around at such a rate. I read that passage of your letter for J Devoy and he laughed as hearty over it as I have heard him laugh in a long time.

…Your letters are not half long enough. You know I suppose how I keep looking out for mail day to arrive till I hear from you. Why, woman if I missed one letter, by all that's holy I would get a divorce. So just you beware.

Your obedient servant, Tom

61
[New York]
August 15 1905

Dear Daly,
Are you having great fun in Limerick Ireland and how many cows have you seen and did they all have ears and tails. Did you see the one that jumped over the moon at all. He must be a great fellow. Does Kattie ever have to whack your botty for being a bad boy. I hope she does if you do not do what she tells you. If you do what she says you and I are great friends and I am going to have twenty nine pieces of candy for you when you come back to Fulton Street where you can see the soldiers hang up the American flag on the pole.

Best love to mama and John Daly Clarke and to Uncle John and to everyone at home in Ireland.

From your papa,
Tom Clarke

62
[New York]
Friday, August 18 05
Dear Kattie,
…When I got home on Tuesday evening last I found a note in the letter box from Maria asking me to send her as much money as I could that night or early next morning. I borrowed a $10 bill and got up to her place before ten next morning. Ed, lying beastly drunk in bed, had only got home at 4 o'clock in the morning. I felt very mad but had

common sense enough to realize that the fellow is too degraded a wretch to risk getting into trouble with. If he were only half decent I think I would have tried to give him a good walloping. However I didn't but talked plainly and squarely to Maria about the situation she is in and left her resolved (she) to write home to Dora and see if she could send her some money to pay her way home. I told her if Dora was unable to do so she must not be uneasy that I would stand by her and borrow whatever was needed. This was after she told me she wouldn't hear of coming to live with us. I also told her if she was in any difficulty about anything where a friend was needed to send me word and I would be with her. She had decided to auction off the furniture as soon as possible and have done with that degenerate at once and for all. Well on yesterday I was called to the phone and got a message that Mrs Fleming wanted to see me. The voice and manner of talking seemed like that of a drunken person and I thought it was Mr Fleming. So I enquired who was talking – "O'Rourke" was the answer. I, suspecting Fleming, cross-questioned and confused whoever it was and felt satisfied it was Mr Ed. I swore at him and banged down the telephone but on reflection thought I might have been mistaken and that O'Rourke might be the name of the janitor who speaks thick and sluggishly. So I determined to go up and see Maria – got there – Maria opened the door – asked her did she send a telephone message to come, "No, but Ed is after telling me he did so". I was out in the corridor and I saw Ed in the dining room, drunk. Maria invited me in. I told her I would not and turned and left.

So Mr Uncle John asks impertinent questions about how long it took me to write a long letter to you. You can tell him with my compliments that writing to my sweetheart is such a pleasant occupation that I never notice how long it takes me and could not tell. Say, Kattie, I miss you very much. Life wouldn't be worth living if I had to face the future "free and unfettered". God Almighty! How fond I am of that chain that binds us to each other. Yes you are my first thoughts in the morning and my last at night are of you and I will make you laugh when I get you back telling you of the fool things I catch myself doing in my lonesomeness. God bless you darling and send you back safe and strong to me, Your Tom

---

63
[New York]
August 22 1905

Dear Kattie,
…I am delighted to know Daly is such a pet – they can now see for themselves that our description of our little lad was not the over drawn picture of fond father or fond mother. Your uncle need be in no way ashamed of his namesake and if he (Daly) only turns out such a fellow when a man as he now gives promise of being, the old land will have one other of her sons in the future with the will and ability to do his full share for her so proudly as his old namesake did in his day.

Good bye, your Tom

64
[New York]
August 29 1905

Dear Kattie,
…As to Egan – has he put on that story of his to any of the others? If he has not, well and good, but if he has, why I won't let him get off with it. It is pretty cheeky, damned cheeky of the little buckeen to try and brazen it out to your face that he did not play as mean and contemptible a part when he came over with you as the cheapest and meanest of cads could play. I am riled at the thought of his gall in trying to put blame on anyone than himself. If he'd frankly own up to it and blame the drink for causing him to act the part he did, I wouldn't have a word to say, but enough of this little…

…Tell that uncle of yours to mind his own business and not to be remarking about how often and at what length I write to my girl – though if he cares he can take the meaning of my regard for you by the frequency and length of my letters to you.

…Good night my girl. I do be lonely and am longing, longing for you. Tom

---

65

[New York]

Haig, Daly Clarke & Co

Friday Sept 1 1905

Dear Kattie,

…Say Kattie, are they serious in talking about you remaining away from me till Spring? I don't by any means like the idea and I certainly wouldn't care to spend six months of this kind of life – not unless indeed it would be necessary for you to remain till Spring to gather what you went over to get (that is mainly to get). If it would be necessary for that then by God Kattie I would put up with the discomfort of the present order of things for a much longer period than six months.

I don't miss you. Oh no, not all, and I'd give a good deal to have you here to tell it to your face darling, Your Tom.

66

[New York]

Sept 4 1905

Dear Kattie,

…As to Ned and your uncle's proposition. I won't give any opinion just now but will have a talk with Brother Stanislaus who has charge of St Anthony's school in Greenpoint and with another fellow who is a teacher in one of the public schools here and who was raised in Ireland. As to the other feature of the proposition, interfering with our "togetherness", well Kattie for your uncle's sake and for the sake of one of Ned's sisters I can bring myself to make the sacrifice and I needn't say another word. I will try and see the two I have mentioned some day this week.

...some time ago I got a "members ticket" from P. J. Conway for Celtic Park. It carries me free at any time into Celtic Park and I was going to go out there today to see the Tailtin Games, but I decided to stay here and write you instead.

Do you know that I am missing you more as the time goes on. At times I feel very lonely.

Good luck, Good health and plenty of pleasure be yours my girl and with Daly may you soon now be safely back with your Tom

---

67
[New York]
Sept 11 1905

Dear Kattie,
...I haven't heard a word from Maria since, so of course she has made it up with Ed again. A letter came for her to me from Joe O'Neill who is out West and I am after sending it on to her with a very brief note from myself just saying I hope she and the baby are well and that I had just heard from you and told her how you are.

I feel very much annoyed at that vixen Dora. Don't bother your head any further. There is evidently very little affection in her composition – she appears to be largely made up of spite and raw egotism. I feel sorry to find her thus.

... I am going to attend to getting out citizen papers this week with a view of having a try for an inspectorship in the City employ. The salaries range from ten to twelve thousand. I will try for one at the latter figure. I had a talk with Gillespie and Tom McGovern about it and they both urge me to do so. I haven't mentioned my intention to any one else and I won't till I see something further into the thing.

Give love to everyone for me and kiss Daly and hug him and tell him to kiss you and hug you for me.
Tom

68

[New York]

Sept 19 1905

Dear Kattie,

…Maria came over to see me on Friday night. Of course she has made it up with Ed who has made her any number of holy religious promises as to his future conduct.

…Good bye my girl,

Tom

69

[New York]

Sept 22 1905

Dear Kattie,

…I wrote to Brother Stanislaus of the St Anthony's school. He has charge there and those schools have the name of being the best parochial schools in Greater New York. Before writing to him I spoke to half a dozen friends whose opinion would be worth taking as to the proposition about Ned coming here for 12 months. All agreed that the parochial schools were in every respect far better than the public schools, pure and simple. Needless to say that opinion was not based upon ecclesiastical reasons. Well I saw Bro Stanislaus. He is a great admirer of your uncle and remembers him in the Mitchel Election in Tipperary. Bro Stanislaus is a Limerick (Co.) man himself and knows the city and was greatly interested in the proposition and talked it over with me for at least an hour. He is strongly of opinion that it would be a good thing for Ned to get a year's course in an American school and will see to it that if he (Ned) is too far advanced for the parochial school to have him placed in a college. He says of course he would be specially interested in Ned for John's sake as well as because Ned was from Limerick and he added "and besides I am not the only Brother here (in Milton St.) from Limerick. There are several others and they of course would feel much as I do". I asked him what would be the probable cost of a year's tuition including books and everything else and he said "not over 75 dollars".

I will write to John next week and go more fully into the thing than I do here.

...As of old, Tom

70

[New York]

Oct 3rd 1905

Dear Kattie,

...Oh I am getting very tired of being alone and it will be many a long day before I leave you go off all by yourself again. Next time I'll be with you when you go to Ireland.

As to that job I was speaking about – 'tis one of the City inspectorships that I have in my head and that I mean to try for. If I get it, it will be upon my own merits and not by any influence, and getting it that way will please me ever so much more. Besides so far as I am able to see, very few folks are around this City who would be disposed to even make the effort to help in the direction of using influence to secure a situation[15]. I haven't seen Maria in some time and fear her keeping away means that Mr Ed is going the pace again.

...We are going to give a mating to Douglas Hyde in Brooklyn on 3rd December at which all the money raised by the Clan in America for the language will be presented to Dr. Hyde. You will of course be home and at the meeting.

...Fondest love to yourself and Daly, Tom

iii 1907-1912

71

Manorville, New York,
28 June 1907

Dear John [Daly],

I hardly know where to begin. Well, first of all let me make note that I will send you enclosed the title deed to the manor property – conveying the property from me and Katty to you. This deed is a similar one to the other you hold of the Calverton property and for you to hold.

...I had quite overlooked the fact that the half yearly payment of interest on the mortgage falls due on June 21. I assumed it would not be due till August 1st – six months after we came up here – but it is due – it amounts to about £14. I have written today to Henry Waterling, the fellow from whom I bought, telling him I will be up to see him with the money about the middle of July and so write you asking to send it on if you can by hook or by crook as early as possible, for to tell the truth I have not on hand just now enough to pay it myself. When sending it if you have no objection send it by international post office money order as that will save me a journey to New York and what is a considerable some 3 or four dollars for railway fare.

Up to the present this has been an exceptionally bad year for the farmers as I suppose you will have seen in the newspapers but the strange part of it is that I haven't been nearly so badly hit as the fellows who have been farming all their life time. I have admittedly the best plot of potatoes in the section – four acres in blossom – have grown as good cauliflower plants as good grade of any and am busy just now transplanting an acre of these.

I had an acre and a quarter of onions but the bad weather of the past three weeks – not a drop of rain – has told on them and they are not going to "pan out" as they ought. I have in about 2½ acres of lina beans. I can't tell just yet how they are going to do. I had to re-plant an acre of them that the cold and rain of the early part of the season spoiled. My corn seems to be doing fairly well – ditto an acre of oats. Now old man if I am doing better than the average farmer of these parts it is simply because I am at it late and early. I get up around half four or five and keep pegging away till after dark. This and the fact that I have studied up the farming from the Agricultural publications and use a little bit of guile and common sense and don't care a damn how the farmers of these parts would be used to doing anything gives you the secret. Of course apart from anything else I feel that I am in honor bound to "make good" and give you the satisfaction of knowing that you were not assisting a worthless dog – or a fellow who did not appreciate a generous and manly kindness.

Jack old man I won't trust myself to tell you how I feel for the way you have helped me in this matter. God knows there does be a great lump rise in my throat when I compare your <u>friendship</u> with the thing that goes by that name among mostly all of my acquaintances in the United States. But I may be talking of this at too great length for your taste so I'll drop it after I have said if it lies with me you will have the satisfaction of hearing of me as a successful farmer.

By the way – a story – my potatoes at the early stages were infected with the flea beetle and they were making such ravages that early blight commenced to show itself. The flea beetle has infected all the potatoes planted around here this season. I got busy at once, made a spray with several ingredients in it – bought a sprayer and went over the plants killing off the fleas and stopping the blight. A fellow who has been farming all his life saw what I had done and asked me to show him how to make that spray. He was astonished at the effect it had on my potatoes. Around here the farmers are a bit curious about me and my methods but they all think I have been at the business before.

Katie is improving in health but slowly though she has a fine appetite. She keeps out in the open as much as possible and the place here and its surroundings are very delightful. She is greatly interested – as becomes a farmer's wife – in having raised the best chickens around these parts. Daly is well and very much in love with the life here – he is getting a very cute little fellow, but very lovable.

...James Reidy[16] will be going home on a visit to Ballingarry next month. He will call to see you of course...He is the fellow that did up those articles in the Gaelic American going for the rotten ones of the Limerick Corporation – just about the time you were finishing up your connection with that august (?) body.

...God bless you old man, as ever Tom

72

176 Gt. Britain St,
Dublin,
Jan 4 1908

Dear Katty,

I have had talks with a number of friends who know the city in order to get information as to good locations for the business and I have myself gone over such locations as were spoken of as good besides walking around and through other business positions. Up to present time I haven't struck the right thing in the matter of a vacant shop in the good business sections. There are numbers of shops vacant, some too large, some double corridored, some too large a window, some too mean looking, etc.

I am just after getting back from a long walk up Harcourt St out Rathmines way, back and along Camden St, Aungier St and Capel St Soon as I finish this I will be off again on the hunt.

My friend that I mentioned I was first to consult says our people are scattered all over and can hardly be said to have any place that could be called central but he says that when I get started he will have a card sent to every one of them asking them to patronize me and cant see any reason why I cant make the business pay.

You will be surprised to hear that Hannah is the most friendly, as well as the most capable, advisor I have in the matter of setting up in the tobacconist line. She would not hear of anything else but that business (one or two others were speaking of other lines than tobacco as better paying). She had a long talk with me in reference to the business itself as she knows it – where and how to buy, discounts, profits, adapting stock to suit the neighbourhood, etc. She is evidently making money hand over fist – a couple of days ago just after I got back after hunting around, my mother said Hannah has done better after the holidays than she expected. She is after counting what she took in these last two days – she took in £10 – it nearly took my breath away…she took in over £3 yesterday. Understand this means cash sales for she has accounts with numbers of people such as publicans, etc and gets (I infer this from a remark she made) over £100 a quarter from the City for papers supplied to the various libraries.

…Good bye my girl – kiss Daly for me. Just as soon as I fix anything you will hear from me…Take good care of yourself, Tom

---

73
176 Gt. Britain St,
Dublin,
Jan 6 1908

Dear Katty,
I have struck what I consider the right thing – a shop and back room both in pretty good condition at 55 Amiens Street – rent free of taxes £36 a year. I have taken it for a year – at the end of that time I have the option of a 21 year's lease at same rent. The lease can if I so wish be discontinued at the end of every 7th year by me giving six months notice. The landlord is Dr Crinson who is Dispensary Dr. for the North Dublin Union. I am after seeing him – Lewis McMullan accompanied me and looked after arranging the terms of letting and leasing. The landlord is to have the document of agreement ready for signature tomorrow or day after – when the key will be turned over to me. Rent to be paid monthly.

The location is a splendid one inasmuch as there is always plenty of people passing and repassing. The crowd was so great on last Saturday night that one could hardly keep on the side walk. The position of the shop is on the opposite side of the street from Amiens Street Station and is about 30 or 40 houses away from that metal railway bridge that crossing Amiens St

The shop is not a big one but has a good front. It was done up and a new window put in about 3 years ago. It has since been a candy, fruit and newspaper store. To put the inside of the place in shape would require an expenditure of about £15 for fixtures, papering and gas alterations – and then with the stock there would be a bright, clean and up to date little concern. I will write to John tomorrow; meanwhile let him know what I am giving now.

I met Ned at the station yesterday morning and we were together till I saw him aboard the boat at half past 6. We had lunch at the Clarence and tea with my mother and Hannah.

I got your letter this morning. Yes, Hannah is certainly a strange woman. She would tear to pieces any one who would say a word about me. Just imagine my being wakened up by her this morning at 10 o'clock to have my breakfast in bed and I had it there. She advises my doing my first business with Murray and introduced me to Murray's traveller and said I was thinking of starting in the tobacconist line. He said if I so decided his firm would be delighted to do business with me and would require no further reference than my sister's introduction.

Katty I am not getting over the lonely feeling a bit. I'm a fish out of water although I have nothing to grumble about with the folks here at 176. Both Hannah and my mother cant do half enough to try and make me feel at home. Did I tell you the old lady said the first time we met that I was not a day older looking and looked as young as Alf. She stands it well – not a bit changed in appearance but I believe she is not nearly as blunt and harsh in manner.

…Goodbye my girl, you have my heart, Tom

74

176 Gt. Britain St,
Dublin,
Jan 14 1908

Dear Katty,

…God knows my girl you are never out of my thoughts and I won't try to tell you how lonely I have felt since ever I came to Dublin and the chilly feeling that comes over me when I start to count up how long it will be till we are together again altho' both my mother and Hannah do everything in their power to make me comfortable they cant understand me sitting for long stretches without a word. Sure my thoughts do be with you and with what concerns our future. I get a big lump in my throat but its choked down and no one knows how my thoughts are running.

I have the key of the place but the lease is not yet signed owing solely to delay of the lawyers. I have been taking measurements etc with a view to getting estimates for fixtures etc. By an expenditure of about £15 the shop can be made a place we need not be ashamed of. The room at the back of the shop is not far off as large as the room in Norman Ave but it is not nearly as old looking. In fact both shop and room looks as if they were only a few years built. There is a fire place in it and also a gas cooking stove. There is a yard or rather a very trim garden at the back where the toilet is (open plumbing). I am greatly pleased with the place no matter from what point of view I look at it. All things considered, I believe if we can't make it "go" no one else in Dublin could. Apart from the ordinary business possibilities of it there is the Jack Hanlon[17] assistance which will be all that I could hope for and also Hannah's assistance which will count for a great deal more than I could expect.

So you and Daly are lucky enough to escape the influenza – good. Kiss the little lad for me. If you have a spare photo of him (you know the one taken in Prospect Park) send it on – my mother will be delighted. They have his picture (the baby with the rubber doll) framed and hanging over the mantel piece.

Good night my love. My heart is with you, Tom

75
176 Gt. Britain St,
Dublin,
Jany 15 1908

Dear Katty,
…Hannah came down with me to examine the shop and locality. She is delighted with both and says I might be here many months before I could have dropped on such a good cheap shop in a splendid location. She noted that among the advantages of the location were a big fine station, Kennedy the baker's big yard and stables, the parcels post office, the Loop line station, Amien's St Station, etc in the immediate neighbourhood.

She gave me some good practical ideas about the fixtures and says when the shop is fixed up and stocked it will be a fine looking and compact shop. Although I tried to give her an idea of what it was like before we went there she was surprised to find that it was in every way better than she thought.

…Good night my girl – I'm missing you, Tom

76
[Jan 1908]
Monday evg,
Dublin

Dear Katty,
…I have quite recovered from the slight influenza attack although there is a very lonely feeling over me all the time that won't be shaken off. No matter where I am or to whom I be talking that loneliness and longing does be over me. At the bottom of it all is my being separated from you

– there is no getting away from the fact. I could not feel happy or even easy if you were not by me. And I miss you too when I am deciding about the arrangements in connection with the shop – for so far I know what I have decided upon would have been OK'd by you were you here to be consulted. All the same the habit of chatting things over with you has grown so strong upon me that I don't feel easy when I haven't the opportunity of getting your advice. Now as to starting the barbering right off as Hagan thinks would be right. I agree with you; in the first place even if we had our own cash to do that, I would be against it as unwise to start it simultaneously with the tobacco and paper business. There would be too many strange irons in the fire. Better wait until we have got somewhat accustomed to those that are connected with the tobacconist and paper business before starting the barbering.

Besides that view of it there is the still more serious consideration to which you allude – the borrowing from U. J. Sometimes when I get athinking of the load already on us and of the generous way John is and has been standing us I feel my heart getting very heavy and that there is no one in the world outside yourself that I could hope to expect such proof of generous friendship. No Katty, let us first get the tobacco etc going and then see where we are at before starting the hair cutting.

I am getting more confident than ever that we will be able to build up a good business in that shop. There are a hundred and one little facts that I could tell you off all pointing to that result.

I haven't see Egan since I parted with him the day we landed but have tried to connect with him from time to time whenever I thought he would be in the city. As far as I know he has made no effort to reach me and I haven't heard that he has made any enquiries. Nor am I going to bother very much more about him. I am thinking from a number of little things I noticed when in Limerick and on the way up that at bottom he feels sore against me – just why I don't know, nor am I going to bother finding out.

…I suspect the shop will be all ready for the stock at the end of the week. Hannah is to sit down with me and suggest kind and quantity of tobacco, cigarettes, etc as well as newspapers that it will be advisable to stock with. Soon as I get this I will be able to see where I am at in the matter of cash and will write to John. Of course you realize that we will have to buy some odds and ends of furniture and cooking utensils. Until you come up I will put up with the minimum number and quantity.

We cannot live in the back room. We can cook and eat there but I'll have to get a room where we can sleep but that will be time enough until you will be ready to come to me.

... All things going well I should be opened in about 9 or 10 days from now.

I mean to get a couple of thousand small business cards for distribution among friends etc (Hanlon etc). I saw Fred Allen today – he asked me to send him 50 such cards when I opened to pass around among City Hall employees. I will also send some up to a number of northern towns. I have procured a register of the ward (the North dock – a Sinn Féiner was returned from it at last election) which came in handy to give me the names and addresses of people in the immediate vicinity of the shop to whom I mean to send a leaflet. Besides that I think it will be well to advertize 3 or four times in Sinn Féin and the Peasant. Later on when the tourist season sets in from the States a couple or three mentions in the Gaelic American will be likely to bring results.

...Good bye Katty. Give my love to Madge, Ag, Laura and all the others as well as to U. J.

I have you in my heart my Girl,

Tom

77
176 Gt Britain St,
Dublin,
Jany 18 1908

Dear Katty,

...The agreement is not yet signed – the landlord's lawyer's delay is the sole cause. On the phone this evening he assured McMullan that he would mail it to him this evening. I have spent 6 or 7 hours of every day since I wrote you down at the shop in Amiens St giving measurements and data to painters, gas fitters and carpenters to enable them to give an estimate on the work required. I have now estimates from several in each trade and can see what the total is going to cost.

I am having the fixtures made up of deal (the cheapest wood) and of simple construction but done in such a way as to make a good appearance, edges rounded on all the shelves and partitions and with a cornice running along the top – the whole wood work to be stained a light mahogany and varnished.

The ceiling is a good level one and will be well whitened – the walls papered with a very nice light green colour paper – but cheap (only 6¹/₂ a piece). This paper has a small white lily pattern with a longish stem running through it but not too thickly – a good deep border – clustered lilies of the same pattern running at the top next the ceiling.

The front of the shop to be painted a deep olive green, picked out with gold; window sash a deep mahogany; the sign board to be black on it "T. J. Clarke" in gaelic characters. In the fan light over the door which is a fine big one will be "Tom Clarke, Tobacconist, etc".

The shop will be lighted by two inverted incandescent gas burners over the counter and by two of the same lights in the window. These inverted lights are better than the electric light bulb, that is they show as strong a light but it is more mellow. Hannah's shop is an exceptionally well lighted one – ours will be still better.

…The figures put in by the various tradesmen seem pretty closely alike for the various jobs and the total comes higher than I was figuring:

	£
Gas alteration and fixtures	2. 12. 0
Shop fixtures, counters, windows, fixtures, etc	10. 15. 0
Painting, paperhanging, etc	5. 15. 0

That makes a total of £19.2 which will cover the fitting up of the shop excepting the floor oil cloth and a couple of lengths of glass for the windows (shelves).

…God Almighty she [Hannah] is a strange woman who is more interested and concerned with me and what I am doing than she is with her own business. We have, neither of us, harked back to anything beyond the day I came in on her. But Katty my girl how different I feel when you and I are together chatting. I am happy when I am with you. I can't help it but with Hannah I am with a stranger who doesn't really know me and I can't feel happy or content. It is only when I am away from you for a while that I fully realize how precious you are to me. Life without you Katty wouldn't be worth living. Daly too has my heart but the love is different to that which centres around your own darling self. There now, I am perhaps writing like a sentimental ass. Anyway if I didn't feel as I do about my wee wife I would be an ass – so there. Love to John and Madge and Ag and Laura and everyone. My heart to yourself, Tom

---

78
Dublin,
Jany 23, 08

Dear Katty,
…As soon as Hannah came in to go into bed I took hold in the shop and ran it all right until she relieved me yesterday morning. I didn't feel the least odd or out of place although I found it bothersome at first to lay my hand on whatever was wanted but by dint of studying up the stock and questioning the boy when he was around and by calling on the assistance of the customers occasionally to tell me where what they were asking for was kept, I got along all right and now have a fairly good grasp of the stock and retail prices.

…I mean to spend a while every day during the rush doing the shop boy for Hannah. She urges me and by the way was quite surprised to find I was able to handle the situation successfully. The mother too was delighted – I'm still her white-haired boy and it is laughable to hear her ruling against Hannah whenever she gets a chance in my favour. My mother seems to me to be a great deal clearer and not so queer as when I left for America.

...I spent part of the day jotting down in a memorandum book the names of tobaccos and cigarettes Hannah keeps in stock with the selling price of each, she dictating them to me.

By the way she does a considerable wholesale trade in tobacco and cigarettes among liquor store men of this neighbourhood. The two days I ran the shop I took in over £6 in cash, the Saturday previous she took in £10.9. There now, I must wind up. I wish I were with you to tell you all that and a lot more, as well as to...but wait, it won't be long now my girl. Good luck and love of my heart to self and Daly,

Tom

79
[Dublin]
Jany 30 '08

Dear Katty,
...Look here Katty since I read your letter this morning there is a strong feeling getting hold of me to go down to Limerick after I have everything fixed up in the shop and before getting in the stock. Lord knows how miserably lonely I do be feeling. I rarely go out at all at night, chat some to the old lady and other some to Hannah, fool with the dog (a lovely retriever and will leave any one for me) or with the cats, try to read the papers...that's how I generally spend the evenings [and] my thoughts do be with you or else combing over our concerns. But apart from that there are some things in connection with the business I'd wish to talk over with you as well as to how we are to fix up for sleeping accommodation when you will be ready to come up here. All this with a view to fix on the sum it will be necessary to get from U.J. to tide us over the getting in of stock and living for a few months. Oh there are a thousand and one things mainly about the business that I am longing to tell you and that will be interesting to you to hear. But even if I hadn't a thing of that nature to tell you and only had boodle to spare, wild horses wouldn't hold me from you for another six weeks. But if I go down now I suppose I could not go again when stock is due.

Anyway here goes – I'll run down and stay at least a day and a night just as soon as the shop is completed and I think that will be about Wednesday next.

Like you I also hear from various quarters how successful some have been in the tobacco business. Everyone who is a person competent to judge says I can get over the 1st twelve months without going under it means success. We appear to have almost everything in our favour at the start off and I am full of hope and confident that we can make it go. At last I think we are going to get a "look in" at the money making game.

The paperhanger has finished his work and so has the gas fitter – the place looks splendid. The fixture man started this morning to put up the fixtures – he already has them all ready for putting together. He has carried out my idea perfectly and when they are completed and linoleum on the floor and the place stocked with goods and dummies it will look very far ahead of Hannah's place. She went down to the Custom House for me today and got the tobacco licence. It cost 2/7 and pays up to July. I stayed in the shop while she was away; in fact I spent some time every day behind the counter and feel quite at home there. Of course I also have a chance of cutting up the tobacco – she uses up several large rolls every week.

At present time I have a slight cold in my head. It only amounts to a nuisance inasmuch as I am continually blowing at my nose. Ever since I came back to Dublin my appetite is not as big as it had been on board ship and while I was in Limerick. Lord knows I was beginning to feel ashamed at the immense meals I was eating at 26 William St.

As to God father and your suggestion – let Alf go for the present. I'll talk it over with you when we meet. By the way I wrote Alf some time ago but like Uncle J. he doesn't love sitting down to write letters and of course I haven't got any reply. He has two kids.

The fellows here (O'Hanlon etc) pressed me very hard to deliver the public lecture at the Emmet Celebration in the Rotunda. Of course I wouldn't do so. I told them they must get a better speaker, one that would do them and the occasion credit, as an orator. They discussed among themselves several others and finally decided to ask Major

McBride. But between ourselves I don't think – even as a lecturer – he is much of an improvement upon myself.

I didn't mention I got the two keys you sent all right. When I go down to Limerick I will take the white silk ties with me. They are all soiled and I would not trust them to my mother's washing although she washes my handkerchiefs and socks.

Good bye girl – 'twont be long now till I'll put my arms around you my darling wife,

Tom

80
[Dublin]
Feb 8 1908

Dear Katty,

…The painter only finished this evening and the fixture man finished the day I got back from Limerick. Katty the shop outside and inside is a perfect gem. It is just what I wanted it to be. All concerned have carried out the work just as I wished them.

Hannah went down last night to look at it and came back delighted with the way everything has been finished – but was very emphatic in her disapproval of the big gold 55 on the window. She never saw that done – nobody did it in Dublin and everybody will be talking about it because of its address, etc, etc.

I told her I was delighted to hear that – that the points she was making in condemning it were the very points – or some of the points I was aiming at reaching by having the big gold letters in figures on the pane. After further explaining she frankly admitted she was wrong and that the number on the window was a real good idea – though its oddity would deter her from doing the same.

…Write me back your opinion about the following by return mail if possible. Hannah is not going to offer a tender for supplying the public libraries for next year (beginning April 1st next). She has her back up against the Corporation for their delay in paying last quarter's mail, but I suspect her chief reason is that she is anxious to give me a chance to go for it – she urges me to do so – if I think I will have the other business sufficiently in hand by the first of April and can see my way from the financial point of view – she says while there is no extraordinary profit in the handling of the libraries that the advertising it gives one's business is very great.

...There is required a number of prepaid subscription papers and periodicals for the libraries...These papers at present amount to £53 a quarter. Next year they may be a couple of £ more or a couple of £ less depending on the revising of the list by the Library committee. Do you think it would be two damned much gall and haggishness to ask John for that much more backing? I really do and would feel it awkward to ask it. Everything considered it would seem that there would be no limit to my pressing on his generosity. Katty, not even you I think realizes how I appreciate such friendship as his has been – and it's this thought that I was abusing it by pressing him and going beyond the limit is the thing that worries me. Look at this all around and tell me my girl what you advise.

...I will have ads in the Peasant and in Sinn Féin next week. I also will be advertised as agent for Sinn Féin stamps in the "Sinn Féin".

I enclose copy of the business card.

Good bye, love Tom

81
55 Amiens Street,
Dublin,
14 February 1908

Dear Katty,
Have opened today.

The shop looks well – stock nicely arranged and so too is the window – not so nice, I am satisfied, as it would have been had you the job on hand. Hannah did both shop and window arrangements. She left her own place in charge of one of her little boys from about 8 o'clock every night during last 3 nights and didn't get home from here till nearly 2 in the morning. She is certainly acting the real true friend in this matter in a way that I could not have conceived in my wildest imagination – but let that go now.

I have been fairly busy, tis now 7 o'clock and I have taken in a little over £1, the most of that I think from general public (I only had about ½ doz of people that I recognized in with me). So taking that into a/c it seems promising as a start but it will take a few days to enable me to form a good idea of just what task its going to be.

I had a short note from Reidy saying that he has attended to the Waterling matter – the draft he says (for £188) was $17.38 short. He says it would be better to send drafts in U. S. money terms and I say so too if that were at all possible...

I felt considerable relieved by your ruling against me attempting to write U. J. in reference to backing library. I appreciate the situation as it is at present down with the business at 26...

Tis now 5 minutes after 11 and I am going up to see my mother who was not well this morning. Hannah left about an hour ago. I find I have taken in today about £1.15.

I will write tomorrow night again,

Love to Daly and self,

Tom

82

[Dublin]

Monday Morn,

Feb 08

Dear Katty,

...I took in only £1.2.6 yesterday but I daresay the week will average up things all right.

That kid...I'm longing to see him and his mother – longing more to see his mother and fondle her though.

I found out last night who one of my U. I. L customers is who seems very friendly and fond of chatting to me. He keeps a drapery shop next door to Alderman Farrell's tobacco shop in Talbot St. He said last night there was every prospect of my being able to build up a good business here – the location of the shop, the appearance of it, bright and clean, and my being able to chat intelligently on any subject made it quite certain as he believed. So, there you are, all my love, Tom

---

83
[Dublin]
Saturday night,
Feb 08

Dear Katty,

…My only news is that the opposition shop is closed. The girl that ran it in the day time came in this evening to buy a paper. I didn't know her, she told me who she was and said they were giving up…She said they only had 5 newspaper customers. I asked what they were.

…Alf is likely to be home this incoming week. He can have a job soon as he gets here in the same department of the Corporation as he was employed in before.

…I was interrupted here by the entrance of three apparently negroes. They wanted cigarettes and soon as I heard them speak I asked them if they were from India. Yes, but I couldn't get them to talk much. They were small fellows and bought some of my best cigarettes. They came from Bombay and told me they are getting stared at by everyone they meet in the street.

…Good night my girl. You are always in my thoughts. Love to our little ones. Tom

---

84

[Dublin]

5 March 1908

Dear Madge [Daly],

…Yes I know how pleased Uncle John is at the way this place is going and I also know how pleased you feel and the pleasure it must be for the others but I don't think you can realize what my feelings of gratitude are to Uncle John. I realize there is only one such man in this world as far as I am concerned.

I haven't started on that memorandum I have to give U. J. showing amount I owe him. I know he is in no hurry about it otherwise I'd let other things slide and get it together. I'll let it stand a little while longer. To give you an idea of how things are going in one direction. For some days after I opened nine evening papers were more than enough for me – I am now getting three dozen – my newspaper and periodical bills last week amounted to about £1/5/0. Mr O'Leary is manager of Hopkins and Hopkins jewelry place in O'Connell Street. During the Exhibition in New York while Katty was home with you Mr O'Leary was in New York with Hopkins exhibit at the exhibition. I made his acquaintance and found him an ardent nationalist and it so happened I was able to show him some samples. He recommended this and brought his wife with him on Sunday to see me and has been circulating my cards amongst a good many people that would not otherwise be reached – besides buying his cigars from me. He is coming to see me on Sunday night with a bunch of friends that he wants to introduce me to. Talking to him today he told me that Griffith had been talking of Sinn Féin having a candidate in me for the Corporation at the next election – but none of that for me.

Good luck Madge, Tom.

I forgot to say if a more lengthy stay at home would be necessary for Katty's health I certainly would not say no.

85

[Dublin]

St Patrick's Day, 08

Katty,

…I am going to turn in for a sleep soon as I finish here and will go to a Gaelic League Concert in Clontarf Town Hall tonight. Most of the boys connected with the Branch there are customers of mine and the president gave me an invitation and of course I go.

…By the way can you send up those red shoes of mine? My feet have swollen with so much standing and I am getting or rather have got some very bad corns that torture me.

…good luck my girl and best love to wife and our boys, Tom

86

[Dublin]

March 27 '08

Dear Katty,

…I only have gone out to the Clontarf concert and twice to H's place during the last three weeks except to dash out to mail letters to you. Truth is I was in torture with my corns – the feet swelled with so much standing and the boots were then not large enough so walking even if I were inclined was a torture. I got the other shoe this morning.

…The end of my financial week wasn't as good as the first part – but the week itself was 13/6 better than last week – that is I took in this week (ending last night) £7/18/0 and is the best week I have had yet – the next best was £7/12.

87

[Dublin]

March 28 1908

Dear Katty,

...I had an old gent in with me today – one of my old customers. He said if I cared to supply the men in the Irish Times office with tobacco – they use about 3lbs a week – he would speak to his son to come and see me. His son got the tobacco for the men from Foley the tobacconist who I had told you had just closed (closed because he took to drink and betting as the old fellow told me). He, the son, used to get the stuff from Foley because they were distant relations. I agreed of course. It means being paid for the tobacco at the end of the week. Hannah has quite a number of shops and offices (Cleary's, the Independent, etc.) where she has the same kind of trade. [no signature at end of letter]

88

[Dublin]

March 29 1908

Dear Katty,

...My mother has been sick for some days – in bed one of them. I was up to see her on Friday night. Talk of Maria being fond of greasy cooking – my mother is worse. She will take rank fat from frying suet and eat it with her potatoes. It would kill me if I did it. Hence her sickness. I don't like the cooking at all but I wouldn't say so of course, even if I dared.

...The fellow from the Irish Times didn't materialize since to give me the order.

Good night girl, my love Tom

89

[Dublin]

March 31 1908

Dear Katty,

…I have been feeling out of sorts today – stomach deranged. I couldn't eat any breakfast so I had a long debate with myself whether I ought to get a bottle of stout for dinner. Common sense prevailed and I sent the boy for 2 bottles – drank one and hold the other in reserve. The bottle toned up my appetite and I am feeling improved ever since.

I was just figuring up how much profit I make on morning and evening papers. You will be surprised to hear I get over 45 dozen a week of morning and evening papers and dispose of them all except about 10 dozen. I find I make about 7 or 8 shillings a week on these alone. Then there is the provincials, the weeklies, the provincial papers and the Sunday papers and the Sporting papers. Someway I think I must be making the rent out of sale of papers alone, but I'll have to figure it out and see exactly what the profit is.

I took in 19/6 yesterday which was 2/- better than the best Monday I had previously since opening.

Today will also be a record Tuesday. As I write I have in 5/- more than any previous Tuesday. Don't worry girl over whether or not we made a mistake in coming home. I feel sure we did not. The only thing that is worrying me is the load of debt that has to be cleared off. If we were only starting fair and anew there would be a nice comfortable living for us here in Dublin.

…I am in a quandary. There's a hole worn in the seat of my pants. I can't bring myself to wear the good ones and I can't see any way to spend money buying new ones. I wish I had you here to clap a piece on these for me. They'd last a couple of months more.

Love to you my girl, Tom

90
[Dublin]
March '08
Thursday night

My Dear Girl,

I am a new man – feeling good because of the good news Madge was able to send me. <u>She</u> is a brick. Two letters a day. You should see me grab the letters from the postman and tear them apart and you should hear me humming to myself – Katty all right and this place going to be a success. At last luck seems to be setting in my direction, not mind you but I have had a few chunks of good luck in my day and the best share of it I ever got was when I got Katty Daly and I think you know it too. Anyway my girl may you still continue to improve and be in a short time up and about and ready for enjoying life and the love of your own man and our own two little darlings.

…Things are going on all right here. This is the best Thursday I have had – took in exactly £1.

…I didn't say anything about God father. Have Ned or anyone you wish and if you carry out your original idea about the name – calling the baby after his dad – I will be delighted, though mind you there may be a danger of his being such a pet that he will cut out Daly – I'm talking of myself now.

…My boy is beginning to be useful. He has secured me several additional customers for delivering papers to. Hannah sent down her boy to go along with my fellow to show how to go about securing new customers. I now have 13 on the list.

…Give my love to all – keep the cream of it for yourself – 'tis yours,
Tom

91

[Dublin]

March '08

Thurs morning

Dear Katty,

…The librarian of Charleville Mall and Clontarf libraries – who is a customer of mine – came to me yesterday morning and asked me to oblige him by letting him have the evening papers for the two libraries and asked if I'd care to give him a figure saying what I would supply the two libraries for the month of April for, explaining that only one tender had been received for supplying all the libraries for the year (beginning 1st April) and that tender was considered so exorbitant that the committee would not accept it and the town clerk was directed to write to each of the librarians and ask them to try and get a news dealer in their own locality to supply the papers for a month. So he came to me with the result that I have been figuring out this all day yesterday and with Hannah last night up to $\frac{1}{2}$ past 1 this morning and my letter has gone off and I offer to do the thing for £8/5 which would give a profit of about £1/12.

Love to all, firstly my girl. I feel tired, my stomach is fighting itself.
Tom

PS This will my best week since I opened by several shillings.

92

[Dublin]

March 08,

Tuesday morning

My Darling,

I got John's telegram telling me you are both well. I am delighted for I have been feeling very anxious for you fearing maybe the operations would tell against your coming through the childbirth labour successfully.

When I read the telegram I dropped what I was doing and went back into the room and burst out crying. I still feel choking – it is the reaction. But at the same time the condensement of delightful satisfaction is keen.

…kiss the little stranger over and over again for me. Love to him and to Daly. My heart to yourself my own dear girl, Tom

PS I didn't expect news so soon at all.

93
[Dublin]
March 08
Sunday evg

Dear Katty,
…As to the receipts and Madge's opinion I shall be in a better position to pass my judgement on that in the course of a few days when I expect to be able to get at a close approximation of just what the profit is or what I take in. We can then figure out how we stand in regard to being able to live out of it. So until then I won't think of being obliged to live without you for another lengthened spell.

…I had Lynch of the New York Gaelic League Soc. in with me today along with a nephew of Anthony Mackay's – a brother to the fellow over in New York but a vastly smarter man. I also had Mr O'Leary of Hopkins and his wife in and spent some time chatting. Of course it has to be in the shop. My back den hasn't the woman's hand over it and it is not usually very presentable. There is to be a Sinn Féin meeting in the Rotunda tomorrow night. Hobson (who was also in today with another friend) and some of the others have been wanting me if possible to be at the meeting to meet Sweetman, Dolan, etc. If I can get Hannah to come down about 9 o'clock I'll go although I have no clean shirt – forgot to send it to the laundry last week. There now, don't read me a lecture. I know I deserve it but has a poor devil nothing to do that he must think of damned cuffs and collars and white shirts.

Goodbye my Girl. Love to my three and to everyone at 26. Yours Tom

PS I have taken in today £1/12/6 as against £1/4/0 this day week.

94

[Dublin]

March 08,

Sat night

Dear Katty,

…I had the best day today that I had yet – took in £2/3 which is 2/- better than this day week which up to today had been the record. By all means let John and Madge know about what B. H. told me in reference to the paper – only ask them to not mention it. H. was in with me today and he thought there was every prospect of their being successful in raising enough cash or selling off stock to start.

…My love to you my girl and kiss the little ones for me. Your Tom

---

95

[Dublin]

March 08,

Sunday night

Dear Katty,

…I had Miss Mary Devoy and John's brother and little Eily in to see me today. They were impressed with the shop etc and very glad I am to know it because of the frightful effect that news is likely to have on Kate [Devoy's sister] when they tell her.

I had been trying to get the address before I opened to go and see them but I wasn't able to manage it. My heart is with you, good night, Tom

PS I got the newspaper with birth notice.

96
[Dublin]
March 08,
Sunday night

Dear Katty,

…We are going to build up a business very rapidly here my girl. It is going on in good fashion and has me very much encouraged. I am certain. I am getting tangible proofs every day that this is the case and speaking of this reminds me that Mr. Whelan the wholesale Sinn Féin stamp man who handles the wholesale agency of the Leitrim Guardian (Dolan's paper) called over with some copies of the Leitrim Guardian I had ordered.

…I must write Daly some time this next week. I'd love to hear his prattle around here and above all I'd love to hear the sound of your own voice and feel the warmth of your arms. God bless you both. Good night my girl, as ever Tom.

97
[Dublin]
March 08

Dear Katty,

…You'd laugh if you saw me this evening getting ready my tea and trying to eat it. When I took off the lid to rinse out the pot – a customer – served him, went back to my teapot – got half the water in – another customer – served him – went back to my teapot – just got to it – another customer, and so on all the while I was eating but I do love the interruptions. Several times this evening I have had $^1/_2$ doz. people at one time in the shop. It looks well.

…Bulmer Hobson and Dolan[18] was down to see me yesterday. Dolan doesn't amount to much either in point of ability or strength of character.

…Goodbye and love you, Tom

98

[Dublin]

April 3, 1908

Dear Katty,

…Now Katty the barber's idea is out of the question[19]. I have my hands too full at present time with the present business. It would be a mistake un-aided and alone to attempt to add on the other. I couldn't attend to the preliminary arrangements concerning the getting of the place ready without neglecting what I have in hand. In fact, I couldn't attempt it without having someone to look after the shop at times and just now no-one can look after the shop and the business as I can myself. I'm building up and doing well, but am doing so mainly because I'm attending with scrupulous attention to everything that is calculated to make for the building up of the business.

…My business week ended last night. I took in during the week £8/13/6 which is 15/6 better than last week and it (the previous one) was the best week I had since opening – so that speaks for itself as to how things are going. I expect the improvement will continue as I now have a line of Carroll's Dundalk tobacco which has been frequently asked for.

…My figure was too high for supplying the library papers for a month – that is the sec. thought the committee would think them so and the librarian was instructed to get other tenders…

…I have just had a letter from Reidy – a very short one – Ballis (the fellow who bought some of the trees and left them), has written to him to say that he wanted them March 30 and Reidy is not sure whether I stipulated as to who was to pay for the digging of them out. He wants to know. I thought I had posted him as to that. He also mentioned that he hasn't heard from Dr. Frayne and says that Dr. Frayne has broken his contract by not paying up rent on time which means of course that Reidy must be out of pocket for the shortage in last instalment. I will write Reidy now and tell him that we will send him cash to recoup himself for that shortage by next mail. I judge John is somewhat tight now in the business. I mean that there is not much to spare just now so I think I will send Reidy £5 myself and write John in reference to the matter. What do you think? I hate that Reidy should be called upon to lay out the cash for any length of time.

...I must now start in to take the stuff out of the window to dress it. Hannah wasn't able to come down last Friday because of my mother being ill so I had to prepare to tackle it myself and the other day when Hannah was out to pay dog licence she called around and had a good laugh at the ra ree show my window was. I wish you were here to do that kind of thing for me. I'm a duffer to spell out the things so as to make an artistic display. But I did my best and I don't worry as long as the main thing is going on all right.

It was a lovely and loving letter I got from wife yesterday morning. Gosh, I'd like to have you here to tell you how good it made me feel and make you feel a good hearty hug and maybe a few kisses and – but no, I'll tell you the rest when we meet. You are in my heart Katty, kisses to the little ones, Tom.

99
[Dublin]
April 4 1908

Dear Katty,
...I didn't get the library contract and on the whole I don't much regret, all things considered. I still keep doing well in the business. The landlord (Dr. Crinson) came in this evening to tell me he had been speaking to Mrs Moran (Moran's Hotel) about having me supply the hotel with papers and that she would do so and asked me to go up and see her and get the list.
...Good night Tom

100

[Dublin]

April 7 08

Dear Katty,

…My mother only comes down once or twice a week, but she occasionally sends me down a hot dinner by the boy. I think both she and Hannah have an idea that I am starving myself and indeed I'm not, though in truth I have never bought a bit of meat or anything of that kind since I came here. Where's the good since I couldn't cook it. But I'm getting enough and feel in good shape only very tired at night – so tired that I often fall asleep taking off my shoes or when undressing. That's one of the things I am promising myself when you are up and ready to go on guard in the shop. I'll turn in and get one good round sleep of about 12 hours – but not on the first night mind you.

Goodbye my ownful, love to you and the babies, Tom.

101

[Dublin]

April 8 08

Dear Katty,

…So you had a letter from Maria and with it the usual good news about Ed. I hope it is true for her sake but I have my doubts.

…Good luck my love. I'm with you in spirit and with the little men and all the others. Tom

102

[Dublin]

April 10 1908

Dear Katty,

…My mother only cooked dinner for me here one or two days. Lately she has not been down often, but I don't know that there is any reason. I never ask. She came and still comes when she likes. I wouldn't ask her for to tell the truth I'd just as soon do for myself. You are the only woman I understand and feel that I wont be misunderstood and the only woman that I will stand meekly and allow any criticism of concerning my affairs…God bless, Tom

---

103
[Dublin]
April 11 1908

Dear Katty,
Sure I forgot about your birthday and I'm reproaching myself for not remembering it.

…I am just after having Hobson and O'Hegarty of London in. [P.S.] O'Hegarty you will best know as "Sarsfield" who wrote for the Republic and sometimes for the old United Irishman – the most dilapidated and careless-looking fellow you'd see – never dream there was anything in him.

…I opened on February 14 and up to March 13th (inclusive) I took in £32/12/2. This month won't end till April 13 (Monday night) but up to the present time – including £2 today – I have taken in £34/14. I expect to do an increased business during the Easter Holidays and this reminds me you asked if I would close on Easter Monday – most emphatically, NO – only close one day in the year, St Pat's day – National Holiday. I don't mean to let any guilty dollar escape.

Good luck my girl – may your future birthdays – every one of them and may they be many – be happier than present one…

Love, yours, Tom

104

[Dublin]

April 15 1908

Dear Katty,

…Katty, I haven't a particle of fear about this business. We may not perhaps be able to live on the profits for a month or two – that is, maybe the profits are not large enough to enable us to do that, but I am not sure about that even and I can't yet say for certain just what the margin of profit is, but sure if the worst came to the worst and that we found after you had come up that we were eating into the stock why you could go down to Limerick for a vacation and stay a month or two but I don't think there will be any fear of that.

…The hopeful feature about the business is that while some of the Irish Ireland trade has fallen away I am getting more of the ordinary trade which more than affects the other.

…A fellow – an old gent – called in yesterday to buy a provincial paper he saw at the door – recognized an American twang in my accent – he introduced himself as from Washington…

Ever since I got to Dublin I feel only part of me is here. I'm missing and longing for my own girl and her company. Good night my love. You are in my heart of hearts. Kiss the little ones for me. Tom

105

[Dublin]

April 17 1908

Dear Katty,

…Hannah is astonished at the fine business I'm doing – so my mother who was down today was telling me. By the way I have several Protestant and English customers and they are among my best. You'd be surprised at the number of English and Scotch who come in to me.

Good night my own girl. Love of the warmest to you and the little ones. Tom

106

[Dublin]

May 4 08

Dear Katty,

…My mother was enquiring about you and asked me to remember her to you. I think she has discovered a tender spot in her nature for you. Hannah enquired never a word. She's an unbearable article.

…Goodbye love, Tom

107

[Dublin]

May 8 08

Dear Katty,

…All the travellers know me – know that I am H's [Hannah's] brother and that I get my stuff through her but Mary's traveller I don't think knows she is letting me have it at same as they give it to her. I am almost sure they'd object and refuse to do further business with her for as a matter of fact they fix the retail price for tobacconists they supply (as do all other manufacturers) and if they find any one selling at less than that price they refuse to supply such a one – so it is, I take it, that where they give exceptional terms, it would be on condition of not re-selling at less than at the ordinary terms. Anyway I'll find out from H and settle that point.

If my new boy only keeps on as he has been doing he will be all ok. For me he is as quick as a yankee boy and is at the door every morning at 6.30 though his time is 7.

…Good luck and love to you and to the little ones, Tom

You'll have to be buying me a white shirt one of these days – the one on me is in ribbons.

108
[Dublin]
May 14 1908

Dear Katty,

…I don't think it would do to have E [James Egan] as a boarder. It would have us in a perpetual state of "expectedness" – staying out all hours – coming in drunk – quarrelling and running the show. No Katty, better a crust in a back room than the misery that would be inflicted on us by his being with us.

   …Good night my love, Tom

109
[Dublin]
May 17 1908

Dear Katty,

…What I did say to Uncle J. was "Tell Katty I am dying to have her here with me". Anything over and above that is his own embellishment. You can tell him that Miss Eglinton, when on paying me her paper bill, told me "Mr Daly is an awful man. Oh he said some terrible things to me – awful things". And the poor girl was blushing all over her face. Somehow I too expect Ned's story to be of the cock and bull kind.

   …goodbye my girl. Love to our little ones, Tom

110

[Dublin]

May 18 1908

Dear Katty,

…Since I opened the monthly receipts have been:

  1st month £32.12.0
  2nd month £37.15.0
  3rd month (last) £42.18.0

So if that rate of success keeps up for a few months we will be on the "pig's back".

  …Good luck my girl, love to our little ones, Tom

111

[Dublin]

May 19 1908

Dear Katty,

…This shirt I have on is worn out and can't be sent to the laundry again but I think 1 cotton shirt will be enough to enable me to pull through till you come up. You might send up some of the white ties I like to change on Sunday.

  …I do feel very lonely here at times when I am not busy and I am longing for Monday week and the change that it will bring to my way of living. I think if this style of thing lasted much longer it would begin to tell on me. Anyway, I am getting tired of it. Still, if I had to stick it I know I could but now that the way seems clear why I want you with me.

  Good night my girl – love to my little ones – my heart to yourself, your Tom

---

112

[Dublin]

May 20 1908

Dear Katty,

…I got your letter this morning. I think the business is now in such shape that by living somewhat economically for a couple of months we can live out of it all right and by the end of a couple of months it should be in such shape that we can have no fear of not being able to live out of it as well as we have ever done.

…I think I sent my mother away mad when she came down when I was sick. I haven't seen her since. You know what I am when I'm sick. She started in to lay down the law about something or another and I gobbled her up and told her I never take anyone's advice or opinion only my own and I didn't want any more advice, etc.

…she's (Hannah) a queer mixture and beyond my understanding – pretty clear head, plenty of common sense but it is warped here and there – generous to those she likes but an unlovable character – very. She has done me much kind turns and is still doing them but I can't cotton to her. I am away at a distance from her and don't want to get nearer. So there, I'll talk this way only to you.

…Love Katty to you and the little ones, Good night, Tom

113

[Dublin]

July 13 1908

Dear Katty,

…read the Gaelic American – U. J. may not have opened it. Tell him to do so in a hurry. I am expecting it to be seized here. 'Tis an awful story.

…love to you and to the little ones. I am missing you. Love to all the others. Tom

114

[Dublin]

July 16 1908

Dear Katty,

Just got your letter and am much disappointed. I was building for certain on you being up today and I am heartily sick of being alone. Still I know you could hardly decline to do what Madge wanted.

…I too would wish that we would be together on the marriage anniversary – and all the time. Life is not worth living now without you.

…You have my love, Tom

115

26 William Street,

Limerick,

Sat Aug 08

Dear Katty,

I got here all right, feeling in good shape with an elephant's appetite. I felt no way cold on the journey and had no occasion to tap the bottle.

…All here are taking the greatest care of me and I feel today unmistakably stronger than at any time since the sickness.

…good luck my girl. Love to you and Daly. I have kissed Tom for you. Your Tom

116

26 William Street,
Limerick,
Monday morning
Aug 08

Dear Katty,

I am feeling immensely improved, eating like a Trojan – an egg flip before I get out of bed and a glass of punch after I get into bed – the bed and my night sheet heated – beef tea or chicken broth during the day and strolling out at intervals. We reckoned it up that altogether I walked 4 miles yesterday – that is I was out 4 different times. My only regret is that you are not here to share in the enjoyment of the holiday.

We start for Crookhaven this morning – your mother, Laura, John and I. The intention is to take a cottage. That will be ever so much more home-like than staying at a hotel. Crookhaven is not far from Queenstown out on the water.

…If I only continue to improve at the same rate that I have since coming here I will, by the time I get back to you, be in shape to fill the bill on that Glasgow proposition.

…Good luck my girl. Tell Daly I send him love. My heart is with you. Tom

117

26 William Street,
Aug 08
Sunday Evg

Dear Katty,

…I am feeling splendidly and am eating as well as while at sea. The weather today was grand here and I had two walks – about 6 miles in all.

…Love my girl. I'll wire you in the morning if Daly comes. Your Tom

118

c/o Mrs Small,
Woodview,
Crookhaven,
Co. Cork,
Sept 8 08

Dear Katty,

…I still continue to improve – still continue to keep the big appetite and enjoy the splendid food I am getting.

…But say, tell it not in Ireland's capital, His majesty king Ned and our previous lady the late Queen Vic my estimable hostess for, as long with some others of high degree, look down on us from the walls of the dining room on us as we eat our meals making us feel lucky to be thus in the blessed odour of loyalty – so there you are. But seriously Katty I am all the time since I came here regretting you are not here sharing the pleasure and benefit of the holiday.

…Good luck my girl and my heart's love to you. Tom

119

c/o Mrs Small,
Woodview,
Crookhaven,
Co. Cork,
Sept 11 08

Dear Katty,

…The weather here is delightful. Yesterday morning I got up and took a walk of 2 miles before breakfast – before any of the others were up. I took the precaution though of drinking $\frac{1}{2}$ glass of the whiskey you put into my bag – but that was the first time I had occasion to touch it. After I got back your mother had my usual morning glass of egg flip ready for me.

…I am still eating with the same big appetite as when I left you and what between beef tea or chicken broth and egg flip and meals I seem to keep eating almost all the time.

…Tis a beautiful quiet place to spend a holiday with lovely walks full of interest in almost every direction. I walked all told yesterday between 7 or 8 miles – the others 2 miles less than that. Laura is improving immensely. She and I squabble all the time as to who is the invalid. She insists on cuddling me and I want to turn the tables on her. She is very jolly.

…Good luck my girl and love to both yourself and Daly. Love of the kind you know of. Remember me to P. McCartan, Bulmer Hobson and the others. Yours Tom

---

120

c/o Mrs Small,
Woodview,
Crookhaven,
Co. Cork,
Tuesday,
Sept 15 08

Dear Katty,

…I am going on in the same way improving and beginning to feel in fine shape swinging along at a rapid stride when walking. I am curious to know what weight I am now as I must have added nearly another 6lbs judging by the fine style I clean up everything in sight at meals.

…love to you my own girl, love to Daly. Your Tom is all right.

121

c/o Mrs Small,
Woodview,
Crookhaven,
Co. Cork,
Thursday,
Sept 17 08

Dear Katty,

…I weighed myself again the other day but only increased another pound – that is altogether I had gained 7lbs.

…I am feeling splendid with more spirits and vigour than I have known in many a day.

Good luck my girl. I'm longing to be back with you my love. Tell Daly I send him love. Tom

---

122

c/o Mrs Small,
Woodview,
Crookhaven,
Co. Cork,
Friday,
Sept 18 08

Dear Katty,

…as to the 6 months limit. I'll just have to get a why and a wherefore – your ipse dixit (that's Latin) will hardly carry sufficient weight. [No name at end]

123

[Limerick]

Sep 08 Wed

Dear Katty,

I am going along just as normal, eating well, sleeping well, and feeling well.

...On the whole I have had a very pleasant time. Every one of the family seemed anxious to do everything in their power to build me up and make me strong and give me a pleasant time. I am full of gratitude to them. Experiences like this would prevent one from losing faith in the unselfish kindness of men and women. I haven't weighed myself since I came back to Limerick but I mean to go over to Will Shanahan's today and find out my correct weight. His sister and himself and Willie Norman and his sister were in with us on Sunday evening. They all say I have improved wonderfully. A number of people that I met say I am looking ever so much better and brighter than when here last before I got sick.

...Goodbye my love. I am longing for Saturday and for you. Tell Daly I send him my love. Tom

124

26 William Street,

Limerick,

Tues evg

Sep 08

Dear Katty,

...I am going along as usual eating and sleeping well and taking plenty of fresh air. I'll be back in great shape by the time I get back to you and will be able to look after you to soothe your longing and send you off to sleep.

...That was characteristic of Egan to turn up full. Poor unfortunate devil. Where is he going to end.

...I will write to John Devoy tomorrow a letter partly sympathy and partly business. I suppose you saw the notice of Kate McBride's death in the Gaelic American[20].

...good night my love. Kiss Daly for me. Tom

125
[Dublin]
25 September 1908

Dear John [Devoy]
...I suppose you heard I had a bad fit of sickness – typhoid fever and several other things. I haven't been at home for a couple of months, for as soon as I got out of hospital I accepted an invitation from John Daly to go and spend some weeks with him at one of the health resorts to get an opportunity to recuperate. We spent a couple of weeks at Crookhaven (beside Queenstown) where I put on 7 lbs. to my weight. For the last week I have been in Limerick.

Yours with sympathy, (commiserating on death of Devoy's sister)
Thos. J. Clarke

126
[Dublin]
17 November 1908
Tuesday morning

My Dear John [Daly],
Kathy has just received a letter from Madge which has given us both a great shock – my God I never expected you were so bad. Madge tells what the illness was and describes how your health suffered – all the while we were thinking it was only a bad cold. But along with the bad news of how seriously ill comes the good word of your being over all danger. If I would act on my present impulse I'd be on the next train for Limerick.

I know that if the care that comes from devoted long service counts for anything in hurrying along your recovery – and that <u>does</u> count – the girls and their mother will have you on your legs again in a short time as strong as a fighting cock.

Madge mentions that the trouble was something like Peritonitis – If I understand aright once the inflammation emboldens that removes all danger and pain. Peritonitis is an inflammation of the membrane of the chamber in which the heart is situated and not the kind of stomach trouble Madge is believing. I mention that so that you can ease your mind a bit and not have her worrying any more than is necessary – with one thing and another God knows she has enough to worry her.

Daly has a bit of a cold – not amounting to much though. Katty is much as usual – so am I.

I know the worriment your sickness will have caused to all at home but I hope they keep well. They can be relied on in such an emergency – so too can you be relied upon to keep the pecker up as we would say when we had to fight against being pulverised between English rocks. You'll be as strong as ever I'm sure. God knows I feel a bit sick at heart though to know it was so bad with you. Good luck old man. If wishes count for anything you'd be well and strong in a hurry and one of the happiest mortals on this earth.

Love to one and all,

Tom

127
Dublin,
19 December 1908

Dear John [Devoy],
…I am in a hell of a rush here. The Aonach is on and is a great success. It has astonished friend and foe. The Committee are this morning looking after securing the entire Rotunda for next year's Aonach.

…John Daly came very near dying a month ago. Gall stones and a touch of appendicitis. He was up here in Dublin in Charlemont Street Hospital. Jim Egan, too, nearly kicked the bucket – spent 7 weeks in hospital. Both are well over their sickness.

Yours,

Tom.

128

Dublin,

Jany 3 1909

Dear James [Reidy],

…First of all, I am not nearly as strong as before my sickness. That sickness has left its mark. In the next place Mrs Clarke (Kathleen) has been knocked out and next week she goes into hospital to undergo another operation. Add to this the fact that I have never been more busy in all my life than since I came to Dublin. The business itself would require all my time and energies to look after it but I can't help doing some work in other directions, such as the Wolfe Tone memorial project, Sinn Féin work, etc, and the whole job has kept me going at as strenuous a pace as a rushing New Yorker.

You will have seen that the ward I live in is giving a good account of itself in connection with the Wolfe Tone monument fund. We have made a start on house to house collections and got in some money. We will resume that work now that the strike appears to be over (the strike affected our ward more than any other in the city). We ran off the most successful ceilidh that was ever held in the mansion house on Dec 26. Two other ceilidhs that were held on same night were failures. We scored well on that and will be able to turn in about £20 into the ward fund (Wolfe Tone monument) as a result of the ceilidh.

I was out tonight and talked over with a few others the idea of starting a branch of the Sinn Féin in our ward. It will be started in the course of a week and as far as I can size up the situation, conditions and men are such in the ward that we won't be very many moons older until we will have as good and as aggressive a branch as any in Dublin.

There is a splendid set of young fellows – earnest, able and energetic – around Dublin, with whom it is a pleasure to work, fellows who believe in <u>doing</u> things, not in gabbing about them only. I'm in great heart with this young, <u>thinking</u> generation. They are men; they'll give a good account of themselves.

You have heard of the Christmas Aonach held in the Rotunda. It was a great success, exceeding all our expectations, and can be taken as an evidence of the strength and spirit of the industrial revival. But after all the one man that may be thanked for its being such a success is young Seaghan McDermott (he was Sinn Féin organiser in Leitrim in the late election contest there). He it was who attended to the securing of exhibitors and looked after the details generally. He is one of Hobson's school and surely bids fair to make a name and a reputation for himself that any Irish man might envy[21]. Hobson is quietly and effectively doing fine work. He appears to be Griffith's black heart. Arthur loves him not and is disposed to sit on him whenever he thinks he has a chance but Bulmer is too strong to be sat upon unfairly.

John Daly of Limerick like myself and Jim Egan came near "passing in the checks" lately. For a couple of days the doctors had held out little hopes of his pulling through but all the same he did pull through but he is still somewhat weak and shaken up.

…On getting your last letter I at once sent it down to Limerick and when John and Madge Daly were up here about a month ago we talked the matter over. There is (interrupted at this point and had to go off in connection with local elections – have been in the jump over them and visit Mrs Clarke in hospital. I resume now January 19th).

First:- Elections have gone splendidly for us. Sinn Féin is 100 per cent stronger in Dublin today than when I commenced writing this letter.

…Now again back to Maple Farm. Dispose of Maple Farm if you can do so for $4,000. If that can be done and it is necessary to give a free and clean title by clearing off the mortgage, John says he can manage to send cash to pay off the balance due on mortgage. Of course he would make no money on the Maple Farm investment by selling at $4,000 but neither would he lose any. If you cannot get that figure for it say what it is likely to sell at now so that John may know exactly how the thing stands but I don't think he would care to part with it at a loss. I think I told you that Waterling some months after I bought the place from him offered me a thousand dollars more than I purchased it for. As far as Calverton property is concerned – hold that – it won't deteriorate. You have of course heard from Madge and got money to pay off instalment of mortgage due.

I am afraid I have put far more work and trouble on your shoulders than I anticipated when asking you to attend to the Long Island property. It is not fair to you and certainly were the thing to be done again and I have the knowledge I now have of what bother and trouble it is meaning I would try to make other arrangements. Anyway if things would only keep running well with me here perhaps I will be able to take a trip across at a not far distant date.

Business is going along well with me. I scored well over the Avomac (I was the first one to engage a space for it). Both Col Everard and Murray's managers were greatly pleased with the way I handled that business and the amount of advertising that came to them out of it apart altogether from the sales. By the way, Col Everard speaks in no mild terms about the English Govt's treatment of Ireland in the matter of manufactures. He left the impression on me of regarding a great many things from the out-and-out Sinn Féiner's point of view.

I was up seeing Mrs Clarke in the hospital today and met Pat McCartan there. He looks quite thin and tired after his campaign but the happy smile of success is on his face. Pat is a grand fellow.

Remember me to all friends and with best of good wishes to yourself, Mrs Reidy and little ones. Believe me as ever, yours sincerely, Tom

---

129
[Dublin]
29 January 1909

Dear John [Daly],
...Business has picked up lately. It is now back again to where it was before I got sick – averaging around £13 per week. Kathy still feels

weak but has much improved. I have been talking to Dr. Crinson (our landlord) about renting me one or two rooms overhead (the place is now vacant). I think he will be disposed to give two rooms and cut them off from the other portion of the house and make an entrance to these two rooms (immediately over shop and room) from the back garden.

…Laura[22] is doing splendidly. She is a great business woman and I think likes the shop work.

…Good luck and every good wish to you and all at home, Tom

130
[Dublin]
8 March 1909

Dear John [Daly],
I received a letter from Reidy a couple of days ago and again another this morning… These are the only letters I have had from him since we talked over putting Maple Farm on the market. I wrote immediately after that talk and went into the details of the thing but you will see by his letters that he doesn't make the smartest reference to the matter.

But the thing that stands out in the first letter is that he has been informed that the Calverton place has been sued for taxes. By God I got a start when I read that for I was under the impression that Reidy had fixed up the taxes – one of his letters left that impression on me. Property over there when sold for taxes <u>can only be sold for the amount of taxes due</u>…Let the reasons be what they may – Reidy is not attending to the business as I expected. When you come up here we will talk this phase of the thing over.

…Yours ever Tom

131
[Dublin]
April 16 1909

Dear James [Reidy],
I have a whole lot I'd like to talk to you about – some of it can't be touched on in a letter. Anyway here goes for "business" first.

Jack Daly has been up here for a spell and we have discussed his estate in America. He thinks, and I agree fully with him, that if it were possible to dispose of both properties without his having to suffer much financial loss it would be the wise thing to get rid of them. Personally, old Friend, I realize how much trouble and bother I have put upon you by asking you to look after that business. At times I could with great satisfaction kick myself for having added still more to an already overloaded back. However, I suppose railing at myself won't mend matters. And anyway the conclusion (as given above) that Jack and myself arrived at has been almost entirely independent of that consideration.

Can you put the properties on the market with any hope of selling them? If so by all means go ahead – using your own judgement whether to do so by direct advertising or through a real estate agent.

Of course we were very pleased – and myself immensely relieved – that your first good opinion of the tenant on Maple Farm has been borne out by his good faith in the matter of paying up and I trust you have been able to straighten out that matter of the Calverton property, if it be really true that it was sold for back taxes.

To get away from that, for the time being at all events. Matt Cummings is here in Dublin staying at the Gresham. I went up to see him last Tuesday along with James Deaken (you may remember the name he delivered a splendid lecture some time ago before the Young Men's Christian Assoc. – subject: Sinn Féin). Cummings gave me some very interesting news.

…Cummings got a real good reception here – more or less spontaneous though some of us – a good many of us – could not quite see our way to "demonstrate" for any representative of any <u>sectarian</u> organization. At the same time quite a number participated in the demonstration because Joe Devlin's Molly Maguires had taken their stand to boycott Cummings and from that point of view I'm glad the affair was a success.

…By the way was word sent over here by any one to throw cold water on Cummings reception? Ask Uncle. <u>Let me know at once</u> if no such word was sent. This won't seem of any great importance to you, but take my word just now I attach great importance to it. This I am asking of myself and for myself and is in connection with something at a very great distance from Cummings or his reception.

Bulmer Hobson is up in Belfast at present for the Easter holidays. I fear the Peasant won't last much longer. Several times since I came home it has been on the verge of going down – friends came to the rescue. This time I fear it will sink. From what I know and see the main cause is bad business management.

The Sinn Féin Daily is to come out in May. I can't meet a single one (and I bump against many including prominent members of the Sinn Féin organization) that does not shake the head about establishing a daily paper in the capital Griffith asks for. Personally, I may whisper you that I doubt it most damdably.

I have met Anthony Macky several times since he got home. He is trying to get started in some business for himself.

When writing to Paddy Lee I mentioned enquiringly about a John Byrne of Boston who is over here and denouncing everything and anybody on your side. After writing I had a visit from the gent and I went for him bald headed, so much so that he got flummoxed and rather panic-stricken. While in that state a decided Lancashire accent became very noticeable. In cross hackling I forced him to admit he has only been taking interest in Irish affairs for the last three years. Without delay I had word passed all round – National Council, AOH, Industrial Development Ass, Wolfe Tone Com, etc. The fellow claims to have belonged to the Dublin Men's Ass of Boston, now defunct, but claims his visit has mainly to do with securing specimens of Celtic ornaments in gold and silver of high grade, literature for an Irish section of a museum to be started in Boston and that he is engaged on this mission at the instance of the Kerry Men's Ass. of Boston…In any case everyone is now on the alert.

PT Daly made a very good fight in the Trinity Ward, lost by only 18 although that was the first time the issue between the UIL and Sinn Féin was tried out in the ward. Daly made a mistake to go forward himself there and went in spite of the advice of his best friends.

The Sinn Féin idea is gaining ground but the National Council seem to be resting on their oars and allowing the movement to drift forward of itself. The opportunity to make it go forward with a whirl is not being availed of by anything like the extent to which it might.

Mrs Clarke has been unwell and hardly able to do anything since Christmas. Just now she is showing a little improvement. As a consequence of her being knocked out I am tied down to the shop and can't do as much as I'd like in some directions. Daly Clarke has improved a great deal and has acquired something of the Irish accent – the other young Clarke is also in good shape.

I was delighted to get that photograph of John – money wouldn't buy it from me. Pat McCartan is in splendid form and has made his mark in the Corporation at committee meetings. Nanette was telling W. J. Ryan that McC is the ablest man among the Sinn Féin members.

Fred Daly has sworn off the tipple and is in great shape – I never saw him look better. I am much as usual. We formed a branch of the Sinn Féin lately in this ward – they elected me president. Only for the way I am tied down, and have that as an excuse, those fellows would keep me busy…

Good luck old Friend, yours as ever Tom

PS In connection with Byrne, the suspicious fellow, I know he gets remittances from Watertown, Mass, they come in the shape of PO money orders for £1 and for £1.10.

242 • Tom Clarke: Life, Liberty, Revolution

132

[Dublin]

21 July 1909

Dear John [Daly],

The enclosed from Reidy – partly satisfactory and partly unsatisfactory…It is [also] satisfactory to have the assurances that what we heard about the Calverton property having been sued for taxes was untrue. The unsatisfactory portion is where he refers to the sale of Manor of Calverton properties – the fellow either didn't read my letter through or else he forgets a good deal of what I wrote. I went into detail about putting the properties on the market – fixing the minimum at $4,000 – that would mean a "margin" of $400 (£80) to cover expenses, not taking into account rental, etc. His logic about a purchaser who would look for a profit on the rental is all right as logic but the fellow who buys property (real estate) in the country parts of New York State with a view to make a profit on its rental is a very rare bird.

…Things are going well in the new place (75 a Great Britain Street) – though last week it was a few shillings behind Amiens Street. But this week for the first five days of the week I have run £2 ahead of Amiens Street. Last week's receipts in Amiens Street was nearly £13 while in Britain St they were £12. There is no question about this place. The possibilities are very great. To my mind it is for me the very best spot in the City and I am going to do my level best to work it up to avail of all the advantages of the location. I am doing a decidedly better class of trade than in Amiens Street.

Love to all and everyone. Hope Egan continues to improve. Ever Tom

133

[Dublin]

13 August 1909

Dear John [Daly],

I sent you a telegram this morning with the news that it is a son [Emmet] and that Katty was splendid. She is continuing in great shape without pain and chatting away as if nothing had happened. Katty says the new kid is very like young Tom. You must take that for granted but I can't figure out the resemblance. She had no bad time on this occasion like the last – the labour didn't last more than an hour and no chloroform or instruments had to be used.

Laura and myself were all anxiety until we had a talk with Katty herself. She is feeling better than ever she has felt for weeks. I mean Katty

…Last week was the Oireachtas week and I took in over £18 here in Britain Street. This week (ending Thursday) I took in almost the same amount but that includes over £3 which came in from a Gaelic League order for the Oireachtas…This place is "going" in great shape. I'll be putting an ad in the papers offering 55 [Amiens St] for sale in the course of a few weeks.

Give my love to everyone, Tom

134

[Dublin]

24 May 1910

Dear John [Daly],

…Tom is as "bowld" as the devil – the blackguard would not shake hands or kiss me – worse still he wouldn't show ordinary friendship for Katty. Daly seems to be full of nothing but talk about him and feels flattered that he was the only one of the family Tom would condescend to treat decently…What think you of this Carnival of flunkeyism and loyalty that is sweeping the country. 'Twas appalling here in Dublin. I believe I was the only one who kept open shop on day of funeral of the King all the way from Talbot Street up and at my Britain Street – but all the same there is a fierce undercurrent of indignation and anger running. I hear that Marlborough Street Cathedral was tarred the night before they pulled off that Mass for the late Edward and I believe there is a police guard around ever since.

Good bye old man…love to every one as ever, Tom

PS Hyde has brought pressure to bear on the students to discontinue their paper – Pat McCartan was editor[23].

135
[Dublin]
Sept 23 1910

Dear John [Daly],
…Katty has been to see the Doctor and he advises her to take a rest away from the business. She is thinking of going to Limerick for a week or two. We have a fairly good girl in Amiens St so by a careful keeping of "tab" upon stock and other supervision I will be able to deal with the situation for a while. At all events Katty must take a rest and as long as she is near the shop she wouldn't allow herself to take that.

…Nanette[24] was in to see me yesterday – just dropped in – Mac Bride seems sure to get the job he is after. The Committee have unanimously recommended him and Clancy, Sherlock, the town clerk, etc are out for him. Even J. D. Nugent of the Board of Erin is out canvassing for him but Nanette says that is because John Redmond gave orders because of his being interested on my behalf. Redmond also wrote Nanette asking him to exert himself to his utmost for me.

Good luck, Yours as ever Tom

136

[Dublin]

27 December 1910

Dear John [Daly],

I hope you and all at home spent a very enjoyable Christmas. We closed both shops for two days and I spent the time at home with Katty and the kids. God almighty what an obstreperous kid I discovered Emmet to be when I was at close quarters with him for the two days. Katty and Daly are about the same as when you were here – Daly full of excitement and big words over his Santa Claus toys which include a hammer (and said hammer can bang!).

…Needless to say I am very much interested in the work of the Gaelic League. As a matter of fact I have been a member for almost twelve years.

…The Christmas business in Britain Street was <u>very</u> good – Amiens Street Christmas was just average – hardly more.

Good luck old man. May health and strength and happiness be yours. Every good wish for each and every one at home. Yours as ever Tom

---

137

Dublin

March 28 1911

Dear Peter [Donnelly] [25],

I regret very much to hear the news that you have to emigrate but I am pleased to be able to be of use to you where you are going. Find enclosed letter of introduction to an old friend of mine and a good old Irishman. That note will interest him sufficiently in you to do whatever may lie in his power. I am glad, in your case, Jack advised asking me for this for I assure you from the evidence I have had of your earnestness on the Irish side of things, giving you an introduction is a pleasure.

Don't be afraid of the future. Keep from drink. Don't be afraid to work at anything and with good health any young fellow sooner or later will "get there", that is be able to make a living. May you soon "get there" and if you only make out as I would wish you, your future need not be feared. Be always true to the old land. Never desert the ship again. Good luck, Yours very sincerely, Thos. J. Clarke

---

138
[Dublin]
18 June 1911

Dear John [Daly],
I got a letter from Jim Reidy – among other things he deals with the Long Island properties. Protzman who has leased the Maple Farm for several years just left on April 1. Reidy says he is just after making a deal with another party leasing it for the balance of this year at $75 and for the two years following at $150 a year and says this was the best he could do. This same party made cash offer of $3,000 for purchase of Maple Farm which Reidy said he could not consider. He told him that he thought the owner would not sell for anything less than $4,500. Reidy says he thinks it will be difficult to get that just now as the real estate market has not swung back to where it was during the boom that preceded the financial crash over there. He asks me to have a talk with you and let him know the lowest figure you are prepared to take for Maple Farm and says of course he will try to get as much as possible but asks you for the lowest he would be at liberty to sell at.

He says that situated as he is he can not give it the attention it should get as it takes a whole day to go there and come back to New York.

There, so for Reidy – will you write direct to him or do it by posting me. I give you what he says without comment but at this juncture I feel it is only right to you to give you my candid opinion. I know Reidy's opinion regarding both the properties. It was a mistake buying so far away from the city, etc and in proof of his contention quotes how a couple of lots he purchased in the suburbs of Brooklyn increased in value in a few years and brought him a very material profit while Maple farm and Calverton would be doing well if they'd bring their own and expense. That's the sum of his reasoning as I heard him at it and is I gathered from yourself that he presented to you.

That reasoning would be all right if it were a question of buying <u>lots</u> in the suburbs of Brooklyn as against buying <u>lots</u> 60 miles away. The Brooklyn lots would be certain to enhance in value much sooner than those 60 miles away – unless indeed some exceptional improvement sent the latter booming. But in any case, either in Brooklyn or 60 miles away the amount of profit that would be likely to accrue for the investment in a few lots would be comparatively small when measured up by what can be expected to accrue from a tract of land containing hundreds – many hundreds – of lots once the active real estate market pushes out there – as push out it certainly will – apart altogether from unforeseen boom resulting from local or general development. Already that almost came to pass when that bunch of millionaires got together to open up the automobile speedway along the whole length of the Island before I left America. But for some reason after running it as far as Jamaica they stopped and abandoned the scheme.

The point is that with 30 acres and 20 acres of property to be subdivided into lots when building lots are in demand in those sections it will not be a question of a few hundreds profit but a profit that would be reckoned by the tens of hundreds many times over.

…In point of value as building lots property there is no comparison between Maple Farm and Calverton. Maple Farm has a main road frontage and also a main road running through it…Manorville is a railway junction – not so Calverton. I have tried to give you my reasons for holding the opinion I do about the properties. I would not argue the matter with Reidy when I heard him talking as it would serve no purpose. Take what I say just as the reasons strike you. I would be sorry if you part with either place now – that is, if you can see your way to hold them. But if you decide to sell I know that will be right as you see it and that old friend is good enough for me and I wouldn't allow myself to say it was wrong. Good luck anyway no matter how you decide.

…I am down at Woodenbridge in County Wicklow since Tuesday but will be going home tomorrow. I have improved immensely. For some time past I have had a bad tension in my nerves – all wound up like. I am eased up very much after this rest – loafed and slept and eat all the time – that and nothing more.

…I have got a good innings in the tobacco war. Col. Everard and several of the representatives of the tobacco manufactory firms complimented me on my handling of the case for the Irish as against the Imperial. The newspaper reports blurred or omitted some of the strongest arguments.

Good luck, Tom

139

[Limerick]

May 2 1912

Dear Katty,

…Your uncle and all here are well. He keeps in extraordinary good spirits. I think Shawn Mac Dermott will stay a week or two longer and I am glad as it will mean much for uncle in not having a complete break with present conditions. Shawn has improved immensely.

…I am feeling immensely improved. Every morning I have been up about 7 and go after a cup of tea and do a walk along the Shannon bank – myself and Shawn the dog. Sometimes Tom with us and such lovely sunny mornings as they have here – sometimes with the cuckoo calling in the distance and a corncrake working away in the meadows. The papers came this morning from Hobson – a day late.

Looking forward to the pleasure of being home with my own girl again and love to Daly and Emmet. Your Tom

140
[Dublin]
14 May 1912

Dear Madge [Daly],
We are pretty well here and I have benefitted immensely by the holiday week with you in Limerick.

I write now just because I wish to tell you I had a long chat with Mr Broderick and explained to him in detail about that turn John got. I wanted to get his private opinion candidly and I knew he would give it without reluctance to me.

He says that was symptomatic and there was no need to worry too much over it – that the chances are U. J. may live to a good old age – that the average of cases of that kind, after they reach the present stage, they progress very slowly. The result of the chat with Broderick has left me feeling much easier about your uncle than I had been.

I hope you feel well and that John keeps in the fine form he appeared to be in excepting for that one turn.

Tom Clarke

141
[Dublin]
24 May 1912

Dear John [Daly],
Since writing to you I find friend Bulmer has "edited out" what really pleased myself best in my last instalment of the prison story. However I must abide by his decision. I have given him a free hand right along with my stuff as I trust in his literary judgement much more than I dared in my own. I enclose you the portion he has deleted[26]. Bulmer's idea is that I was too "gushy" in that portion. Yet God knows it was "gush" straight from the heart and conveyed just what my innermost feelings are on the subject. However, maybe I can get another occasion

in the course of the story to have my say in another style. For the first time Katty disputes friend Bulmer's word in matters of that kind.

…As ever, Tom

142
Dublin,
July 22 1912

Dear Katty,
Lane the tobacconist and newsagent who started about a year ago some half dozen doors away from us in Parnell St closed shop last week… I am getting the front of 75 Parnell St washed and varnished tomorrow. It looks very dingy at present.

…Good luck, love to yourself and the kids and to everyone in Limerick and Kilkee. Tom

---

143
75 Parnell Street, Dublin,
26 December 1912

Dear John [Daly],
I meant to have written you for Christmas Day – for old time's sake, for the sake of many things and many memories of these times as well as the old times – memories and recollections that are knit into my heart and are treasured there with a few others (and they are few) like sacred things. Good luck to you old man anyway. I didn't write as I meant and the reason was that I didn't want to merely dash off a hasty scribble and I found myself so busy ever since Saturday until yesterday that I had no opportunity to do anything more than a hasty scribble.

…Of course I heard from Bulmer and read in the Leader with great interest of your opening of the Fianna Hall and how you presided and made several speeches. Bulmer gave a great account of the fine shape you were in. 'Tis grand to find that you have made the Fianna such a success in Limerick. You are away ahead of anything else in Ireland. In

Dublin they haven't yet got the length of even thinking about building a hall. Bulmer was up in Belfast for the Christmas and got back to Dublin today. He is kept busy with one thing and another.

Shawn Mac Dermott didn't go from Dublin at all for the holidays. Instead he spent the time with one of his old friends here. I wanted him to come down and spend it with us but the other friend had asked him some time ago and it wouldn't do if he had ignored his invitation. His health is none too bad – is now just recovering from a bout of influenza. In fact that kept him to Dublin for the Christmas.

...I am sending you enclosed an advance of January Irish Freedom. I would give something to hear your opinion as to how I have handled the description of the Silent System. As far as I know this is the first time any one has attempted to enumerate the causes and trace their effects. I found this instalment more difficult to write than any that preceded it. Hobson says it is very good but I'd lay more store upon your opinion. You have experienced what it is – he has not.

...With every kind and good wish for yourself in the first place and for all at home in Barrington St.

As ever, Tom

144
Limerick,
March 20 1915

Dear K,
...I'll be home on Monday all right unless indeed I find U. J. taking a hand in and getting any way annoyed over my going. U. J. is in good shape ever since the day after my arriving here.

I am still eating and sleeping splendidly and feeling improved day by day – am now better than I have felt for months.

...give my love to Daly, Emmet, and Tom and keep biggest share for yourself. Tom

Political

145

On board SS Severin,
4 October 1899

Dear Jim [Bermingham] [27],

We expect to land tomorrow and this to be mailed first thing for I want to get from you that note we talked about giving what Lord Mayor Tallon[28] stated about his anxiety that a closer connection should exist between the Castle and the Mansion House. <u>Send me that note at once</u>. I see such a note is likely to strike the truth home to our people here as to what manner of Nationalist (?) Mr Tallon is – with far greater force than a statement or hearsay by myself. You were there and heard it. I really ought to have got this note from you before leaving and I had intended to do so but one thing or another knocked it out of my head.

You might also mention on the strength of some of the upstarts who were present at the Tourists' Banquet – the fact of Tallon proposing the health of the Queen and indeed anything else that you know of and that will help to kill his mission over here. Jim Egan will give you the names of the reporters who were present at the Banquet – catch one of them and put the question and then you can give it on your oath as coming from him. I am writing hastily and none too clever but you'll quite understand me I know.

It was rather a disagreeable voyage owing to bad weather but Maria and I are both feeling tip top.

There are three detectives abroad this ship one of them birthed in my cabin and sits at the same table with me. Nobody else on board appears to know me and of course I keep my identity dark. I am playing the fool with my big Kerry detectives but tomorrow I'll give him some information about myself free gratis and for nothing.

Best wishes to Mrs Bermingham and family and Jim Egan and my old mob.

Yours faithfully,
Thos. J. Clarke.

146
363 West 36 St,
New York City, U. S. A.
Sunday night,
28th January 1900

Dear Jim [Bermingham],
I had a letter from Egan the day before yesterday and he tells me you
are contesting the Mansion House Ward against Phil Little – Success
Old Man – Success and I am sure you will be successful[29]. My only
regret about the thing is that your opponent is not that flabby-souled
creature Dan Tallon instead of Little. However by the time next year's
elections come round I expect to hear that Mr Dan has got the "quit-
ters" and will have to take himself off to lie in some out of the way
shelf for the remainder of his natural life – Sir Daniel or no Sir Daniel.

Is Pile Lord Mayor now? Or who? We get very little Irish news over
here at all except what I get out of the papers you send me – not only
do I benefit by them but I pass them round to other friends here.

I also got the Amnesty Assn's final audit. It was very interesting to
me and some parts of it surprising to me.

Things here are not satisfactory – by no means. I am sick of a good
deal of what I see. The demoralization has taken place here as on your
side. Here we are "getting ready" – making preparations, when we
should be acting. But where's the good. A fellow can do nothing but
keep on churning his wrath[30].

Jim told you, of course that I am working and what at and the wages
I get etc, so I needn't repeat it here.

Maria keeps house for me and we are pretty nicely fixed in a small
flat close to my work (that is close for New York which in this case
means about two miles of a tram ride).

Maud Gonne was to arrive here today and I have just been writing to a friend to send me on her address soon as he gets it. I mean to call and see her and assist her in some things that she ought to know. She is in the hands of about half a dozen of fellows who are exaggerated specimens of the genus "Tom Kelly" [31] – cranks of the first order who go around doing whatever they are at with a fighting shoulder up and wanting fight. I mean these are the moving spirits in the Reception Commt. tho' of course there are others such as Rossa whose names are in the Committee, but only their names, the other class are "bossing" the show. All Miss Gonne's old friends here are very much dissatisfied with the present arrangements which gives over the management of her tour into the hands of the men who are running it.

We are going to have a big Boer meeting tomorrow in the Grand Central Palace. Of course I'll be there, occupying a back seat but as hearty and earnest a sympathiser with the gallant farmers of the Transvaal as will be in the hall. Holy God but aren't they surprising the world! Yes almost as much as they are surprising the English. Talk of Washington and the American patriots of the Revolution! Those Boers and their old Oom Paul [President Paul Kruger] are knocking them completely into the shade. Washington and the United States of America are "not in it" with my brave old Oom Paul and his United States of Africa. Success to him and them and the prayers of every exiled Irishman here in these States.

Except Egan I have heard from none of my old Dublin friends for several months. How is McGinn and McMullan? [32] Don't fail to remember me to them and Tom and every one – also to the Capt and the Misses Harpers and Mrs Meagher – did she get that position?

I sent a letter to Jim addressed to Babs. I find the P. O. people there are holding some letters of mine and delaying most of those I do get.

…I met Jim Featherston with Rossa at a meeting of the Maud Gonne reception commte. that I attended about a fortnight ago. Jim is as usual. Rossa looks as spry and hearty as a young fellow. He's a lovable old man and I took to him directly.

I hope all the family are well. Remember me in the warmest way to Mrs Bermingham also to the boys and to Matty and Babs and the little ones. Now old man don't fail, soon as you get this election over, to drop me a line. My next letter will have the initials T. C. I hope on the envelope after your name. Goodbye old man with every good wish to you and Mrs.

Believe me Yours sincerely Thos. J. Clarke

147
[New York]
13 May 1901

My Dear Major [McBride],
…Daly speaks highly of your lecture and of your manner of telling it – "a <u>very</u> interesting story and told in fine style" was his reply to a question I put to him about it. He says he himself was not in good shape in Chicago and didn't at all satisfy himself. But he has satisfied himself and even the old "soreheads" here with the speech he made on Sunday night. It was <u>great</u>, with the true "John Daly of Limerick" ring about it. It was a speech of the same kind that I have heard him at times make on an Irish hillside to "the Boys" away back in the old days only it was told with more snap and fire than ever.

…With best wishes and apologies for this roughly written scrawl. I remain yours very sincerely, Thos. J. Clarke

---

148
1305 Brook Ave,
New York,
June 18, 1901

My Dear Major McBride,
I have been shown a letter which was sent on here from San Francisco. The letter was written by P. O'B Kennedy ex-political prisoner to a member of the organization in that city and would be by no means a credit to a sane Irishman's pen. As you have alluded to in the letter referred to – indeed you and your lecture tour is the main subject of it. I take it

you will be almost sure to hear something about Kennedy's queer style of talking and I want to set your mind clear about poor Kennedy.

Very few know him better than I. We spent upwards of fifteen years together in the various convict prisons of England in close contact with each other and with every opportunity of "sizing" each other "up". He is as honest as God's daylight at bottom – that is honest in his loyalty to Ireland. But he was a nuisance to all his fellow Irish prisoners by his morose disposition and his inability to see virtue and goodness in anything or anybody outside himself. Never once have I heard his good word for any living Irishman. Sometimes I have heard him speak disparagingly of Irishmen – dear and fast friends of my own and men I would trust with implicit faith. That used to make me mad and Irish-like when I'm mad I've got to say right out what I mean and I did to Kennedy – told him how mean and contemptible he was to go in for trying to run down and blacken men whose shoes he wasn't worthy to black. In the end I got him educated up to the point that in my presence he would refrain from indulging in that offensive style of talk. That of course was in prison where…I had to nip the matter in the bud or the nuisance would keep on growing and I had no way of getting away from it…For your life don't notice anything he may say. There is really a "screw loose" somewhere or another in his mental make-up and no man of ordinary intelligence can talk to him for one quarter of an hour without finding it out…There now I have tried to give you an idea of the man's disposition and the peculiar faults of his character and I do so because I don't want you to feel hurt by anything he may say. I don't want you to take him seriously. The opinion I give you of him is the self same opinion that John Daly and James F Egan have of him and their opinions were formed under the same circumstances and based upon the same sort of facts as my own.

I saw Miss Nally a few days ago and had quite a long chat with her about various matters. It was down at the prison. Dicky Gill was also there and of course where Dicky is, there is bound to be fun in some shape or form. I made an appointment with him to be at the Napper Tandy Club meeting last night in order to show him how we do things

there. He turned up all right and I think what he saw and heard has
made him more determined than ever to get a transfer. It was a splendid meeting – packed like sardines in a box and among the candidates
initiated was Victor J Dowling, who was Chairman of the Albany
lecture meeting. Things are now humming in the District – not a jar
and physical force and physical force alone is the word that gets
stronger day by day. [Daniel] Cohalan is doing magnificent work – he
won't stand for any nonsense.

…With best wishes,

Yours Very sincerely,

Thomas J. Clarke

149

William Street,

Limerick,

28 December 1907

Dear James [Reidy],

We got across home safe and well and were met at Queenstown by
Daly; he looks in fine shape – much better than when I was here last.

After a few days spent in Limerick (during which time I met Rosy's
acquaintance and acted in the capacity of your ambassador) I took a
trip Northward, spending several days in Dublin – met a number of
friends there including P.T. Daly, Major McB, Fred Allan, Jack, Jim Egan
etc. I had a long chat with PT and Jack and gave them the pictures you
sent. They and the others are well. After Dublin I ran on to Derry and
had a pleasant time with McGill and Flanagan (the Editor of the Derry
People) and several other of the Sinn Féin party. The young fellows I
met there and in Dublin who take the lead in the Sinn Féin movement
impressed me very much by their earnestness and ability. I am delighted
to find them away above what I had expected. After Derry I went
across to Mount Charles and Seamus Mac Manus, found him well and
busy…After getting back to Derry I found I had to curtail my program
and cut out visiting Hobson – the reason for this was that the Dublin

boys had made me promise to be at a Sinn Féin meeting in Castlebar. However, I was unable to be there after all, as I was unable to make train connections to get to Castlebar in time when I got as far as Dungannon, so I stayed there a couple of days and then got back to Dublin and ran back here and have spent a very enjoyable Christmas, Daly, Egan and myself having great fun. This is really the first enjoyable holiday I have spent in many, many years. Egan is still here and between himself and Daly we have had a very happy Christmas indeed. Egan leaves for Dublin on Monday and I am going up with him. I have made up my mind to stay on this side if I can possibly do so; in any case I would not think of returning till middle of summer as Katty tells me there will be a visit from the stork in March – so there you are – there's what living the simple life – "close to nature" – brings on a fellow.

The G men give me no bother at all, although after Egan and myself got back here we had a fellow standing in the hallway next door one whole day, but only for that one day.

Daly and Egan are in the room with me as I write this and I am unable to get my thoughts down to writing you anything more than the brief sketch of how things have been going with me since I parted with you.

I will write to you in the course of a few days about other matters. Good bye and good luck to you, Mrs R and the little ones, Yours etc Tom

PS Tell uncle I will write him in a day or so

———————————

150

55 Amiens Street,
Dublin,
Jany 23 1909

Dear James [Reidy],

I wrote you for last mail and forgot to ask you to try and get me as soon as you can 2 A. O. H buttons. I want them for a particular purpose and it is important to get them as soon as possible. I enclose rules of the Insurance Scheme. The first rule gives the key to what the object of the scheme is. If we can make the scheme "go" and the opinion of those behind it (the progressive Sinn Féiners) is that it will succeed, then you may look out for a quickening of the pace…John McGarry (late manager of the Republic) did up a story about the municipal elections and sent it on to John.

Good luck, Tom

151
[Dublin]
25 May 1909

Dear John [Devoy],
I take advantage of bearer's trip to your side to speak on something I couldn't well do in the ordinary way. He knows nothing about subject I'll touch on. I told you in my last that I was asked by friends to be present during their interview with Neponset [Clan na Gael visitor]. In the course of the interview, and in reply to some question, Neponset referred to the amount of cash sent over during the two years preceding middle of last year. No such amount had been received, they told him. He was positive about its having been charged up to them. The discrepancy runs into hundreds of £. Friends much worried over this. The principal one came to me later on to see me and advising my passing you word of what I heard, and that you would then know what to do to locate the trouble – that is if what Neponset states is correct. That's the thing in a nut shell. Now my own opinion about the matter. I am afraid there may be something at bottom of this, and that all the money sent across did not reach its destination. I am basing that opinion upon one or two things I became aware of before Neponset came on the scene at all. I won't, even in this, explain just what I mean – won't risk it.

I have not mentioned this to any one here – nor will I – now that I mention it to you. For the present don't let a single one, more than is necessary to sift the matter, know anything of it[33].

T.

152

[Dublin]

Oct 5 1910

Dear John [Daly],

…I hope Katty got down all right. She needed a rest away from the shop for a spell – I am very lonely though.

I told her to tell you about the starting of a paper here in November – a monthly on the same lines as the United Irishman or rather on a higher level. Pat McCartan will be editor – Hobson, O'Hegarty, Lynd and all the good writers of the Republic, the United Irishman (Griffith excepted) and the Irish Student will be contributors. It certainly will not lack literary ability. It will ring true to national principles also. The scheme has been organised on the basis of a few hundred people guaranteeing to put down 1/- a month as a fund to put the paper in the field. Already far more than had been calculated upon have responded. Of course I put your name down. I know you'd "beat" me if I didn't.

Shawn McDermott is employed on the business end to look after advertising, etc.

The idea is to convert the paper into a weekly as soon as the financial strength of the monthly will admit of it. For already there will be more than is needed to bring out the early issues. Whatever is over will go into a sinking fund with a view to go towards the starting of the weekly.

…Good luck old friend. Love to all. Tell Katty business going on satisfactory.

Yours as ever, Tom

153
Dublin,
10 February 1911

Dear John [Devoy],

I am sending on by this mail $100 to Mr. Lennon to be credited to my Gaelic American account. For a long while past, from time to time, I had meant to have something done in this direction and mentioned about it to you, but sickness of one kind or another at home with us and its consequences in the shape of doctors' and surgeons' bills – together with the fact that my sister's business went wrong and I couldn't help giving her a hand, has led me to putting the G.A. a/c. on the long finger and kept me at low water[34]. As a matter of fact I am doing exceptionally well in business and were it not for the drain referred to above, I would have been feeling fairly easy for some time back. As it is I have the business fairly in hand and prospects look very promising so that by June or July I will be able to send on a remittance to clear off the entire balance.

John Daly is up in Dublin at present in Dr. Sigerson's hands for treatment of his legs, which have "gone back" on him badly. He is stopping with me and excepting for his legs he is in splendid shape. He has had a letter in some of the papers here which is characteristic. I send you a clipping from the Limerick Leader.

The [Irish] Nation ceased publication in December and the plant and offices are at present under seizure for debt.

We have secured the Mansion House for 22 June (Coronation Day) to hold a nationalist demonstration – by way of celebrating Wolfe Tone's birthday. I was on the deputation that waited on [Lord Mayor] Farrell to ask him for the Mansion House and I think we will be able to get him, the Lord Mayor, to preside and some of us will try to get every available man in Dublin to line up in opposition to "the enemy" – that is, we will try and get the Molly Maguires, Sherlock, etc., to go in with us on that occasion. This, of course, is all on the quiet for the present.

262 • Tom Clarke: Life, Liberty, Revolution

Jer. Lynch [Diarmuid Lynch] of the Gaelic League, N.Y., at present is in Cork City and doing well managing the seed and hard-ware dept. of the biggest firm in that line in Cork. Pat [McCartan] is doing exceptionally well at his profession and is otherwise in good shape but kept very busy. Mrs. Clarke just now as well as the kids are well, I am as usual. Things go fairly well in other directions.

Good luck and every good wish.

Yours sincerely,

Thomas J. Clarke

154

[Dublin]

10 June 1912

Dear John [Daly],

...Good luck old man. Yours ever, Tom

PS A friend of ours Reynolds[35] (the auditor) will be in Limerick tomorrow and will call on you. He is secretary of our new Irish Insurance Scheme which has been started – as the lesser of two evils – to safeguard our young fellows from the contaminating influence of un-national societies they would be compelled to go to.

155

[Dublin]

11 May 1913

Dear John [Daly],

...Now about that Kilkenny and Limerick match. I have talked the matter over with a number of the GAA people with a view to get them to fix the thing up. But it wasn't until I got a hold of Tom Kenny[36] of Craughwell that I got an intelligent grip of the situation. I find there has been very strained relations existing between Kilkenny and Limerick sections – strained relations existing between the Central Council and Limerick and all dating back to that match in Dublin which Crowe referred over a year ago when Limerick was marked defeated. Then there is trouble in Limerick itself between rival boards here and the whole thing is in such a tangle that the Central Council is disposed to "go slow" in the matter of trying to put things right. This being the situation it is impossible to make the arrangements we have been trying to lead up to. On getting this line of things from Kenny I saw the others that had been interesting themselves in the matter and found out from them that what Kenny said was exactly true and I promptly cursed and damd their stupidity in not letting me know this and not be wasting energy on an impossible proposition. I asked each of them to suggest some way out – something that would in its results work out as the other idea (Kilkenny v Limerick in Limerick) would have done. Various suggestions were given me – the most practical and definite being that from Mick Crowe. He says he can arrange to bring down a Dublin Hurling team or a Dublin Football team – or two teams – to play in Limerick for the object you wish. How would that do? Let me know. If it will be all right drop a line no matter how short to Crowe – 58 Cabra Park, Dublin. He is a slippery – a damd slippery – duck but we will keep him up to this and do so more effectively if the complexion can be put upon it that you are directly connected with him in the negotiations.

…Shawn Mac Dermott was away for a spell but got back last Sunday. He will be going off again the latter end of the week I think to Limerick and Kilkee to spend a few weeks with you. He left here yesterday and won't be back till Tuesday morning – gone West I think.

Hobson has been in Belfast for the past week or ten days and I am not sure when he is likely to get back. He had been feeling unwell and went home to rest up for a spell. A letter came from Limerick for him on Sat which Shawn and I identified as in your hand-writing on the envelope which I have of course forwarded to Bulmer.

…Good luck, as ever Tom

156

Dublin,
18 June 1913

Dear John [Daly],

Just a hurried note. We are getting the memorial project well to the front at last. Things are moving in various directions as indicated by enclosed clippings from to-night's Evening Telegraph. We have a majority of the central council of G.A.A. pledged in favour of the next opportunity for a big tournament. It was touch and go for us to get the reply of the Louth v. Kerry match in Jones's Road on Sunday week next.

The cinematograph picture showing in the various towns (Pilgrimage procession, etc) will count for much in getting the project, etc., before the minds of the younger element. I saw A. Griffith the other day and he was pleased to stand in with us on the General Purposes Committee and also to give us whatever space we need for reports of meetings, etc…I know it will please you to see that there is a good spirit amongst the workers of the Committee in charge of the memorial work.

Jameson the picture show man was very reluctant to touch the [Bodenstown] pilgrimage – didn't think it would be so very popular. I went up and had a talk with him. The argument that carried weight with him was that I would be able to get an advertisement about the film in Irish Freedom, Sinn Féin and the Gaelic American…I forgot to say Jameson has a number of picture show places in a number of towns in Ireland. He is an Irish man and the only man in the business in a big way in Ireland.

Yours in haste,
Thos. J. Clarke

157
Dublin,
25 June 1913

Dear John [Devoy],
Don't publish anything about Pilgrimage to Bodenstown until you hear from me by next mail. We have a good report and pictures for you. 'Twas an immense success, at least 5,000 people around the grave.

The march was very imposing, inspiring. Went off with military precision all the way to the graveside. Jameson, Cinematograph man, there, took pictures, these have been exhibited twice or thrice nightly since (22nd inst.) in the Rotunda and Rathmines. No pictures he has ever shown (and he has been 14 years in the business) ever received such tremendous applause. The old round room appeared to shake. The pictures are grand. He is to show them next in Galway, then in Tralee. Afterwards Queenstown, then Cork, then the Curragh, then back to Rathmines and Rotunda.

…Don't say a single word about that sketch of a suggested design in Freedom. 'Tis a horrible thing entirely and we and members are all of one opinion on that. So don't think that is our idea of the monument that will be erected to Wolfe Tone and the United Irishmen and put us down as a pack of thick mugs (I mean don't say a single word reproaching us).

Poor [John] Daly is completely paralysed in both legs, Can't move at all now, as far as they are concerned. I'm going down to see him in a couple of weeks. Maybe it will be our last meeting. They tell me he thinks he is going fast and they fear he may be right, so they sent me up word to come. Shawn MacDermott has been down in Limerick with Daly for several weeks past. Comes back this evening.

There is an old "Bags" over her at present from Providence, R.I. – name Gibbons – tell my friend J.L. that if he has any more in that town of this kind will he for God's own sake keep them at home or put them into some high-walled lunatic asylum. In fact I feel like sending across a request for some one to come over and lug him back quick. There now! I'll feel easier after relieving myself of some super-heated steam.

There will probably be a general election before the Home Rule Bill is placed on the Statute Book. Even suppose it passes, a general election must in the ordinary course take place soon after. If by any chance, and it is not unlikely, a Unionist Government comes into power they'll suspend its [Home Rule] operation. This is not so much my own opinion as that of most of the well-informed folk here with whom I am in contact.

…Good luck. Hope you keep well.

Tom

PS I made reference to Col. Ric. [Burke] and to John Devoy's cablegrams at the graveside (when I had to preside) and both names were wildly cheered. I'm feeling ten years younger since Sunday. At last we see tangible results from the patient, plodding work of sowing the seed. The tide is running strongly in our direction. <u>We have the rising generation</u>.

158

Letter published in *Irish Freedom*, October 1913

75 Parnell Street

I have witnessed a number of fierce riots in Ulster in bye-gone times, was present when buck-shot was fired into an unarmed crowd in Dungannon, which so infuriated them that in their frenzy they closed in on a strong *posse* of police who were sweeping through them with fixed bayonets, and the crowd, with naked hands, came to grips with the police and put them to flight. I saw brutal things done that day on both sides. As might be expected there was much bloodshed – one killed outright and a long list of wounded was the toll. Later on I witnessed the Bowery hooligans and New York police have a "set to." The fight was fierce and some savage acts were witnessed.

It has fallen to my lot to get considerable first hand knowledge of the ruffianism of the criminal classes of London's underworld. Yet nothing I know of during my whole career can match the downright inhuman savagery that was witnessed recently in the streets and some of the homes of our city, when the police were let loose to run amok and indiscriminately bludgeon every man, woman and child they came across, in many cases kicking them on the ground after felling them with the baton. They have wrecked the homes of dozens of our citizens, smashing windows, fanlights, doors, furniture, china, pictures – everything breakable; murderously assaulting the inmates, irrespective of age or sex. The new-born babe at its mother's breast wasn't safe any more than the sick mother herself; in one instance she was dragged out of bed and clubbed, and the poor wee babe got it, too, and showed the result in a black eye. An avalanche of evidence is just now available to sustain everything I am stating.

Dublin, with its people the most easy-going and peaceful of any city I know, is staggered by what has happened. Totting up the "casualties", we find two dead and about a thousand maimed and battered citizens have received treatment in the public hospitals and private surgeries of the city! A bloody holocaust, surely! But a fitting one to be dedicated to Dublin Castle and its idea of "Law and order".

In the course of my business I have occasion to come in contact with all classes of our citizens – Catholic and Protestant – journalists and other professional men, as well as business men and tradesmen and the ordinary working man. Almost everyone I have met during the last week or so has spoken about the action of the police, and only one note have I heard – that of wrathful indignation against Dublin Castle and its methods.

When Dublin Castle is mentioned in this connection let it not be forgotten that the recent shocking exhibition of police brutality is nothing new in our city. There are still people amongst us who carry on their person scars and infirmities – results of the Police Riot in Phoenix Park on August 6th, 1871, when the people were bludgeoned right and left there; the bludgeoning was carried on right down into the city. But very few are aware that it is on record that Mr. John Mallon (Assistant Commissioner of Police) has stated that "the police were to blame for the riot," and that "the two senior officers (of police) were drunk" that day. Then, again, in 1881, Mr Frederick Moir Bussy, a prominent English journalist connected with the London Press, writing later about what he witnessed, states:- "In Dublin…I have seen the police smash the heads of the people and kick women and girls on the side-walk of the principal street"… "As we were well aware that most of these fellows (the police) had changed uniforms before leaving barracks that evening so that they should not be indentified in case of accidents, or at least be able to provide an alibi in the event of being summoned according to their numbers."

This statement of Mr. Bussy is startlingly significant in the light of "conflicting evidence" in the coroner's Court the other day.

An enquiry into the conduct of the police has been demanded by the Lord Mayor and Corporation of the City. Is this "enquiry", my Lord Mayor and City fathers, to be engineered by Dublin Castle? Is that what you want? Is that what the great bulk of the citizens want? I would undertake to say that 80 per cent of the citizens would answer "No; we know what the result of such a machined enquiry would be."

The interests of the city – the lives and property of the citizens – not to speak of national dignity and the dictates of common humanity demand that there should be and must be an independent enquiry – free of Castle control – an enquiry free to probe and search in every direction – even up to the private chambers of Dublin Castle, and bring out into the light of day and before the gaze of he world's opinion whoever and whatever was responsible for this blood lust of official hooliganism in our midst.

Even as it is, the machinery of the police department of Dublin Castle is busy at work. We can see it operating in various directions. For instance (apart from the Police Court incidents), a D.M.P. Inspector called upon a friend of mine, who is a B.A. of Trinity College, and tendered him an apology for two policemen who had without the slightest provocation brutally assaulted him in the presence of several witnesses. The Inspector gave this written apology on condition that the gentleman would drop the matter.

Thos. J. Clarke

———————————————

159
Dublin,
10 October 1913

Dear John [Daly],
…W. J. Ryan is talking about going down for a weekend to have a chat. He will have a few days to spare and mentioned that he didn't know just where to spend them. Katty suggested his going down to Limerick and spending a couple of days with you. Ryan was delighted with the suggestion for he has a great regard for you and all the time is making enquiries how you are getting on.

The town is quiet – very quiet – business is rotten all over although with us up to the present it hasn't affected the receipts very much – if anything they are better. The improvement in this respect coincides with one of the assistants leaving about a month ago in Amiens Street.

I set a trap for Seaghan Mac Dermott some time ago. I knew he suspected Seamus O'Connor of being concerned in sending that love letter from Limerick. So I quietly told Seamus to ask Seaghan the first time he met him "What about that letter you got?" Later on they met in the shop and Seamus asked the question (of course knowing nothing at all about the matter at the time) and Seaghan went for him and cursed him up and down and let loose the vials of his wrath upon Seamus who was completely mystified over the thing and could do nothing but laugh and roar and laugh and this only made Seaghan all the hotter. It was a good farcical bit of business for nearly half an hour. In a day or two after I gave Seaghan a drop by telling him Seamus knew nothing about it and that he only gave the game away to him.

There is a contribution of mine in last Gaelic American to hand signed "Rory the Rover"[37]. Did you read it?

Love to all, Good luck old friend, as ever Tom

160
Dublin,
8 December 1913

Friend Joe [McGarrity],

Your letter received OK and a very encouraging one it was for all of us. I read it to the Wolfe Tone Committee – Shawn MacDermott our vice-president being to the fore and Shawn was directed to attend to the matter of the certificates – he and Chas. K. Kickham (nephew of the Chas. J. Kickham of '67 fame) our secretary being associated in the work – Shawn will probably communicate with you in the course of the week.

Joe, it is worth living in Ireland these times – there is an awakening – the slow, silent, plodding and the open preaching is at last showing results, things are in full swing on the up grade – and we are breathing air that compels one to fling up his head and stand more erect.

I can't – I won't try to give you a history of the causes that have brought about what I refer to – just take for granted that the prospect today – from the national point of view is brighter than it has been in many a long year – certainly as far back as my memory goes – and remember I am no spring chicken and some of the boys here have no scruple about keeping me reminded of the fact by referring to me as 'the old chap'.

You will see in the Gaelic American what was done in Dublin to commemorate the anniversary of the deaths of Allen, Larkin and O'Brien. It was a magnificent demonstration – the finest thing of its kind I ever witnessed in Dublin or anywhere else – and let me tell you no other party in Ireland today could have brought the people together – so many different and opposing sections for the purpose except ourselves. My friend the heart of Ireland is sound in spite of Redmond and his people and their ranting about being loyal to the British Empire.

The volunteer movement caught on in great style here in Dublin. Such an outpouring of young fellows was never seen. They filled the Rink in the Rotunda Gardens (which holds 7,000), filled the adjacent

garden, overflowed into the large Concert Hall in the Rotunda buildings and packed the street around the entrances and upwards 5,000
people at least had tried to get up to entrance and had to go back home.
The places were packed too closely to enable the stewards to move
around inside and have enrolment forms filled, but even as it was there
were about 4,000 enrolled that night. Then the drills – every hall packed
since – too much packed to allow of satisfactory drilling – then the class
of fellows who are there – and the enthusiasm and the National note in
the atmosphere! – 'tis good to be in Ireland these times.

The government has taken alarm and issued a proclamation forbid-
ding importation of arms. I hoped they wouldn't do so for some
months, but the drilling will go ahead and already we know it is not
going to cause any panicky feeling among the volunteers – hundreds
of young fellows who could not be interested in the National
Movement, even on the milk and water side, are in these volunteers and
are saying things which proves that the right spot has been touched in
them by the volunteering. Wait till they get their fist clutching the steel
barrel of a business rifle and then Irish instincts and Irish manhood can
be relied upon...

Yours as ever, Tom

161
[Dublin]
26 January 1914

Dear John [Daly],
...Sir Roger Casement called this evening and told me of the meeting
yesterday and how delighted he was with his stay with you. Both he
and Pearse say your Limerick meeting was the best in many respects of
any they have been at yet. That's grand.

The various Companies here during the last week and tonight have
been out route marching and the members are delighted at the way
they have acquitted themselves. Their instructors – mostly ex-army
non-commissioned officers – also speak in high terms of the extraor-

dinary progress the men have made in learning the drill. They say they have made more progress in a couple of weeks than the ordinary British Army recruit would make in 6 or 9 months.

…We had a collector with a Wolfe Tone Fund can down at Waterford yesterday. He tells me there were at least 200 police in a cordon surrounding the platform John Redmond etc were speaking from and no-one was allowed to get near the platform. How is that for Nationality!

…Good luck and still more rapid progress be yours.

Love to all, Tom

___

162
[Dublin]
29 April 1914

Dear John [Daly],
…Great God how I do rail against providence that you are not in shape to be around and about. Never in our recollection has there ever been such an opportunity to get results from intelligent National effort and work as in these days and no-one alive in Ireland today could give a better account of himself in work of this kind as yourself – record – reputation – sincerity of purpose. You would tower away above any one else who is working on our National work…

Anyway I will get to the point. Redmond and Co are thoroughly alarmed at the wildfire-like spread of the Volunteer Movement. We were prepared for some attempt on his part to make his peace with the influential ones of the Provisional committee when Easter recess came around. That anticipation was correct. Redmond (John) had a meeting with John McNeill and to make a long story short offered to finance the Volunteer Movement if 'the party' would be allowed to have a controlling "say" upon the Irish Volunteers – not agreed to by McNeill, John left after failing.

Simultaneously with this Joe Devlin had an interview with Sir R. Casement. His proposition to him was practically the same as

Redmond's to McNeill. You can judge of the result when Devlin at the conclusion of the interview put the situation thus: "well the young men of the country are flocking into the Volunteer Movement and of course as a consequence are drawn away from 'the party' and this is going on at such a rate that it means the smashing of the party – unless we smash the Volunteer Movement". Joe went off to report failure.

Now Joe is contemplating starting a boys' organisation on the same lines as the Ancient Order of Hibernians – a sectarian boys' organisation. This were he to succeed would be a very serious affair but already steps are being taken to counteract his work and bowl over his attempts. The machinery of the Irish Volunteers will be utilized to organise an Irish Volunteer boys' organisation on the same lines and upon the same principles as the Irish Volunteer organisation. McNeill and the majority of the Provisional Committee are sound upon this as they are upon the national question generally and in spite of Joe and the support of the priests throughout the country which he is endeavouring to enlist in his attempt, he will not succeed.

With a view of preventing the possibility of Redmond or Joe attempting in the near future any tricks to capture the Irish Volunteers organisation it has been quietly decided to have no more co-options on the Provisional Committee. I asked Pat Mc Cartan to come down last week. I wanted to consult him in a few matters…His most interesting news is that the Volunteers – Irish Volunteers – are being formed in almost every parish and hamlet and town in Ulster and while the Carsonites regard the Hibernians with fierce hatred and detestation they have a somewhat friendly face for the Irish Volunteers. He is in the confidence of the leading Carsonites of his own district and was able to tell me before-hand of the landing of arms at Larne, etc. He also told me they were expecting a ship-load of ammunition to be landed somewhere on the Donegal coast in a few days (this is evidently the ship-load which the papers have twisted to be a load of arms for the Irish Volunteers).

I have a letter from Eamonn Blythe in Belfast…He and some others of those young north of Ireland Protestant Nationalists with our own

274 • Tom Clarke: Life, Liberty, Revolution

papishes are preparing the way for a big anti-partition meeting in Belfast in order to set the pace for the rest of Ireland. They have been addressing the mob at street corners and distributing handbills and supplying paragraphs to the papers with the result that last night they held a meeting at Clonard St (off the Falls Rd) at which there were 2,000 persons and they had the whole meeting with them a unit for anti-partition and the ground has been prepared to such an extent that they are going to hold an anti-Home Rule meeting.

By the way, what I tell you of Joe Devlin and John Redmond's interview is strictly private – none of the members of the Provisional committee outside a couple of our own friends know nothing of it – nor will they know.

For strategic purposes it is necessary to keep the matter quiet for the present.

We are going to have a great pilgrimage this year to Bodenstown. I have written across and urgently requested a loan of Col. Ric Burke to put the finishing touch upon the completeness of our arrangements. Should we get him over he must go down and spend a while with you.

It is 11 o'clock. Good luck Tom

163
Dublin,
14 May 1914

Dear Uncle[38] [John Devoy],
I know with what interest you follow things in the old country and how you hanker after reliable information regarding conditions, so I am going to try and give you a "line" upon the situation here at present writing.

The country is electrified with the volunteering business – never in my recollection have I known in any former movement anything to compare with the spontaneous rush that is being made all over to get into the movement and start drill and get hold of a rifle. John E. Redmond and Co. were panic-stricken at what was happening, and when too late for themselves privately opened negotiations with the leading members of the Irish Volunteer Provisional Committee. These members didn't rise to the bait and still the volunteering went on at a gallop.

The Home Rule Bill will pass as it stands, but an amending Bill re Exclusion [of Ulster], will be introduced as a result of an understanding between the Government and the Opposition (Redmond and Co. quite ignored in this). We have known of this for some weeks, so that there were more pourparlers between the Irish Volunteer people and Redmond, Devlin & Co. to consider what should be done in face of this new development. I believe a programme was mapped out by the I. V. people and has been approved of by the other people, with the result that a "private and confidential" circular has been issued by the National Secretary of the A. O. H. [John D. Nugent, Nat. Secretary of the Ancient Order of Hibernians, Board of Erin] to all the divisions directing all the members to join the Volunteers – join the companies that are already formed and form committees to start new companies and regiments, where they don't already exist, and emphasising the necessity of sinking all minor points and join hands in this work with all creeds and classes of the people who are working in the movement. This circular was only sent out this week, but I saw a copy of it, and upon my word one would think it was written by an ultra Sinn Féiner.

…Volunteering is going on at a rather rapid rate in Ulster (I mean Irish volunteering). I know this from an old friend up there named Carrick [Pat McCartan] from whom I hear often; and the strange thing about it is that in some sections the Carsonites regard the Irish Volunteers with a friendly face, and in fact some of the influential ones in conversation with prominent Volunteer men say that if it comes to a scrap between them (Carsonites) and the English they know that the Irish Volunteers would fight with them and not against them. This is an extraordinary change in the attitude of the one-time Orangeman, when he even allows himself to entertain the thought of himself and the papists fighting together in any circumstances. However, seeing with what lightening-like rapidity things are developing in various directions, one needn't be surprised at anything now.

And the change that has come over the young men of the country who are volunteering! Erect, Heads up in the air, the glint in the eye, and then the talent and ability that had been latent and is now being discovered! Young fellows who had been regarded as something like wastrels now changed to energetic soldiers and absorbed in the work, and taking pride that at last they feel they can do something for their country that will count. Tis good to be alive in Ireland these times.

[James] Larkin's people for some time past have been making war on the Irish Volunteers. I think this is largely inspired by a disgruntled fellow named O'Casey[39]. By this attitude they have antagonised the sympathy of all sections of the country and none more than the advanced section. Liberty Hall is now a negligible quantity here.

…The family are well and in real good health and business is splendid. Good-bye. Trusting you keep strong and in good health, with all sorts of kind wishes to old friends.

T. James.

P.S. Since finishing my letter last night I was talking to a lady belonging to the Lady Volunteer Committee…Two Limerick ladies [Madge and Laura Daly] were present to get information, etc., in order to start a committee in that city. Those ladies, by the way, are nieces of the old Rebel, John Daly. Another married sister [Kathleen Clarke] was with them who is a member of the Dublin Committee

----

164
Dublin,
3 June 1914

Dear John [Devoy],
Enclosed clippings from the Clare Champion. I had a lot more but have mislaid them. However, this will serve your purpose. If you can see your way to tackle [Colonel Arthur] Lynch[40] in another article, we will see to it that it will be reprinted and circulated all through Co. Clare. We have Lynch nearly flattened out as it is. Tom Hayes, Ben

Parsons and others here in Dublin have been going for his scalp, and Maguire, Editor of the Clare Champion, is after him. So between us we will do for the s- of a b- (as Curtayne would put it).

Everything goes well here, but the old age appears to be creeping on me. Most of the time I feel 'moidered' and can't cope with all the work that is crying out to be attended to on my doorstep. But I'll peg away in any case, and like my friends the Carsonites, do what is right and damn the consequences.

Yours sy.,

Thos. J. Clarke

P.S. Eoin Mac Neill will be speaker at Bodenstown, June 21.

165

[Dublin]

7 July 1914

Dear Uncle [John Devoy],

Got your letter all right. You've did quite right in regard to that money. When we found you were sending it we figured out why and I see by your letter that we got very close to the exact situation.

This morning's Independent gives the American Committee's cablegram to Eoin Mac Neill and to John Redmond – both given in full. These cablegrams will have a powerful effect for good upon the volunteers and upon the Country. The Independent has a circulation of 70,000 daily.

The Freeman and the Irish Times only give an extract with an editorial foot-note in both cases. The Irish Times does not circulate very much amongst our side of the house and the Freeman's Journal has only a circulation of 10,000.

A letter was sent to McGarrity last Wednesday from the Provisional committee per Eoin Mac Neill asking you to send no more money, instead to buy arms and send them. The sending will be a matter of arrangement that must be attended to in the very near future and on which you may expect to hear something before long. This is a question of the utmost importance which we here realize as well as you on your side.

That letter to McGarrity from the Provisional committee should have the effect of strengthening your hand over there as much as your cablegrams have strengthened the hands of the Volunteers against Redmond's designs.

You have sized up the situation here correctly. The program that Redmond is working upon is just what you have mapped out, but he will fail and will be smashed. Day by day the situation has improved since the Provisional Committee's betrayal. That Betrayal was almost entirely due to Hobson and Mac Neill. The O'Rahilly and others made no bones about it and say it was only Hobson's attitude that swayed them at the last moment. They believed he spoke for and represented the virile section of the Volunteer movement. They now recognize the terrible mistake they made and are full of regrets. Hobson expresses no regret. On the contrary boasts of the part he played. At a hastily summoned meeting of the paper committee he was accused of selling out (he objected to the word but admitted the fact). Result – his connection with the paper completely severed – the friendship of all his old colleagues gone too. He will be before long an outcast. Even his standing on the Provisional Committee will be a more or less impossible one. 'Tis a great pity. He with his great ability and in some respects he has ability in greater measure than any one in Ireland. But it is some satisfaction to know that in spite of all his ability and popularity he was promptly put in his place when he showed the cloven hoof. He and I had been more intimate than any other two men in this town so you can judge of the feeling against him in other directions when you find me speak as I do. It has been a terrible stab to me.

We are standing in the ranks of the Volunteers to a man – a splendid spirit. The cities and towns are quite safe and some whole counties and a great many country sections. This I know from first-hand information. Take it for granted Redmond cannot control this movement. Even now in spite of the decision of the Provisional Committee he no more controls the cities and towns than a man in Timbuctoo – 95 per cent of the Dublin Volunteers are right. Cork held elections for Company Commanders. Six of the eight were elected on a straight issue against Redmonite control, the other two are against it but the issue did not enter into the elections. Limerick is the only case where that was made an issue in the recent elections for the permanent Committee. Geo. Clancy, a friend of ours, got over 400 votes against Lalor (Redmonite) who polled only 60 votes. Practically the whole of the Limerick Provisional committee was elected on the permanent committee. Belfast had a meeting of its elected Volunteer officers – 68 officers present, representing about 3,000 men, Denny McCullough elected permanent Chairman, motion approving Redmonite control was proposed but had to be withdrawn owing to the indignant opposition offered by the majority. This I got from Denny. Pat McCartan assures me Tyrone is completely lost to Redmond and Devlin. My friend Reilly, Vice-Chairman of the Cavan County Council tells me that Cavan, Fermanagh and Monaghan stands 75 per cent. of the best men in the Irish Volunteers against Redmondite control. You must understand we had a big temperance demonstration last Sunday week and we had people from all parts of Ireland here. I saw a great many old friends. Derry, Strabane, Dungannon, Omagh, Newry, etc., etc., from places in the other three Provinces. Every one speaks in much the same strain and in almost every case real good men with the real Volunteer spirit if they don't control, they influence their respective committees.

Any of our friends on your side who are holding aloof from the I. V. Fund Committee there fearing Redmond's control are making a mistake. He is not controlling, he won't be allowed control it. That movement will smash him into little pieces in a five months time. Already the A. O. H. is practically smashed all over the country. The moribund U. I. L. can only be seen in the ramshackle Machine that tries to pass resolutions etc., in different parts of the country.

I am feeling very much run down, over work and worriment is leaving its mark on me and I am feeling it within myself. But I must peg away. Flynn [Seán MacDiarmada] is exactly in the same class and P.

Cove [P. S. O'Higgins] looks even worse. Denny McCullough has been ordered away by the doctor, he is threatened with consumption. Magnificent workers are these young men.

Good luck. Tom.

166
27 July 1914
[Dublin]

Special cable to the *Gaelic American*

The authorities outwitted. Two thousand rifles landed at Howth yesterday. Slight skirmish returning to Dublin. Lost twenty rifles. Otherwise all well.

167
Hotel St George,
51 Clarke Street,
Brooklyn Heights,
New York,
23 September 1914

Coded letter to John Devoy

Dear Sister,
You will be anxious to hear that I arrived safely without ever being questioned. I gave the gold ear-rings to the New York Gaelic Leaguer who was with me but they merely took his name and address.

Things look fairly good regarding the establishment of the mission which we all discussed. Our friend reached Rome and found those interested at the Vatican very friendly. As you know ere this he went on to see the Superior but unfortunately did not see him personally. The fathers here think Father Roger should go to Rome at once as he can do most there. The say a capital of five thousand would be useless. It must be at least twenty five thousand or better fifty thousand. Better they think have as few converts as possible along – as they would be safer on the foreign mission. A plan of the building for which Father John asked (marked in pencil "Athlone") is being sent to him and Father Roger should take a copy or copies of same with him. The prayer books will be ready in a week or two. His friend here (marked in pencil "Bulmer") took charge of them and is following his advice regarding them.

Many good Catholics would object to the project if it were made public as it would be misunderstood. Fr Roger must rush the superiors into making the public statement we spoke of. It will clear the air considerably. The anti-Catholics will oppose the new mission strongly but their voice will not count for much if the friends at Fr Roger's disposal are large enough.

Your fond sister,

Mary

168

[Dublin]

October 20 1914,

Dear John [Daly],

Katty was telling you about the new daily paper it is the intention to start – Griffith, Beaslai and three or four other journalists interested in it. Probably W. J. Ryan chief Editor – if he accepts it.

The business end will receive careful attention and the best available man will be put in charge. With £300 we calculate the paper can be kept going until about January or Feb. About £200 of this will be on hand at the end of the week.

At this juncture, with the daily press of Dublin closed on all Irish news, where it is not outrageously garbled, the crying need of some daily paper to give reliable news as far as it will be possible to secure it, as well as to present to the public happenings at home and abroad from the point of view of how such news affect Irish National interests is obvious.

You will of course wish to be with us in this.

I remember that incident lately – "Anthony Mackey v Sinn Féin" when you were speaking of sending £50 to Griffith. In this present case I would suggest that even half of that should be the very highest limit to which you should go.. Under no circumstances, I would say, should you exceed £25. I venture to say that knowing your generosity might likely imperil you to do more than you should.

I saw the lawyer who acts for the Landlord of 77 Amiens St and I had a very satisfactory interview with him. He is to write to the Landlord to release me from the lease and promised to let us have word in the course of a couple of days. Soon as I hear from him we will shift up to rooms overhead the 75 Parnell St shop. I suppose it will take a week or so to straighten those rooms out which will keep Katty busy.

As soon as that is finished I mean to take a week off and go down and spend it with you. I do need a rest very badly. I feel almost done up. I have a great big budget of news to give you and have been very anxious to chat over things with you.

…With every good wish, as ever Tom

169

[Dublin]

2 June 1915

Dear John [Daly],

You will like to hear about Sean Mac D. I saw him today in the Court house dock. He looked remarkably well and quite bright and seemed pleased to recognise a good many friends amongst those present.

You will have seen by tonight's paper that the case has been adjourned for a week. This was at the insistence of his counsel Tim Healy. The case seems to be creating considerable interest in Dublin but very few seem to think that he won't be jailed. I will go up to Mountjoy tomorrow and have a chat with him in the cage.

…Daly's finger is all right again. He and everyone as usual. Good luck as ever, Tom

170

Coded letter to John Devoy

[Dublin]

1915

I am in receipt of yours of May last. I need hardly tell you how glad I am to see that America isn't going to let the Huns off so easy for the great crime they committed against civilization in sinking the Lusitania. I see where they now allege that she had ammunition on board which Sam Hughes very promptly denies.

Nothing is too bad for them to do and the sooner conscription is put in place in these countries the sooner the war will be over.

By the way I suppose you saw how Redmond and Co have been tricked over the Home Rule Bill. Sir Edward has the best of him by odds and is now a Cabinet minister. It has given a great setback to Redmond altogether and I think the worst of it will be it will set all the young men of the country back to O'Leary's policy. It is all very fine for us Orangemen now but if it changes the humbug policy of Redmond to the dangerous and forward policy of O'Leary and Donovan I don't know what to say and a person who was down south in Munster says the people have turned altogether already. They also say that John had the Liberals in the palm of his hand for the past 7 years and now instead he has only a handful of broken pledges. Only for the Defence of the Realm Act Ireland would be at the mercy of the wretched physical force party but as it is I don't think there is any great fear of them pushing their policy to extremes as we have them too well watched.

Jack and Jim are to be tried again on Monday. It is too bad the way these 2 boys were misled. They say it was all owing to a few they got in with down in Enniscorthy that was the cause of it.

Anyhow, I hope they will get out of this and shall be better citizens in future. It is all nonsense this crying down of the Allies and besides it is a shame to see the leisurely way the youth of the country, that is the farmer's sons, are treating this serious business. One would never think that the Huns were almost within rifle shot of London as they were in the air raid during this week. There are a great many Belgians up and down the country just now. They are a hardy vigorous lot and one would think if they had any nationality in them they would be out in the trenches instead of living on charity in this country.

It knocks the bottom out of the "cause" for which our brave boys are pouring their life blood in Flanders – that of revenging Belgium.

I am sending you a paper that will interest you.

There are no celebrations to be held up north this Twelfth which will make matters for us rather dull this year. The Volunteers are going ahead – the "Ulster" division, as there are now 3 Divisions – the Ulster (our own) – the National (Redmond's) and the Irish (the Sinn Féin or physical force party as they call them).

But our boys are by far the best of the crowd they are earnest and now that Sir Ed is on the Cabinet there is no standing them on drill nights with enthusiasm. The only things we are short of are arms but we have been promised these from "Canada" by the brotherhood there acting under Lodge 67.

Bye the way the Government made a great capture last Sunday week a fellow named McDermott he is one of those blood thirsty good for nothing thunder and turf fellows who is always spouting sedition and who at one time ran a rag I think he called Mr Freedom. Well this lad went down to Tuam and there commenced to give out against our glorious Empire when the DI reached for him. Now he is awaiting his trial on Wed next when they say he will have something to think of for the rest of his shortened span.

I am anxious to get that orange paper you promised some time ago which I never received.

With best wishes and kindest regards,

Yours fraternally,

Tee Dee

171

O'Donovan Rossa Funeral Committee,
Dublin,
18 July 1915

Dear Madge [Daly],

Katty is over in Liverpool – she and Sean McGarry as a deputation from the Funeral Committee – to meet Mrs. O'Donovan Rossa when she lands today. Mrs. Rossa had written to me, placing in my hands the matter of funeral arrangements and gave me a general authorization. Already before receiving that letter we had started work and divided the work of the funeral arrangements into departments, placing a sub-committee in charge of each (we have 11 sub-committees at work up to present) the whole supervised by the executive of the Wolfe Tone Memorial Association. At present from the reports we are receiving from different parts of the country the funeral promises to be the largest ever seen here since that of the Manchester Martyrs. The Southern and G. W. Railway will run cheap excursions from all over the system – all the other railways are doing much the same except the Northern – they want a money guarantee – which we will not give them.

At present there seems every likelihood that the remains will lie in state in the Cathedral here (with armed guard of honor, etc). The Obsequies sub Committee is in communication with the Archbishop and it seems likely from the correspondence that he will make a departure from precedent in such cases. Rossa's remains will leave New York on 17th inst and the funeral take place on Sunday August 1st. When Katty gets back we will know who will be on the delegation that accompanies the remains. Miss O'Donovan Rossa will be with her mother.

I saw those four men who got orders to "get off the earth" – all four were here in Dublin during the week[41]. I see they held a big mutiny in the heart of Joe Devlin's district in Belfast and had the support of the crowd with them in the stand they are taking. I hear from Sean fairly often – he is in great health and spirits.

I am writing this to you as I owe you several letters, but of course Uncle John will understand that I have him in my mind's eye as I write and he will understand. You may be blaming me for neglect in some things you asked me to do in your letters. With one thing and another I am rushed as I never have been before and am sometimes "moidered" as to which thing of the heap should receive attention first. Just now a good deal of extra work is coming my way and as things must be made a success I am not disposed to shirk anything. Tom and Emmet are with Mrs Holohan. Daly is keeping house with me. Katty may be home tomorrow. Come up for the funeral – it will be worth attending. We are getting out a souvenir of it – all our best writers engaged on the work. Oh God, if Uncle J were only able to be with us in these times. Many and many a time do I regret that he is knocked out. He would be worth a whole army corps of the ordinary workers.

Love to him and to yourself and to all at home.

Yours, as ever,

Tom

172

[Dublin]

Sunday,

Dec 19 1915

Dear Madge [Daly],

I am sending you down some Anti-Conscription badges – about 2,000. The Cumann na mBan in other parts of the country and in Dublin have been selling them like wild fire and making money on them. They cost about 13/6 per 1,000.

If you don't require them I can take them back with me after Christmas.

All as usual here. Hope U. J. and every one same as when we last heard.

Yours as ever, Tom

173

[Dublin]

2 May 1916

Dear K,

I am in better health and more satisfied than for many a day – all will be well eventually – but this is my good-bye and now you are ever before me to cheer me – God bless you and the boys, let them be proud to follow same path – Sean [MacDiarmada] is with me and McG [Sean McGarry], all well they all heroes – I'm full of pride my love.

    Yours Tom

    Love to John and Madge, etc

174

Kilmainham Jail

3 May 1916

'Message to the Irish People'

I and my fellow-signatories believe we have struck the first successful blow for Freedom. The next blow, which we have no doubt Ireland will strike, will win through. In this belief we die happy.

    Thomas James Clarke

Notes to Letters

The letters in this collection were obtained from the following sources:

1, 128, 131, 149, 150, the National Museum of Ireland; **2** and **3**, the National Archives, Kew, London, Home Office Papers (hereafter HO), 45/9739/A55037and HO 144/195/A46664C/220; **4** and **6**, Thomas J. Clarke, *Glimpses of an Irish Felon's Prison Life* (Dublin: Maunsel and Roberts, 1922; 1970); **5**, Mealys' Auction, April 2006, accession lot 365. (This letter was purchased by a private buyer and not made available to the author. Consequently it has only been possible to use an excerpt given in the catalogue.); **7–70, 72–83, 85–124, 139, 142, 144**, National Library of Ireland (hereafter NLI), Thomas Clarke Papers, ACC 6410; **71, 84, 126, 129, 130, 132-6, 138, 140, 141, 143, 145, 146, 152, 154, 155, 159, 161, 162, 168, 169, 171, 172**, University of Limerick Archives, Daly Papers; **125, 127, 151, 153, 156, 157, 163, 164**, William O'Brien and Desmond Ryan (eds), *Devoy's Post Bag, 1871–1928, Volume II, 1880–1928*, (Dublin: C.J. Fallon Ltd, 1948); **137**, I am grateful to Peter O'Curry, Bottle Cottage, Finch Lane, Amersham, Buckinghamshire, England, for providing me with this letter; **147**, NLI, Fred Allan Papers, Ms 26,761; **148**, Kilmainham Gaol Archive; **158**, *Irish Freedom*, October 1913; **160**, Seán Cronin, *The McGarrity Papers*, (Tralee: Anvil Books, 1992); **165, 167, 170**, NLI, Joseph McGarrity Papers, Ms 17,609 (9) and 17,647 (3); **166**, NLI, John Devoy Papers, Ms 18,137 (4); **173** and **174**, Piaras F. MacLochlainn (ed.), *Last Words, Letters and Statements of the Leaders Executed after the Rising at Easter 1916* (Dublin: The Stationery Office, 1990).

1. The prison authorities remarked that this letter was written to a J [Joseph] Hart [originally from Donaghmore, County Tyrone] but was 'apparently intended for a Mr Done of New York'. Consequently it was felt necessary to 'call attention to the nature of the letter and ask whether it should be sent'. In a letter dated 23 November 1893 the prison authorities asked the advice of the Under Secretary of State at the Home Department as to whether the letter should be forwarded to the person to whom it was addressed. They noted how 'the whole letter relates to the failure of the United States Government to intervene to prevent the release of the prisoner and only the last two lines are really intended for Mr Hart'. In a minute written on the following day at the Home Office it was stated that even though the letter appeared to be written 'to urge on the movement for his release rather than for purely "political purposes"' there were 'strong objections' to allowing 'these prisoners' to communicate 'under cover to their friends with individuals, unknown and of unknown address'. Hence it was decided that the letter should not be sent.
2. Clarke's inexperience at public speaking was alluded to in the reply from Katty (12 April 1899) when, in wishing him success with his lecture, she assured him that 'you will not be so nervous when speaking about your "Prison Life" you know it was nervousness here in Limerick as anyone could see'.
3. Katty's reply (August 1899) was strong evidence of her love for Tom: 'It's ridiculous for you to think that because a lecturing tour fell through my love for you must change. Things may look black at present but if they looked as black again I cannot take back what I gave. As it is I am very glad it happened the time it did for if you had not high hopes you would not I know speak to me. You'd go off to America leaving me to the humiliating thought that I had given my love unasked unsought so you see there's a bright side to everything if we could only see it. I felt a bit dazed when I read your letter. I got it before Devoy's, not on my own account but on yours, knowing partly all you had built on that tour. I thought of your mother and sisters. What they must feel about it. For myself I'm no worse off than I was before. I have all I care about, your love and so long as I have that I'm all right'.
4. Tom's father, James Clarke, died of pneumonia, aged 64, on 3 March 1894.
5. James Stephens (1825–1901) was one of the founding members of the IRB in 1858. Charles Stewart Parnell approached the British government about the possibility of Stephens being allowed to return to Ireland from America. Permission was granted on the basis that no public demonstrations occurred and he came home on 25 September 1891. He lived in a cottage in Dublin and died on 29 March 1901.
6. The Boer War (October 1899–May 1902) was also a hot topic in Ireland as illustrated by Katty's letter of 30 October 1899: 'What do you think of the War? Isn't it grand the slating the English are getting? There's great excitement over it. You hear nothing on all sides from morning 'till night but war. Uncle John is threatening us he'll go off to the Transvaal. I can quite understand his wish to go but 'twould be very foolish of him as he would not be able to stand any hardship'.
7. In her reply (27 Nov 1899) Katty assured Tom that she also remembered their first intimate contact: 'I do remember the morning in the dining room very well and surprise for what was done faded in the surprise for who did it. I never at the time would suspect you guilty of such conduct'.
8. Henry Dalton was a fellow prisoner of Clarke's in Chatham and Portland prisons.
9. Expressing surprise that Tom had moved to a new address Katty commented 'I thought you were quite satisfied where you were but I suppose those niggers were too much for you. I must say I've an objection to them myself...' (28 March 1900).
10. Dora was the family's affectionate name for Hannah Clarke.
11. The 'National Election' to which Clarke referred was the United States Presidential Election of 1900 in which Republican William McKinley triumphed over the Democratic candidate William Jennings Bryan.

12. Katty's reply (18 March 1901) gave a strong indication that Maria would be disappointed in her hopes of marriage improving Tom's attitude to religion: 'It was kind of her to think of it. You can tell Maria from me that I'm afraid 'twill be all the other way. That instead of I making you a good Catholic you'll make me a bad one. I can't boast of ever being a very good one'.

13. The Daughters of Erin (Inghinidhe na hÉireann) was founded in 1900 with Maud Gonne as president and Annie Egan (wife of James) one of the vice-presidents. From that date until 1914 it was the main nationalist organisation for women in Ireland. Around the time this letter was written Madge Daly was attempting to establish a branch of the organisation in Limerick.

14. Tom's frustration was shared by Katty and she made her feelings clear in a letter dated 5 May 1901: 'Sometimes I think its U.J. I should blame. If he let me go back with you all this would be saved. 'Twould be rank heresy to say that here though I do feel he is more to blame than anyone else. Madge ate me when I said so to her. I said so to himself once too'.

15. Kathleen remembered how Tom had passed the exam and 'we were both delighted as we thought we were settled there for life'. However, he was advised by a friend named Fitzgerald who worked in the Civil Service not to take any subsequent offer of employment as the authorities might then investigate his past. She remembered how Tom 'thought it best to take his advice, with which I did not agree; personally, I thought Mr Fitzgerald was no friend'.

16. James Reidy (1873–1953) was born in Knockfierna, Ballingary, Co. Limerick, 23 January 1873. He was reputed to be a member of the IRB before emigrating to America in May 1896 where he secured employment as a journalist for the *New Era*. By 1902 he was an active member of Clan na Gael and had befriended John Devoy. With the establishment of the Devoy's *Gaelic American* in 1903 he was appointed assistant editor. From 1908 Devoy shared a house with Reidy and in 1916 he ciphered for Devoy the secret IRB supreme council document sent to him in February 1916, announcing that a rising had been decided upon. During the 1920s he was chairman of the United Irish-American Societies of New York and an active member of the American-Irish Historical Society.

17. Jack O'Hanlon was the Leinster representative on the supreme council of the IRB.

18. In 1907 Charles J. Dolan resigned from his position as Irish Parliamentary Party (IPP) MP for North Leitrim. In the subsequent by-election, in February 1908, he stood on a Sinn Féin ticket, losing to IPP candidate Francis Meehan.

19. The reference to 'the barber's idea' was in reply to Katty's letter of 10 February 1908 when she informed Tom that Madge was 'very anxious that you should get into the barbering business and believes that £40-£50 invested that way would bring better returns than the libraries'.

20. Kate McBride was the sister of John Devoy. On hearing of her death Kathleen wrote to Tom: 'I suppose I will go up to the sisters tomorrow. It gave me a kind of shock. I feel a bit unnerved over it. Strange isn't it when I did not care a rap for her – it may be the suddenness of it'.

21. This letter is important in that it illustrates the high regard in which Clarke held Seán MacDiarmada. However, an attempt was made at one stage to erase the words 'He is one of Hobson's school'. MacDiarmada and Hobson had been very close at one stage but Hobson's actions in relation to the Volunteers drove a wedge between both men. Indeed, it was MacDiarmada who arranged for him to be kidnapped on the eve of the Rising due to his outspoken opposition to the venture. It may well be that somebody wished to eliminate any evidence of a connection between both men and so tried to erase these words.

22. Laura was one of Kathleen's seven sisters.

23. The paper referred to was the *Irish Student* which had been initiated by Clarke and McCartan in order to give succour to the idea that the Irish language should be made

compulsory in the National University. It received financial backing from Joe McGarrity but after Douglas Hyde, President of the Gaelic League, promised that the language would be 'made essential' in the University, the journal was terminated after just two issues.

24. Joseph Patrick Nannetti (1851–1915) was first elected to Dublin city council as a councillor for the Rotunda ward in 1898 and remained a member until his death. He was twice lord mayor of Dublin (1906–7, 1907–8). In 1900 he was elected MP for Dublin (College Green) and was subsequently re-elected in 1906 and 1910.

25. Peter Donnelly sailed on the SS *California* from Glasgow on 1 April 1911 giving his address as Irish St Dungannon. He lived in Philadelphia where he had a grocery business in Delancy Street until his death about 1964. Donnelly was the brother-in-law of Patrick the IRB district centre in Maryhill, Glasgow in 1905. He was a member of a committee established in Dungannon on the instructions of Clarke to contribute to the support of the elderly parents of William Philip Allen, one of the 'Manchester Martyrs', executed in 1867.

26. Clarke enclosed the deleted excerpt with his letter. It read as follows: 'Jim! You are gone. May the sod rest lightly upon you my noble friend. Ireland lost a faithful son when you left us. And dear old friend Jack – self-reliant and courageous as any man could wish – ever true to Ireland – ever hopeful. I knew you in your prime, before I knew you in the British dungeons, old Fenian. Then you were full of energy and resourcefulness – doing and daring for Ireland. But now, alas, for Ireland's sake at this time you are an invalid. Oh the pity of it! But the poison they gave you that day, curse them, in the penal cells of Chatham, though it failed to kill you at the time, it has succeeded now. Their belladonna has succeeded in its stealthy work and placed you in an invalid's chair'.

27. James Bermingham (1853–1907) was a veteran of the 1867 Fenian rising and, as a member of the IRB, took part in an attack on the police barracks at Tallaght, near Dublin. He later became honorary treasurer of the Irish National Amnesty Association from 1892 until 1899.

28. Daniel Tallon (1836–1908), wine merchant and nationalist politician, was elected to Dublin Corporation for the Mansion House ward in 1890 and the following year joined the board of the Parnellite *Irish Daily Independent*. In 1895 he became High Sheriff of Dublin City and in 1897 was elected lord mayor for 1898 and 1899. Tallon was regarded as being responsible for undermining a proposed pro-Boer resolution brought before the Corporation in 1899, arguing that if passed it might cause the British parliament to reject legislation to extend the corporation boundaries. He supported loyal addresses when Dublin was visited by British monarchs Queen Victoria (1900) and Edward VII (1903). When Clarke wrote this letter Tallon was embarking on what turned out to be a successful tour of the United States with John Redmond to raise funds for a Parnell statue in Dublin. As well as dining with President McKinley at the White House both men managed to raise more than $30,000 for the project. (See *New York Times*, 3 December 1899). In a letter to Jim Bermingham on 25 October 1899 John Daly referred to Dan Tallon as a 'True blue Briton'. (See University of Limerick Archives, Daly Papers, Box 2, Folder 57 (2)). Clarke was probably unaware of the fact that Tallon had been a member of a deputation representing Dublin Corporation which, on 29 October 1894, had urged the Chief Secretary to grant an amnesty to Irish political prisoners.

29. The election referred to by Clarke was the Dublin Municipal election and Little, no doubt to Clarke's regret, beat Bermingham by 656 votes to 463 (See *Freeman's Journal* of 6, 13 and 20 July 1900).

30. In a letter to Jim Bermingham on 25 October 1899 John Daly commented on his disenchantment with the Irish in New York: 'In truth Jim I find that a goodly number of those professing advanced Nationalists here in this city of New York are Parliamentarians and partisans of Parliamentarians in the first place and advanced men after that … The worst of it is such men have great influence and they use it to boost up any one who starts to

jiggle with Mr. Parnell's name'. See University of Limerick Archives, Daly Papers, Box 2, Number 57 (2).

31. Colonel Tom Kelly (1833–1908) was an Irish-American Fenian, a veteran of the American Civil War and an associate of James Stephens. His rescue from police custody in Manchester in 1867 led to the death of a police sergeant and the consequent execution on 23 November that year of William Philip Allen, Michael Larkin and Michael O'Brien who became immortalised as the 'Manchester Martyrs'.

32. Michael McGinn and Lewis McMullan had been sworn into the IRB in Dungannon along with Clarke.

33. This letter from Clarke to Devoy concerned funds sent by the Clan na Gael in the USA to the IRB in Ireland. 'Neponset' was the code name of the Clan representative to the supreme council of the IRB that year. As Clarke mentioned, there was a discrepancy between the amount sent and that received by the supreme council – a total of £300. In 1910, the following year, another Clan visitor came over to Ireland with exact particulars of the amount sent, and attended a special meeting of the supreme council which had been summoned to meet him. P.T. Daly, Secretary of the latter body, did not come to the meeting, but sent a letter in which he admitted that he had received the missing £300 during his official visit to the Clan in the USA in 1908. He was removed from office and expelled from the organisation. These facts became public in December 1924 when a libel action brought by P.T. Daly against the Irish Transport and General Workers' Union and its official organ, *The Voice of Labour*, was tried. P.S. O'Hegarty, a member of the supreme council of the IRB from 1908 to 1915, who was personally acquainted with all the circumstances, gave evidence. Daly's action was dismissed.

34. It appears that Clarke's help could not save his sister's business and Hannah and her mother moved to Glasgow shortly after this.

35. John R. Reynolds, accountant, was a member of the IRB and treasurer for the Volunteers (see Bureau of Military History, Witness Statement 195, Molly Reynolds). He acted for Kathleen Clarke in dealing with Tom's estate.

36. Tom Kenny was an IRB member who had been arrested in connection with the killing of an RIC man in Craughwell, County Galway in 1908. After the split in the Volunteer movement he denied the Redmondites access to the pitch at Castlerea, County Roscommon on the grounds that the GAA was a non-partisan organisation.

37. Clarke's article under the pseudonym 'Rory the Rover' appeared in the *Gaelic American* of 27 September 1913 and included the letter he had written to *Irish Freedom*. However, the following addition appeared in the American paper: 'From a national point of view the police brutality we have just witnessed has been a good thing – one of the best things that has happened in this city for years. It has been brought home to even the milk and water Parliamentarians that the leopard has not changed his spots, that Dublin Castle, the citadel of English Government in this land of ours, is as brutal and tyrannical as ever it was. It speaks volumes that the Irish Parliamentary Party – that contemptible tail to the present English Government – up to the present time has been taking no more interest in what has been happening here in our city than if it occurred in Timbuctoo. But the handwriting is on the wall: they are doomed!'

38. In *Recollections of an Irish Rebel* Devoy comments (pp.394-6): 'Tom Clarke's letters to me during that period … threw an interesting light on the situation in Ireland and the hopes which the men who were executed in 1916 based on that situation … When communicating with us in America, Tom always addressed me as "Uncle", and wrote as though himself and his "uncle" were merely interested onlookers with respect to political developments'.

39. Seán O'Casey, future dramatist, had written some severe criticisms of the Irish Volunteers in the *Irish Worker*.

40. Colonel Arthur Lynch fought on the side of the Boers but his exaggerated claims to have been a major participant rankled with those who had fought with MacBride's Irish Brigade during the war.

41. Four men, Herbert Moore Pim, Denis McCullough, Liam Mellows and Ernest Blythe, had been issued with deportation orders by the British Government in July 1915. However, Clarke advised them to remain in the country with the result that McCullough was imprisoned for four months while the others received sentences of three months each.

Bibliography

Primary Sources

Archives of the University College Dublin
Irish Volunteers.
Denis McCullough Papers.

General Registrar's Office, Roscommon
Death certificate of James Clarke.

Kilmainham Gaol
Letters written by Thomas Clarke.

Leitrim County Library
Local Studies Collection, File 1598, Correspondence between Michael Whelan and Kathleen and Emmet Clarke.

National Archives Dublin
General Prison Board Ledgers.
1901 Census of Ireland.
1911 Census of Ireland.
Bureau of Military History Witness Statements.

National Library Dublin
Bulmer Hobson Papers.
Thomas Clarke Papers.
John Devoy Papers.
Pat McCartan Papers.
Denis McCullough Papers.
Joseph McGarrity Papers.
P. T. Madden Papers.
John Redmond Papers.

O'Fiaich Library and Archive, Armagh
Material collected by Father Louis O'Kane including Witness Statement of
William Kelly Senior.
University of Limerick Archives
Daly Papers.

English National Archives, Kew, London
Colonial Office Papers.
Home Office Papers.
War Office Papers.

Official Publications
*Minutes of Evidence taken before the visitors of her Majesty's Convict Prison at
Chatham as to the Treatment of certain prisoners convicted of Treason Felony, H. C.,
1890, xxxii.*
Hansard Parliamentary Debates.
*Thom's Official Directory of the United Kingdom of Great Britain and Ireland for
the year 1904.*

Articles
Bill Forsythe, 'Loneliness and Cellular confinement in English Prisons
1878–1921', *British Journal of Criminology* (2004) 44 (5) 7 May 2004.
Francis McKiernan, 'Carrigallen parish in 1821', *Breifne Journal*, 1962, vol ii
no 5.
Ciarán Ó Gríofa, 'John Daly The Fenian Mayor of Limerick', in David Lee
(ed.), *Remembering Limerick: Historical Essays Celebrating the 800th Anniversary
of Limerick's First Charter Produced in 1197* (1997).
Michael Whelan, 'Clarke's Leitrim Background', in *The Leitrim Guardian*,
1969 (2).

Newspapers
Belfast Morning News
Catholic Bulletin
Freeman's Journal
Irish Daily Independent
Irish Freedom
Irish Press
Irish Times
Irish Volunteer
Limerick Leader
Southern Star
Tyrone Courier

Online Resources

www.ancestry.com
www.oldbaileyonline.org

Interviews
Sister Mary Benignus and Bertie Foley, Dungannon, 22 April 2005.
Mairead and Nora de Hóir, Limerick, 29 November 2011.

Books

Barton, B., *From Behind a Closed Door, Secret Court Martial Records of the 1916 Rising* (Belfast: Blackstaff Press, 2002).

Barton, B. and M. Foy, *The Easter Rising* (Stroud: Sutton Publishing, 1999).

Buckland, P., *Irish Unionism 1885–1922: A Documentary History* (London: Historical Association, 1973).

Clarke, T.J., *Glimpses of an Irish Felon's Prison Life. With an introduction by P.S. O'Hegarty*, (Dublin: Maunsel and Roberts, 1922, 1970).

Coogan, T.P., *1916: The Easter Rising* (London: Cassell & Co., 2002).

Cronin, S., *The McGarrity Papers* (Tralee: Anvil Books, 1992).

Devoy, J., *Recollections of an Irish Rebel – A Personal Narrative* (New York: Chas. D. Young, 1929).

Hay, M., *Bulmer Hobson and the Nationalist Movement in Twentieth-Century Ireland* (Manchester: Manchester University Press, 2009).

Hobson, B., *Ireland Yesterday and Tomorrow* (Tralee: Anvil Books, 1968).

Le Roux, L., *Tom Clarke and the Irish Freedom Movement* (Dublin: The Talbot Press, 1936).

Levenson, S., *Maud Gonne* (London: Cassell & Co., 1977).

Litton, H. (ed.), *Kathleen Clarke, Revolutionary Woman, An Autobiography* (Dublin: The O'Brien Press, 1991).

MacAtasney, G., *Seán MacDiarmada, The Mind of the Revolution* (Leitrim: Drumlin Publications, 2004).

McConville, S., *Irish Political Prisoners, 1848–1922 – Theatres of War* (London: Routledge, 2003).

McGarry, F., *The Rising, Ireland: Easter 1916* (Oxford: Oxford University Press, 2011).

McGarry, F., *Rebels: Voices from the Easter Rising* (London: Penguin Publishing Ltd, 2011).

McGarry, F., and J. McConnel (eds), *The Black Hand of Republicanism: Fenianism in Modern Ireland* (Dublin: Irish Academic Press, 2009).

McGee, O., *The IRB – The Irish Republican Brotherhood From The Land League To Sinn Féin*, (Dublin: Four Courts Press, 2005).

MacLochlainn, P.F. (ed.), *Last Words, Letters and Statements of the Leaders Executed after the Rising at Easter 1916* (Dublin: The Stationery Office, 1990).

298 • Tom Clarke: Life, Liberty, Revolution

Martin, F. X., *The Irish Volunteers 1913–1915: Recollections and Documents* (Dublin: J. Duffy, 1963).

Martin, F. X., *The Easter Rising and University College Dublin* (Dublin: Browne and Nolan, 1966).

Meleady, D., *Redmond: The Parnellite* (Cork: Cork University Press, 2007).

O'Brien, W., and Ryan, D., *Devoy's Post Bag, 1871–1928, Volume II, 1880–1928* (Dublin: C.J. Fallon Ltd, 1948).

O'Hegarty, P.S. (ed.), *A Bibliography of Books by the O'Rahilly, Tom Clarke, Michael O'Hannracháin, and the Countess de Markievicz* (Dublin, 1936).

Walker, B.M., *Parliamentary Election Results in Ireland, 1801–1922* (Dublin: Royal Irish Academy, 1978).

Ward, M., *Maud Gonne: Ireland's Joan of Arc* (London: Pandora, 1990).

Wren, J., *St Laurence O'Toole G. A. C. Centenary History* (Dublin, 2001).

Index

180, 181, 182, 183, 184, 187, 188, 189, 190, 191, 192, 209, 215, 246, 253, 255, 266, 280, 285
  cleansing department 56
  Gaelic League Society 215
  state 242
  'United Irish Societies' 161
New York Press 29
Nicolson, Dr 27, 28
Norman, William, J. (alias Joseph William Lynch) 9, 121, 122
Norman Avenue (New York) 197
Norman, Willie 232
North Dublin Union 195
North Wall (Dublin) 45, 70
Northern Railway Co. 285
Northland Row (Dungannon) 3
Norton, Capt (MP) 38
Nugent, John D. 244, 275

O'Brien, Rocky Mountain 155
O'Casey, Seán 276
O'Connell Street (Dublin) 89, 209
O'Connor, Dalton 130
O'Connor, John (MP) 21
O'Connor, Patrick 6
O'Connor, Seamus 269
O'Hanlon, Jack 60, 74, 197, 200, 204, 257
O'Hegarty, P. S. 74, 77, 85, 99, 105, 221, 260
O'Higgins, P. S. 280
O'Kelly, Sean T 85, 90
O'Leary, John 72, 102
  condemns Jeremiah O'Donovan Rossa 6
  policy of 283
O'Leary, Mr 209, 215
O'Neil, Joe 189
O'Rahilly, Michael (The) 278
O'Riordan, Timothy 8
O'Rourke, William 4
O'Sullivan, Gearóid 71
Oireachtas 243
Old Bailey (Central Criminal Court) 9
Oldham, Mr 25
Omagh (Co. Tyrone) 279
Orangeman 103, 114, 275
Orangemen 283
Ottomans 2

Palm Sunday 88
Palmer, Mary 2
Paris 31, 36
Parliament Bill 73
Parnell, Charles Stewart 4, 20, 21
Parnell Commission 20-1, 49
Parnellites 24
Parnell Street (Dublin) 66, 102, 250, 266, 282
Parsons, Ben 277
Pearse, Patrick xiii, 63, 73, 76, 82, 85, 89, 90, 91, 94, 102, 271
  oration at funeral of Jeremiah O'Donovan Rossa (1915) 84
Peasant 200, 206, 240
Pelham Bay (New York) 183
Penal servitude 124
Pentonville Prison 40
People's Budget (1909) 73
Philadelphia 60, 170
Phoenix Park (1871 riot in) 267
Pigott, Richard 21
Pile, Lord Mayor 253
Plunkett, Joseph 76, 85, 90, 91

Portland Prison 27, 31, 36, 40, 52, 98, 109, 118, 120, 123, 125, 127, 140
Prisoners' Aid Society 40
Progressive Review 29
Pro-Cathedral (Dublin) 84
Proclamation of the Irish Republic 89, 104, 115
Prospect Park (New York) 197
Protestant (customers) 222, 267
Protestants 4, 252, 273
  in support of Clarke's release 23
Protzman, Mr 246
Providence (Rhode Island) 265

Quaker 60, 103
Queen Victoria 22, 226
  diamond jubilee of 31
Queenstown 60, 143, 145, 146, 166, 174, 228, 233, 257, 265

Rankin, Patrick 102
Rathdown Board of Guardians 50, 131, 133
Rathdown Poor Law Union 49, 140
Rathmines (Co. Dublin) 194, 265
Redmond, John (MP) 21, 27, 31, 38, 72, 73, 78, 81, 86, 99 120, 125, 244, 270, 272, 273, 274, 275, 277, 278, 279, 281, 283, 284
  demands release of Irish prisoners 22
  acts as prisoners' legal advisor 28
  questions medical opinion of prison doctors 28
  importance of role acknowledged by Clarke 41-2
  supports Clarke's application for employment 50
  ultimatum re Irish Volunteers 76
  makes Woodenbridge speech (1914) 80
Redmond, William (MP) (father of John) 22
Redmond, William (MP) (brother of John) 25, 38
Redmondites 80, 114, 279
Reidy, James 60, 62, 70, 71, 72, 114, 183, 194, 207, 218, 219, 235, 238, 239, 242, 246, 247, 257, 258
Reidy, Mrs 237, 258
Reilly, Mr 279
Republic 72, 99, 221, 259, 260
Republic of Ireland 101
Reynolds, James (MP) 24, 25
Reynolds, John 262
Ridley, Sir Matthew 40
Riot Act 4
River Liffey (Dublin) 91
Rossa, Jeremiah O'Donovan 100, 102, 254, 285
  funds bombing campaign in Britain 6, 7
  funeral of 82-4
  funeral committee 285
Rossa, O'Donovan, (Mrs) 83, 285
Rossa, O'Donovan, Eileen 83, 285
Rotunda, 45, 94, 204, 215, 234, 236, 265, 271
Rotunda Gardens 270
Rotunda Hospital 92
Royal Hospital (Chelsea) 3
Royal Irish Constabulary (RIC) 4
Royal Regiment of Artillery 3
Russell, O'Neill, T. (MP) 22
Russell, Whitworth 11
Russians 2
Ryan, Jim (Dr) 90
Ryan, Mark (Dr) 40
Ryan, Min 101, 103
Ryan, Tom (Fr) 94
Ryan, W. J. 241, 269, 281